The first**writer**.com

Writers' Handbook

2016

The firstwriter.com

Writers' Handbook 2016

EDITOR

J. PAUL DYSON

Published in 2015 by JP&A Dyson

http://www.firstwriter.com

ISBN 978-1-909935-09-9

Foreword

The firstwriter.com Writers' Handbook returns for its 2016 edition with over 1,400 listings of literary agents, publishers, and magazines, updated in firstwriter.com's online databases between 2013 and 2015, including revised and updated listings from the previous edition and over 40% new entries.

Previous editions of this handbook have been bought by writers across the United States, Canada, and Europe; and ranked in the United Kingdom as the number one bestselling writing and publishing directory on Amazon. The 2016 edition continues this international outlook, giving writers all over the English-speaking world access to the global publishing markets.

Readers of this edition can also benefit from insights from Andrew Lownie, of the Andrew Lownie Literary Agency Ltd, who describes how literary agencies sell their authors.

The handbook also provides free online access to the entire current firstwriter.com databases, including over 850 literary agencies, over 1,700 book publishers, over 2,000 magazines, and constantly updated listings of current writing competitions, with typically more than 50 added each month.

For details on how to claim your free access please see the back of this book.

Included in the subscription

A subscription to the full website is not only free with this book, but comes packed with all the following features:

Advanced search features

- Save searches and save time – set up to 15 search parameters specific to your work, save them, and then access the search results with a single click whenever you log in. You can even save multiple different searches if you have different types of work you are looking to place.
- Add personal notes to listings, visible only to you and fully searchable – helping you to organise your actions.
- Set reminders on listings to notify you when to submit your work, when to follow up, when to expect a reply, or any other custom action.
- Track which listings you've viewed and when, to help you organise your search – any listings which have changed since you last viewed them will be highlighted for your attention.

Daily email updates

As a subscriber you will be able to take advantage of our email alert service, meaning you can specify your particular interests and we'll send you automatic email updates when we change or add a listing that matches them. So if you're interested in agents dealing in romantic fiction in the United States you can have us send you emails with the latest updates about them – keeping you up to date without even having to log in.

User feedback

Our agent, publisher, and magazine databases all include a user feedback feature that allows our subscribers to leave feedback on each listing – giving you not only the chance to have your say about the markets you contact, but giving a unique authors' perspective on the listings.

Save on copyright protection fees

If you're sending your work away to publishers, competitions, or literary agents, it's vital that you first protect your copyright. As a subscriber to firstwriter.com you can do this through our site and save 10% on the copyright registration fees normally payable for protecting your work internationally through the Intellectual Property Rights Office (http://www.CopyrightRegistrationService.com).

firstwriter.magazine

firstwriter.magazine showcases the best in new poetry and fiction from around the world. If you're interested in writing and want to get published, the most important thing you can do is read contemporary writing that's getting into print now. Our magazine helps you do that.

Half price competitions

As well as saving money on copyright registration, subscribers to firstwriter.com can also make further savings by entering writing competitions at a special reduced rate. Subscribers can enter the firstwriter.com International Poetry Competition and International Short Story Contest for half price.

Monthly newsletter

When you subscribe to firstwriter.com you also receive our monthly email newsletter – described by one publishing company as "the best in the business" – including articles, news, and interviews for writers. And the best part is that you can continue to receive the newsletter even after you stop your paid subscription – at no cost!

For details on how to claim your free access please see the back of this book.

Contents

Magazines

Free Access

Glossary of Terms

This section explains common terms used in this handbook, and in the publishing industry more generally.

Academic

Listings in this book will be marked as targeting the academic market only if they publish material of an academic nature; e.g. academic theses, scientific papers, etc. The term is not used to indicate publications that publish general material aimed at people who happen to be in academia, or who are described as academic by virtue of being educated.

Adult

In publishing, "adult" simply refers to books that are aimed at adults, as opposed to books that are aimed at children, or young adults, etc. It is not a euphemism for pornographic or erotic content. Nor does it necessarily refer to content which is unsuitable for children; it is just not targeted at them. In this book, most ordinary mainstream publishers will be described as "adult", unless their books are specifically targeted at other groups (such as children, professionals, etc.).

Agented

An *agented* submission is one which is submitted by a literary agent. If a publisher accepts only *agented* submissions then you will need a literary agent to submit the work on your behalf.

Author bio

A brief description of you and your life – normally in relation to your writing activity, but if intended for publication (particularly in magazines) may be broader in scope. May be similar to *Curriculum Vitae* (CV) or résumé, depending on context.

Bio

See *Author bio.*

Curriculum Vitae

A brief description of you, your qualifications, and accomplishments – normally in this context in relation to writing (any previous publications, or awards, etc.), but in the case of nonfiction proposals may also include relevant experience that qualifies you to write on the subject. Commonly abbreviated to "CV". May also be referred to as a résumé. May be similar to *Author bio*, depending on context.

CV

See *Curriculum Vitae*.

International Reply Coupon

When submitting material overseas you may be required to enclose *International Reply Coupons*, which will enable the recipient to send a response and/or return your material at your cost. Not applicable/available in all countries, so check with your local Post Office for more information.

IRC

See *International Reply Coupon.*

Manuscript

Your complete piece of work – be it a novel, short story, or article, etc. – will be referred to as your manuscript. Commonly abbreviated to "ms" (singular) or "mss" (plural).

MS
See *Manuscript*.

MSS
See *Manuscript*.

Professional
Listings in this book will be marked as targeting the professional market if they publish material serving a particular profession: e.g. legal journals, medical journals, etc. The term is not used to indicate publications that publish general material aimed at a notional "professional class".

Proposal
A proposal is normally requested for nonfiction projects (where the book may not yet have been completed, or even begun). Proposals can consist of a number of components, such as an outline, table of contents, CV, marketing information, etc. but the exact requirements will vary from one publisher to another.

Query
Many agents and publishers will prefer to receive a query in the first instance, rather than your full *manuscript*. A query will typically consist of a cover letter accompanied by a *synopsis* and/or sample chapter(s). Specific requirements will vary, however, so always check on a case by case basis.

SAE
See *Stamped Addressed Envelope*. Can also be referred to as SASE.

SASE
Self-Addressed Stamped Envelope. Variation of SAE. See *Stamped Addressed Envelope*.

Stamped Addressed Envelope
Commonly abbreviated to "SAE". Can also be referred to as Self-Addressed Stamped Envelope, or SASE. When supplying an SAE, ensure that the envelope and postage is adequate for a reply or the return of your material, as required. If you are submitting overseas, remember that postage from your own country will not be accepted, and you may need to provide an *International Reply Coupon*.

Synopsis
A short outline of your story. This should cover all the main characters and events, including the ending. It is not the kind of "teaser" found on a book's back cover. The length of synopsis required can vary, but is generally between one and three pages.

TOC
Table of Contents. These are often requested as part of nonfiction proposals.

Unagented
An unagented submission is one which is not submitted through a literary agent. If a publisher accepts unagented submissions then you can approach them directly.

Unsolicited mss
A manuscript which has not been requested. Many agents and publishers will not accept unsolicited mss, but this does not necessarily mean they are closed to approaches – many will prefer to receive a short *query* in the first instance. If they like the idea, they will request the full work, which will then be a solicited manuscript.

Youth
The term "Youth" in this book is used to indicate the Young Adult market.

Formatting Your Manuscript

Before submitting a manuscript to an agent, magazine, or publisher, it's important that you get the formatting right. There are industry norms covering everything from the size of your margins to the font you choose – get them wrong and you'll be marking yourself out as an amateur. Get them right, and agents and editors will be far more likely to take you seriously.

Fonts

Don't be tempted to "make your book stand out" by using fancy fonts. It *will* stand out, but not for any reason you'd want. Your entire manuscript should be in a monospaced font like Courier (not a proportional font, like Times Roman) at 12 points. (A monospaced font is one where each character takes up the same amount of space; a proportional font is where the letter "i" takes up less space than the letter "m".)

This goes for your text, your headings, your title, your name – everything. Your objective is to produce a manuscript that looks like it has been produced on a simple typewriter.

Italics / bold

Your job as the author is to indicate words that require emphasis, not to pick particular styles of font. This will be determined by the house style of the publisher in question. You indicate emphasis by underlining text; the publisher will decide whether they will use bold or italic to achieve this emphasis – you shouldn't use either in your text.

Margins

You should have a one inch (2.5 centimetre) margin around your entire page: top, bottom, left, and right.

Spacing

In terms of line spacing, your entire manuscript should be double spaced. Your word processor should provide an option for this, so you don't have to insert blank lines manually.

While line spacing should be double, spaces after punctuation should be single. If you're in the habit of putting two spaces after full stops this is the time to get out of that habit, and remove them from your manuscript. You're just creating extra work for the editor who will have to strip them all out.

Do not put blank lines between paragraphs. Start every paragraph (even those at the start of chapters) with an indent equivalent to five spaces. If you want a scene break then create a line with the "#" character centred in the middle. You don't need blank lines above or below this line.

Word count

You will need to provide an estimated word count on the front page of your manuscript. Tempting as it will be to simply use the word processor's word counting function to tell you exactly how many words there are in your manuscript, this is not what you should do. Instead, you should work out the maximum number of characters on a line, divide this number by six, and then multiply by the total number of lines in your manuscript.

Once you have got your estimated word count you need to round it to an approximate value. How you round will depend on the overall length of your manuscript:

- up to 1,500 words: round to the nearest 100;
- 1,500–10,000 words: round to the nearest 500;
- 10,000–25,000 words: round to the nearest 1,000;
- Over 25,000 words: round to the nearest 5,000.

The reason an agent or editor will need to know your word count is so that they can estimate how many pages it will make. Since actual pages include varying amounts of white space due to breaks in paragraphs, sections of speech, etc. the formula above will actually provide a better idea of how many pages will be required than an exact word count would.

And – perhaps more importantly – providing an exact word count will highlight you immediately as an amateur.

Layout of the front page

On the first page of the manuscript, place your name, address, and any other relevant contact details (such as phone number, email address, etc.) in the top left-hand corner. In the top right-hand corner write your approximate word count.

If you have registered your work for copyright protection, place the reference number two single lines (one double line) beneath your contact details. Since your manuscript will only be seen by agents or editors, not the public, this should be done as discreetly as possible, and you should refrain from using any official seal you may have been granted permissions to use. (For information on registering for copyright protection see "Protecting Your Copyright", below.)

Place your title halfway down the front page. Your title should be centred and would normally be in capital letters. You can make it bold or underlined if you want, but it should be the same size as the rest of the text.

From your title, go down two single lines (or one double line) and insert your byline. This should be centred and start with the word "By", followed by the name you are writing under. This can be your name or a pen name, but should be the name you want the work published under. However, make sure that the name in the top left-hand corner is your real, legal name.

From your byline, go down four single lines (or two double lines) and begin your manuscript.

Layout of the text

Print on only one side of the paper, even if your printer can print on both sides.

In the top right-hand corner of all pages except the first should be your running head. This should be comprised of the surname used in your byline; a keyword from your title, and the page number, e.g. "Myname / Mynovel Page 5".

Text should be left-aligned, *not* justified. This means that you should have a ragged right-hand edge to the text, with lines ending at different points. Make sure you don't have any sort of hyphenation function switched on in your word processor: if a word is too long to fit on a line it should be taken over to the next.

Start each new chapter a third of the way down the page with the centred chapter number / title, underlined. Drop down four single lines (two double lines) to the main text.

At the end of the manuscript you do not need to indicate the ending in any way: you don't need to write "The End", or "Ends", etc. The only exception to this is if your manuscript happens to end at the bottom of a page, in which case you can handwrite the word "End" at the bottom of the last page, after you have printed it out.

Protecting Your Copyright

Protecting your copyright is by no means a requirement before submitting your work, but you may feel that it is a prudent step that you would like to take before allowing strangers to see your material.

These days, you can register your work for copyright protection quickly and easily online. The Intellectual Property Rights Office operates a website called the "Copyright Registration Service" which allows you to do this:

- *http://www.CopyrightRegistrationService.com*

This website can be used for material created in any nation signed up to the Berne Convention. This includes the United States, United Kingdom, Canada, Australia, Ireland, New Zealand, and most other countries. There are around 180 countries in the world, and over 160 of them are part of the Berne Convention.

Provided you created your work in one of the Berne Convention nations, your work should be protected by copyright in all other Berne Convention nations. You can therefore protect your copyright around most of the world with a single registration, and because the process is entirely online you can have your work protected in a matter of minutes, without having to print and post a copy of your manuscript.

How an Agency Sells Its Authors

Andrew Lownie, the best-selling literary agent in the world according to Publishers Marketplace, and short-listed for The Bookseller UK literary agent of the year for the last three years, explains how the agency goes about selling its authors.

There are three elements to selling books to publishers. An agency needs to have saleable books in the first place, the proposals need to be the best they can be, and one needs to know the right editors to approach and not give up too easily.

The agency spends a lot of time and effort on the website, as it's a crucial tool in presenting the public face of the agency, in attracting potential authors and in selling rights. The website runs to several thousand pages with individual pages for each author – with a photo and link to their own website – and each book with the jacket cover, a précis of the book, review extracts and the rights sold. There are also pages for latest news, current submissions, publishing tips, forthcoming releases, and much more.

Details of what books have been sold, important reviews, short-listings for prizes etc are posted on a daily basis in the news section. These postings are also carried over onto the agency's Facebook pages and Twitter account which has some 7,000 followers. There are also commissioned articles, such as the popular annual feature "What Editors Want", which tend to be picked up on social media. The result is we receive an enormous number of visits to the website – over 20,000 in January, for example – and, as a consequence, some 500 submissions each week.

From those 20,000 submissions each year, we'll pick maybe 20 authors. This isn't a simple or cheap process but we take submissions very seriously, from the standpoint of how can we make them work, rather than why we should reject them. Every single submission is read by the agency and a response sent with perhaps two proposals or manuscripts a day sent for further readings by external experts. These reports do not come cheap and constitute the agency's biggest annual bill. Quite often this development process can go through a dozen readings over a period of years but it's time well spent as the more polished the proposal, the easier it is to sell.

Once we have our ducks in a row, we need to attract the interest of publishers. Every book is pitched by phone, or more often, a personalised email to a dozen appropriate editors and, if they don't respond by either declining or calling it in, then they are politely chased. The agency also sends out a newsletter to some 4,000 subscribers, with links through to the website entries, the first weekend of every month, giving agency news for the previous month, details of books sold in all territories, a pitch for all books on current submission, links to articles on the website and links to books to be published that month. Many editors don't subscribe so it's individually emailed to them a week later asking if there is anything they would like to call in.

Both my fiction colleague David Haviland and I also make a point of meeting editors, especially the younger editors just starting out, for coffee, drinks or lunch on a regular basis to pitch ideas. It's important to know and deal with a wide range of editors from every possible publishing house as one never knows where they might end up and what they might buy. It's important, too, to be patient and not give up on editors who never buy from one – I sold my first book to one editor, whom I had known since university, almost thirty years after I first submitted to him. Finally, we make the general trade aware of our books by rights posting or announcing deals on Publishers Marketplace and this is particularly good at bringing in film and US enquiries from companies and editors unknown to us. That current buzzword "discoverability" can also be applied to authors' books before they are published and our aim, often using scouts, is to ensure as many people in publishing know about our books as early as possible.

The agency tends to submit in waves so that there is always scope to try new publishers in the light of the comments on why the proposal was turned down. Sometimes it's simply a matter of revising the proposal or building the profile/platform of the author. Sometimes it's a matter of timing and withdrawing the proposal for a future date or new proposal. Often we will submit twenty times trying to find the right editor and I've occasionally sold a book to an editor who'd forgotten they'd already rejected it! With *The Girl with No Name: the Incredible True Story of the Girl Raised by Monkeys* by Marina Chapman, I persevered for five years of due diligence to make her case and five different ghosts worked on the book but it became an international bestseller sold to seventeen countries including separately to Australia, Canada and the United States. Daniel Tammet's autism memoir *Born on a Blue Day* took as long and was even more successful, selling to twenty-five countries. I make the analogy to authors that sometimes one needs to kiss a lot of frogs before one meets one's prince.

Authors don't just come in on the "slush pile". Both David and I network extensively by speaking and attending writer conferences and events, taking part in Guardian Masterclasses and the London Author Fair, using LinkedIn and Twitter to target interesting authors and approaching writers who have appeared in the media, though we never knowingly approach a writer whom we know to be already represented.

We also suggest projects to authors. A good example is Clare Mulley's *The Spy Who Loved* about the SOE agent Christine Granville, now optioned to a Hollywood studio and sold in a range of countries. Recently I put an idea to an author of mine, which he researched with seed money I arranged through a national newspaper, and we now have a book to sell with a serial already tied to it. Naturally, we are always open to finding authors for book ideas put up by editors – especially since those ideas usually tend to be commissioned. Recently an editor said they wanted a teacher's memoir from an inner city comprehensive and I duly worked through educational columnists to find someone.

I also make a point of approaching agents in other fields, whether it is speaker agencies or those managing celebrities or sports stars. They can often do something for my authors and vice versa. Such partnerships have brought the memoirs of such reality stars as Sam Faiers, Kirk Norcross and Nanny Pat of *The Only Way is Essex* and Spencer Matthews of *Made in Chelsea*. My own involvement in the Biographers Club and Biographers International Organisation has brought several successful writers to the agency.

Increasingly the agency has taken to "establishing" a book by either selling it in another territory first – we've recently done this successfully in the United States, Germany, Australia and South Africa – or through the agency imprint Thistle Publishing. When, for example, no publisher was interested in Monica Porter's "yummy-grand-mummy" memoir *Raven: My Year of Dating Dangerously*, the agency published the book through its own imprint Thistle, sold a serial to the Mail on Sunday for a three-week run and used the interest to attract interest from foreign publishers and film companies.

Thistle, under the management of David Haviland, has now published some two hundred books over the last year – a mixture of agency backlist and frontlist – as well as several Thistle "shorts". A good example is *Guardian* correspondent Shaun Walker's *Odessa Dreams: The Dark Heart of Ukraine's Online Marriage Industry*, published in conjunction with Amazon Kindle Singles, which is currently number one in Russian travel guides on Amazon! I've just signed an audio deal as a result of another Thistle "short" in partnership with Kindle Singles – Katharine Quarmby's account of her search for her birth father *Blood & Water: An Anglo-Iranian Love Story*. Indeed, a real focus in recent months, as part of the agency's mission to develop as many revenue streams as possible for authors, has been to exploit unsold territorial and subsidiary rights in agency books and seek reversion when publishers are not exploiting those rights themselves.

The agency has always been responsive to the market. Having initially specialised in serious nonfiction, especially biography and history, the agency quickly also moved into memoirs, seeing that publishers' commissioning policy was being shaped by the growing importance of the supermarkets. The result is the agency now represents many of the leading authors of inspirational memoir, including bestselling authors Cathy Glass and Casey Watson, and the success of these authors brings in other authors in the field. Given the importance of ghost writers to work with such authors, the agency developed a strong brand as an agency for ghost writers with their very own themed "ghosts" party every Halloween. The agency now represents over thirty ghost writers who have their own dedicated section on the website. As a result, publishers will often approach the agency looking for ghosts where they have a project in need of some editorial help, and it means the agency can "package" books in-house, linking agency authors with the right ghost giving greater control. Every two months, editors who commission books which require ghost writers, receive a "ghost newsletter".

It isn't easy selling books and there are no shortcuts to success – it's taken me thirty years of agenting to get to where I am now – but if one is nimble, responsive, pleasant, prepared to think outside the box, reads proposals and manuscripts diligently, attends events and responds to every email, phone call and letter the deals will come. It's important to be courteous – but also firm – and to always put the needs of the book first. Agenting requires imagination, flexibility, a thick skin to cope with constant rejection and hard work – both David and I work over 70-hour weeks and rarely take any holiday – but it is rewarding to feel that one has given a life to a writer's prose and how the lives of both authors and readers can be changed by publication. Even after over 1,500 deals, I take pleasure in every deal done and in the launching and nurturing of writers' careers.

The Andrew Lownie Literary Agency Ltd, founded in 1988, is one of the UK's leading boutique literary agencies, with some two hundred nonfiction and fiction authors handled respectively by Andrew Lownie and David Haviland. It prides itself on its personal attention to its clients and specialises both in launching new writers and taking established writers to a new level of recognition. Andrew Lownie remains the top selling agent worldwide, according to Publishers

Marketplace, and was short-listed for Literary Agent of the Year at the 2013 and 2014 Bookseller Awards.

Books represented have included: The Cambridge Guide to Literature in English; The Oxford Classical Dictionary; The Penguin Companion to the European Union; Norma Major's history of Chequers; the memoirs of Sir John Mills, Alan Whicker, Gloria Hunniford, David Hasselhoff, Emily Lloyd, Kerry Katona and Patrick MacNee; the best-selling fostering series by Cathy Glass and Casey Watson; Sam Faiers' Living Life the Essex Way; Daniel Tammet's international best-seller Born on a Blue Day; Laurence Gardner'sThe Magdalene Legacy and The Shadow of Solomon, the literary estates of Joyce Cary and Julian MacLaren-Ross; the historians Juliet Barker, Roger Crowley, Tom Devine, Robert Hutchinson, Sean McMeekin, Linda Porter, Geoff Roberts ,Desmond Seward, David Stafford and Christian Wolmar; the wine writer Michael Schuster; crime writers, such as Mei Trow and David Roberts, and thriller writers such as Duncan Falconer.

US Literary Agents

For the most up-to-date listings of these and hundreds of other literary agents, visit http://www.firstwriter.com/Agents

*To claim your **free** access to the site, please see the back of this book.*

A+B Works

Email: query@aplusbworks.com
Website: http://www.aplusbworks.com

Handles: Fiction; Nonfiction; *Areas:* Women's Interests; *Markets:* Adult; Children's; Youth

Specialises in young adult and middle grade fiction, women's fiction, and select narrative nonfiction. No thrillers, literary fiction, erotica, cook books, picture books, poetry, short fiction, or screenplays. Query by email only. Response not guaranteed. Accepts very few new clients.

Abbot Management

PO Box 430, S Pasadena, CA 91031
Tel: +1 (626) 441-4410
Email: a@abbotent.com
Website: http://www.abbotmanagement.com

Handles: Scripts; *Areas:* Adventure; Anthropology; Antiques; Archaeology; Architecture; Arts; Autobiography; Beauty and Fashion; Biography; Business; Cookery; Crafts; Crime; Criticism; Culture; Current Affairs; Design; Drama; Entertainment; Erotic; Fantasy; Film; Finance; Gardening; Gothic; Health; Historical; Hobbies; Horror; How-to; Humour; Legal; Leisure; Lifestyle; Literature; Media; Medicine; Men's Interests; Military; Music; Mystery; Nature; New Age; Philosophy; Photography; Politics; Psychology; Radio; Religious; Romance; Science; Sci-Fi; Self-Help; Short Stories; Sociology; Spiritual; Sport; Suspense; Technology; Theatre; Thrillers; Translations; Travel; TV; Westerns; Women's Interests; *Markets:* Academic; Adult; Children's; Family; Professional; Youth; *Treatments:* Commercial; Contemporary; Cynical; Dark; Experimental; In-depth; Light; Literary; Mainstream; Niche; Popular; Positive; Progressive; Satirical; Serious; Traditional

Our mission is simple: to provide a steady flow of high quality film and television screenplays to Producers and Production Companies in the New York City and Los Angeles areas. Scripts must be an industry standard final draft (properly formatted; grammatically correct; 88-125 pages; written without camera angles) created on screenwriting software. Approach via screenplay submission form on website.

Dominick Abel Literary Agency, Inc

146 W. 82nd Street, #1B, New York, NY 10024
Tel: +1 (212) 877-0710
Fax: +1 (212) 595-3133
Email: dominick@dalainc.com

Handles: Fiction; Nonfiction; *Markets:* Adult

Handles adult fiction and nonfiction. 100 clients. Not accepting submissions as at September 2013.

Abrams Artists Agency

275 Seventh Ave, 26th Floor, New York, NY 10001
Tel: +1 (646) 486-4600
Fax: +1 (646) 486-2358
Email: literary@abramsartny.com
Website: http://www.abramsartists.com

Handles: Scripts; *Areas:* Drama; Film; Humour; Music; Mystery; Romance; Suspense; TV; *Markets:* Adult

Send query with SASE via industry professional only. Specialises in film, TV, theatre, and publishing.

Adler & Robin Books, Inc

3000 Connecticut Avenue, NW, Suite 317, Washington DC, 20008
Tel: +1 (202) 986-9275
Fax: +1 (202) 986-9485
Email: submissions@adlerrobin.com
Website: http://www.adlerrobin.com

Handles: Nonfiction; Reference; *Areas:* Autobiography; Biography; Culture; Historical; How-to; Humour; Lifestyle; Self-Help; Technology; *Markets:* Adult; Children's

Send queries by email only.

The Agency Group, Ltd

142 West 57th Street, Sixth Floor, New York, NY 10019
Tel: +1 (310) 385-2800
Fax: +1 (310) 385-1220
Email: marcgerald@theagencygroup.com
Website: http://www.theagencygroup.com

Handles: Fiction; Nonfiction; *Areas:* Anthropology; Archaeology; Architecture; Arts; Autobiography; Biography; Business; Cookery; Crime; Culture; Design; Entertainment; Finance; Health; Historical; How-to; Humour; Legal; Lifestyle; Medicine; Music; Nature; Politics; Psychology; Self-Help; Sport; *Markets:* Adult

Multimedia agency representing recording artists, celebrities, and with a literary agency operating out of the New York office. Takes on new clients by referral only.

Agency for the Performing Arts (APA)

405 S. Beverly Dr , Beverly Hills, CA 90212
Tel: +1 (310) 888-4200
Fax: +1 (310) 888-4242
Website: http://www.apa-agency.com

Handles: Fiction; Nonfiction; Scripts; *Areas:* Film; Theatre; TV; *Markets:* Adult

Handles nonfiction, novels, scripts for film, theatre, and TV, as well as musicians and other performing artists.

The Ahearn Agency, Inc

2021 Pine St., New Orleans, LA 70118-5456
Tel: +1 (504) 861-8395
Fax: +1 (504) 866-6434
Email: pahearn@aol.com
Website: http://www.ahearnagency.com

Handles: Fiction; Nonfiction; *Areas:* Autobiography; Biography; Crime; Current Affairs; Health; Historical; Humour; Lifestyle; Mystery; Nature; Romance; Short Stories; Suspense; Thrillers; Women's Interests; *Markets:* Adult; *Treatments:* Literary

Send one page query with SASE, description, length, market info, and any writing credits. Accepts email queries without attachments. Response in 2-3 months.

Specialises in women's fiction and suspense. No nonfiction, poetry, juvenile material or science fiction.

Aimee Entertainment Agency

15840 Ventura Blvd., Ste. 215, Encino, CA 91436
Tel: +1 (818) 783-3831
Fax: +1 (818) 783-4447

Email: info@onlinemediapublications.com
Website:
http://www.aimeeentertainment.com

Handles: Fiction; Scripts; *Areas:* Film; *Markets:* Adult

Handles film scripts and book-length works.

Alive Communications, Inc

7680 Goodard Street, Suite 200, Colorado Springs, CO 80920
Tel: +1 (719) 260-7080
Fax: +1 (719) 260-8223
Email: Submissions@aliveliterary.com
Website: http://aliveliterary.com

Handles: Fiction; Nonfiction; *Areas:* Adventure; Autobiography; Biography; Business; Crime; Historical; How-to; Humour; Lifestyle; Mystery; Religious; Self-Help; Short Stories; Spiritual; Sport; Suspense; Thrillers; Westerns; Women's Interests; *Markets:* Adult; Children's; *Treatments:* Commercial; Literary; Mainstream; Popular

Accepts queries from referred authors only. Works primarily with well-established, best-selling, and career authors. Referred authors may submit query by email with bio, name of the client referring you, synopsis, and first three chapters. See website for full details.

Miriam Altshuler Literary Agency

53 Old Post Road North, Red Hook, NY 12571
Tel: +1 (845) 758-9408
Fax: +1 (845) 758-3118
Email: query@maliterary.com
Website: http://www.miriamaltshuler literaryagency.com

Handles: Fiction; Nonfiction; *Areas:* Autobiography; Culture; Fantasy; How-to; Psychology; Self-Help; Sociology; Spiritual; *Markets:* Adult; Children's; Youth; *Treatments:* Commercial; Literary

Send query by post or by email. If submitting by post, include email address for reply. Only include SASE if no email address available, but note that a response is not guaranteed, even with an SASE. Include brief author bio, synopsis, and the first chapter, pasted into the body of the email (no attachments). See website for full guidelines. No Mystery, Romance, Poetry, Fantasy, Science Fiction, Thrillers, Screenplays, Horror, or Westerns.

Ambassador Speakers Bureau & Literary Agency

PO Box 50358, Nashville, TN 37205
Tel: +1 (615) 370-4700
Fax: +1 (615) 661-4344
Email: info@ambassadorspeakers.com
Website:
http://www.ambassadorspeakers.com

Handles: Fiction; Nonfiction; *Areas:* Adventure; Autobiography; Biography; Culture; Current Affairs; Finance; Health; Historical; How-to; Legal; Lifestyle; Medicine; Politics; Religious; Self-Help; Women's Interests; *Markets:* Adult; *Treatments:* Contemporary; Literary; Mainstream

Represents select authors and writers who are published by religious and general market publishers in the US and Europe.No short stories, children's books, screenplays, or poetry. Send query by email with short description. Submit work on invitation only.

Betsy Amster Literary Enterprises

6312 SW Capitol Hwy. #503, Portland, OR 97239
Email: b.amster.assistant@gmail.com
Website: http://amsterlit.com

Handles: Fiction; Nonfiction; Poetry; *Areas:* Autobiography; Biography; Cookery; Culture; Fantasy; Gardening; Health; Historical; Humour; Lifestyle; Medicine; Mystery; Psychology; Self-Help; Sociology; Thrillers; Travel; Women's Interests; *Markets:* Adult; Children's; Youth; *Treatments:* Commercial; Contemporary; Literary

Send query by email only. For fiction and memoirs include the first three pages in the body of your email; for nonfiction include your proposal, again in the body of the email. See website for different email addresses for adult and children's/YA submissions. No unsolicited attachments or queries by phone or fax.

No romances, screenplays, adult poetry, westerns, adult fantasy, horror, science fiction, techno thrillers, spy capers, apocalyptic scenarios, or political or religious arguments.

Marcia Amsterdam Agency

41 W. 82nd St., New York, NY 10024-5613
Tel: +1 (212) 873-4945

Handles: Fiction; Scripts; *Areas:* Adventure; Crime; Film; Historical; Horror; Humour; Mystery; Romance; Science; Thrillers; TV; *Markets:* Adult; Youth; *Treatments:* Contemporary; Mainstream

Send query with SASE. No poetry, how-to, books for the 8-10 age-group, or unsolicited MSS. Response to queries usually in one month.

Anonymous Content

588 Broadway, Suite 308, New York, NY 10012
Tel: +1 (212) 925-0055
Fax: +1 (212) 925-5030
Email: litmanagement@anonymouscontent.com
Website: http://www.anonymouscontent.com

Handles: Scripts; *Areas:* Film; TV; *Markets:* Adult

Works in the areas of film, TV, adverts, and music videos.

Arcadia

31 Lake Place North, Danbury, CT 06810
Email: arcadialit@sbcglobal.net

Handles: Nonfiction; *Areas:* Autobiography; Biography; Current Affairs; Health; Historical; Lifestyle; Music; Nature; Politics; Psychology; Science; Self-Help; Spiritual; Technology; Women's Interests; *Markets:* Adult; *Treatments:* Commercial; Literary

Send query with proposal or up to 50 sample pages by email (no attachments) or by post with SASE. No fiction.

Movable Type Management

244 Madison Avenue, Suite 334, New York, NY 10016
Tel: +1 (646) 431-6134
Email: AChromy@MovableTM.com
Website: http://www.mtmgmt.net

Handles: Fiction; Nonfiction; Culture; *Markets:* Adult; Family

Works with authors in a wide variety of categories and genres. Aims to develop properties for distribution across platforms, devices, and territories. Send queries by email only. For nonfiction send query describing topic, approach, and bio. For fiction send query with first 10 pages. Include "Query" in the subject line. No attachments or approaches by post.

Audrey A. Wolf Literary Agency

2510 Virginia Avenue NW, #702N, Washington, DC 20037
Email: audreyrwolf@gmail.com

Handles: Nonfiction; *Areas:* Autobiography; Biography; Business; Current Affairs; Finance; Health; Historical; Lifestyle; Politics; Self-Help; Sport; *Markets:* Adult

Send query by post or email, including synopsis up to two pages long showing the full structure of the book: beginning, middle, and end. Also include chapter outline.

The August Agency LLC

Email: submissions@augustagency.com
Website: http://www.augustagency.com

Handles: Fiction; Nonfiction; *Areas:* Arts; Autobiography; Biography; Business; Culture; Current Affairs; Entertainment; Finance; Historical; Media; Politics; Sociology; Technology; Women's Interests; *Markets:* Adult; Family; Literary

Accepts queries by referral or by request at a writers' conference only.

The Axelrod Agency

55 Main Street, P.O. Box 357, Chatham, NY 12037
Tel: +1 (518) 392-2100
Fax: +1 (518) 392-2944
Email: steve@axelrodagency.com
Website: http://axelrodagency.com

Handles: Fiction; *Areas:* Crime; Erotic; Mystery; Romance; Thrillers; Women's Interests; *Markets:* Adult

Send query by email only. No nonfiction, African-American, Christian, comedy, humour, comics, graphic novels, gay/lesbian, historical, horror, literary, poetry, puzzles, games, science fiction, fantasy, or westerns.

Ayesha Pande Literary

128 West 132 Street, New York, NY 10027
Email: queries@pandeliterary.com
Website: http://pandeliterary.com

Handles: Fiction; Nonfiction; *Areas:* Autobiography; Biography; Culture; Finance; Historical; Humour; Women's Interests; *Markets:* Adult; Youth; *Treatments:* Literary; Popular

Send query describing your project in a paragraph, with brief author bio and any publishing history. Prefers queries by email with first five pages pasted into the body of the email (no attachments). Also accepts submissions by post with SASE and first five pages. No fantasy, science fiction, romance, poetry, screenplays or children's books including middle grade fiction. Will consider young adult and graphic novels. See website for full guidelines.

Baldi Agency

233 West 99th Street, 19C, New York, NY 10025
Tel: +1 (212) 222-3213
Email: info@baldibooks.com
Website: http://www.baldibooks.com

Handles: Fiction; Nonfiction; Reference; *Areas:* Autobiography; Biography; Business; Cookery; Culture; Historical; Lifestyle; Science; Spiritual; Technology; Travel; *Markets:* Adult; *Treatments:* Literary

Send one page query by email, or by post with SASE.

Barbara Hogenson Agency

165 West End Ave., Suite 19-C, New York, NY 10023
Tel: +1 (212) 874-8084
Fax: +1 (212) 362-3011
Email: Bhogenson@aol.com

Handles: Fiction; Nonfiction; Scripts; *Areas:* Theatre; *Markets:* Adult

Represents fiction, nonfiction, and stage plays. Send query by email only. No unsolicited MSS.

Belcastro Agency

721 Virginia Ave, Tarpon Springs, FL 34689
Tel: +1 (330) 766-4885
Email: queries@belcastroagency.com
Website: http://www.belcastroagency.com

Handles: Fiction; *Areas:* Adventure; Crime; Erotic; Fantasy; Mystery; Romance; Sci-Fi; Suspense; Thrillers; Women's Interests; *Markets:* Adult; Children's; Youth; *Treatments:* Commercial; Contemporary; Literary; Mainstream

We are a passionate, hands-on, editorially-focused boutique agency with a focus on women's fiction and YA. We work closely with our writers in developing manuscripts and proposals for submission. Queries welcome by email.

The Bent Agency

204 Park Place, Number Two, Brooklyn, NY 11238
Email: queries@thebentagency.com
Website: http://www.thebentagency.com

Handles: Fiction; Nonfiction; *Areas:* Adventure; Autobiography; Cookery; Crime; Culture; Fantasy; Historical; Horror; Humour; Lifestyle; Mystery; Romance;

Science; Sci-Fi; Suspense; Thrillers; Women's Interests; *Markets:* Adult; Children's; Youth; *Treatments:* Commercial; Contemporary; Literary; Popular

Accepts email queries only. See website for agent bios and specific interests and email addresses, then query one agent only. See website for full submission guidelines.

Meredith Bernstein Literary Agency, Inc.

2095 Broadway, Suite 505, New York, NY 10023
Tel: +1 (212) 799-1007
Fax: +1 (212) 799-1145
Email: mgoodbern@aol.com
Website: http://www.meredithbernstein literaryagency.com

Handles: Fiction; Nonfiction; *Areas:* Mystery; Romance; Thrillers; *Markets:* Adult; Youth; *Treatments:* Literary

Send query with SASE. An eclectic agency which does not specialise in any one particular area. Accepts queries by post, or via form on website. No poetry or screenplays. See website for full guidelines.

Bidnick & Company

Email: bidnick@comcast.net

Handles: Nonfiction; *Areas:* Cookery; *Markets:* Adult

Handles cookbooks and narrative nonfiction. Send query by email only.

Vicky Bijur Literary Agency

333 West End Avenue, Apt. 5B, New York, NY 10023
Email: queries@vickybijuragency.com
Website: http://www.vickybijuragency.com

Handles: Fiction; Nonfiction; *Areas:* Biography; Cookery; Health; Historical; Politics; Psychology; Science; Self-Help; Sociology; *Markets:* Adult

Send query by email or by post with SASE. For fiction include synopsis and first chapter (pasted into the body of the email if submitting electronically). For nonfiction include proposal. No attachments or queries by phone or fax. No children's books, poetry, science fiction, fantasy, horror, or romance.

David Black Literary Agency

335 Adams Street, Suite 2707, Brooklyn, NY 11201
Tel: +1 (718) 852-5500
Fax: +1 (718) 852-5539
Email: dblack@dblackagency.com
Website: http://www.davidblackagency.com

Handles: Fiction; Nonfiction; *Areas:* Autobiography; Biography; Business; Cookery; Crafts; Current Affairs; Entertainment; Finance; Health; Historical; Humour; Legal; Lifestyle; Military; Mystery; Politics; Psychology; Romance; Science; Self-Help; Spiritual; Sport; Thrillers; Women's Interests; *Markets:* Adult; Children's; Youth; *Treatments:* Commercial; Literary; Mainstream

See website for details of different agents, and specific interests and submission guidelines of each. Otherwise, query the agency generally by post only and allow 8 weeks for a response. See website for full details.

Bleecker Street Associates, Inc.

217 Thompson Street, #519, New York, NY 10012
Tel: +1 (212) 677-4492
Fax: +1 (212) 388-0001
Email: bleeckerst@hotmail.com

Handles: Fiction; Nonfiction; *Areas:* Autobiography; Biography; Business; Cookery; Crime; Culture; Current Affairs; Entertainment; Erotic; Health; Historical; Horror; How-to; Humour; Lifestyle; Military; Mystery; Nature; New Age; Politics; Psychology; Religious; Romance; Science; Self-Help; Sociology; Spiritual; Sport; Technology; Thrillers; Women's Interests; *Markets:* Adult; Youth; *Treatments:* Literary

Send query with SASE for response. No poetry, plays, scripts, short stories, academic, scholarly, professional, science fiction, westerns, children's books, or phone calls, faxes, or emails.

The Book Group

20 West 20th Street, Suite 601, New York, NY 10011
Tel: +1 (212) 803-3360
Email: submissions@thebookgroup.com
Website: http://www.thebookgroup.com

Handles: Fiction; Nonfiction; *Areas:* Autobiography; Biography; Cookery; Historical; Lifestyle; Psychology; *Markets:* Adult; Children's; Youth; *Treatments:* Commercial; Literary

Represents a broad range of fiction and nonfiction. No poetry or screenplays. Send query by email only with ten sample pages and the first and last name of the agent you are querying in the subject line (see website for individual agent interests). No attachments. Include all material in the body of the email. See website for full guidelines. Response only if interested.

BookEnds, LLC

Tel: +1 (908) 362-0090
Email: submissions@bookends-inc.com
Website: http://www.bookends-inc.com

Handles: Fiction; Nonfiction; Reference; *Areas:* Business; Culture; Current Affairs; Erotic; Fantasy; Historical; Lifestyle; Mystery; Romance; Sci-Fi; Suspense; Women's Interests; *Markets:* Adult; Youth; *Treatments:* Contemporary

Accepts queries from both published and unpublished authors by email only. No postal approaches. Send query directly to specific agent (see website for specific interests and email addresses). No children's picture books, short fiction, poetry, screenplays, or techno-thrillers.

Books & Such Literary Agency

52 Mission Circle, Suite 122, PMB 170, Santa Rosa, CA 95409-5370
Email: representation@booksandsuch.com
Website: http://www.booksandsuch.biz

Handles: Fiction; Nonfiction; *Areas:* Historical; Humour; Lifestyle; Religious; Romance; Women's Interests; *Markets:* Adult; Children's; Youth

Send query by email only. No attachments. Query should be up to one page detailing your book, your market, your experience, etc., as well as why you chose to contact this agency and if you are contacting others. Particularly interested in material for the Christian market. No queries by post or phone. See website for full details.

Georges Borchardt, Inc.

136 East 57th Street, New York, NY 10022
Tel: +1 (212) 753-5785
Fax: +1 (212) 838-6518
Email: office@gbagency.com
Website: http://www.gbagency.com

Handles: Fiction; Nonfiction; *Areas:* Autobiography; Biography; Historical; *Markets:* Adult; Youth; *Treatments:* Commercial; Literary

New York based literary agency founded in 1967. No unsolicited MSS or screenplays.

Brandt & Hochman Literary Agents, Inc.

1501 Broadway, Suite 2310, New York, NY 10036
Tel: +1 (212) 840-5760
Fax: +1 (212) 840-5776
Email: ghochman@bromasite.com
Website: http://brandthochman.com

Handles: Fiction; Nonfiction; *Areas:* Arts; Autobiography; Culture; Current Affairs; Health; Historical; Lifestyle; Mystery; Science; Thrillers; *Markets:* Adult; Children's; Youth; *Treatments:* Commercial; Literary; Popular

Send query by post with SASE or by email with query letter up to two pages long, including overview and author details and writing credits. See website for full submission guidelines and for details of individual agents' interests and direct contact details, then approach one agent specifically. No screenplays or textbooks. Response to email queries not guaranteed.

The Helen Brann Agency, Inc.

94 Curtis Road, Bridgewater, CT 06752
Fax: +1 (860) 355-2572
Email: helenbrannagency@earthlink.net

Handles: Fiction; Nonfiction; *Markets:* Adult

Send query with SASE. Works mostly with established writers and referrals.

Barbara Braun Associates, Inc.

7 East 14th St #19F, New York, NY 10003
Email: bbasubmissions@gmail.com
Website: http://www.barbarabraunagency.com

Handles: Fiction; Nonfiction; *Areas:* Architecture; Arts; Beauty and Fashion; Biography; Criticism; Culture; Design; Film; Historical; Mystery; Photography; Politics; Psychology; Sociology; Thrillers; Women's Interests; *Markets:* Adult; *Treatments:* Commercial; Literary; Serious

Send query by email only, with "Query" in the subject line, including brief summary, word count, genre, any relevant publishing experience, and the first five pages pasted into the body of the email. No attachments. No poetry, science fiction, fantasy, horror, or screenplays. Particularly interested in stories for women, art-related fiction, historical and multicultural stories, and to a lesser extent mysteries and thrillers. Also interested in narrative nonfiction and current affairs books by journalists.

Marie Brown Associates, Inc.

412 W. 154th Street, New York, NY 10032
Tel: +1 (212) 939-9725
Fax: +1 (212) 939-9728
Email: mbrownlit@aol.com

Handles: Fiction; Nonfiction; *Areas:* Biography; Business; Culture; Historical; Music; Religious; Women's Interests; *Markets:* Adult; Youth; *Treatments:* Literary; Mainstream

Send query with SASE. Particularly interested in multicultural and African-American writers. MSS should preferably not be submitted elsewhere simultaneously.

Tracy Brown Literary Agency

P.O. Box 88, Scarsdale, NY 10583
Tel: +1 (914) 400-4147
Fax: +1 (914) 931-1746
Email: tracy@brownlit.com

Handles: Fiction; Nonfiction; *Areas:* Biography; Current Affairs; Health; Historical; Humour; Nature; Psychology; Sport; Travel; Women's Interests; *Markets:* Adult; *Treatments:* Contemporary; Literary; Mainstream; Serious

Send query with author bio, outline/proposal, synopsis, and one sample chapter. Queries accepted by email but not by fax. No Young Adult, Science Fiction, or Romance.

Browne & Miller Literary Associates

410 S. Michigan Avenue, Suite 460, Chicago, IL 60605
Tel: +1 (312) 922-3063
Fax: +1 (312) 922-1905
Email: mail@browneandmiller.com
Website: http://www.browneandmiller.com

Handles: Fiction; Nonfiction; *Areas:* Anthropology; Archaeology; Autobiography; Biography; Business; Cookery; Crafts; Crime; Culture; Current Affairs; Finance; Health; Historical; Hobbies; How-to; Humour; Lifestyle; Medicine; Mystery; Nature; Psychology; Religious; Science; Self-Help; Sociology; Sport; Technology; Women's Interests; *Markets:* Adult; Youth; *Treatments:* Commercial; Literary; Satirical

Particularly interested in literary/commercial fiction/women's fiction, women's historical fiction, literary-leaning crime fiction, romance, Amish fiction, time travel stories, Christian/inspirational fiction by established authors, literary and commercial Young Adult fiction, nonfiction by nationally-recognised, platformed author/experts. No children's picture books, horror or sci-fi novels, short stories, poetry, original screenplays, articles, or software. Send query by email with synopsis and first five chapters for fiction, or proposal and three chapters for nonfiction, in the body of the email (attachments will not be opened). See website for full details.

Marcus Bryan & Associates Inc.

1500 Skokie Boulevard, Suite 310,
Northbrook, IL 60068
Tel: +1 (847) 412-9394
Fax: +1 (847) 412-9394
Email: mba3308@aol.com
Website: http://marcusbryan.com

Handles: Fiction; Scripts; *Markets:* Adult

Note: Not accepting new clients as at July 2013. Check website for current status.

Accepts query letters from book authors and screenwriters.

Kelvin C. Bulger and Associates

4540 W. Washington Blvd , Suite 101,
Chicago, IL 60624
Tel: +1 (312) 218-1943
Fax: +1 (773) 261-5950
Email: bulgerassociates@gmail.com
Website: http://bulgerandassociates.biz

Handles: Scripts; *Areas:* Adventure; Film; Humour; Religious; TV; *Markets:* Adult

Send query by post with SASE, or by fax or email. Include first ten pages of your screenplay, one-page plot synopsis and one-page logline.

Sheree Bykofsky Associates, Inc.

4326 Harbor Beach Boulevard, PO Box 706,
Brigantine, NJ 08203
Email: submitbee@aol.com
Website: http://www.shereebee.com

Handles: Fiction; Nonfiction; Reference; *Areas:* Biography; Business; Cookery; Culture; Current Affairs; Film; Hobbies; Humour; Lifestyle; Mystery; Psychology; Self-Help; Spiritual; Women's Interests; *Markets:* Adult; *Treatments:* Commercial; Literary

Send query by email only. Include one page query, and for fiction a one page synopsis, and first page of manuscript, all in the body of the email. No attachments. Always looking for a bestseller in any category, but generally not interested in poetry, thrillers, westerns, romances, occult, science fiction, fantasy, children's or young adult.

Carnicelli Literary Management

7 Kipp Road, Rhinebeck, NY 12572
Email: queries@carnicellilit.com
Website: http://www.carnicellilit.com

Handles: Fiction; Nonfiction; *Areas:* Autobiography; Biography; Business; Culture; Current Affairs; Health; Historical; Psychology; Science; Spiritual; Sport; *Markets:* Adult; *Treatments:* Commercial; Literary; Popular; Serious

Handles mainly nonfiction. Send query by email, or using form on website. Restrict queries to one page. If approaching by email, include the word "Query" in the subject line and do not include attachments. See website for full guidelines. No poetry, plays, screenplays, or books for children.

Maria Carvainis Agency, Inc.

1270 Avenue of the Americas, Suite 2320,
New York, NY 10020
Tel: +1 (212) 245-6365
Fax: +1 (212) 245-7196
Email: mca@mariacarvainisagency.com
Website: http://mariacarvainisagency.com

Handles: Fiction; Nonfiction; *Areas:* Autobiography; Biography; Business; Culture; Finance; Historical; Mystery; Psychology; Science; Suspense; Technology; Thrillers; Women's Interests; *Markets:*

Adult; Children's; Youth; *Treatments:* Contemporary; Literary; Mainstream; Popular

Send query with synopsis, two sample chapters, and details of any previous writing credits, by post or by email. If sending by post and return of the material is required, include SASE; otherwise include email address for response, usually within 5-10 days. If submitting by email, all documents must be Word or PDF. No screenplays, children's picture books, science fiction, or poetry.

Castiglia Literary Agency

1155 Camino Del Mar, Suite 510, Del Mar, CA 92014
Tel: +1 (858) 755-8761
Fax: +1 (858) 755-7063
Email: CastigliaAgency-query@yahoo.com
Website: http://www.castigliaagency.com

Handles: Fiction; Nonfiction; *Areas:* Architecture; Biography; Business; Cookery; Crime; Culture; Current Affairs; Design; Finance; Health; Lifestyle; Mystery; Science; Sci-Fi; Thrillers; *Markets:* Adult; Youth; *Treatments:* Contemporary; Literary; Mainstream

Send one-page query by email, including brief description / synopsis and background / short bio of author. See website for full guidelines.

Chalberg & Sussman

115 West 29th St, Third Floor , New York, NY 10001
Email: rachel@chalbergsussman.com
Website: http://www.chalbergsussman.com

Handles: Fiction; Nonfiction; *Areas:* Autobiography; Culture; Historical; Psychology; Science; Self-Help; Suspense; Thrillers; Women's Interests; *Markets:* Adult; Children's; *Treatments:* Commercial; Dark; Literary; Popular

Send query by email. See website for specific agent interests and email addresses.

Jane Chelius Literary Agency, Inc.

548 Second Street, Brooklyn, NY 11215
Tel: +1 (718) 499-0236
Fax: +1 (718) 832-7335
Email: queries@janechelius.com
Website: http://www.janechelius.com

Handles: Fiction; Nonfiction; *Areas:* Biography; Culture; Humour; Lifestyle; Medicine; *Markets:* Adult; *Treatments:* Satirical

Note: Not currently accepting submissions as at February 2015

Send query by email with query letter, one-page synopsis, and first ten pages in the body of the email. No email attachments. Considers all genres except children's books, poetry, science fiction, fantasy, category romance, stage plays or screenplays. Response only if interested.

Elyse Cheney Literary Associates, LLC

78 Fifth Avenue, 3rd Floor, New York, NY 10011
Tel: +1 (212) 277-8007
Fax: +1 (212) 614-0728
Email: submissions@cheneyliterary.com
Website: http://www.cheneyliterary.com

Handles: Fiction; Nonfiction; *Areas:* Autobiography; Biography; Business; Culture; Current Affairs; Finance; Historical; Horror; Literature; Politics; Romance; Science; Sport; Suspense; Thrillers; Women's Interests; *Markets:* Adult; *Treatments:* Commercial; Contemporary; Literary

Send query only by post with SASE, or by email (no attachments).

Linda Chester & Associates

630 Fifth Avenue, Suite 2000, Rockefeller Center, New York, NY 10111
Tel: +1 (212) 218-3350
Fax: +1 (212) 218-3343
Email: submissions@lindachester.com
Website: http://www.lindachester.com

Handles: Fiction; Nonfiction; *Markets:* Adult; *Treatments:* Commercial; Literary

Send query by email only with short bio and first five pages pasted directly into the body of the email. Response within 4 weeks if interested only. No submissions by post.

The Chudney Agency

72 North State Road, Suite 501, Briarcliff Manor , NY 10510
Tel: +1 (914) 488-5008
Email: mail@thechudneyagency.com
Website: http://www.thechudneyagency.com

Handles: Fiction; *Areas:* Historical; Mystery; Suspense; *Markets:* Children's; Youth; *Treatments:* Commercial; Literary; Mainstream

Handles children's and young adult books. Send query only in first instance. Happy to accept queries by email. Submit material upon invitation only. See website for full guidelines.

Cine/Lit Representation

PO Box 802918, Santa Clarita, CA 91380-2918
Tel: +1 (661) 513-0268
Fax: +1 (661) 513-0915
Email: makier@msn.com

Handles: Fiction; Nonfiction; *Areas:* Adventure; Biography; Culture; Horror; Mystery; Nature; Thrillers; Travel; *Markets:* Adult; *Treatments:* Mainstream; Popular

Handles nonfiction and novels. Send query with SASE. No romance, westerns, or science fiction.

The Collective

8383 Wilshire Boulevard, Suite 1050, Beverly Hills, CA 90211
Tel: +1 (323) 370-1500
Website: http://www.thecollective-la.com

Handles: Scripts; *Areas:* Film; TV; *Markets:* Adult

A full-service entertainment management, media and content production company, with offices in Beverly Hills, New York, Nashville, and San Francisco. Handles scripts for film and TV.

Frances Collin Literary Agent

PO Box 33, Wayne, PA 19087-0033
Tel: +1 (610) 254-0555
Fax: +1 (610) 254-5029
Email: queries@francescollin.com
Website: http://www.francescollin.com

Handles: Fiction; Nonfiction; *Areas:* Autobiography; Biography; Culture; Fantasy; Historical; Nature; Sci-Fi; Travel; Women's Interests; *Markets:* Adult; *Treatments:* Literary

Send query by email (no attachments) or by post with SASE or IRCs if outside the US. No queries by phone or fax.

Don Congdon Associates, Inc.

110 William St. Suite 2202, New York, NY 10038
Tel: +1 (212) 645-1229
Fax: +1 (212) 727-2688
Email: dca@doncongdon.com
Website: http://doncongdon.com

Handles: Fiction; Nonfiction; *Areas:* Adventure; Anthropology; Archaeology; Autobiography; Biography; Cookery; Crime; Culture; Current Affairs; Film; Health; Historical; Humour; Legal; Lifestyle; Literature; Medicine; Military; Music; Mystery; Nature; Politics; Psychology; Science; Technology; Theatre; Thrillers; Travel; Women's Interests; *Markets:* Adult; *Treatments:* Literary; Mainstream

Send query by email (no attachments) or by post with SASE. Include one-page synopsis, relevant background info, and first chapter, all within the body of the email if submitting by email. Include the word "Query" in the subject line. See website for full guidelines. No unsolicited MSS.

Connor Literary Agency

2911 West 71st Street, Minneapolis, MN 55423

Tel: +1 (612) 866-1486
Email: connoragency@aol.com
Website:
http://www.connorliteraryagency.webs.com

Handles: Fiction; Nonfiction; *Areas:* Autobiography; Cookery; Crafts; Crime; Criticism; Culture; Current Affairs; Design; Finance; Health; Historical; Hobbies; Horror; How-to; Humour; Legal; Lifestyle; Literature; Medicine; Photography; Politics; Self-Help; Women's Interests; *Markets:* Adult; Children's; *Treatments:* Contemporary; Literary; Mainstream; Satirical

Send query by email or via contact form on website. Seeking previously published authors and talented new writers. Prefers writers who have or have the potential to gain national exposure through their own efforts. No unsolicited MSS.

The Doe Coover Agency

PO Box 668, Winchester, MA 01890
Tel: +1 (781) 721-6000
Fax: +1 (781) 721-6727
Email: info@doecooveragency.com
Website: http://doecooveragency.com

Handles: Fiction; Nonfiction; Reference; *Areas:* Autobiography; Biography; Business; Cookery; Finance; Gardening; Health; Historical; Music; Politics; Psychology; Science; Sociology; Sport; Technology; *Markets:* Adult; *Treatments:* Commercial; Literary; Popular

Send query by email only with (for nonfiction) a detailed proposal, including overview, table of contents or detailed outline, author biography, and pertinent marketing information; or (for fiction) a detailed synopsis, the first 50 pages, and author bio. Specialises in cookery, general nonfiction (particularly interested in books on social issues), and journalism, as well as both commercial and literary fiction. No children's books, or queries by fax or by post.

CowlesRyan Agency

Email: katherine@cowlesryan.com
Website: http://www.cowlesryan.com

Handles: Fiction; Nonfiction; *Areas:* Arts; Autobiography; Biography; Cookery; Culture; Current Affairs; Historical; Literature; Mystery; Nature; Psychology; Science; Self-Help; Spiritual; *Markets:* Adult; Children's; *Treatments:* Commercial; Contemporary; Literary; Mainstream; Popular; Satirical

We specialise in quality fiction and non-fiction. Our primary areas of interest include literary and selected commercial fiction, history, journalism, culture, biography, memoir, science, natural history, spirituality, cooking, gardening, building and design, and young adult and children's books. We also work with institutions and organisations to develop books and book programs. We do not represent authors in a number of categories, e.g. romance and westerns, and we do not represent screenplays. See website for full submission guidelines.

Crawford Literary Agency

92 Evans Road, Barnstead, NH 03218
Tel: +1 (603) 269-5851
Fax: +1 (603) 269-2533
Email: crawfordlit@att.net

Handles: Fiction; Nonfiction; *Areas:* Adventure; Crime; Entertainment; How-to; Legal; Media; Medicine; Psychology; Romance; Self-Help; Suspense; Thrillers; Women's Interests; *Markets:* Adult; *Treatments:* Commercial

No poetry or short stories. Send query with SASE.

Creative Trust, Inc.

5141 Virginia Way, Suite 320, Brentwood, TN 37027
Tel: +1 (615) 297-5010
Fax: +1 (615) 297-5020
Email: info@creativetrust.com
Website: http://www.creativetrust.com

Handles: Fiction; Scripts; *Areas:* Film; *Markets:* Adult

Literary division founded in 2001 to handle

authors with particular potential in cross-media development, including movie scripts, graphic novels, etc. Accepts queries by email from previously published authors only. No attachments.

Crichton & Associates, Inc.

6940 Carroll Avenue, Takoma Park, MD 20912
Tel: +1 (301) 495-9663
Fax: +1 (202) 318-0050
Email: query@crichton-associates.com
Website: http://crichton-associates.com

Handles: Fiction; Nonfiction; *Areas:* Crime; Culture; Legal; Mystery; Politics; Religious; Romance; Suspense; Women's Interests; *Markets:* Adult; *Treatments:* Literary; Mainstream

Send query by email with description of project and author bio, and proposal for nonfiction or synopsis and first three chapters for fiction, all in the body of the email (no attachments). Indicate in subject line if fiction or nonfiction. Postal submissions also accepted, but include email address for response. No poetry, screenplays, children's, young adult, or science fiction.

Criterion Group, Inc.

4842 Sylmar Avenue , Sherman Oaks, CA 91423
Tel: +1 (818) 995-1485
Fax: +1 (818) 995-1085
Email: info@criterion-group.com
Website: http://www.criterion-group.com

Handles: Scripts; *Areas:* Film; Theatre; *Markets:* Adult

Note: Reports that this agency is not accepting scripts as at July 19, 2013. Check website for current status.

Handles film and stage scripts. Send query by post only. No unsolicited material accepted.

The Croce Agency

PO Box 3161, Fort Lee, NJ 07024
Tel: +1 (201) 248-3175
Email: submissions@thecroceagency.com
Website: http://www.thecroceagency.com

Handles: Fiction; Nonfiction; *Areas:* Autobiography; Biography; Historical; Mystery; Science; Suspense; Thrillers; Travel; Women's Interests; *Markets:* Adult; *Treatments:* Commercial; Literary; Mainstream

Note: not accepting submissions as at February 2013. Check website for current situation.

Represents character-driven upmarket fiction and plot-driven commercial fiction (including chick lit). Also represents narrative nonfiction. Searching for strong, unique writing with commercial appeal, even it falls outside their usual categories of work.

Actively seeking submissions, which must be made by email and include: brief synopsis; word count; stage of completion; explanation of what makes your book unique; first chapter (if written); author credentials.

Curtis Brown Ltd

10 Astor Place, New York, NY 10003
Tel: +1 (212) 473-5400
Fax: +1 (212) 598-0917
Email: gc@cbltd.com
Website: http://www.curtisbrown.com

Handles: Fiction; Nonfiction; *Markets:* Adult; Children's; Youth

Handles material for adults and children in all genres. Send query with SASE, synopsis, CV and a sample chapter. No unsolicited MSS. No scripts.

Richard Curtis Associates, Inc.

171 East 74th Street, Floor 2, New York, NY 10021
Tel: +1 (212) 772-7363
Fax: +1 (212) 772-7393
Email: info@curtisagency.com
Website: http://www.curtisagency.com

Handles: Fiction; Nonfiction; *Areas:*

Autobiography; Biography; Business; Fantasy; Finance; Health; Historical; Medicine; Mystery; Romance; Science; Sci-Fi; Technology; Thrillers; Westerns; *Markets:* Adult; Children's; Youth

Accepts approaches from authors previously published with national publishing houses only.

Laura Dail Literary Agency

350 Seventh Avenue, Suite 2003, New York, NY 10001
Tel: +1 (212) 239-7477
Fax: +1 (212) 947-0460
Email: queries@ldlainc.com
Website: http://www.ldlainc.com

Handles: Fiction; Nonfiction; *Areas:* Autobiography; Biography; Cookery; Crime; Fantasy; Historical; Humour; Mystery; Science; Sci-Fi; Technology; Thrillers; Women's Interests; *Markets:* Adult; Children's; Youth; *Treatments:* Commercial; Light; Literary; Serious

Send query by email (preferred) with the word "query" in the subject line, or by post with SASE. You may optionally include a synopsis and up to 10 pages. Particularly interested in historical and high-concept fiction, funny YA, humour, and serious nonfiction. Also considers graphical novels. No children's picture books, new age, screenplays, poetry, or unsolicited Spanish material.

Daniel Literary Group

1701 Kingsbury Drive, Suite 100, Nashville, TN 37215
Tel: +1 (615) 730-8207
Email: submissions@danielliterarygroup.com
Website: http://www.danielliterarygroup.com

Handles: Nonfiction; *Markets:* Adult

Specialises in nonfiction and is closed to submissions of fiction. No Children's literature, Romance, Science fiction, Screenplays, Poetry, or Short stories. Query by email only, including brief synopsis, key selling points, author biography, and publishing history, all pasted into the body of the email. No attachments, or queries by post or telephone. Response not guranteed if guidelines are not adhered to.

Darhansoff & Verrill Literary Agents

133 West 72nd Street, Room 304, New York, NY 10023
Tel: +1 (917) 305-1300
Fax: +1 (917) 305-1400
Email: submissions@dvagency.com
Website: http://www.dvagency.com

Handles: Fiction; Nonfiction; *Areas:* Mystery; Suspense; *Markets:* Adult; Children's; Youth; *Treatments:* Literary

Particularly interested in literary fiction, narrative nonfiction, memoir, sophisticated suspense, and fiction and nonfiction for younger readers. No theatrical plays or film scripts. Send queries by post or email. See website for full submission guidelines.

Liza Dawson Associates

350 Seventh Avenue, Suite 2003, New York, NY 10001
Tel: +1 (212) 465-9071
Fax: +1 (212) 947-0460
Email: queryliza@LizaDawsonAssociates.com
Website: http://www.lizadawsonassociates.com

Handles: Fiction; Nonfiction; *Areas:* Autobiography; Business; Culture; Current Affairs; Fantasy; Historical; Humour; Lifestyle; Medicine; Military; Mystery; Politics; Psychology; Religious; Romance; Science; Sci-Fi; Self-Help; Sociology; Spiritual; Suspense; Theatre; Thrillers; Women's Interests; *Markets:* Academic; Adult; Children's; Youth; *Treatments:* Commercial; Literary; Mainstream; Popular

See website for specific agent interests and query appropriate agent directly. Specific agent submission guidelines and contact details are available on website.

The Jennifer DeChiara Literary Agency

31 East 32nd Street, Suite 300, New York, NY 10016
Tel: +1 (212) 481-8484
Fax: +1 (212) 481-9582
Email: jenndec@aol.com
Website: http://www.jdlit.com

Handles: Fiction; Nonfiction; *Areas:* Autobiography; Biography; Cookery; Culture; Fantasy; Film; Health; Historical; How-to; Humour; Lifestyle; Literature; Mystery; Science; Self-Help; Sociology; Sport; Suspense; Theatre; Thrillers; Travel; Women's Interests; *Markets:* Adult; Children's; Youth; *Treatments:* Commercial; Contemporary; Literary; Mainstream; Popular

Send query by email only. Posted submissions will be discarded. See website for full guidelines and for specific agent interests and email addresses.

DeFiore and Company

47 East 19th Street, 3rd Floor, New York, NY 10003
Tel: +1 (212) 925-7744
Fax: +1 (212) 925-9803
Email: submissions@defioreandco.com
Website: http://www.defioreandco.com

Handles: Fiction; Nonfiction; *Areas:* Arts; Biography; Culture; Current Affairs; Historical; Lifestyle; Literature; Medicine; Military; Music; Nature; Philosophy; Politics; Psychology; Romance; Science; Short Stories; Sociology; Technology; Thrillers; *Markets:* Adult; Children's; Youth; *Treatments:* Commercial; Literary; Mainstream

Always looking for exciting, fresh, new talent, and currently accepting queries for both fiction and nonfiction. Send query with summary, description of why you're writing the book, any specific credentials, and (for fiction) first five pages. Send by email (with all material in the body of the text; no attachments; and the word "Query" in the subject line) or post with SASE. See website for specific agent interests and methods of approach. No scripts for film, TV, or theatre.

Joëlle Delbourgo Associates, Inc.

101 Park St., Montclair, Montclair, NJ 07042
Tel: +1 (973) 773-0836
Email: submissions@delbourgo.com
Website: http://www.delbourgo.com

Handles: Fiction; Nonfiction; Reference; *Areas:* Autobiography; Biography; Business; Culture; Current Affairs; Fantasy; Health; Historical; Lifestyle; Mystery; Psychology; Science; Sci-Fi; Thrillers; Women's Interests; *Markets:* Adult; Children's; Youth; *Treatments:* Commercial; Popular

We are a highly selective agency, broad in our interests. No category romance, Westerns, early readers, or picture books. Send query by email to specific agent (see website for interests and email addresses) or to generic submissions address. Submittions must include the word "QUERY" in the subject line. See website for full guidelines.

Sandra Dijkstra Literary Agency

PMB 515, 1155 Camino Del Mar, Del Mar, CA 92014
Tel: +1 (858) 755-3115
Fax: +1 (858) 794-2822
Email: queries@dijkstraagency.com
Website: http://www.dijkstraagency.com

Handles: Fiction; Nonfiction; *Areas:* Autobiography; Business; Cookery; Culture; Current Affairs; Design; Fantasy; Health; Historical; Humour; Lifestyle; Music; Mystery; Politics; Religious; Romance; Science; Sci-Fi; Self-Help; Short Stories; Sociology; Sport; Thrillers; Travel; Women's Interests; *Markets:* Adult; Children's; Youth; *Treatments:* Commercial; Contemporary; Literary

Check author bios on website and submit query by email to one agent only. For fiction, include a one-page synopsis, brief bio, and first 10-15 pages. For nonfiction, include overview, chapter outline, brief bio, and first 10-15 pages. All material must be in the body of the email. No attachments. See website for full submission guidelines.

Janis A. Donnaud & Associates, Inc.

525 Broadway, 2nd Floor, New York, NY 10012
Tel: +1 (212) 431-2664
Fax: +1 (212) 431-2667
Email: jdonnaud@aol.com

Handles: Nonfiction; *Areas:* Beauty and Fashion; Biography; Business; Cookery; Finance; Gardening; Health; Lifestyle; Science; Sport; Travel; Women's Interests; *Markets:* Adult

The agency represents, develops, and packages a wide range of commercially successful properties. It negotiates publishing agreements with the top trade houses in the U.S., licenses all subsidiary rights, arranges foreign editions and translation rights, and licenses film and performance rights. The agency has a working relationship with Artists Agency to handle television clients. The agency's varied list is concentrated mainly on nonfiction, with a special emphasis on the culinary.

Jim Donovan Literary

5635 SMU Boulevard, Suite 201, Dallas, TX 75206
Email: jdliterary@sbcglobal.net

Handles: Fiction; Nonfiction; Reference; *Areas:* Adventure; Autobiography; Biography; Business; Crime; Culture; Current Affairs; Finance; Health; Historical; How-to; Legal; Lifestyle; Medicine; Military; Music; Mystery; Nature; Politics; Sport; Suspense; Thrillers; Women's Interests; *Markets:* Adult; *Treatments:* Commercial; Contemporary; Literary; Mainstream; Popular

Send query with SASE or by email. For fiction, include first 30-50 pages and a 2-5 page outline. Handles mainly nonfiction, and specialises in commercial fiction and nonfiction. No poetry, children's, short stories, or inspirational.

Doyen Literary Services, Inc.

1931 660th Street, Newell, IA 50568-7613
Tel: +1 (712) 272-3300
Email: bestseller@barbaradoyen.com
Website: http://www.barbaradoyen.com

Handles: Nonfiction; *Areas:* Anthropology; Archaeology; Architecture; Arts; Autobiography; Biography; Business; Cookery; Crafts; Crime; Culture; Current Affairs; Design; Film; Finance; Gardening; Health; How-to; Leisure; Lifestyle; Politics; Psychology; Science; Self-Help; Sociology; Technology; Theatre; Women's Interests; *Markets:* Adult

Send query by email. Handles adult trade nonfiction only. No poetry, screenplays, children's books, or teen books.

Dunham Literary, Inc.

110 William Street, Suite 2202, New York, NY 10038
Tel: +1 (212) 929-0994
Fax: +1 (212) 929-0904
Email: query@dunhamlit.com
Website: http://www.dunhamlit.com

Handles: Fiction; Nonfiction; *Areas:* Autobiography; Biography; Culture; Current Affairs; Fantasy; Historical; Lifestyle; Music; Nature; Politics; Science; Sci-Fi; Spiritual; Technology; Travel; Women's Interests; *Markets:* Adult; Children's; Youth; *Treatments:* Literary

Handles quality fiction and nonfiction for adults and children. Send query by email or by post with SASE. See website for full guidelines. No genre romance, Westerns, poetry, or approaches by phone or fax. No email attachments.

Dystel & Goderich Literary Management

One Union Square West, Suite 904, New York, NY 10003
Tel: +1 (212) 627-9100
Fax: +1 (212) 627-9313
Email: miriam@dystel.com
Website: http://www.dystel.com

Handles: Fiction; Nonfiction; *Areas:*

Adventure; Anthropology; Archaeology; Autobiography; Biography; Business; Cookery; Crime; Culture; Current Affairs; Fantasy; Finance; Health; Historical; Humour; Lifestyle; Military; Mystery; New Age; Politics; Psychology; Religious; Romance; Science; Sci-Fi; Spiritual; Suspense; Technology; Thrillers; Women's Interests; *Markets:* Adult; Children's; Youth; *Treatments:* Commercial; Contemporary; Literary; Mainstream; Popular

Prefers email approaches, but will also still accept queries by post with brief synopsis and sample chapter with SASE. Email queries should include the cover letter in the body of the email, and synopsis and sample material (a chapter or the first 25 pages) either below the query letter or in an attached document. Attachments to blank emails will not be opened.. Queries should be brief, devoid of gimmicks, and professionally presented, including author details and any writing credits. See website for more details.

Eames Literary Services, LLC

4117 Hillsboro Road, Suite 251, Nashville, TN 37215
Fax: +1 (615) 463-9361
Email: info@eamesliterary.com
Website: http://www.eamesliterary.com

Handles: Fiction; Nonfiction; *Areas:* Religious; *Markets:* Adult; Youth

Handles adult and young adult fiction and nonfiction that supports a Christian perspective on life. Send query by email with book proposal; author bio (including publishing history); plot synopsis or chapter summary; and 2-3 chapters of sample content (attached as a Microsoft Word document). Incomplete enquiries will not be responded to. No queries by post.

Anne Edelstein Literary Agency

404 Riverside Drive, New York, NY 10025
Tel: +1 (212) 414-4923
Fax: +1 (212) 414-2930
Email: info@aeliterary.com
Website: http://www.aeliterary.com

Handles: Fiction; Nonfiction; *Areas:* Autobiography; Historical; Psychology; Religious; *Markets:* Adult; *Treatments:* Commercial; Literary

Note: Note accepting approaches as at August 2014

Send query letter with SASE and for fiction a summary of your novel plus the first 25 pages, or for nonfiction an outline of your book and one or two sample chapters. No queries by email.

Ethan Ellenberg Literary Agency

548 Broadway, #5E, New York, NY 10012
Tel: +1 (212) 431-4554
Fax: +1 (212) 941-4652
Email: agent@ethanellenberg.com
Website: http://www.ethanellenberg.com

Handles: Fiction; Nonfiction; *Areas:* Adventure; Autobiography; Biography; Cookery; Crime; Culture; Current Affairs; Fantasy; Health; Historical; Mystery; New Age; Psychology; Romance; Science; Sci-Fi; Spiritual; Thrillers; Women's Interests; *Markets:* Adult; Children's; *Treatments:* Commercial; Literary

Actively looking for established and new writers in a wide range of genres. Send query by email (no attachments; paste material into the body of the email) or by post with SASE. For fiction send synopsis and first 50 pages. For nonfiction send proposal, author bio, and sample chapters. For picture books send complete MS. No poetry, short stories, scripts, or queries by fax.

We have been in business for over 17 years. We are a member of the AAR. We accept unsolicited submissions and, of course, do not charge reading fees.

Nicholas Ellison, Inc.

55 Fifth Avenue, 15th Floor, New York, NY 10003
Tel: +1 (212) 206-5600
Fax: +1 (212) 436-8718
Email: nellison@sjga.com
Website: http://www.greenburger.com

Handles: Fiction; Nonfiction; *Markets:* Adult; *Treatments:* Literary; Mainstream

Represents primarily fiction, along with a select list of nonfiction. Send queries by email including brief descriptiona and any relevant credentials in the body of the email, and attach at least 50 pages along with any other relevant material. Assume rejection if no response within 6 weeks.

Ann Elmo Agency, Inc.

305 Seventh Avenue, #1101, New York, NY 10001
Tel: +1 (212) 661-2880
Fax: +1 (212) 661-2883
Email: aalitagent@aol.com

Handles: Fiction; Nonfiction; *Areas:* Biography; Culture; Current Affairs; Gothic; Health; Historical; How-to; Romance; Science; Thrillers; Women's Interests; *Markets:* Adult; Family; *Treatments:* Contemporary; Mainstream

No unsolicited mss.

Energy Entertainment

9107 Wilshire Boulevard, 6th Floor, Los Angeles, CA 90069
Email: info@energyentertainment.net
Website: http://www.energyentertainment.net

Handles: Scripts; *Areas:* Film; TV; *Markets:* Adult

Agency specialising in discovering new and edgy screenwriters. No unsolicited MSS or calls; send query only.

Evatopia, Inc.

8447 Wilshire Boulevard, Suite 401, Beverly Hills, CA 90211
Email: submissions@evatopia.com
Website: http://www.evatopia.com

Handles: Fiction; Nonfiction; Scripts; *Areas:* Adventure; Autobiography; Biography; Crime; Drama; Fantasy; Film; Historical; Horror; Humour; Mystery; Romance; Sport; Suspense; Thrillers; Women's Interests; *Markets:* Adult; Children's; Youth; *Treatments:* Contemporary; Mainstream

Send query by email only. Handles scripts, TV/reality series; fictionl graphic novels, nonfiction, and music, aimed at women, teens, and children. See website for full guidelines.

Fairbank Literary Representation

P.O. Box 6, Hudson, NY 12534-0006
Tel: +1 (617) 576-0030
Fax: +1 (617) 576-0030
Email: queries@fairbankliterary.com
Website: http://www.fairbankliterary.com

Handles: Fiction; Nonfiction; Reference; *Areas:* Architecture; Biography; Cookery; Culture; Design; Humour; Lifestyle; Mystery; Science; Sport; Thrillers; *Markets:* Adult; *Treatments:* Literary; Mainstream

No romance, poetry, screenplays, science fiction or fantasy, paranormal, young adult, children's books, or novels set before 1900. Send one-page query outlining work by post or email. If sending by post a sample chapter may be included, plus SASE if return is required. If sending by email, do not include attachments, but you may include up to the first three pages pasted into the email. No queries by fax, or phone calls. Works over 120,000 by unpublished authors are probably too long to be accepted.

Farris Literary Agency, Inc.

PO Box 570069, Dallas, Texas 75357-0069
Tel: +1 (972) 203-8804
Email: farris1@airmail.net
Website: http://www.farrisliterary.com

Handles: Fiction; Nonfiction; Scripts; *Areas:* Adventure; Autobiography; Biography; Business; Crime; Culture; Current Affairs; Entertainment; Finance; Health; Historical; How-to; Humour; Legal; Lifestyle; Military; Music; Mystery; Politics; Religious; Romance; Self-Help; Spiritual; Sport; Suspense; Thrillers; Travel; Women's Interests; *Markets:* Adult; *Treatments:* Mainstream; Satirical

NOTE: As at April 2, 2013, only accepting submissions by referral or writers' conferences. Check website for current status.

Send query by post with SASE, or by email. Include title, description of project, author bio, and (for fiction) the genre and word count, or (for nonfiction) the type of book and your qualifications for writing it. No science fiction, fantasy, gay and lesbian, erotica, young adult, children's, or email attachments.

The Fielding Agency, LLC

269 South Beverly Drive, #341, Beverly Hills, CA 90212
Tel: +1 (323) 461-4791
Email: wlee@fieldingagency.com
Website: http://fieldingagency.com

Handles: Fiction; Nonfiction; *Areas:* Adventure; Anthropology; Archaeology; Architecture; Arts; Autobiography; Biography; Business; Cookery; Crafts; Crime; Culture; Current Affairs; Design; Fantasy; Finance; Health; Historical; Horror; How-to; Humour; Legal; Lifestyle; Literature; Medicine; Military; Mystery; Nature; Politics; Psychology; Romance; Science; Self-Help; Short Stories; Sociology; Sport; Technology; Thrillers; Translations; Women's Interests; *Markets:* Adult; Children's; Youth; *Treatments:* Literary; Mainstream; Satirical

Send query with SASE or by email (no attachments), including detailed outline / proposal of your book, and brief description of your writing background. Handles all genres of fiction and nonfiction, but need to feel passionately about a book to accept it. Handles film rights to books already represented only. No screenplays or queries by phone.

Diana Finch Literary Agency

116 West 23rd Street, Suite 500, New York, NY 10011
Tel: +1 (917) 544-4470
Email: diana.finch@verizon.net
Website: http://dianafinchliteraryagency.blogspot.com

Handles: Fiction; Nonfiction; *Areas:* Adventure; Autobiography; Biography; Business; Crime; Culture; Current Affairs; Film; Finance; Health; Historical; How-to; Humour; Legal; Lifestyle; Medicine; Military; Music; Nature; Photography; Politics; Psychology; Science; Self-Help; Sport; Technology; Theatre; Thrillers; Translations; Women's Interests; *Markets:* Academic; Adult; Youth; *Treatments:* Literary; Mainstream; Satirical

Approach using online submission system – see website for link. Particularly interested in narrative nonfiction, health, and popular science, however actively looking for new fiction to balance the list. No children's picture books, romance, or mysteries.

Fine Literary

1236 Comstock Avenue, Los Angeles, CA 90024
Email: asst@FineLiterary.com
Website: http://www.FineLiterary.com

Handles: Fiction; Nonfiction; *Areas:* Adventure; Antiques; Architecture; Arts; Autobiography; Beauty and Fashion; Biography; Business; Cookery; Crafts; Crime; Culture; Current Affairs; Design; Drama; Entertainment; Gardening; Health; Historical; How-to; Humour; Leisure; Lifestyle; Literature; Men's Interests; Music; Mystery; Psychology; Romance; Science; Self-Help; Spiritual; Sport; Suspense; Technology; Theatre; Thrillers; Travel; Women's Interests; *Markets:* Adult; Youth; *Treatments:* Commercial; Contemporary; Cynical; Dark; Light; Literary; Mainstream; Niche; Popular; Positive; Progressive; Satirical; Serious; Traditional

Literary agency based in Los Angeles, focused on the development of Literary careers.

Interested in queries of all kinds: from Romance and Thrillers to Literary Fiction and Cookbooks. Our interests are vast but our attention is micro-focused on selling your work to the right publisher.

Accepts submissions by post or by email. Send query with brief synopsis along with first 20 pages for fiction, or details of why you are writing the book and its place in the market for nonfiction. See website for full guidelines. Response to email queries not guaranteed.

FinePrint Literary Management

115 West 29th Street, 3rd Floor, New York, NY 10001
Tel: +1 (212) 279-1282
Email: peter@fineprintlit.com
Website: http://www.fineprintlit.com

Handles: Fiction; Nonfiction; Reference; *Areas:* Autobiography; Beauty and Fashion; Biography; Business; Cookery; Crime; Culture; Entertainment; Fantasy; Health; Historical; Horror; How-to; Humour; Lifestyle; Military; Music; Mystery; Nature; Religious; Romance; Science; Sci-Fi; Self-Help; Spiritual; Suspense; Technology; Thrillers; Travel; Women's Interests; *Markets:* Adult; Children's; Youth; *Treatments:* Contemporary; Dark; Literary; Serious

Consult agent profiles on website for individual interests and approach appropriate agent for your work. Send query by email (no attachments) with proposal and sample chapters for nonfiction, or synopsis and first two chapters for fiction.

Flannery Literary

1140 Wickfield Court, Naperville, IL 60563-3300
Tel: +1 (630) 428-2682
Fax: +1 (630) 428-2683
Email: jennifer@flanneryliterary.com
Website: http://flanneryliterary.com

Handles: Fiction; Nonfiction; *Markets:* Children's; Youth

Send query with SASE. Deals exclusively in children's and young adults' fiction and nonfiction, including picture books. No queries by fax or email. See website for full guidelines.

Peter Fleming Agency

PO Box 458, Pacific Palisades, CA 90272
Tel: +1 (310) 454-1373
Email: peterfleming@earthlink.net

Handles: Nonfiction; *Markets:* Adult; *Treatments:* Commercial

Send query with SASE. Seeks one-of-a-kind nonfiction books that unearth innovative and uncomfortable truths, and which have bestseller potential. Must be backed up by author's expertise in given area.

Fletcher & Company

78 Fifth Avenue, Third Floor, New York, NY 10011
Tel: +1 (212) 614-0778
Fax: +1 (212) 614-0728
Email: info@fletcherandco.com
Website: http://www.fletcherandco.com

Handles: Fiction; Nonfiction; *Areas:* Autobiography; Biography; Business; Current Affairs; Health; Historical; Humour; Lifestyle; Science; Sport; Travel; *Markets:* Adult; Youth; *Treatments:* Commercial; Literary

Full-service literary agency representing writers of nonfiction and commercial and literary fiction. Send query with brief synopsis by post with SASE, or by email (no attachments). No genre fiction. Query only one agent at a time and allow 4-6 weeks before following up.

Folio Literary Management, LLC

630 9th Avenue, Suite 1101 , New York, NY 10036
Email: jeff@foliolit.com
Website: http://www.foliolit.com

Handles: Fiction; Nonfiction; Reference; *Areas:* Autobiography; Business; Cookery; Crime; Culture; Entertainment; Fantasy; Health; Historical; Horror; How-to; Humour; Lifestyle; Media; Military; Music; Mystery; Politics; Psychology; Religious; Romance; Science; Sci-Fi; Self-Help; Spiritual; Sport; Suspense; Technology; Thrillers; Women's Interests; *Markets:* Adult; Children's; Youth;

Treatments: Commercial; Contemporary; Dark; Literary; Popular; Serious

Read agent bios on website and decide which agent to approach. Do not submit to multiple agents simultaneously. Each agent has different submission requirements: consult website for details. No unsolicited MSS or multiple submissions.

Foundry Literary + Media

33 West 17th Street, PH, New York, NY 10011
Tel: +1 (212) 929-5064
Fax: +1 (212) 929-5471
Email: info@foundrymedia.com
Website: http://www.foundrymedia.com

Handles: Fiction; Nonfiction; *Areas:* Adventure; Autobiography; Biography; Business; Culture; Current Affairs; Health; Historical; How-to; Humour; Lifestyle; Music; Psychology; Religious; Science; Sci-Fi; Sport; Thrillers; Travel; Women's Interests; *Markets:* Adult; Children's; Youth; *Treatments:* Commercial; Literary; Niche; Popular

Queries should be addressed to a specific agent (see website) and sent by email or by post with SASE, according to requirements of individual agent (se website). For fiction queries, send letter with synopsis, First Three Chapters of Manuscript, and Author Bio. For nonfiction approaches send letter with Sample Chapters, Table of Contents, and Author Bio.

Fox Chase Agency, Inc.

701 Lee Road, Suite 102, Chesterbrook Corporate Center, Chesterbrook, PA 19087

Handles: Fiction; Nonfiction; *Markets:* Adult

Handles novels and nonfiction. Send query with SASE.

Jeanne Fredericks Literary Agency, Inc.

221 Benedict Hill Road, New Canaan, CT 06840
Tel: +1 (203) 972-3011
Fax: +1 (203) 972-3011
Email: jeanne.fredericks@gmail.com
Website: http://jeannefredericks.com

Handles: Nonfiction; Reference; *Areas:* Antiques; Arts; Biography; Business; Cookery; Crafts; Design; Finance; Gardening; Health; Historical; How-to; Legal; Leisure; Lifestyle; Medicine; Nature; Photography; Psychology; Science; Self-Help; Sport; Travel; Women's Interests; *Markets:* Adult

Send query by email (no attachments) or post with SASE. Specialises in adult nonfiction by authorities in their fields. No fiction, true crime, juvenile, textbooks, poetry, essays, screenplays, short stories, science fiction, pop culture, guides to computers and software, politics, horror, pornography, books on overly depressing or violent topics, romance, teacher's manuals, or memoirs. See website for full guidelines.

Grace Freedson's Publishing Network

375 North Broadway, Suite 102, Jericho, NY 11753
Tel: +1 (516) 931-7757
Fax: +1 (516) 931-7759
Email: gfreedson@worldnet.att.net

Handles: Nonfiction; *Areas:* Business; Cookery; Crafts; Culture; Current Affairs; Finance; Health; Historical; Hobbies; How-to; Humour; Lifestyle; Medicine; Nature; Psychology; Religious; Science; Self-Help; Sport; Technology; *Markets:* Adult; Children's; Youth

Handles nonfiction from qualified authors with credentials and platforms only. No fiction. Send query with synopsis and SASE.

Samuel French, Inc.

235 Park Avenue South, Fifth Floor, New York, NY 10003
Tel: +1 (212) 206-8990
Fax: +1 (212) 206-1429
Email: info@samuelfrench.com
Website: http://www.samuelfrench.com

Handles: Scripts; *Areas:* Crime; Fantasy; Horror; Humour; Mystery; Theatre; Thrillers; *Markets:* Adult

Note: Not accepting unsolicited submissions as at March 2015

Publishes plays and represents writers of plays. Deals in well-known plays from Broadway and London's West End.

Sarah Jane Freymann Literary Agency

59 West 71st Street, New York, NY 10023
Tel: +1 (212) 362-9277
Fax: +1 (212) 501-8240
Email: Submissions@SarahJaneFreymann.com
Website: http://www.sarahjanefreymann.com

Handles: Fiction; Nonfiction; *Areas:* Autobiography; Business; Cookery; Crime; Culture; Health; Historical; Humour; Lifestyle; Men's Interests; Nature; Psychology; Science; Self-Help; Spiritual; Sport; Thrillers; Travel; Women's Interests; *Markets:* Adult; Youth; *Treatments:* Literary; Mainstream

Prefers to receive queries by email. Include pitch letter and first ten pages pasted into the body of the email (no attachments). See website for full details.

Full Throttle Literary Agency

P.O.Box 5, Greenwich, Ohio 44837
Tel: +1 (419) 752-0444
Email: fullthrottlelit@aol.com
Website: http://www.fullthrottleliterary.com

Handles: Fiction; Scripts; *Areas:* Adventure; Drama; Film; Horror; Humour; Mystery; Short Stories; Suspense; Thrillers; Westerns; *Markets:* Adult; Children's; Family; *Treatments:* Contemporary; Light; Mainstream; Traditional

We are an independent agency that specializes in fiction material. Accepting new clients for manuscripts,screenplays and short stories. No e-mail queries. Send query through regular mail along with S.A.S.E. and short bio.

The G Agency, LLC

PO Box 374, Bronx, NY 10471
Tel: +1 (718) 664-4505
Email: gagencyquery@gmail.com

Handles: Fiction; Nonfiction; *Areas:* Biography; Business; Culture; Finance; Historical; Military; Mystery; Sport; Technology; *Markets:* Adult; *Treatments:* Commercial; Literary; Mainstream; Serious

Send queries by post or by email (prefers email submissions) with sample chapters or proposal. Write "QUERY" in the subject line or on the envelope of postal queries. Email submissions get priority. No screenplays, sci-fi, or romance.

Don Gastwirth & Associates

265 College Street, New Haven, CT 06510
Tel: +1 (203) 562-7600
Fax: +1 (203) 562-4300
Email: Donlit@snet.net

Handles: Fiction; Nonfiction; *Areas:* Business; Crime; Culture; Current Affairs; Historical; Military; Music; Mystery; Nature; Psychology; Thrillers; Translations; *Markets:* Academic; Adult

Highly selective agency which rarely takes on clients who are not referred to the agency by an industry professional.

Gelfman Schneider Literary Agents, Inc.

850 Seventh Avenue, Suite 903, New York, NY 10019
Tel: +1 (212) 245-1993
Email: mail@gelfmanschneider.com
Website: http://www.gelfmanschneider.com

Handles: Fiction; Nonfiction; *Areas:* Autobiography; Culture; Current Affairs; Historical; Mystery; Politics; Science; Suspense; Thrillers; Women's Interests; *Markets:* Adult; *Treatments:* Commercial; Literary; Mainstream; Popular

Different agents within the agency have different submission guidelines. See website for full details. No screenplays, or poetry.

The Gernert Company

136 East 57th Street, New York, NY 10022
Tel: +1 (212) 838-7777
Fax: +1 (212) 838-6020
Email: info@thegernertco.com
Website: http://www.thegernertco.com

Handles: Fiction; Nonfiction; *Areas:* Adventure; Arts; Autobiography; Biography; Crafts; Current Affairs; Fantasy; Historical; Politics; Science; Sci-Fi; Sociology; Sport; Thrillers; *Markets:* Academic; Adult; Children's; Youth; *Treatments:* Commercial; Literary; Popular

Send query describing work by post with SASE or email with author info and sample chapter. If querying by email, send to generic email and indicate which agent you would like to query. No queries by fax. Response only if interested.

Global Lion Intellectual Property Management, Inc.

PO BOX 669238, Pompano Beach, FL 33066
Email: queriesgloballionmgt@gmail.com
Website: http://www.globallionmanagement.com

Handles: Fiction; Nonfiction; *Markets:* Adult

Looks for cutting-edge authors of both fiction and nonfiction with global marketing and motion picture/television production potential. Authors must not only have a great book and future, but also a specific game-plan of how to use social media to grow their fan base. Send query by email only with synopsis, up to 20 pages if available (otherwise, chapter synopsis), author bio, and any social media outlets. See website for full details.

Frances Goldin Literary Agency, Inc.

57 E. 11th Street, Suite 5B, New York, NY 10003
Tel: +1 (212) 777-0047
Fax: +1 (212) 228-1660
Email: agency@goldinlit.com
Website: http://www.goldinlit.com

Handles: Fiction; Nonfiction; *Areas:* Arts; Autobiography; Culture; Current Affairs; Entertainment; Film; Historical; Nature; Philosophy; Science; Sociology; Sport; Technology; *Markets:* Adult; Children's; Youth; *Treatments:* Commercial; Literary; Progressive

Submit through online system available at website. No screenplays, illustrated books, genre fiction, romance, science fiction, cookery, business, diet, racism, sexism, ageism, homophobia, or pornography.

Goodman Associates

500 West End Avenue, New York, NY 10024
Tel: +1 (212) 873-4806

Handles: Fiction; Nonfiction; *Areas:* Adventure; Anthropology; Archaeology; Autobiography; Biography; Business; Cookery; Crime; Criticism; Culture; Current Affairs; Erotic; Film; Finance; Health; Historical; Legal; Leisure; Literature; Medicine; Military; Music; Mystery; Nature; Philosophy; Politics; Psychology; Science; Sociology; Sport; Suspense; Technology; Theatre; Thrillers; Translations; Travel; Women's Interests; *Markets:* Adult; *Treatments:* Contemporary; Literary; Mainstream

Send query with SASE. Accepting new clients by recommendation only. No poetry, articles, children's, young adult, or individual stories.

Sanford J. Greenburger Associates, Inc

15th Floor, 55 Fifth Avenue, New York, NY 10003
Tel: +1 (212) 206-5600
Fax: +1 (212) 463-8718
Email: queryHL@sjga.com
Website: http://www.greenburger.com

Handles: Fiction; Nonfiction; Reference; *Areas:* Arts; Autobiography; Biography; Business; Entertainment; Fantasy; Health; Historical; Humour; Lifestyle; Music;

Mystery; Nature; Politics; Psychology; Romance; Science; Sci-Fi; Self-Help; Sociology; Sport; Thrillers; Women's Interests; *Markets:* Adult; Children's; Youth; *Treatments:* Commercial; Literary; Popular

Check website for specific agent interests, guidelines, and contact details. Most will not accept submissions by post. Aims to respond to queries within 6-8 weeks.

Blanche C. Gregory Inc.

2 Tudor City Place, New York, NY 10017
Tel: +1 (212) 697-0828
Email: info@bcgliteraryagency.com
Website: http://www.bcgliteraryagency.com

Handles: Fiction; Nonfiction; *Markets:* Adult; Children's

Specialises in adult fiction and nonfiction, but will also consider children's literature. Send query describing your background with SASE and synopsis. No stage, film or TV scripts, or queries by fax or email.

Greyhaus Literary Agency

3021 20th St. Pl. SW, Puyallup, WA 98373
Email: scott@greyhausagency.com
Website: http://www.greyhausagency.com

Handles: Fiction; *Areas:* Historical; Romance; Suspense; Women's Interests; *Markets:* Adult; *Treatments:* Contemporary; Traditional

ONLY focuses on traditional romance and traditional women's fiction.

Opens to submissions on May 20, 2013.

We only focus on Romance Writers in the following sub-genres: Contemporary, Mainstream Paranormal/Time Travel, Regency, Historical, Inspirational, Romantic Suspense. Send query by email or through submission form on website. Only considers writers with completed manuscript ready for publication. No Fantasy, Single Title Inspirational, YA or Middle Grade, Picture Books, Memoirs, Biographies, Erotica, Urban Fantasy, Science Fiction, Screenplays, Poetry, Authors interested in only e-publishing or self-publishing, or Works that have already been published.

Jill Grosjean Literary Agency

1390 Millstone Road, Sag Harbor, NY 11963-2214
Tel: +1 (631) 725-7419
Fax: +1 (631) 725-8632
Email: JillLit310@aol.com

Handles: Fiction; *Areas:* Crime; Gardening; Historical; Humour; Mystery; Nature; Romance; Suspense; Thrillers; Travel; Women's Interests; *Markets:* Adult; Literary

Prefers email queries. No attachments. Particularly interested in literary novels and mysteries. Editorial assistance offered.

The Mitchell J. Hamilburg Agency

149 South Barrington Avenue #732, Los Angeles, CA 90049-2930
Tel: +1 (310) 471-4024
Fax: +1 (310) 471-9588

Handles: Fiction; Nonfiction; Poetry; *Areas:* Adventure; Anthropology; Architecture; Autobiography; Biography; Business; Cookery; Crime; Current Affairs; Fantasy; Finance; Gardening; Health; Historical; Horror; Humour; Leisure; Lifestyle; Military; Mystery; Nature; New Age; Politics; Psychology; Religious; Romance; Science; Sci-Fi; Self-Help; Short Stories; Sociology; Spiritual; Sport; Suspense; Thrillers; Travel; Women's Interests; *Markets:* Adult; Children's; *Treatments:* Experimental; Literary; Mainstream

Send query with SASE, outline, and 2 sample chapters.

Hannigan Salky Getzler (HSG) Agency

37 West 28th St, 8th floor, New York, NY 10001
Tel: +1 (646) 442-5770
Email: channigan@hsgagency.com
Website: http://hsgagency.com

Handles: Fiction; Nonfiction; *Areas:*

Adventure; Business; Cookery; Current Affairs; Finance; Historical; Lifestyle; Mystery; Photography; Politics; Psychology; Science; Sociology; Thrillers; Travel; Women's Interests; *Markets:* Adult; Children's; Youth; *Treatments:* Commercial; Literary

Send query by email only with first five pages pasted into the body of hte email (no attachments), or the full ms for picture books. See website for agent interests and individual email addresses, and contact one agent only. No screenplays, romance fiction, science fiction, or religious fiction.

Joy Harris Literary Agency, Inc.

381 Park Avenue South, Suite 428, New York, NY 10016
Tel: +1 (212) 924-6269
Fax: +1 (212) 725-5275
Email: submissions@joyharrisliterary.com
Website: http://www.joyharrisliterary.com

Handles: Fiction; Nonfiction; *Areas:* Autobiography; Biography; Culture; Historical; Humour; Media; Mystery; Short Stories; Spiritual; Suspense; Translations; Women's Interests; *Markets:* Adult; Youth; *Treatments:* Experimental; Literary; Mainstream; Satirical

Send query by post with SASE or by email, including sample chapter or outline. Prefers submissions by email. No poetry, screenplays, genre fiction, self-help, or unsolicited mss.

John Hawkins & Associates, Inc.

80 Maiden Lane, STE 1503, New York, NY 10038
Tel: +1 (212) 807-7040
Fax: +1 (212) 807-9555
Email: jha@jhalit.com
Website: http://www.jhalit.com

Handles: Fiction; Nonfiction; *Areas:* Autobiography; Biography; Business; Crime; Current Affairs; Fantasy; Gardening; Health; Historical; Lifestyle; Mystery; Nature; Politics; Psychology; Science; Sci-Fi; Short Stories; Technology; Thrillers; Travel; Women's Interests; *Markets:* Adult

Send query by email with details about you and your writing, and for fiction the first three chapters as a single Word attachment, or for nonfiction include proposal as a single attachment. Include the word "Query" in the subject line. See website for full guidelines.

Heacock Hill Literary Agency, LLC

1020 Hollywood Way, #439, Burbank, CA 91505
Tel: +1 (818) 951-6788
Email: Agent@HeacockHill.com
Website: http://www.heacockliteraryagency.com

Handles: Fiction; Nonfiction; *Areas:* Anthropology; Arts; Business; Crafts; Culture; Gardening; Health; Lifestyle; Nature; Politics; Science; Spiritual; *Markets:* Adult; Children's; Youth

Fiction: Juvenile, middle grade children's, picture books, young adult. No juvenile nonfiction. No adult fiction at this time. Please check website for updates. Open to all kinds of adult nonfiction, particularly those outlined above. Query by email only. See website for full details.

The Jeff Herman Agency, LLC

PO Box 1522, Stockbridge, MA 01262
Tel: +1 (413) 298-0077
Fax: +1 (413) 298-8188
Email: submissions@jeffherman.com
Website: http://www.jeffherman.com

Handles: Nonfiction; Reference; *Areas:* Autobiography; Business; Crime; Culture; Health; Historical; How-to; Lifestyle; Psychology; Self-Help; Spiritual; *Markets:* Academic; Adult

Send query by post with SASE, or by email. With few exceptions, handles nonfiction only, with particular interest in the genres given above. No scripts or unsolicited MSS.

Hill Nadell Literary Agency

8899 Beverly Bl., Suite 805, Los Angeles, CA 90048
Tel: +1 (310) 860-9605
Fax: +1 (310) 860-9672
Email: queries@hillnadell.com
Website: http://www.hillnadell.com

Handles: Fiction; Nonfiction; *Areas:* Autobiography; Biography; Cookery; Culture; Current Affairs; Health; Historical; Legal; Nature; Politics; Science; Thrillers; Women's Interests; *Markets:* Adult; Youth; *Treatments:* Literary; Mainstream

Handles current affairs, food, memoirs and other narrative nonfiction, fiction, thrillers, upmarket women's fiction, literary fiction, genre fiction, graphic novels, and occasional young adult novels. No scripts or screenplays. Accepts queries both by post and by email. See website for full submission guidelines.

Hopkins Literary Associates

2117 Buffalo Road, Ste. 327, Rochester, NY 14624
Tel: +1 (585) 352-6268
Email: hlasubmissions@rochester.rr.com

Handles: Fiction; *Areas:* Historical; Romance; Women's Interests; *Markets:* Adult; Youth; *Treatments:* Contemporary; Mainstream

Send query by email only. Specialises in women's fiction, particularly historical and contemporary romance. No queries by fax or email.

Hornfischer Literary Management, L.P.

PO Box 50544, Austin, Texas 78763
Email: queries@hornfischerlit.com
Website: http://www.hornfischerlit.com

Handles: Nonfiction; *Areas:* Anthropology; Archaeology; Autobiography; Biography; Business; Crime; Culture; Current Affairs; Finance; Health; Historical; How-to; Humour; Legal; Lifestyle; Medicine; Military; Nature; Politics; Psychology; Religious; Science; Self-Help; Sociology; Sport; Technology; *Markets:* Adult; *Treatments:* Commercial; Satirical; Serious

Send query by email, or by post with SASE. Response to email queries only if interested.

Hudson Agency

3 Travis Lane, Montrose, NY 10548
Tel: +1 (914) 737-1475
Fax: +1 (914) 736-3064
Email: hudsonagency@optonline.net
Website: http://www.hudsonagency.net

Handles: Scripts; *Areas:* Crime; Drama; Fantasy; Film; Humour; Mystery; Romance; TV; Westerns; *Markets:* Adult; Children's; Family; Youth; *Treatments:* Contemporary

Send query with SASE. Most new clients taken on by recommendation from industry professionals.

Andrea Hurst Literary Management

PO Box 1467, Coupeville, WA 98239
Email: info@andreahurst.com
Website: http://www.andreahurst.com

Handles: Fiction; Nonfiction; *Areas:* Adventure; Autobiography; Business; Cookery; Crime; Current Affairs; Fantasy; Historical; How-to; Humour; Politics; Psychology; Religious; Romance; Science; Sci-Fi; Self-Help; Thrillers; Westerns; Women's Interests; *Markets:* Adult; Youth; *Treatments:* Commercial; Contemporary

Check website for submission guidelines. Different genres handled by different agents, so check website for correct agent to query. Query only one agent. Queries accepted by email only (email addresses for each agent available on website). Do not include any attachments, proposals, sample chapters, etc.

InkWell Management

521 Fifth Avenue, 26th Floor, New York, NY 10175
Tel: +1 (212) 922-3500
Fax: +1 (212) 922-0535
Email: submissions@inkwellmanagement.com

Website:
http://www.inkwellmanagement.com

Handles: Fiction; Nonfiction; Business; Crime; Current Affairs; Finance; Health; Historical; Medicine; Mystery; Psychology; Self-Help; Thrillers; *Markets:* Adult; *Treatments:* Contemporary; Literary; Mainstream

Send query by email with up to two sample chapters. No large attachments. Response not guaranteed. Response within two months if interested. See website for full guidelines.

J de S Associates Inc

9 Shagbark Road, Wilson Point, South Norwalk, CT 06854
Tel: +1 (203) 838-7571
Fax: +1 (203) 866-2713
Email: jdespoel@aol.com
Website: http://www.jdesassociates.com

Handles: Fiction; *Areas:* Autobiography; Biography; Business; Crime; Culture; Current Affairs; Finance; Health; Historical; How-to; Legal; Lifestyle; Medicine; Military; Mystery; New Age; Politics; Self-Help; Sociology; Sport; Suspense; Thrillers; Translations; Westerns; *Markets:* Adult; Children's; Youth; *Treatments:* Literary; Mainstream

Welcomes brief queries by post and by email, but no samples or other material unless requested.

Jabberwocky Literary Agency

49 West 45th Street, 12th Floor North, New York, NY 10036
Tel: +1 (917) 388-3010
Fax: +1 (917) 388-2998
Email: queryeddie@awfulagent.com
Website: http://awfulagent.com

Handles: Fiction; Nonfiction; *Areas:* Fantasy; Historical; Science; Sci-Fi; *Markets:* Adult; Children's; Youth; *Treatments:* Literary

Handles a broad range of fiction and nonfiction intended for general audiences, but no series romance or poetry. Book-length material only. Also considers graphic novels and comics. Send query by post with SASE or IRC, or by email. No queries by phone or by fax. See website for full guidelines.

The Joan Brandt Agency

788 Wesley Drive, Atlanta, GA 30305-3933
Tel: +1 (404) 351-8877

Handles: Fiction; Nonfiction; *Areas:* How-to; Mystery; Suspense; Women's Interests; *Markets:* Adult; *Treatments:* Literary; Mainstream

Send query with SASE. Simultaneous submissions are accepted.

Ken Sherman & Associates

1275 N. Hayworth, Suite 103, Los Angeles, CA 90046
Tel: +1 (310) 273-8840
Fax: +1 (310) 271-2875
Email: ken@kenshermanassociates.com
Website:
http://www.kenshermanassociates.com

Handles: Fiction; Nonfiction; Scripts; *Areas:* Film; TV; *Markets:* Adult

Handles fiction, nonfiction, and writers for film and TV. Query by referral only.

Kimberley Cameron & Associates (Formerly Reece Halsey North)

1550 Tiburon Blvd #704, Tiberon, CA 94920
Tel: +1 (415) 789-9191
Fax: +1 (415) 789-9177
Email: info@kimberleycameron.com
Website: http://www.kimberleycameron.com

Handles: Fiction; Nonfiction; *Areas:* Mystery; Thrillers; *Markets:* Adult; Family; *Treatments:* Contemporary; Literary; Mainstream

Send query by email only with "Author Submission" in the subject line, and one-page synopsis and writing sample of up to 50 pages as separate Word file attachments. No screenplays, Children's Literature, poetry, novels in a foreign language, or teleplays. Approach one agent specifically – direct email address available for each agent on website.

Harvey Klinger, Inc

300 West 55th Street, Suite 11V, New York, NY 10019
Tel: +1 (212) 581-7068
Fax: +1 (212) 315-3823
Email: david@harveyklinger.com
Website: http://www.harveyklinger.com

Handles: Fiction; Nonfiction; *Areas:* Adventure; Autobiography; Biography; Cookery; Crime; Culture; Fantasy; Health; How-to; Humour; Medicine; Music; Mystery; Psychology; Romance; Science; Sci-Fi; Self-Help; Spiritual; Sport; Suspense; Technology; Thrillers; Women's Interests; *Markets:* Adult; Children's; Youth; *Treatments:* Literary; Mainstream; Popular

Send query by email or through submission form on website. No submissions by post. Include short synopsis, author bio, and first five pages, pasted into the body of your email. No attachments. Do not query more than one agent at the agency at a time. See website for individual agent interests and email addresses. No screenplays, or queries by phone or fax. See website for full submission guidelines.

Kneerim & Williams

90 Canal Street, Boston, MA 02114
Tel: +1 (617) 303-1650
Fax: +1 (617) 542-1660
Email: jill@kwlit.com
Website: http://www.kwlit.com

Handles: Fiction; Nonfiction; *Areas:* Adventure; Anthropology; Archaeology; Autobiography; Biography; Business; Crime; Culture; Current Affairs; Finance; Health; Historical; Legal; Lifestyle; Literature; Medicine; Nature; Politics; Psychology; Religious; Science; Sociology; Sport; Technology; Women's Interests; *Markets:* Adult; *Treatments:* Commercial; Literary; Mainstream; Serious

Send query by email to individual agent. See website for specific agent interests and email addresses.

The Knight Agency

Email: submissions@knightagency.net
Website: http://www.knightagency.net

Handles: Fiction; *Areas:* Autobiography; Business; Culture; Entertainment; Fantasy; Finance; Health; How-to; Lifestyle; Media; Mystery; Psychology; Romance; Sci-Fi; Self-Help; Suspense; Thrillers; Women's Interests; *Markets:* Adult; Youth; *Treatments:* Commercial; Literary

Send one-page query by email, providing details of your awards and affiliations, an explanation of what makes your book unique, and a synopsis. No paper or phone queries. Any unsolicited material will not be returned.

Not accepting Screen Plays, Short Story Collections, Poetry Collections, Essay Collections, Photography, Film Treatments, Picture Books (excluding graphic novels), Children's Books (excluding young adult and middle grade), Biographies, Nonfiction Historical Treatments.

Linda Konner Literary Agency

10 West 15 Street, Suite 1918, New York, NY 10011
Tel: +1 (212) 691-3419
Email: ldkonner@cs.com
Website: http://www.lindakonnerliteraryagency.com

Handles: Nonfiction; Reference; *Areas:* Biography; Business; Cookery; Culture; Entertainment; Finance; Health; How-to; Lifestyle; Psychology; Science; Self-Help; Women's Interests; *Markets:* Adult; *Treatments:* Popular

Send one-two page query by email or by post with SASE, synopsis, and author bio. Attachments from unknown senders will be deleted unread. Nonfiction only. Books must be written by or with established experts in their field. No Fiction, Memoir, Religion, Spiritual/Christian, Children's/young adult, Games/puzzles, Humour, History, Politics, or unsolicited MSS. See website for full guidelines.

Elaine Koster Literary Agency LLC

55 Central Park West Suite 6, New York, NY 10023
Tel: +1 (212) 362-9488
Fax: +1 (212) 712-0164
Email: ElaineKost@aol.com

Handles: Fiction; Nonfiction; *Areas:* Biography; Business; Cookery; Culture; Current Affairs; Finance; Health; Historical; How-to; Mystery; Nature; Psychology; Self-Help; Spiritual; Thrillers; Women's Interests; *Markets:* Adult; *Treatments:* Literary; Mainstream

Send query with SASE. No science fiction, children's, screenplays, simultaneous submissions, or queries by fax or email.

Barbara S. Kouts, Literary Agent

PO Box 560, Bellport, NY 11713
Tel: +1 (631) 286-1278
Fax: +1 (631) 286-1538
Email: bkouts@aol.com

Handles: Fiction; *Areas:* Autobiography; Biography; Crime; Current Affairs; Health; Historical; Lifestyle; Mystery; Nature; Psychology; Suspense; Thrillers; Women's Interests; *Markets:* Adult; Children's; *Treatments:* Literary

Send query with SASE. Postal queries only. Particularly interested in adult fiction and nonfiction and children's books.

Bert P. Krages

6665 S.W. Hampton Street, Suite 200, Portland, Oregon 97223
Tel: +1 (503) 597-2525
Fax: +1 (503) 597-2549
Email: krages@onemain.com
Website: http://www.krages.com/lvaserv.htm

Handles: Nonfiction; *Areas:* Health; Historical; Psychology; Science; *Markets:* Adult

Send query by email, with outline, similar books and how yours will compete with them, and your relevant qualifications and writing experience. Query letters should not exceed one page. Particularly interested in science, health, psychology, and history. Not currently accepting fiction. Do not call or send MS instead of query.

The LA Literary Agency

PO Box 46370, Los Angeles, CA 90046
Tel: +1 (323) 654-5288
Email: ann@laliteraryagency.com
Website: http://www.laliteraryagency.com

Handles: Fiction; Nonfiction; *Areas:* Autobiography; Biography; Business; Cookery; Health; Historical; Lifestyle; Psychology; Science; Sport; *Markets:* Adult; *Treatments:* Commercial; Contemporary; Literary; Mainstream

Send query with proposal (nonfiction) or full ms (fiction) by email. Response only if interested. Sister company offers editorial services.

Peter Lampack Agency, Inc

The Empire State Building, 350 Fifth Avenue, Suite 5300, New York, NY 10118
Tel: +1 (212) 687-9106
Fax: +1 (212) 687-9109
Email: andrew@peterlampackagency.com
Website: http://www.peterlampackagency.com

Handles: Fiction; Nonfiction; *Markets:* Adult; *Treatments:* Commercial; Literary; Mainstream

Specialises in commercial and literary fiction as well as nonfiction by recognised experts in a given field. Send query by email only, with cover letter, author bio, sample chapter, and 1-2 page synopsis. No children's books, horror, romance, westerns, science fiction or screenplays.

Laura Langlie, Literary Agent

147-149 Green Street, Hudson, NY 12534
Tel: +1 (518) 828-4708
Fax: +1 (518) 828-4787

Email: laura@lauralanglie.com

Handles: Fiction; Nonfiction; *Areas:* Autobiography; Biography; Crime; Culture; Current Affairs; Film; Historical; Humour; Legal; Literature; Mystery; Nature; Politics; Psychology; Suspense; Theatre; Thrillers; Women's Interests; *Markets:* Adult; Children's; Youth; *Treatments:* Literary; Mainstream

Send query by post with SASE, or by fax. No poetry, children's picture books, hardcore science fiction, men's adventure, how-to, or erotica. Simultaneous submissions accepted.

Larsen Pomada Literary Agents

1029 Jones Street, San Francisco, CA 94109-5023
Tel: +1 (415) 673-0939
Fax: +1 (415) 673-0367
Email: larsenpoma@aol.com
Website: http://www.Larsen-Pomada.com

Handles: Fiction; Nonfiction; *Areas:* Anthropology; Architecture; Arts; Autobiography; Biography; Business; Cookery; Crime; Culture; Current Affairs; Design; Fantasy; Film; Finance; Health; Historical; How-to; Humour; Legal; Lifestyle; Medicine; Music; Mystery; Nature; New Age; Politics; Psychology; Religious; Romance; Science; Self-Help; Sociology; Sport; Suspense; Thrillers; Travel; Women's Interests; *Markets:* Adult; Children's; *Treatments:* Commercial; Literary; Mainstream; Satirical

See website for detailed submission guidelines.

The Steve Laube Agency

5025 N. Central Ave., #635, Phoenix, AZ 85012-1502
Email: krichards@stevelaube.com
Website: http://www.stevelaube.com

Handles: Fiction; Nonfiction; *Areas:* Religious; *Markets:* Adult; Youth

Handles quality Christian fiction and nonfiction in all genres, except poetry, personal biographies, personal stories, end-times literature (either fiction or nonfiction), and children's picture books. Accepts submissions by post or by email. See website for extensive information on making submissions.

Lenhoff & Lenhoff

830 Palm Avenue, West Hollywood, CA 90069
Tel: +1 (310) 855-2411
Fax: +1 (310) 855-2412
Email: charles@lenhoff.com
Website: http://www.lenhoff.com

Handles: Scripts; *Areas:* Film; *Markets:* Adult

No unsolicited material. Approach via conference or referral only.

Levine Greenberg Literary Agency, Inc.

307 Seventh Ave., Suite 2407, New York, NY 10001
Tel: +1 (212) 337-0934
Fax: +1 (212) 337-0948
Email: submit@levinegreenberg.com
Website: http://www.levinegreenberg.com

Handles: Fiction; Nonfiction; *Areas:* Arts; Autobiography; Biography; Business; Cookery; Crafts; Crime; Culture; Finance; Gardening; Health; Historical; Hobbies; Humour; Leisure; Lifestyle; Mystery; Nature; New Age; Politics; Psychology; Religious; Romance; Science; Self-Help; Sociology; Spiritual; Sport; Suspense; Technology; Thrillers; Travel; Women's Interests; *Markets:* Adult; Children's; Youth; *Treatments:* Literary; Mainstream; Popular

No queries by mail. Send query using online form at website, or send email attaching no more than 50 pages. See website for detailed submission guidelines. No response to submissions by post.

The Lisa Ekus Group, LLC

57 North Street, Hatfield, MA 01038
Tel: +1 (413) 247-9325
Email: info@lisaekus.com

Website: http://www.lisaekus.com

Handles: Nonfiction; *Areas:* Cookery; *Markets:* Adult

Send query with table of contents, summary of chapters, one complete sample chapter, author bio, explanation of concept, potential market, and potential competition. Handles cookery books only. See website for full submission guidelines.

Literary & Creative Artists Inc.

3543 Albemarle Street NW, Washington, DC 20008-4213
Tel: +1 (202) 362-4688
Fax: +1 (202) 362-8875
Email: lca9643@lcadc.com
Website: http://www.lcadc.com

Handles: Fiction; Nonfiction; *Areas:* Arts; Autobiography; Biography; Business; Cookery; Crime; Current Affairs; Drama; Health; Historical; How-to; Legal; Lifestyle; Medicine; Nature; Philosophy; Politics; Religious; Spiritual; *Markets:* Adult

Send query by post with SASE, or by email without attachments. No poetry, academic / educational textbooks, or unsolicited MSS. Currently only accepts projects from established authors.

The Literary Group

330 W 38th Street, Suite 408, New York, NY 10018
Tel: +1 (646) 442-5896
Fax: +1 (646) 792-3969
Email: js@theliterarygroup.com
Website: http://www.theliterarygroup.com

Handles: Fiction; Nonfiction; *Areas:* Autobiography; Biography; Cookery; Crime; Current Affairs; Fantasy; Health; Historical; Horror; Humour; Lifestyle; Military; Mystery; Nature; Psychology; Religious; Romance; Science; Sport; Suspense; Thrillers; Women's Interests; *Markets:* Adult

Send query by email or by post with SASE, writing credentials, 2 page synopsis, and 50-page writing sample. Response only if interested. Asks for a 30-day exclusivity period, beginning from the date the material is received.

Sterling Lord Literistic, Inc.

65 Bleecker Street, New York, NY 10012
Tel: +1 (212) 780-6050
Fax: +1 (212) 780-6095
Email: sterling@sll.com
Website: http://www.sll.com

Handles: Fiction; Nonfiction; *Areas:* Autobiography; Biography; Business; Culture; Current Affairs; Health; Historical; Lifestyle; Science; Self-Help; Women's Interests; *Markets:* Adult; Children's; Youth; *Treatments:* Commercial; Literary

Send query with SASE, synopsis, brief author bio, and first three chapters. Literary value considered above all else. No response to unsolicited email queries.

Julia Lord Literary Management

38 W. Ninth Street, New York, NY 10011
Tel: +1 (212) 995-2333
Fax: +1 (212) 995-2332
Email: query@julialordliterary.com
Website: http://julialordliterary.com

Handles: Fiction; Nonfiction; Reference; *Areas:* Adventure; Autobiography; Biography; Crafts; Crime; Current Affairs; Entertainment; Health; Historical; Hobbies; Humour; Lifestyle; Music; Mystery; Politics; Science; Self-Help; Sport; Technology; Thrillers; Women's Interests; *Markets:* Adult; Youth

Send query by post or by email. If sending by email, include synopsis and first five pages in the body of the email. Responds only if interested and does not open or respond to emails with attachments.

If sending by post include synopsis, first five pages, and SASE for response. Responds to all postal submissions.

Lowenstein Associates, Inc.

115 East 23rd Street, 4th Floor, New York, NY 10010

Tel: +1 (212) 206-1630
Email: assistant@bookhaven.com
Website:
http://www.lowensteinassociates.com

Handles: Fiction; Nonfiction; *Areas:* Autobiography; Business; Crime; Fantasy; Health; Lifestyle; Literature; Psychology; Science; Sci-Fi; Sociology; Spiritual; Thrillers; Women's Interests; *Markets:* Adult; *Treatments:* Commercial; Literary

Send query by email with one-page query letter and first ten pages pasted into the body of the email (fiction) or table of contents and (if available) proposal. See website for full guidelines. No Westerns, textbooks, children's picture books, or books in need of translation.

The Jennifer Lyons Literary Agency, LLC

151 West 19th Street 3rd floor, New York, NY 10011
Tel: +1 (212) 368-2812
Email: jenniferlyonsagency@gmail.com
Website:
http://www.jenniferlyonsliteraryagency.com

Handles: Fiction; Nonfiction; *Areas:* Autobiography; Biography; Current Affairs; Finance; Historical; Science; Sport; Thrillers; *Markets:* Adult; Children's; Youth

See website for agent preferences and submission policies, plus specific email addresses.

Donald Maass Literary Agency

Suite 801, 121 West 27th Street, New York, NY 10001
Tel: +1 (212) 727-8383
Fax: +1 (212) 727-3271
Email: info@maassagency.com
Website: http://www.maassagency.com

Handles: Fiction; *Areas:* Crime; Fantasy; Historical; Horror; Humour; Mystery; Romance; Sci-Fi; Suspense; Westerns; Women's Interests; *Markets:* Adult; Youth; *Treatments:* Dark; Literary; Mainstream

Welcomes all genres, in particular science fiction, fantasy, mystery, suspense, horror, romance, historical, literary and mainstream novels. Send query to a specific agent, by email, with "query" in the subject line, or by post with SASE, with synopsis and first five pages. Prefers electronic approaches, but no attachments (include all material within the body of the email). No screenplays, poetry or picture books. See website for individual agent interests and email addresses.

Gina Maccoby Agency

PO Box 60, Chappaqua, NY 10514
Tel: +1 (914) 238-5630
Email: query@maccobylit.com

Handles: Fiction; Nonfiction; *Areas:* Autobiography; Biography; Culture; Current Affairs; Entertainment; Health; Historical; Lifestyle; Mystery; Nature; Politics; Self-Help; Thrillers; Women's Interests; *Markets:* Adult; Children's; Youth; *Treatments:* Literary; Mainstream

Send query by post with SASE, or by email with "Query" in the subject line. No attachments. Response not guaranteed.

Ricia Mainhardt Agency (RMA)

85 Lincoln Street, First Floor, Meriden, CT 06451
Email: ricia@ricia.com
Website: http://www.ricia.com

Handles: Fiction; Nonfiction; *Areas:* Adventure; Autobiography; Biography; Crime; Culture; Current Affairs; Erotic; Fantasy; Gothic; Historical; Horror; Humour; Leisure; Mystery; New Age; Romance; Sci-Fi; Self-Help; Spiritual; Sport; Suspense; Thrillers; Westerns; Women's Interests; *Markets:* Adult; Children's; Family; Youth; *Treatments:* Commercial; Contemporary; Cynical; Dark; Light; Literary; Mainstream; Niche; Popular; Progressive; Serious; Traditional

Send complete MS as an attachment by email. In the body of the email, include a brief one-paragraph pitch. No poetry, shildren's picture books, or screenplays (except from existing clients). See website for full guidelines.

Carol Mann Agency

55 Fifth Avenue, New York, NY 10003
Tel: +1 (212) 206-5635
Fax: +1 (212) 674-4809
Email: submissions@carolmannagency.com
Website: http://www.carolmannagency.com

Handles: Fiction; Nonfiction; *Areas:* Anthropology; Archaeology; Architecture; Arts; Autobiography; Biography; Business; Culture; Current Affairs; Design; Finance; Health; Historical; Humour; Legal; Lifestyle; Medicine; Music; Nature; Politics; Psychology; Religious; Self-Help; Sociology; Spiritual; Sport; Women's Interests; *Markets:* Adult; Youth; *Treatments:* Commercial; Literary

Send query by email only, including synopsis, brief bio, and (in the case of fiction and memoir) first 25 pages. No submissions by post, or phone calls. Allow 3-4 weeks for response.

Manus & Associates Literary Agency, Inc.

425 Sherman Avenue, Suite 200, Palo Alto, CA 94306
Tel: +1 (650) 470-5151
Fax: +1 (650) 470-5159
Email: ManusLit@ManusLit.com
Website: http://www.ManusLit.com

Handles: Fiction; Nonfiction; *Areas:* Autobiography; Biography; Business; Culture; Current Affairs; Finance; Health; How-to; Lifestyle; Mystery; Nature; Psychology; Romance; Science; Self-Help; Suspense; Thrillers; Women's Interests; *Markets:* Adult; *Treatments:* Literary; Mainstream

Send query letter describing your project and giving pertinent biographical info only by fax or email, or send query letter by post with SASE and include complete proposal (nonfiction), or first 30 pages (fiction). When querying by email use one of the direct personal emails of a specific agent as given on the website, not the generic inbox shown on this page. Approach only one agent. No horror, romance, science fiction, fantasy, western, young adult, children's, poetry, cookbooks, or magazine articles. See website for full guidelines.

March Tenth, Inc.

24 Hillside Terrace, Montvale, NJ 07645
Tel: +1 (201) 387-6551
Fax: +1 (201) 387-6552
Email: schoron@aol.com
Website: http://www.marchtenthinc.com

Handles: Fiction; Nonfiction; Reference; *Areas:* Autobiography; Biography; Culture; Current Affairs; Film; Health; Historical; Humour; Literature; Medicine; Music; Theatre; *Markets:* Adult; *Treatments:* Literary; Satirical

Send query by email or by post with SASE. In your query, include the genre of your work, a brief description of the project, and the approximate word count; your qualifications and previous writing or publishing experience or some basic information about your background; all your contact information; a one to two page synopsis if you are submitting a novel as well as the first three chapters; and state whether or not your work has been previously shown to publishers.

No poetry, scripts, children's or young adult novels.

Denise Marcil Literary Agency, Inc.

110 William Street, Suite 2202, New York, NY 10038
Tel: +1 (212) 337-3402
Email: dmla@denisemarcilagency.com
Website: http://www.denisemarcilagency.com

Handles: Fiction; Nonfiction; Reference; *Areas:* Biography; Business; Health; Lifestyle; Self-Help; Spiritual; Suspense; Thrillers; Women's Interests; *Markets:* Adult; *Treatments:* Contemporary; Popular

Send query by email or by post with SASE.

No science fiction, children's books, or political nonfiction. No queries by fax.

Elaine Markson Literary Agency

450 Seventh Ave, Suite 1408, New York, NY 10123
Tel: +1 (212) 243-8480
Fax: +1 (212) 691-9014
Email: gary@marksonagency.com
Website: http://www.marksonagency.com

Handles: Fiction; Nonfiction; *Markets:* Adult; *Treatments:* Literary

Most new clients obtained through recommendation.

The Martell Agency

1350 Avenue of the Americas, Suite 1205, New York, NY 10019
Tel: +1 (212) 317-2672
Email: submissions@themartellagency.com
Website: http://www.themartellagency.com

Handles: Fiction; Nonfiction; *Areas:* Autobiography; Business; Finance; Health; Historical; Medicine; Mystery; Psychology; Self-Help; Suspense; Thrillers; Women's Interests; *Markets:* Adult; *Treatments:* Commercial

Send query by post or by email, including summary, short bio, any information, if appropriate, as to why you are qualified to write on the subject of your book, any publishing credits, the year of publication and the publisher. No original screenplays or poetry.

Martin Literary Management

7683 SE 27th Street, #307, Mercer Island, WA 98040
Tel: +1 (206) 466-1773
Fax: +1 (206) 466-1774
Email: Sharlene@martinliterarymanagement.com
Website: http://www.martinliterarymanagement.com

Handles: Fiction; Nonfiction; *Areas:* Autobiography; Biography; Business; Crime; Current Affairs; Entertainment; Health; How-to; Lifestyle; Media; Self-Help; Women's Interests; *Markets:* Adult; Children's; Youth; *Treatments:* Commercial; Literary; Mainstream; Popular; Positive; Traditional

This agency has strong ties to film/TV. Actively seeking nonfiction that is highly commercial and that can be adapted to film. Please review our website carefully to make sure we're a good match for your work. How to contact: Completely electronic: emails and MS Word only. No attachments on queries. Place letter in body of email. See submission requirements on website. Do not send materials unless requested. We give very serious consideration to the material requested. We are actively seeing new submissions. We only ask to see materials that we intend to offer representation for – IF the work is saleable. Therefore, in exchange for that close evaluation, we require a two week exclusive consideration period, whereby your agree if we offer representation, you are already certain you are willing to accept pending our contract.

No adult fiction. Principal agent handles adult nonfiction only. See website for submission guidelines and separate email address for submissions of picture books, middle grade, and young adult fiction and nonfiction.

The Marton Agency, Inc.

1 Union Square West, Suite 815, New York, NY 10003-3303
Tel: +1 (212) 255-1908
Fax: +1 (212) 691-9061
Email: info@martonagency.com
Website: http://www.martonagency.com

Handles: Scripts; *Areas:* Theatre; Translations; *Markets:* Adult

International literary rights agency, specialising in foreign-language licensing.

Margret McBride Literary Agency

PO Box 9128, La Jolla, CA 92037
Tel: +1 (858) 454-1550

Fax: +1 (858) 459-0550
Email: staff@mcbridelit.com
Website: http://www.mcbrideliterary.com

Handles: Fiction; Nonfiction; *Areas:* Business; Health; Self-Help; *Markets:* Adult; *Treatments:* Commercial

Represents commercial fiction and nonfiction, business, health, and self-help. No poetry or romance. As at December 2013 accepting submission by referral only. See website for current status and detailed submission guidelines.

McIntosh & Otis, Inc

353 Lexington Avenue, New York, NY 10016
Tel: +1 (212) 687-7400
Fax: +1 (212) 687-6894
Email: info@mcintoshandotis.com
Website: http://www.mcintoshandotis.com

Handles: Fiction; Nonfiction; *Areas:* Adventure; Culture; Current Affairs; Fantasy; Historical; Horror; Humour; Music; Mystery; Nature; Psychology; Romance; Sci-Fi; Self-Help; Spiritual; Sport; Suspense; Thrillers; Travel; Women's Interests; *Markets:* Adult; Children's; Youth; *Treatments:* Commercial; Contemporary; Literary; Mainstream; Popular

Prefers submissions by email. See website for specific agent interests and email addresses, and query appropriate agent. Also accepts submissions by post, see website for full details.

Mendel Media Group, LLC

115 West 30th Street, Suite 800, New York, NY 10001
Tel: +1 (646) 239-9896
Fax: +1 (212) 685-4717
Email: scott@mendelmedia.com
Website: http://www.mendelmedia.com

Handles: Fiction; Nonfiction; *Areas:* Autobiography; Biography; Culture; Current Affairs; Entertainment; Finance; Historical; How-to; Humour; Literature; Media; Mystery; Politics; Religious; Science; Self-Help; Spiritual; Thrillers; Women's Interests; *Markets:* Adult; Children's; Youth; *Treatments:* Contemporary; Literary; Mainstream

Send query by regular mail. Works mainly with established authors, but accepts queries from unpublished authors who have researched the publishing industry and have a polished proposal or manuscript ready for consideration.

Represents a wide range of fiction and nonfiction. In fiction, particularly interested in historical and contemporary multicultural fiction, contemporary thrillers and mainstream women's fiction. In nonfiction, represents both individual authors and institutions. Also accepts young adult fiction and nonfiction, Chapter Books and Picture Books. No poetry, screenplays, or queries by fax or email. See website for full guidelines.

Martha Millard Literary Agency

50 West 67th Street #1G, New York, NY 10023
Tel: +1 (212) 662-1030
Email: marmillink@aol.com

Handles: Fiction; Nonfiction; *Areas:* Architecture; Arts; Autobiography; Biography; Business; Cookery; Crime; Culture; Current Affairs; Design; Fantasy; Film; Finance; Health; Historical; Horror; How-to; Lifestyle; Music; Mystery; New Age; Photography; Psychology; Romance; Sci-Fi; Self-Help; Short Stories; Suspense; Theatre; Thrillers; Women's Interests; *Markets:* Adult; Children's; Youth

No unsolicited queries or queries by fax or email. Authors wishing to approach this agency will need to be recommended to the agent by someone else in the profession.

The Miller Agency

630 Ninth Ave., Suite 1102, New York, NY 10036
Tel: +1 (212) 206-0913
Email: info@milleragency.net
Website: http://www.milleragency.net

Handles: Nonfiction; *Areas:* Arts;

Autobiography; Biography; Cookery; Culture; Psychology; Self-Help; Sport; Travel; *Markets:* Adult

No unsolicited MSS. Any unsolicited MSS submitted will not be responded to or returned.

William Morris Endeavor Entertainment

1325 Avenue of the Americas, New York, NY 10019
Tel: +1 (212) 586-5100
Fax: +1 (212) 246-3583
Email: jrw@wmeentertainment.com
Website: http://www.wma.com

Handles: Fiction; Nonfiction; Scripts; *Areas:* Film; TV; *Markets:* Adult

Send query with publishing history, synopsis, and SASE.

Nelson Literary Agency, LLC

1732 Wazee Street, Suite 207, Denver, CO 80202
Tel: +1 (303) 292-2805
Email: querykristin@nelsonagency.com
Website: http://www.nelsonagency.com

Handles: Fiction; *Areas:* Fantasy; Historical; Romance; Sci-Fi; Women's Interests; *Markets:* Adult; Children's; Youth; *Treatments:* Commercial; Literary; Mainstream

Handles young adult, upper-level middle grade, "big crossover novels with one foot squarely in genre", literary commercial novesl, upmarket women's fiction, single-title romances (especially historicals), and lead title or hardcover science fiction and fantasy. No nonfiction, screenplays, short story collections, poetry, children's picture books or chapter books, or material for the Christian/inspirational market. No queries by post, phone, in person, or through Facebook. No email attachments. See website for full submission guidelines.

Northern Lights Literary Services

762 State Road 458, Bedford, IN 47421
Email: queries@northernlightsls.com
Website: http://www.northernlightsls.com

Handles: Fiction; Nonfiction; *Areas:* Biography; Business; Health; Historical; How-to; Lifestyle; Medicine; Mystery; New Age; Psychology; Romance; Self-Help; Suspense; Women's Interests; *Markets:* Adult

Our goal is to provide personalized service to clients and create a bond that will endure throughout your career. We seriously consider each query we receive and will accept hardworking new authors who are willing to develop their talents and skills.

Encourages email queries but responds only if interested (within 5 working days). No horror or books for children.

Harold Ober Associates

425 Madison Avenue, New York, NY 10017
Tel: +1 (212) 759-8600
Fax: +1 (212) 759-9428
Email: phyllis@haroldober.com
Website: http://www.haroldober.com

Handles: Fiction; Nonfiction; *Markets:* Adult; Children's

Send query addressed to a specific agent by post only, including first five pages and SASE for reply. No plays, screenplays, or queries by fax.

Objective Entertainment

609 Greenwich St. 6th Floor, New York, NY 10014
Tel: +1 (212) 431-5454
Fax: +1 (917) 464-6394
Email: IK@objectiveent.com
Website: http://www.objectiveent.com

Handles: Fiction; Nonfiction; Scripts; *Areas:* Autobiography; Biography; Business; Cookery; Culture; Current Affairs; Fantasy; Film; Lifestyle; Music; Mystery; Politics; Sci-Fi; Sport; Thrillers; TV; Women's Interests; *Markets:* Adult; Children's; Youth;

Treatments: Commercial; Literary

We represent over 100 celebrities, musicians, authors and bestselling writers.

Fifi Oscard Agency, Inc.

110 West 40th Street, 16th Floor, New York, NY 10018
Tel: +1 (212) 764-1100
Fax: +1 (212)840-5019
Email: agency@fifioscard.com
Website: http://www.fifioscard.com

Handles: Fiction; Nonfiction; Scripts; *Areas:* Biography; Business; Cookery; Finance; Health; Historical; Lifestyle; Religious; Science; Spiritual; Sport; Technology; Theatre; Women's Interests; *Markets:* Adult

Send query via online submission form. No unsolicited MSS. Due to volume of queries, unable to acknowledge each one.

The Richard Parks Agency

P.O. Box 693, Salem, NY 12865
Tel: +1 (518) 854-9466
Fax: +1 (518) 854-9466
Email: rp@richardparksagency.com
Website: http://www.richardparksagency.com

Handles: Fiction; Nonfiction; *Areas:* Adventure; Anthropology; Archaeology; Arts; Autobiography; Biography; Business; Cookery; Crafts; Culture; Current Affairs; Film; Finance; Gardening; Health; Historical; Hobbies; How-to; Humour; Legal; Lifestyle; Medicine; Military; Music; Nature; Politics; Psychology; Science; Self-Help; Sociology; Technology; Theatre; Travel; Women's Interests; *Markets:* Adult; *Treatments:* Commercial; Literary

Send query by post only, including SASE. No children's books, poetry, plays, screenplays, unsolicited MSS, or queries by fax or email. Fiction considered by referral only.

Kathi J. Paton Literary Agency

PO Box 2236, Radio City Station, New York, NY 10101-2236
Tel: +1 (212) 265-6586
Email: kjplitbiz@optonline.net

Handles: Fiction; Nonfiction; *Areas:* Biography; Business; Culture; Current Affairs; Finance; Health; Historical; Humour; Lifestyle; Politics; Religious; Science; Sport; Technology; *Markets:* Adult; *Treatments:* Literary; Mainstream; Popular

Send query with brief description by email only. No attachments or referrals to websites. Specialises in adult nonfiction. No science fiction, fantasy, horror, category romance, juvenile, young adult or self-published books. Response only if interested.

Peregrine Whittlesey Agency

279 Central Park West, New York, NY 10024
Tel: +1 (212) 787-1802
Fax: +1 (212) 787-4985
Email: pwwagy@aol.com

Handles: Scripts; *Areas:* Film; Theatre; TV; *Markets:* Adult

Handles mainly theatre scripts, plus a small number of film/TV scripts by playwrights who also write for screen. Send query with SASE. No simultaneous submissions.

L. Perkins Associates

5800 Arlington Ave, Riverdale, NY 10471
Tel: +1 (718) 543-5344
Fax: +1 (718) 543-5354
Email: submissions@lperkinsagency.com
Website: http://lperkinsagency.com

Handles: Fiction; Nonfiction; *Areas:* Biography; Cookery; Culture; Erotic; Fantasy; Film; Historical; Horror; Humour; Music; Mystery; Psychology; Science; Sci-Fi; Theatre; Thrillers; *Markets:* Adult; Youth; *Treatments:* Commercial; Dark; Literary; Popular

Send query by email with synopsis, bio, and first five pages of your novel / proposal in the body of the email. No email attachments and no queries by post or any other means apart from email. Pitch only one book at a time, and to only one agent. Specific agent email addresses are available at website, or use general address provided below. No screenplays, short story collections, or poetry.

James Peter Associates, Inc.

PO Box 358, New Canaan, CT 06840
Tel: +1 (203) 972-1070
Fax: +1 (203) 972-1759
Email: gene_brissie@msn.com
Website:
http://www.jamespeterassociates.com

Handles: Nonfiction; Reference; *Areas:* Autobiography; Biography; Business; Cookery; Culture; Film; Finance; Health; Historical; Humour; Leisure; Nature; Politics; Sport; Travel; TV; *Markets:* Adult

Send query with brief outline of project, CV and writing samples. Prefers to read material exclusively. Specialises in business, popular culture, history, health, biography, general, reference, and politics. No poetry, fiction, children's books, young adult, or unsolicited MSS.

Pinder Lane & Garon-Brooke Associates Ltd

159 West 53rd Street, Suite 14-E, New York, NY 10019
Tel: +1 (212) 489-0880
Fax: +1 (212) 489-7104
Email: pinderlanegaronbrooke@gmail.com
Website: http://www.pinderlane.com

Handles: Fiction; Nonfiction; *Areas:* Arts; Autobiography; Biography; Business; Cookery; Crime; Culture; Current Affairs; Entertainment; Erotic; Fantasy; Film; Health; Historical; Horror; Humour; Music; Mystery; Photography; Politics; Romance; Sci-Fi; Self-Help; Spiritual; Sport; Theatre; Thrillers; Travel; Westerns; Women's Interests; *Markets:* Adult; Children's; Youth; *Treatments:* Mainstream

Send query by email or by post with SASE, including brief synopsis and first three chapters only. No film, TV, or theatre scripts, or unsolicited MSS.

The Poynor Group

13454 Yorktown Drive, Bowie, MD 20715
Tel: +1 (301)805-6788
Email: jpoynor@aol.com

Handles: Fiction; Nonfiction; *Areas:* Autobiography; Biography; Business; Cookery; Culture; Finance; Health; Medicine; Mystery; Religious; Romance; Suspense; *Markets:* Adult; Children's; Youth

Send query by post with SASE, or by email.

Rebecca Pratt Literary Group

Seven Mile House, PO Box 77, Lititz, PA 17543
Tel: +1 (717) 625-2186
Fax: +1 (717) 625-3754
Email: Query@agentR.com
Website: http://www.agentr.com

Handles: Fiction; Nonfiction; *Areas:* Adventure; Autobiography; Biography; Fantasy; Historical; Horror; How-to; Mystery; Sci-Fi; Self-Help; Thrillers; *Markets:* Adult; *Treatments:* Literary; Mainstream

Send query in first instance by email only. No attachments (unsolicited email attachments will not be opened). No previously published works; juvenile, young adult, or children's; scripts; poetry, graphic novels; short stories; anything not between 70,000 and 120,000 words. See website for full guidelines.

Linn Prentis Literary

c/o Trodayne Northern, Acquisitions Director, for: Amy Hayden, Acquisitions, Linn Prentis Literary, PO Box 674, New York, NY 10035
Tel: +1 (212) 875-8557
Fax: +1 (425) 489-2809
Email: ahayden@linnprentis.com
Website: http://www.linnprentis.com

Handles: Fiction; Nonfiction; *Areas:* Autobiography; Fantasy; Mystery; Sci-Fi; Women's Interests; *Markets:* Adult; Youth; *Treatments:* Contemporary; Literary; Mainstream

Particularly interested in science fiction and fantasy, but willing to consider any fiction of interest. Send query by email or by post with SASE, including synopsis and first ten pages. No books for small children, or queries by fax or phone.

Aaron M. Priest Literary Agency

708 Third Avenue, 23rd Floor, New York, NY 10017-4201
Tel: +1 (212) 818-0344
Fax: +1 (212) 573-9417
Email: querypriest@aaronpriest.com
Website: http://www.aaronpriest.com

Handles: Fiction; Nonfiction; *Areas:* Autobiography; Biography; Crime; Culture; Fantasy; Gothic; Historical; How-to; Mystery; Politics; Suspense; Thrillers; Translations; Women's Interests; *Markets:* Adult; Youth; *Treatments:* Commercial; Contemporary; Literary

Send one-page query by email, describing your work and your background. No attachments, but you may paste the first chapter into the body of the email. Query one agent only. See website for specific agent interests and email addresses. No poetry, screenplays, sci-fi, or horror.

Prospect Agency

551 Valley Rd., PMB 377, Upper Montclair, NJ 07043
Tel: +1 (718) 788-3217
Fax: +1 (718) 360-9582
Email: esk@prospectagency.com
Website: http://www.prospectagency.com

Handles: Fiction; Nonfiction; *Areas:* Adventure; Autobiography; Crime; Erotic; Fantasy; Mystery; Romance; Science; Sci-Fi; Suspense; Thrillers; Westerns; Women's Interests; *Markets:* Adult; Children's; Youth; *Treatments:* Contemporary; Literary; Mainstream

Handles very little nonfiction. Specialises in romance, women's fiction, literary fiction, young adult/children's literature, and science fiction. Send submissions via website submission system **only** (no email queries – **email queries are not accepted or responded to** – or queries by post (these will be recycled). No poetry, short stories, text books, screenplays, or most nonfiction.

Susan Rabiner, Literary Agent, Inc.

315 West 39th Street, Suite 1501, New York, NY 10018
Tel: +1 (212) 279-0316
Fax: +1 (212) 279-0932
Email: susan@rabiner.net
Website: http://www.rabiner.net

Handles: Fiction; Nonfiction; *Areas:* Arts; Autobiography; Entertainment; Finance; Historical; Humour; Politics; Science; Sport; *Markets:* Adult

Send query by email only. Response within two weeks if interested. See website for details and email addresses of individual agents.

Rebecca Friedman Literary Agency

Email: brandie@rfliterary.com
Website: http://rfliterary.com

Handles: Fiction; Nonfiction; *Areas:* Autobiography; Fantasy; Mystery; Romance; Sci-Fi; Suspense; Thrillers; Women's Interests; *Markets:* Adult; Youth; *Treatments:* Commercial; Contemporary; Literary

See website for full submission guidelines and specific agent interests and contact details. Aims to respond in 6-8 weeks, but may take longer.

Regina Ryan Publishing Enterprises

251 Central Park West, #7D, New York, NY 10024
Tel: +1 (212) 787-5589
Email: queries@reginaryanbooks.com
Website: http://www.reginaryanbooks.com

Handles: Nonfiction; Reference; *Areas:* Adventure; Architecture; Autobiography; Business; Cookery; Gardening; Health;

Historical; Legal; Leisure; Lifestyle; Nature; Politics; Psychology; Science; Spiritual; Sport; Travel; Women's Interests; *Markets:* Adult; *Treatments:* Popular

Send query by email, stating what your books is about, why you are qualified to write it, your plans for promotion, and analysis of competing books. See website for full guidelines.

Ann Rittenberg Literary Agency

15 Maiden Lane, Suite 206, New York, NY 10038
Email: info@rittlit.com
Website: http://www.rittlit.com

Handles: Fiction; Nonfiction; *Areas:* Autobiography; Biography; Culture; Historical; Sociology; Women's Interests; *Markets:* Adult; *Treatments:* Literary

Send three sample chapters with outline by email (pasted into the body of the email) or by post with SASE. Email queries receive a response only if interested. No Screenplays, Genre fiction, Poetry, or Self-help. No queries by fax.

RLR Associates

Literary Department, 7 West 51st Street, New York, NY 10019
Tel: +1 (212) 541-8641
Fax: +1 (212) 262-7084
Email: sgould@rlrassociates.net
Website: http://www.rlrliterary.net

Handles: Fiction; Nonfiction; *Areas:* Adventure; Anthropology; Arts; Biography; Business; Cookery; Crime; Culture; Current Affairs; Health; Historical; Horror; Humour; Music; Mystery; Nature; Photography; Politics; Psychology; Religious; Science; Self-Help; Short Stories; Sociology; Sport; Thrillers; Translations; Travel; Women's Interests; *Markets:* Academic; Adult; Children's; Family; *Treatments:* Commercial; Experimental; Literary; Mainstream

Represents literary and commercial fiction, genre fiction, and narrative nonfiction. Particularly interested in history, pop culture, humour, food and beverage, biography, and sports. Also represents all types of children's literature. Send query or proposal by post or by email. For fiction, include writing sample (normally the first few chapters). If no response after three months, assume rejection.

B.J. Robbins Literary Agency

5130 Bellaire Avenue, North Hollywood, CA 91607
Tel: +1 (818) 760-6602
Fax: +1 (818) 760-6616
Email: Robbinsliterary@gmail.com

Handles: Fiction; Nonfiction; *Areas:* Autobiography; Biography; Crime; Culture; Current Affairs; Film; Health; Humour; Medicine; Music; Mystery; Psychology; Self-Help; Sociology; Sport; Suspense; Theatre; Thrillers; Travel; Women's Interests; *Markets:* Adult; *Treatments:* Literary; Mainstream

Send query with outline / proposal and three sample chapters by post with SASE or by email (no attachments).

Linda Roghaar Literary Agency, Inc.

133 High Point Drive, Amherst, MA 01002
Tel: +1 (413) 256-1921
Fax: +1 (413) 256-2636
Email: contact@lindaroghaar.com
Website: http://www.LindaRoghaar.com

Handles: Fiction; Nonfiction; *Areas:* Anthropology; Biography; Culture; Historical; Nature; Religious; Self-Help; Women's Interests; *Markets:* Adult

Send query by email (mentioning "query" in the subject line) or by post with SASE. For fiction, include the first five pages. Specialises in nonfiction. No romance, science fiction, or horror. Scripts handled through sub-agents.

Rita Rosenkranz Literary Agency

440 West End Ave, Suite 15D, New York,

NY 10024
Tel: +1 (212) 873-6333
Email: rrosenkranz@mindspring.com
Website: http://www.ritarosenkranz literaryagency.com

Handles: Nonfiction; *Areas:* Anthropology; Arts; Autobiography; Biography; Business; Cookery; Crafts; Culture; Current Affairs; Design; Finance; Health; Historical; Hobbies; How-to; Humour; Legal; Lifestyle; Literature; Medicine; Military; Music; Nature; Photography; Politics; Psychology; Religious; Science; Self-Help; Sport; Technology; Theatre; Women's Interests; *Markets:* Adult

Send query only by post or email. Submit proposal on request only. Deals specifically in adult nonfiction. No screenplays, poetry, fiction, children's or YA books. No queries by fax.

Ross Yoon Agency

1666 Connecticut Avenue, NW, Suite 500, Washington, DC 20009
Tel: +1 (202) 328-3282
Fax: +1 (202) 328-9162
Email: submissions@rossyoon.com
Website: http://www.rossyoon.com

Handles: Nonfiction; *Areas:* Autobiography; Biography; Business; Culture; Current Affairs; Historical; Psychology; Science; *Markets:* Adult; *Treatments:* Commercial; Popular; Serious

Handles nonfiction only. Send query by email only with proposal in body of email or as .doc or .docx attachment. No unsolicited MSS or approaches by post or phone.

Andy Ross Agency

767 Santa Ray Avenue, Oakland, CA 94610
Tel: +1 (510) 238-8965
Email: andyrossagency@hotmail.com
Website: http://www.andyrossagency.com

Handles: Fiction; Nonfiction; *Areas:* Culture; Current Affairs; Historical; Religious; Science; *Markets:* Adult; Children's; Youth; *Treatments:* Commercial; Contemporary; Literary

We encourage queries for material in our fields of interest.

The agent has worked in the book business for 36 years, all of his working life. He was owner and general manager of Cody's Books in Berkeley, California from 1977-2006. Cody's has been recognised as one of America's great independent book stores.

During this period, the agent was the primary trade book buyer. This experience has given him a unique understanding of the retail book market, of publishing trends and, most importantly and uniquely, the hand selling of books to book buyers.

The agent is past president of the Northern California Booksellers Association, a board member and officer of the American Booksellers Association and a national spokesperson for issues concerning independent businesses. He has had signifcant profiles in the Wall Street Journal, Time Magazine, and the San Francisco Chronicle.

Queries by email only. See website for full guidelines.

Jane Rotrosen Agency

318 East 51st Street, New York, NY 10022
Tel: +1 (212) 593-4330
Fax: +1 (212) 935-6985
Email: acirillo@janerotrosen.com
Website: http://www.janerotrosen.com

Handles: Fiction; Nonfiction; *Areas:* Autobiography; Historical; Mystery; Romance; Suspense; Thrillers; Women's Interests; *Markets:* Adult; Youth; *Treatments:* Commercial; Mainstream

Send query by email to one of the agent email addresses provided on the agency bios page of the website, or by post with SASE, describing your work and giving relevant biographical details and publishing history, along with synopsis and the first three chapters in the case of fiction, or proposal in the case of nonfiction. Submissions without an SASE will be recycled without response. Attachments to a blank email will not be opened. See website for full guidelines and individual agent details.

The Damaris Rowland Agency

420 East 23rd Street, Suite 6F, New York, NY 10010-5040

Handles: Fiction; Nonfiction; *Areas:* Women's Interests; *Markets:* Adult; *Treatments:* Literary; Popular

Closed to queries as at August 2014.

The Rudy Agency

825 Wildlife Lane, Estes Park, CO 80517
Tel: +1 (970) 577-8500
Fax: +1 (970) 577-8600
Email: mak@rudyagency.com
Website: http://www.rudyagency.com

Handles: Fiction; Nonfiction; *Areas:* Autobiography; Biography; Business; Culture; Health; Historical; Medicine; Military; Science; Technology; *Markets:* Adult

Concentrates on adult nonfiction in the areas listed above. Not accepting fiction submissions, except historical fiction. No poetry, children's or young adult, religion books, parenting how-to books, or screenplays. Send query letter only in first instance, by email or by fax.

The Sagalyn Literary Agency

1250 Connecticut Ave NW, 7th Floor, Washington, DC 20036
Email: query@sagalyn.com
Website: http://www.sagalyn.com

Handles: Fiction; Nonfiction; Historical; Science; *Markets:* Adult; *Treatments:* Mainstream

Some fiction, but mainly upmarket nonfiction. No romance, westerns, science fiction, poetry, children's books, or screenplays. Query by email only, but no attachments. Visit website for details on submissions.

Victoria Sanders & Associates LLC

241 Avenue of the Americas, Suite 11H, New York, NY 10014
Tel: +1 (212) 633-8811
Fax: +1 (212) 633-0525
Email: queriesvsa@gmail.com
Website: http://www.victoriasanders.com

Handles: Fiction; Nonfiction; *Areas:* Adventure; Arts; Autobiography; Biography; Crime; Culture; Current Affairs; Fantasy; Film; Historical; Humour; Legal; Literature; Music; Mystery; Politics; Psychology; Sociology; Suspense; Theatre; Thrillers; Translations; Women's Interests; *Markets:* Adult; Children's; Youth; *Treatments:* Commercial; Contemporary; Light; Literary; Mainstream; Satirical

Send one-page query describing the work and the author by email only, with the first 25 pages pasted into the body of the email. No attachments.

Schiavone Literary Agency

236 Trails End, West Palm Beach, FL 33413-2135
Tel: +1 (561) 966-9294
Fax: +1 (561) 966-9294
Email: profschia@aol.com

Handles: Fiction; Nonfiction; *Areas:* Biography; Business; Cookery; Crime; Culture; Fantasy; Finance; Health; Historical; Mystery; Politics; Religious; Romance; Science; Sci-Fi; Spiritual; Sport; Suspense; Thrillers; Travel; *Markets:* Academic; Adult; Children's; Family; Youth; *Treatments:* Literary; Mainstream

Send one-page query letter only by email or by post with SASE. No proposals, sample chapters, etc. unless requested. No poetry, short stories, anthologies or children's picture books, unsolicited MSS, or email attachments. No previously published or self-published material. Prefers to work with authors already published by major New York publishing houses.

Susan Schulman, A Literary Agency

454 West 44th Street, New York, NY 10036
Tel: +1 (212) 713-1633
Fax: +1 (212) 581-8830
Email: queries@schulmanagency.com
Website: http://schulmanagency.com

Handles: Fiction; Nonfiction; Scripts; *Areas:* Adventure; Anthropology; Archaeology; Arts; Autobiography; Biography; Business; Cookery; Crafts; Crime; Culture; Current Affairs; Entertainment; Film; Finance; Health; Historical; Hobbies; How-to; Humour; Legal; Lifestyle; Literature; Medicine; Music; Mystery; Nature; Photography; Politics; Psychology; Religious; Science; Self-Help; Sociology; Spiritual; Sport; Suspense; Technology; Theatre; Thrillers; Travel; Women's Interests; *Markets:* Adult; Children's; Youth; *Treatments:* Commercial; Literary; Mainstream

Send query with synopsis by email in the body of the email or by post with SASE. Include author resume and outline. For fiction, include three sample chapters. For nonfiction, include at least one. No poetry, TV scripts, concepts for TV, email attachments, submissions via UPS or FedEx, or unsolicited MSS.

Scovil Galen Ghosh Literary Agency, Inc.

276 Fifth Avenue, Suite 708, New York, NY 10001
Tel: +1 (212) 679-8686
Fax: +1 (212) 679-6710
Email: info@sgglit.com
Website: http://www.sgglit.com

Handles: Fiction; Nonfiction; *Areas:* Adventure; Arts; Autobiography; Biography; Cookery; Culture; Health; Historical; Nature; Psychology; Religious; Science; Sociology; Women's Interests; *Markets:* Adult; Children's; Youth; *Treatments:* Commercial; Literary

Send query letter only in first instance. Prefers contact by email, but no attachments. If contacting by post include letter only, with email address for response rather than an SASE.

The Seven Bridges Group

5000 Birch Street, Suite 3000, Newport Beach, CA 92660
Tel: +1 (949) 260-2099
Fax: +1 (650) 249-1612
Email: travis.bell@sevenbridgesgroup.com
Website: http://www.sevenbridgesgroup.com

Handles: Fiction; Scripts; *Areas:* Adventure; Autobiography; Biography; Crime; Culture; Current Affairs; Drama; Entertainment; Literature; Men's Interests; Military; Music; Politics; Short Stories; Sport; Suspense; Travel; TV; Westerns; Women's Interests; *Markets:* Adult; Family; Professional; *Treatments:* Commercial; Contemporary; In-depth; Light; Literary; Mainstream; Niche; Popular; Traditional

No upfront fees will be incurred by writer (Client).

The Seymour Agency

475 Miner Street Road, Canton, NY 13617
Tel: +1 (315) 386-1831
Email: marysue@theseymouragency.com
Website: http://www.theseymouragency.com

Handles: Fiction; Nonfiction; *Areas:* Adventure; Fantasy; Historical; Mystery; Religious; Romance; Sci-Fi; Suspense; Thrillers; Women's Interests; *Markets:* Adult; Children's; Youth

Brief email queries accepted (no attachments), including first five pages pasted into the bottom of your email. No poetry or erotica. All agents prefer queries by email and one accepts email queries only. See website for full submission guidelines and specific interests of each agent.

Denise Shannon Literary Agency, Inc.

20 West 22nd Street, Suite 1603, New York, NY 10010
Tel: +1 (212) 414-2911
Fax: +1 (212) 414-2930
Email:

submissions@deniseshannonagency.com
Website: http://deniseshannonagency.com

Handles: Fiction; Nonfiction; *Areas:* Autobiography; Biography; Business; Current Affairs; Health; Historical; Politics; Sociology; *Markets:* Adult; *Treatments:* Literary

Send query by email, or by post with SASE, including outline and bio listing any previous publishing credits. Notify if simultaneous submission. No unsolicited MSS, or queries for incomplete fiction MSS.

Wendy Sherman Associates, Inc.

27 West 24th Street, Suite 700B, New York, NY 10010
Tel: +1 (212) 279-9027
Email: submissions@wsherman.com
Website: http://www.wsherman.com

Handles: Fiction; Nonfiction; *Areas:* Autobiography; Biography; Cookery; Culture; Entertainment; Health; Historical; Lifestyle; Nature; Psychology; Self-Help; Spiritual; Sport; Suspense; Women's Interests; *Markets:* Adult; Youth; *Treatments:* Literary

Send queries by email only, including query letter and (for fiction) first ten pages pasted into the body of the email, or (for nonfiction) author bio. No unsolicited attachments. Do not send emails to personal agent addresses (these are deleted unread). Response only if interested.

Rosalie Siegel, International Literary Agency, Inc.

1 Abbey Drive, Pennington, NJ 08534
Tel: +1 (609) 737-1007
Fax: +1 (609) 737-3708
Email: rosalie@rosaliesiegel.com
Website: http://www.rosaliesiegel.com

Handles: Fiction; Nonfiction; *Areas:* Biography; Current Affairs; Historical; Nature; Psychology; Science; Short Stories; *Markets:* Adult

Not currently accepting unsolicited MSS or queries. Any unsolicited material will not be returned. Accepts new authors by referral only.

Signature Literary Agency

101 W. 23rd St, Suite 346, New York, NY 10011
Tel: +1 (201) 435-8334
Fax: +1 (202) 478-1623
Email: ellen@signaturelit.com
Website: http://www.signaturelit.com

Handles: Fiction; Nonfiction; Reference; *Areas:* Beauty and Fashion; Biography; Crime; Criticism; Culture; Current Affairs; Historical; Military; Politics; Science; Technology; Thrillers; Women's Interests; *Markets:* Adult; Children's; Youth; *Treatments:* Commercial; Literary; Popular

Agency established in Washington DC. The principal agent formerly worked at the Graybill and English Literary Agency. She has a law degree from George Washington University and extensive editorial experience.

Send query by email to specific agent (see website for individual contact details and "wishlists").

Offices in both New York and Washington DC.

SLW Literary Agency

4100 Ridgeland Avenue, Northbrook, IL 60062
Tel: +1 (847) 509-0999
Fax: +1 (847) 509-0996
Email: shariwenk@gmail.com

Handles: Nonfiction; *Areas:* Sport; *Markets:* Adult

Handles sports celebrities and sports writers only.

Valerie Smith, Literary Agent

1746 Route 44/55 RR, Box 160, Modena, NY 12548

Handles: Fiction; Nonfiction; *Areas:*

Cookery; Fantasy; Historical; How-to; Mystery; Sci-Fi; Self-Help; Suspense; Women's Interests; *Markets:* Adult; Youth; *Treatments:* Contemporary; Literary; Mainstream

Send query with SASE, synopsis, author bio, and three sample chapters, by post only. No unsolicited MSS, or queries by fax or email. Strong ties to science fiction, fantasy, and young adult.

Solow Literary Enterprises, Inc.

769 Center Blvd., #148, Fairfax, CA 94930
Email: info@solowliterary.com
Website: http://www.solowliterary.com

Handles: Nonfiction; *Areas:* Autobiography; Business; Culture; Finance; Health; Historical; Nature; Psychology; Science; *Markets:* Adult

Handles nonfiction in the stated areas only. Send single-page query by email or by post with SASE, providing information on what your book is about; why you think it has to be written; and why you are the best person to write it.

Spectrum Literary Agency

320 Central Park West, Suite 1-D, New York, NY 10025
Tel: +1 (212) 362-4323
Fax: +1 (212) 362-4562
Email: ruddigore1@aol.com
Website: http://www.spectrumliteraryagency.com

Handles: Fiction; Nonfiction; *Areas:* Fantasy; Historical; Mystery; Romance; Sci-Fi; Suspense; *Markets:* Adult; *Treatments:* Contemporary; Mainstream

Send query with SASE describing your book and providing background information, publishing credits, and relevant qualifications. The first 10 pages of the work may also be included. Response within three months. No unsolicited MSS or queries by fax, email, or phone.

Spencerhill Associates

PO Box 374, Chatham, NY 12037
Tel: +1 (518) 392-9293
Fax: +1 (518) 392-9554
Email: submission@spencerhillassociates.com
Website: http://spencerhillassociates.com

Handles: Fiction; Nonfiction; *Areas:* Erotic; Fantasy; Mystery; Romance; Thrillers; *Markets:* Adult; Youth; *Treatments:* Commercial; Literary

Handles commercial, general-interest fiction, romance including historical romance, paranormal romance, urban fantasy, erotic fiction, category romance, literary fiction, thrillers and mysteries, young adult, and nonfiction. No children's. Send query by email with synopsis and first three chapters attached in .doc / .rtf / .txt format. See website for full details.

The Spieler Agency

27 West 20th Street, Suite 305, New York, NY 10011
Tel: +1 (212) 757-4439, ext.1
Fax: +1 (212) 333.2019
Email: thespieleragency@gmail.com
Website: http://thespieleragency.com

Handles: Fiction; Nonfiction; Poetry; *Areas:* Autobiography; Biography; Business; Cookery; Crime; Culture; Current Affairs; Film; Finance; Health; Historical; Humour; Legal; Lifestyle; Music; Mystery; Nature; Photography; Politics; Science; Sociology; Spiritual; Theatre; Thrillers; Travel; Women's Interests; *Markets:* Adult; Children's; Youth; *Treatments:* Literary; Popular

Consult website for details of specific agents' interests and contact details. Send query by email or by post with SASE. Response not guaranteed if not interested. No response to postal submissions without SASE.

Philip G. Spitzer Literary Agency, Inc.

50 Talmage Farm Lane, East Hampton, NY 11937

Tel: +1 (631) 329-3650
Fax: +1 (631) 329-3651
Email: Luc.Hunt@spitzeragency.com
Website: http://spitzeragency.com

Handles: Fiction; Nonfiction; *Areas:* Biography; Current Affairs; Historical; Mystery; Politics; Short Stories; Sport; Suspense; Thrillers; Travel; *Markets:* Adult; *Treatments:* Literary

Full client list, but will consider queries regarding work you believe is absolutely right for the agency. Send query by email or by post.

Nancy Stauffer Associates

PO Box 1203, Darien, CT 06820
Tel: +1 (203) 202-2500
Fax: +1 (203) 655-3704
Email: nancy@staufferliterary.com

Handles: Fiction; Nonfiction; *Areas:* Culture; Current Affairs; *Markets:* Adult; Youth; *Treatments:* Contemporary; Literary

Specialises in literary fiction, young adult, and narrative nonfiction. Send query by email only inlcuding first 10 pages. Most new clients taken on via referral by existing clients. No genre fiction (mysteries, science fiction/fantasy, romance), historical fiction, thrillers, or action/adventure. Does not respond to all queries.

Sternig & Byrne Literary Agency

2370 S. 107th Street, Apt 4, Milwaukee, Wisconsin 53227-2036
Tel: +1 (414) 328-8034
Fax: +1 (414) 328-8034
Email: jackbyrne@hotmail.com
Website: http://sff.net/people/jackbyrne

Handles: Fiction; Nonfiction; *Areas:* Fantasy; Horror; Mystery; Sci-Fi; Suspense; *Markets:* Adult; Youth

Send brief query by post or email in first instance (if sending by email send in the body of the mail, do not send attachments). Will request further materials if interested. Currently only considering science fiction, fantasy, and mysteries. Preference given to writers with a publishing history.

Robin Straus Agency, Inc.

229 East 79th Street, Suite 5A, New York, NY 10075
Tel: +1 (212) 472-3282
Fax: +1 (212) 472-3833
Email: info@robinstrausagency.com
Website: http://www.robinstrausagency.com

Handles: Fiction; Nonfiction; *Areas:* Autobiography; Biography; Cookery; Culture; Current Affairs; Historical; Lifestyle; Nature; Psychology; Science; Women's Interests; *Markets:* Adult; *Treatments:* Commercial; Literary

Send query with SASE, bio, synopsis or outline, submission history, and market information. You may also include the opening chapter. Approaches by email are accepted, but all material must be in the body of the email. No attachments. No juvenile, young adult, science fiction/fantasy, horror, romance, westerns, poetry or screenplays. No response to approaches without SASE. No metered postage. If no response after 6 weeks, assume rejection.

Stuart Krichevsky Literary Agency, Inc.

381 Park Avenue South, Suite 428, New York, NY 10016
Tel: +1 (212) 725-5288
Fax: +1 (212) 725-5275
Email: query@skagency.com
Website: http://www.skagency.com

Handles: Fiction; Nonfiction; *Areas:* Adventure; Autobiography; Biography; Business; Culture; Current Affairs; Fantasy; Historical; Nature; Politics; Science; Sci-Fi; Technology; *Markets:* Adult; Youth; *Treatments:* Commercial; Literary

Send query by email with first few pages of your manuscript (up to 10) pasted into body of the email (no attachments). See website for complete submission guidelines and appropriate submission addresses for each agent.

The Stuart Agency

260 West 52 Street, Suite. 24-C, New York, NY 10019
Tel: +1 (212) 586-2711
Fax: +1 (212) 977-1488
Email: andrew@stuartagency.com
Website: http://www.stuartagency.com

Handles: Fiction; Nonfiction; *Areas:* Autobiography; Business; Current Affairs; Health; Historical; Lifestyle; Psychology; Religious; Science; Sport; *Markets:* Adult; *Treatments:* Commercial; Literary

Send query using submission form on website.

Susanna Lea Associates

331 West 20th Street, New York, NY 10011
Tel: +1 (646) 638-1435
Fax: +1 (646) 638 1436
Email: us-submission@susannalea.com
Website: http://www.susannaleaassociates.com

Handles: Fiction; Nonfiction; *Markets:* Adult

Agency based in France with US office in New York and UK office in London. No poetry, plays, screenplays, science fiction, educational text books, short stories, illustrated works, or queries by fax or post. Submit by email. See website for specific email addresses for US, UK, and French submissions. Include query letter, brief synopsis, first three chapters and/or proposal. Response not guaranteed.

Talcott Notch Literary

2 Broad Street, Second Floor, Suites 1,2 & 10, Milford, Connecticut 06460
Tel: +1 (203) 876-4959
Fax: +1 (203) 876-9517
Email: editorial@talcottnotch.net
Website: http://www.talcottnotch.net

Handles: Fiction; Nonfiction; *Areas:* Autobiography; Business; Cookery; Crafts; Crime; Fantasy; Gardening; Historical; Horror; Lifestyle; Mystery; Nature; Science; Sci-Fi; Suspense; Technology; Thrillers; Women's Interests; *Markets:* Adult; Children's; Family; Youth; *Treatments:* Mainstream

Rapidly growing literary agency seeking fresh voices in fiction and expert nonfiction authors. Our President has over fifteen years in the publishing industry. Send query by email or by post with SASE, including outline or synopsis and first ten pages. No email attachments. See website for full guidelines.

Talent Source

1711 Dean Forest Road, Suite H, Savannah, Georgia 31408
Tel: +1 (912) 232-9390
Fax: +1 (912) 232-8213
Email: michael@talentsource.com
Website: http://www.talentsource.com

Handles: Scripts; *Areas:* Drama; Humour; Religious; *Markets:* Adult

Send query with synopsis covering Exposition, Conflict and Resolution, by email. It should not tease the reader, but be an outline of the complete story.

Interested only in character-driven comedies and dramas, e.g.: Something about Mary, Sex, Lies and Videotape, SlingBlade, The Spitfire Grill, The Apostle, Chasing Amy, Pulp Fiction, Monster's Ball, Clerks, Reservoir Dogs, My Big Fat Greek Wedding, etc. Also handles TV movies, series, and one-off specials.

No unsolicited MSS, books, poetry, science fiction, horror, period/costume, road pictures, or big budget special effects/CGI feature films.

Patricia Teal Literary Agency

2036 Vista Del Rosa, Fullerton, CA 92831-1336
Tel: +1 (714) 738-8333
Fax: +1 (714) 738-8333

Handles: Fiction; Nonfiction; *Areas:* Biography; Crime; Health; Historical; How-to; Lifestyle; Mystery; Nature; Psychology; Romance; Self-Help; Women's Interests; *Markets:* Adult; *Treatments:* Commercial;

Contemporary; Mainstream

Deals with published authors only. Send query with SASE in first instance. Specialises in women's fiction, and commercial how-to and self-help. No short stories, poetry, articles, regency romance, science fiction, fantasy, or queries by fax or email.

Tessler Literary Agency

27 West 20th Street, Suite 1003, New York, NY 10011
Tel: +1 (212) 242-0466
Fax: +1 (212) 242-2366
Website: http://www.tessleragency.com

Handles: Fiction; Nonfiction; *Areas:* Autobiography; Biography; Business; Cookery; Historical; Psychology; Science; Travel; Women's Interests; *Markets:* Adult; *Treatments:* Commercial; Literary; Popular

Welcomes appropriate queries. Handles quality nonfiction and literary and commercial fiction. No genre fiction or children's fiction. Send query via form on website only.

Tom Lee

716 Kishwaukee Street #D, Rockford, IL 61104
Tel: +1 (815) 505-9147 or +1 (815) 708-7123
Fax: +1 (815) 964-3061
Email: chicagocatorange@yahoo.com

Handles: Fiction; Poetry; Scripts; *Areas:* Adventure; Anthropology; Antiques; Archaeology; Arts; Autobiography; Crime; Drama; Erotic; Fantasy; Film; Historical; Horror; Literature; Mystery; Religious; Sci-Fi; Short Stories; Theatre; Thrillers; *Markets:* Adult; Professional; *Treatments:* Commercial; Dark; Experimental; In-depth; Literary; Mainstream; Progressive; Serious

Want writers who have educated capability in handling their material. Meet the structural and syntactical demands of the publishers and producers, and must be easy to work with, know the industries, and not be playing the self-possessed, eccentric artiste, so to say.

Scott Treimel NY

434 Lafayette Street, New York, NY 10003
Tel: +1 (212) 505-8353
Email: general@scotttreimelny.com
Website: http://www.scotttreimelny.com

Handles: Fiction; Nonfiction; *Markets:* Children's; Youth

Children's books only – from concept / board books to teen fiction. Accepts submissions only by referral from contacts, and from attendees at conferences.

TriadaUS Literary Agency, Inc.

P.O.Box 561, Sewickley, PA 15143
Tel: +1 (412) 401-3376
Email: uwe@triadaus.com
Website: http://www.triadaus.com

Handles: Fiction; Nonfiction; *Areas:* Adventure; Autobiography; Biography; Cookery; Crime; Culture; Current Affairs; Health; How-to; Mystery; Psychology; Romance; Sci-Fi; Self-Help; Sport; Thrillers; Travel; *Markets:* Adult; Children's; Youth; *Treatments:* Commercial; Literary

Actively seeking established and new writers in a wide range of genres. Will only respond to approaches following the guidelines outlined on the website. Only responds to postal queries that include an SASE. Prefers email approaches, but no attachments.

Trident Media Group, LLC

41 Madison Avenue, 36th Fl., New York, NY 10010
Tel: +1 (212) 333-1511
Email: info@tridentmediagroup.com
Website: http://www.tridentmediagroup.com

Handles: Fiction; Nonfiction; *Areas:* Adventure; Autobiography; Biography; Business; Crime; Culture; Current Affairs; Film; Health; Historical; Humour; Lifestyle; Music; Mystery; Politics; Romance; Science; Sport; Suspense; Thrillers; Women's Interests; *Markets:* Adult; Children's; Youth;

Treatments: Commercial; Literary

Send query using form on website. Check website for details and interests of specific agents and approach one agent only. Do not approach more than one agent at a time. No unsolicited MSS.

2M Literary Agency Ltd

33 West 17 Street, PH, New York, NY 10011
Tel: +1 (212) 741-1509
Fax: +1 (212) 691-4460
Email: morel@2mcommunications.com
Website:
http://www.2mcommunications.com

Handles: Nonfiction; *Areas:* Autobiography; Beauty and Fashion; Business; Cookery; Crime; Culture; Film; Health; Lifestyle; Medicine; Music; Politics; Psychology; Science; Sport; *Markets:* Adult; Family; *Treatments:* Contemporary; Mainstream; Niche; Popular; Progressive; Traditional

Only accepts queries from established ghostwriters, collaborators, and editors with experience in the fields of business; film, music and television; health and fitness; medicine and psychology; parenting; politics; science; sport; true crime; or the world of food.

Venture Literary

2683 Via de la Valle, G-714, Del Mar, CA 92014
Tel: +1 (619) 807-1887
Fax: +1 (772) 365-8321
Email: submissions@ventureliterary.com
Website: http://www.ventureliterary.com

Handles: Fiction; Nonfiction; *Areas:* Adventure; Anthropology; Antiques; Archaeology; Architecture; Arts; Autobiography; Beauty and Fashion; Biography; Business; Cookery; Crafts; Crime; Criticism; Culture; Current Affairs; Design; Drama; Entertainment; Erotic; Film; Finance; Gardening; Gothic; Health; Historical; Hobbies; Horror; How-to; Humour; Legal; Leisure; Lifestyle; Literature; Media; Medicine; Men's Interests; Military; Music; Mystery; Nature; New Age; Philosophy; Photography; Politics; Psychology; Radio; Religious; Science; Self-Help; Short Stories; Sociology; Spiritual; Sport; Suspense; Technology; Theatre; Thrillers; Translations; Travel; TV; Women's Interests; *Markets:* Adult

Willing to consider queries in all genres except fantasy, sci-fi, romance, children's picture books, and westerns. Send query letter by email only. First 50 pages will be requested by email if interested in proposal. Unsolicited queries, proposals, or manuscripts via snail mail, and all snail mail submissions will be discarded unopened.

Veritas Literary Agency

601 Van Ness Avenue, Opera Plaza Suite E, San Francisco, CA 94102
Tel: +1 (415) 647-6964
Fax: +1 (415) 647-6965
Email: submissions@veritasliterary.com
Website: http://www.veritasliterary.com

Handles: Fiction; Nonfiction; *Areas:* Business; Crime; Culture; Erotic; Fantasy; Health; Historical; Lifestyle; Mystery; Nature; Science; Sci-Fi; Self-Help; Thrillers; Women's Interests; *Markets:* Adult; Children's; Youth; *Treatments:* Commercial; Literary

Send query or proposal by email only. Submit further information on request only. For fiction, include cover letter listing previously published work, one-page summary and first two chapters. For nonfiction, include author bio, overview, chapter-by-chapter summary, and analysis of competing titles.

Wales Literary Agency, Inc

PO Box 9426, Seattle, WA 98109
Tel: +1 (206) 284-7114
Email: waleslit@waleslit.com
Website: http://www.waleslit.com

Handles: Fiction; Nonfiction; *Areas:* Culture; Politics; *Markets:* Adult; *Treatments:* Progressive

Represents quality works of fiction and narrative nonfiction. The Agency is especially interested in story-driven narratives, new voices, and progressive cultural and political points of view. No self-help, how-to, children's books, romance, genre in general (including mysteries), or screenplays. Send query by post with SASE, or by email (must be no longer than one page and must not include attachments), explaining who you are, what your book is about, and why other readers might be interested. No unsolicited MSS, or queries by fax or phone.

Waterside Productions, Inc

2055 Oxford Avenue, Cardiff, CA 92007
Tel: +1 (760) 632-9190
Fax: +1 (760) 632-9295
Email: admin@waterside.com
Website: http://www.waterside.com

Handles: Nonfiction; *Areas:* Business; Cookery; Health; Hobbies; How-to; Lifestyle; Sociology; Spiritual; Sport; Technology; *Markets:* Adult

Described itself as the world's premiere literary agency for computer and technology authors. Send query by post or fill in online form. You are expected to show knowledge of your market, established titles you will be competing with, and to have researched the niche for your book thoroughly. See website for full proposal guidelines. No unsolicited MSS.

Watkins / Loomis Agency, Inc.

PO Box 20925, New York, NY 10025
Tel: +1 (212) 532-0080
Fax: +1 (646) 383-2449
Email: assistant@watkinsloomis.com
Website: http://www.watkinsloomis.com

Handles: Fiction; Nonfiction; *Areas:* Autobiography; Biography; Culture; Current Affairs; Historical; Nature; Politics; Short Stories; Technology; Travel; *Markets:* Adult; Youth; *Treatments:* Contemporary; Literary; Popular

Specialises in literary fiction, memoir, biography, essay, travel, and political journalism. No unsolicited MSS and does not guarantee a response to queries.

Waxman Leavell Literary Agency

443 Park Ave South, #1004, New York, NY 10016
Tel: +1 (212) 675-5556
Fax: +1 (212) 675-1381
Email: scottsubmit@waxmanleavell.com
Website: http://www.waxmanleavell.com

Handles: Fiction; Nonfiction; *Areas:* Adventure; Autobiography; Biography; Business; Culture; Entertainment; Fantasy; Historical; Humour; Military; Mystery; Romance; Sci-Fi; Sport; Thrillers; Women's Interests; *Markets:* Adult; Children's; Youth; *Treatments:* Commercial; Contemporary; Literary

Send query by email to one of the agent-specific addresses on the website. Do not query more than one agent at a time. For details of what each agent is looking for, see details on website. No attachments, but for fiction include 5-10 pages in the body of the email.

Weed Literary LLC

Email: info@weedliterary.com

Handles: Fiction; *Areas:* Women's Interests; *Markets:* Adult

Agency specialising in upmarket women's fiction. No picture books, romance, YA, middle-grade, or nonfiction. No submissions by post. Send query by email only. See website for more information.

The Wendy Weil Agency, Inc.

232 Madison Avenue, Suite 1300, New York, NY 10016
Tel: +1 (212) 685-0030
Fax: +1 (212) 685-0765
Email: wweil@wendyweil.com
Website: http://www.wendyweil.com

Handles: Fiction; Nonfiction; *Areas:* Arts; Autobiography; Culture; Current Affairs; Health; Historical; Lifestyle; Mystery; Science; Thrillers; *Markets:* Adult; *Treatments:* Commercial; Literary

Note: The status of this agency is

uncertain. The principal agent died in 2012, but the website is still up and still shows the same information as prior to her death. The two remaining agents are reported to have moved to another agency with the intention of taking their clients with them, while the agency itself has been sold to a third party.

Send query by post (up to two pages, plus synopsis and SASE) or by email (response not guaranteed). Response in 4-6 weeks. No screenplays or textbooks.

The Weingel-Fidel Agency

310 East 46th Street, Suite 21-E, New York, NY 10017
Tel: +1 (212) 599-2959
Email: lwf@theweingel-fidelagency.com

Handles: Fiction; Nonfiction; *Areas:* Arts; Autobiography; Biography; Music; Psychology; Science; Sociology; Technology; Women's Interests; *Markets:* Adult; *Treatments:* Commercial; Literary; Mainstream

Accepts new clients by referral only – approach only via an existing client or industry contact. Specialises in commercial and literary fiction and nonfiction. Particularly interested in investigative journalism. No genre fiction, science fiction, fantasy, or self-help.

Whimsy Literary Agency, LLC

310 East 12th Street, Suite 2C, New York, NY 10003
Tel: +1 (212) 674-7162
Email: whimsynyc@aol.com
Website: http://whimsyliteraryagency.com

Handles: Nonfiction; *Areas:* Beauty and Fashion; Business; Cookery; Culture; Entertainment; Health; How-to; Humour; Politics; Psychology; Religious; Self-Help; Spiritual; *Markets:* Adult; *Treatments:* Commercial

No unsolicited mss. Send query by email in first instance.

Wolfson Literary Agency

Email: query@wolfsonliterary.com
Website: http://www.wolfsonliterary.com

Handles: Fiction; Nonfiction; *Areas:* Culture; Health; How-to; Humour; Lifestyle; Medicine; Mystery; Romance; Suspense; Thrillers; Women's Interests; *Markets:* Adult; Youth; *Treatments:* Mainstream; Popular

Accepts queries by email only. Response only if interested. See website for full submission guidelines.

Writers House, LLC.

21 West 26th Street, New York, NY 10010
Tel: +1 (212) 685-2400
Fax: +1 (212) 685-1781
Email: Azuckerman@writershouse.com
Website: http://writershouse.com

Handles: Fiction; Nonfiction; *Areas:* Autobiography; Biography; Business; Cookery; Fantasy; Finance; Historical; How-to; Lifestyle; Psychology; Science; Sci-Fi; Self-Help; Women's Interests; *Markets:* Adult; Children's; Youth; *Treatments:* Commercial; Literary

Handles adult and juvenile fiction and nonfiction, commercial and literary, including picture books. Send query letter of no more than two pages with SASE, synopsis, and CV. No scripts, professional, poetry, or scholarly. Does not guarantee a response to electronic queries. Policies of individual agents vary. Do not query more than one agent at a time. See website for full details.

Writers' Representatives, LLC

116 W. 14th St., 11th Fl., New York, NY 10011-7305
Tel: +1 (212) 620-0023
Fax: +1 (212) 620-0023
Email: transom@writersreps.com
Website: http://www.writersreps.com

Handles: Fiction; Nonfiction; Poetry; Reference; *Areas:* Autobiography; Biography; Business; Cookery; Criticism; Current Affairs; Finance; Historical;

Humour; Legal; Literature; Mystery; Philosophy; Politics; Science; Self-Help; Thrillers; *Markets:* Adult; *Treatments:* Literary; Serious

Send email describing your project and yourself, or send proposal, outline, CV, and sample chapters, or complete unsolicited MS, with SASE. See website for submission requirements in FAQ section. Specialises in serious and literary fiction and nonfiction. No screenplays. No science fiction or children's or young adult fiction unless it aspires to serious literature.

Yates & Yates

1100 Town and Country Road, Suite 1300, Orange, CA 92868
Tel: +1 (714) 480-4000
Fax: +1 (714) 480-4001
Email: email@yates2.com
Website: http://www.yates2.com

Handles: Fiction; Nonfiction; *Areas:* Autobiography; Biography; Business; Current Affairs; Legal; Politics; Religious; Sport; Thrillers; Women's Interests; *Markets:* Adult; *Treatments:* Literary

Literary agency based in California. Takes a holistic approach, combining agency representation, expert legal advice, marketing guidance, career coaching, creative counseling, and business management consulting.

The Zack Company, Inc

PMB 525, 4653 Carmel Mountain Rd, Ste 308, San Diego, CA 92130-6650
Website: http://www.zackcompany.com

Handles: Fiction; Nonfiction; Reference; *Areas:* Adventure; Autobiography; Biography; Business; Cookery; Crime; Current Affairs; Entertainment; Erotic; Fantasy; Film; Finance; Gardening; Health; Historical; Horror; Humour; Lifestyle; Medicine; Military; Music; Mystery; Nature; Politics; Religious; Romance; Science; Sci-Fi; Self-Help; Spiritual; Sport; Suspense; Technology; Thrillers; Translations; TV; Women's Interests; *Markets:* Adult; *Treatments:* Commercial; Literary; Popular

IMPORTANT: This agency objects to being listed on firstwriter.com and has in the past threatened to reject any submission from a writer who found his details through this site. We therefore suggest that if you approach this agency you do not state where you found its contact details.

The agent has also stated that his requirements change frequently, so it is important to check the agency website before approaching. Fully consult the agency's requirements for material and queries before approaching.

While external reports indicate that this agency is legitimate and has made confirmed sales to royalty-paying publishers, please note that it appears to have been formerly listed as "not recommended" on another site. It no longer appears to be part of the AAR. It also offers Editorial Services, which we believe would contravene the AAR canon of ethics, which state "the practice of literary agents charging clients or potential clients for reading and evaluating literary works (including outlines, proposals, and partial or complete manuscripts) is subject to serious abuse that reflects adversely on our profession".

See website at http://www.zackcompany.com for full guidelines on querying. Please note that approaches are not accepted to the former submissions email address (submissions@zackcompany.com). Electronic approaches must be made via the form on the website.

UK Literary Agents

For the most up-to-date listings of these and hundreds of other literary agents, visit http://www.firstwriter.com/Agents

*To claim your **free** access to the site, please see the back of this book.*

A & B Personal Management Ltd

PO Box 64671, London, NW3 9LH
Tel: +44 (0) 20 7794 3255
Email: b.ellmain@aandb.co.uk

Handles: Fiction; Nonfiction; Scripts; *Areas:* Film; Theatre; TV; *Markets:* Adult

Handles full-length mss and scripts for film, TV, and theatre. No unsolicited mss. Query by email or by phone in first instance.

A for Authors

73 Hurlingham Road, Bexleyheath, Kent DA7 5PE
Email: enquiries@aforauthors.co.uk
Website: http://aforauthors.co.uk

Handles: Fiction; Nonfiction; *Markets:* Adult; Children's; *Treatments:* Commercial; Literary

Query by email only. Include synopsis and first three chapters (or up to 50 pages) and short author bio. All attachments must be Word format documents. No scripts, poetry, fantasy, SF, horror, short stories, adult illustrated books on art, architecture, design, visual culture, or submissions by post, hand delivery, or on discs, memory sticks, or other electronic devices. See website for full details.

Sheila Ableman Literary Agency

36 Duncan House, Fellows Road, London, NW3 3LZ
Tel: +44 (0) 20 7586 2339
Email: sheila@sheilaableman.co.uk
Website: http://www.sheilaableman.com

Handles: Nonfiction; *Areas:* Autobiography; Biography; Historical; Science; TV; *Markets:* Adult; *Treatments:* Commercial; Popular

Send query with SAE, brief bio, one-page synopsis, and two sample chapters. Specialises in popular history, science, biography, autobiography, general narrative and 'quirky' nonfiction with strong commercial appeal, TV tie-ins and celebrity ghost writing. No poetry, children's books, gardening, or sport.

The Agency (London) Ltd

24 Pottery Lane, Holland Park, London, W11 4LZ
Tel: +44 (0) 20 7727 1346
Fax: +44 (0) 20 7727 9037
Email: info@theagency.co.uk
Website: http://www.theagency.co.uk

Handles: Fiction; Nonfiction; Scripts; *Areas:* Film; Radio; Theatre; TV; *Markets:* Adult; Children's

Represents writers and authors for film, television, radio and the theatre. Also represents directors, producers, composers, and film and television rights in books, as well as authors of children's books from picture books to teen fiction. **Handles adult fiction and nonfiction for existing clients only**. Does not consider adult fiction or nonfiction from writers who are not already clients. For script writers, only considers unsolicited material if it has been recommended by a producer, development executive or course tutor. If this is the case send CV, covering letter and details of your referee to the relevant agent, or to the email address below. Do not email more than one agent at a time. For directors, send CV, showreel and cover letter by email. For children's authors, send query by email with synopsis and first three chapters (middle grade and teen) or complete ms (picture books) to address given on website.

Aitken Alexander Associates

18–21 Cavaye Place, London, SW10 9PT
Tel: +44 (0) 20 7373 8672
Fax: +44 (0) 20 7373 6002
Email: submissions@aitkenalexander.co.uk
Website: http://www.aitkenalexander.co.uk

Handles: Fiction; Nonfiction; *Markets:* Adult

Send query by email, with short synopsis, and first 30 pages as a Word document. No illustrated children's books, poetry or screenplays. No submissions or queries by post.

The Ampersand Agency Ltd

Ryman's Cottages, Little Tew, Chipping Norton, Oxfordshire OX7 4JJ
Tel: +44 (0) 1608 683677 / 683898
Fax: +44 (0) 1608 683449
Email: amd@theampersandagency.co.uk
Website: http://www.theampersandagency.co.uk

Handles: Fiction; Nonfiction; *Areas:* Autobiography; Biography; Crime; Current Affairs; Fantasy; Historical; Horror; Sci-Fi; Thrillers; Women's Interests; *Markets:* Adult; Youth; *Treatments:* Commercial; Contemporary; Literary

We handle literary and commercial fiction and nonfiction, including contemporary and historical novels, crime, thrillers, biography, women's fiction, history, current affairs, and memoirs. Send query by post or email with brief bio, outline, and first two chapters. Also accepts science fiction, fantasy, horror, and Young Adult material to separate email address listed on website. No scripts except those by existing clients, no poetry, self-help or illustrated children's books. No unpublished American writers, because in our experience British and European publishers aren't interested unless there is an American publisher on board. And we'd like to make it clear that American stamps are no use outside America!

Darley Anderson Children's

Estelle House, 11 Eustace Road, London, SW6 1JB
Tel: +44 (0) 20 7386 2674
Fax: +44 (0) 20 7386 5571
Email: childrens@darleyanderson.com
Website: http://www.darleyandersonchildrens.com

Handles: Fiction; Nonfiction; *Markets:* Children's

Handles fiction and nonfiction for children. Send query by email or by post with SAE, short synopsis, and first three consecutive chapters. For picture books, send complete text or picture book. Prefers to read material exclusively, but will accept simultaneous submissions if notice given on cover letter.

Anne Clark Literary Agency

PO Box 1221 , Harlton, Cambridge , CB23 1WW
Tel: +44 (0) 1223 262160
Email: submissions@anneclarkliteraryagency.co.uk
Website: http://www.anneclarkliteraryagency.co.uk

Handles: Fiction; *Markets:* Children's; Youth

Handles fiction and picture books for

children and young adults. Send query by email only with first 20 pages, or complete ms for picture books. No submissions by post. See website for full guidelines.

Anthony Sheil in Association with Aitken Alexander Associates

18-21 Cavaye Place, London, SW10 9PT
Tel: +44 (0) 20 7373 8672
Fax: +44 (0) 20 7373 6002
Website:
http://www.aitkenalexander.co.uk/agents/anthony-sheil/

Handles: Fiction; Nonfiction; *Markets:* Adult

Handles fiction and nonfiction. No scripts, poetry, short stories, or children's fiction. Send query by post with SAE, synopsis up to half a page, and first 30 pages.

Anubis Literary Agency

6 Birdhaven Close, Lighthorne Heath, CV35 0BE
Tel: +44 (0) 1926 642588
Fax: +44 (0) 1926 642588
Email: writerstuff2@btopenworld.com

Handles: Fiction; *Areas:* Fantasy; Horror; Sci-Fi; *Markets:* Adult

No children's books, poetry, short stories, journalism, TV or film scripts, academic or nonfiction. Only considers genre fiction as listed above. Send a covering letter with one-page synopsis and 50-page sample. SAE essential. No telephone calls, or email / fax queries. Simultaneous queries accepted, but no material returned without SAE. Usually responds in six weeks to queries and three months to MSS. Runs regular writers' workshops/seminars to help writers. Email for details.

AP Watt at United Agents LLP

12-26 Lexington Street, London, W1F 0LE
Tel: +44 (0) 20 3214 0800
Fax: +44 (0) 20 3214 0801
Email: info@unitedagents.co.uk
Website: http://www.apwatt.co.uk

Handles: Fiction; Nonfiction; Scripts; *Areas:* Autobiography; Biography; Business; Cookery; Crime; Film; Gardening; Health; Historical; Medicine; Music; Politics; Psychology; Romance; Science; Sport; Technology; Thrillers; Translations; Travel; TV; *Markets:* Adult; Children's; *Treatments:* Commercial; Literary

No poetry, academic, specialist, or unsolicited MSS. Send query letter by post or by email for the attention of a specific agent, including full plot synopsis. See website for details of agents and their interests.

Artellus Limited

30 Dorset House, Gloucester Place, London, NW1 5AD
Tel: +44 (0) 20 7935 6972
Fax: +44 (0) 20 8609 0347
Email: leslie@artellusltd.co.uk
Website: http://www.artellusltd.co.uk

Handles: Fiction; Nonfiction; *Areas:* Arts; Beauty and Fashion; Biography; Crime; Culture; Current Affairs; Entertainment; Fantasy; Historical; Military; Science; Sci-Fi; *Markets:* Adult; Youth; *Treatments:* Contemporary; Literary

Welcomes submissions from new fiction and nonfiction writers. Send first three chapters and synopsis in first instance. No film or TV scripts. If you would prefer to submit electronically send query by email in advance.

Author Literary Agents

53 Talbot Road, Highgate, London, N6 4QX
Tel: +44 (0) 20 8341 0442
Fax: +44 (0) 20 8341 0442
Email: a@authors.co.uk

Handles: Fiction; Nonfiction; Scripts; *Areas:* Thrillers; *Markets:* Adult; Children's

Send query with SAE, one-page outline and first chapter, scene, or writing sample. Handles fiction, nonfiction, novels, thrillers, graphic novels, children's books, and media entertainment concepts. Handles material for book publishers, screen producers, and graphic media ideas.

Bath Literary Agency

5 Gloucester Road, Bath, BA1 7BH
Email: gill.mclay@bathliteraryagency.com
Website: http://bathliteraryagency.com

Handles: Fiction; Nonfiction; *Markets:* Children's; Youth

Handles fiction and nonfiction for children, from picture books to Young Adult. Send query by post with SAE for reply and return of materials if required, along with the first three chapters (fiction) or the full manuscript (picture books). See website for full details.

Lorella Belli Literary Agency (LBLA)

54 Hartford House, 35 Tavistock Crescent, Notting Hill, London, W11 1AY
Tel: +44 (0) 20 7727 8547
Fax: +44 (0) 870 787 4194
Email: info@lorellabelliagency.com
Website: http://www.lorellabelliagency.com

Handles: Fiction; Nonfiction; *Markets:* Adult; *Treatments:* Literary

Send query by post or by email in first instance. No attachments. Particularly interested in multicultural / international writing, and books relating to Italy, or written in Italian; first novelists, and journalists; successful sel-published authors. Welcomes queries from new authors and will suggest revisions where appropriate. No poetry, children's, original scripts, academic, SF, or fantasy.

Berlin Associates

7 Tyers Gate, London , SE1 3HX
Tel: +44 (0) 20 7836 1112
Fax: +44 (0) 20 7632 5296
Email: submissions@berlinassociates.com
Website: http://www.berlinassociates.com

Handles: Scripts; *Areas:* Film; Radio; Theatre; TV; *Markets:* Adult

Most clients through recommendation or invitation, but accepts queries by email with CV, experience, and outline of work you would like to submit.

The Blair Partnership

Middlesex House, 4th Floor, 34-42 Cleveland Street , London, W1T 4JE
Tel: +44 (0) 20 7504 2520
Fax: +44 (0) 20 7504 2521
Email: submissions@theblairpartnership.com
Website: http://www.theblairpartnership.com

Handles: Fiction; Nonfiction; *Markets:* Adult; Children's; Family; Youth

Open to all genres of fiction and nonfiction. Send query by email with one-page synopsis and first ten pages, including some detail about yourself.

Blake Friedmann Literary Agency Ltd

First Floor, Selous House, 5-12 Mandela Street, London, NW1 0DU
Tel: +44 (0) 20 7387 0842
Fax: +44 (0) 20 7691 9626
Email: info@blakefriedmann.co.uk
Website: http://www.blakefriedmann.co.uk

Handles: Fiction; Nonfiction; Scripts; *Areas:* Biography; Film; Radio; Thrillers; Travel; TV; Women's Interests; *Markets:* Adult; Youth; *Treatments:* Commercial; Literary

Send query by email to a specific agent best suited to your work. See website for full submission guidelines, details of agents, and individual agent contact details.

No poetry or plays. Short stories and journalism for existing clients only.

Media department currently only accepting submissions from writers with produced credits.

Reply not guaranteed.

Luigi Bonomi Associates Ltd

91 Great Russell Street, London, WC1 3PS
Tel: +44 (0) 20 7637 1234

Fax: +44 (0) 20 7637 2111
Email: info@lbabooks.com
Website: http://www.lbabooks.com

Handles: Fiction; Nonfiction; *Areas:* Crime; Health; Historical; Lifestyle; Science; Thrillers; TV; Women's Interests; *Markets:* Adult; Youth; *Treatments:* Commercial; Literary

Keen to find new authors. Send query with synopsis and first three chapters by post with SAE (if return of material required) or email address for response, or by email (Word or PDF attachments only). See website for specific agents' interests and email addresses. No scripts, poetry, children's, science fiction, or fantasy.

Bookseeker Agency

PO Box 7535, Perth, PH2 1AF
Tel: +44 (0) 1738 620688
Email: bookseeker@blueyonder.co.uk
Website: http://bookseekeragency.com

Handles: Fiction; Poetry; *Markets:* Adult

Handles poetry and general creative writing. No nonfiction. Send query by post or email outlining what you have written and your current projects, along with synopsis and sample chapter (novels) or half a dozen poems.

The Bright Literary Academy

Studio 102, 250 York Road, London, SW11 1RJ
Tel: +44 (0) 20 7326 9140
Email: literarysubmissions@brightgroupinternational.com
Website: http://www.brightgroupinternational.com

Handles: Fiction; *Areas:* Autobiography; Entertainment; Literature; Mystery; Sci-Fi; Self-Help; Short Stories; Thrillers; TV; Women's Interests; *Markets:* Children's; Youth; *Treatments:* Commercial; Contemporary; Mainstream; Positive

A boutique literary agency representing the most fabulous new talent to grace the publishing industry in recent years. Born out of the success of a leading illustration agency with an outstanding global client list this agency aims to produce sensational material across all genres of children's publishing, including novelty, picture books, fiction and adult autobiographies, in order to become a one-stop-shop for publishers looking for something extra special to fit into their lists.

Prides itself on nurturing the creativity of its authors and illustrators so that they can concentrate on their craft rather than negotiate their contracts. As a creative agency we develop seeds of ideas into something extraordinary, before searching for the right publisher with which to develop them further to create incredible and unforgettable books.

We are fortunate enough to have a never-ending source of remarkable material at our fingertips and a stable of exceptional creators who are all united by one common goal – a deep passion and dedication to children's books and literature in all its shapes and forms.

Alan Brodie Representation Ltd

Paddock Suite, The Courtyard, 55 Charterhouse Street, London, EC1M 6HA
Tel: +44 (0) 20 7253 6226
Fax: +44 (0) 20 7183 7999
Email: ABR@alanbrodie.com
Website: http://www.alanbrodie.com

Handles: Scripts; *Areas:* Film; Radio; Theatre; TV; *Markets:* Adult

Handles scripts only. No books. Approach with preliminary letter, recommendation from industry professional, CV, and SAE. Do not send a sample of work unless requested. No fiction, nonfiction, or poetry.

Jenny Brown Associates

33 Argyle Place, Edinburgh, Scotland EH9 1JT
Tel: +44 (0) 1312 295334
Email: info@jennybrownassociates.com
Website: http://www.jennybrownassociates.com

Handles: Fiction; Nonfiction; *Areas:* Biography; Crime; Culture; Finance; Historical; Humour; Music; Romance; Science; Sport; Thrillers; Women's Interests; *Markets:* Adult; Children's; *Treatments:* Commercial; Literary; Popular

Strongly prefers queries by email. Approach by post only if not possible to do so by email. Send query with market information, bio, synopsis and first 50 pages in one document (fiction) or sample chapter and info on market and your background (nonfiction). No academic, poetry, short stories, science fiction, or fantasy. Responds only if interested. If no response in 8 weeks assume rejection. See website for individual agent interests and email addresses.

Felicity Bryan

2a North Parade Avenue, Banbury Road, Oxford, OX2 6LX
Tel: +44 (0) 1865 513816
Fax: +44 (0) 1865 310055
Email: submissions@felicitybryan.com
Website: http://www.felicitybryan.com

Handles: Fiction; Nonfiction; *Areas:* Biography; Current Affairs; Historical; Science; *Markets:* Adult; Children's; Youth; *Treatments:* Commercial; Literary

Particularly interested in commercial and literary fiction and nonfiction for the adult market, children's fiction for 8+, and Young Adult. Send query by post with sufficient return postage, or by email with Word or PDF attachmnets. See website for detailed submission guidelines. No adult science fiction, horror, fantasy, light romance, self-help, memoir, film and TV scripts, plays, poetry or picture/illustrated books.

Juliet Burton Literary Agency

2 Clifton Avenue, London, W12 9DR
Tel: +44 (0) 20 8762 0148
Fax: +44 (0) 20 8743 8765
Email: juliet.burton@btinternet.com

Handles: Fiction; Nonfiction; *Areas:* Crime; Women's Interests; *Markets:* Adult

Send query with SAE, synopsis, and two sample chapters. No poetry, plays, film scripts, children's, articles, academic material, science fiction, fantasy, unsolicited MSS, or email submissions.

Capel & Land Ltd

29 Wardour Street, London, W1D 6PS
Tel: +44 (0) 20 7734 2414
Fax: +44 (0) 20 7734 8101
Email: georgina@capelland.co.uk
Website: http://www.capelland.com

Handles: Fiction; Nonfiction; *Areas:* Biography; Film; Historical; Radio; TV; *Markets:* Adult; *Treatments:* Commercial; Literary

Handles general fiction and nonfiction. Send query outlining writing history (for nonfiction, what qualifies you to write your book), with synopsis around 500 words and first three chapters, plus SAE or email address for reply. Submissions are not returned. Mark envelope for the attention of the Submissions Department. Response only if interested, normally within 6 weeks.

CardenWright Literary Agency

27 Khyber Road, London, SW11 2PZ
Tel: +44 (0) 20 7771 0012
Email: gen@cardenwright.com
Website: http://www.cardenwright.com

Handles: Fiction; Nonfiction; Scripts; *Areas:* Theatre; *Markets:* Adult; Youth; *Treatments:* Commercial; Literary

Handles commercial and literary fiction and nonfiction, plus theatre scripts. Will consider teenage / young adult. No poetry, screenplays, or children's books. See website for submission guidelines.

Celia Catchpole

56 Gilpin Avenue, London, SW14 8QY
Tel: +44 (0) 20 8255 4835
Email: catchpolesubmissions@googlemail.com
Website: http://www.celiacatchpole.co.uk

Handles: Fiction; *Markets:* Children's

Works on children's books with both artists and writers. Send query by email with sample pasted directly into the body of the email (no attachments). See website for full guidelines.

Catherine Pellegrino & Associates

148 Russell Court, Woburn Place, London, WC1H 0LR
Email: catherine@catherinepellegrino.co.uk
Website: http://catherinepellegrino.co.uk

Handles: Fiction; *Markets:* Children's; Youth; *Treatments:* Commercial; Literary

Handles children's books, from picture books to young adult. Send query by email with some background on you and the book, plus synopsis and first three chapters or approximately 50 pages, up to a natural break. See website for full details.

Teresa Chris Literary Agency Ltd

43 Musard Road, London, W6 8NR
Tel: +44 (0) 20 7386 0633
Email: teresachris@litagency.co.uk
Website: http://www.teresachrisliteraryagency.co.uk

Handles: Fiction; Nonfiction; *Areas:* Biography; Cookery; Crafts; Crime; Gardening; Historical; Lifestyle; Women's Interests; *Markets:* Adult; *Treatments:* Commercial; Literary

Welcomes submissions. Overseas authors may approach by email, otherwise hard copy submissions preferred. For fiction, send query with SAE, first three chapters, and one-page synopsis. For nonfiction, send overview with two sample chapters. Specialises in crime fiction and commercial women's fiction. No poetry, short stories, fantasy, science fiction, horror, children's fiction or young adult.

Mary Clemmey Literary Agency

6 Dunollie Road, London, NW5 2XP
Tel: +44 (0) 20 7267 1290
Fax: +44 (0) 20 7813 9757
Email: mcwords@googlemail.com

Handles: Fiction; Nonfiction; Scripts; *Areas:* Film; Radio; Theatre; TV; *Markets:* Adult

Send query with SAE and description of work only. Handles high-quality work with an international market. No children's books, science fiction, fantasy, or unsolicited MSS or submissions by email. Scripts handled for existing clients only. Do not submit a script or idea for a script unless you are already a client.

Jonathan Clowes Ltd

10 Iron Bridge House, Bridge Approach, London, NW1 8BD
Tel: +44 (0) 20 7722 7674
Fax: +44 (0) 20 7722 7677
Email: olivia@jonathanclowes.co.uk
Website: http://www.jonathanclowes.co.uk

Handles: Fiction; Nonfiction; Scripts; *Areas:* Film; Radio; Theatre; TV; *Markets:* Adult; *Treatments:* Commercial; Literary

Send query with synopsis and three chapters (or equivalent sample) by email. No science fiction, poetry, short stories, academic. Only considers film/TV clients with previous success in TV/film/theatre. If no response within six weeks, assume rejection.

Rosica Colin Ltd

1 Clareville Grove Mews, London, SW7 5AH
Tel: +44 (0) 20 7370 1080
Fax: +44 (0) 20 7244 6441

Handles: Fiction; Nonfiction; Scripts; *Areas:* Autobiography; Beauty and Fashion; Biography; Cookery; Crime; Current Affairs; Erotic; Fantasy; Film; Gardening; Health; Historical; Horror; Humour; Leisure; Lifestyle; Men's Interests; Military; Mystery; Nature; Psychology; Radio; Religious; Romance; Science; Sport; Suspense; Theatre; Thrillers; Travel; TV; Women's Interests; *Markets:* Academic; Adult; Children's; *Treatments:* Literary

Send query with SAE, CV, synopsis, and list

of other agents and publishers where MSS has already been sent. Considers any full-length mss (except science fiction and poetry), plus scripts, but few new writers taken on. Responds in 3-4 months to full mss – synopsis preferred in first instance.

Conville & Walsh Ltd

5th Floor, Haymarket House, 28-29 Haymarket, London, SW1Y 4SP
Tel: +44 (0) 20 7393 4200
Email: submissions@convilleandwalsh.com
Website: http://www.convilleandwalsh.com

Handles: Fiction; Nonfiction; *Areas:* Biography; Crime; Current Affairs; Historical; Humour; Leisure; Lifestyle; Men's Interests; Military; Mystery; Psychology; Science; Sport; Suspense; Thrillers; Travel; Women's Interests; *Markets:* Adult; Children's; Youth; *Treatments:* Literary

See website for agent profiles and submit to one particular agent only. Send submissions by email as Word .doc files, or by post. For fiction, please submit the first three sample chapters of the completed manuscript (or about 50 pages) with a one to two page synopsis. For nonfiction, send 30-page proposal. No poetry or scripts. See website for full guidelines.

Jane Conway-Gordon Ltd

38 Cromwell Grove, London, W6 7RG
Tel: +44 (0) 20 7371 6939
Email: jane@conway-gordon.co.uk

Handles: Fiction; Nonfiction; *Markets:* Adult

Handles fiction and general nonfiction. Send query with SAE (essential) in first instance. Associate agencies in America, Europe, and Japan. No poetry, short stories, children's, or science fiction.

Coombs Moylett Literary Agency

120 New Kings Road, London, SW6 4LZ
Email: lisa@coombsmoylett.com
Website: http://www.coombsmoylett.com

Handles: Fiction; *Areas:* Crime; Historical; Mystery; Suspense; Thrillers; Women's Interests; *Markets:* Adult; *Treatments:* Commercial; Contemporary; Literary

Send query with synopsis and first three chapters by post. No submissions by fax, but accepts email queries. No nonfiction, poetry, plays or scripts for film and TV.

Please note that this agency also offers editorial services for which writers are charged. Caution should be exercised in relation to these services, particularly if they are pushed as a condition of representation.

The Creative Rights Agency

17 Prior Street, London, SE10 8SF
Tel: +44 (0) 20 8149 3955
Email: info@creativerightsagency.co.uk
Website: http://www.creativerightsagency.co.uk

Handles: Fiction; Nonfiction; *Areas:* Autobiography; Culture; Men's Interests; Sport; *Markets:* Adult; *Treatments:* Contemporary

Specialises in men's interests. Send query by email with sample chapters, synopsis, and author bio.

Creative Authors Ltd

11A Woodlawn Street, Whitstable, Kent CT5 1HQ
Tel: +44 (0) 01227 770947
Email: write@creativeauthors.co.uk
Website: http://www.creativeauthors.co.uk

Handles: Fiction; Nonfiction; *Areas:* Arts; Autobiography; Biography; Business; Cookery; Crafts; Crime; Culture; Health; Historical; Humour; Nature; Women's Interests; *Markets:* Adult; Children's; *Treatments:* Commercial; Literary

As at March 2014 not accepting new fiction clients. See website for current situation.

We are a dynamic literary agency – established to provide an attentive and unique platform for writers and scriptwriters and representing a growing list of clients. We're on the lookout for fresh talent and books with strong commercial potential. No unsolicited MSS, but considers queries by email. No paper submissions. Do not telephone regarding submissions.

Rupert Crew Ltd

6 Windsor Road, London, N3 3SS
Tel: +44 (0) 20 8346 3000
Fax: +44 (0) 20 8346 3009
Email: info@rupertcrew.co.uk
Website: http://www.rupertcrew.co.uk

Handles: Fiction; Nonfiction; *Markets:* Adult

Send query with SAE, synopsis, and first two or three consecutive chapters. International representation, handling volume and subsidiary rights in fiction and nonfiction properties. No Short Stories, Science Fiction, Fantasy, Horror, Poetry or original scripts for Theatre, Television and Film. Email address for correspondence only. No response by post and no return of material with insufficient return postage.

Curtis Brown Group Ltd

Haymarket House, 28/29 Haymarket, London, SW1Y 4SP
Tel: +44 (0) 20 7393 4400
Fax: +44 (0) 20 7393 4401
Email: cb@curtisbrown.co.uk
Website: http://www.curtisbrowncreative.co.uk

Handles: Fiction; Nonfiction; Scripts; *Areas:* Biography; Crime; Fantasy; Film; Historical; Radio; Science; Suspense; Theatre; Thrillers; TV; *Markets:* Adult; Children's; Youth; *Treatments:* Literary; Mainstream; Popular

Renowned and long established London agency. Handles general fiction and nonfiction, and scripts. Also represents directors, designers, and presenters. No longer accepts submissions by post or email – all submissions must be made using online submissions manager. Also offers services such as writing courses for which authors are charged.

The Darley Anderson Agency

Estelle House, 11 Eustace Road, London, SW6 1JB
Tel: +44 (0) 20 7385 6652
Email: enquiries@darleyanderson.com
Website: http://www.darleyanderson.com

Handles: Fiction; Nonfiction; *Areas:* Adventure; Arts; Autobiography; Beauty and Fashion; Biography; Business; Cookery; Crafts; Crime; Criticism; Culture; Current Affairs; Design; Drama; Entertainment; Erotic; Fantasy; Film; Finance; Gardening; Gothic; Health; Historical; Hobbies; Horror; How-to; Humour; Legal; Leisure; Lifestyle; Literature; Media; Medicine; Men's Interests; Military; Music; Mystery; Nature; New Age; Philosophy; Photography; Politics; Psychology; Radio; Religious; Romance; Science; Sci-Fi; Self-Help; Sociology; Spiritual; Sport; Suspense; Technology; Theatre; Thrillers; Translations; Travel; TV; Westerns; Women's Interests; *Markets:* Adult; Children's; Family; Youth; *Treatments:* Commercial; Contemporary; Dark; Light; Mainstream; Popular; Positive; Serious; Traditional

We do not accept Scripts, Screenplays, TV programme ideas, short stories or poetry.

Accepts submissions by email and by post. See website for individual agent requirements, submission guidelines, and contact details.

David Luxton Associates

23 Hillcourt Avenue, London, N12 8EY
Tel: +44 (0) 20 8922 3942
Email: david@davidluxtonassociates.co.uk
Website: http://www.davidluxtonassociates.co.uk

Handles: Nonfiction; *Areas:* Autobiography; Biography; Culture; Historical; Politics; Sport; *Markets:* Adult

Send query by email with brief outline. No unsolicited MSS or sample chapters. Handles little in the way of fiction or children's books. No screenplays or scripts.

Caroline Davidson Literary Agency

5 Queen Anne's Gardens, London, W4 1TU
Tel: +44 (0) 20 8995 5768
Fax: +44 (0) 20 8994 2770
Email: enquiries@cdla.co.uk
Website: http://www.cdla.co.uk

Handles: Fiction; Nonfiction; Reference; *Areas:* Archaeology; Architecture; Arts; Biography; Cookery; Culture; Design; Gardening; Health; Historical; Lifestyle; Medicine; Nature; Politics; Psychology; Science; *Markets:* Adult

Send query with CV, SAE, outline and history of work, and (for fiction) the first 50 pages of novel with 3-sentence description. For nonfiction, include table of contents, detailed chapter-by-chapter synopsis, description of sources and / or research for the book, market and competition analysis, and (if possible) one or two sample chapters.

Submissions without adequate return postage are neither returned or considered. No Chick lit, romance, erotica, Crime and thrillers, Science fiction, fantasy, Poetry, Individual short stories, Children's, Young Adult, Misery memoirs or fictionalised autobiography. Completed and polished first novels positively welcomed. See website for more details. No submissions by fax and only in exceptional circumstances accepts submissions by email.

See website for full details.

Felix de Wolfe

103 Kingsway, London, WC2B 6QX
Tel: +44 (0) 20 7242 5066
Fax: +44 (0) 20 7242 8119
Email: info@felixdewolfe.com
Website: http://www.felixdewolfe.com

Handles: Fiction; Scripts; *Areas:* Film; Theatre; TV; *Markets:* Adult

Send query letter with SAE, short synopsis, and CV by post only, unless alternative arrangements have been made with the agency in advance. Quality fiction and scripts only. No nonfiction, children's books, or unsolicited MSS.

Diamond Kahn and Woods (DKW) Literary Agency Ltd

Top Floor, 66 Onslow Gardens, London, N10 3JX
Tel: +44 (0) 20 3514 6544
Email:
submissions.bryony@dkwlitagency.co.uk
Website: http://dkwlitagency.co.uk

Handles: Fiction; Nonfiction; *Areas:* Adventure; Archaeology; Biography; Crime; Culture; Fantasy; Gothic; Historical; Sci-Fi; Sociology; Suspense; Thrillers; *Markets:* Adult; Children's; Youth; *Treatments:* Commercial; Contemporary; Literary

Send submissions by email. See website for specific agent interests and contact details.

Diane Banks Associates Literary Agency

Email: submissions@dianebanks.co.uk
Website: http://www.dianebanks.co.uk

Handles: Fiction; Nonfiction; *Areas:* Autobiography; Beauty and Fashion; Business; Crime; Culture; Current Affairs; Entertainment; Health; Historical; Lifestyle; Psychology; Science; Self-Help; Thrillers; Women's Interests; *Markets:* Adult; Youth; *Treatments:* Commercial; Literary; Popular

Send query with author bio, synopsis, and the first three chapters by email as Word or Open Document attachments. No poetry, plays, scripts, academic books, short stories or children's books, with the exception of young adult fiction. Hard copy submissions are not accepted will not be read or returned.

Dorian Literary Agency (DLA)

32 Western Road, St Marychurch, Torquay, Devon TQ1 4RL
Tel: +44 (0) 1803 320934
Email: doriandot@compuserve.com

Handles: Fiction; *Areas:* Crime; Fantasy; Historical; Horror; Romance; Sci-Fi;

Thrillers; Women's Interests; *Markets:* Adult; *Treatments:* Popular

Principal agent passed away in October, 2013 – continues to be listed as a member of the AAA, but a user reports submissions being returned by solicitors advising that no new submissions are being accepted.

Concentrates on popular genre fiction. Send query by post with SAE or email address for response, including outline and up to three sample chapters. No queries or submissions by fax, telephone, or email. No poetry, scripts, short stories, nonfiction, children's, young adult, or comic material.

Toby Eady Associates Ltd

Third Floor, 9 Orme Court, London, W2 4RL
Tel: +44 (0) 20 7792 0092
Fax: +44 (0) 20 7792 0879
Email: submissions@tobyeadyassociates.co.uk
Website: http://www.tobyeadyassociates.co.uk

Handles: Fiction; Nonfiction; *Markets:* Adult

Send first 50 pages of your fiction or nonfiction work by email, with a synopsis, and a letter including biographical information. If submitting by post, include SAE for return of material, if required. No film / TV scripts or poetry. Particular interest in China, Middle East, India, and Africa.

Eddison Pearson Ltd

West Hill House, 6 Swains Lane, London, N6 6QS
Tel: +44 (0) 20 7700 7763
Fax: +44 (0) 20 7700 7866
Email: enquiries@eddisonpearson.com
Website: http://www.eddisonpearson.com

Handles: Fiction; Nonfiction; Poetry; *Markets:* Children's; Youth; *Treatments:* Literary

Send query by email only (or even blank email) for auto-response containing up-to-date submission guidelines and email address for submissions. No unsolicited MSS. No longer accepts submissions or enquiries by post. Send query with first two chapters by email only to address provided in auto-response. Response in 6-10 weeks. If no response after 10 weeks send email query.

Edwards Fuglewicz

49 Great Ormond Street, London, WC1N 3HZ
Tel: +44 (0) 20 7405 6725
Fax: +44 (0) 20 7405 6726
Email: info@efla.co.uk

Handles: Fiction; Nonfiction; *Areas:* Biography; Crime; Culture; Historical; Humour; Mystery; Romance; Thrillers; *Markets:* Adult; *Treatments:* Commercial; Literary

Handles literary and commercial fiction, and nonfiction. No children's, science fiction, horror, or email submissions.

Elise Dillsworth Agency (EDA)

9 Grosvenor Road, London, N10 2DR
Email: submissions@elisedillsworthagency.com
Website: http://elisedillsworthagency.com

Handles: Fiction; Nonfiction; Autobiography; Biography; *Markets:* Adult; *Treatments:* Commercial; Literary

Represents writers from around the world. Looking for literary and commercial fiction, and nonfiction (especially memoir and autobiography). No science fiction, fantasy, or children's. Send query by email or by post with SAE or email address for response. Include synopsis up to two pages and first three chapters, up to about 50 pages, as Word or PDF attachments. See website for full guidelines. Response in 6-8 weeks.

Elizabeth Roy Literary Agency

White Cottage, Greatford, Stamford, Lincolnshire PE9 4PR
Tel: +44 (0) 1778 560672
Website: http://www.elizabethroy.co.uk

Handles: Fiction; Nonfiction; *Markets:* Children's

Handles fiction and nonfiction for children. Particularly interested in funny fiction, gentle romance for young teens, picture book texts for pre-school children, and books with international market appeal. Send query by post with return postage, synopsis, and sample chapters. No science fiction, poetry, plays or adult books.

Faith Evans Associates

27 Park Avenue North, London, N8 7RU
Tel: +44 (0) 20 8340 9920
Fax: +44 (0) 20 8340 9410
Email: faith@faith-evans.co.uk

Handles: Fiction; Nonfiction; *Markets:* Adult

Small agency accepting new clients by personal recommendation only. No scripts, phone calls, or unsolicited MSS.

The Feldstein Agency

123-125 Main Street, 2nd Floor, Bangor, Northern Ireland BT20 4AE
Tel: +44 (0) 2891 472823
Email: paul@thefeldsteinagency.co.uk
Website: http://www.thefeldsteinagency.co.uk

Handles: Fiction; Nonfiction; *Areas:* Adventure; Autobiography; Biography; Business; Cookery; Crime; Criticism; Current Affairs; Historical; Humour; Leisure; Lifestyle; Media; Military; Music; Mystery; Philosophy; Politics; Sociology; Sport; Thrillers; Travel; Women's Interests; *Markets:* Adult; *Treatments:* Commercial; Literary

Handles adult fiction and nonfiction only. No children's, young adult, romance, science fiction, fantasy, poetry, or short stories. Send query by email with 1-2 pages synopsis. No reading fees or evaluation fees. The only instance in which an author would be charged a fee is for ghost-writing.

Film Rights Ltd in association with Laurence Fitch Ltd

Suite 306 Belsize Business Centre, 258 Belsize Road, London, NW6 4BT
Tel: +44 (0) 20 7316 1837
Fax: +44 (0) 20 7624 3629
Email: information@filmrights.ltd.uk
Website: http://filmrights.ltd.uk

Handles: Fiction; Scripts; *Areas:* Film; Horror; Radio; Theatre; TV; *Markets:* Adult; Children's

Represents films, plays, and novels, for adults and children.

Jill Foster Ltd (JFL)

48 Charlotte Street, London, W1T 2NS
Tel: +44 (0) 20 3137 8182
Email: agents@jflagency.com
Website: http://www.jflagency.com

Handles: Scripts; *Areas:* Drama; Film; Humour; Radio; Theatre; TV; *Markets:* Adult

Handles scripts only (for television, film, theatre and radio). Considers approaches from established writers with broadcast experience, but only accepts submissions from new writers during specific periods – consult website for details.

Fox Mason Ltd

36-38 Glasshouse Street, London, W1B 5DL
Tel: +44 (0) 20 7287 0972
Email: info@foxmason.com
Website: http://www.foxmason.com

Handles: Fiction; Nonfiction; *Areas:* Adventure; Arts; Autobiography; Biography; Cookery; Crime; Culture; Fantasy; Film; Historical; Horror; Music; Mystery; Philosophy; Psychology; Sci-Fi; Sport; Suspense; Thrillers; Travel; *Markets:* Adult; Youth; *Treatments:* Commercial; Literary

Handles up-market, literary, and commercial fiction, along with narrative nonfiction. No children's authors, bog-standard genre authors, poets, playwrights, or screenwriters. See website for more details, and for online submission form. No submissions by post.

Fox & Howard Literary Agency

39 Eland Road, London, SW11 5JX
Tel: +44 (0) 20 7352 8691
Email: fandhagency@googlemail.com
Website: http://www.foxandhoward.co.uk

Handles: Nonfiction; Reference; *Areas:* Biography; Business; Culture; Health; Historical; Lifestyle; Psychology; Self-Help; Spiritual; *Markets:* Adult

Closed to submissions as at May 2014. Please check website for current status.

Send query with synopsis and SAE for response. Small agency specialising in nonfiction that works closely with its authors. No unsolicited MSS.

Fraser Ross Associates

6/2 Wellington Place, Edinburgh, Scotland EH6 7EQ
Tel: +44 (0) 1316 574412
Email: fraserrossassociates@gmail.com
Website: http://www.fraserross.co.uk

Handles: Fiction; *Markets:* Adult; Children's; *Treatments:* Commercial; Literary; Mainstream

Send query by email or by post with SAE, including CV, the first three chapters and synopsis for fiction, or a one page proposal and the opening and a further two chapters for nonfiction. For picture books, send complete MS, without illustrations. Rarely accept poetry, playscripts or short stories.

Furniss Lawton

James Grant Group Ltd, 94 Strand on the Green, Chiswick, London, W4 3NN
Tel: +44 (0) 20 8987 6804
Email: info@furnisslawton.co.uk
Website: http://furnisslawton.co.uk

Handles: Fiction; Nonfiction; *Areas:* Autobiography; Biography; Business; Cookery; Crime; Fantasy; Historical; Politics; Psychology; Science; Sociology; Suspense; Thrillers; Women's Interests; *Markets:* Adult; Children's; Youth; *Treatments:* Commercial; Literary

Send query with synopsis and first 10,000 words / three chapters as a Word or PDF document by email. Include the word "Submission" in the subject line, and your name and the title of the work in any attachments. No submissions by post. Does not handle screenwriters for film or TV. See website for full details.

Noel Gay

19 Denmark Street, London, WC2H 8NA
Tel: +44 (0) 20 7836 3941
Email: info@noelgay.com
Website: http://www.noelgay.com

Handles: Scripts; *Markets:* Adult

Agency representing writers, directors, performers, presenters, comedians, etc. Send query with SASE.

Eric Glass Ltd

25 Ladbroke Crescent, London, W11 1PS
Tel: +44 (0) 20 7229 9500
Fax: +44 (0) 20 7229 6220
Email: eglassltd@aol.com

Handles: Fiction; Nonfiction; Scripts; *Areas:* Film; Theatre; TV; *Markets:* Adult

Handles full-length mss and scripts for film, TV, and theatre. Send query with SAE. No children's books, short stories, poetry, or unsolicited MSS.

Graham Maw Christie Literary Agency

19 Thornhill Crescent, London, N1 1BJ
Tel: +44 (0) 20 7609 1326
Email:
submissions@grahammawchristie.com
Website:
http://www.grahammawchristie.com

Handles: Fiction; Nonfiction; Reference; *Areas:* Autobiography; Business; Cookery; Crafts; Health; Historical; Humour; Lifestyle; Philosophy; Science; Self-Help; *Markets:* Adult; Children's

Specialises in adult nonfiction, but also has a small children's list, including fiction for children. Particularly interested in fiction for 6–9 year olds. Send query with one-page summary, a paragraph on the contents of each chapter, your qualifications for writing it, market analysis, and what you could do to help promote your book. Accepts approaches by email. No poetry, film scripts, or fiction for adults.

Christine Green Authors' Agent

6 Whitehorse Mews, Westminster Bridge Road, London, SE1 7QD
Tel: +44 (0) 20 7401 8844
Fax: +44 (0) 20 7401 8860
Email: info@christinegreen.co.uk
Website: http://www.christinegreen.co.uk

Handles: Fiction; Nonfiction; *Markets:* Adult; Youth; *Treatments:* Commercial; Literary

Focusses on fiction for adult and young adult, and also considers narrative nonfiction. No children's books, genre science-fiction/fantasy, poetry or scripts. Send query by email or by post with SAE. See website for full submission guidelines.

Louise Greenberg Books Ltd

The End House, Church Crescent, London, N3 1BG
Tel: +44 (0) 20 8349 1179
Fax: +44 (0) 20 8343 4559
Email: louisegreenberg@msn.com

Handles: Fiction; Nonfiction; *Markets:* Adult; *Treatments:* Literary; Serious

Handles full-length literary fiction and serious nonfiction only. All approaches must be accompanied by SAE. No approaches by telephone.

Greene & Heaton Ltd

37 Goldhawk Road, London, W12 8QQ
Tel: +44 (0) 20 8749 0315
Fax: +44 (0) 20 8749 0318
Email: submissions@greeneheaton.co.uk
Website: http://www.greeneheaton.co.uk

Handles: Fiction; Nonfiction; *Areas:* Arts; Autobiography; Biography; Cookery; Crime; Culture; Current Affairs; Gardening; Health; Historical; Humour; Philosophy; Politics; Romance; Science; Sci-Fi; Thrillers; Travel; *Markets:* Adult; Children's; *Treatments:* Commercial; Contemporary; Literary; Traditional

Send query by email or by post with SAE, including synopsis and three chapters or approximately 50 pages. No response to unsolicited MSS with no SAE or inadequate means of return postage provided. No response to email submissions unless interested. Handles all types of fiction and nonfiction, but no scripts.

The Greenhouse Literary Agency

Stanley House, St Chad's Place, London, WC1X 9HH
Tel: +44 (0) 20 7841 3959
Email: submissions@greenhouseliterary.com
Website: http://www.greenhouseliterary.com

Handles: Fiction; *Markets:* Children's; Youth

Transatlantic agency with offices in the US and London. Handles children's and young adult fiction only. For novels, send query by email with first chapter or first five pages (whichever is shorter) pasted into the body of the email. For picture books (maximum 1,000 words) paste full text into the boxy of the email. No illustrations required at this stage, unless you are an author/illustrator. No attachments or hard copy submissions.

Gregory & Company, Authors' Agents

3 Barb Mews, London, W6 7PA
Tel: +44 (0) 20 7610 4676
Fax: +44 (0) 20 7610 4686
Email: maryjones@gregoryandcompany.co.uk
Website: http://www.gregoryandcompany.co.uk

Handles: Fiction; *Areas:* Crime; Historical; Thrillers; *Markets:* Adult; *Treatments:* Commercial

Particularly interested in Crime, Family Sagas, Historical Fiction, Thrillers and Upmarket Commercial Fiction.
Send query with CV, one-page synopsis, future writing plans, and first ten pages, by post with SAE, or by email. No unsolicited MSS, Business Books, Children's, Young Adult Fiction, Plays, Screeplays, Poetry, Science Fiction, Future Fiction, Fantasy, Self Help, Lifestyle books, Short Stories, Spiritual, New Age, Philosophy, Supernatural, Paranormal, Horror, Travel, or True Crime.

David Grossman Literary Agency Ltd

118b Holland Park Avenue, London, W11 4UA
Tel: +44 (0) 20 7221 2770
Fax: +44 (0) 20 7221 1445
Email: david@dglal.co.uk

Handles: Fiction; Nonfiction; *Markets:* Adult

Send preliminary letter before making a submission. No approaches or submissions by fax or email. Usually works with published fiction writers, but well-written and original work from beginners considered. No poetry, scripts, technical books for students, or unsolicited MSS.

Gunn Media Associates

50 Albemarle Street, London, W1S 4BD
Tel: +44 (0) 20 7529 3745
Email: ali@gunnmedia.co.uk
Website: http://www.gunnmedia.co.uk

Handles: Fiction; Nonfiction; *Areas:* Autobiography; Entertainment; Thrillers; *Markets:* Adult; *Treatments:* Commercial; Literary

Handles commercial fiction and nonfiction, including literary, thrillers, and celebrity autobiographies.

Hardman & Swainson

4 Kelmscott Road, London, SW11 6QY
Tel: +44 (0) 20 7223 5176
Email: submissions@hardmanswainson.com
Website: http://www.hardmanswainson.com

Handles: Fiction; Nonfiction; *Areas:* Autobiography; Crime; Historical; Horror; Philosophy; Science; Thrillers; Women's Interests; *Markets:* Adult; Children's; Youth; *Treatments:* Literary; Popular

Agency launched June 2012 by former colleagues at an established agency. Welcomes submissions of fiction and nonfiction. No poetry, plays / screenplays / scripts, or very young children's / picture books. No submissions by post. See website for full submission guidelines.

Antony Harwood Limited

103 Walton Street, Oxford, OX2 6EB
Tel: +44 (0) 1865 559615
Fax: +44 (0) 1865 310660
Email: mail@antonyharwood.com
Website: http://www.antonyharwood.com

Handles: Fiction; Nonfiction; *Areas:* Adventure; Anthropology; Antiques; Archaeology; Architecture; Arts; Autobiography; Beauty and Fashion; Biography; Business; Cookery; Crafts; Crime; Criticism; Culture; Current Affairs; Design; Drama; Entertainment; Erotic; Fantasy; Film; Finance; Gardening; Gothic; Health; Historical; Hobbies; Horror; How-to; Humour; Legal; Leisure; Lifestyle; Literature; Media; Medicine; Men's Interests; Military; Music; Mystery; Nature; New Age; Philosophy; Photography; Politics; Psychology; Radio; Religious; Romance; Science; Sci-Fi; Self-Help; Short Stories; Sociology; Spiritual; Sport; Suspense; Technology; Theatre; Thrillers; Translations; Travel; TV; Westerns; Women's Interests; *Markets:* Adult; Children's; Youth

Handles fiction and nonfiction in every genre and category, except for screenwriting and poetry. Send brief outline and first 50 pages by email, or by post with SASE.

A M Heath & Company Limited, Author's Agents

6 Warwick Court, Holborn, London, WC1R 5DJ

Tel: +44 (0) 20 7242 2811
Fax: +44 (0) 20 7242 2711
Email: enquiries@amheath.com
Website: http://www.amheath.com

Handles: Fiction; Nonfiction; *Areas:* Biography; Cookery; Crime; Historical; Nature; Psychology; Sport; Suspense; Thrillers; Women's Interests; *Markets:* Adult; Children's; Youth; *Treatments:* Commercial; Literary

Handles general commercial and literary fiction and nonfiction. Submit work with cover letter and synopsis via online submission system only. No paper submissions. Aims to respond within six weeks.

Rupert Heath Literary Agency

50 Albemarle Street, London, W1S 4BD
Tel: +44 (0) 20 7060 3385
Email: emailagency@rupertheath.com
Website: http://www.rupertheath.com

Handles: Fiction; Nonfiction; *Areas:* Arts; Autobiography; Biography; Cookery; Crime; Culture; Current Affairs; Historical; Lifestyle; Nature; Politics; Science; Sci-Fi; Thrillers; Women's Interests; *Markets:* Adult; *Treatments:* Commercial; Literary; Popular

Send query giving some information about yourself and the work you would like to submit. Prefers queries by email. Response only if interested.

hhb agency ltd

6 Warwick Court, London, WC1R 5DJ
Tel: +44 (0) 20 7405 5525
Email: jack@hhbagency.com
Website: http://www.hhbagency.com

Handles: Fiction; Nonfiction; *Areas:* Adventure; Autobiography; Biography; Business; Cookery; Crime; Culture; Entertainment; Historical; Humour; Politics; Travel; TV; Women's Interests; *Markets:* Adult; *Treatments:* Commercial; Contemporary; Literary; Popular

Represents nonfiction writers, particularly in the areas of journalism, history and politics, travel and adventure, contemporary autobiography and biography, books about words and numbers, popular culture and quirky humour, entertainment and television, business, family memoir, food and cookery. Also handles commercial fiction. Send query by email with cover letter, synopsis, and first three chapters. If unable to submit by email, send by post with SAE. No international postal vouchers. Does not represent writers outside Europe.

David Higham Associates Ltd

7th Floor, Waverley House, 7–12 Noel Street, London, W1F 8GQ
Tel: +44 (0) 20 7434 5900
Fax: +44 (0) 20 7437 1072
Email: dha@davidhigham.co.uk
Website: http://www.davidhigham.co.uk

Handles: Fiction; Nonfiction; Scripts; *Areas:* Autobiography; Biography; Cookery; Crime; Current Affairs; Drama; Film; Historical; Humour; Nature; Theatre; Thrillers; TV; *Markets:* Adult; Children's; *Treatments:* Commercial; Literary; Serious

For adult fiction and nonfiction contact "Adult Submissions Department" by post only with SASE, covering letter, CV, and synopsis (fiction)/proposal (nonfiction) and first two or three chapters. For children's fiction prefers submissions by email to the specific children's submission address given on the website, with covering letter, synopsis, CV, and first two or three chapters (or complete MS if a picture book). See website for complete guidelines. Scripts by referral only.

Vanessa Holt Ltd

59 Crescent Road, Leigh-on-Sea, Essex SS9 2PF
Tel: +44 (0) 1702 473787
Email: v.holt791@btinternet.com

Handles: Fiction; Nonfiction; *Markets:* Adult

General fiction and nonfiction. No unsolicited mss or overseas approaches.

Kate Hordern Literary Agency

18 Mortimer Road, Clifton, Bristol, BS8 4EY
Tel: +44 (0) 117 923 9368
Email: katehordern@blueyonder.co.uk
Website: http://www.katehordern.co.uk

Handles: Fiction; Nonfiction; Reference; *Areas:* Autobiography; Business; Crime; Culture; Current Affairs; Historical; Sociology; Thrillers; Women's Interests; *Markets:* Adult; Children's; Youth; *Treatments:* Commercial; Contemporary; Literary; Popular

Send query by email only with pitch, outline or synopsis, and first three chapters. No submissions by post, or from authors not resident in the UK.

Valerie Hoskins Associates

20 Charlotte Street, London, W1T 2NA
Tel: +44 (0) 20 7637 4490
Fax: +44 (0) 20 7637 4493
Email: info@vhassociates.co.uk
Website: http://www.vhassociates.co.uk

Handles: Scripts; *Areas:* Film; Radio; TV; *Markets:* Adult

Always on the lookout for screenwriters with an original voice and creatives with big ideas. Query by email or by phone. Allow up to eight weeks for response to submissions.

Amanda Howard Associates Ltd

74 Clerkenwell Road, London, EC1M 5QA
Tel: +44 (0) 20 7250 1760
Email: mail@amandahowardassociates.co.uk
Website: http://www.amandahowardassociates.co.uk

Handles: Nonfiction; Scripts; *Areas:* Autobiography; How-to; Humour; *Markets:* Adult; *Treatments:* Popular

Handles actors, writers, creatives, and voice-over artsts. Send query with return postage, CV/bio, and 10-page writing sample. No poetry.

Independent Talent Group Ltd

40 Whitfield Street, London, W1T 2RH
Tel: +44 (0) 20 7636 6565
Fax: +44 (0) 20 7323 0101
Email: laurarourke@independenttalent.com
Website: http://www.independenttalent.com

Handles: Scripts; *Areas:* Film; Radio; Theatre; TV; *Markets:* Adult

Specialises in scripts and works in association with agencies in Los Angeles and New York. No unsolicited MSS. Materials submitted will not be returned.

Intercontinental Literary Agency

Centric House, 390-391 Strand, London, WC2R 0LT
Tel: +44 (0) 20 7379 6611
Fax: +44 (0) 20 7240 4724
Email: ila@ila-agency.co.uk
Website: http://www.ila-agency.co.uk

Handles: Fiction; Nonfiction; *Areas:* Translations; *Markets:* Adult; Children's

Handles translation rights only for, among others, the authors of LAW Ltd, London; Harold Matson Co. Inc., New York; PFD, London. Submissions accepted via client agencies and publishers only – no submissions from writers seeking agents.

Isabel White Literary Agent

Tel: +44 (0) 20 3070 1602
Email: query.isabelwhite@googlemail.com

Handles: Fiction; Nonfiction; *Markets:* Adult

Selective one-woman agency, not taking on new clients as at June 2015.

Janet Fillingham Associates

52 Lowther Road , London, SW13 9NU
Tel: +44 (0) 20 8748 5594
Fax: +44 (0) 20 8748 7374
Email: info@janetfillingham.com
Website: http://www.janetfillingham.com

Handles: Scripts; *Areas:* Film; Theatre; TV;

Markets: Adult; Children's; Youth

Represents writers and directors for stage, film and TV, as well as librettists, lyricists and composers in musical theatre. Does not represent books. Prospective clients may register via website.

Johnson & Alcock

Clerkenwell House, 45/47 Clerkenwell Green, London, EC1R 0HT
Tel: +44 (0) 20 7251 0125
Fax: +44 (0) 20 7251 2172
Email: info@johnsonandalcock.co.uk
Website: http://www.johnsonandalcock.co.uk

Handles: Fiction; Nonfiction; Poetry; *Areas:* Arts; Autobiography; Biography; Crime; Culture; Current Affairs; Design; Film; Health; Historical; Lifestyle; Music; Nature; Psychology; Science; Sci-Fi; Self-Help; Sport; Suspense; Thrillers; Women's Interests; *Markets:* Adult; Children's; Youth; *Treatments:* Commercial; Literary; Popular

For children's fiction, ages 9+ only. Send query by post with SASE, synopsis and approximately first 50 pages. Accepts email submission, but replies only if interested. Email submissions should go to specific agents. See website for list of agents and full submission guidelines. No poetry, screenplays, children's books 0-7, or board or picture books.

Michelle Kass Associates

85 Charing Cross Road, London, WC2H 0AA
Tel: +44 (0) 20 7439 1624
Fax: +44 (0) 20 7734 3394
Email: office@michellekass.co.uk
Website: http://www.michellekass.co.uk

Handles: Fiction; Scripts; *Areas:* Film; Literature; TV; *Markets:* Adult; *Treatments:* Literary

No email submissions. Approach by telephone in first instance.

Frances Kelly

111 Clifton Road, Kingston upon Thames, Surrey KT2 6PL
Tel: +44 (0) 20 8549 7830
Fax: +44 (0) 20 8547 0051

Handles: Nonfiction; Reference; *Areas:* Arts; Biography; Business; Cookery; Finance; Health; Historical; Lifestyle; Medicine; Self-Help; *Markets:* Academic; Adult; Professional

Send query with SAE, CV, and synopsis or brief description of work. Scripts handled for existing clients only. No unsolicited MSS.

Ki Agency Ltd

48-56 Bayham Place, London, NW1 0EU
Tel: +44 (0) 20 3214 8287
Email: meg@ki-agency.co.uk
Website: http://www.ki-agency.co.uk

Handles: Fiction; Scripts; *Areas:* Film; Theatre; TV; *Markets:* Adult

Represents novelists and scriptwriters in all media. No nonfiction, children's, or poetry. Accepts unsolicited mss by post or by email.

Kilburn Literary Agency

Belsize Road, Kilburn, London, NW6 4BT
Email: info@kilburnlit.com
Website: http://kilburnlit.com

Handles: Fiction; Nonfiction; Scripts; *Areas:* Adventure; Arts; Autobiography; Biography; Business; Health; Literature; Medicine; Mystery; Politics; Psychology; Religious; Romance; Science; Short Stories; Sociology; Spiritual; Thrillers; Women's Interests; *Markets:* Adult; Youth; *Treatments:* Commercial; Contemporary; Literary; Mainstream; Popular; Positive

We are an agency founded in 2013 and offer a window of opportunity while we build up our list.

All submissions and queries must be by e-mail initially.

We are international in outlook.

Knight Hall Agency

Lower Ground Floor, 7 Mallow Street, London, EC1Y 8RQ
Tel: +44 (0) 20 3397 2901
Fax: +44 (0) 871 918 6068
Email: office@knighthallagency.com
Website: http://www.knighthallagency.com

Handles: Scripts; *Areas:* Drama; Film; Theatre; TV; *Markets:* Adult

Note: Closed to submissions on February 19, 2014. Check website for current status.

Send query by post or email (no attachments). Only send sample if requested. Represents playwrights, screenwriters and writer-directors. Handles adaptation rights for novels, but does not handle books directly.

Barbara Levy Literary Agency

64 Greenhill, Hampstead High Street, London, NW3 5TZ
Tel: +44 (0) 20 7435 9046
Fax: +44 (0) 20 7431 2063
Email: blevysubmissions@gmail.com

Handles: Fiction; Nonfiction; *Markets:* Adult

Send query with synopsis by email or by post with SAE.

Limelight Management

10 Filmer Mews, 75 Filmer Road , London, SW6 7JF
Tel: +44 (0) 20 7384 9950
Fax: +44 (0) 20 7384 9955
Email: mail@limelightmanagement.com
Website: http://www.limelightmanagement.com

Handles: Fiction; Nonfiction; *Areas:* Lifestyle; *Markets:* Adult; *Treatments:* Commercial; Literary

Particularly interested in lifestyle nonfiction, and commercial and literary fiction for the adult market. For nonfiction send query with 3-4 page outline. For fiction send query with synopsis and first three or four consecutive chapters. Accepts queries by email, but no large attachments – emails with large attachments will be deleted unread. No scripts. See website for full submission guidelines.

Lindsay Literary Agency

East Worldham House, East Worldham, Alton GU34 3AT
Tel: +44 (0) 0142 083143
Email: info@lindsayliteraryagency.co.uk
Website: http://www.lindsayliteraryagency.co.uk

Handles: Fiction; Nonfiction; *Markets:* Adult; Children's; *Treatments:* Literary; Serious

Send query by post with SASE or by email, including single-page synopsis and first three chapters. For picture books send complete ms.

The Christopher Little Literary Agency

48 Walham Grove, London, SW6 1QR
Tel: +44 (0) 20 7736 4455
Fax: +44 (0) 20 7736 4490
Email: submissions@christopherlittle.net
Website: http://www.christopherlittle.net

Handles: Fiction; Nonfiction; *Markets:* Adult; *Treatments:* Commercial; Literary

Handles commercial and literary full-length fiction and nonfiction. Film scripts handled for existing clients only (no submissions of film scripts). Send query by email (preferred) or by post with SAE or IRCs. Attach one-page synopsis and three consecutive chapters (fiction) or proposal (nonfiction). No poetry, plays, textbooks, short stories, illustrated children's books, science fiction, fantasy, or submissions by email.

London Independent Books

26 Chalcot Crescent, London, NW1 8YD
Tel: +44 (0) 20 7722 7160

Handles: Fiction; Nonfiction; *Areas:* Fantasy; *Markets:* Adult; Youth; *Treatments:* Commercial

Send query with synopsis, SASE, and first two chapters. All fiction and nonfiction subjects considered if treatment is strong and saleable, but no computer books, young children's, or unsolicited MSS. Particularly interested in commercial fiction, fantasy, and teen fiction. Scripts handled for existing clients only.

Andrew Lownie Literary Agency Ltd

36 Great Smith Street, London, SW1P 3BU
Tel: +44 (0) 20 7222 7574
Fax: +44 (0) 20 7222 7576
Email: mail@andrewlownie.co.uk
Website: http://www.andrewlownie.co.uk

Handles: Fiction; Nonfiction; *Areas:* Autobiography; Biography; Crime; Culture; Current Affairs; Fantasy; Finance; Health; Historical; Horror; How-to; Lifestyle; Literature; Media; Medicine; Men's Interests; Military; Music; Mystery; Politics; Psychology; Romance; Science; Sci-Fi; Self-Help; Sport; Suspense; Technology; Thrillers; Translations; Westerns; *Markets:* Academic; Adult; Family; Professional; *Treatments:* Commercial; Mainstream; Popular; Serious; Traditional

This agency, founded in 1988, is now one of the UK's leading boutique literary agencies with some two hundred nonfiction and fiction authors and is actively building its fiction list through its new agent (see website for specific contact address for fiction submissions). It prides itself on its personal attention to its clients and specialises both in launching new writers and taking established writers to a new level of recognition.

Lutyens and Rubinstein

21 Kensington Park Road, London, W11 2EU
Tel: +44 (0) 20 7792 4855
Email: submissions@lutyensrubinstein.co.uk
Website: http://www.lutyensrubinstein.co.uk

Handles: Fiction; Nonfiction; *Markets:* Adult; *Treatments:* Commercial; Literary

Send up to 5,000 words or first three chapters by email with covering letter and short synopsis. No film or TV scripts, or unsolicited submissions by hand or by post.

Macnaughton Lord Representation

44 South Molton Street, London, W1K 5RT
Tel: +44 (0) 20 7499 1411
Email: info@mlrep.com
Website: http://www.mlrep.com

Handles: Scripts; *Areas:* Arts; Film; Theatre; TV; *Markets:* Adult

Theatrical and literary agency representing established names and emerging talent in theatre, film, tv and the performing arts. Send query by email with CV and a sample of your work.

Madeleine Milburn Literary Agency

42A Great Percy Street, Bloomsbury, London, WC1X 9QR
Tel: +44 (0) 20 3602 6425
Fax: +44 (0) 20 3602 6425
Email: submissions@madeleinemilburn.com
Website: http://madeleinemilburn.co.uk

Handles: Fiction; Nonfiction; Scripts; *Areas:* Autobiography; Crime; Film; Mystery; Suspense; Thrillers; TV; Women's Interests; *Markets:* Adult; Children's; Youth; *Treatments:* Literary

Send query by email only, with synopsis and first three chapters as Word or PDF attachments. See website for full submission guidelines. Film and TV scripts for established clients only.

Andrew Mann Ltd

39 – 41 North Road, London, N7 9DP
Tel: +44 (0) 20 7609 6218
Email: info@andrewmann.co.uk
Website: http://www.andrewmann.co.uk

Handles: Fiction; Nonfiction; *Areas:* Film; Radio; Theatre; TV; *Markets:* Adult; Children's; Youth

Interested in literary and commercial fiction, nonfiction, and children's fiction (middle grade, teen, youg adult, and picture books). Send query by email, or by post if absolutely necessary with SAE, with brief synopsis and first three chapters or 30 pages. No poetry, spiritual or new age philosophy, short stories, misery memoirs, screenplays, science fiction, vampires, or dystopian fiction. See website for full submission guidelines.

Marjacq Scripts Ltd

Box 412, 19/21 Crawford St, London, W1H 1PJ
Tel: +44 (0) 20 7935 9499
Fax: +44 (0) 20 7935 9115
Email: subs@marjacq.com
Website: http://www.marjacq.com

Handles: Fiction; Nonfiction; Scripts; *Areas:* Biography; Crime; Film; Health; Historical; Radio; Sci-Fi; Sport; Thrillers; Travel; TV; Women's Interests; *Markets:* Adult; Children's; *Treatments:* Commercial; Literary

For books, send query with synopsis and three sample chapters. For scripts, send short treatment and entire screenplay. All queries must include an SAE for response, if sent by post. If sent by email send only Word or PDF documents less than 2MB. Do not paste work into the body of the email. See website for full details. No poetry, short stories, or stage plays. Do not send queries without including samples of the actual work.

The Marsh Agency

50 Albemarle Street, London, W1S 4BD
Tel: +44 (0) 20 7493 4361
Fax: +44 (0) 20 7495 8961
Email: english.language@marsh-agency.co.uk
Website: http://www.marsh-agency.co.uk

Handles: Fiction; Nonfiction; *Markets:* Adult; Youth; *Treatments:* Literary

Use online submission system to send brief query letter with contact details, relevant information, details of any previously published work, and any experience which relates to the book's subject matter; an outline of the plot and main characters for fiction, or a summary of the work and chapter outlines for nonfiction. Include three consecutive chapters up to 100 pages, and your CV. See website for full guidelines and online submission system. No TV, film, radio or theatre scripts, poetry, or children's/picture books. Does not handle US authors as a primary English Language Agent. Do not call or email until at least 8 weeks have elapsed from submission date.

MBA Literary Agents Ltd

62 Grafton Way, London, W1T 5DW
Tel: +44 (0) 20 7387 2076
Fax: +44 (0) 20 7387 2042
Email: submissions@mbalit.co.uk
Website: http://www.mbalit.co.uk

Handles: Fiction; Nonfiction; Scripts; *Areas:* Arts; Biography; Crafts; Film; Health; Historical; Lifestyle; Radio; Self-Help; Theatre; TV; *Markets:* Adult; Children's; Youth; *Treatments:* Commercial; Literary

For books, send query with synopsis and first three chapters. For scripts, send query with synopsis, CV, and finished script. Submissions by email only. No submissions by post. See website for full submission guidelines. Works in conjunction with agents in most countries.

Duncan McAra

28 Beresford Gardens, Edinburgh, Scotland EH5 3ES
Tel: +44 (0) 131 552 1558
Email: duncanmcara@mac.com

Handles: Fiction; Nonfiction; *Areas:* Archaeology; Architecture; Arts; Biography; Historical; Military; Travel; *Markets:* Adult; *Treatments:* Literary

Also interested in books of Scottish interest. Send query letter with SAE in first instance.

McKernan Agency

Studio 50, Out of the Blue Drill Hall, 36 Dalmeny Street, Edinburgh, EH6 8RG
Tel: +44 (0) 1315 571771
Email: info@mckernanagency.co.uk
Website: http://www.mckernanagency.co.uk

Handles: Fiction; Nonfiction; *Areas:* Autobiography; Biography; Crime; Current Affairs; Historical; *Markets:* Adult; Children's; Family; Youth; *Treatments:* Literary

Handles high quality literary fiction including historical and crime and high quality nonfiction, including memoirs, biography, history, current affairs etc. Also considers fiction for older children. Submit through online webform only. No submissions by post or email.

Miles Stott Children's Literary Agency

East Hook Farm, Lower Quay Road, Hook, Haverfordwest, Pembrokeshire SA62 4LR
Tel: +44 (0) 1437 890570
Email: submissions@milesstottagency.co.uk
Website: http://www.milesstottagency.co.uk

Handles: Fiction; *Markets:* Children's

Handles picture books, novelty books, and children's fiction. No poetry or nonfiction. Not accepting new fiction submissions as at July 2015, however this is due to be reviewed in late 2015. Check website for current status. For picture book submissions, send query by email only, with short covering letter, details about you and your background, and up to three stories a Word or PDF attachments. See website for full guidelines.

Mulcahy Associates

First Floor, 7 Meard Street, London, W1F 0EW
Email: submissions@ma-agency.com
Website: http://www.ma-agency.com

Handles: Fiction; Nonfiction; *Areas:* Biography; Crime; Finance; Historical; Lifestyle; Sport; Thrillers; Women's Interests; *Markets:* Adult; Children's; Youth; *Treatments:* Commercial; Literary

Send query with synopsis and first three chapters by email only. See website for full guidelines.

Judith Murdoch Literary Agency

19 Chalcot Square, London, NW1 8YA
Tel: +44 (0) 20 7722 4197
Email: jmlitag@btinternet.com
Website: http://www.judithmurdoch.co.uk

Handles: Fiction; *Areas:* Crime; Women's Interests; *Markets:* Adult; *Treatments:* Commercial; Literary; Popular

Send query by post with SAE or email address for response, brief synopsis, and and first three chapters. Provides editorial advice. No short stories, children's books, science fiction, email submissions, or unsolicited MSS.

MNLA (Maggie Noach Literary Agency)

7 Peacock Yard, Iliffe Street, London, SE17 3LH
Tel: +44 (0) 20 7708 3073
Email: info@mnla.co.uk
Website: http://www.mnla.co.uk

Handles: Fiction; Nonfiction; *Areas:* Biography; Historical; Travel; *Markets:* Adult; Children's

Note: As at June 2013 not accepting submissions. Check website for current situation.

Deals with UK residents only. Send query with SAE, outline, and two or three sample chapters. No email attachments or fax queries. Very few new clients taken on. Deals in general adult nonfiction and non-illustrated children's books for ages 8 and upwards. No poetry, scripts, short stories, cookery, gardening, mind, body, and spirit, scientific, academic, specialist nonfiction, or unsolicited MSS.

Andrew Nurnberg Associates, Ltd

20-23 Greville Street, London, EC1N 8SS
Tel: +44 (0) 20 3327 0400
Fax: +44 (0) 20 7430 0801
Email: submissions@andrewnurnberg.com
Website: http://www.andrewnurnberg.com

Handles: Fiction; Nonfiction; *Markets:* Adult; Children's

Handles adult fiction and nonfiction, and children's fiction. No poetry, or scripts for film, TV, radio or theatre. Send query with one-page synopsis and first three chapters by post with SAE (if return required) or by email as attachments.

Deborah Owen Ltd

78 Narrow Street, Limehouse, London, E14 8BP
Tel: +44 (0) 20 7987 5119 / 5441

Handles: Fiction; Nonfiction

Represents only two authors worldwide. Not accepting any new authors.

John Pawsey

8 Snowshill Court, Giffard Park, Milton Keynes, MK14 5QG
Tel: +44 (0) 1908 611841
Email: john.pawsey@virgin.net

Handles: Nonfiction; *Areas:* Biography; Sport; *Markets:* Adult

No fiction, poetry, scripts, journalism, academic, or children's books. Particularly interested in sport and biography. Send query by email only, with synopsis and opening chapter.

PBJ and JBJ Management

22 Rathbone Street, London, W1T 1LA
Tel: +44 (0) 20 7287 1112
Fax: +44 (0) 20 7637 0899
Email: general@pbjmanagement.co.uk
Website: http://www.pbjmgt.co.uk

Handles: Scripts; *Areas:* Drama; Film; Humour; Radio; Theatre; TV; *Markets:* Adult

Handles scripts for film, TV, theatre, and radio. Send complete MS with cover letter and CV, if you have one. Send one script only. No submissions by email. Particularly interested in comedy and comedy drama.

Maggie Pearlstine Associates Ltd

31 Ashley Gardens, Ambrosden Avenue, London, SW1P 1QE
Tel: +44 (0) 20 7828 4212
Fax: +44 (0) 20 7834 5546
Email: maggie@pearlstine.co.uk

Handles: Fiction; Nonfiction; *Areas:* Biography; Current Affairs; Health; Historical; *Markets:* Adult

Small, selective agency, not currently taking on new clients.

Jonathan Pegg Literary Agency

32 Batoum Gardens, London, W6 7QD
Tel: +44 (0) 20 7603 6830
Fax: +44 (0) 20 7348 0629
Email: submissions@jonathanpegg.com
Website: http://www.jonathanpegg.com

Handles: Fiction; Nonfiction; *Areas:* Arts; Autobiography; Biography; Culture; Current Affairs; Historical; Lifestyle; Nature; Psychology; Science; Thrillers; *Markets:* Adult; *Treatments:* Commercial; Literary; Popular

Established by the agent after twelve years at Curtis Brown. The agency's main areas of interest are:
Fiction: literary fiction, thrillers and quality commercial in general
Non-Fiction: current affairs, memoir and biography, history, popular science, nature, arts and culture, lifestyle, popular psychology

Rights:
Aside from the UK market, the agency will work in association with translation, US, TV & film agents according to each client's best interests.

If you're looking for an agent:
I accept submissions by email. Please include a 1-page mini-synopsis, a half-page cv, a longer synopsis (for non-fiction) and the first three chapters, or around 50 pages to a natural break. Please ensure it is via 'word document' attachments, 1.5 line spacing.

See website for full submission guidelines.

Pendle Hill Literary Agency

1 Farm Cottages; Offices 1a Brockhall Village, Old Langho Clitheroe Ribble Valley, Blackburn BB6 8BB
Tel: +44 (0) 1254 230000
Email: submissions@PendleHillLiteraryAgency.com
Website: http://www.pendlehillliteraryagency.com

Handles: Fiction; Nonfiction; Scripts; *Areas:* Adventure; Autobiography; Biography; Crime; Erotic; Fantasy; Film; Gothic; Historical; Hobbies; Horror; Mystery; Philosophy; Psychology; Romance; Sci-Fi; Short Stories; Spiritual; Suspense; Thrillers; *Markets:* Adult; Children's; Family; Youth; *Treatments:* Commercial; Dark; Literary; Mainstream; Popular

Not accepting submissions as at July 2015. Check website for current status.

A Lancashire-based literary agency set in the heart of the Ribble Valley market town of Clitheroe. Our ambition is to find new writers while elevating the careers for already, published authors. Literary agent Lee Woodcock drives a wide range of children's, young adult and adult fiction. Passionate about extending its authors capacity, we work closely with a wide range of publishing houses throughout the UK and globally, as well as directly with editorial, writing mentors and self-publishing houses.

The Peters Fraser & Dunlop Group Ltd (PFD)

Drury House, 34-43 Russell Street, London, WC2B 5HA
Tel: +44 (0) 20 7344 1000
Fax: +44 (0) 20 7836 9523
Email: info@pfd.co.uk
Website: http://www.pfd.co.uk

Handles: Fiction; Nonfiction; Scripts; *Areas:* Film; Radio; Theatre; TV; *Markets:* Adult; Children's

Send query with SAE, CV, synopsis and three sample chapters. Currently not accepting children's and illustrators submissions, or fantasy or science fiction. Submissions by post only. No fax or email submissions. Film, stage, and TV department is accepting new writers by referral only. No unsolicited scripts or pitches.

Shelley Power Literary Agency Ltd

20 Powell Gardens, South Heighton, Newhaven, BN9 0PS
Tel: +44 (0) 1273 512347
Email: sp@shelleypower.co.uk

Handles: Fiction; Nonfiction; *Markets:* Adult

Send query by post with return postage. No attachments. No poetry, scripts, or children's books.

Redhammer

186 Bickenhall Mansions, Bickenhall Street, London, W1U 6BX
Tel: +44 (0) 20 7486 3465
Fax: +44 (0) 20 7000 1249
Email: admin@redhammer.info
Website: http://redhammer.info

Handles: Fiction; Nonfiction; *Areas:* Autobiography; Crime; Entertainment; Mystery; Thrillers; *Markets:* Adult

Handles fiction and nonfiction. Would love to discover a big, sprawling crime / mystery / thriller with international blockbuster potential. Also keen on autobiographies, whistleblowers, and celebrity tales. Submit first ten pages of manuscript using online form on website only.

Richford Becklow Literary Agency

Tel: +44 (0)7510 023823
Email: enquiries@richfordbecklow.co.uk
Website: http://www.richfordbecklow.com

Handles: Fiction; Nonfiction; *Areas:* Arts; Autobiography; Biography; Cookery; Crime; Fantasy; Gardening; Gothic; Historical; Horror; Lifestyle; Literature; Romance; Sci-Fi; Self-Help; Women's Interests; *Markets:*

Adult; Youth; *Treatments:* Commercial; Contemporary; Literary; Satirical; Serious

Company founded in 2011 by an experienced agent, previously at the longest established literary agency in the world. Interested in fiction and nonfiction. Email submissions only. Does not accept postal submissions and cannot currently offer to represent American or Australian authors. No picture book texts for babies and toddlers, or erotica. No submissions in April or October. See website for full submission guidelines.

Robert Dudley Agency

135A Bridge Street, Ashford, Kent TN25 5DP
Email: info@robertdudleyagency.co.uk
Website: http://www.robertdudleyagency.co.uk

Handles: Nonfiction; *Areas:* Adventure; Biography; Business; Current Affairs; Historical; Medicine; Military; Sport; Technology; Travel; *Markets:* Adult; *Treatments:* Popular

Specialises in nonfiction. No fiction submissions. Send query outlining your idea by post or by email in first instance. See website for full guidelines.

Robin Jones Literary Agency

6b Marmora Road, London, SE22 0RX
Tel: +44 (0) 20 8693 6062
Email: robijones@gmail.com

Handles: Fiction; Nonfiction; *Markets:* Adult; Children's; *Treatments:* Commercial; Literary

London-based literary agency founded in 2007 by an agent who has previously worked at four other agencies, and was the UK scout for international publishers in 11 countries. Handles commercial and literary fiction and nonfiction for adults, and occasional children's for ages 8 and over. Welcomes Russian language fiction and nonfiction. No poetry, young adult, academic, religious, or original scripts. Accepts full mss or query with synopsis and 50-page sample.

Rochelle Stevens & Co.

2 Terretts Place, Upper Street, London, N1 1QZ
Tel: +44 (0) 20 7359 3900
Email: info@rochellestevens.com
Website: http://www.rochellestevens.com

Handles: Scripts; *Areas:* Film; Radio; Theatre; TV; *Markets:* Adult

Handles script writers for film, television, theatre, and radio. No longer handles writers of fiction, nonfiction, or children's books. Submit by post only. See website for full submission guidelines.

Rocking Chair Books

2 Rudgwick Terrace, St Stephens Close, London, NW8 6BR
Tel: +44 (0) 7809 461342
Email: representme@rockingchairbooks.com
Website: http://www.rockingchairbooks.com

Handles: Fiction; Nonfiction; *Areas:* Adventure; Arts; Crime; Culture; Current Affairs; Entertainment; Historical; Horror; Lifestyle; Literature; Mystery; Nature; Romance; Thrillers; Translations; Travel; Women's Interests; *Markets:* Adult; *Treatments:* Commercial; Contemporary; Cynical; Dark; Experimental; In-depth; Light; Literary; Mainstream; Popular; Positive; Progressive; Satirical; Serious; Traditional

Founded in 2011 after the founder worked for five years as a Director at an established London literary agency. Send complete ms or a few chapters by email only. No Children's, YA or Science Fiction / Fantasy.

Uli Rushby-Smith Literary Agency

72 Plimsoll Road, London, N4 2EE
Tel: +44 (0) 20 7354 2718
Fax: +44 (0) 20 7354 2718
Email: uli.rushby-smith@btconnect.com

Handles: Fiction; Nonfiction; *Markets:* Adult; Children's; *Treatments:* Commercial; Literary

Send query with SAE, outline, and two or

three sample chapters. Film and TV rights handled in conjunction with a sub-agent. No disks, poetry, picture books, films, or plays.

Sayle Screen Ltd

11 Jubilee Place, London, SW3 3TD
Tel: +44 (0) 20 7823 3883
Fax: +44 (0) 20 7823 3363
Email: info@saylescreen.com
Website: http://www.saylescreen.com

Handles: Scripts; *Areas:* Film; Radio; Theatre; TV; *Markets:* Adult

Only considers material which has been recommended by a producer, development executive or course tutor. In this case send query by email with cover letter and details of your referee to the relevant agent. Query only one agent at a time.

The Science Factory

Scheideweg 34C, Hamburg, Germany 20253
Tel: +44 (0) 20 7193 7296 (Skype)
Email: info@sciencefactory.co.uk
Website: http://www.sciencefactory.co.uk

Handles: Fiction; Nonfiction; *Areas:* Autobiography; Biography; Current Affairs; Historical; Medicine; Politics; Science; Technology; Travel; *Markets:* Adult

Specialises in science, technology, medicine, and natural history, but will also consider other areas of nonfiction. Novelists handled only occasionally, and if there is some special relevance to the agency (e.g. a thriller about scientists, or a novel of ideas). See website for full submission guidelines.

Please note that the agency address is in Germany, but the country is listed as United Kingdom, as the company is registered in the United Kingdom.

Linda Seifert Management

Screenworks Room 315, 22 Highbury Grove, Islington, London, N5 2ER
Tel: +44 (0) 20 3214 8293
Email: contact@lindaseifert.com
Website: http://www.lindaseifert.com

Handles: Scripts; *Areas:* Film; TV; *Markets:* Adult; Children's

A London-based management company representing screenwriters and directors for film and television. Our outstanding client list ranges from the highly established to the new and exciting emerging talent of tomorrow. Represents UK-based writers and directors only. Accepts submissions by post only. No novels or short stories. See website for full submission guidelines.

Sheil Land Associates Ltd

52 Doughty Street, London, WC1N 2LS
Tel: +44 (0) 20 7405 9351
Fax: +44 (0) 20 7831 2127
Email: info@sheilland.co.uk
Website: http://www.sheilland.co.uk

Handles: Fiction; Nonfiction; Scripts; *Areas:* Autobiography; Biography; Cookery; Crime; Drama; Fantasy; Film; Gardening; Historical; Humour; Lifestyle; Military; Mystery; Politics; Psychology; Radio; Romance; Science; Sci-Fi; Self-Help; Theatre; Thrillers; Travel; TV; Women's Interests; *Markets:* Adult; Children's; Youth; *Treatments:* Commercial; Contemporary; Literary

Send query with synopsis, CV, and first three chapters (or around 50 pages), by post addressed to "The Submissions Dept", or by email. Do not include SAE or return postage with postal submissions as all submissions are recycled.

Caroline Sheldon Literary Agency

71 Hillgate Place, London, W8 7SS
Tel: +44 (0) 20 7727 9102
Email: carolinesheldon@carolinesheldon.co.uk
Website: http://www.carolinesheldon.co.uk

Handles: Fiction; Nonfiction; *Areas:* Autobiography; Historical; Humour; Women's Interests; *Markets:* Adult; Children's; Youth; *Treatments:* Commercial; Contemporary; Literary

Send query by email only. Do not query both

agents. See website for both email addresses and appropriate subject line to include. Handles fiction and human-interest nonfiction for adults, and fiction for children, including full-length and picture books.

Shelley Instone Literary Agency

Tel: +44 (0) 20 8876 8209
Email: info@shelleyinstoneliteraryagency.co.uk
Website: http://www.shelleyinstoneliteraryagency.co.uk

Handles: Fiction; Nonfiction; *Areas:* Adventure; Autobiography; Cookery; Crime; Erotic; Fantasy; Gothic; Historical; Horror; Literature; Mystery; Romance; Sci-Fi; Thrillers; Women's Interests; *Markets:* Adult; Children's; Family; Youth; *Treatments:* Commercial; Contemporary; Dark; In-depth; Light; Literary; Mainstream; Niche; Popular; Positive

Agency established in 2014. We support, nurture and develop debut and established writers of children's fiction, adult fiction alongside nonfiction. In order to sign you to our agency, we need to feel thrilled and inspired by your manuscript. If you have an ability for vivid, descriptive and well – structured storytelling, please submit your work to us.

Dorie Simmonds Agency

Riverbank House, 1 Putney Bridge Approach, London, SW6 3JD
Tel: +44 (0) 20 7736 0002
Fax: +44 (0) 20 7736 0010
Email: info@doriesimmonds.com
Website: http://doriesimmonds.com

Handles: Fiction; Nonfiction; *Areas:* Biography; Historical; Women's Interests; *Markets:* Adult; Children's; *Treatments:* Commercial; Contemporary

Send query by email as Word or PDF attachments or by post with SAE. Include details on your background and relevant writing experience, and first three chapters or fifty pages. See website for full details.

Jeffrey Simmons

15 Penn House, Mallory Street, London, NW8 8SX
Tel: +44 (0) 20 7224 8917
Email: jasimmons@unicombox.co.uk

Handles: Fiction; Nonfiction; *Areas:* Autobiography; Biography; Crime; Current Affairs; Entertainment; Film; Historical; Legal; Politics; Psychology; Sport; Theatre; *Markets:* Adult; *Treatments:* Commercial; Literary

Send query with brief bio, synopsis, history of any prior publication, and list of any publishers or agents to have already seen the MSS. Particularly interested in personality books of all kinds and fiction from young writers (under 40) with a future. No children's books, science fiction, fantasy, cookery, crafts, gardening, or hobbies. Film scripts handled for existing book clients only.

Sinclair-Stevenson

3 South Terrace, London, SW7 2TB
Tel: +44 (0) 20 7581 2550
Fax: +44 (0) 20 7581 2550

Handles: Fiction; Nonfiction; *Areas:* Arts; Biography; Current Affairs; Historical; Travel; *Markets:* Adult

Send query with synopsis and SAE. No children's books, scripts, academic, science fiction, or fantasy.

Robert Smith Literary Agency Ltd

12 Bridge Wharf, 156 Caledonian Road, London, N1 9UU
Tel: +44 (0) 20 7278 2444
Fax: +44 (0) 20 7833 5680
Email: robertsmith.literaryagency@virgin.net
Website: http://www.robertsmithliteraryagency.com

Handles: Nonfiction; *Areas:* Autobiography; Biography; Crime; Culture; Current Affairs; Health; Historical; Humour; Lifestyle; Military; Self-Help; *Markets:* Adult; *Treatments:* Mainstream; Popular

Send query with synopsis initially and sample chapter if available, by post or by email. No poetry, fiction, scripts, children's books, academic, or unsolicited MSS. Will suggest revision. See website for full guidelines.

Standen Literary Agency

4 Winton Avenue, London, N11 2AT
Tel: +44 (0) 20 8245 2606
Fax: +44 (0) 20 8245 2606
Email: submissions@standenliteraryagency.com
Website: http://www.standenliteraryagency.com

Handles: Fiction; Nonfiction; *Markets:* Adult; Children's; Youth; *Treatments:* Commercial; Literary

Based in London. For fiction, send synopsis and first three chapters by email only. Responds if interested only. If no response in 12 weeks assume rejection. For nonfiction, query in first instance.

Elaine Steel

49 Greek Street, London, W1D 4EG
Tel: +44 (0) 1273 739022
Email: info@elainesteel.com
Website: http://www.elainesteel.com

Handles: Fiction; Nonfiction; Scripts; *Areas:* Film; Radio; TV; *Markets:* Adult

Send query by email with CV and outline, along with details of experience. No unsolicited mss.

Abner Stein

10 Roland Gardens, London, SW7 3PH
Tel: +44 (0) 20 7373 0456
Fax: +44 (0) 20 7370 6316
Email: caspian@abnerstein.co.uk
Website: http://www.abnerstein.co.uk

Handles: Fiction; Nonfiction; *Markets:* Adult; Children's

Agency based in London. Handles fiction, general nonfiction, and children's.

Steph Roundsmith Agent and Editor

3 Bowes Road, Billingham, Stockton-on-Tees TS23 2BU
Email: agent@stephroundsmith.co.uk
Website: http://www.stephroundsmith.co.uk

Handles: Fiction; *Areas:* Adventure; Fantasy; Historical; Humour; Literature; Mystery; Sci-Fi; *Markets:* Children's; *Treatments:* Commercial; Literary; Mainstream

I only represent children's authors and I am currently looking for new clients. If you would like to submit your work for consideration then please send me a one page synopsis (including age range and word count), a paragraph or two about yourself, and your first three chapters. Please send everything by email and I will endeavour to get back to you within two weeks.

Ideally, I'm looking for writers who write for children (up to 12 years) in any genre. Whether it's a picture book or a full-length novel, I'd love to see your work. If you'd like to ask any questions then please don't hesitate to contact me.

Shirley Stewart Literary Agency

3rd Floor, 21 Denmark Street, London, WC2H 8NA
Tel: +44 (0) 20 7836 4440
Fax: +44 (0) 20 7836 3482
Email: shirleystewart@btinternet.com

Handles: Fiction; Nonfiction; *Markets:* Adult; *Treatments:* Literary

Paricularly interested in literary fiction and general nonfiction. Send query with SAE and two or three sample chapters. Unsolicited material considered, but no submissions by fax or on disk. No poetry, scripts, children's books, science fiction, or fantasy.

Sarah Such Literary Agency

81 Arabella Drive, London, SW15 5LL
Tel: +44 (0) 20 8876 4228
Fax: +44 (0) 20 8878 8705

Email: info@sarah-such.com
Website: http://www.sarahsuch.com

Handles: Fiction; Nonfiction; *Areas:* Autobiography; Biography; Culture; Historical; Humour; *Markets:* Adult; Children's; Youth; *Treatments:* Commercial; Literary; Popular

Handles literary and commercial nonfiction and fiction for adults, young adults and children. Particularly interested in debut novels, biography, memoir, history, popular culture and humour. Works mainly by recommendation, but does also accept unsolicited approaches, by email only. Send synopsis, author bio, and sample chapter as Word attachment. No unsolicited mss or queries by phone. Handles TV and film scripts for existing clients, but no radio or theatre scripts. No poetry, fantasy, self-help or short stories.

Susanna Lea Associates (UK)

34 Lexington Street, London, W1F 0LH
Tel: +44 (0) 20 7287 7757
Fax: +44 (0) 20 7287 7775
Email: uk-submission@susannalea.com
Website: http://www.susannalea.com

Handles: Fiction; Nonfiction; *Markets:* Adult

Literary agency with offices in Paris, London, and New York. Always on the lookout for exciting new talent. No poetry, plays, screen plays, science fiction, educational text books, short stories or illustrated works. No queries by fax or post. Accepts queries by email only. Include cover letter, synopsis, and first three chapters or proposal. Response not guaranteed.

The Susijn Agency

820 Harrow Road, London, NW10 5JU
Tel: +44 (0) 20 8968 7435
Fax: +44 (0) 20 7580 8626
Email: submissions@thesusijnagency.com
Website: http://www.thesusijnagency.com

Handles: Fiction; Nonfiction; *Markets:* Adult; *Treatments:* Literary

Send query with synopsis and three sample chapters only by post or by email. Include SASE if return of material required. Response in 8-10 weeks. Specialises in selling rights worldwide and also represents non-English language authors and publishers for US, UK, and translation rights worldwide. No self-help, science-fiction, fantasy, romance, children's, illustrated, business, screenplays, or theatre plays.

SYLA – Susan Yearwood Literary Agency

2 Knebworth House, Londesborough Road, Stoke Newington, London N16 8RL
Tel: +44 (0) 20 7503 0954
Email: fiction@susanyearwood.com
Website: http://www.susanyearwood.com

Handles: Fiction; Nonfiction; *Areas:* Autobiography; Biography; Business; Crime; Lifestyle; Psychology; Thrillers; Women's Interests; *Markets:* Adult; Children's; Youth; *Treatments:* Commercial; Literary; Popular

Send query by email, including synopsis and first thirty pages in one Word file attachment. No poetry or screenwriting, or submissions by post. Check website for specific email address to query, as this differs by genre.

The Tennyson Agency

10 Cleveland Avenue, Wimbledon Chase, London, SW20 9EW
Tel: +44 (0) 20 8543 5939
Email: enquiries@tenagy.co.uk
Website: http://www.tenagy.co.uk

Handles: Scripts; *Areas:* Drama; Film; Radio; Theatre; TV; *Markets:* Adult

Mainly deals in scripts for film, TV, theatre, and radio, along with related material on an ad-hoc basis. Handles writers in the European Union only. Send query with CV and outline of work. Prefers queries by email. No nonfiction, poetry, short stories, science fiction and fantasy or children's writing, or unsolicited MSS.

Jane Turnbull

Barn Cottage, Veryan, Truro TR2 5QA
Tel: +44 (0) 20 7727 9409 / +44 (0) 1872 501317
Email: jane@janeturnbull.co.uk
Website: http://www.janeturnbull.co.uk

Handles: Fiction; Nonfiction; *Areas:* Biography; Current Affairs; Entertainment; Gardening; Historical; Humour; Lifestyle; Nature; TV; *Markets:* Adult; *Treatments:* Commercial; Literary; Mainstream

Agency with offices in London and Cornwall. New clients always welcome and a few taken on every year. Send query by post to Cornwall office with short description of your book or idea. No unsolicited MSS.

United Agents

12–26 Lexington Street, London, W1F 0LE
Tel: +44 (0) 20 3214 0800
Fax: +44 (0) 20 3214 0802
Email: info@unitedagents.co.uk
Website: http://unitedagents.co.uk

Handles: Fiction; Nonfiction; Scripts; *Areas:* Biography; Film; Radio; Theatre; TV; *Markets:* Adult; Children's; Youth

Do not approach the book department generally. Consult website and view details of each agent before selecting a specific agent to approach personally. Accepts submissions by email only. Submissions by post will not be returned or responded to.

Ed Victor Ltd

6 Bayley Street, Bedford Square, London, WC1B 3HE
Tel: +44 (0) 20 7304 4100
Fax: +44 (0) 20 7304 4111
Email: info@edvictor.com
Website: http://www.edvictor.com

Handles: Fiction; Nonfiction; *Areas:* Autobiography; Biography; Cookery; Historical; Politics; Travel; *Markets:* Adult; Children's; *Treatments:* Commercial; Literary

Handles authors of both literary and commercial fiction, as well as children's books and nonfiction in areas including biography, memoir, politics, travel, food and history. Send query by email with synopsis/outline and first five chapters as an attachment – do not include in the body of the email. Response not guaranteed unless interested.

Wade & Co Literary Agency

33 Cormorant Lodge, Thomas More Street, London, E1W 1AU
Tel: +44 (0) 20 7488 4171
Fax: +44 (0) 20 7488 4172
Email: rw@rwla.com
Website: http://www.rwla.com

Handles: Fiction; Nonfiction; *Markets:* Adult; Youth

New full-length proposals for adult and young adult fiction and nonfiction always welcome. Send query with detailed 1–6 page synopsis, brief biography, and first 10,000 words via email as Word documents (.doc) or PDF; or by post with SAE if return required. We much prefer to correspond by email. Actively seeking new writers across the literary spectrum. No poetry, children's, short stories, scripts or plays.

Cecily Ware Literary Agents

19C John Spencer Square, London, N1 2LZ
Tel: +44 (0) 20 7359 3787
Fax: +44 (0) 20 7226 9828
Email: info@cecilyware.com
Website: http://www.cecilyware.com

Handles: Scripts; *Areas:* Drama; Film; Humour; TV; *Markets:* Adult; Children's

Handles film and TV scripts only. No books or theatre scripts. Submit complete script with covering letter, CV, and SAE. No email submissions or return of material without SAE and correct postage.

Watson, Little Ltd

Suite 315, ScreenWorks, 22 Highbury Grove, London, N5 2ER
Tel: +44 (0) 20 7388 7529
Fax: +44 (0) 20 7388 8501

Email: submissions@watsonlittle.com
Website: http://www.watsonlittle.com

Handles: Fiction; Nonfiction; *Areas:* Business; Crime; Film; Historical; Humour; Leisure; Music; Psychology; Science; Self-Help; Sport; Technology; Women's Interests; *Markets:* Adult; Children's; Youth; *Treatments:* Commercial; Literary; Popular

Send query by post with SAE (if return required) or email (preferred) with synopsis and sample material, addressed to a specific agent. See website for full guidelines and details of specific agents. No scripts, poetry, or unsolicited MSS.

Whispering Buffalo Literary Agency Ltd

97 Chesson Road, London, W14 9QS
Tel: +44 (0) 20 7565 4737
Email: info@whisperingbuffalo.com
Website: http://www.whisperingbuffalo.com

Handles: Fiction; Nonfiction; *Areas:* Adventure; Anthropology; Arts; Autobiography; Beauty and Fashion; Design; Entertainment; Film; Health; Humour; Lifestyle; Music; Nature; Politics; Romance; Sci-Fi; Self-Help; Thrillers; *Markets:* Adult; Children's; Youth; *Treatments:* Commercial; Literary

Handles commercial/literary fiction/nonfiction and children's/YA fiction with special interest in book to film adaptations. No TV, film, radio or theatre scripts, or poetry or academic. Accepts submissions by email only. For fiction, send query with CV, synopsis, and first three chapters. For nonfiction, send proposal and sample chapter. Response only if interested.

Eve White: Literary Agent

54 Gloucester Street, London, SW1V 4EG
Tel: +44 (0) 20 7630 1155
Email: eve@evewhite.co.uk
Website: http://www.evewhite.co.uk

Handles: Fiction; Nonfiction; *Markets:* Adult; Children's; *Treatments:* Commercial; Literary

Important! Check and follow website submission guidelines before contacting!

DO NOT send submissions to email address listed on this page – see website for specific submission email addresses for different areas.

QUERIES ONLY to the email address on this page.

This agency requests that you go to their website for up-to-date submission procedure.

Commercial and literary fiction, nonfiction, children's fiction and picture books ages 7+ (home 15%, overseas 20%). No reading fee. No poetry, short stories, novellas, screenplays, or science fiction/fantasy for adults. Does not consider approaches from US writers. See website for detailed submission guidelines. Submission by email only.

Dinah Wiener Ltd

12 Cornwall Grove, Chiswick, London, W4 2LB
Tel: +44 (0) 20 8994 6011
Fax: +44 (0) 20 8994 6044
Email: dinah@dwla.co.uk

Handles: Fiction; Nonfiction; *Areas:* Autobiography; Biography; Cookery; Science; *Markets:* Adult

Send preliminary query letter with SAE. No poetry, scripts, or children's books.

William Morris Endeavor (WME) London

100 New Oxford Street, London, WC1A 1HB
Tel: +44 (0) 20 7534 6800
Fax: +44 (0) 20 7534 6900
Email: ldnsubmissions@wmeentertainment.com
Website: http://www.wmeauthors.co.uk

Handles: Fiction; Nonfiction; *Areas:* Autobiography; Biography; Crime; Culture; Historical; Thrillers; *Markets:* Adult; Youth; *Treatments:* Commercial; Literary

London office of a worldwide theatrical and literary agency, with offices in New York, Beverly Hills, Nashville, Miami, and Shanghai, as well as associates in Sydney. No unsolicited scripts for film, TV, or theatre. No self-help, poetry or picture books. Send query by email, using link on website. See website for full guidelines.

Writers House UK

25 Gerrard Street, London, W1D 6JL
Email: akowal@writershouse.com
Website: http://www.writershouse.com

Handles: Fiction; Nonfiction; *Areas:* Autobiography; Biography; Business; Cookery; Fantasy; Finance; Historical; How-to; Lifestyle; Psychology; Science; Sci-Fi; Self-Help; Women's Interests; *Markets:* Adult; Children's; Youth; *Treatments:* Commercial; Literary

UK branch of established US agency with offices in New York and California.

The Wylie Agency (UK) Ltd

17 Bedford Square, London, WC2B 3JA
Tel: +44 (0) 20 7908 5900
Fax: +44 (0) 20 7908 5901
Email: mail@wylieagency.co.uk
Website: http://www.wylieagency.co.uk

Handles: Fiction; Nonfiction; *Markets:* Adult

Note: Not accepting unsolicited mss as at June 2015

Send query by post or email before submitting. All submissions must include adequate return postage. No scripts, children's books, or unsolicited MSS.

Zeno Agency Ltd

Primrose Hill Business Centre, 110 Gloucester Avenue, London, NW1 3LH
Tel: +44 (0) 20 7096 0927
Email: info@zenoagency.com
Website: http://zenoagency.com

Handles: Fiction; *Areas:* Crime; Fantasy; Historical; Horror; Sci-Fi; Thrillers; *Markets:* Adult; Youth; *Treatments:* Commercial

London-based literary agency specialising in Science Fiction, Fantasy, and Horror. Temporarily closed to submissions of science fiction and fantasy as at June 2015 (check website for current status), but accepting approaches regarding completed horror, crime, or thriller fiction of over 75,000 words. No crossover fiction. Submissions by email only. See website for full guidelines.

Canadian Literary Agents

For the most up-to-date listings of these and hundreds of other literary agents, visit http://www.firstwriter.com/Agents

*To claim your **free** access to the site, please see the back of this book.*

Abela Literature

39 King St, Box 20039 Brunswick Square, Saint John, New Brunswick E2L 5B2
Email: submissions@abela-lit.com
Website: http://www.abela-lit.com

Handles: Fiction; *Areas:* Adventure; Crime; Drama; Fantasy; Gothic; Historical; Horror; Literature; Mystery; Sci-Fi; Suspense; Thrillers; Westerns; *Markets:* Adult; Family; *Treatments:* Literary; Popular; Traditional

Happy to work with both first time and previously published authors. We are not currently looking for any nonfiction projects, but would be interested in queries for manuscripts in a variety of fiction categories.

Rick Broadhead & Associates Literary Agency

47 St. Clair Avenue West, Suite 501, Toronto, Ontario M4V 3A5
Tel: +1 (416) 929-0516
Fax: +1 (416) 927-8732
Email: submissions@rbaliterary.com
Website: http://www.rbaliterary.com

Handles: Nonfiction; *Areas:* Biography; Business; Culture; Current Affairs; Health; Historical; Humour; Lifestyle; Medicine; Military; Nature; Politics; Science; Self-Help; *Markets:* Adult; *Treatments:* Popular

Prefers queries by email. Send brief query outlining your project and your credentials. Responds only if interested. No screenplays, poetry, children's books, or fiction.

The Characters Talent Agency

8 Elm Street, Toronto, Ontario M3H 1Y9
Tel: +1 (416) 964-8522
Fax: +1 (416) 964-8206
Email: litsubmissionsto@thecharacters.com
Website: http://www.thecharacters.com

Handles: Scripts; *Areas:* Biography; Drama; Erotic; Fantasy; Film; Historical; Horror; Humour; Mystery; Romance; Science; Sport; Thrillers; TV; Westerns; Women's Interests; *Markets:* Adult; Children's; Youth; *Treatments:* Contemporary; Mainstream

Approach by email. Response only if interested.

The Cooke Agency

75 Sherbourne Street., Suite 501, Toronto, Ontario M5A 2P9
Tel: +1 (647) 788-4010
Email: egriffin@cookeagency.ca
Website: http://www.cookeagency.ca

Handles: Fiction; Nonfiction; *Areas:* Crime; Culture; Fantasy; Historical; Nature; Politics; Romance; Science; Sci-Fi; Spiritual; *Markets:* Adult; Children's; Youth; *Treatments:* Commercial; Literary

Send query by email only with "Author Query" in the subject line (no attachments). No illustrated, photographic or children's picture books, US political thrillers, or poetry. No queries or submissions by post. Consult website before making contact.

Anne McDermid & Associates Ltd

64 Bloem Avenue, Toronto, Ontario M6E 1S1
Tel: +1 (416) 324-8845
Fax: +1 (416) 324-8870
Email: info@mcdermidagency.com
Website: http://www.mcdermidagency.com

Handles: Fiction; Nonfiction; *Areas:* Autobiography; Biography; Fantasy; Historical; Science; Sci-Fi; Travel; *Markets:* Adult; Children's; Youth; *Treatments:* Commercial; Literary

Send query by post or email, describing you and your project. You may also include the first 5 pages of your mss only. No unsolicited mss or queries by telephone.

P.S. Literary Agency

20033-520 Kerr Street, Oakville, Ontario L6K 3C7
Tel: +1 (416) 907-8325
Email: query@psliterary.com
Website: http://www.PSLiterary.com

Handles: Fiction; Nonfiction; *Areas:* Autobiography; Business; Current Affairs; Health; Historical; Humour; Literature; Mystery; Politics; Psychology; Romance; Science; Sport; Suspense; Thrillers; Women's Interests; *Markets:* Adult; Children's; Youth; *Treatments:* Commercial; Contemporary; Literary; Mainstream; Popular

A literary agency representing both fiction and nonfiction for adults, young adults, and children. Does not handle poetry or screenplays. Send one-page query by email only. No attachments. See website for full submission guidelines.

Seventh Avenue Literary Agency

2052 – 124th Street , South Surrey, BC V4A 9K3
Tel: +1 (604) 538-7252
Fax: +1 (604) 538-7252
Email: info@seventhavenuelit.com
Website: http://www.seventhavenuelit.com

Handles: Nonfiction; *Markets:* Adult

Handles nonfiction only and takes on few new clients. Send query by email with 2-3 paragraph description of your project and one paragraph about you; or by post with decsription of your book and its catefory, its potential market, table of contents with short description of each chapter, one sample chapter, and author bio, including previously published material and your qualifications on the subject you have written on.

Transatlantic Literary Agency, Inc.

2 Bloor Street East, Suite 3500, Toronto, Ontario M4W 1A8
Tel: +1 (416) 488-9214
Fax: +1 (416) 929-3174
Email: info@transatlanticagency.com
Website: http://transatlanticagency.com

Handles: Fiction; Nonfiction; *Areas:* Autobiography; Biography; Crime; Historical; Humour; Mystery; Nature; Politics; Travel; Women's Interests; *Markets:* Adult; Children's; Youth; *Treatments:* Commercial; Contemporary; Literary

Canadian branch of international agency with agents in Canada, the US, and the UK, founded in Canada in 1993. The different agents have different interests and different submission requirements, so essential to consult website before submitting.

Westwood Creative Artists

94 Harbord Street, Toronto , Ontario M5S 1G6
Tel: +1 (416) 964-3302
Fax: +1 (416) 975-9209
Email: wca_office@wcaltd.com

Website: http://www.wcaltd.com

Handles: Fiction; Nonfiction; *Areas:* Autobiography; Biography; Current Affairs; Historical; Mystery; Science; Thrillers; *Markets:* Adult; Children's; Youth;

Treatments: Commercial; Literary

Send query by email with your credentials, a synopsis, and short sample up to ten pages in the body of the email. No attachments.

Irish Literary Agents

For the most up-to-date listings of these and hundreds of other literary agents, visit http://www.firstwriter.com/Agents

*To claim your **free** access to the site, please see the back of this book.*

Author Rights Agency

20 Victoria Road, Rathgar, Dublin, 6
Tel: +353 1 4922112
Email: submissions@authorrightsagency.com
Website: http://www.authorrightsagency.com

Handles: Fiction; Nonfiction; *Areas:* Crime; Fantasy; Historical; Sci-Fi; Women's Interests; *Markets:* Adult; Children's; Youth; *Treatments:* Contemporary; Literary

Welcomes submissions in English, particularly from Irish and American writers. Send query by email only with synopsis, ideally one page long, and writing sample up to 10 pages or about 3,000 words, as a Word or RTF attachment. Do not include in the body of the email, or send full manuscripts. See website for full guidelines. No phone calls.

Marianne Gunn O'Connor Literary Agency

Morrison Chambers, Suite 17, 32 Nassau Street,, Dublin, 2
Tel: 353 1 677 9100
Fax: 353 1 677 9101
Email: mgoclitagency@eircom.net

Handles: Fiction; Nonfiction; *Areas:* Biography; Health; *Markets:* Adult; Children's; *Treatments:* Commercial; Literary

Send query with half-page synopsis by email.

The Lisa Richards Agency

108 Upper Leeson Street, Dublin, 4
Tel: +353 1 637 5000
Fax: +353 1 667 1256
Email: info@lisarichards.ie
Website: http://www.lisarichards.ie

Handles: Fiction; Nonfiction; Scripts; *Areas:* Autobiography; Biography; Culture; Historical; Humour; Lifestyle; Self-Help; Sport; Theatre; *Markets:* Adult; Children's; *Treatments:* Commercial; Literary; Popular

Send query by email or by post with SASE, including three or four sample chapters in the case of fiction, or proposal and sample chapter for nonfiction. No horror, science fiction, screenplays, or children's picture books.

Australian Literary Agents

For the most up-to-date listings of these and hundreds of other literary agents, visit http://www.firstwriter.com/Agents

To claim your ***free*** *access to the site, please see the back of this book.*

The Mary Cunnane Agency Pty Ltd

PO Box 336, Bermagui, NSW 2546
Tel: +61 (0) 2 6493 3880
Fax: +61 (0) 2 6493 3881
Email: mary@cunnaneagency.com
Website: http://www.cunnaneagency.com

Handles: Fiction; Nonfiction; *Markets:* Adult

Make initial query by post, phone, or email. If querying by email, copy in both agents. Does not handle North American writers. No science fiction, fantasy, romance novels, new age/spiritual books, or children's books.

Literary Agents Subject Index

This section lists literary agents by their subject matter, with directions to the section of the book where the full listing can be found.

You can create your own customised lists of literary agents using different combinations of these subject areas, plus over a dozen other criteria, instantly online at http://www.firstwriter.com.

*To claim your **free** access to the site, please see the back of this book.*

Alive Communications, Inc (*US*)
Miriam Altshuler Literary Agency (*US*)
Ambassador Speakers Bureau & Literary Agency (*US*)
The Ampersand Agency Ltd (*UK*)
Betsy Amster Literary Enterprises (*US*)
AP Watt at United Agents LLP (*UK*)
Arcadia (*US*)
Audrey A. Wolf Literary Agency (*US*)
The August Agency LLC (*US*)
Ayesha Pande Literary (*US*)
Baldi Agency (*US*)
The Bent Agency (*US*)
David Black Literary Agency (*US*)
Bleecker Street Associates, Inc. (*US*)
The Book Group (*US*)
Georges Borchardt, Inc. (*US*)
Brandt & Hochman Literary Agents, Inc. (*US*)
The Bright Literary Academy (*UK*)
Browne & Miller Literary Associates (*US*)
Carnicelli Literary Management (*US*)
Maria Carvainis Agency, Inc. (*US*)
Chalberg & Sussman (*US*)
Elyse Cheney Literary Associates, LLC (*US*)
Rosica Colin Ltd (*UK*)
Frances Collin Literary Agent (*US*)
Don Congdon Associates, Inc. (*US*)
Connor Literary Agency (*US*)
The Doe Coover Agency (*US*)
CowlesRyan Agency (*US*)
The Creative Rights Agency (*UK*)
Creative Authors Ltd (*UK*)
The Croce Agency (*US*)
Richard Curtis Associates, Inc. (*US*)
Laura Dail Literary Agency (*US*)
The Darley Anderson Agency (*UK*)
David Luxton Associates (*UK*)
Liza Dawson Associates (*US*)
The Jennifer DeChiara Literary Agency (*US*)
Joëlle Delbourgo Associates, Inc. (*US*)
Diane Banks Associates Literary Agency (*UK*)
Sandra Dijkstra Literary Agency (*US*)
Jim Donovan Literary (*US*)
Doyen Literary Services, Inc. (*US*)
Dunham Literary, Inc. (*US*)
Dystel & Goderich Literary Management (*US*)
Anne Edelstein Literary Agency (*US*)
Elise Dillsworth Agency (EDA) (*UK*)
Ethan Ellenberg Literary Agency (*US*)
Evatopia, Inc. (*US*)
Farris Literary Agency, Inc. (*US*)
The Feldstein Agency (*UK*)
The Fielding Agency, LLC (*US*)
Diana Finch Literary Agency (*US*)
Fine Literary (*US*)
FinePrint Literary Management (*US*)
Fletcher & Company (*US*)
Folio Literary Management, LLC (*US*)
Foundry Literary + Media (*US*)
Fox Mason Ltd (*UK*)
Sarah Jane Freymann Literary Agency (*US*)
Furniss Lawton (*UK*)
Gelfman Schneider Literary Agents, Inc. (*US*)
The Gernert Company (*US*)
Frances Goldin Literary Agency, Inc. (*US*)
Goodman Associates (*US*)
Graham Maw Christie Literary Agency (*UK*)
Sanford J. Greenburger Associates, Inc (*US*)
Greene & Heaton Ltd (*UK*)
Gunn Media Associates (*UK*)
The Mitchell J. Hamilburg Agency (*US*)
Hardman & Swainson (*UK*)
Joy Harris Literary Agency, Inc. (*US*)
Antony Harwood Limited (*UK*)
John Hawkins & Associates, Inc. (*US*)
Rupert Heath Literary Agency (*UK*)
The Jeff Herman Agency, LLC (*US*)
hhb agency ltd (*UK*)
David Higham Associates Ltd (*UK*)
Hill Nadell Literary Agency (*US*)
Kate Hordern Literary Agency (*UK*)
Hornfischer Literary Management, L.P. (*US*)
Amanda Howard Associates Ltd (*UK*)
Andrea Hurst Literary Management (*US*)
J de S Associates Inc (*US*)
Johnson & Alcock (*UK*)
Kilburn Literary Agency (*UK*)
Harvey Klinger, Inc (*US*)
Kneerim & Williams (*US*)
The Knight Agency (*US*)
Barbara S. Kouts, Literary Agent (*US*)
The LA Literary Agency (*US*)
Laura Langlie, Literary Agent (*US*)
Larsen Pomada Literary Agents (*US*)
Levine Greenberg Literary Agency, Inc. (*US*)
Literary & Creative Artists Inc. (*US*)
The Literary Group (*US*)
Sterling Lord Literistic, Inc. (*US*)
Julia Lord Literary Management (*US*)
Lowenstein Associates, Inc. (*US*)
Andrew Lownie Literary Agency Ltd (*UK*)
The Jennifer Lyons Literary Agency, LLC (*US*)
Gina Maccoby Agency (*US*)
Madeleine Milburn Literary Agency (*UK*)
Ricia Mainhardt Agency (RMA) (*US*)
Carol Mann Agency (*US*)
Manus & Associates Literary Agency, Inc. (*US*)
March Tenth, Inc. (*US*)
The Martell Agency (*US*)
Martin Literary Management (*US*)
Anne McDermid & Associates Ltd (*Can*)
McKernan Agency (*UK*)
Mendel Media Group, LLC (*US*)
Martha Millard Literary Agency (*US*)
The Miller Agency (*US*)
Objective Entertainment (*US*)
P.S. Literary Agency (*Can*)
The Richard Parks Agency (*US*)
Jonathan Pegg Literary Agency (*UK*)
Pendle Hill Literary Agency (*UK*)
James Peter Associates, Inc. (*US*)
Pinder Lane & Garon-Brooke Associates Ltd (*US*)
The Poynor Group (*US*)
Rebecca Pratt Literary Group (*US*)
Linn Prentis Literary (*US*)

Aaron M. Priest Literary Agency (*US*)
Prospect Agency (*US*)
Susan Rabiner, Literary Agent, Inc. (*US*)
Rebecca Friedman Literary Agency (*US*)
Redhammer (*UK*)
Regina Ryan Publishing Enterprises (*US*)
The Lisa Richards Agency (*Ire*)
Richford Becklow Literary Agency (*UK*)
Ann Rittenberg Literary Agency (*US*)
B.J. Robbins Literary Agency (*US*)
Rita Rosenkranz Literary Agency (*US*)
Ross Yoon Agency (*US*)
Jane Rotrosen Agency (*US*)
The Rudy Agency (*US*)
Victoria Sanders & Associates LLC (*US*)
Susan Schulman, A Literary Agency (*US*)
The Science Factory (*UK*)
Scovil Galen Ghosh Literary Agency, Inc. (*US*)
The Seven Bridges Group (*US*)
Denise Shannon Literary Agency, Inc. (*US*)
Sheil Land Associates Ltd (*UK*)
Caroline Sheldon Literary Agency (*UK*)
Shelley Instone Literary Agency (*UK*)
Wendy Sherman Associates, Inc. (*US*)
Jeffrey Simmons (*UK*)
Robert Smith Literary Agency Ltd (*UK*)
Solow Literary Enterprises, Inc. (*US*)
The Spieler Agency (*US*)
Robin Straus Agency, Inc. (*US*)
Stuart Krichevsky Literary Agency, Inc. (*US*)
The Stuart Agency (*US*)
Sarah Such Literary Agency (*UK*)
SYLA – Susan Yearwood Literary Agency (*UK*)
Talcott Notch Literary (*US*)
Tessler Literary Agency (*US*)
Tom Lee (*US*)
Transatlantic Literary Agency, Inc. (*Can*)
TriadaUS Literary Agency, Inc. (*US*)
Trident Media Group, LLC (*US*)
2M Literary Agency Ltd (*US*)
Venture Literary (*US*)
Ed Victor Ltd (*UK*)
Watkins / Loomis Agency, Inc. (*US*)
Waxman Leavell Literary Agency (*US*)
The Wendy Weil Agency, Inc. (*US*)
The Weingel-Fidel Agency (*US*)
Westwood Creative Artists (*Can*)
Whispering Buffalo Literary Agency Ltd (*UK*)
Dinah Wiener Ltd (*UK*)
William Morris Endeavor (WME) London (*UK*)
Writers House UK (*UK*)
Writers House, LLC. (*US*)
Writers' Representatives, LLC (*US*)
Yates & Yates (*US*)
The Zack Company, Inc (*US*)

Beauty and Fashion

Abbot Management (*US*)
Artellus Limited (*UK*)
Barbara Braun Associates, Inc. (*US*)
Rosica Colin Ltd (*UK*)
The Darley Anderson Agency (*UK*)
Diane Banks Associates Literary Agency (*UK*)
Janis A. Donnaud & Associates, Inc. (*US*)
Fine Literary (*US*)
FinePrint Literary Management (*US*)
Antony Harwood Limited (*UK*)
Signature Literary Agency (*US*)
2M Literary Agency Ltd (*US*)
Venture Literary (*US*)
Whimsy Literary Agency, LLC (*US*)
Whispering Buffalo Literary Agency Ltd (*UK*)

Biography

Abbot Management (*US*)
Sheila Ableman Literary Agency (*UK*)
Adler & Robin Books, Inc (*US*)
The Agency Group, Ltd (*US*)
The Ahearn Agency, Inc (*US*)
Alive Communications, Inc (*US*)
Ambassador Speakers Bureau & Literary Agency (*US*)
The Ampersand Agency Ltd (*UK*)
Betsy Amster Literary Enterprises (*US*)
AP Watt at United Agents LLP (*UK*)
Arcadia (*US*)
Artellus Limited (*UK*)
Audrey A. Wolf Literary Agency (*US*)
The August Agency LLC (*US*)
Ayesha Pande Literary (*US*)
Baldi Agency (*US*)
Vicky Bijur Literary Agency (*US*)
David Black Literary Agency (*US*)
Blake Friedmann Literary Agency Ltd (*UK*)
Bleecker Street Associates, Inc. (*US*)
The Book Group (*US*)
Georges Borchardt, Inc. (*US*)
Barbara Braun Associates, Inc. (*US*)
Rick Broadhead & Associates Literary Agency (*Can*)
Jenny Brown Associates (*UK*)
Marie Brown Associates, Inc. (*US*)
Tracy Brown Literary Agency (*US*)
Browne & Miller Literary Associates (*US*)
Felicity Bryan (*UK*)
Sheree Bykofsky Associates, Inc. (*US*)
Capel & Land Ltd (*UK*)
Carnicelli Literary Management (*US*)
Maria Carvainis Agency, Inc. (*US*)
Castiglia Literary Agency (*US*)
The Characters Talent Agency (*Can*)
Jane Chelius Literary Agency, Inc. (*US*)
Elyse Cheney Literary Associates, LLC (*US*)
Teresa Chris Literary Agency Ltd (*UK*)
Cine/Lit Representation (*US*)
Rosica Colin Ltd (*UK*)
Frances Collin Literary Agent (*US*)
Don Congdon Associates, Inc. (*US*)
Conville & Walsh Ltd (*UK*)
The Doe Coover Agency (*US*)
CowlesRyan Agency (*US*)
Creative Authors Ltd (*UK*)
The Croce Agency (*US*)
Curtis Brown Group Ltd (*UK*)
Richard Curtis Associates, Inc. (*US*)
Laura Dail Literary Agency (*US*)
The Darley Anderson Agency (*UK*)
David Luxton Associates (*UK*)

Caroline Davidson Literary Agency (*UK*)
The Jennifer DeChiara Literary Agency (*US*)
DeFiore and Company (*US*)
Joëlle Delbourgo Associates, Inc. (*US*)
Diamond Kahn and Woods (DKW) Literary Agency Ltd (*UK*)
Janis A. Donnaud & Associates, Inc. (*US*)
Jim Donovan Literary (*US*)
Doyen Literary Services, Inc. (*US*)
Dunham Literary, Inc. (*US*)
Dystel & Goderich Literary Management (*US*)
Edwards Fuglewicz (*UK*)
Elise Dillsworth Agency (EDA) (*UK*)
Ethan Ellenberg Literary Agency (*US*)
Ann Elmo Agency, Inc. (*US*)
Evatopia, Inc. (*US*)
Fairbank Literary Representation (*US*)
Farris Literary Agency, Inc. (*US*)
The Feldstein Agency (*UK*)
The Fielding Agency, LLC (*US*)
Diana Finch Literary Agency (*US*)
Fine Literary (*US*)
FinePrint Literary Management (*US*)
Fletcher & Company (*US*)
Foundry Literary + Media (*US*)
Fox Mason Ltd (*UK*)
Fox & Howard Literary Agency (*UK*)
Jeanne Fredericks Literary Agency, Inc. (*US*)
Furniss Lawton (*UK*)
The G Agency, LLC (*US*)
The Gernert Company (*US*)
Goodman Associates (*US*)
Sanford J. Greenburger Associates, Inc (*US*)
Greene & Heaton Ltd (*UK*)
Marianne Gunn O'Connor Literary Agency (*Ire*)
The Mitchell J. Hamilburg Agency (*US*)
Joy Harris Literary Agency, Inc. (*US*)
Antony Harwood Limited (*UK*)
John Hawkins & Associates, Inc. (*US*)
A M Heath & Company Limited, Author's Agents (*UK*)
Rupert Heath Literary Agency (*UK*)
hhb agency ltd (*UK*)
David Higham Associates Ltd (*UK*)
Hill Nadell Literary Agency (*US*)
Hornfischer Literary Management, L.P. (*US*)
J de S Associates Inc (*US*)
Johnson & Alcock (*UK*)
Frances Kelly (*UK*)
Kilburn Literary Agency (*UK*)
Harvey Klinger, Inc (*US*)
Kneerim & Williams (*US*)
Linda Konner Literary Agency (*US*)
Elaine Koster Literary Agency LLC (*US*)
Barbara S. Kouts, Literary Agent (*US*)
The LA Literary Agency (*US*)
Laura Langlie, Literary Agent (*US*)
Larsen Pomada Literary Agents (*US*)
Levine Greenberg Literary Agency, Inc. (*US*)
Literary & Creative Artists Inc. (*US*)
The Literary Group (*US*)
Sterling Lord Literistic, Inc. (*US*)
Julia Lord Literary Management (*US*)
Andrew Lownie Literary Agency Ltd (*UK*)
The Jennifer Lyons Literary Agency, LLC (*US*)
Gina Maccoby Agency (*US*)
Ricia Mainhardt Agency (RMA) (*US*)
Carol Mann Agency (*US*)
Manus & Associates Literary Agency, Inc. (*US*)
March Tenth, Inc. (*US*)
Denise Marcil Literary Agency, Inc. (*US*)
Marjacq Scripts Ltd (*UK*)
Martin Literary Management (*US*)
MBA Literary Agents Ltd (*UK*)
Duncan McAra (*UK*)
Anne McDermid & Associates Ltd (*Can*)
McKernan Agency (*UK*)
Mendel Media Group, LLC (*US*)
Martha Millard Literary Agency (*US*)
The Miller Agency (*US*)
Mulcahy Associates (*UK*)
MNLA (Maggie Noach Literary Agency) (*UK*)
Northern Lights Literary Services (*US*)
Objective Entertainment (*US*)
Fifi Oscard Agency, Inc. (*US*)
The Richard Parks Agency (*US*)
Kathi J. Paton Literary Agency (*US*)
John Pawsey (*UK*)
Maggie Pearlstine Associates Ltd (*UK*)
Jonathan Pegg Literary Agency (*UK*)
Pendle Hill Literary Agency (*UK*)
L. Perkins Associates (*US*)
James Peter Associates, Inc. (*US*)
Pinder Lane & Garon-Brooke Associates Ltd (*US*)
The Poynor Group (*US*)
Rebecca Pratt Literary Group (*US*)
Aaron M. Priest Literary Agency (*US*)
The Lisa Richards Agency (*Ire*)
Richford Becklow Literary Agency (*UK*)
Ann Rittenberg Literary Agency (*US*)
RLR Associates (*US*)
B.J. Robbins Literary Agency (*US*)
Robert Dudley Agency (*UK*)
Linda Roghaar Literary Agency, Inc. (*US*)
Rita Rosenkranz Literary Agency (*US*)
Ross Yoon Agency (*US*)
The Rudy Agency (*US*)
Victoria Sanders & Associates LLC (*US*)
Schiavone Literary Agency (*US*)
Susan Schulman, A Literary Agency (*US*)
The Science Factory (*UK*)
Scovil Galen Ghosh Literary Agency, Inc. (*US*)
The Seven Bridges Group (*US*)
Denise Shannon Literary Agency, Inc. (*US*)
Sheil Land Associates Ltd (*UK*)
Wendy Sherman Associates, Inc. (*US*)
Rosalie Siegel, International Literary Agency, Inc. (*US*)
Signature Literary Agency (*US*)
Dorie Simmonds Agency (*UK*)
Jeffrey Simmons (*UK*)
Sinclair-Stevenson (*UK*)
Robert Smith Literary Agency Ltd (*UK*)
The Spieler Agency (*US*)
Philip G. Spitzer Literary Agency, Inc. (*US*)

Robin Straus Agency, Inc. (*US*)
Stuart Krichevsky Literary Agency, Inc. (*US*)
Sarah Such Literary Agency (*UK*)
SYLA – Susan Yearwood Literary Agency (*UK*)
Patricia Teal Literary Agency (*US*)
Tessler Literary Agency (*US*)
Transatlantic Literary Agency, Inc. (*Can*)
TriadaUS Literary Agency, Inc. (*US*)
Trident Media Group, LLC (*US*)
Jane Turnbull (*UK*)
United Agents (*UK*)
Venture Literary (*US*)
Ed Victor Ltd (*UK*)
Watkins / Loomis Agency, Inc. (*US*)
Waxman Leavell Literary Agency (*US*)
The Weingel-Fidel Agency (*US*)
Westwood Creative Artists (*Can*)
Dinah Wiener Ltd (*UK*)
William Morris Endeavor (WME) London (*UK*)
Writers House UK (*UK*)
Writers House, LLC. (*US*)
Writers' Representatives, LLC (*US*)
Yates & Yates (*US*)
The Zack Company, Inc (*US*)

Business

Abbot Management (*US*)
The Agency Group, Ltd (*US*)
Alive Communications, Inc (*US*)
AP Watt at United Agents LLP (*UK*)
Audrey A. Wolf Literary Agency (*US*)
The August Agency LLC (*US*)
Baldi Agency (*US*)
David Black Literary Agency (*US*)
Bleecker Street Associates, Inc. (*US*)
BookEnds, LLC (*US*)
Rick Broadhead & Associates Literary Agency (*Can*)
Marie Brown Associates, Inc. (*US*)
Browne & Miller Literary Associates (*US*)
Sheree Bykofsky Associates, Inc. (*US*)
Carnicelli Literary Management (*US*)
Maria Carvainis Agency, Inc. (*US*)
Castiglia Literary Agency (*US*)
Elyse Cheney Literary Associates, LLC (*US*)
The Doe Coover Agency (*US*)
Creative Authors Ltd (*UK*)
Richard Curtis Associates, Inc. (*US*)
The Darley Anderson Agency (*UK*)
Liza Dawson Associates (*US*)
Joëlle Delbourgo Associates, Inc. (*US*)
Diane Banks Associates Literary Agency (*UK*)
Sandra Dijkstra Literary Agency (*US*)
Janis A. Donnaud & Associates, Inc. (*US*)
Jim Donovan Literary (*US*)
Doyen Literary Services, Inc. (*US*)
Dystel & Goderich Literary Management (*US*)
Farris Literary Agency, Inc. (*US*)
The Feldstein Agency (*UK*)
The Fielding Agency, LLC (*US*)
Diana Finch Literary Agency (*US*)
Fine Literary (*US*)
FinePrint Literary Management (*US*)
Fletcher & Company (*US*)
Folio Literary Management, LLC (*US*)
Foundry Literary + Media (*US*)
Fox & Howard Literary Agency (*UK*)
Jeanne Fredericks Literary Agency, Inc. (*US*)
Grace Freedson's Publishing Network (*US*)
Sarah Jane Freymann Literary Agency (*US*)
Furniss Lawton (*UK*)
The G Agency, LLC (*US*)
Don Gastwirth & Associates (*US*)
Goodman Associates (*US*)
Graham Maw Christie Literary Agency (*UK*)
Sanford J. Greenburger Associates, Inc (*US*)
The Mitchell J. Hamilburg Agency (*US*)
Hannigan Salky Getzler (HSG) Agency (*US*)
Antony Harwood Limited (*UK*)
John Hawkins & Associates, Inc. (*US*)
Heacock Hill Literary Agency, LLC (*US*)
The Jeff Herman Agency, LLC (*US*)
hhb agency ltd (*UK*)
Kate Hordern Literary Agency (*UK*)
Hornfischer Literary Management, L.P. (*US*)
Andrea Hurst Literary Management (*US*)
InkWell Management (*US*)
J de S Associates Inc (*US*)
Frances Kelly (*UK*)
Kilburn Literary Agency (*UK*)
Kneerim & Williams (*US*)
The Knight Agency (*US*)
Linda Konner Literary Agency (*US*)
Elaine Koster Literary Agency LLC (*US*)
The LA Literary Agency (*US*)
Larsen Pomada Literary Agents (*US*)
Levine Greenberg Literary Agency, Inc. (*US*)
Literary & Creative Artists Inc. (*US*)
Sterling Lord Literistic, Inc. (*US*)
Lowenstein Associates, Inc. (*US*)
Carol Mann Agency (*US*)
Manus & Associates Literary Agency, Inc. (*US*)
Denise Marcil Literary Agency, Inc. (*US*)
The Martell Agency (*US*)
Martin Literary Management (*US*)
Margret McBride Literary Agency (*US*)
Martha Millard Literary Agency (*US*)
Northern Lights Literary Services (*US*)
Objective Entertainment (*US*)
Fifi Oscard Agency, Inc. (*US*)
P.S. Literary Agency (*Can*)
The Richard Parks Agency (*US*)
Kathi J. Paton Literary Agency (*US*)
James Peter Associates, Inc. (*US*)
Pinder Lane & Garon-Brooke Associates Ltd (*US*)
The Poynor Group (*US*)
Regina Ryan Publishing Enterprises (*US*)
RLR Associates (*US*)
Robert Dudley Agency (*UK*)
Rita Rosenkranz Literary Agency (*US*)
Ross Yoon Agency (*US*)
The Rudy Agency (*US*)
Schiavone Literary Agency (*US*)
Susan Schulman, A Literary Agency (*US*)
Denise Shannon Literary Agency, Inc. (*US*)
Solow Literary Enterprises, Inc. (*US*)

The Spieler Agency (*US*)
Stuart Krichevsky Literary Agency, Inc. (*US*)
The Stuart Agency (*US*)
SYLA – Susan Yearwood Literary Agency (*UK*)
Talcott Notch Literary (*US*)
Tessler Literary Agency (*US*)
Trident Media Group, LLC (*US*)
2M Literary Agency Ltd (*US*)
Venture Literary (*US*)
Veritas Literary Agency (*US*)
Waterside Productions, Inc (*US*)
Watson, Little Ltd (*UK*)
Waxman Leavell Literary Agency (*US*)
Whimsy Literary Agency, LLC (*US*)
Writers House UK (*UK*)
Writers House, LLC. (*US*)
Writers' Representatives, LLC (*US*)
Yates & Yates (*US*)
The Zack Company, Inc (*US*)

Cookery

Abbot Management (*US*)
The Agency Group, Ltd (*US*)
Betsy Amster Literary Enterprises (*US*)
AP Watt at United Agents LLP (*UK*)
Baldi Agency (*US*)
The Bent Agency (*US*)
Bidnick & Company (*US*)
Vicky Bijur Literary Agency (*US*)
David Black Literary Agency (*US*)
Bleecker Street Associates, Inc. (*US*)
The Book Group (*US*)
Browne & Miller Literary Associates (*US*)
Sheree Bykofsky Associates, Inc. (*US*)
Castiglia Literary Agency (*US*)
Teresa Chris Literary Agency Ltd (*UK*)
Rosica Colin Ltd (*UK*)
Don Congdon Associates, Inc. (*US*)
Connor Literary Agency (*US*)
The Doe Coover Agency (*US*)
CowlesRyan Agency (*US*)
Creative Authors Ltd (*UK*)
Laura Dail Literary Agency (*US*)
The Darley Anderson Agency (*UK*)
Caroline Davidson Literary Agency (*UK*)
The Jennifer DeChiara Literary Agency (*US*)
Sandra Dijkstra Literary Agency (*US*)
Janis A. Donnaud & Associates, Inc. (*US*)
Doyen Literary Services, Inc. (*US*)
Dystel & Goderich Literary Management (*US*)
Ethan Ellenberg Literary Agency (*US*)
Fairbank Literary Representation (*US*)
The Feldstein Agency (*UK*)
The Fielding Agency, LLC (*US*)
Fine Literary (*US*)
FinePrint Literary Management (*US*)
Folio Literary Management, LLC (*US*)
Fox Mason Ltd (*UK*)
Jeanne Fredericks Literary Agency, Inc. (*US*)
Grace Freedson's Publishing Network (*US*)
Sarah Jane Freymann Literary Agency (*US*)
Furniss Lawton (*UK*)
Goodman Associates (*US*)
Graham Maw Christie Literary Agency (*UK*)
Greene & Heaton Ltd (*UK*)
The Mitchell J. Hamilburg Agency (*US*)
Hannigan Salky Getzler (HSG) Agency (*US*)
Antony Harwood Limited (*UK*)
A M Heath & Company Limited, Author's Agents (*UK*)
Rupert Heath Literary Agency (*UK*)
hhb agency ltd (*UK*)
David Higham Associates Ltd (*UK*)
Hill Nadell Literary Agency (*US*)
Andrea Hurst Literary Management (*US*)
Frances Kelly (*UK*)
Harvey Klinger, Inc (*US*)
Linda Konner Literary Agency (*US*)
Elaine Koster Literary Agency LLC (*US*)
The LA Literary Agency (*US*)
Larsen Pomada Literary Agents (*US*)
Levine Greenberg Literary Agency, Inc. (*US*)
The Lisa Ekus Group, LLC (*US*)
Literary & Creative Artists Inc. (*US*)
The Literary Group (*US*)
Martha Millard Literary Agency (*US*)
The Miller Agency (*US*)
Objective Entertainment (*US*)
Fifi Oscard Agency, Inc. (*US*)
The Richard Parks Agency (*US*)
L. Perkins Associates (*US*)
James Peter Associates, Inc. (*US*)
Pinder Lane & Garon-Brooke Associates Ltd (*US*)
The Poynor Group (*US*)
Regina Ryan Publishing Enterprises (*US*)
Richford Becklow Literary Agency (*UK*)
RLR Associates (*US*)
Rita Rosenkranz Literary Agency (*US*)
Schiavone Literary Agency (*US*)
Susan Schulman, A Literary Agency (*US*)
Scovil Galen Ghosh Literary Agency, Inc. (*US*)
Sheil Land Associates Ltd (*UK*)
Shelley Instone Literary Agency (*UK*)
Wendy Sherman Associates, Inc. (*US*)
Valerie Smith, Literary Agent (*US*)
The Spieler Agency (*US*)
Robin Straus Agency, Inc. (*US*)
Talcott Notch Literary (*US*)
Tessler Literary Agency (*US*)
TriadaUS Literary Agency, Inc. (*US*)
2M Literary Agency Ltd (*US*)
Venture Literary (*US*)
Ed Victor Ltd (*UK*)
Waterside Productions, Inc (*US*)
Whimsy Literary Agency, LLC (*US*)
Dinah Wiener Ltd (*UK*)
Writers House UK (*UK*)
Writers House, LLC. (*US*)
Writers' Representatives, LLC (*US*)
The Zack Company, Inc (*US*)

Crafts

Abbot Management (*US*)
David Black Literary Agency (*US*)
Browne & Miller Literary Associates (*US*)
Teresa Chris Literary Agency Ltd (*UK*)
Connor Literary Agency (*US*)

Creative Authors Ltd (*UK*)
The Darley Anderson Agency (*UK*)
Doyen Literary Services, Inc. (*US*)
The Fielding Agency, LLC (*US*)
Fine Literary (*US*)
Jeanne Fredericks Literary Agency, Inc. (*US*)
Grace Freedson's Publishing Network (*US*)
The Gernert Company (*US*)
Graham Maw Christie Literary Agency (*UK*)
Antony Harwood Limited (*UK*)
Heacock Hill Literary Agency, LLC (*US*)
Levine Greenberg Literary Agency, Inc. (*US*)
Julia Lord Literary Management (*US*)
MBA Literary Agents Ltd (*UK*)
The Richard Parks Agency (*US*)
Rita Rosenkranz Literary Agency (*US*)
Susan Schulman, A Literary Agency (*US*)
Talcott Notch Literary (*US*)
Venture Literary (*US*)

Crime

Abbot Management (*US*)
Abela Literature (*Can*)
The Agency Group, Ltd (*US*)
The Ahearn Agency, Inc (*US*)
Alive Communications, Inc (*US*)
The Ampersand Agency Ltd (*UK*)
Marcia Amsterdam Agency (*US*)
AP Watt at United Agents LLP (*UK*)
Artellus Limited (*UK*)
Author Rights Agency (*Ire*)
The Axelrod Agency (*US*)
Belcastro Agency (*US*)
The Bent Agency (*US*)
Bleecker Street Associates, Inc. (*US*)
Luigi Bonomi Associates Ltd (*UK*)
Jenny Brown Associates (*UK*)
Browne & Miller Literary Associates (*US*)
Juliet Burton Literary Agency (*UK*)
Castiglia Literary Agency (*US*)
Teresa Chris Literary Agency Ltd (*UK*)
Rosica Colin Ltd (*UK*)
Don Congdon Associates, Inc. (*US*)
Connor Literary Agency (*US*)
Conville & Walsh Ltd (*UK*)
The Cooke Agency (*Can*)
Coombs Moylett Literary Agency (*UK*)
Crawford Literary Agency (*US*)
Creative Authors Ltd (*UK*)
Crichton & Associates, Inc. (*US*)
Curtis Brown Group Ltd (*UK*)
Laura Dail Literary Agency (*US*)
The Darley Anderson Agency (*UK*)
Diamond Kahn and Woods (DKW) Literary Agency Ltd (*UK*)
Diane Banks Associates Literary Agency (*UK*)
Jim Donovan Literary (*US*)
Dorian Literary Agency (DLA) (*UK*)
Doyen Literary Services, Inc. (*US*)
Dystel & Goderich Literary Management (*US*)
Edwards Fuglewicz (*UK*)
Ethan Ellenberg Literary Agency (*US*)
Evatopia, Inc. (*US*)
Farris Literary Agency, Inc. (*US*)
The Feldstein Agency (*UK*)
The Fielding Agency, LLC (*US*)
Diana Finch Literary Agency (*US*)
Fine Literary (*US*)
FinePrint Literary Management (*US*)
Folio Literary Management, LLC (*US*)
Fox Mason Ltd (*UK*)
Samuel French, Inc. (*US*)
Sarah Jane Freymann Literary Agency (*US*)
Furniss Lawton (*UK*)
Don Gastwirth & Associates (*US*)
Goodman Associates (*US*)
Greene & Heaton Ltd (*UK*)
Gregory & Company, Authors' Agents (*UK*)
Jill Grosjean Literary Agency (*US*)
The Mitchell J. Hamilburg Agency (*US*)
Hardman & Swainson (*UK*)
Antony Harwood Limited (*UK*)
John Hawkins & Associates, Inc. (*US*)
A M Heath & Company Limited, Author's Agents (*UK*)
Rupert Heath Literary Agency (*UK*)
The Jeff Herman Agency, LLC (*US*)
hhb agency ltd (*UK*)
David Higham Associates Ltd (*UK*)
Kate Hordern Literary Agency (*UK*)
Hornfischer Literary Management, L.P. (*US*)
Hudson Agency (*US*)
Andrea Hurst Literary Management (*US*)
InkWell Management (*US*)
J de S Associates Inc (*US*)
Johnson & Alcock (*UK*)
Harvey Klinger, Inc (*US*)
Kneerim & Williams (*US*)
Barbara S. Kouts, Literary Agent (*US*)
Laura Langlie, Literary Agent (*US*)
Larsen Pomada Literary Agents (*US*)
Levine Greenberg Literary Agency, Inc. (*US*)
Literary & Creative Artists Inc. (*US*)
The Literary Group (*US*)
Julia Lord Literary Management (*US*)
Lowenstein Associates, Inc. (*US*)
Andrew Lownie Literary Agency Ltd (*UK*)
Donald Maass Literary Agency (*US*)
Madeleine Milburn Literary Agency (*UK*)
Ricia Mainhardt Agency (RMA) (*US*)
Marjacq Scripts Ltd (*UK*)
Martin Literary Management (*US*)
McKernan Agency (*UK*)
Martha Millard Literary Agency (*US*)
Mulcahy Associates (*UK*)
Judith Murdoch Literary Agency (*UK*)
Pendle Hill Literary Agency (*UK*)
Pinder Lane & Garon-Brooke Associates Ltd (*US*)
Aaron M. Priest Literary Agency (*US*)
Prospect Agency (*US*)
Redhammer (*UK*)
Richford Becklow Literary Agency (*UK*)
RLR Associates (*US*)
B.J. Robbins Literary Agency (*US*)
Rocking Chair Books (*UK*)
Victoria Sanders & Associates LLC (*US*)

Schiavone Literary Agency (*US*)
Susan Schulman, A Literary Agency (*US*)
The Seven Bridges Group (*US*)
Sheil Land Associates Ltd (*UK*)
Shelley Instone Literary Agency (*UK*)
Signature Literary Agency (*US*)
Jeffrey Simmons (*UK*)
Robert Smith Literary Agency Ltd (*UK*)
The Spieler Agency (*US*)
SYLA – Susan Yearwood Literary Agency (*UK*)
Talcott Notch Literary (*US*)
Patricia Teal Literary Agency (*US*)
Tom Lee (*US*)
Transatlantic Literary Agency, Inc. (*Can*)
TriadaUS Literary Agency, Inc. (*US*)
Trident Media Group, LLC (*US*)
2M Literary Agency Ltd (*US*)
Venture Literary (*US*)
Veritas Literary Agency (*US*)
Watson, Little Ltd (*UK*)
William Morris Endeavor (WME) London (*UK*)
The Zack Company, Inc (*US*)
Zeno Agency Ltd (*UK*)

Criticism

Abbot Management (*US*)
Barbara Braun Associates, Inc. (*US*)
Connor Literary Agency (*US*)
The Darley Anderson Agency (*UK*)
The Feldstein Agency (*UK*)
Goodman Associates (*US*)
Antony Harwood Limited (*UK*)
Signature Literary Agency (*US*)
Venture Literary (*US*)
Writers' Representatives, LLC (*US*)

Culture

Abbot Management (*US*)
Adler & Robin Books, Inc (*US*)
The Agency Group, Ltd (*US*)
Miriam Altshuler Literary Agency (*US*)
Ambassador Speakers Bureau & Literary Agency (*US*)
Betsy Amster Literary Enterprises (*US*)
Artellus Limited (*UK*)
Movable Type Management (*US*)
The August Agency LLC (*US*)
Ayesha Pande Literary (*US*)
Baldi Agency (*US*)
The Bent Agency (*US*)
Bleecker Street Associates, Inc. (*US*)
BookEnds, LLC (*US*)
Brandt & Hochman Literary Agents, Inc. (*US*)
Barbara Braun Associates, Inc. (*US*)
Rick Broadhead & Associates Literary Agency (*Can*)
Jenny Brown Associates (*UK*)
Marie Brown Associates, Inc. (*US*)
Browne & Miller Literary Associates (*US*)
Sheree Bykofsky Associates, Inc. (*US*)
Carnicelli Literary Management (*US*)
Maria Carvainis Agency, Inc. (*US*)
Castiglia Literary Agency (*US*)
Chalberg & Sussman (*US*)
Jane Chelius Literary Agency, Inc. (*US*)
Elyse Cheney Literary Associates, LLC (*US*)
Cine/Lit Representation (*US*)
Frances Collin Literary Agent (*US*)
Don Congdon Associates, Inc. (*US*)
Connor Literary Agency (*US*)
The Cooke Agency (*Can*)
CowlesRyan Agency (*US*)
The Creative Rights Agency (*UK*)
Creative Authors Ltd (*UK*)
Crichton & Associates, Inc. (*US*)
The Darley Anderson Agency (*UK*)
David Luxton Associates (*UK*)
Caroline Davidson Literary Agency (*UK*)
Liza Dawson Associates (*US*)
The Jennifer DeChiara Literary Agency (*US*)
DeFiore and Company (*US*)
Joëlle Delbourgo Associates, Inc. (*US*)
Diamond Kahn and Woods (DKW) Literary Agency Ltd (*UK*)
Diane Banks Associates Literary Agency (*UK*)
Sandra Dijkstra Literary Agency (*US*)
Jim Donovan Literary (*US*)
Doyen Literary Services, Inc. (*US*)
Dunham Literary, Inc. (*US*)
Dystel & Goderich Literary Management (*US*)
Edwards Fuglewicz (*UK*)
Ethan Ellenberg Literary Agency (*US*)
Ann Elmo Agency, Inc. (*US*)
Fairbank Literary Representation (*US*)
Farris Literary Agency, Inc. (*US*)
The Fielding Agency, LLC (*US*)
Diana Finch Literary Agency (*US*)
Fine Literary (*US*)
FinePrint Literary Management (*US*)
Folio Literary Management, LLC (*US*)
Foundry Literary + Media (*US*)
Fox Mason Ltd (*UK*)
Fox & Howard Literary Agency (*UK*)
Grace Freedson's Publishing Network (*US*)
Sarah Jane Freymann Literary Agency (*US*)
The G Agency, LLC (*US*)
Don Gastwirth & Associates (*US*)
Gelfman Schneider Literary Agents, Inc. (*US*)
Frances Goldin Literary Agency, Inc. (*US*)
Goodman Associates (*US*)
Greene & Heaton Ltd (*UK*)
Joy Harris Literary Agency, Inc. (*US*)
Antony Harwood Limited (*UK*)
Heacock Hill Literary Agency, LLC (*US*)
Rupert Heath Literary Agency (*UK*)
The Jeff Herman Agency, LLC (*US*)
hhb agency ltd (*UK*)
Hill Nadell Literary Agency (*US*)
Kate Hordern Literary Agency (*UK*)
Hornfischer Literary Management, L.P. (*US*)
J de S Associates Inc (*US*)
Johnson & Alcock (*UK*)
Harvey Klinger, Inc (*US*)
Kneerim & Williams (*US*)
The Knight Agency (*US*)
Linda Konner Literary Agency (*US*)
Elaine Koster Literary Agency LLC (*US*)
Laura Langlie, Literary Agent (*US*)

Larsen Pomada Literary Agents (*US*)
Levine Greenberg Literary Agency, Inc. (*US*)
Sterling Lord Literistic, Inc. (*US*)
Andrew Lownie Literary Agency Ltd (*UK*)
Gina Maccoby Agency (*US*)
Ricia Mainhardt Agency (RMA) (*US*)
Carol Mann Agency (*US*)
Manus & Associates Literary Agency, Inc. (*US*)
March Tenth, Inc. (*US*)
McIntosh & Otis, Inc (*US*)
Mendel Media Group, LLC (*US*)
Martha Millard Literary Agency (*US*)
The Miller Agency (*US*)
Objective Entertainment (*US*)
The Richard Parks Agency (*US*)
Kathi J. Paton Literary Agency (*US*)
Jonathan Pegg Literary Agency (*UK*)
L. Perkins Associates (*US*)
James Peter Associates, Inc. (*US*)
Pinder Lane & Garon-Brooke Associates Ltd (*US*)
The Poynor Group (*US*)
Aaron M. Priest Literary Agency (*US*)
The Lisa Richards Agency (*Ire*)
Ann Rittenberg Literary Agency (*US*)
RLR Associates (*US*)
B.J. Robbins Literary Agency (*US*)
Rocking Chair Books (*UK*)
Linda Roghaar Literary Agency, Inc. (*US*)
Rita Rosenkranz Literary Agency (*US*)
Ross Yoon Agency (*US*)
Andy Ross Agency (*US*)
The Rudy Agency (*US*)
Victoria Sanders & Associates LLC (*US*)
Schiavone Literary Agency (*US*)
Susan Schulman, A Literary Agency (*US*)
Scovil Galen Ghosh Literary Agency, Inc. (*US*)
The Seven Bridges Group (*US*)
Wendy Sherman Associates, Inc. (*US*)
Signature Literary Agency (*US*)
Robert Smith Literary Agency Ltd (*UK*)
Solow Literary Enterprises, Inc. (*US*)
The Spieler Agency (*US*)
Nancy Stauffer Associates (*US*)
Robin Straus Agency, Inc. (*US*)
Stuart Krichevsky Literary Agency, Inc. (*US*)
Sarah Such Literary Agency (*UK*)
TriadaUS Literary Agency, Inc. (*US*)
Trident Media Group, LLC (*US*)
2M Literary Agency Ltd (*US*)
Venture Literary (*US*)
Veritas Literary Agency (*US*)
Wales Literary Agency, Inc (*US*)
Watkins / Loomis Agency, Inc. (*US*)
Waxman Leavell Literary Agency (*US*)
The Wendy Weil Agency, Inc. (*US*)
Whimsy Literary Agency, LLC (*US*)
William Morris Endeavor (WME) London (*UK*)
Wolfson Literary Agency (*US*)

Current Affairs

Abbot Management (*US*)
The Ahearn Agency, Inc (*US*)
Ambassador Speakers Bureau & Literary Agency (*US*)
The Ampersand Agency Ltd (*UK*)
Arcadia (*US*)
Artellus Limited (*UK*)
Audrey A. Wolf Literary Agency (*US*)
The August Agency LLC (*US*)
David Black Literary Agency (*US*)
Bleecker Street Associates, Inc. (*US*)
BookEnds, LLC (*US*)
Brandt & Hochman Literary Agents, Inc. (*US*)
Rick Broadhead & Associates Literary Agency (*Can*)
Tracy Brown Literary Agency (*US*)
Browne & Miller Literary Associates (*US*)
Felicity Bryan (*UK*)
Sheree Bykofsky Associates, Inc. (*US*)
Carnicelli Literary Management (*US*)
Castiglia Literary Agency (*US*)
Elyse Cheney Literary Associates, LLC (*US*)
Rosica Colin Ltd (*UK*)
Don Congdon Associates, Inc. (*US*)
Connor Literary Agency (*US*)
Conville & Walsh Ltd (*UK*)
CowlesRyan Agency (*US*)
The Darley Anderson Agency (*UK*)
Liza Dawson Associates (*US*)
DeFiore and Company (*US*)
Joëlle Delbourgo Associates, Inc. (*US*)
Diane Banks Associates Literary Agency (*UK*)
Sandra Dijkstra Literary Agency (*US*)
Jim Donovan Literary (*US*)
Doyen Literary Services, Inc. (*US*)
Dunham Literary, Inc. (*US*)
Dystel & Goderich Literary Management (*US*)
Ethan Ellenberg Literary Agency (*US*)
Ann Elmo Agency, Inc. (*US*)
Farris Literary Agency, Inc. (*US*)
The Feldstein Agency (*UK*)
The Fielding Agency, LLC (*US*)
Diana Finch Literary Agency (*US*)
Fine Literary (*US*)
Fletcher & Company (*US*)
Foundry Literary + Media (*US*)
Grace Freedson's Publishing Network (*US*)
Don Gastwirth & Associates (*US*)
Gelfman Schneider Literary Agents, Inc. (*US*)
The Gernert Company (*US*)
Frances Goldin Literary Agency, Inc. (*US*)
Goodman Associates (*US*)
Greene & Heaton Ltd (*UK*)
The Mitchell J. Hamilburg Agency (*US*)
Hannigan Salky Getzler (HSG) Agency (*US*)
Antony Harwood Limited (*UK*)
John Hawkins & Associates, Inc. (*US*)
Rupert Heath Literary Agency (*UK*)
David Higham Associates Ltd (*UK*)
Hill Nadell Literary Agency (*US*)
Kate Hordern Literary Agency (*UK*)
Hornfischer Literary Management, L.P. (*US*)
Andrea Hurst Literary Management (*US*)
InkWell Management (*US*)
J de S Associates Inc (*US*)

Design

Drama

Entertainment

Gunn Media Associates (*UK*)
Antony Harwood Limited (*UK*)
hhb agency ltd (*UK*)
The Knight Agency (*US*)
Linda Konner Literary Agency (*US*)
Julia Lord Literary Management (*US*)
Gina Maccoby Agency (*US*)
Martin Literary Management (*US*)
Mendel Media Group, LLC (*US*)
Pinder Lane & Garon-Brooke Associates Ltd (*US*)
Susan Rabiner, Literary Agent, Inc. (*US*)
Redhammer (*UK*)
Rocking Chair Books (*UK*)
Susan Schulman, A Literary Agency (*US*)
The Seven Bridges Group (*US*)
Wendy Sherman Associates, Inc. (*US*)
Jeffrey Simmons (*UK*)
Jane Turnbull (*UK*)
Venture Literary (*US*)
Waxman Leavell Literary Agency (*US*)
Whimsy Literary Agency, LLC (*US*)
Whispering Buffalo Literary Agency Ltd (*UK*)
The Zack Company, Inc (*US*)

Erotic

Abbot Management (*US*)
The Axelrod Agency (*US*)
Belcastro Agency (*US*)
Bleecker Street Associates, Inc. (*US*)
BookEnds, LLC (*US*)
The Characters Talent Agency (*Can*)
Rosica Colin Ltd (*UK*)
The Darley Anderson Agency (*UK*)
Goodman Associates (*US*)
Antony Harwood Limited (*UK*)
Ricia Mainhardt Agency (RMA) (*US*)
Pendle Hill Literary Agency (*UK*)
L. Perkins Associates (*US*)
Pinder Lane & Garon-Brooke Associates Ltd (*US*)
Prospect Agency (*US*)
Shelley Instone Literary Agency (*UK*)
Spencerhill Associates (*US*)
Tom Lee (*US*)
Venture Literary (*US*)
Veritas Literary Agency (*US*)
The Zack Company, Inc (*US*)

Fantasy

Abbot Management (*US*)
Abela Literature (*Can*)
Miriam Altshuler Literary Agency (*US*)
The Ampersand Agency Ltd (*UK*)
Betsy Amster Literary Enterprises (*US*)
Anubis Literary Agency (*UK*)
Artellus Limited (*UK*)
Author Rights Agency (*Ire*)
Belcastro Agency (*US*)
The Bent Agency (*US*)
BookEnds, LLC (*US*)
The Characters Talent Agency (*Can*)
Rosica Colin Ltd (*UK*)
Frances Collin Literary Agent (*US*)
The Cooke Agency (*Can*)
Curtis Brown Group Ltd (*UK*)
Richard Curtis Associates, Inc. (*US*)
Laura Dail Literary Agency (*US*)
The Darley Anderson Agency (*UK*)
Liza Dawson Associates (*US*)
The Jennifer DeChiara Literary Agency (*US*)
Joëlle Delbourgo Associates, Inc. (*US*)
Diamond Kahn and Woods (DKW) Literary Agency Ltd (*UK*)
Sandra Dijkstra Literary Agency (*US*)
Dorian Literary Agency (DLA) (*UK*)
Dunham Literary, Inc. (*US*)
Dystel & Goderich Literary Management (*US*)
Ethan Ellenberg Literary Agency (*US*)
Evatopia, Inc. (*US*)
The Fielding Agency, LLC (*US*)
FinePrint Literary Management (*US*)
Folio Literary Management, LLC (*US*)
Fox Mason Ltd (*UK*)
Samuel French, Inc. (*US*)
Furniss Lawton (*UK*)
The Gernert Company (*US*)
Sanford J. Greenburger Associates, Inc (*US*)
The Mitchell J. Hamilburg Agency (*US*)
Antony Harwood Limited (*UK*)
John Hawkins & Associates, Inc. (*US*)
Hudson Agency (*US*)
Andrea Hurst Literary Management (*US*)
Jabberwocky Literary Agency (*US*)
Harvey Klinger, Inc (*US*)
The Knight Agency (*US*)
Larsen Pomada Literary Agents (*US*)
The Literary Group (*US*)
London Independent Books (*UK*)
Lowenstein Associates, Inc. (*US*)
Andrew Lownie Literary Agency Ltd (*UK*)
Donald Maass Literary Agency (*US*)
Ricia Mainhardt Agency (RMA) (*US*)
Anne McDermid & Associates Ltd (*Can*)
McIntosh & Otis, Inc (*US*)
Martha Millard Literary Agency (*US*)
Nelson Literary Agency, LLC (*US*)
Objective Entertainment (*US*)
Pendle Hill Literary Agency (*UK*)
L. Perkins Associates (*US*)
Pinder Lane & Garon-Brooke Associates Ltd (*US*)
Rebecca Pratt Literary Group (*US*)
Linn Prentis Literary (*US*)
Aaron M. Priest Literary Agency (*US*)
Prospect Agency (*US*)
Rebecca Friedman Literary Agency (*US*)
Richford Becklow Literary Agency (*UK*)
Victoria Sanders & Associates LLC (*US*)
Schiavone Literary Agency (*US*)
The Seymour Agency (*US*)
Sheil Land Associates Ltd (*UK*)
Shelley Instone Literary Agency (*UK*)
Valerie Smith, Literary Agent (*US*)
Spectrum Literary Agency (*US*)
Spencerhill Associates (*US*)
Steph Roundsmith Agent and Editor (*UK*)
Sternig & Byrne Literary Agency (*US*)

Eames Literary Services, LLC (*US*)
Eddison Pearson Ltd (*UK*)
Anne Edelstein Literary Agency (*US*)
Edwards Fuglewicz (*UK*)
Elise Dillsworth Agency (EDA) (*UK*)
Elizabeth Roy Literary Agency (*UK*)
Ethan Ellenberg Literary Agency (*US*)
Nicholas Ellison, Inc. (*US*)
Ann Elmo Agency, Inc. (*US*)
Faith Evans Associates (*UK*)
Evatopia, Inc. (*US*)
Fairbank Literary Representation (*US*)
Farris Literary Agency, Inc. (*US*)
The Feldstein Agency (*UK*)
The Fielding Agency, LLC (*US*)
Film Rights Ltd in association with Laurence Fitch Ltd (*UK*)
Diana Finch Literary Agency (*US*)
Fine Literary (*US*)
FinePrint Literary Management (*US*)
Flannery Literary (*US*)
Fletcher & Company (*US*)
Folio Literary Management, LLC (*US*)
Foundry Literary + Media (*US*)
Fox Chase Agency, Inc. (*US*)
Fox Mason Ltd (*UK*)
Fraser Ross Associates (*UK*)
Sarah Jane Freymann Literary Agency (*US*)
Full Throttle Literary Agency (*US*)
Furniss Lawton (*UK*)
The G Agency, LLC (*US*)
Don Gastwirth & Associates (*US*)
Gelfman Schneider Literary Agents, Inc. (*US*)
The Gernert Company (*US*)
Eric Glass Ltd (*UK*)
Global Lion Intellectual Property Management, Inc. (*US*)
Frances Goldin Literary Agency, Inc. (*US*)
Goodman Associates (*US*)
Graham Maw Christie Literary Agency (*UK*)
Christine Green Authors' Agent (*UK*)
Louise Greenberg Books Ltd (*UK*)
Sanford J. Greenburger Associates, Inc (*US*)
Greene & Heaton Ltd (*UK*)
The Greenhouse Literary Agency (*UK*)
Gregory & Company, Authors' Agents (*UK*)
Blanche C. Gregory Inc. (*US*)
Greyhaus Literary Agency (*US*)
Jill Grosjean Literary Agency (*US*)
David Grossman Literary Agency Ltd (*UK*)
Marianne Gunn O'Connor Literary Agency (*Ire*)
Gunn Media Associates (*UK*)
The Mitchell J. Hamilburg Agency (*US*)
Hannigan Salky Getzler (HSG) Agency (*US*)
Hardman & Swainson (*UK*)
Joy Harris Literary Agency, Inc. (*US*)
Antony Harwood Limited (*UK*)
John Hawkins & Associates, Inc. (*US*)
Heacock Hill Literary Agency, LLC (*US*)
A M Heath & Company Limited, Author's Agents (*UK*)
Rupert Heath Literary Agency (*UK*)
hhb agency ltd (*UK*)
David Higham Associates Ltd (*UK*)
Hill Nadell Literary Agency (*US*)
Vanessa Holt Ltd (*UK*)
Hopkins Literary Associates (*US*)
Kate Hordern Literary Agency (*UK*)
Andrea Hurst Literary Management (*US*)
InkWell Management (*US*)
Intercontinental Literary Agency (*UK*)
Isabel White Literary Agent (*UK*)
J de S Associates Inc (*US*)
Jabberwocky Literary Agency (*US*)
The Joan Brandt Agency (*US*)
Johnson & Alcock (*UK*)
Michelle Kass Associates (*UK*)
Ken Sherman & Associates (*US*)
Ki Agency Ltd (*UK*)
Kilburn Literary Agency (*UK*)
Kimberley Cameron & Associates (Formerly Reece Halsey North) (*US*)
Harvey Klinger, Inc (*US*)
Kneerim & Williams (*US*)
The Knight Agency (*US*)
Elaine Koster Literary Agency LLC (*US*)
Barbara S. Kouts, Literary Agent (*US*)
The LA Literary Agency (*US*)
Peter Lampack Agency, Inc (*US*)
Laura Langlie, Literary Agent (*US*)
Larsen Pomada Literary Agents (*US*)
The Steve Laube Agency (*US*)
Levine Greenberg Literary Agency, Inc. (*US*)
Barbara Levy Literary Agency (*UK*)
Limelight Management (*UK*)
Lindsay Literary Agency (*UK*)
Literary & Creative Artists Inc. (*US*)
The Literary Group (*US*)
The Christopher Little Literary Agency (*UK*)
London Independent Books (*UK*)
Sterling Lord Literistic, Inc. (*US*)
Julia Lord Literary Management (*US*)
Lowenstein Associates, Inc. (*US*)
Andrew Lownie Literary Agency Ltd (*UK*)
Lutyens and Rubinstein (*UK*)
The Jennifer Lyons Literary Agency, LLC (*US*)
Donald Maass Literary Agency (*US*)
Gina Maccoby Agency (*US*)
Madeleine Milburn Literary Agency (*UK*)
Ricia Mainhardt Agency (RMA) (*US*)
Carol Mann Agency (*US*)
Andrew Mann Ltd (*UK*)
Manus & Associates Literary Agency, Inc. (*US*)
March Tenth, Inc. (*US*)
Denise Marcil Literary Agency, Inc. (*US*)
Marjacq Scripts Ltd (*UK*)
Elaine Markson Literary Agency (*US*)
The Marsh Agency (*UK*)
The Martell Agency (*US*)
Martin Literary Management (*US*)
MBA Literary Agents Ltd (*UK*)
Duncan McAra (*UK*)
Margret McBride Literary Agency (*US*)
Anne McDermid & Associates Ltd (*Can*)
McIntosh & Otis, Inc (*US*)
McKernan Agency (*UK*)

Mendel Media Group, LLC (*US*)
Miles Stott Children's Literary Agency (*UK*)
Martha Millard Literary Agency (*US*)
William Morris Endeavor Entertainment (*US*)
Mulcahy Associates (*UK*)
Judith Murdoch Literary Agency (*UK*)
Nelson Literary Agency, LLC (*US*)
MNLA (Maggie Noach Literary Agency) (*UK*)
Northern Lights Literary Services (*US*)
Andrew Nurnberg Associates, Ltd (*UK*)
Harold Ober Associates (*US*)
Objective Entertainment (*US*)
Fifi Oscard Agency, Inc. (*US*)
Deborah Owen Ltd (*UK*)
P.S. Literary Agency (*Can*)
The Richard Parks Agency (*US*)
Kathi J. Paton Literary Agency (*US*)
Maggie Pearlstine Associates Ltd (*UK*)
Jonathan Pegg Literary Agency (*UK*)
Pendle Hill Literary Agency (*UK*)
L. Perkins Associates (*US*)
The Peters Fraser & Dunlop Group Ltd (PFD) (*UK*)
Pinder Lane & Garon-Brooke Associates Ltd (*US*)
Shelley Power Literary Agency Ltd (*UK*)
The Poynor Group (*US*)
Rebecca Pratt Literary Group (*US*)
Linn Prentis Literary (*US*)
Aaron M. Priest Literary Agency (*US*)
Prospect Agency (*US*)
Susan Rabiner, Literary Agent, Inc. (*US*)
Rebecca Friedman Literary Agency (*US*)
Redhammer (*UK*)
The Lisa Richards Agency (*Ire*)
Richford Becklow Literary Agency (*UK*)
Ann Rittenberg Literary Agency (*US*)
RLR Associates (*US*)
B.J. Robbins Literary Agency (*US*)
Robin Jones Literary Agency (*UK*)
Rocking Chair Books (*UK*)
Linda Roghaar Literary Agency, Inc. (*US*)
Andy Ross Agency (*US*)
Jane Rotrosen Agency (*US*)
The Damaris Rowland Agency (*US*)
The Rudy Agency (*US*)
Uli Rushby-Smith Literary Agency (*UK*)
The Sagalyn Literary Agency (*US*)
Victoria Sanders & Associates LLC (*US*)
Schiavone Literary Agency (*US*)
Susan Schulman, A Literary Agency (*US*)
The Science Factory (*UK*)
Scovil Galen Ghosh Literary Agency, Inc. (*US*)
The Seven Bridges Group (*US*)
The Seymour Agency (*US*)
Denise Shannon Literary Agency, Inc. (*US*)
Sheil Land Associates Ltd (*UK*)
Caroline Sheldon Literary Agency (*UK*)
Shelley Instone Literary Agency (*UK*)
Wendy Sherman Associates, Inc. (*US*)
Rosalie Siegel, International Literary Agency, Inc. (*US*)
Signature Literary Agency (*US*)
Dorie Simmonds Agency (*UK*)
Jeffrey Simmons (*UK*)
Sinclair-Stevenson (*UK*)
Valerie Smith, Literary Agent (*US*)
Spectrum Literary Agency (*US*)
Spencerhill Associates (*US*)
The Spieler Agency (*US*)
Philip G. Spitzer Literary Agency, Inc. (*US*)
Standen Literary Agency (*UK*)
Nancy Stauffer Associates (*US*)
Elaine Steel (*UK*)
Abner Stein (*UK*)
Steph Roundsmith Agent and Editor (*UK*)
Sternig & Byrne Literary Agency (*US*)
Shirley Stewart Literary Agency (*UK*)
Robin Straus Agency, Inc. (*US*)
Stuart Krichevsky Literary Agency, Inc. (*US*)
The Stuart Agency (*US*)
Sarah Such Literary Agency (*UK*)
Susanna Lea Associates (*US*)
Susanna Lea Associates (UK) (*UK*)
The Susijn Agency (*UK*)
SYLA – Susan Yearwood Literary Agency (*UK*)
Talcott Notch Literary (*US*)
Patricia Teal Literary Agency (*US*)
Tessler Literary Agency (*US*)
Tom Lee (*US*)
Transatlantic Literary Agency, Inc. (*Can*)
Scott Treimel NY (*US*)
TriadaUS Literary Agency, Inc. (*US*)
Trident Media Group, LLC (*US*)
Jane Turnbull (*UK*)
United Agents (*UK*)
Venture Literary (*US*)
Veritas Literary Agency (*US*)
Ed Victor Ltd (*UK*)
Wade & Co Literary Agency (*UK*)
Wales Literary Agency, Inc (*US*)
Watkins / Loomis Agency, Inc. (*US*)
Watson, Little Ltd (*UK*)
Waxman Leavell Literary Agency (*US*)
Weed Literary LLC (*US*)
The Wendy Weil Agency, Inc. (*US*)
The Weingel-Fidel Agency (*US*)
Westwood Creative Artists (*Can*)
Whispering Buffalo Literary Agency Ltd (*UK*)
Eve White: Literary Agent (*UK*)
Dinah Wiener Ltd (*UK*)
William Morris Endeavor (WME) London (*UK*)
Wolfson Literary Agency (*US*)
Writers House UK (*UK*)
Writers House, LLC. (*US*)
Writers' Representatives, LLC (*US*)
The Wylie Agency (UK) Ltd (*UK*)
Yates & Yates (*US*)
The Zack Company, Inc (*US*)
Zeno Agency Ltd (*UK*)

Film

A & B Personal Management Ltd (*UK*)
Abbot Management (*US*)
Abrams Artists Agency (*US*)
The Agency (London) Ltd (*UK*)
Agency for the Performing Arts (APA) (*US*)

Aimee Entertainment Agency (*US*)
Marcia Amsterdam Agency (*US*)
Anonymous Content (*US*)
AP Watt at United Agents LLP (*UK*)
Berlin Associates (*UK*)
Blake Friedmann Literary Agency Ltd (*UK*)
Barbara Braun Associates, Inc. (*US*)
Alan Brodie Representation Ltd (*UK*)
Kelvin C. Bulger and Associates (*US*)
Sheree Bykofsky Associates, Inc. (*US*)
Capel & Land Ltd (*UK*)
The Characters Talent Agency (*Can*)
Mary Clemmey Literary Agency (*UK*)
Jonathan Clowes Ltd (*UK*)
Rosica Colin Ltd (*UK*)
The Collective (*US*)
Don Congdon Associates, Inc. (*US*)
Creative Trust, Inc. (*US*)
Criterion Group, Inc. (*US*)
Curtis Brown Group Ltd (*UK*)
The Darley Anderson Agency (*UK*)
The Jennifer DeChiara Literary Agency (*US*)
Felix de Wolfe (*UK*)
Doyen Literary Services, Inc. (*US*)
Energy Entertainment (*US*)
Evatopia, Inc. (*US*)
Film Rights Ltd in association with Laurence Fitch Ltd (*UK*)
Diana Finch Literary Agency (*US*)
Jill Foster Ltd (JFL) (*UK*)
Fox Mason Ltd (*UK*)
Full Throttle Literary Agency (*US*)
Eric Glass Ltd (*UK*)
Frances Goldin Literary Agency, Inc. (*US*)
Goodman Associates (*US*)
Antony Harwood Limited (*UK*)
David Higham Associates Ltd (*UK*)
Valerie Hoskins Associates (*UK*)
Hudson Agency (*US*)
Independent Talent Group Ltd (*UK*)
Janet Fillingham Associates (*UK*)
Johnson & Alcock (*UK*)
Michelle Kass Associates (*UK*)
Ken Sherman & Associates (*US*)
Ki Agency Ltd (*UK*)
Knight Hall Agency (*UK*)
Laura Langlie, Literary Agent (*US*)
Larsen Pomada Literary Agents (*US*)
Lenhoff & Lenhoff (*US*)
Macnaughton Lord Representation (*UK*)
Madeleine Milburn Literary Agency (*UK*)
Andrew Mann Ltd (*UK*)
March Tenth, Inc. (*US*)
Marjacq Scripts Ltd (*UK*)
MBA Literary Agents Ltd (*UK*)
Martha Millard Literary Agency (*US*)
William Morris Endeavor Entertainment (*US*)
Objective Entertainment (*US*)
The Richard Parks Agency (*US*)
PBJ and JBJ Management (*UK*)
Pendle Hill Literary Agency (*UK*)
Peregrine Whittlesey Agency (*US*)
L. Perkins Associates (*US*)
James Peter Associates, Inc. (*US*)
The Peters Fraser & Dunlop Group Ltd (PFD) (*UK*)
Pinder Lane & Garon-Brooke Associates Ltd (*US*)
B.J. Robbins Literary Agency (*US*)
Rochelle Stevens & Co. (*UK*)
Victoria Sanders & Associates LLC (*US*)
Sayle Screen Ltd (*UK*)
Susan Schulman, A Literary Agency (*US*)
Linda Seifert Management (*UK*)
Sheil Land Associates Ltd (*UK*)
Jeffrey Simmons (*UK*)
The Spieler Agency (*US*)
Elaine Steel (*UK*)
The Tennyson Agency (*UK*)
Tom Lee (*US*)
Trident Media Group, LLC (*US*)
2M Literary Agency Ltd (*US*)
United Agents (*UK*)
Venture Literary (*US*)
Cecily Ware Literary Agents (*UK*)
Watson, Little Ltd (*UK*)
Whispering Buffalo Literary Agency Ltd (*UK*)
The Zack Company, Inc (*US*)

Finance

Abbot Management (*US*)
The Agency Group, Ltd (*US*)
Ambassador Speakers Bureau & Literary Agency (*US*)
Audrey A. Wolf Literary Agency (*US*)
The August Agency LLC (*US*)
Ayesha Pande Literary (*US*)
David Black Literary Agency (*US*)
Jenny Brown Associates (*UK*)
Browne & Miller Literary Associates (*US*)
Maria Carvainis Agency, Inc. (*US*)
Castiglia Literary Agency (*US*)
Elyse Cheney Literary Associates, LLC (*US*)
Connor Literary Agency (*US*)
The Doe Coover Agency (*US*)
Richard Curtis Associates, Inc. (*US*)
The Darley Anderson Agency (*UK*)
Janis A. Donnaud & Associates, Inc. (*US*)
Jim Donovan Literary (*US*)
Doyen Literary Services, Inc. (*US*)
Dystel & Goderich Literary Management (*US*)
Farris Literary Agency, Inc. (*US*)
The Fielding Agency, LLC (*US*)
Diana Finch Literary Agency (*US*)
Jeanne Fredericks Literary Agency, Inc. (*US*)
Grace Freedson's Publishing Network (*US*)
The G Agency, LLC (*US*)
Goodman Associates (*US*)
The Mitchell J. Hamilburg Agency (*US*)
Hannigan Salky Getzler (HSG) Agency (*US*)
Antony Harwood Limited (*UK*)
Hornfischer Literary Management, L.P. (*US*)
InkWell Management (*US*)
J de S Associates Inc (*US*)
Frances Kelly (*UK*)
Kneerim & Williams (*US*)
The Knight Agency (*US*)

Linda Konner Literary Agency (*US*)
Elaine Koster Literary Agency LLC (*US*)
Larsen Pomada Literary Agents (*US*)
Levine Greenberg Literary Agency, Inc. (*US*)
Andrew Lownie Literary Agency Ltd (*UK*)
The Jennifer Lyons Literary Agency, LLC (*US*)
Carol Mann Agency (*US*)
Manus & Associates Literary Agency, Inc. (*US*)
The Martell Agency (*US*)
Mendel Media Group, LLC (*US*)
Martha Millard Literary Agency (*US*)
Mulcahy Associates (*UK*)
Fifi Oscard Agency, Inc. (*US*)
The Richard Parks Agency (*US*)
Kathi J. Paton Literary Agency (*US*)
James Peter Associates, Inc. (*US*)
The Poynor Group (*US*)
Susan Rabiner, Literary Agent, Inc. (*US*)
Rita Rosenkranz Literary Agency (*US*)
Schiavone Literary Agency (*US*)
Susan Schulman, A Literary Agency (*US*)
Solow Literary Enterprises, Inc. (*US*)
The Spieler Agency (*US*)
Venture Literary (*US*)
Writers House UK (*UK*)
Writers House, LLC. (*US*)
Writers' Representatives, LLC (*US*)
The Zack Company, Inc (*US*)

Gardening

Abbot Management (*US*)
Betsy Amster Literary Enterprises (*US*)
AP Watt at United Agents LLP (*UK*)
Teresa Chris Literary Agency Ltd (*UK*)
Rosica Colin Ltd (*UK*)
The Doe Coover Agency (*US*)
The Darley Anderson Agency (*UK*)
Caroline Davidson Literary Agency (*UK*)
Janis A. Donnaud & Associates, Inc. (*US*)
Doyen Literary Services, Inc. (*US*)
Fine Literary (*US*)
Jeanne Fredericks Literary Agency, Inc. (*US*)
Greene & Heaton Ltd (*UK*)
Jill Grosjean Literary Agency (*US*)
The Mitchell J. Hamilburg Agency (*US*)
Antony Harwood Limited (*UK*)
John Hawkins & Associates, Inc. (*US*)
Heacock Hill Literary Agency, LLC (*US*)
Levine Greenberg Literary Agency, Inc. (*US*)
The Richard Parks Agency (*US*)
Regina Ryan Publishing Enterprises (*US*)
Richford Becklow Literary Agency (*UK*)
Sheil Land Associates Ltd (*UK*)
Talcott Notch Literary (*US*)
Jane Turnbull (*UK*)
Venture Literary (*US*)
The Zack Company, Inc (*US*)

Gothic

Abbot Management (*US*)
Abela Literature (*Can*)
The Darley Anderson Agency (*UK*)
Diamond Kahn and Woods (DKW) Literary Agency Ltd (*UK*)
Ann Elmo Agency, Inc. (*US*)
Antony Harwood Limited (*UK*)
Ricia Mainhardt Agency (RMA) (*US*)
Pendle Hill Literary Agency (*UK*)
Aaron M. Priest Literary Agency (*US*)
Richford Becklow Literary Agency (*UK*)
Shelley Instone Literary Agency (*UK*)
Venture Literary (*US*)

Health

Abbot Management (*US*)
The Agency Group, Ltd (*US*)
The Ahearn Agency, Inc (*US*)
Ambassador Speakers Bureau & Literary Agency (*US*)
Betsy Amster Literary Enterprises (*US*)
AP Watt at United Agents LLP (*UK*)
Arcadia (*US*)
Audrey A. Wolf Literary Agency (*US*)
Vicky Bijur Literary Agency (*US*)
David Black Literary Agency (*US*)
Bleecker Street Associates, Inc. (*US*)
Luigi Bonomi Associates Ltd (*UK*)
Brandt & Hochman Literary Agents, Inc. (*US*)
Rick Broadhead & Associates Literary Agency (*Can*)
Tracy Brown Literary Agency (*US*)
Browne & Miller Literary Associates (*US*)
Carnicelli Literary Management (*US*)
Castiglia Literary Agency (*US*)
Rosica Colin Ltd (*UK*)
Don Congdon Associates, Inc. (*US*)
Connor Literary Agency (*US*)
The Doe Coover Agency (*US*)
Creative Authors Ltd (*UK*)
Richard Curtis Associates, Inc. (*US*)
The Darley Anderson Agency (*UK*)
Caroline Davidson Literary Agency (*UK*)
The Jennifer DeChiara Literary Agency (*US*)
Joëlle Delbourgo Associates, Inc. (*US*)
Diane Banks Associates Literary Agency (*UK*)
Sandra Dijkstra Literary Agency (*US*)
Janis A. Donnaud & Associates, Inc. (*US*)
Jim Donovan Literary (*US*)
Doyen Literary Services, Inc. (*US*)
Dystel & Goderich Literary Management (*US*)
Ethan Ellenberg Literary Agency (*US*)
Ann Elmo Agency, Inc. (*US*)
Farris Literary Agency, Inc. (*US*)
The Fielding Agency, LLC (*US*)
Diana Finch Literary Agency (*US*)
Fine Literary (*US*)
FinePrint Literary Management (*US*)
Fletcher & Company (*US*)
Folio Literary Management, LLC (*US*)
Foundry Literary + Media (*US*)
Fox & Howard Literary Agency (*UK*)
Jeanne Fredericks Literary Agency, Inc. (*US*)
Grace Freedson's Publishing Network (*US*)
Sarah Jane Freymann Literary Agency (*US*)
Goodman Associates (*US*)
Graham Maw Christie Literary Agency (*UK*)
Sanford J. Greenburger Associates, Inc (*US*)
Greene & Heaton Ltd (*UK*)
Marianne Gunn O'Connor Literary Agency (*Ire*)

The Mitchell J. Hamilburg Agency (*US*)
Antony Harwood Limited (*UK*)
John Hawkins & Associates, Inc. (*US*)
Heacock Hill Literary Agency, LLC (*US*)
The Jeff Herman Agency, LLC (*US*)
Hill Nadell Literary Agency (*US*)
Hornfischer Literary Management, L.P. (*US*)
InkWell Management (*US*)
J de S Associates Inc (*US*)
Johnson & Alcock (*UK*)
Frances Kelly (*UK*)
Kilburn Literary Agency (*UK*)
Harvey Klinger, Inc (*US*)
Kneerim & Williams (*US*)
The Knight Agency (*US*)
Linda Konner Literary Agency (*US*)
Elaine Koster Literary Agency LLC (*US*)
Barbara S. Kouts, Literary Agent (*US*)
Bert P. Krages (*US*)
The LA Literary Agency (*US*)
Larsen Pomada Literary Agents (*US*)
Levine Greenberg Literary Agency, Inc. (*US*)
Literary & Creative Artists Inc. (*US*)
The Literary Group (*US*)
Sterling Lord Literistic, Inc. (*US*)
Julia Lord Literary Management (*US*)
Lowenstein Associates, Inc. (*US*)
Andrew Lownie Literary Agency Ltd (*UK*)
Gina Maccoby Agency (*US*)
Carol Mann Agency (*US*)
Manus & Associates Literary Agency, Inc. (*US*)
March Tenth, Inc. (*US*)
Denise Marcil Literary Agency, Inc. (*US*)
Marjacq Scripts Ltd (*UK*)
The Martell Agency (*US*)
Martin Literary Management (*US*)
MBA Literary Agents Ltd (*UK*)
Margret McBride Literary Agency (*US*)
Martha Millard Literary Agency (*US*)
Northern Lights Literary Services (*US*)
Fifi Oscard Agency, Inc. (*US*)
P.S. Literary Agency (*Can*)
The Richard Parks Agency (*US*)
Kathi J. Paton Literary Agency (*US*)
Maggie Pearlstine Associates Ltd (*UK*)
James Peter Associates, Inc. (*US*)
Pinder Lane & Garon-Brooke Associates Ltd (*US*)
The Poynor Group (*US*)
Regina Ryan Publishing Enterprises (*US*)
RLR Associates (*US*)
B.J. Robbins Literary Agency (*US*)
Rita Rosenkranz Literary Agency (*US*)
The Rudy Agency (*US*)
Schiavone Literary Agency (*US*)
Susan Schulman, A Literary Agency (*US*)
Scovil Galen Ghosh Literary Agency, Inc. (*US*)
Denise Shannon Literary Agency, Inc. (*US*)
Wendy Sherman Associates, Inc. (*US*)
Robert Smith Literary Agency Ltd (*UK*)
Solow Literary Enterprises, Inc. (*US*)
The Spieler Agency (*US*)
The Stuart Agency (*US*)
Patricia Teal Literary Agency (*US*)
TriadaUS Literary Agency, Inc. (*US*)
Trident Media Group, LLC (*US*)
2M Literary Agency Ltd (*US*)
Venture Literary (*US*)
Veritas Literary Agency (*US*)
Waterside Productions, Inc (*US*)
The Wendy Weil Agency, Inc. (*US*)
Whimsy Literary Agency, LLC (*US*)
Whispering Buffalo Literary Agency Ltd (*UK*)
Wolfson Literary Agency (*US*)
The Zack Company, Inc (*US*)

Historical

Abbot Management (*US*)
Abela Literature (*Can*)
Sheila Ableman Literary Agency (*UK*)
Adler & Robin Books, Inc (*US*)
The Agency Group, Ltd (*US*)
The Ahearn Agency, Inc (*US*)
Alive Communications, Inc (*US*)
Ambassador Speakers Bureau & Literary Agency (*US*)
The Ampersand Agency Ltd (*UK*)
Betsy Amster Literary Enterprises (*US*)
Marcia Amsterdam Agency (*US*)
AP Watt at United Agents LLP (*UK*)
Arcadia (*US*)
Artellus Limited (*UK*)
Audrey A. Wolf Literary Agency (*US*)
The August Agency LLC (*US*)
Author Rights Agency (*Ire*)
Ayesha Pande Literary (*US*)
Baldi Agency (*US*)
The Bent Agency (*US*)
Vicky Bijur Literary Agency (*US*)
David Black Literary Agency (*US*)
Bleecker Street Associates, Inc. (*US*)
Luigi Bonomi Associates Ltd (*UK*)
The Book Group (*US*)
BookEnds, LLC (*US*)
Books & Such Literary Agency (*US*)
Georges Borchardt, Inc. (*US*)
Brandt & Hochman Literary Agents, Inc. (*US*)
Barbara Braun Associates, Inc. (*US*)
Rick Broadhead & Associates Literary Agency (*Can*)
Jenny Brown Associates (*UK*)
Marie Brown Associates, Inc. (*US*)
Tracy Brown Literary Agency (*US*)
Browne & Miller Literary Associates (*US*)
Felicity Bryan (*UK*)
Capel & Land Ltd (*UK*)
Carnicelli Literary Management (*US*)
Maria Carvainis Agency, Inc. (*US*)
Chalberg & Sussman (*US*)
The Characters Talent Agency (*Can*)
Elyse Cheney Literary Associates, LLC (*US*)
Teresa Chris Literary Agency Ltd (*UK*)
The Chudney Agency (*US*)
Rosica Colin Ltd (*UK*)
Frances Collin Literary Agent (*US*)
Don Congdon Associates, Inc. (*US*)
Connor Literary Agency (*US*)

The Lisa Richards Agency (*Ire*)
Richford Becklow Literary Agency (*UK*)
Ann Rittenberg Literary Agency (*US*)
RLR Associates (*US*)
Robert Dudley Agency (*UK*)
Rocking Chair Books (*UK*)
Linda Roghaar Literary Agency, Inc. (*US*)
Rita Rosenkranz Literary Agency (*US*)
Ross Yoon Agency (*US*)
Andy Ross Agency (*US*)
Jane Rotrosen Agency (*US*)
The Rudy Agency (*US*)
The Sagalyn Literary Agency (*US*)
Victoria Sanders & Associates LLC (*US*)
Schiavone Literary Agency (*US*)
Susan Schulman, A Literary Agency (*US*)
The Science Factory (*UK*)
Scovil Galen Ghosh Literary Agency, Inc. (*US*)
The Seymour Agency (*US*)
Denise Shannon Literary Agency, Inc. (*US*)
Sheil Land Associates Ltd (*UK*)
Caroline Sheldon Literary Agency (*UK*)
Shelley Instone Literary Agency (*UK*)
Wendy Sherman Associates, Inc. (*US*)
Rosalie Siegel, International Literary Agency, Inc. (*US*)
Signature Literary Agency (*US*)
Dorie Simmonds Agency (*UK*)
Jeffrey Simmons (*UK*)
Sinclair-Stevenson (*UK*)
Robert Smith Literary Agency Ltd (*UK*)
Valerie Smith, Literary Agent (*US*)
Solow Literary Enterprises, Inc. (*US*)
Spectrum Literary Agency (*US*)
The Spieler Agency (*US*)
Philip G. Spitzer Literary Agency, Inc. (*US*)
Steph Roundsmith Agent and Editor (*UK*)
Robin Straus Agency, Inc. (*US*)
Stuart Krichevsky Literary Agency, Inc. (*US*)
The Stuart Agency (*US*)
Sarah Such Literary Agency (*UK*)
Talcott Notch Literary (*US*)
Patricia Teal Literary Agency (*US*)
Tessler Literary Agency (*US*)
Tom Lee (*US*)
Transatlantic Literary Agency, Inc. (*Can*)
Trident Media Group, LLC (*US*)
Jane Turnbull (*UK*)
Venture Literary (*US*)
Veritas Literary Agency (*US*)
Ed Victor Ltd (*UK*)
Watkins / Loomis Agency, Inc. (*US*)
Watson, Little Ltd (*UK*)
Waxman Leavell Literary Agency (*US*)
The Wendy Weil Agency, Inc. (*US*)
Westwood Creative Artists (*Can*)
William Morris Endeavor (WME) London (*UK*)
Writers House UK (*UK*)
Writers House, LLC. (*US*)
Writers' Representatives, LLC (*US*)
The Zack Company, Inc (*US*)
Zeno Agency Ltd (*UK*)

Hobbies

Abbot Management (*US*)
Browne & Miller Literary Associates (*US*)
Sheree Bykofsky Associates, Inc. (*US*)
Connor Literary Agency (*US*)
The Darley Anderson Agency (*UK*)
Grace Freedson's Publishing Network (*US*)
Antony Harwood Limited (*UK*)
Levine Greenberg Literary Agency, Inc. (*US*)
Julia Lord Literary Management (*US*)
The Richard Parks Agency (*US*)
Pendle Hill Literary Agency (*UK*)
Rita Rosenkranz Literary Agency (*US*)
Susan Schulman, A Literary Agency (*US*)
Venture Literary (*US*)
Waterside Productions, Inc (*US*)

Horror

Abbot Management (*US*)
Abela Literature (*Can*)
The Ampersand Agency Ltd (*UK*)
Marcia Amsterdam Agency (*US*)
Anubis Literary Agency (*UK*)
The Bent Agency (*US*)
Bleecker Street Associates, Inc. (*US*)
The Characters Talent Agency (*Can*)
Elyse Cheney Literary Associates, LLC (*US*)
Cine/Lit Representation (*US*)
Rosica Colin Ltd (*UK*)
Connor Literary Agency (*US*)
The Darley Anderson Agency (*UK*)
Dorian Literary Agency (DLA) (*UK*)
Evatopia, Inc. (*US*)
The Fielding Agency, LLC (*US*)
Film Rights Ltd in association with Laurence Fitch Ltd (*UK*)
FinePrint Literary Management (*US*)
Folio Literary Management, LLC (*US*)
Fox Mason Ltd (*UK*)
Samuel French, Inc. (*US*)
Full Throttle Literary Agency (*US*)
The Mitchell J. Hamilburg Agency (*US*)
Hardman & Swainson (*UK*)
Antony Harwood Limited (*UK*)
The Literary Group (*US*)
Andrew Lownie Literary Agency Ltd (*UK*)
Donald Maass Literary Agency (*US*)
Ricia Mainhardt Agency (RMA) (*US*)
McIntosh & Otis, Inc (*US*)
Martha Millard Literary Agency (*US*)
Pendle Hill Literary Agency (*UK*)
L. Perkins Associates (*US*)
Pinder Lane & Garon-Brooke Associates Ltd (*US*)
Rebecca Pratt Literary Group (*US*)
Richford Becklow Literary Agency (*UK*)
RLR Associates (*US*)
Rocking Chair Books (*UK*)
Shelley Instone Literary Agency (*UK*)
Sternig & Byrne Literary Agency (*US*)
Talcott Notch Literary (*US*)
Tom Lee (*US*)
Venture Literary (*US*)
The Zack Company, Inc (*US*)

Larsen Pomada Literary Agents (*US*)
Levine Greenberg Literary Agency, Inc. (*US*)
The Literary Group (*US*)
Julia Lord Literary Management (*US*)
Donald Maass Literary Agency (*US*)
Ricia Mainhardt Agency (RMA) (*US*)
Carol Mann Agency (*US*)
March Tenth, Inc. (*US*)
McIntosh & Otis, Inc (*US*)
Mendel Media Group, LLC (*US*)
P.S. Literary Agency (*Can*)
The Richard Parks Agency (*US*)
Kathi J. Paton Literary Agency (*US*)
PBJ and JBJ Management (*UK*)
L. Perkins Associates (*US*)
James Peter Associates, Inc. (*US*)
Pinder Lane & Garon-Brooke Associates Ltd (*US*)
Susan Rabiner, Literary Agent, Inc. (*US*)
The Lisa Richards Agency (*Ire*)
RLR Associates (*US*)
B.J. Robbins Literary Agency (*US*)
Rita Rosenkranz Literary Agency (*US*)
Victoria Sanders & Associates LLC (*US*)
Susan Schulman, A Literary Agency (*US*)
Sheil Land Associates Ltd (*UK*)
Caroline Sheldon Literary Agency (*UK*)
Robert Smith Literary Agency Ltd (*UK*)
The Spieler Agency (*US*)
Steph Roundsmith Agent and Editor (*UK*)
Sarah Such Literary Agency (*UK*)
Talent Source (*US*)
Transatlantic Literary Agency, Inc. (*Can*)
Trident Media Group, LLC (*US*)
Jane Turnbull (*UK*)
Venture Literary (*US*)
Cecily Ware Literary Agents (*UK*)
Watson, Little Ltd (*UK*)
Waxman Leavell Literary Agency (*US*)
Whimsy Literary Agency, LLC (*US*)
Whispering Buffalo Literary Agency Ltd (*UK*)
Wolfson Literary Agency (*US*)
Writers' Representatives, LLC (*US*)
The Zack Company, Inc (*US*)

Legal

Abbot Management (*US*)
The Agency Group, Ltd (*US*)
Ambassador Speakers Bureau & Literary Agency (*US*)
David Black Literary Agency (*US*)
Don Congdon Associates, Inc. (*US*)
Connor Literary Agency (*US*)
Crawford Literary Agency (*US*)
Crichton & Associates, Inc. (*US*)
The Darley Anderson Agency (*UK*)
Jim Donovan Literary (*US*)
Farris Literary Agency, Inc. (*US*)
The Fielding Agency, LLC (*US*)
Diana Finch Literary Agency (*US*)
Jeanne Fredericks Literary Agency, Inc. (*US*)
Goodman Associates (*US*)
Antony Harwood Limited (*UK*)
Hill Nadell Literary Agency (*US*)
Hornfischer Literary Management, L.P. (*US*)
J de S Associates Inc (*US*)
Kneerim & Williams (*US*)
Laura Langlie, Literary Agent (*US*)
Larsen Pomada Literary Agents (*US*)
Literary & Creative Artists Inc. (*US*)
Carol Mann Agency (*US*)
The Richard Parks Agency (*US*)
Regina Ryan Publishing Enterprises (*US*)
Rita Rosenkranz Literary Agency (*US*)
Victoria Sanders & Associates LLC (*US*)
Susan Schulman, A Literary Agency (*US*)
Jeffrey Simmons (*UK*)
The Spieler Agency (*US*)
Venture Literary (*US*)
Writers' Representatives, LLC (*US*)
Yates & Yates (*US*)

Leisure

Abbot Management (*US*)
Rosica Colin Ltd (*UK*)
Conville & Walsh Ltd (*UK*)
The Darley Anderson Agency (*UK*)
Doyen Literary Services, Inc. (*US*)
The Feldstein Agency (*UK*)
Fine Literary (*US*)
Jeanne Fredericks Literary Agency, Inc. (*US*)
Goodman Associates (*US*)
The Mitchell J. Hamilburg Agency (*US*)
Antony Harwood Limited (*UK*)
Levine Greenberg Literary Agency, Inc. (*US*)
Ricia Mainhardt Agency (RMA) (*US*)
James Peter Associates, Inc. (*US*)
Regina Ryan Publishing Enterprises (*US*)
Venture Literary (*US*)
Watson, Little Ltd (*UK*)

Lifestyle

Abbot Management (*US*)
Adler & Robin Books, Inc (*US*)
The Agency Group, Ltd (*US*)
The Ahearn Agency, Inc (*US*)
Alive Communications, Inc (*US*)
Ambassador Speakers Bureau & Literary Agency (*US*)
Betsy Amster Literary Enterprises (*US*)
Arcadia (*US*)
Audrey A. Wolf Literary Agency (*US*)
Baldi Agency (*US*)
The Bent Agency (*US*)
David Black Literary Agency (*US*)
Bleecker Street Associates, Inc. (*US*)
Luigi Bonomi Associates Ltd (*UK*)
The Book Group (*US*)
BookEnds, LLC (*US*)
Books & Such Literary Agency (*US*)
Brandt & Hochman Literary Agents, Inc. (*US*)
Rick Broadhead & Associates Literary Agency (*Can*)
Browne & Miller Literary Associates (*US*)
Sheree Bykofsky Associates, Inc. (*US*)
Castiglia Literary Agency (*US*)
Jane Chelius Literary Agency, Inc. (*US*)
Teresa Chris Literary Agency Ltd (*UK*)
Rosica Colin Ltd (*UK*)

Susan Schulman, A Literary Agency (*US*)
The Seven Bridges Group (*US*)
Shelley Instone Literary Agency (*UK*)
Steph Roundsmith Agent and Editor (*UK*)
Tom Lee (*US*)
Venture Literary (*US*)
Writers' Representatives, LLC (*US*)

Media

Abbot Management (*US*)
The August Agency LLC (*US*)
Crawford Literary Agency (*US*)
The Darley Anderson Agency (*UK*)
The Feldstein Agency (*UK*)
Folio Literary Management, LLC (*US*)
Joy Harris Literary Agency, Inc. (*US*)
Antony Harwood Limited (*UK*)
The Knight Agency (*US*)
Andrew Lownie Literary Agency Ltd (*UK*)
Martin Literary Management (*US*)
Mendel Media Group, LLC (*US*)
Venture Literary (*US*)

Medicine

Abbot Management (*US*)
The Agency Group, Ltd (*US*)
Ambassador Speakers Bureau & Literary Agency (*US*)
Betsy Amster Literary Enterprises (*US*)
AP Watt at United Agents LLP (*UK*)
Rick Broadhead & Associates Literary Agency (*Can*)
Browne & Miller Literary Associates (*US*)
Jane Chelius Literary Agency, Inc. (*US*)
Don Congdon Associates, Inc. (*US*)
Connor Literary Agency (*US*)
Crawford Literary Agency (*US*)
Richard Curtis Associates, Inc. (*US*)
The Darley Anderson Agency (*UK*)
Caroline Davidson Literary Agency (*UK*)
Liza Dawson Associates (*US*)
DeFiore and Company (*US*)
Jim Donovan Literary (*US*)
The Fielding Agency, LLC (*US*)
Diana Finch Literary Agency (*US*)
Jeanne Fredericks Literary Agency, Inc. (*US*)
Grace Freedson's Publishing Network (*US*)
Goodman Associates (*US*)
Antony Harwood Limited (*UK*)
Hornfischer Literary Management, L.P. (*US*)
InkWell Management (*US*)
J de S Associates Inc (*US*)
Frances Kelly (*UK*)
Kilburn Literary Agency (*UK*)
Harvey Klinger, Inc (*US*)
Kneerim & Williams (*US*)
Larsen Pomada Literary Agents (*US*)
Literary & Creative Artists Inc. (*US*)
Andrew Lownie Literary Agency Ltd (*UK*)
Carol Mann Agency (*US*)
March Tenth, Inc. (*US*)
The Martell Agency (*US*)
Northern Lights Literary Services (*US*)
The Richard Parks Agency (*US*)
The Poynor Group (*US*)
B.J. Robbins Literary Agency (*US*)
Robert Dudley Agency (*UK*)
Rita Rosenkranz Literary Agency (*US*)
The Rudy Agency (*US*)
Susan Schulman, A Literary Agency (*US*)
The Science Factory (*UK*)
2M Literary Agency Ltd (*US*)
Venture Literary (*US*)
Wolfson Literary Agency (*US*)
The Zack Company, Inc (*US*)

Men's Interests

Abbot Management (*US*)
Rosica Colin Ltd (*UK*)
Conville & Walsh Ltd (*UK*)
The Creative Rights Agency (*UK*)
The Darley Anderson Agency (*UK*)
Fine Literary (*US*)
Sarah Jane Freymann Literary Agency (*US*)
Antony Harwood Limited (*UK*)
Andrew Lownie Literary Agency Ltd (*UK*)
The Seven Bridges Group (*US*)
Venture Literary (*US*)

Military

Abbot Management (*US*)
Artellus Limited (*UK*)
David Black Literary Agency (*US*)
Bleecker Street Associates, Inc. (*US*)
Rick Broadhead & Associates Literary Agency (*Can*)
Rosica Colin Ltd (*UK*)
Don Congdon Associates, Inc. (*US*)
Conville & Walsh Ltd (*UK*)
The Darley Anderson Agency (*UK*)
Liza Dawson Associates (*US*)
DeFiore and Company (*US*)
Jim Donovan Literary (*US*)
Dystel & Goderich Literary Management (*US*)
Farris Literary Agency, Inc. (*US*)
The Feldstein Agency (*UK*)
The Fielding Agency, LLC (*US*)
Diana Finch Literary Agency (*US*)
FinePrint Literary Management (*US*)
Folio Literary Management, LLC (*US*)
The G Agency, LLC (*US*)
Don Gastwirth & Associates (*US*)
Goodman Associates (*US*)
The Mitchell J. Hamilburg Agency (*US*)
Antony Harwood Limited (*UK*)
Hornfischer Literary Management, L.P. (*US*)
J de S Associates Inc (*US*)
The Literary Group (*US*)
Andrew Lownie Literary Agency Ltd (*UK*)
Duncan McAra (*UK*)
The Richard Parks Agency (*US*)
Robert Dudley Agency (*UK*)
Rita Rosenkranz Literary Agency (*US*)
The Rudy Agency (*US*)
The Seven Bridges Group (*US*)
Sheil Land Associates Ltd (*UK*)
Signature Literary Agency (*US*)
Robert Smith Literary Agency Ltd (*UK*)
Venture Literary (*US*)
Waxman Leavell Literary Agency (*US*)

The Zack Company, Inc (*US*)

Music

Abbot Management (*US*)
Abrams Artists Agency (*US*)
The Agency Group, Ltd (*US*)
AP Watt at United Agents LLP (*UK*)
Arcadia (*US*)
Jenny Brown Associates (*UK*)
Marie Brown Associates, Inc. (*US*)
Don Congdon Associates, Inc. (*US*)
The Doe Coover Agency (*US*)
The Darley Anderson Agency (*UK*)
DeFiore and Company (*US*)
Sandra Dijkstra Literary Agency (*US*)
Jim Donovan Literary (*US*)
Dunham Literary, Inc. (*US*)
Farris Literary Agency, Inc. (*US*)
The Feldstein Agency (*UK*)
Diana Finch Literary Agency (*US*)
Fine Literary (*US*)
FinePrint Literary Management (*US*)
Folio Literary Management, LLC (*US*)
Foundry Literary + Media (*US*)
Fox Mason Ltd (*UK*)
Don Gastwirth & Associates (*US*)
Goodman Associates (*US*)
Sanford J. Greenburger Associates, Inc (*US*)
Antony Harwood Limited (*UK*)
Johnson & Alcock (*UK*)
Harvey Klinger, Inc (*US*)
Larsen Pomada Literary Agents (*US*)
Julia Lord Literary Management (*US*)
Andrew Lownie Literary Agency Ltd (*UK*)
Carol Mann Agency (*US*)
March Tenth, Inc. (*US*)
McIntosh & Otis, Inc (*US*)
Martha Millard Literary Agency (*US*)
Objective Entertainment (*US*)
The Richard Parks Agency (*US*)
L. Perkins Associates (*US*)
Pinder Lane & Garon-Brooke Associates Ltd (*US*)
RLR Associates (*US*)
B.J. Robbins Literary Agency (*US*)
Rita Rosenkranz Literary Agency (*US*)
Victoria Sanders & Associates LLC (*US*)
Susan Schulman, A Literary Agency (*US*)
The Seven Bridges Group (*US*)
The Spieler Agency (*US*)
Trident Media Group, LLC (*US*)
2M Literary Agency Ltd (*US*)
Venture Literary (*US*)
Watson, Little Ltd (*UK*)
The Weingel-Fidel Agency (*US*)
Whispering Buffalo Literary Agency Ltd (*UK*)
The Zack Company, Inc (*US*)

Mystery

Abbot Management (*US*)
Abela Literature (*Can*)
Abrams Artists Agency (*US*)
The Ahearn Agency, Inc (*US*)
Alive Communications, Inc (*US*)
Betsy Amster Literary Enterprises (*US*)
Marcia Amsterdam Agency (*US*)
The Axelrod Agency (*US*)
Belcastro Agency (*US*)
The Bent Agency (*US*)
Meredith Bernstein Literary Agency, Inc. (*US*)
David Black Literary Agency (*US*)
Bleecker Street Associates, Inc. (*US*)
BookEnds, LLC (*US*)
Brandt & Hochman Literary Agents, Inc. (*US*)
Barbara Braun Associates, Inc. (*US*)
The Bright Literary Academy (*UK*)
Browne & Miller Literary Associates (*US*)
Sheree Bykofsky Associates, Inc. (*US*)
Maria Carvainis Agency, Inc. (*US*)
Castiglia Literary Agency (*US*)
The Characters Talent Agency (*Can*)
The Chudney Agency (*US*)
Cine/Lit Representation (*US*)
Rosica Colin Ltd (*UK*)
Don Congdon Associates, Inc. (*US*)
Conville & Walsh Ltd (*UK*)
Coombs Moylett Literary Agency (*UK*)
CowlesRyan Agency (*US*)
Crichton & Associates, Inc. (*US*)
The Croce Agency (*US*)
Richard Curtis Associates, Inc. (*US*)
Laura Dail Literary Agency (*US*)
Darhansoff & Verrill Literary Agents (*US*)
The Darley Anderson Agency (*UK*)
Liza Dawson Associates (*US*)
The Jennifer DeChiara Literary Agency (*US*)
Joëlle Delbourgo Associates, Inc. (*US*)
Sandra Dijkstra Literary Agency (*US*)
Jim Donovan Literary (*US*)
Dystel & Goderich Literary Management (*US*)
Edwards Fuglewicz (*UK*)
Ethan Ellenberg Literary Agency (*US*)
Evatopia, Inc. (*US*)
Fairbank Literary Representation (*US*)
Farris Literary Agency, Inc. (*US*)
The Feldstein Agency (*UK*)
The Fielding Agency, LLC (*US*)
Fine Literary (*US*)
FinePrint Literary Management (*US*)
Folio Literary Management, LLC (*US*)
Fox Mason Ltd (*UK*)
Samuel French, Inc. (*US*)
Full Throttle Literary Agency (*US*)
The G Agency, LLC (*US*)
Don Gastwirth & Associates (*US*)
Gelfman Schneider Literary Agents, Inc. (*US*)
Goodman Associates (*US*)
Sanford J. Greenburger Associates, Inc (*US*)
Jill Grosjean Literary Agency (*US*)
The Mitchell J. Hamilburg Agency (*US*)
Hannigan Salky Getzler (HSG) Agency (*US*)
Joy Harris Literary Agency, Inc. (*US*)
Antony Harwood Limited (*UK*)
John Hawkins & Associates, Inc. (*US*)
Hudson Agency (*US*)
InkWell Management (*US*)
J de S Associates Inc (*US*)
The Joan Brandt Agency (*US*)

Nature

Regina Ryan Publishing Enterprises (*US*)
RLR Associates (*US*)
Rocking Chair Books (*UK*)
Linda Roghaar Literary Agency, Inc. (*US*)
Rita Rosenkranz Literary Agency (*US*)
Susan Schulman, A Literary Agency (*US*)
Scovil Galen Ghosh Literary Agency, Inc. (*US*)
Wendy Sherman Associates, Inc. (*US*)
Rosalie Siegel, International Literary Agency, Inc. (*US*)
Solow Literary Enterprises, Inc. (*US*)
The Spieler Agency (*US*)
Robin Straus Agency, Inc. (*US*)
Stuart Krichevsky Literary Agency, Inc. (*US*)
Talcott Notch Literary (*US*)
Patricia Teal Literary Agency (*US*)
Transatlantic Literary Agency, Inc. (*Can*)
Jane Turnbull (*UK*)
Venture Literary (*US*)
Veritas Literary Agency (*US*)
Watkins / Loomis Agency, Inc. (*US*)
Whispering Buffalo Literary Agency Ltd (*UK*)
The Zack Company, Inc (*US*)

New Age

Abbot Management (*US*)
Bleecker Street Associates, Inc. (*US*)
The Darley Anderson Agency (*UK*)
Dystel & Goderich Literary Management (*US*)
Ethan Ellenberg Literary Agency (*US*)
The Mitchell J. Hamilburg Agency (*US*)
Antony Harwood Limited (*UK*)
J de S Associates Inc (*US*)
Larsen Pomada Literary Agents (*US*)
Levine Greenberg Literary Agency, Inc. (*US*)
Ricia Mainhardt Agency (RMA) (*US*)
Martha Millard Literary Agency (*US*)
Northern Lights Literary Services (*US*)
Venture Literary (*US*)

Nonfiction

A & B Personal Management Ltd (*UK*)
A for Authors (*UK*)
A+B Works (*US*)
Dominick Abel Literary Agency, Inc (*US*)
Sheila Ableman Literary Agency (*UK*)
Adler & Robin Books, Inc (*US*)
The Agency (London) Ltd (*UK*)
The Agency Group, Ltd (*US*)
Agency for the Performing Arts (APA) (*US*)
The Ahearn Agency, Inc (*US*)
Aitken Alexander Associates (*UK*)
Alive Communications, Inc (*US*)
Miriam Altshuler Literary Agency (*US*)
Ambassador Speakers Bureau & Literary Agency (*US*)
The Ampersand Agency Ltd (*UK*)
Betsy Amster Literary Enterprises (*US*)
Darley Anderson Children's (*UK*)
Anthony Sheil in Association with Aitken Alexander Associates (*UK*)
AP Watt at United Agents LLP (*UK*)
Arcadia (*US*)
Artellus Limited (*UK*)
Movable Type Management (*US*)
Audrey A. Wolf Literary Agency (*US*)
The August Agency LLC (*US*)
Author Literary Agents (*UK*)
Author Rights Agency (*Ire*)
Ayesha Pande Literary (*US*)
Baldi Agency (*US*)
Barbara Hogenson Agency (*US*)
Bath Literary Agency (*UK*)
Lorella Belli Literary Agency (LBLA) (*UK*)
The Bent Agency (*US*)
Meredith Bernstein Literary Agency, Inc. (*US*)
Bidnick & Company (*US*)
Vicky Bijur Literary Agency (*US*)
David Black Literary Agency (*US*)
The Blair Partnership (*UK*)
Blake Friedmann Literary Agency Ltd (*UK*)
Bleecker Street Associates, Inc. (*US*)
Luigi Bonomi Associates Ltd (*UK*)
The Book Group (*US*)
BookEnds, LLC (*US*)
Books & Such Literary Agency (*US*)
Georges Borchardt, Inc. (*US*)
Brandt & Hochman Literary Agents, Inc. (*US*)
The Helen Brann Agency, Inc. (*US*)
Barbara Braun Associates, Inc. (*US*)
Rick Broadhead & Associates Literary Agency (*Can*)
Jenny Brown Associates (*UK*)
Marie Brown Associates, Inc. (*US*)
Tracy Brown Literary Agency (*US*)
Browne & Miller Literary Associates (*US*)
Felicity Bryan (*UK*)
Juliet Burton Literary Agency (*UK*)
Sheree Bykofsky Associates, Inc. (*US*)
Capel & Land Ltd (*UK*)
CardenWright Literary Agency (*UK*)
Carnicelli Literary Management (*US*)
Maria Carvainis Agency, Inc. (*US*)
Castiglia Literary Agency (*US*)
Chalberg & Sussman (*US*)
Jane Chelius Literary Agency, Inc. (*US*)
Elyse Cheney Literary Associates, LLC (*US*)
Linda Chester & Associates (*US*)
Teresa Chris Literary Agency Ltd (*UK*)
Cine/Lit Representation (*US*)
Mary Clemmey Literary Agency (*UK*)
Jonathan Clowes Ltd (*UK*)
Rosica Colin Ltd (*UK*)
Frances Collin Literary Agent (*US*)
Don Congdon Associates, Inc. (*US*)
Connor Literary Agency (*US*)
Conville & Walsh Ltd (*UK*)
Jane Conway-Gordon Ltd (*UK*)
The Cooke Agency (*Can*)
The Doe Coover Agency (*US*)
CowlesRyan Agency (*US*)
Crawford Literary Agency (*US*)
The Creative Rights Agency (*UK*)
Creative Authors Ltd (*UK*)
Rupert Crew Ltd (*UK*)
Crichton & Associates, Inc. (*US*)
The Croce Agency (*US*)
The Mary Cunnane Agency Pty Ltd (*Aus*)

Waterside Productions, Inc (*US*)
Watkins / Loomis Agency, Inc. (*US*)
Watson, Little Ltd (*UK*)
Waxman Leavell Literary Agency (*US*)
The Wendy Weil Agency, Inc. (*US*)
The Weingel-Fidel Agency (*US*)
Westwood Creative Artists (*Can*)
Whimsy Literary Agency, LLC (*US*)
Whispering Buffalo Literary Agency Ltd (*UK*)
Eve White: Literary Agent (*UK*)
Dinah Wiener Ltd (*UK*)
William Morris Endeavor (WME) London (*UK*)
Wolfson Literary Agency (*US*)
Writers House UK (*UK*)
Writers House, LLC. (*US*)
Writers' Representatives, LLC (*US*)
The Wylie Agency (UK) Ltd (*UK*)
Yates & Yates (*US*)
The Zack Company, Inc (*US*)

Philosophy

Abbot Management (*US*)
The Darley Anderson Agency (*UK*)
DeFiore and Company (*US*)
The Feldstein Agency (*UK*)
Fox Mason Ltd (*UK*)
Frances Goldin Literary Agency, Inc. (*US*)
Goodman Associates (*US*)
Graham Maw Christie Literary Agency (*UK*)
Greene & Heaton Ltd (*UK*)
Hardman & Swainson (*UK*)
Antony Harwood Limited (*UK*)
Literary & Creative Artists Inc. (*US*)
Pendle Hill Literary Agency (*UK*)
Venture Literary (*US*)
Writers' Representatives, LLC (*US*)

Photography

Abbot Management (*US*)
Barbara Braun Associates, Inc. (*US*)
Connor Literary Agency (*US*)
The Darley Anderson Agency (*UK*)
Diana Finch Literary Agency (*US*)
Jeanne Fredericks Literary Agency, Inc. (*US*)
Hannigan Salky Getzler (HSG) Agency (*US*)
Antony Harwood Limited (*UK*)
Martha Millard Literary Agency (*US*)
Pinder Lane & Garon-Brooke Associates Ltd (*US*)
RLR Associates (*US*)
Rita Rosenkranz Literary Agency (*US*)
Susan Schulman, A Literary Agency (*US*)
The Spieler Agency (*US*)
Venture Literary (*US*)

Poetry

Betsy Amster Literary Enterprises (*US*)
Bookseeker Agency (*UK*)
Eddison Pearson Ltd (*UK*)
The Mitchell J. Hamilburg Agency (*US*)
Johnson & Alcock (*UK*)
The Spieler Agency (*US*)
Tom Lee (*US*)
Writers' Representatives, LLC (*US*)

Politics

Abbot Management (*US*)
The Agency Group, Ltd (*US*)
Ambassador Speakers Bureau & Literary Agency (*US*)
AP Watt at United Agents LLP (*UK*)
Arcadia (*US*)
Audrey A. Wolf Literary Agency (*US*)
The August Agency LLC (*US*)
Vicky Bijur Literary Agency (*US*)
David Black Literary Agency (*US*)
Bleecker Street Associates, Inc. (*US*)
Barbara Braun Associates, Inc. (*US*)
Rick Broadhead & Associates Literary Agency (*Can*)
Elyse Cheney Literary Associates, LLC (*US*)
Don Congdon Associates, Inc. (*US*)
Connor Literary Agency (*US*)
The Cooke Agency (*Can*)
The Doe Coover Agency (*US*)
Crichton & Associates, Inc. (*US*)
The Darley Anderson Agency (*UK*)
David Luxton Associates (*UK*)
Caroline Davidson Literary Agency (*UK*)
Liza Dawson Associates (*US*)
DeFiore and Company (*US*)
Sandra Dijkstra Literary Agency (*US*)
Jim Donovan Literary (*US*)
Doyen Literary Services, Inc. (*US*)
Dunham Literary, Inc. (*US*)
Dystel & Goderich Literary Management (*US*)
Farris Literary Agency, Inc. (*US*)
The Feldstein Agency (*UK*)
The Fielding Agency, LLC (*US*)
Diana Finch Literary Agency (*US*)
Folio Literary Management, LLC (*US*)
Furniss Lawton (*UK*)
Gelfman Schneider Literary Agents, Inc. (*US*)
The Gernert Company (*US*)
Goodman Associates (*US*)
Sanford J. Greenburger Associates, Inc (*US*)
Greene & Heaton Ltd (*UK*)
The Mitchell J. Hamilburg Agency (*US*)
Hannigan Salky Getzler (HSG) Agency (*US*)
Antony Harwood Limited (*UK*)
John Hawkins & Associates, Inc. (*US*)
Heacock Hill Literary Agency, LLC (*US*)
Rupert Heath Literary Agency (*UK*)
hhb agency ltd (*UK*)
Hill Nadell Literary Agency (*US*)
Hornfischer Literary Management, L.P. (*US*)
Andrea Hurst Literary Management (*US*)
J de S Associates Inc (*US*)
Kilburn Literary Agency (*UK*)
Kneerim & Williams (*US*)
Laura Langlie, Literary Agent (*US*)
Larsen Pomada Literary Agents (*US*)
Levine Greenberg Literary Agency, Inc. (*US*)
Literary & Creative Artists Inc. (*US*)
Julia Lord Literary Management (*US*)
Andrew Lownie Literary Agency Ltd (*UK*)
Gina Maccoby Agency (*US*)
Carol Mann Agency (*US*)
Mendel Media Group, LLC (*US*)
Objective Entertainment (*US*)

Victoria Sanders & Associates LLC (*US*)
Susan Schulman, A Literary Agency (*US*)
Scovil Galen Ghosh Literary Agency, Inc. (*US*)
Sheil Land Associates Ltd (*UK*)
Wendy Sherman Associates, Inc. (*US*)
Rosalie Siegel, International Literary Agency, Inc. (*US*)
Jeffrey Simmons (*UK*)
Solow Literary Enterprises, Inc. (*US*)
Robin Straus Agency, Inc. (*US*)
The Stuart Agency (*US*)
SYLA – Susan Yearwood Literary Agency (*UK*)
Patricia Teal Literary Agency (*US*)
Tessler Literary Agency (*US*)
TriadaUS Literary Agency, Inc. (*US*)
2M Literary Agency Ltd (*US*)
Venture Literary (*US*)
Watson, Little Ltd (*UK*)
The Weingel-Fidel Agency (*US*)
Whimsy Literary Agency, LLC (*US*)
Writers House UK (*UK*)
Writers House, LLC. (*US*)

Radio

Abbot Management (*US*)
The Agency (London) Ltd (*UK*)
Berlin Associates (*UK*)
Blake Friedmann Literary Agency Ltd (*UK*)
Alan Brodie Representation Ltd (*UK*)
Capel & Land Ltd (*UK*)
Mary Clemmey Literary Agency (*UK*)
Jonathan Clowes Ltd (*UK*)
Rosica Colin Ltd (*UK*)
Curtis Brown Group Ltd (*UK*)
The Darley Anderson Agency (*UK*)
Film Rights Ltd in association with Laurence Fitch Ltd (*UK*)
Jill Foster Ltd (JFL) (*UK*)
Antony Harwood Limited (*UK*)
Valerie Hoskins Associates (*UK*)
Independent Talent Group Ltd (*UK*)
Andrew Mann Ltd (*UK*)
Marjacq Scripts Ltd (*UK*)
MBA Literary Agents Ltd (*UK*)
PBJ and JBJ Management (*UK*)
The Peters Fraser & Dunlop Group Ltd (PFD) (*UK*)
Rochelle Stevens & Co. (*UK*)
Sayle Screen Ltd (*UK*)
Sheil Land Associates Ltd (*UK*)
Elaine Steel (*UK*)
The Tennyson Agency (*UK*)
United Agents (*UK*)
Venture Literary (*US*)

Reference

Adler & Robin Books, Inc (*US*)
Baldi Agency (*US*)
BookEnds, LLC (*US*)
Sheree Bykofsky Associates, Inc. (*US*)
The Doe Coover Agency (*US*)
Caroline Davidson Literary Agency (*UK*)
Joëlle Delbourgo Associates, Inc. (*US*)
Jim Donovan Literary (*US*)
Fairbank Literary Representation (*US*)
FinePrint Literary Management (*US*)
Folio Literary Management, LLC (*US*)
Fox & Howard Literary Agency (*UK*)
Jeanne Fredericks Literary Agency, Inc. (*US*)
Graham Maw Christie Literary Agency (*UK*)
Sanford J. Greenburger Associates, Inc (*US*)
The Jeff Herman Agency, LLC (*US*)
Kate Hordern Literary Agency (*UK*)
Frances Kelly (*UK*)
Linda Konner Literary Agency (*US*)
Julia Lord Literary Management (*US*)
March Tenth, Inc. (*US*)
Denise Marcil Literary Agency, Inc. (*US*)
James Peter Associates, Inc. (*US*)
Regina Ryan Publishing Enterprises (*US*)
Signature Literary Agency (*US*)
Writers' Representatives, LLC (*US*)
The Zack Company, Inc (*US*)

Religious

Abbot Management (*US*)
Alive Communications, Inc (*US*)
Ambassador Speakers Bureau & Literary Agency (*US*)
Bleecker Street Associates, Inc. (*US*)
Books & Such Literary Agency (*US*)
Marie Brown Associates, Inc. (*US*)
Browne & Miller Literary Associates (*US*)
Kelvin C. Bulger and Associates (*US*)
Rosica Colin Ltd (*UK*)
Crichton & Associates, Inc. (*US*)
The Darley Anderson Agency (*UK*)
Liza Dawson Associates (*US*)
Sandra Dijkstra Literary Agency (*US*)
Dystel & Goderich Literary Management (*US*)
Eames Literary Services, LLC (*US*)
Anne Edelstein Literary Agency (*US*)
Farris Literary Agency, Inc. (*US*)
FinePrint Literary Management (*US*)
Folio Literary Management, LLC (*US*)
Foundry Literary + Media (*US*)
Grace Freedson's Publishing Network (*US*)
The Mitchell J. Hamilburg Agency (*US*)
Antony Harwood Limited (*UK*)
Hornfischer Literary Management, L.P. (*US*)
Andrea Hurst Literary Management (*US*)
Kilburn Literary Agency (*UK*)
Kneerim & Williams (*US*)
Larsen Pomada Literary Agents (*US*)
The Steve Laube Agency (*US*)
Levine Greenberg Literary Agency, Inc. (*US*)
Literary & Creative Artists Inc. (*US*)
The Literary Group (*US*)
Carol Mann Agency (*US*)
Mendel Media Group, LLC (*US*)
Fifi Oscard Agency, Inc. (*US*)
Kathi J. Paton Literary Agency (*US*)
The Poynor Group (*US*)
RLR Associates (*US*)
Linda Roghaar Literary Agency, Inc. (*US*)
Rita Rosenkranz Literary Agency (*US*)
Andy Ross Agency (*US*)
Schiavone Literary Agency (*US*)
Susan Schulman, A Literary Agency (*US*)

Scovil Galen Ghosh Literary Agency, Inc. (*US*)
The Seymour Agency (*US*)
The Stuart Agency (*US*)
Talent Source (*US*)
Tom Lee (*US*)
Venture Literary (*US*)
Whimsy Literary Agency, LLC (*US*)
Yates & Yates (*US*)
The Zack Company, Inc (*US*)

Romance

Abbot Management (*US*)
Abrams Artists Agency (*US*)
The Ahearn Agency, Inc (*US*)
Marcia Amsterdam Agency (*US*)
AP Watt at United Agents LLP (*UK*)
The Axelrod Agency (*US*)
Belcastro Agency (*US*)
The Bent Agency (*US*)
Meredith Bernstein Literary Agency, Inc. (*US*)
David Black Literary Agency (*US*)
Bleecker Street Associates, Inc. (*US*)
BookEnds, LLC (*US*)
Books & Such Literary Agency (*US*)
Jenny Brown Associates (*UK*)
The Characters Talent Agency (*Can*)
Elyse Cheney Literary Associates, LLC (*US*)
Rosica Colin Ltd (*UK*)
The Cooke Agency (*Can*)
Crawford Literary Agency (*US*)
Crichton & Associates, Inc. (*US*)
Richard Curtis Associates, Inc. (*US*)
The Darley Anderson Agency (*UK*)
Liza Dawson Associates (*US*)
DeFiore and Company (*US*)
Sandra Dijkstra Literary Agency (*US*)
Dorian Literary Agency (DLA) (*UK*)
Dystel & Goderich Literary Management (*US*)
Edwards Fuglewicz (*UK*)
Ethan Ellenberg Literary Agency (*US*)
Ann Elmo Agency, Inc. (*US*)
Evatopia, Inc. (*US*)
Farris Literary Agency, Inc. (*US*)
The Fielding Agency, LLC (*US*)
Fine Literary (*US*)
FinePrint Literary Management (*US*)
Folio Literary Management, LLC (*US*)
Sanford J. Greenburger Associates, Inc (*US*)
Greene & Heaton Ltd (*UK*)
Greyhaus Literary Agency (*US*)
Jill Grosjean Literary Agency (*US*)
The Mitchell J. Hamilburg Agency (*US*)
Antony Harwood Limited (*UK*)
Hopkins Literary Associates (*US*)
Hudson Agency (*US*)
Andrea Hurst Literary Management (*US*)
Kilburn Literary Agency (*UK*)
Harvey Klinger, Inc (*US*)
The Knight Agency (*US*)
Larsen Pomada Literary Agents (*US*)
Levine Greenberg Literary Agency, Inc. (*US*)
The Literary Group (*US*)
Andrew Lownie Literary Agency Ltd (*UK*)
Donald Maass Literary Agency (*US*)
Ricia Mainhardt Agency (RMA) (*US*)
Manus & Associates Literary Agency, Inc. (*US*)
McIntosh & Otis, Inc (*US*)
Martha Millard Literary Agency (*US*)
Nelson Literary Agency, LLC (*US*)
Northern Lights Literary Services (*US*)
P.S. Literary Agency (*Can*)
Pendle Hill Literary Agency (*UK*)
Pinder Lane & Garon-Brooke Associates Ltd (*US*)
The Poynor Group (*US*)
Prospect Agency (*US*)
Rebecca Friedman Literary Agency (*US*)
Richford Becklow Literary Agency (*UK*)
Rocking Chair Books (*UK*)
Jane Rotrosen Agency (*US*)
Schiavone Literary Agency (*US*)
The Seymour Agency (*US*)
Sheil Land Associates Ltd (*UK*)
Shelley Instone Literary Agency (*UK*)
Spectrum Literary Agency (*US*)
Spencerhill Associates (*US*)
Patricia Teal Literary Agency (*US*)
TriadaUS Literary Agency, Inc. (*US*)
Trident Media Group, LLC (*US*)
Waxman Leavell Literary Agency (*US*)
Whispering Buffalo Literary Agency Ltd (*UK*)
Wolfson Literary Agency (*US*)
The Zack Company, Inc (*US*)

Science

Abbot Management (*US*)
Sheila Ableman Literary Agency (*UK*)
Marcia Amsterdam Agency (*US*)
AP Watt at United Agents LLP (*UK*)
Arcadia (*US*)
Artellus Limited (*UK*)
Baldi Agency (*US*)
The Bent Agency (*US*)
Vicky Bijur Literary Agency (*US*)
David Black Literary Agency (*US*)
Bleecker Street Associates, Inc. (*US*)
Luigi Bonomi Associates Ltd (*UK*)
Brandt & Hochman Literary Agents, Inc. (*US*)
Rick Broadhead & Associates Literary Agency (*Can*)
Jenny Brown Associates (*UK*)
Browne & Miller Literary Associates (*US*)
Felicity Bryan (*UK*)
Carnicelli Literary Management (*US*)
Maria Carvainis Agency, Inc. (*US*)
Castiglia Literary Agency (*US*)
Chalberg & Sussman (*US*)
The Characters Talent Agency (*Can*)
Elyse Cheney Literary Associates, LLC (*US*)
Rosica Colin Ltd (*UK*)
Don Congdon Associates, Inc. (*US*)
Conville & Walsh Ltd (*UK*)
The Cooke Agency (*Can*)
The Doe Coover Agency (*US*)
CowlesRyan Agency (*US*)
The Croce Agency (*US*)
Curtis Brown Group Ltd (*UK*)
Richard Curtis Associates, Inc. (*US*)

Laura Dail Literary Agency (*US*)
The Darley Anderson Agency (*UK*)
Caroline Davidson Literary Agency (*UK*)
Liza Dawson Associates (*US*)
The Jennifer DeChiara Literary Agency (*US*)
DeFiore and Company (*US*)
Joëlle Delbourgo Associates, Inc. (*US*)
Diane Banks Associates Literary Agency (*UK*)
Sandra Dijkstra Literary Agency (*US*)
Janis A. Donnaud & Associates, Inc. (*US*)
Doyen Literary Services, Inc. (*US*)
Dunham Literary, Inc. (*US*)
Dystel & Goderich Literary Management (*US*)
Ethan Ellenberg Literary Agency (*US*)
Ann Elmo Agency, Inc. (*US*)
Fairbank Literary Representation (*US*)
The Fielding Agency, LLC (*US*)
Diana Finch Literary Agency (*US*)
Fine Literary (*US*)
FinePrint Literary Management (*US*)
Fletcher & Company (*US*)
Folio Literary Management, LLC (*US*)
Foundry Literary + Media (*US*)
Jeanne Fredericks Literary Agency, Inc. (*US*)
Grace Freedson's Publishing Network (*US*)
Sarah Jane Freymann Literary Agency (*US*)
Furniss Lawton (*UK*)
Gelfman Schneider Literary Agents, Inc. (*US*)
The Gernert Company (*US*)
Frances Goldin Literary Agency, Inc. (*US*)
Goodman Associates (*US*)
Graham Maw Christie Literary Agency (*UK*)
Sanford J. Greenburger Associates, Inc (*US*)
Greene & Heaton Ltd (*UK*)
The Mitchell J. Hamilburg Agency (*US*)
Hannigan Salky Getzler (HSG) Agency (*US*)
Hardman & Swainson (*UK*)
Antony Harwood Limited (*UK*)
John Hawkins & Associates, Inc. (*US*)
Heacock Hill Literary Agency, LLC (*US*)
Rupert Heath Literary Agency (*UK*)
Hill Nadell Literary Agency (*US*)
Hornfischer Literary Management, L.P. (*US*)
Andrea Hurst Literary Management (*US*)
Jabberwocky Literary Agency (*US*)
Johnson & Alcock (*UK*)
Kilburn Literary Agency (*UK*)
Harvey Klinger, Inc (*US*)
Kneerim & Williams (*US*)
Linda Konner Literary Agency (*US*)
Bert P. Krages (*US*)
The LA Literary Agency (*US*)
Larsen Pomada Literary Agents (*US*)
Levine Greenberg Literary Agency, Inc. (*US*)
The Literary Group (*US*)
Sterling Lord Literistic, Inc. (*US*)
Julia Lord Literary Management (*US*)
Lowenstein Associates, Inc. (*US*)
Andrew Lownie Literary Agency Ltd (*UK*)
The Jennifer Lyons Literary Agency, LLC (*US*)
Manus & Associates Literary Agency, Inc. (*US*)
Anne McDermid & Associates Ltd (*Can*)
Mendel Media Group, LLC (*US*)
Fifi Oscard Agency, Inc. (*US*)
P.S. Literary Agency (*Can*)
The Richard Parks Agency (*US*)
Kathi J. Paton Literary Agency (*US*)
Jonathan Pegg Literary Agency (*UK*)
L. Perkins Associates (*US*)
Prospect Agency (*US*)
Susan Rabiner, Literary Agent, Inc. (*US*)
Regina Ryan Publishing Enterprises (*US*)
RLR Associates (*US*)
Rita Rosenkranz Literary Agency (*US*)
Ross Yoon Agency (*US*)
Andy Ross Agency (*US*)
The Rudy Agency (*US*)
The Sagalyn Literary Agency (*US*)
Schiavone Literary Agency (*US*)
Susan Schulman, A Literary Agency (*US*)
The Science Factory (*UK*)
Scovil Galen Ghosh Literary Agency, Inc. (*US*)
Sheil Land Associates Ltd (*UK*)
Rosalie Siegel, International Literary Agency, Inc. (*US*)
Signature Literary Agency (*US*)
Solow Literary Enterprises, Inc. (*US*)
The Spieler Agency (*US*)
Robin Straus Agency, Inc. (*US*)
Stuart Krichevsky Literary Agency, Inc. (*US*)
The Stuart Agency (*US*)
Talcott Notch Literary (*US*)
Tessler Literary Agency (*US*)
Trident Media Group, LLC (*US*)
2M Literary Agency Ltd (*US*)
Venture Literary (*US*)
Veritas Literary Agency (*US*)
Watson, Little Ltd (*UK*)
The Wendy Weil Agency, Inc. (*US*)
The Weingel-Fidel Agency (*US*)
Westwood Creative Artists (*Can*)
Dinah Wiener Ltd (*UK*)
Writers House UK (*UK*)
Writers House, LLC. (*US*)
Writers' Representatives, LLC (*US*)
The Zack Company, Inc (*US*)

Sci-Fi

Abbot Management (*US*)
Abela Literature (*Can*)
The Ampersand Agency Ltd (*UK*)
Anubis Literary Agency (*UK*)
Artellus Limited (*UK*)
Author Rights Agency (*Ire*)
Belcastro Agency (*US*)
The Bent Agency (*US*)
BookEnds, LLC (*US*)
The Bright Literary Academy (*UK*)
Castiglia Literary Agency (*US*)
Frances Collin Literary Agent (*US*)
The Cooke Agency (*Can*)
Richard Curtis Associates, Inc. (*US*)
Laura Dail Literary Agency (*US*)
The Darley Anderson Agency (*UK*)
Liza Dawson Associates (*US*)
Joëlle Delbourgo Associates, Inc. (*US*)

Diamond Kahn and Woods (DKW) Literary Agency Ltd (*UK*)
Sandra Dijkstra Literary Agency (*US*)
Dorian Literary Agency (DLA) (*UK*)
Dunham Literary, Inc. (*US*)
Dystel & Goderich Literary Management (*US*)
Ethan Ellenberg Literary Agency (*US*)
FinePrint Literary Management (*US*)
Folio Literary Management, LLC (*US*)
Foundry Literary + Media (*US*)
Fox Mason Ltd (*UK*)
The Gernert Company (*US*)
Sanford J. Greenburger Associates, Inc (*US*)
Greene & Heaton Ltd (*UK*)
The Mitchell J. Hamilburg Agency (*US*)
Antony Harwood Limited (*UK*)
John Hawkins & Associates, Inc. (*US*)
Rupert Heath Literary Agency (*UK*)
Andrea Hurst Literary Management (*US*)
Jabberwocky Literary Agency (*US*)
Johnson & Alcock (*UK*)
Harvey Klinger, Inc (*US*)
The Knight Agency (*US*)
Lowenstein Associates, Inc. (*US*)
Andrew Lownie Literary Agency Ltd (*UK*)
Donald Maass Literary Agency (*US*)
Ricia Mainhardt Agency (RMA) (*US*)
Marjacq Scripts Ltd (*UK*)
Anne McDermid & Associates Ltd (*Can*)
McIntosh & Otis, Inc (*US*)
Martha Millard Literary Agency (*US*)
Nelson Literary Agency, LLC (*US*)
Objective Entertainment (*US*)
Pendle Hill Literary Agency (*UK*)
L. Perkins Associates (*US*)
Pinder Lane & Garon-Brooke Associates Ltd (*US*)
Rebecca Pratt Literary Group (*US*)
Linn Prentis Literary (*US*)
Prospect Agency (*US*)
Rebecca Friedman Literary Agency (*US*)
Richford Becklow Literary Agency (*UK*)
Schiavone Literary Agency (*US*)
The Seymour Agency (*US*)
Sheil Land Associates Ltd (*UK*)
Shelley Instone Literary Agency (*UK*)
Valerie Smith, Literary Agent (*US*)
Spectrum Literary Agency (*US*)
Steph Roundsmith Agent and Editor (*UK*)
Sternig & Byrne Literary Agency (*US*)
Stuart Krichevsky Literary Agency, Inc. (*US*)
Talcott Notch Literary (*US*)
Tom Lee (*US*)
TriadaUS Literary Agency, Inc. (*US*)
Veritas Literary Agency (*US*)
Waxman Leavell Literary Agency (*US*)
Whispering Buffalo Literary Agency Ltd (*UK*)
Writers House UK (*UK*)
Writers House, LLC. (*US*)
The Zack Company, Inc (*US*)
Zeno Agency Ltd (*UK*)

Scripts

A & B Personal Management Ltd (*UK*)
Abbot Management (*US*)
Abrams Artists Agency (*US*)
The Agency (London) Ltd (*UK*)
Agency for the Performing Arts (APA) (*US*)
Aimee Entertainment Agency (*US*)
Marcia Amsterdam Agency (*US*)
Anonymous Content (*US*)
AP Watt at United Agents LLP (*UK*)
Author Literary Agents (*UK*)
Barbara Hogenson Agency (*US*)
Berlin Associates (*UK*)
Blake Friedmann Literary Agency Ltd (*UK*)
Alan Brodie Representation Ltd (*UK*)
Marcus Bryan & Associates Inc. (*US*)
Kelvin C. Bulger and Associates (*US*)
CardenWright Literary Agency (*UK*)
The Characters Talent Agency (*Can*)
Mary Clemmey Literary Agency (*UK*)
Jonathan Clowes Ltd (*UK*)
Rosica Colin Ltd (*UK*)
The Collective (*US*)
Creative Trust, Inc. (*US*)
Criterion Group, Inc. (*US*)
Curtis Brown Group Ltd (*UK*)
Felix de Wolfe (*UK*)
Energy Entertainment (*US*)
Evatopia, Inc. (*US*)
Farris Literary Agency, Inc. (*US*)
Film Rights Ltd in association with Laurence Fitch Ltd (*UK*)
Jill Foster Ltd (JFL) (*UK*)
Samuel French, Inc. (*US*)
Full Throttle Literary Agency (*US*)
Noel Gay (*UK*)
Eric Glass Ltd (*UK*)
David Higham Associates Ltd (*UK*)
Valerie Hoskins Associates (*UK*)
Amanda Howard Associates Ltd (*UK*)
Hudson Agency (*US*)
Independent Talent Group Ltd (*UK*)
Janet Fillingham Associates (*UK*)
Michelle Kass Associates (*UK*)
Ken Sherman & Associates (*US*)
Ki Agency Ltd (*UK*)
Kilburn Literary Agency (*UK*)
Knight Hall Agency (*UK*)
Lenhoff & Lenhoff (*US*)
Macnaughton Lord Representation (*UK*)
Madeleine Milburn Literary Agency (*UK*)
Marjacq Scripts Ltd (*UK*)
The Marton Agency, Inc. (*US*)
MBA Literary Agents Ltd (*UK*)
William Morris Endeavor Entertainment (*US*)
Objective Entertainment (*US*)
Fifi Oscard Agency, Inc. (*US*)
PBJ and JBJ Management (*UK*)
Pendle Hill Literary Agency (*UK*)
Peregrine Whittlesey Agency (*US*)
The Peters Fraser & Dunlop Group Ltd (PFD) (*UK*)
The Lisa Richards Agency (*Ire*)
Rochelle Stevens & Co. (*UK*)
Sayle Screen Ltd (*UK*)

Susan Schulman, A Literary Agency (*US*)
Linda Seifert Management (*UK*)
The Seven Bridges Group (*US*)
Sheil Land Associates Ltd (*UK*)
Elaine Steel (*UK*)
Talent Source (*US*)
The Tennyson Agency (*UK*)
Tom Lee (*US*)
United Agents (*UK*)
Cecily Ware Literary Agents (*UK*)

Self-Help

Abbot Management (*US*)
Adler & Robin Books, Inc (*US*)
The Agency Group, Ltd (*US*)
Alive Communications, Inc (*US*)
Miriam Altshuler Literary Agency (*US*)
Ambassador Speakers Bureau & Literary Agency (*US*)
Betsy Amster Literary Enterprises (*US*)
Arcadia (*US*)
Audrey A. Wolf Literary Agency (*US*)
Vicky Bijur Literary Agency (*US*)
David Black Literary Agency (*US*)
Bleecker Street Associates, Inc. (*US*)
The Bright Literary Academy (*UK*)
Rick Broadhead & Associates Literary Agency (*Can*)
Browne & Miller Literary Associates (*US*)
Sheree Bykofsky Associates, Inc. (*US*)
Chalberg & Sussman (*US*)
Connor Literary Agency (*US*)
CowlesRyan Agency (*US*)
Crawford Literary Agency (*US*)
The Darley Anderson Agency (*UK*)
Liza Dawson Associates (*US*)
The Jennifer DeChiara Literary Agency (*US*)
Diane Banks Associates Literary Agency (*UK*)
Sandra Dijkstra Literary Agency (*US*)
Doyen Literary Services, Inc. (*US*)
Farris Literary Agency, Inc. (*US*)
The Fielding Agency, LLC (*US*)
Diana Finch Literary Agency (*US*)
Fine Literary (*US*)
FinePrint Literary Management (*US*)
Folio Literary Management, LLC (*US*)
Fox & Howard Literary Agency (*UK*)
Jeanne Fredericks Literary Agency, Inc. (*US*)
Grace Freedson's Publishing Network (*US*)
Sarah Jane Freymann Literary Agency (*US*)
Graham Maw Christie Literary Agency (*UK*)
Sanford J. Greenburger Associates, Inc (*US*)
The Mitchell J. Hamilburg Agency (*US*)
Antony Harwood Limited (*UK*)
The Jeff Herman Agency, LLC (*US*)
Hornfischer Literary Management, L.P. (*US*)
Andrea Hurst Literary Management (*US*)
InkWell Management (*US*)
J de S Associates Inc (*US*)
Johnson & Alcock (*UK*)
Frances Kelly (*UK*)
Harvey Klinger, Inc (*US*)
The Knight Agency (*US*)
Linda Konner Literary Agency (*US*)
Elaine Koster Literary Agency LLC (*US*)
Larsen Pomada Literary Agents (*US*)
Levine Greenberg Literary Agency, Inc. (*US*)
Sterling Lord Literistic, Inc. (*US*)
Julia Lord Literary Management (*US*)
Andrew Lownie Literary Agency Ltd (*UK*)
Gina Maccoby Agency (*US*)
Ricia Mainhardt Agency (RMA) (*US*)
Carol Mann Agency (*US*)
Manus & Associates Literary Agency, Inc. (*US*)
Denise Marcil Literary Agency, Inc. (*US*)
The Martell Agency (*US*)
Martin Literary Management (*US*)
MBA Literary Agents Ltd (*UK*)
Margret McBride Literary Agency (*US*)
McIntosh & Otis, Inc (*US*)
Mendel Media Group, LLC (*US*)
Martha Millard Literary Agency (*US*)
The Miller Agency (*US*)
Northern Lights Literary Services (*US*)
The Richard Parks Agency (*US*)
Pinder Lane & Garon-Brooke Associates Ltd (*US*)
Rebecca Pratt Literary Group (*US*)
The Lisa Richards Agency (*Ire*)
Richford Becklow Literary Agency (*UK*)
RLR Associates (*US*)
B.J. Robbins Literary Agency (*US*)
Linda Roghaar Literary Agency, Inc. (*US*)
Rita Rosenkranz Literary Agency (*US*)
Susan Schulman, A Literary Agency (*US*)
Sheil Land Associates Ltd (*UK*)
Wendy Sherman Associates, Inc. (*US*)
Robert Smith Literary Agency Ltd (*UK*)
Valerie Smith, Literary Agent (*US*)
Patricia Teal Literary Agency (*US*)
TriadaUS Literary Agency, Inc. (*US*)
Venture Literary (*US*)
Veritas Literary Agency (*US*)
Watson, Little Ltd (*UK*)
Whimsy Literary Agency, LLC (*US*)
Whispering Buffalo Literary Agency Ltd (*UK*)
Writers House UK (*UK*)
Writers House, LLC. (*US*)
Writers' Representatives, LLC (*US*)
The Zack Company, Inc (*US*)

Short Stories

Abbot Management (*US*)
The Ahearn Agency, Inc (*US*)
Alive Communications, Inc (*US*)
The Bright Literary Academy (*UK*)
DeFiore and Company (*US*)
Sandra Dijkstra Literary Agency (*US*)
The Fielding Agency, LLC (*US*)
Full Throttle Literary Agency (*US*)
The Mitchell J. Hamilburg Agency (*US*)
Joy Harris Literary Agency, Inc. (*US*)
Antony Harwood Limited (*UK*)
John Hawkins & Associates, Inc. (*US*)
Kilburn Literary Agency (*UK*)
Martha Millard Literary Agency (*US*)
Pendle Hill Literary Agency (*UK*)
RLR Associates (*US*)

The Seven Bridges Group (*US*)
Rosalie Siegel, International Literary Agency, Inc. (*US*)
Philip G. Spitzer Literary Agency, Inc. (*US*)
Tom Lee (*US*)
Venture Literary (*US*)
Watkins / Loomis Agency, Inc. (*US*)

Sociology

Abbot Management (*US*)
Miriam Altshuler Literary Agency (*US*)
Betsy Amster Literary Enterprises (*US*)
The August Agency LLC (*US*)
Vicky Bijur Literary Agency (*US*)
Bleecker Street Associates, Inc. (*US*)
Barbara Braun Associates, Inc. (*US*)
Browne & Miller Literary Associates (*US*)
The Doe Coover Agency (*US*)
The Darley Anderson Agency (*UK*)
Liza Dawson Associates (*US*)
The Jennifer DeChiara Literary Agency (*US*)
DeFiore and Company (*US*)
Diamond Kahn and Woods (DKW) Literary Agency Ltd (*UK*)
Sandra Dijkstra Literary Agency (*US*)
Doyen Literary Services, Inc. (*US*)
The Feldstein Agency (*UK*)
The Fielding Agency, LLC (*US*)
Furniss Lawton (*UK*)
The Gernert Company (*US*)
Frances Goldin Literary Agency, Inc. (*US*)
Goodman Associates (*US*)
Sanford J. Greenburger Associates, Inc (*US*)
The Mitchell J. Hamilburg Agency (*US*)
Hannigan Salky Getzler (HSG) Agency (*US*)
Antony Harwood Limited (*UK*)
Kate Hordern Literary Agency (*UK*)
Hornfischer Literary Management, L.P. (*US*)
J de S Associates Inc (*US*)
Kilburn Literary Agency (*UK*)
Kneerim & Williams (*US*)
Larsen Pomada Literary Agents (*US*)
Levine Greenberg Literary Agency, Inc. (*US*)
Lowenstein Associates, Inc. (*US*)
Carol Mann Agency (*US*)
The Richard Parks Agency (*US*)
Ann Rittenberg Literary Agency (*US*)
RLR Associates (*US*)
B.J. Robbins Literary Agency (*US*)
Victoria Sanders & Associates LLC (*US*)
Susan Schulman, A Literary Agency (*US*)
Scovil Galen Ghosh Literary Agency, Inc. (*US*)
Denise Shannon Literary Agency, Inc. (*US*)
The Spieler Agency (*US*)
Venture Literary (*US*)
Waterside Productions, Inc (*US*)
The Weingel-Fidel Agency (*US*)

Spiritual

Abbot Management (*US*)
Alive Communications, Inc (*US*)
Miriam Altshuler Literary Agency (*US*)
Arcadia (*US*)
Baldi Agency (*US*)
David Black Literary Agency (*US*)
Bleecker Street Associates, Inc. (*US*)
Sheree Bykofsky Associates, Inc. (*US*)
Carnicelli Literary Management (*US*)
The Cooke Agency (*Can*)
CowlesRyan Agency (*US*)
The Darley Anderson Agency (*UK*)
Liza Dawson Associates (*US*)
Dunham Literary, Inc. (*US*)
Dystel & Goderich Literary Management (*US*)
Ethan Ellenberg Literary Agency (*US*)
Farris Literary Agency, Inc. (*US*)
Fine Literary (*US*)
FinePrint Literary Management (*US*)
Folio Literary Management, LLC (*US*)
Fox & Howard Literary Agency (*UK*)
Sarah Jane Freymann Literary Agency (*US*)
The Mitchell J. Hamilburg Agency (*US*)
Joy Harris Literary Agency, Inc. (*US*)
Antony Harwood Limited (*UK*)
Heacock Hill Literary Agency, LLC (*US*)
The Jeff Herman Agency, LLC (*US*)
Kilburn Literary Agency (*UK*)
Harvey Klinger, Inc (*US*)
Elaine Koster Literary Agency LLC (*US*)
Levine Greenberg Literary Agency, Inc. (*US*)
Literary & Creative Artists Inc. (*US*)
Lowenstein Associates, Inc. (*US*)
Ricia Mainhardt Agency (RMA) (*US*)
Carol Mann Agency (*US*)
Denise Marcil Literary Agency, Inc. (*US*)
McIntosh & Otis, Inc (*US*)
Mendel Media Group, LLC (*US*)
Fifi Oscard Agency, Inc. (*US*)
Pendle Hill Literary Agency (*UK*)
Pinder Lane & Garon-Brooke Associates Ltd (*US*)
Regina Ryan Publishing Enterprises (*US*)
Schiavone Literary Agency (*US*)
Susan Schulman, A Literary Agency (*US*)
Wendy Sherman Associates, Inc. (*US*)
The Spieler Agency (*US*)
Venture Literary (*US*)
Waterside Productions, Inc (*US*)
Whimsy Literary Agency, LLC (*US*)
The Zack Company, Inc (*US*)

Sport

Abbot Management (*US*)
The Agency Group, Ltd (*US*)
Alive Communications, Inc (*US*)
AP Watt at United Agents LLP (*UK*)
Audrey A. Wolf Literary Agency (*US*)
David Black Literary Agency (*US*)
Bleecker Street Associates, Inc. (*US*)
Jenny Brown Associates (*UK*)
Tracy Brown Literary Agency (*US*)
Browne & Miller Literary Associates (*US*)
Carnicelli Literary Management (*US*)
The Characters Talent Agency (*Can*)
Elyse Cheney Literary Associates, LLC (*US*)
Rosica Colin Ltd (*UK*)
Conville & Walsh Ltd (*UK*)
The Doe Coover Agency (*US*)
The Creative Rights Agency (*UK*)

The Darley Anderson Agency (*UK*)
David Luxton Associates (*UK*)
The Jennifer DeChiara Literary Agency (*US*)
Sandra Dijkstra Literary Agency (*US*)
Janis A. Donnaud & Associates, Inc. (*US*)
Jim Donovan Literary (*US*)
Evatopia, Inc. (*US*)
Fairbank Literary Representation (*US*)
Farris Literary Agency, Inc. (*US*)
The Feldstein Agency (*UK*)
The Fielding Agency, LLC (*US*)
Diana Finch Literary Agency (*US*)
Fine Literary (*US*)
Fletcher & Company (*US*)
Folio Literary Management, LLC (*US*)
Foundry Literary + Media (*US*)
Fox Mason Ltd (*UK*)
Jeanne Fredericks Literary Agency, Inc. (*US*)
Grace Freedson's Publishing Network (*US*)
Sarah Jane Freymann Literary Agency (*US*)
The G Agency, LLC (*US*)
The Gernert Company (*US*)
Frances Goldin Literary Agency, Inc. (*US*)
Goodman Associates (*US*)
Sanford J. Greenburger Associates, Inc (*US*)
The Mitchell J. Hamilburg Agency (*US*)
Antony Harwood Limited (*UK*)
A M Heath & Company Limited, Author's Agents (*UK*)
Hornfischer Literary Management, L.P. (*US*)
J de S Associates Inc (*US*)
Johnson & Alcock (*UK*)
Harvey Klinger, Inc (*US*)
Kneerim & Williams (*US*)
The LA Literary Agency (*US*)
Larsen Pomada Literary Agents (*US*)
Levine Greenberg Literary Agency, Inc. (*US*)
The Literary Group (*US*)
Julia Lord Literary Management (*US*)
Andrew Lownie Literary Agency Ltd (*UK*)
The Jennifer Lyons Literary Agency, LLC (*US*)
Ricia Mainhardt Agency (RMA) (*US*)
Carol Mann Agency (*US*)
Marjacq Scripts Ltd (*UK*)
McIntosh & Otis, Inc (*US*)
The Miller Agency (*US*)
Mulcahy Associates (*UK*)
Objective Entertainment (*US*)
Fifi Oscard Agency, Inc. (*US*)
P.S. Literary Agency (*Can*)
Kathi J. Paton Literary Agency (*US*)
John Pawsey (*UK*)
James Peter Associates, Inc. (*US*)
Pinder Lane & Garon-Brooke Associates Ltd (*US*)
Susan Rabiner, Literary Agent, Inc. (*US*)
Regina Ryan Publishing Enterprises (*US*)
The Lisa Richards Agency (*Ire*)
RLR Associates (*US*)
B.J. Robbins Literary Agency (*US*)
Robert Dudley Agency (*UK*)
Rita Rosenkranz Literary Agency (*US*)
Schiavone Literary Agency (*US*)
Susan Schulman, A Literary Agency (*US*)
The Seven Bridges Group (*US*)
Wendy Sherman Associates, Inc. (*US*)
Jeffrey Simmons (*UK*)
SLW Literary Agency (*US*)
Philip G. Spitzer Literary Agency, Inc. (*US*)
The Stuart Agency (*US*)
TriadaUS Literary Agency, Inc. (*US*)
Trident Media Group, LLC (*US*)
2M Literary Agency Ltd (*US*)
Venture Literary (*US*)
Waterside Productions, Inc (*US*)
Watson, Little Ltd (*UK*)
Waxman Leavell Literary Agency (*US*)
Yates & Yates (*US*)
The Zack Company, Inc (*US*)

Suspense

Abbot Management (*US*)
Abela Literature (*Can*)
Abrams Artists Agency (*US*)
The Ahearn Agency, Inc (*US*)
Alive Communications, Inc (*US*)
Belcastro Agency (*US*)
The Bent Agency (*US*)
BookEnds, LLC (*US*)
Maria Carvainis Agency, Inc. (*US*)
Chalberg & Sussman (*US*)
Elyse Cheney Literary Associates, LLC (*US*)
The Chudney Agency (*US*)
Rosica Colin Ltd (*UK*)
Conville & Walsh Ltd (*UK*)
Coombs Moylett Literary Agency (*UK*)
Crawford Literary Agency (*US*)
Crichton & Associates, Inc. (*US*)
The Croce Agency (*US*)
Curtis Brown Group Ltd (*UK*)
Darhansoff & Verrill Literary Agents (*US*)
The Darley Anderson Agency (*UK*)
Liza Dawson Associates (*US*)
The Jennifer DeChiara Literary Agency (*US*)
Diamond Kahn and Woods (DKW) Literary Agency Ltd (*UK*)
Jim Donovan Literary (*US*)
Dystel & Goderich Literary Management (*US*)
Evatopia, Inc. (*US*)
Farris Literary Agency, Inc. (*US*)
Fine Literary (*US*)
FinePrint Literary Management (*US*)
Folio Literary Management, LLC (*US*)
Fox Mason Ltd (*UK*)
Full Throttle Literary Agency (*US*)
Furniss Lawton (*UK*)
Gelfman Schneider Literary Agents, Inc. (*US*)
Goodman Associates (*US*)
Greyhaus Literary Agency (*US*)
Jill Grosjean Literary Agency (*US*)
The Mitchell J. Hamilburg Agency (*US*)
Joy Harris Literary Agency, Inc. (*US*)
Antony Harwood Limited (*UK*)
A M Heath & Company Limited, Author's Agents (*UK*)
J de S Associates Inc (*US*)
The Joan Brandt Agency (*US*)

Johnson & Alcock (*UK*)
Harvey Klinger, Inc (*US*)
The Knight Agency (*US*)
Barbara S. Kouts, Literary Agent (*US*)
Laura Langlie, Literary Agent (*US*)
Larsen Pomada Literary Agents (*US*)
Levine Greenberg Literary Agency, Inc. (*US*)
The Literary Group (*US*)
Andrew Lownie Literary Agency Ltd (*UK*)
Donald Maass Literary Agency (*US*)
Madeleine Milburn Literary Agency (*UK*)
Ricia Mainhardt Agency (RMA) (*US*)
Manus & Associates Literary Agency, Inc. (*US*)
Denise Marcil Literary Agency, Inc. (*US*)
The Martell Agency (*US*)
McIntosh & Otis, Inc (*US*)
Martha Millard Literary Agency (*US*)
Northern Lights Literary Services (*US*)
P.S. Literary Agency (*Can*)
Pendle Hill Literary Agency (*UK*)
The Poynor Group (*US*)
Aaron M. Priest Literary Agency (*US*)
Prospect Agency (*US*)
Rebecca Friedman Literary Agency (*US*)
B.J. Robbins Literary Agency (*US*)
Jane Rotrosen Agency (*US*)
Victoria Sanders & Associates LLC (*US*)
Schiavone Literary Agency (*US*)
Susan Schulman, A Literary Agency (*US*)
The Seven Bridges Group (*US*)
The Seymour Agency (*US*)
Wendy Sherman Associates, Inc. (*US*)
Valerie Smith, Literary Agent (*US*)
Spectrum Literary Agency (*US*)
Philip G. Spitzer Literary Agency, Inc. (*US*)
Sternig & Byrne Literary Agency (*US*)
Talcott Notch Literary (*US*)
Trident Media Group, LLC (*US*)
Venture Literary (*US*)
Wolfson Literary Agency (*US*)
The Zack Company, Inc (*US*)

Technology

Abbot Management (*US*)
Adler & Robin Books, Inc (*US*)
AP Watt at United Agents LLP (*UK*)
Arcadia (*US*)
The August Agency LLC (*US*)
Baldi Agency (*US*)
Bleecker Street Associates, Inc. (*US*)
Browne & Miller Literary Associates (*US*)
Maria Carvainis Agency, Inc. (*US*)
Don Congdon Associates, Inc. (*US*)
The Doe Coover Agency (*US*)
Richard Curtis Associates, Inc. (*US*)
Laura Dail Literary Agency (*US*)
The Darley Anderson Agency (*UK*)
DeFiore and Company (*US*)
Doyen Literary Services, Inc. (*US*)
Dunham Literary, Inc. (*US*)
Dystel & Goderich Literary Management (*US*)
The Fielding Agency, LLC (*US*)
Diana Finch Literary Agency (*US*)
Fine Literary (*US*)
FinePrint Literary Management (*US*)
Folio Literary Management, LLC (*US*)
Grace Freedson's Publishing Network (*US*)
The G Agency, LLC (*US*)
Frances Goldin Literary Agency, Inc. (*US*)
Goodman Associates (*US*)
Antony Harwood Limited (*UK*)
John Hawkins & Associates, Inc. (*US*)
Hornfischer Literary Management, L.P. (*US*)
Harvey Klinger, Inc (*US*)
Kneerim & Williams (*US*)
Levine Greenberg Literary Agency, Inc. (*US*)
Julia Lord Literary Management (*US*)
Andrew Lownie Literary Agency Ltd (*UK*)
Fifi Oscard Agency, Inc. (*US*)
The Richard Parks Agency (*US*)
Kathi J. Paton Literary Agency (*US*)
Robert Dudley Agency (*UK*)
Rita Rosenkranz Literary Agency (*US*)
The Rudy Agency (*US*)
Susan Schulman, A Literary Agency (*US*)
The Science Factory (*UK*)
Signature Literary Agency (*US*)
Stuart Krichevsky Literary Agency, Inc. (*US*)
Talcott Notch Literary (*US*)
Venture Literary (*US*)
Waterside Productions, Inc (*US*)
Watkins / Loomis Agency, Inc. (*US*)
Watson, Little Ltd (*UK*)
The Weingel-Fidel Agency (*US*)
The Zack Company, Inc (*US*)

Theatre

A & B Personal Management Ltd (*UK*)
Abbot Management (*US*)
The Agency (London) Ltd (*UK*)
Agency for the Performing Arts (APA) (*US*)
Barbara Hogenson Agency (*US*)
Berlin Associates (*UK*)
Alan Brodie Representation Ltd (*UK*)
CardenWright Literary Agency (*UK*)
Mary Clemmey Literary Agency (*UK*)
Jonathan Clowes Ltd (*UK*)
Rosica Colin Ltd (*UK*)
Don Congdon Associates, Inc. (*US*)
Criterion Group, Inc. (*US*)
Curtis Brown Group Ltd (*UK*)
The Darley Anderson Agency (*UK*)
Liza Dawson Associates (*US*)
The Jennifer DeChiara Literary Agency (*US*)
Felix de Wolfe (*UK*)
Doyen Literary Services, Inc. (*US*)
Film Rights Ltd in association with Laurence Fitch Ltd (*UK*)
Diana Finch Literary Agency (*US*)
Fine Literary (*US*)
Jill Foster Ltd (JFL) (*UK*)
Samuel French, Inc. (*US*)
Eric Glass Ltd (*UK*)
Goodman Associates (*US*)
Antony Harwood Limited (*UK*)
David Higham Associates Ltd (*UK*)
Independent Talent Group Ltd (*UK*)
Janet Fillingham Associates (*UK*)

Harvey Klinger, Inc (*US*)
The Knight Agency (*US*)
Elaine Koster Literary Agency LLC (*US*)
Barbara S. Kouts, Literary Agent (*US*)
Laura Langlie, Literary Agent (*US*)
Larsen Pomada Literary Agents (*US*)
Levine Greenberg Literary Agency, Inc. (*US*)
The Literary Group (*US*)
Julia Lord Literary Management (*US*)
Lowenstein Associates, Inc. (*US*)
Andrew Lownie Literary Agency Ltd (*UK*)
The Jennifer Lyons Literary Agency, LLC (*US*)
Gina Maccoby Agency (*US*)
Madeleine Milburn Literary Agency (*UK*)
Ricia Mainhardt Agency (RMA) (*US*)
Manus & Associates Literary Agency, Inc. (*US*)
Denise Marcil Literary Agency, Inc. (*US*)
Marjacq Scripts Ltd (*UK*)
The Martell Agency (*US*)
McIntosh & Otis, Inc (*US*)
Mendel Media Group, LLC (*US*)
Martha Millard Literary Agency (*US*)
Mulcahy Associates (*UK*)
Objective Entertainment (*US*)
P.S. Literary Agency (*Can*)
Jonathan Pegg Literary Agency (*UK*)
Pendle Hill Literary Agency (*UK*)
L. Perkins Associates (*US*)
Pinder Lane & Garon-Brooke Associates Ltd (*US*)
Rebecca Pratt Literary Group (*US*)
Aaron M. Priest Literary Agency (*US*)
Prospect Agency (*US*)
Rebecca Friedman Literary Agency (*US*)
Redhammer (*UK*)
RLR Associates (*US*)
B.J. Robbins Literary Agency (*US*)
Rocking Chair Books (*UK*)
Jane Rotrosen Agency (*US*)
Victoria Sanders & Associates LLC (*US*)
Schiavone Literary Agency (*US*)
Susan Schulman, A Literary Agency (*US*)
The Seymour Agency (*US*)
Sheil Land Associates Ltd (*UK*)
Shelley Instone Literary Agency (*UK*)
Signature Literary Agency (*US*)
Spencerhill Associates (*US*)
The Spieler Agency (*US*)
Philip G. Spitzer Literary Agency, Inc. (*US*)
SYLA – Susan Yearwood Literary Agency (*UK*)
Talcott Notch Literary (*US*)
Tom Lee (*US*)
TriadaUS Literary Agency, Inc. (*US*)
Trident Media Group, LLC (*US*)
Venture Literary (*US*)
Veritas Literary Agency (*US*)
Waxman Leavell Literary Agency (*US*)
The Wendy Weil Agency, Inc. (*US*)
Westwood Creative Artists (*Can*)
Whispering Buffalo Literary Agency Ltd (*UK*)
William Morris Endeavor (WME) London (*UK*)
Wolfson Literary Agency (*US*)
Writers' Representatives, LLC (*US*)
Yates & Yates (*US*)
The Zack Company, Inc (*US*)
Zeno Agency Ltd (*UK*)

Translations

Abbot Management (*US*)
AP Watt at United Agents LLP (*UK*)
The Darley Anderson Agency (*UK*)
The Fielding Agency, LLC (*US*)
Diana Finch Literary Agency (*US*)
Don Gastwirth & Associates (*US*)
Goodman Associates (*US*)
Joy Harris Literary Agency, Inc. (*US*)
Antony Harwood Limited (*UK*)
Intercontinental Literary Agency (*UK*)
J de S Associates Inc (*US*)
Andrew Lownie Literary Agency Ltd (*UK*)
The Marton Agency, Inc. (*US*)
Aaron M. Priest Literary Agency (*US*)
RLR Associates (*US*)
Rocking Chair Books (*UK*)
Victoria Sanders & Associates LLC (*US*)
Venture Literary (*US*)
The Zack Company, Inc (*US*)

Travel

Abbot Management (*US*)
Betsy Amster Literary Enterprises (*US*)
AP Watt at United Agents LLP (*UK*)
Baldi Agency (*US*)
Blake Friedmann Literary Agency Ltd (*UK*)
Tracy Brown Literary Agency (*US*)
Cine/Lit Representation (*US*)
Rosica Colin Ltd (*UK*)
Frances Collin Literary Agent (*US*)
Don Congdon Associates, Inc. (*US*)
Conville & Walsh Ltd (*UK*)
The Croce Agency (*US*)
The Darley Anderson Agency (*UK*)
The Jennifer DeChiara Literary Agency (*US*)
Sandra Dijkstra Literary Agency (*US*)
Janis A. Donnaud & Associates, Inc. (*US*)
Dunham Literary, Inc. (*US*)
Farris Literary Agency, Inc. (*US*)
The Feldstein Agency (*UK*)
Fine Literary (*US*)
FinePrint Literary Management (*US*)
Fletcher & Company (*US*)
Foundry Literary + Media (*US*)
Fox Mason Ltd (*UK*)
Jeanne Fredericks Literary Agency, Inc. (*US*)
Sarah Jane Freymann Literary Agency (*US*)
Goodman Associates (*US*)
Greene & Heaton Ltd (*UK*)
Jill Grosjean Literary Agency (*US*)
The Mitchell J. Hamilburg Agency (*US*)
Hannigan Salky Getzler (HSG) Agency (*US*)
Antony Harwood Limited (*UK*)
John Hawkins & Associates, Inc. (*US*)
hhb agency ltd (*UK*)
Larsen Pomada Literary Agents (*US*)
Levine Greenberg Literary Agency, Inc. (*US*)
Marjacq Scripts Ltd (*UK*)
Duncan McAra (*UK*)
Anne McDermid & Associates Ltd (*Can*)

McIntosh & Otis, Inc (*US*)
The Miller Agency (*US*)
MNLA (Maggie Noach Literary Agency) (*UK*)
The Richard Parks Agency (*US*)
James Peter Associates, Inc. (*US*)
Pinder Lane & Garon-Brooke Associates Ltd (*US*)
Regina Ryan Publishing Enterprises (*US*)
RLR Associates (*US*)
B.J. Robbins Literary Agency (*US*)
Robert Dudley Agency (*UK*)
Rocking Chair Books (*UK*)
Schiavone Literary Agency (*US*)
Susan Schulman, A Literary Agency (*US*)
The Science Factory (*UK*)
The Seven Bridges Group (*US*)
Sheil Land Associates Ltd (*UK*)
Sinclair-Stevenson (*UK*)
The Spieler Agency (*US*)
Philip G. Spitzer Literary Agency, Inc. (*US*)
Tessler Literary Agency (*US*)
Transatlantic Literary Agency, Inc. (*Can*)
TriadaUS Literary Agency, Inc. (*US*)
Venture Literary (*US*)
Ed Victor Ltd (*UK*)
Watkins / Loomis Agency, Inc. (*US*)

TV

A & B Personal Management Ltd (*UK*)
Abbot Management (*US*)
Sheila Ableman Literary Agency (*UK*)
Abrams Artists Agency (*US*)
The Agency (London) Ltd (*UK*)
Agency for the Performing Arts (APA) (*US*)
Marcia Amsterdam Agency (*US*)
Anonymous Content (*US*)
AP Watt at United Agents LLP (*UK*)
Berlin Associates (*UK*)
Blake Friedmann Literary Agency Ltd (*UK*)
Luigi Bonomi Associates Ltd (*UK*)
The Bright Literary Academy (*UK*)
Alan Brodie Representation Ltd (*UK*)
Kelvin C. Bulger and Associates (*US*)
Capel & Land Ltd (*UK*)
The Characters Talent Agency (*Can*)
Mary Clemmey Literary Agency (*UK*)
Jonathan Clowes Ltd (*UK*)
Rosica Colin Ltd (*UK*)
The Collective (*US*)
Curtis Brown Group Ltd (*UK*)
The Darley Anderson Agency (*UK*)
Felix de Wolfe (*UK*)
Energy Entertainment (*US*)
Film Rights Ltd in association with Laurence Fitch Ltd (*UK*)
Jill Foster Ltd (JFL) (*UK*)
Eric Glass Ltd (*UK*)
Antony Harwood Limited (*UK*)
hhb agency ltd (*UK*)
David Higham Associates Ltd (*UK*)
Valerie Hoskins Associates (*UK*)
Hudson Agency (*US*)
Independent Talent Group Ltd (*UK*)
Janet Fillingham Associates (*UK*)
Michelle Kass Associates (*UK*)
Ken Sherman & Associates (*US*)
Ki Agency Ltd (*UK*)
Knight Hall Agency (*UK*)
Macnaughton Lord Representation (*UK*)
Madeleine Milburn Literary Agency (*UK*)
Andrew Mann Ltd (*UK*)
Marjacq Scripts Ltd (*UK*)
MBA Literary Agents Ltd (*UK*)
William Morris Endeavor Entertainment (*US*)
Objective Entertainment (*US*)
PBJ and JBJ Management (*UK*)
Peregrine Whittlesey Agency (*US*)
James Peter Associates, Inc. (*US*)
The Peters Fraser & Dunlop Group Ltd (PFD) (*UK*)
Rochelle Stevens & Co. (*UK*)
Sayle Screen Ltd (*UK*)
Linda Seifert Management (*UK*)
The Seven Bridges Group (*US*)
Sheil Land Associates Ltd (*UK*)
Elaine Steel (*UK*)
The Tennyson Agency (*UK*)
Jane Turnbull (*UK*)
United Agents (*UK*)
Venture Literary (*US*)
Cecily Ware Literary Agents (*UK*)
The Zack Company, Inc (*US*)

Westerns

Abbot Management (*US*)
Abela Literature (*Can*)
Alive Communications, Inc (*US*)
The Characters Talent Agency (*Can*)
Richard Curtis Associates, Inc. (*US*)
The Darley Anderson Agency (*UK*)
Full Throttle Literary Agency (*US*)
Antony Harwood Limited (*UK*)
Hudson Agency (*US*)
Andrea Hurst Literary Management (*US*)
J de S Associates Inc (*US*)
Andrew Lownie Literary Agency Ltd (*UK*)
Donald Maass Literary Agency (*US*)
Ricia Mainhardt Agency (RMA) (*US*)
Pinder Lane & Garon-Brooke Associates Ltd (*US*)
Prospect Agency (*US*)
The Seven Bridges Group (*US*)

Women's Interests

A+B Works (*US*)
Abbot Management (*US*)
The Ahearn Agency, Inc (*US*)
Alive Communications, Inc (*US*)
Ambassador Speakers Bureau & Literary Agency (*US*)
The Ampersand Agency Ltd (*UK*)
Betsy Amster Literary Enterprises (*US*)
Arcadia (*US*)
The August Agency LLC (*US*)
Author Rights Agency (*Ire*)
The Axelrod Agency (*US*)
Ayesha Pande Literary (*US*)
Belcastro Agency (*US*)
The Bent Agency (*US*)

David Black Literary Agency (*US*)
Blake Friedmann Literary Agency Ltd (*UK*)
Bleecker Street Associates, Inc. (*US*)
Luigi Bonomi Associates Ltd (*UK*)
BookEnds, LLC (*US*)
Books & Such Literary Agency (*US*)
Barbara Braun Associates, Inc. (*US*)
The Bright Literary Academy (*UK*)
Jenny Brown Associates (*UK*)
Marie Brown Associates, Inc. (*US*)
Tracy Brown Literary Agency (*US*)
Browne & Miller Literary Associates (*US*)
Juliet Burton Literary Agency (*UK*)
Sheree Bykofsky Associates, Inc. (*US*)
Maria Carvainis Agency, Inc. (*US*)
Chalberg & Sussman (*US*)
The Characters Talent Agency (*Can*)
Elyse Cheney Literary Associates, LLC (*US*)
Teresa Chris Literary Agency Ltd (*UK*)
Rosica Colin Ltd (*UK*)
Frances Collin Literary Agent (*US*)
Don Congdon Associates, Inc. (*US*)
Connor Literary Agency (*US*)
Conville & Walsh Ltd (*UK*)
Coombs Moylett Literary Agency (*UK*)
Crawford Literary Agency (*US*)
Creative Authors Ltd (*UK*)
Crichton & Associates, Inc. (*US*)
The Croce Agency (*US*)
Laura Dail Literary Agency (*US*)
The Darley Anderson Agency (*UK*)
Liza Dawson Associates (*US*)
The Jennifer DeChiara Literary Agency (*US*)
Joëlle Delbourgo Associates, Inc. (*US*)
Diane Banks Associates Literary Agency (*UK*)
Sandra Dijkstra Literary Agency (*US*)
Janis A. Donnaud & Associates, Inc. (*US*)
Jim Donovan Literary (*US*)
Dorian Literary Agency (DLA) (*UK*)
Doyen Literary Services, Inc. (*US*)
Dunham Literary, Inc. (*US*)
Dystel & Goderich Literary Management (*US*)
Ethan Ellenberg Literary Agency (*US*)
Ann Elmo Agency, Inc. (*US*)
Evatopia, Inc. (*US*)
Farris Literary Agency, Inc. (*US*)
The Feldstein Agency (*UK*)
The Fielding Agency, LLC (*US*)
Diana Finch Literary Agency (*US*)
Fine Literary (*US*)
FinePrint Literary Management (*US*)
Folio Literary Management, LLC (*US*)
Foundry Literary + Media (*US*)
Jeanne Fredericks Literary Agency, Inc. (*US*)
Sarah Jane Freymann Literary Agency (*US*)
Furniss Lawton (*UK*)
Gelfman Schneider Literary Agents, Inc. (*US*)
Goodman Associates (*US*)
Sanford J. Greenburger Associates, Inc (*US*)
Greyhaus Literary Agency (*US*)
Jill Grosjean Literary Agency (*US*)
The Mitchell J. Hamilburg Agency (*US*)
Hannigan Salky Getzler (HSG) Agency (*US*)
Hardman & Swainson (*UK*)
Joy Harris Literary Agency, Inc. (*US*)
Antony Harwood Limited (*UK*)
John Hawkins & Associates, Inc. (*US*)
A M Heath & Company Limited, Author's Agents (*UK*)
Rupert Heath Literary Agency (*UK*)
hhb agency ltd (*UK*)
Hill Nadell Literary Agency (*US*)
Hopkins Literary Associates (*US*)
Kate Hordern Literary Agency (*UK*)
Andrea Hurst Literary Management (*US*)
The Joan Brandt Agency (*US*)
Johnson & Alcock (*UK*)
Kilburn Literary Agency (*UK*)
Harvey Klinger, Inc (*US*)
Kneerim & Williams (*US*)
The Knight Agency (*US*)
Linda Konner Literary Agency (*US*)
Elaine Koster Literary Agency LLC (*US*)
Barbara S. Kouts, Literary Agent (*US*)
Laura Langlie, Literary Agent (*US*)
Larsen Pomada Literary Agents (*US*)
Levine Greenberg Literary Agency, Inc. (*US*)
The Literary Group (*US*)
Sterling Lord Literistic, Inc. (*US*)
Julia Lord Literary Management (*US*)
Lowenstein Associates, Inc. (*US*)
Donald Maass Literary Agency (*US*)
Gina Maccoby Agency (*US*)
Madeleine Milburn Literary Agency (*UK*)
Ricia Mainhardt Agency (RMA) (*US*)
Carol Mann Agency (*US*)
Manus & Associates Literary Agency, Inc. (*US*)
Denise Marcil Literary Agency, Inc. (*US*)
Marjacq Scripts Ltd (*UK*)
The Martell Agency (*US*)
Martin Literary Management (*US*)
McIntosh & Otis, Inc (*US*)
Mendel Media Group, LLC (*US*)
Martha Millard Literary Agency (*US*)
Mulcahy Associates (*UK*)
Judith Murdoch Literary Agency (*UK*)
Nelson Literary Agency, LLC (*US*)
Northern Lights Literary Services (*US*)
Objective Entertainment (*US*)
Fifi Oscard Agency, Inc. (*US*)
P.S. Literary Agency (*Can*)
The Richard Parks Agency (*US*)
Pinder Lane & Garon-Brooke Associates Ltd (*US*)
Linn Prentis Literary (*US*)
Aaron M. Priest Literary Agency (*US*)
Prospect Agency (*US*)
Rebecca Friedman Literary Agency (*US*)
Regina Ryan Publishing Enterprises (*US*)
Richford Becklow Literary Agency (*UK*)
Ann Rittenberg Literary Agency (*US*)
RLR Associates (*US*)
B.J. Robbins Literary Agency (*US*)
Rocking Chair Books (*UK*)
Linda Roghaar Literary Agency, Inc. (*US*)
Rita Rosenkranz Literary Agency (*US*)

US Publishers

For the most up-to-date listings of these and hundreds of other publishers, visit http://www.firstwriter.com/publishers

*To claim your **free** access to the site, please see the back of this book.*

Abrams ComicArts

115 West 18th Street, 6th Floor
New York, NY 10011
Tel: +1 (212) 206-7715
Fax: +1 (212) 519-1210
Email: abrams@abramsbooks.com
Website: http://www.abramsbooks.com

Publishes: Fiction; Nonfiction; *Markets:* Adult; Children's

Contact: Abrams ComicArts Editorial

Publishes graphic novels, illustrated books, and nonfiction books about comics and comic history. Send submissions by post with SASE.

Ahsahta Press

Department of English
Boise State University
1910 University Drive
Boise, ID 83725-1525
Tel: +1 (208) 426-3134
Email: ahsahta@boisestate.edu
Website: http://ahsahtapress.org

Publishes: Poetry; *Markets:* Adult; *Treatments:* Literary

Contact: Janet Holmes

Submit poetry manuscripts between 50 and 100 pages long via online submissions system. Accepts open submissions during March each year only. Charges $5 per submission. Also runs poetry competitions at other times of the year.

Alexander Hamilton Institute

Business Management Daily
PO Box 9070
McLean, VA 22102-0070
Tel: +1 (800) 543-2055
Fax: +1 (703) 905-8040
Email: Editor@BusinessManagementDaily.com
Website: http://www.legalworkplace.com

Publishes: Nonfiction; *Areas:* Business; Legal; *Markets:* Professional

Publishes material for executives, upper management, and HR managers.

Alice James Books

238 Main St.
Farmington, ME 04936
Tel: +1 (207) 778-7071
Fax: +1 (207) 778-7766
Email: info@alicejamesbooks.org
Website: http://alicejamesbooks.org

Publishes: Poetry; *Markets:* Adult

Poetry press accepting submissions through its various competitions only. Competitions include large cash prizes and reasonable entry fees.

Alondra Press

4119 Wildacres Drive
Houston, TX 77072
Email: lark@alondrapress.com
Website: http://www.alondrapress.com

Publishes: Fiction; Nonfiction; *Areas:* Anthropology; Archaeology; Historical; Philosophy; Psychology; Translations; *Markets:* Adult; *Treatments:* Literary

Contact: Fiction: "Editor"; Nonfiction: Armando Benitez, Solomon Tager, or Henry Hollenbaugh

Send query by email, with synopsis up to 300 words and sample or full manuscript. See website for full guidelines.

Amadeus Press

33 Plymouth Street, Suite 302
Montclair, NJ 07042
Email: jcerullo@halleonard.com
Website: http://www.amadeuspress.com

Publishes: Nonfiction; *Areas:* Music; *Markets:* Adult

Contact: John Cerullo

Publishes books on classical music and opera. Send query with outline or table of contents, one or two sample chapters, sample illustrations, and your schedule for completion. Prefers contact early in the project, but cannot guarantee a response. See website for full details.

Amakella Publishing

Arlington, VA
Email: info@amakella.com
Website: http://www.amakella.com

Publishes: Fiction; Nonfiction; *Areas:* Adventure; Anthropology; Biography; Business; Culture; Current Affairs; Historical; Hobbies; How-to; Leisure; Lifestyle; Literature; Media; Men's Interests; Nature; Psychology; Romance; Self-Help; Short Stories; Sociology; Spiritual; Travel; Women's Interests; *Markets:* Academic; Family; Professional; *Treatments:* Commercial; Contemporary; Literary; Mainstream; Niche; Popular; Positive; Progressive; Serious

An independent publisher currently particularly interested in publishing books in areas such as social sciences, international development, environmental conservation, and current affairs.

American Press

60 State Street #700
Boston, MA 02109
Tel: +1 (617) 247- 0022
Email: americanpress@flash.net
Website: http://www.americanpresspublishers.com

Publishes: Nonfiction; *Areas:* Anthropology; Architecture; Arts; Business; Drama; Finance; Health; Historical; Legal; Music; Philosophy; Politics; Psychology; Religious; Science; Sociology; Sport; Technology; Theatre; *Markets:* Academic; Professional

Welcomes proposals for academic and professional titles in all subject areas. Accepts textbooks, handbooks, laboratory manuals, workbooks, study guides, journal research, reference books, DVDs, CDs and software programs and materials for college level courses. See website for more details.

AMG Publishers

6815 Shallowford Road
Chattanooga, TN 37421
Tel: +1 (423) 894-6060 (ext. 275)
Fax: +1 (423) 894-9511
Email: ricks@amgpublishers.com
Website: http://www.amgpublishers.com

Publishes: Fiction; Nonfiction; Reference; *Areas:* Fantasy; Lifestyle; Politics; Religious; Spiritual; *Markets:* Adult

Contact: Rick Steele

Publishes biblically oriented books including: Biblical Reference, Applied Theology and Apologetics, Christian

Ministry, Bible Study Books in the Following God series format, Christian Living, Women/Men/Family Issues, Single/Divorce Issues, Contemporary Issues, (unique) Devotionals, Inspirational, Prayer, and Gift books. Introducing young adult fiction titles. Send query letter by email or by post, including proposed page count, brief description of the proposed book, market info, and author details. See website for full guidelines.

Amira Press

Email: submissions@amirapress.com
Website: http://www.amirapress.com

Publishes: Fiction; *Areas:* Erotic; Fantasy; Historical; Horror; Romance; Sci-Fi; Suspense; Travel; Westerns; *Markets:* Adult; *Treatments:* Contemporary

Contact: Y. Lynn; Dahlia Rose

Small ebook publisher of erotic romance. Send complete ms by email. See website for more details.

Anaiah Press, LLC

7780 49th St. N #129
Pinellas Park, FL 33781
Email: submissions@anaiahpress.com
Website: http://www.anaiahpress.com

Publishes: Fiction; Nonfiction; *Areas:* Adventure; Drama; Fantasy; Historical; Horror; Humour; Lifestyle; Literature; Mystery; New Age; Religious; Romance; Science; Sci-Fi; Spiritual; Suspense; Thrillers; Women's Interests; *Markets:* Adult; Children's; Family; Youth; *Treatments:* Contemporary; Literary; Mainstream; Positive; Traditional

Contact: Eden Plantz

A Christian digital-first publishing house dedicated to presenting quality faith-based fiction and nonfiction books to the public. Our goal is to provide our authors with the close-knit, hands-on experience of working with a small press, while making sure they don't have to sacrifice quality editing, cover art, and marketing.

Our first books will be released in digital formats beginning in Summer 2014.

Currently, we do not accept proposals for works yet to be written. Please, only query us if your manuscript is complete.

As a Christian press, we publish books with a strong inspirational theme and/ or a message of faith. We do not accept manuscripts with the following:

-- Anti-Christian propaganda/ themes
-- Gratuitous sex
-- Messages of religious or social intolerance

We do respond personally to every query received. Please allow 6-8 weeks for a response.

Simultaneous submissions are fine, but we do ask that out of professional courtesy, you let us know if you receive an offer from another publisher or agent.

Ankerwycke

American Bar Association
321 North Clark Street
Chicago, IL 60654
Tel: +1 (312) 988-5000
Website: http://www.ababooks.org

Publishes: Fiction; Nonfiction; *Areas:* Crime; Legal; *Markets:* Adult; *Treatments:* Popular

Publishes books that bring law to the general public, including legal fiction, true crime, popular legal histories, handbooks, and guides.

Arcade Publishing

307 West 36th Street, 11th Floor
New York, NY 10018
Tel: +1 (212) 643-6816
Fax: +1 (212) 643-6819
Email:
arcadesubmissions@skyhorsepublishing.com
Website: http://www.arcadepub.com

Publishes: Fiction; Nonfiction; *Areas:* Adventure; Arts; Autobiography; Business; Cookery; Current Affairs; Historical;

Military; Nature; Science; Travel; *Markets:* Adult; *Treatments:* Literary

Send query by email with a brief cover letter; one-to-two page synopsis; annotated chapter outline; market analysis, including competitive research; 1-2 sample chapters; author bio, including list of all previous publishing credits.

Arch Street Press

1429 South 9th Street
Philadelphia, PA 19147
Tel: +1 (877) 732-ARCH
Email: contact@archstreetpress.org
Website: http://archstreetpress.org

Publishes: Fiction; Nonfiction; *Areas:* Arts; Autobiography; Biography; Business; Criticism; Culture; Finance; Historical; Legal; Literature; Music; Nature; Philosophy; Politics; Sociology; Spiritual; Translations; Women's Interests; *Markets:* Adult; *Treatments:* Contemporary; Literary

Independent nonprofit publisher dedicated to the collaborative work of creative visionaries, social entrepreneurs and leading scholars worldwide. Send query with SASE, outline, and three sample chapters.

Arrow Publications, LLC

20411 Sawgrass Drive
Montgomery Village, MD 20886
Tel: +1 (301) 299-9422
Fax: +1 (301) 632-8477
Email: arrow_info@arrowpub.com
Website: http://www.arrowpub.com

Publishes: Fiction; *Areas:* Adventure; Crime; Fantasy; Humour; Mystery; Romance; Suspense; Women's Interests; *Markets:* Adult

Contact: Tom King; Maryan Gibson

Publishes romance fiction and selective nonfiction, including women's interests. Also considers supernatural, mystery, crime and other genres if the story has a strong romance element. Send query by email with outline, word count, brief description, one chapter (usually the first), and promotional plan. See website for full guidelines.

The Backwater Press

3502 North 52nd Street
Omaha, NE 68104-3506
Tel: +1 (402) 451-4052
Email: thebackwaterspress@gmail.com
Website: http://thebackwaterspress.com

Publishes: Poetry; *Markets:* Adult; *Treatments:* Literary

Publishes poetry. Currently closed to general submissions, and is accepting work only through its poetry competition, for which there is a reading fee of $25. Submit online via website.

Bailiwick Press

309 East Mulberry Street
Fort Collins, Colorado 80524
Tel: +1 (970) 672-4878
Fax: +1 (970) 672-4731
Email: aldozelnick@gmail.com
Website: http://www.bailiwickpress.com

Publishes: Fiction; *Areas:* Humour; *Markets:* Children's; Youth

Publishes smart, funny, and layered writing for children and young adult. Looking for hysterically funny. Illustrated fiction is desired but not required. Approach through online form, where you will be required to submit the funniest part of your book, and display a knowledge of the publisher's existing work.

Barbarian Books

PO Box 170881
Boise, ID 83717-0881
Email: submissions@barbarianbooks.com
Website: http://www.barbarianbooks.com

Publishes: Fiction; *Areas:* Adventure; Crime; Fantasy; Historical; Humour; Mystery; Romance; Sci-Fi; Suspense; Westerns; *Markets:* Adult; *Treatments:* Contemporary; Mainstream

Contact: Conda Douglas; Kathy McIntosh

Ebook publisher of genre fiction, including Science Fiction, Western, Mystery/Crime, Horror, Romance, and cross-genre. Submit online through submission form on website, or by email. See website for full details.

Barron's Educational Series, Inc.

250 Wireless Blvd
Hauppauge, NY 11788
Tel: +1 (800) 645-3476
Email: waynebarr@barronseduc.com
Website: http://www.barronseduc.com

Publishes: Fiction; Nonfiction; *Areas:* Arts; Beauty and Fashion; Business; Cookery; Crafts; Finance; Health; Hobbies; Legal; Lifestyle; New Age; Photography; Sport; Travel; *Markets:* Adult; Children's; Youth

Contact: Wayne Barr, Acquisitions Editor

Particularly interested in children and young adult fiction and nonfiction books, foreign language learning books, New Age books, cookbooks, business and financial advice books, parenting advice books, art instruction books, sports, fashion, crafts, and study guides. No poetry. Send query by email or by post with SASE (if return of materials required). Only queries accepted by email. See website for full guidelines.

BelleBooks

PO Box 300921
Memphis, TN 38130
Tel: +1 (901) 344-9024
Fax: +1 (901) 344-9068
Email: query@BelleBooks.com
Website: http://www.bellebooks.com

Publishes: Fiction; *Areas:* Fantasy; Historical; Horror; Mystery; Romance; Sci-Fi; Short Stories; Suspense; Thrillers; Women's Interests; *Markets:* Adult; Children's; Youth

Publishes women's fiction, cozy mysteries, well-researched civil war fiction, young adult fiction, urban fantasy and horror, young adult fantasy fiction, and fantasy. Send query by email with brief synopsis and credentials/credits. See website for full guidelines.

Bellevue Literary Press

Department of Medicine
NYU School of Medicine
550 First Avenue, OBV A612
New York, NY 10016
Tel: +1 (212) 263-7802
Email: blpsubmissions@gmail.com
Website: http://blpress.org

Publishes: Fiction; Nonfiction; *Markets:* Adult; *Treatments:* Literary

Contact: Erika Goldman, Publisher and Editorial Director

Publisher of literary fiction and narrative nonfiction. No poetry, single short stories, plays, screenplays, or self-help/instructional books. Send submissions by email. For fiction submissions, attach complete ms. For nonfiction, send complete ms or proposal. See website for full guidelines.

Bethany House Publishers

Baker Publishing Group
6030 East Fulton Road
Ada, MI 49301
Tel: +1 (616) 676-9185
Fax: +1 (616) 676-9573
Website: http://bakerpublishinggroup.com/bethanyhouse

Publishes: Fiction; Nonfiction; *Areas:* Fantasy; Historical; Mystery; Religious; Romance; Suspense; Women's Interests; *Markets:* Adult; Children's; Youth; *Treatments:* Contemporary; Literary

Publishes Christian fiction and nonfiction. No poetry, memoirs, picture books, Western, End-Times, Spiritual Warfare, or Chick-Lit. No unsolicited manuscripts, proposals or queries by mail, telephone, email, or fax. Approach through a literary agent, at a conference, or through an online manuscript service (see website for more details).

Bick Publishing House

16 Marion Road

Branford, CT 06405
Tel: +1 (203) 208-5253
Fax: +1 (203) 208-5253
Email: bickpubhse@aol.com
Website: http://www.bickpubhouse.com

Publishes: Fiction; Nonfiction; *Areas:* Arts; Health; Philosophy; Psychology; Science; Sci-Fi; Self-Help; *Markets:* Adult; Youth

Publishes Life Sciences and Self-Help Books for Teens; Young Adult: Psychology, Science and Philosophy; Science Fiction for Teens; Adult Health and Recovery; Meditation; Living with Disabilities; Wildlife Rehabilitation. See website for submission guidelines. No submissions by email.

Bilingual Review Press

Hispanic Research Center
Arizona State University
PO Box 875303
Tempe, AZ 85287-5303
Email: brp@asu.edu
Website: http://bilingualpress.clas.asu.edu/

Publishes: Fiction; Nonfiction; Poetry; Scripts; *Areas:* Short Stories; Translations; *Markets:* Academic; Adult; *Treatments:* Literary; Serious

Contact: Gary Francisco Keller

Publishes hardcover and paperback originals and reprints on US Hispanic themes, including creative literature (novels, short story collections, poetry, drama, translations), scholarly monographs and edited compilations, and other nonfiction. Particularly interested in Chicano, Puerto Rican, Cuban American, and other US Hispanic themes with strong and serious literary qualities and distinctive and intellectually important topics. Send query by post with SASE and sample chapter or sample poems, plot summary / TOC, marketing info and brief bio. Accepts simultaneous submissions, but no electronic submissions. See website for full guidelines.

Black Lawrence Press

Email: editors@blacklawrencepress.com
Website:
http://blacklawrence.homestead.com

Publishes: Fiction; Nonfiction; Poetry; *Areas:* Autobiography; Biography; Culture; Literature; Short Stories; Translations; *Markets:* Adult; *Treatments:* Contemporary; Literary

Idependent press specialising in books of contemporary literature and creative nonfiction, including novels, memoirs, short story collections, poetry, biographies, and cultural studies. Also publishes occasional translations from German and French. Submit online via website submission system.

Black Lyon Publishing, LLC

PO Box 567
Baker City, OR 97814
Email: Queries@BlackLyonPublishing.com
Website:
http://www.blacklyonpublishing.com

Publishes: Fiction; Nonfiction; *Areas:* Adventure; Historical; Romance; Self-Help; Women's Interests; *Markets:* Adult; *Treatments:* Contemporary; Literary

Small, independent publishing house, publishing mainly romance (contemporary, paranormal, historical, inspirational, adventure, literary, and novellas), as well as self-help. Send query by email. See website for full submission guidelines.

Black Ocean

Email: carrie@blackocean.org
Website: http://www.blackocean.org

Publishes: Poetry; Translations; *Markets:* Adult; *Treatments:* Literary

Contact: Carrie O. Adams (Poetry Editor)

Publishes new poetry, and out-of-print or translated texts. Reading period runs from June 1 to June 30 each year. During reading period, submit via link on website.

Blurbeo

509 7th St
Sultan, WA 98294
Email: alleywolf@gmail.com
Website: http://www.blurbeo.com

Publishes: Fiction; *Areas:* Adventure; Anthropology; Crime; Drama; Entertainment; Horror; Humour; Lifestyle; Literature; Men's Interests; Military; Mystery; Religious; Romance; Sci-Fi; Short Stories; Spiritual; Suspense; Thrillers; Women's Interests; *Markets:* Adult; Children's; Family; Youth; *Treatments:* Mainstream

Contact: Chris Vaughn

A small whiteboard video company that assists authors with promoting their books through the power of video. Founded by an author for authors, Blurbeo is now accepting manuscripts for publication

We are currently seeking works of fiction in the following genres:

Holiday themed short fiction
Thriller/Action Adventure
Horror
Romance short fiction
YA fiction, short and long

Writers interested in submitting work should do so via email and should follow the directions closely. Please put your name and the word "submission" in the email's subject line. Your email should include a brief letter of interest and author bio. Please attached the first 2,000 words or the first 2 chapters of your story.

Please allow up to 3 weeks for a response as there are multiple submissions being sent in. We will attempt to respond to all who contact us.

Why publish with us? Simple! We not only offer a 20% royalty to our authors but we also include our deluxe video promotion package absolutely FREE. That way you can get a jump start on promoting your book!
20% Royalties on sales of digital and print copies
10% Royalties on all merchandise sales (T-shirts, poster, etc)
FREE deluxe video package
120 second promotional whiteboard video
Promotion on Blurbeo, Youtube, Vimeo, and more
Internet radio advertising services
Author-2-Author interview
Dedicated author support (Your success is our success)

We will never ask our authors to pay fees for any part of the publishing process, and no publisher should.

Bold Strokes Books

PO Box 249
Valley Falls, NY 12185
Tel: +1 (518) 677-5127
Fax: +1 (518) 677-5291
Email: submissions@boldstrokesbooks.com
Website: http://www.boldstrokesbooks.com

Publishes: Fiction; Nonfiction; *Areas:* Adventure; Crime; Erotic; Fantasy; Historical; Horror; Mystery; Romance; Sci-Fi; *Markets:* Adult; Youth

Contact: Len Barot, Selections Director

Publishes LesbianGayBiTransQueer general and genre fiction, and nonfiction. Accepts unsolicited mss by email with one-page synopsis. See website for full guidelines.

Bracket Books

PO Box 286098
New York, NY 10128-9991
Email: info@bracketbooks.com
Website: http://bracketbooks.com

Publishes: Fiction; Nonfiction; *Areas:* Culture; Photography; *Markets:* Adult; Family; *Treatments:* Commercial; Contemporary; Literary; Mainstream

Contact: Sam Majors

Based in New York, New York. The company was established to fill a niche, a publishing void that grows larger as traditional print publishers continue to consolidate, struggle to maintain their narrow profit margins, and hold onto outmoded methods of distribution and old-fashioned book marketing techniques. Our business model embraces digital distribution and online marketing, and although we love to design and devour books that are produced in a printed form, we understand that the key to succeeding in the book industry in the coming decades won't be price points or corporate alliances; the key will be, as it always has been, matching the right author with the right audience, and doing so in an efficient, intelligent way.

Although we publish fiction, our focus is non-fiction, and we'll be releasing approximately four non-fiction titles for each fiction title we publish. At this time, we do not publish coffee table books, art books, or children's books, and we cannot imagine ever being interested in publishing poetry or plays. We are primarily interested in books about the art of photography or about photographers, but we will also publish fiction that is connected, in an important way, to pop culture, particularly to movements in film or genres of popular music (think, for instance, of Michael Chabon's The Amazing Adventures of Kavalier & Clay).

Bronze Man Books

Millikin University
1184 W. Main St.
Decatur, Illinois 62522
Tel: +1 (217) 424-6264
Email: rbrooks@millikin.edu
Website: http://www.bronzemanbooks.com

Publishes: Fiction; Poetry; Scripts; *Areas:* Drama; Short Stories; *Markets:* Adult; *Treatments:* Literary

Contact: Dr. Randy Brooks

Publishes 1-2 chapbooks per year of various genres (poetry, prose, drama, etc.). Always open to proposals. Poetry chapbooks should consist of 18-30 poems with a connecting theme or notion; fiction chapbooks should be 32-72 pages and may be short story collections or one or two longer works. Send proposal by email or by post with SASE in first instance. See website for more details.

Bullitt Publishing

Email: submissions@bullittpublishing.com
Website: http://bullittpublishing.com

Publishes: Fiction; *Areas:* Romance; *Markets:* Adult; *Treatments:* Contemporary

Publishes contemporary romance. Submissions by email only – see website for full guidelines.

By Light Unseen Media

PO Box 1233
Pepperell, MA 01463-3233
Email: vyrdolak@bylightunseenmedia.com
Website:
http://www.bylightunseenmedia.com

Publishes: Fiction; Nonfiction; Culture; Fantasy; Historical; Horror; Sci-Fi; *Markets:* Adult; Youth

Publishes vampire fiction and nonfiction.

Fiction should be full-length novels 75,000 to 150,000 words in length. No short story collections. Interested in dramatic fiction with a realistic tone. All work must be entirely the author's work (not using any elements of other, established worlds). No slayers, hunters, etc.

Nonfiction of 50,000 words to 150,000 words exploring vampires in folklore, cultural tradition, occult theory and as a modern social subgroup or counter-culture are also sought.

Accepts approaches by post or email. See website for full guidelines.

Canterbury House Publishing, Ltd

7350 S. Tamiami Trail
Sarasota, FL 34231
Tel: +1 (941) 312-6912
Website:
http://www.canterburyhousepublishing.com

Publishes: Fiction; Nonfiction; *Areas:* Autobiography; Mystery; Romance; Suspense; *Markets:* Adult

Publishes manuscripts that have a strong Southeastern US regional setting. Gives preference to stories along the southern Appalachian trail. Seeks fiction with an unusual protagonist that could be part of a romance/suspense or mystery series. Will consider memoirs or inspirational novels wuth strong regional appeal. No spy thrillers, explicit material, or books for children or young adults. Make contact via web form in first instance, requesting editorial email address. See website for full guidelines. Also provides ebook formatting services.

Capstone

1710 Roe Crest Drive
North Mankato, MN 56003
Email: author.sub@capstonepub.com
Website: http://www.capstonepub.com

Publishes: Fiction; Nonfiction; Poetry; *Areas:* Adventure; Autobiography; Biography; Drama; Fantasy; Historical; Humour; Military; Mystery; Sci-Fi; Sport; *Markets:* Children's; Youth

Publishes fiction and nonfiction for children and young adults. Send query by email with CV, sample chapters, and list of any previous publishing credits. Response only if interested. See website for full submission guidelines.

The Catholic University of America Press

240 Leahy Hall
620 Michigan Avenue NE
Washington, DC 20064
Email: Lipscombe@cua.edu
Website: http://cuapress.cua.edu

Publishes: Nonfiction; *Areas:* Historical; Literature; Philosophy; Politics; Religious; Sociology; *Markets:* Academic; Professional

Contact: Trevor Lipscombe, Director

Publishes books disseminating scholarship in the areas of theology, philosophy, church history, and medieval studies. Send query with outline, CV, sample chapter, and publishing history.

Centerstream Publishing

Email: Centerstrm@aol.com
Website: http://www.centerstream-usa.com

Publishes: Nonfiction; Reference; *Areas:* Biography; How-to; Music; *Markets:* Adult

Publishes music books on instruments, instructional, reference, and biographies.

Chicago Review Press

814 North Franklin Street
Chicago, Illinois 60610
Tel: +1 (312) 337-0747
Fax: +1 (312) 337-5110
Email: frontdesk@chicagoreviewpress.com
Website: http://www.chicagoreviewpress.com

Publishes: Fiction; Nonfiction; *Areas:* Autobiography; Biography; Crafts; Culture; Film; Gardening; Historical; Lifestyle; Music; Politics; Science; Sport; Travel; Women's Interests; *Markets:* Adult; Children's; Youth

Publishes nonfiction through all imprints, and fiction through specific imprint listed above. Also publishes children's and young adult titles, but no picture books. See website for full submission guidelines.

Church Publishing Incorporated

445 Fifth Avenue
New York, NY 10016
Email: nabryan@cpg.org
Website: https://www.churchpublishing.org

Publishes: Nonfiction; *Areas:* Religious; *Markets:* Adult; Professional

Contact: Nancy Bryan, Editorial Director

Publishes worship materials and resources for The Episcopal Church, including works on church leadership, pastoral care and Christian formation.

Conari Press

665 Third Street, Suite 400
San Francisco, CA 94107

Email: submissions@rwwbooks.com
Website: http://redwheelweiser.com

Publishes: Nonfiction; *Areas:* Cookery; Health; Humour; Lifestyle; Self-Help; Spiritual; Women's Interests; *Markets:* Adult

Contact: Pat Bryce

Publishes inspirational books: mind, body, spirit; health; food; wellness; women's; spirituality; parenting; social issues. Send query post or by email with proposal and sample illustrations or photographs is appropriate. See website for full guidelines.

Continental

520 East Bainbridge Street
Elizabethtown, PA 17022
Tel: +1 (800) 233-0759
Fax: +1 (888) 834-1303
Email: bspencer@continentalpress.com
Website: https://www.continentalpress.com

Publishes: Fiction; Nonfiction; *Areas:* Arts; Science; Sociology; Technology; *Markets:* Academic; Children's

Publishes educational materials for grades K–12, specialising in reading, mathematics, and test preparation materials. Also publishes fiction and nonfiction leveled readers and other materials that support early literacy in kindergarten through to second grade. See website for full submission guidelines.

Craigmore Creations

Attn: Submissions
2900 SE Stark St, Suite 1A
Portland, OR 97214
Tel: +1 (503) 477-9562
Email: info@craigmorecreations.com
Website: http://www.craigmorecreations.com

Publishes: Fiction; Nonfiction; *Areas:* Nature; Science; *Markets:* Children's

Graphic novel and children's book publisher, publishing books focussed on science and natural history. For picture books submit complete ms; otherwise send query with one or two sample chapters. Include SASE for reply. No submissions by fax or email. No approaches by phone. See website for full submission guidelines.

Cup of Tea Books

Email: weditor@pagespringpublishing.com
Website: http://cupofteabooks.com

Publishes: Fiction; *Areas:* Mystery; Romance; Women's Interests; *Markets:* Adult; *Treatments:* Commercial

Publishes fiction for women, including cozy mysteries, upmarket commercial fiction, and romance. Send query by email with synopsis and the first thirty pages in the body of the email. Include title and the word "Submission" in the subject line. Aims to respond within four weeks – follow up if no response in that time. No submissions or queries by post.

Cyclotour Guide Books

PO Box 10585
Rochester, NY 14610
Tel: +1 (585) 244-6157
Email: cyclotour@cyclotour.com
Website: http://www.cyclotour.com

Publishes: Nonfiction; *Areas:* Sport; Travel; *Markets:* Adult

Publishes bicycle touring guide books.

Darkhouse Books

Email: submissions@darkhousebooks.com
Website: http://darkhousebooks.com

Publishes: Fiction; *Areas:* Crime; Mystery; Short Stories; *Markets:* Adult

Publishes crime and mystery novels and anthologies. See website for current calls for submissions.

Dog-Eared Publications

PO Box 620863
Middleton, WI 53562-0863
Tel: +1 (608) 831-1410
Fax: +1 (608) 831-1410
Email: field@dog-eared.com
Website: http://www.dog-eared.com

Publishes: Nonfiction; *Areas:* Nature; *Markets:* Children's

Publishes nature books for children.

Dragonfairy Press

Email: info@dragonfairypress.com
Website: http://www.dragonfairypress.com

Publishes: Fiction; *Areas:* Fantasy; Romance; Sci-Fi; *Markets:* Adult; Youth

Please follow submission instructions on website. We want manuscripts that stretch beyond the world as we know it. That means fantasy and science fiction, including their various subgenres, such as urban fantasy, paranormal romance/erotica, cyberpunk, supernatural horror, and others. Don't worry about sex, gore, or foul language. While we certainly do not require these, we don't shy away from them either. Although we don't expect manuscripts to be publication-ready, we strongly recommend that your manuscript be clean enough (and in our manuscript format) to minimize distractions as we read. We look for strong writing and well-paced stories.

Dufour Editions

PO Box 7
124 Byers Road
Chester Springs, PA 19425
Tel: +1 (610) 458-5005
Fax: +1 (610) 458-7103
Email: info@dufoureditions.com
Website: http://www.dufoureditions.com

Publishes: Fiction; Nonfiction; Poetry; *Areas:* Biography; Historical; Short Stories; Translations; *Markets:* Adult; *Treatments:* Literary

Contact: Christopher May

Publishes fiction, poetry, and nonfiction for a sophisticated, literate audience. Particularly focuses on distributing the output of British and Irish publishers across the US and Canada, and translating foreign literature, as well as publishing American writers. Strong Irish-Celtic focus. Check website to see if you're material is suitable, and, if so, send query with SASE.

Eakin Press

PO Box 331779
Fort Worth, Texas 76163
Tel: +1 (817) 344-7036
Fax: +1 (817) 344-7036
Website: http://www.eakinpress.com

Publishes: Fiction; Nonfiction; *Areas:* Biography; Business; Cookery; Culture; Finance; Historical; Military; Sport; *Markets:* Adult; Children's; Youth

Publishes books on the history and culture of the Southwest, especially Texas and Oklahoma. Publishes nonfiction for adults, and books for children. Send query with outline/synopsis, or use author inquiry form on website.

William B. Eerdmans Publishing Co.

2140 Oak Industrial Dr. NE
Grand Rapids, MI 49505
Tel: +1 (616) 459-4591
Fax: +1 (616) 459-6540
Email: info@eerdmans.com
Website: http://www.eerdmans.com

Publishes: Nonfiction; Reference; *Areas:* Historical; Philosophy; Religious; Spiritual; *Markets:* Adult; Children's

Contact: Jon Pott, Editor-in-Chief

Publishes some regional books and other nonreligious titles, but essentially a religious publisher whose titles range from the academic to the semi-popular. It is now publishing a growing number of books in the areas of spirituality and the Christian life. It has long specialised, however, in biblical studies and Religious and in religious approaches to philosophy, history, art, literature, ethics, and contemporary social and cultural issues. See website for full submission guidelines.

Enete Enterprises

Tel: +1 (619) 618-0224

Email: EneteEnterprises@gmail.com
Website: http://www.eneteenterprises.com

Publishes: Nonfiction; *Areas:* Autobiography; Travel; *Markets:* Adult

Publishes travel, guide books, and memoir genres. Send query by email with the subject line "Query", with marketing plan and sample chapters as a PDF attachment. Accepts simultaneous submissions and unagented authors. See website for full details.

Facts on File, Inc.

Infobase Publishing
132 West 31st Street, 17th Floor
New York, NY 10001
Tel: +1 (800) 322-8755
Fax: +1 (800) 678-3633
Email: editorial@factsonfile.com
Website: http://www.factsonfile.com

Publishes: Nonfiction; Reference; *Markets:* Academic; Adult; Youth

Publishes print, eBooks, and online reference materials for the school and library market. Send query or manuscript proposal by post or by email. Publishes reference books, general trade, young adult trade, and academic, for the school and library markets; atlases, encyclopedias, biographical dictionaries, etc. No fiction, popular nonfiction, or cookery.

Farrar, Straus & Giroux, Inc.

18 West 18th Street
New York, NY 10011
Tel: +1 (646)307-5151
Email: fsg.editorial@fsgbooks.com
Website: http://www.fsgbooks.com

Publishes: Fiction; Nonfiction; Poetry; *Markets:* Adult; Children's; Youth

Send query describing submission with first 50 pages (fiction and nonfiction), complete ms (picture books), or 3-4 poems. Submissions by mail only – no queries or mss by email.

Fiction Collective Two (FC2)

University of Alabama Press
Box 870380
Tuscaloosa, AL 35487-0380
Tel: +1 (773) 702-7000
Email: fc2.cmu@gmail.com
Website: http://www.fc2.org

Publishes: Fiction; *Markets:* Adult; *Treatments:* Experimental

An author-run, not-for-profit publisher of artistically adventurous, non-traditional fiction. Publishes the work of the members of the Collective, and is committed to finding new and innovative work and continuously expanding the membership of the Collective. New members are acquired through contests (see website) and through member-sponsored submissions.

Filbert Publishing

140 3rd Street North
Kandiyohi, MN 56251-0326
Tel: +1 (320) 444-5080
Email: FilbertPublishing@FilbertPublishing.com
Website: http://filbertpublishing.com

Publishes: Fiction; Nonfiction; *Areas:* Cookery; Health; How-to; Lifestyle; Self-Help; *Markets:* Adult

Publishes mainly nonfiction and a small amount of fiction every year. Particularly interested in books that help creative people make a living following their dream; healthy living; plant based cooking; but will also consider other topics. Considers manuscripts from 25,000 to 85,000 words (minimum for cookbooks is 5,000 words). Prefers conversational writing. Send query by email with synopsis and information about your ms. See website for full details.

Fodor's Travel Publications

1745 Broadway, 15th floor
New York, NY 10019
Email: editors@fodors.com
Website: http://www.fodors.com

Publishes: Nonfiction; *Areas:* Travel; *Markets:* Adult

Publishes travel books. Send query by email or by post with resume and writing clips. Writers generally live in the area they are covering. No unsolicited mss.

Foreign Policy Association

470 Park Avenue South
New York, NY 10016
Email: info@fpa.org
Website: http://www.fpa.org

Publishes: Nonfiction; *Areas:* Historical; Legal; Politics; *Markets:* Adult

Publishes books that develop awareness, understanding, and informed opinion on US foreign policy and global issues.

Frederic C. Beil, Publisher

609 Whitaker Street
Savannah, GA 31401
Tel: +1 (912) 233-2446
Email: editor@beil.com
Website: http://www.beil.com

Publishes: Fiction; Nonfiction; *Areas:* Biography; Historical; *Markets:* Adult

Publishes general trade books in the fields of history, biography, and fiction. Will respond to email queries, but prefers queries by post with SASE. No unsolicited mss.

Free Spirit Publishing

217 Fifth Avenue North, Suite 200
Minneapolis, MN 55401-1299
Tel: +1 (800) 735-7323
Fax: +1 (866) 419-5199
Email: acquisitions@freespirit.com
Website: http://www.freespirit.com

Publishes: Fiction; Nonfiction; *Areas:* How-to; Lifestyle; Self-Help; Sociology; *Markets:* Academic; Adult; Children's; Youth

Publishes nonfiction books and learning materials for children and teens, parents, educators, counselors, and others who live and work with young people. Also publishes fiction relevant to the mission of providing children and teens with the tools they need to succeed in life, e.g.: self-esteem; conflict resolution, etc. No general fiction or storybooks; books with animal or mythical characters; books with religious or New Age content; or single biographies, autobiographies, or memoirs. No submissions by fax or email. See website for full submission guidelines.

Geostar Publishing & Services LLC

6423 Woodbine Court
St. Louis, MO 63109
Tel: +1 (314) 260-9978
Email: opportunities@geostarpublishing.com
Website: http://www.geostarpublishing.com/opportunities.htm

Publishes: Nonfiction; Reference; *Areas:* Adventure; Anthropology; Antiques; Archaeology; Architecture; Arts; Autobiography; Beauty and Fashion; Biography; Business; Cookery; Crafts; Crime; Criticism; Culture; Current Affairs; Design; Drama; Entertainment; Erotic; Fantasy; Film; Finance; Gardening; Gothic; Health; Historical; Hobbies; Horror; How-to; Humour; Legal; Leisure; Lifestyle; Literature; Media; Medicine; Men's Interests; Military; Music; Mystery; Nature; New Age; Philosophy; Photography; Politics; Psychology; Radio; Religious; Romance; Science; Sci-Fi; Self-Help; Short Stories; Sociology; Spiritual; Sport; Suspense; Technology; Theatre; Thrillers; Translations; Travel; TV; Westerns; Women's Interests; *Markets:* Academic; Adult; Children's; Family; Professional; Youth; *Treatments:* Commercial; Contemporary; Cynical; Dark; Experimental; In-depth; Light; Mainstream; Niche; Popular; Positive; Progressive; Satirical; Serious; Traditional

Contact: Richard J. Runion

We invite SMEs (Subject Matter Experts), Small Businesspersons and Niche Service Providers to visit our site.

We market your services, worldwide!
Absolutely Free!!
...And Pay You Too!!!

How Can Anyone Do That?
Sounds Too Good To Be True?
Is Geostar A Charity?
Is There A Catch?
...Read On!

We are a UNIQUE Publisher. Unlike Any Other! We're like Venture Capital Investor of the Publishing Industry. We publish eBooks on topics people are desperately looking for. We don't publish on a topic just because we can find writers. We do extensive & intensive research, secondary & primary, on every topic we publish on. Our customers for eBooks (like the ones on Waste Water Treatment and Content Management Systems) are more than eBook buyers; many of them are actively looking for a product/ service/ help from experts: some are looking for Consultancy, some for services, even on a long term basis.

We have evolved business models that will work like a charm for you, fetching you pre-qualified business leads, at no cost to you, from across the globe. (Or locally if you so prefer.)

If you want to work with us, please fill in the form on our site, or contact us thru email/ phone.

Gibbs Smith, Publisher

PO Box 667
Layton, Utah, 84041
Tel: +1 (801) 544-9800
Fax: +1 (801) 544-5582
Email: DUribe@gibbs-smith.com
Website: http://www.gibbs-smith.com

Publishes: Nonfiction; *Areas:* Architecture; Arts; Cookery; Crafts; Design; Humour; *Markets:* Adult; Children's

Send query by email only. Main emphasis is on interior design, architecture, children's activities, and cookbooks. Will also accept submissions of: Arts & Crafts, western humour with general appeal, general humour, gift books, and children's activity books and board books. See website for full submission guidelines. At this time not accepting fiction, poetry, or picture books.

Gival Press, LLC

PO Box 3812
Arlington, VA 22203
Tel: +1 (703) 351-0079
Email: givalpress@yahoo.com
Website: http://www.givalpress.com

Publishes: Fiction; Nonfiction; Poetry; *Areas:* Culture; Philosophy; Sociology; Translations; Women's Interests; *Markets:* Adult; *Treatments:* Literary

Publishes fiction, nonfiction (including essays and educational texts) and poetry by poets and writers from many walks of life whose work has a philosophical or social message. See website for full submission guidelines.

The Glencannon Press

P.O. Box 1428
El Cerrito, CA 94530
Tel: +1 (510) 528-4216
Fax: +1 (510) 528-3194
Email: info@glencannon.com
Website: http://www.glencannon.com

Publishes: Fiction; Nonfiction; *Areas:* Adventure; Military; Travel; *Markets:* Adult; Children's

Publishes nonfiction and fiction about ships and the sea; including World War I and II, steamships, battleships, sailing ships, and true adventure.

Great Potential Press, Inc.

1325 N. Wilmot Ave., #300
Tucson, AZ 85712
Tel: +1 (520) 777-6161
Fax: +1 (520) 777-6217
Email: info@greatpotentialpress.com
Website: http://www.greatpotentialpress.com

Publishes: Nonfiction; *Markets:* Academic; Adult; Children's

Publishes books that support the academic, social, or emotional needs of gifted children and adults. No fiction, poetry, or K-12 classroom materials. Approach via proposal submission form on website.

Gulf Publishing Company

2 Greenway Plaza, Suite 1020
Houston, Texas 77046
Tel: +1 (713) 529-4301
Fax: +1 (713) 520-4433
Email: store@gulfpub.com
Website: http://www.gulfpub.com

Publishes: Nonfiction; *Areas:* Design; Science; Technology; *Markets:* Academic; Professional

Oil and gas industry publisher, producing books for engineers, students, well managers, academics, etc. Submit outline with 1-2 sample chapters, or complete ms.

Gun Digest Books

F+W Media
700 East State Street
Iola, WI 54990
Website: http://www.gundigest.com

Publishes: Nonfiction; Reference; *Areas:* Historical; Hobbies; How-to; Technology; *Markets:* Adult; *Treatments:* Mainstream

Publishes firearms books with mainstream appeal. Send complete ms or query with outline, author bio and two sample chapters.

Heritage Books, Inc.

5810 Ruatan Street
Berwyn Heights, MD 20740
Tel: +1 (800) 876-6103
Fax: +1 (410) 558-6574
Email: submissions@HeritageBooks.com
Website: http://www.heritagebooks.com

Publishes: Fiction; Nonfiction; Reference; *Areas:* Autobiography; Historical; Military; *Markets:* Academic; Adult

Publishes nonfiction in genealogy, history, military history, historical fiction, and memoirs. Also some fact-rich historical novels. Send query with SASE or submit outline by email.

Hadley Rille Books

PO Box 25466
Overland Park KS 66225
Email: subs@hadleyrillebooks.com
Website: http://www.hadleyrillebooks.com

Publishes: Fiction; *Areas:* Archaeology; Fantasy; Historical; Sci-Fi; *Markets:* Adult

Contact: Eric T. Reynolds, Editor/Publisher

Publishes Science Fiction stories with an emphasis on space, archaeology, climate and other science-related topics. Opens to submissions in specific months. See website for details.

Harry N. Abrams, Inc.

115 West 18th Street
New York, NY 10011
Tel: +1 (212) 206-7715
Fax: +1 (212) 519-1210
Email: abrams@abramsbooks.com
Website: http://www.abramsbooks.com

Publishes: Fiction; Nonfiction; Reference; *Areas:* Architecture; Arts; Beauty and Fashion; Crafts; Culture; Design; Entertainment; Film; Gardening; Hobbies; Humour; Leisure; Lifestyle; Music; Nature; Photography; Religious; Science; Sport; *Markets:* Adult; Children's; Youth

In general, does not accept unsolicited manuscripts or book proposals without a literary agent, except for two imprints: one of comic art and one of crafts. Email approaches accepted only by crafts imprint. See website for full details.

The Harvard Common Press

535 Albany Street
Boston, MA 02118
Tel: +1 (617) 423-5803
Fax: +1 (617) 695-9794
Email: editorial@harvardcommonpress.com
Website:
http://www.harvardcommonpress.com

Publishes: Nonfiction; *Areas:* Cookery; Lifestyle; *Markets:* Adult

Independent publisher of books on cookery and parenting. See website for full guidelines on submitting a proposal. No phone calls. Postal submissions cannot be returned.

Harvest House Publishers

990 Owen Loop North
Eugene, OR 97402-9173
Tel: +1 (800) 547-8979
Fax: +1 (888) 501-6012
Email:
ContactRep@harvesthousepublishers.com
Website: http://harvesthousepublishers.com

Publishes: Fiction; Nonfiction; *Areas:* Health; Historical; Humour; Lifestyle; Men's Interests; Mystery; Religious; Romance; Suspense; Westerns; Women's Interests; *Markets:* Adult; Children's; Youth

Publisher of Christian literature. Does not accept submissions directly, but is a member of an association which accepts proposals to share with their members. See website for full details.

Hayes School Publishing Co., Inc.

321 Pennwood Avenue
Pittsburgh, PA 15221

Tel: +1 (800) 245-6234
Email: chayes@hayespub.com
Website: http://www.hayespub.com

Publishes: Nonfiction; *Markets:* Academic; Children's

Publishes school books for children. Welcomes manuscripts and ideas for new products. Send query by email to receive a copy of the author's guide.

Hearts 'N Tummies Cookbook Co. / Quixote Press

3544 Blakslee Street
Wever, IA 52658
Tel: +1 (800) 571 2665
Website: http://www.heartsntummies.com

Publishes: Fiction; Nonfiction; *Areas:* Cookery; Humour; Short Stories; Markets

Publishes books on cookery, ghosts, humour, and folklore. Send query with SASE. Also offers services for which writers are charged.

Highland Press

Submissions Department
PO Box 2292
High Springs, FL 32655
Email: Submissions.hp@gmail.com
Website: http://www.highlandpress.org

Publishes: Fiction; Nonfiction; Reference; *Areas:* Fantasy; Historical; Mystery; Romance; Suspense; *Markets:* Adult; Children's; Youth; *Treatments:* Contemporary

Has previously focused on publishing historical fictions, but currently open to all genres except erotic. Particularly interested in both contemporary and historical Christian / Inspirational / family. Accepts queries by post and email, but any approaches not adhering to the submission guidelines will be discarded. See website for full submission guidelines.

Hill and Wang

Farrar Straus & Giroux, Inc.
19 Union Square West
New York, NY 10003
Email: fsg.editorial@fsgbooks.com
Website: http://us.macmillan.com/fsg

Publishes: Nonfiction; Historical; Politics; Science; Sociology; *Markets:* Adult; *Treatments:* Serious

Publisher of serious nonfiction covering history, maths, science, and the social sciences. No fiction, poetry, or drama. Send query with SASE, outline, and sample chapters.

Homestead Publishing

Acquisitions
Box 193
Moose, Wyoming 83012
Tel: +1 (307) 733-6248
Fax: +1 (307) 733-6248
Email: homesteadpublishing@mac.com
Website:
http://www.homesteadpublishing.net

Publishes: Fiction; Nonfiction; *Areas:* Architecture; Arts; Biography; Cookery; Design; Literature; Nature; Photography;

Travel; *Markets:* Adult; *Treatments:* Literary

Publishes fine art, design, photography, and architecture; full-color nature books; national park guide books: cookbooks; biographies and literary fiction; Western Americana; regional and international travel guides, including Yellowstone, Grand Teton, Glacier-Waterton and Banff-Jasper national parks. Particularly interested in outdoor guide—hiking, climbing, bicycling, canoeing, mountaineering—and travel books. Accepts queries with samples. See website for full submission guidelines.

Hopewell Publications

PO Box 11
Titusville, NJ 08560-0011
Tel: +1 (609) 818-1049
Fax: +1 (609) 964-1718
Email: submissions@hopepubs.com
Website: http://www.hopepubs.com

Publishes: Fiction; Nonfiction; *Markets:* Adult; Youth

Publishes fiction and nonfiction. Specialises in classic reprints but also considers new titles. See website for submission guidelines. Queries which do not follow them will be deleted unread.

HOW Books

10151 Carver Road, Ste. #200
Blue Ash, OH 45242
Tel: +1 (513) 531-2690
Email: editorial@howdesign.com
Website: http://www.howdesign.com

Publishes: Nonfiction; *Areas:* Arts; Culture; Design; Technology; *Markets:* Adult

Contact: Scott Francis

Publishes books on graphic design, web design, and pop culture. Send query by email with proposal, sample chapter, and sample image(s) as PDFs.

Humanics Publishing Group

12 S. Dixie Hwy, Ste. 203
Lake Worth, FL 33460
Tel: +1 (800) 874-8844
Fax: +1 (888) 874-8844
Email: humanics@mindspring.com
Website: http://www.humanicspub.com

Publishes: Nonfiction; Finance; How-to; New Age; Religious; Science; Self-Help; *Markets:* Adult; Children's

Contact: W. Arthur Bligh, Acquisitions Editor

Started in 1969, in response to the need from the education community for quality classroom materials to support parents as the prime educators of their children. In 1984 launched a New Age imprint. Accepts unsolicited mss by post with SASE. See website for full submission guidelines.

IBEX Publishers, Inc.

Post Office Box 30087
Bethesda, MD 20824
Tel: +1 (301) 718-8188
Fax: +1 (301) 907-8707
Email: info@ibexpub.com
Website: http://ibexpub.com

Publishes: Nonfiction; Poetry; Reference; *Areas:* Arts; Autobiography; Cookery; Criticism; Historical; Humour; Literature; Music; Philosophy; Politics; Religious; Translations; *Markets:* Adult; Children's

Publishes books which introduce the best of the Persian language, literature, culture and history to the world. Accepts initial queries by email but the actual submission must be sent by post. See "Authors" section of website for full guidelines. May consider translations of Persian poetry, but generally does not publish original poetry or fiction by unknown authors.

Ideals Publications

2630 Elm Hill Pike, Suite 100
Nashville, TN 37214
Tel: +1 (615) 781-1451
Email: kwest@guideposts.org
Website: http://www.idealsbooks.com

Publishes: Fiction; Nonfiction; *Markets:* Children's

Publishes fiction and nonfiction picture books for children aged 4-8 (up to 800 words), and board and novelty books for children 2-5 (up to 250 words). Subjects include holiday, inspirational, and patriotic themes; relationships and values; and general fiction. Submit complete mss only – no queries or proposals. No submissions by email or computer disk. See website for full guidelines.

Ig Publishing

392 Clinton Ave
Brooklyn, NY 11238
Tel: +1 (718) 797-0676
Email: robert@igpub.com
Website: http://igpub.com

Publishes: Fiction; Nonfiction; *Areas:* Culture; *Markets:* Adult; Youth; *Treatments:* Literary

Contact: Robert Lasner, Editor-in-Chief

Publishes original literary fiction from writers who are perceived to have been overlooked by the mainstream publishing establishment, plus political and cultural nonfiction. Young adult imprint is devoted to bringing back young adult literature from as far back as the '30s and '40s and as recently as the '70s and '80s. No unsolicited mss. Send query by email only.

Ignatius Press

1348 10th Avenue
San Francisco, CA 94122
Email: info@ignatius.com
Website: http://www.ignatius.com

Publishes: Nonfiction; *Areas:* Religious; *Markets:* Adult

Christian publisher. Submit complete ms. No phone calls or emails. See webite for full submission guidelines.

Impact Books

F+W Media, Inc.
10151 Carver Road, Suite 200
Blue Ash, OH 45242
Email: Pam.wissman@fwpubs.com
Website: http://www.impact-books.com

Publishes: Nonfiction; Reference; *Areas:* Arts; How-to; *Markets:* Adult

Contact: Pamela Wissman, Acquisitions Editor

Publishes books to assist artists drawing comics, superheroes, Japanese-style manga, fantasy, creatures, action, caricature, anime, etc.

Impact Publishers

PO Box 6016
Atascadero, CA 93423-6016
Tel: +1 (805) 466-5917
Email: submissions@impactpublishers.com
Website: http://impactpublishers.com

Publishes: Nonfiction; *Areas:* Psychology; Self-Help; *Markets:* Adult; *Treatments:* Popular

Publishes popular psychology and self-help written by professionals. Send query by post or email. See website for detailed submission guidelines.

International Foundation of Employee Benefit Plans

18700 West Bluemound Road
Brookfield, WI 53045
Tel: +1 (888) 334-3327
Email: bookstore@ifebp.org
Website: http://www.ifebp.org

Publishes: Nonfiction; *Areas:* Business; Health; *Markets:* Adult; Professional

Nonprofit organisation publishing material relating to employee benefits, health care, pensions, etc. Send query with outline.

International Press

PO Box 43502
Somerville, MA 02143
Tel: +1 (617) 623-3855
Fax: +1 (617) 623-3101
Email: ipb-info@intlpress.com
Website: http://www.intlpress.com

Publishes: Nonfiction; Science; *Markets:* Academic

Contact: Mr Lixin Qin

Academic publisher of high-level mathematics and mathematical physics book titles, including monographs, textbooks, and more.

Ion Imagination Entertainment, Inc.

PO Box 210943
Nashville, TN 37221-0943
Tel: +1 (615) 646-6276
Email: ionimagin@aol.com
Website: http://www.flumpa.com

Publishes: Fiction; *Areas:* Science; *Markets:* Children's

Publishes science-related fiction for children. Send query with SASE, bio, and publishing history. No unsolicited mss.

Jewish Lights Publishing

Sunset Farm Offices
Route 4, PO Box 237
Woodstock, VT 05091
Tel: +1 (802) 457-4000
Fax: +1 (802) 457-4004
Email: editorial@jewishlights.com
Website: http://jewishlights.com

Publishes: Fiction; Nonfiction; *Areas:* Crime; Historical; Men's Interests; Mystery; Philosophy; Religious; Sci-Fi; Spiritual; Women's Interests; *Markets:* Adult; Children's; Youth

Publishes books for people of all faiths and backgrounds, drawing on the Jewish wisdom tradition. Books are almost exclusively nonfiction, covering topics such as religion, Jewish life cycle, theology, philosophy, history, and spirituality, however does publish some fiction, including children's books and graphic novels. No biography, haggadot, or poetry. Send proposal by post only – no email submissions or unsolicited mss. See website for full details.

JIST Publishing

875 Montreal Way
St Paul, MN 55102
Email: educate@emcp.com
Website: http://jist.emcp.com

Publishes: Nonfiction; Reference; *Areas:* Business; How-to; Self-Help; *Markets:* Adult

Published books to assist job finding and career development. Send query with proposal, one sample chapter, author CV, competitive analysis, and marketing ideas.

Jupiter Gardens Press

Email: submissions@jupitergardens.com
Website: http://jupitergardenspress.com

Publishes: Fiction; Nonfiction; *Areas:* Erotic; Fantasy; New Age; Romance; Sci-Fi; Short Stories; *Markets:* Adult; Children's; Youth

Send query by email with 2-4 pages synopsis, author bio, and first three chapters as .DOC or .RTF attachments.

Just Us Books

Submissions Manager
Just Us Books
356 Glenwood Avenue
East Orange, NJ 07017
Tel: +1 (973) 672-7701
Fax: +1 (973) 677-7570
Email: cheryl_hudson@justusbooks.com
Website: http://justusbooks.com

Publishes: Fiction; Nonfiction; Poetry; *Markets:* Children's; Youth

Publishes Black-interest books for young people, including picture books, chapter books for middle readers, poetry, nonfiction series, biographies and young adult fiction. Currently accepting queries for young adult titles only. Send query with SAE, author bio, 1-2 page synopsis, and 3-5 page sample. See website for full submission guidelines.

Kalmbach Publishing Co.

21027 Crossroads Circle

PO Box 1612
Waukesha, WI 53187-1612
Tel: +1 (262) 796-8776 Ext. 421
Fax: +1 (262) 796-1615
Email: books@kalmbach.com
Website: http://www.kalmbach.com

Publishes: Nonfiction; Reference; *Areas:* Crafts; Hobbies; How-to; *Markets:* Adult

Publishes books on arts and crafts, model-making, jewellery-making, toy trains, etc. Send query with 2-3 page outline, plus sample chapter with photos.

Kamehameha Publishing

567 South King Street, Suite 118
Honolulu, HI 96813
Tel: +1 (808) 523-6200
Email: publishing@ksbe.edu
Website:
http://www.kamehamehapublishing.org

Publishes: Fiction; Nonfiction; *Areas:* Biography; Culture; Historical; *Markets:* Academic; Adult; Children's; Youth

Publishes books on Hawaiian language, culture, history, and community, for children, young people, and adults. See website for full details and submission guidelines.

Kane Miller Books

4901 Morena Boulevard, Ste 213
San Diego, CA 92117
Tel: +1 (800) 475-4522
Email: submissions@kanemiller.com
Website: http://www.kanemiller.com

Publishes: Fiction; *Areas:* Adventure; Fantasy; Historical; Mystery; *Markets:* Children's; Youth

This publisher is committed to expanding their picture book, chapter book, and middle-grade fiction lists. Particularly interested in engaging characters and American subjects. Send query by email with complete ms (picture books) or synopsis and two sample chapters in the body of the email. No attachments or links to websites.

Kansas City Star Books

The Kansas City Star
1729 Grand Boulevard
Kansas City, MO 64108
Email: dweaver@kcstar.com
Website: http://kansascitystarquilts.com

Publishes: Nonfiction; *Areas:* Crafts; Design; Hobbies; Markets

Contact: Doug Weaver

Publishes books on quilting. See website for full submission guidelines and downloadable author form and book proposal form.

Kearney Street Books

PO Box 2021
Bellingham, WA 98227
Tel: +1 (360) 738-1355
Email: garyrmc@mac.com
Website: http://kearneystreetbooks.com

Publishes: Fiction; *Areas:* Music; *Markets:* Adult; *Treatments:* Niche

Publishes fiction by or about musicians or music. Publishes very few titles a year. Send query by email or send complete ms by post with SASE for reply only.

Kelly Point Publishing LLC

Martin Sisters Publishing LLC
PO Box 1154
Barbourville, KY 40906
Email:
submissions@kellypointpublishing.com
Website:
http://www.kellypointpublishing.com

Publishes: Fiction; *Areas:* Adventure; Fantasy; Historical; Humour; Mystery; Religious; Romance; Sci-Fi; Short Stories; Spiritual; Sport; Westerns; Women's Interests; *Markets:* Adult; Children's; Youth; *Treatments:* Contemporary; Literary; Mainstream

Open to all genres of fiction. No nonfiction or poetry. Send query by email, with marketing plan and first three chapters pasted into the body of the email. No attachments. See website for full guidelines.

Kind of a Hurricane Press

Email: kindofahurricanepress@yahoo.com
Website:
http://www.kindofahurricanepress.com

Publishes: Fiction; Poetry; *Areas:* Short Stories; *Markets:* Adult

Eclectic small press publishing anthologies of poetry and flash fiction. See website for calls for current anthologies and submission guidelines.

Kirkbride Bible Company

1102 Deloss Street
Indianapolis, IN 46203
Tel: +1 (800) 428-4385
Fax: +1 (317) 633-1444
Email: info@kirkbride.com
Website: http://www.kirkbride.com

Publishes: Nonfiction; Reference; *Areas:* Religious; *Markets:* Adult

Publisher of bible reference titles.

Knox Robinson Publishing (US)

244 5th Avenue, Suite 1861
New York, NY 10001
Tel: +1 (646) 652-6980
Email: subs@knoxrobinsonpublishing.com
Website:
http://www.knoxrobinsonpublishing.com

Publishes: Fiction; *Areas:* Fantasy; Historical; Romance; *Markets:* Adult

Publishes historical fiction, historical romance (pre-1960), and medieval fantasy. No science fiction, time travel, or fantasy with children and/or animal protagonists. Send query by email only, with detailed synopsis and the first three chapters. No approaches by fax or post. See website for full details.

Legacy Press

Rainbow Publishers
PO Box 261129
San Diego, CA 92196
Tel: +1 (800) 638-4428
Fax: +1 (800) 331-0297
Email:
john.gregory@rainbowpublishers.com
Website: http://www.legacypresskids.com

Publishes: Fiction; Nonfiction; *Areas:* Religious; *Markets:* Children's

Publishes devotions, instructional books, and faith-based fiction for kids. See website for submission guidelines.

Lawyers & Judges Publishing Co.

917 N Swan, Suite 300
Tucson, AZ 85711
Tel: +1 (520) 323-1500
Fax: +1 (520) 323-0055
Email: steve@lawyersandjudges.com
Website: http://www.lawyersandjudges.com

Publishes: Nonfiction; Reference; *Areas:* Legal; Medicine; *Markets:* Professional

Contact: Steve Weintraub

Publishes legal and medical books for professionals. See website for submission guidelines.

Leapfrog Press

PO Box 505
Fredonia, NY 14063
Email: acquisitions@leapfrogpress.com
Website: http://www.leapfrogpress.com

Publishes: Fiction; Nonfiction; Poetry; *Markets:* Adult; Children's; *Treatments:* Literary

Publisher with an eclectic list of fiction, poetry, and nonfiction, including paperback originals of adult and middle-grade fiction and nonfiction. Closed to submissions between January 15 and May each year. Accepts queries by email only: send query letter and short sample within the email itself. No attachments. See website for full guidelines.

Ledge Hill Publishing

PO Box 337

Alton, NH 03809
Tel: +1 (603) 998-6801
Email: info@ledgehillpublishing.com
Website:
http://www.ledgehillpublishing.com

Publishes: Fiction; Nonfiction; Poetry; *Areas:* Short Stories; *Markets:* Adult

Publishes short fiction, poetry, and creative nonfiction. Electronic approaches only. Send short query via webform on website, or send complete ms with covering letter by email. See website for full details.

Leisure Arts, Inc.

104 Champs Boulevard, Suite 100
Maumelle, AR 72113
Tel: +1 (800) 643-8030
Email: submissions@leisurearts.com
Website: http://www.leisurearts.com

Publishes: Nonfiction; *Areas:* Crafts; Hobbies; How-to; Lifestyle; *Markets:* Adult

Publisher of lifestyle and instructional craft publications. Publishes books and leaflets in virtually all craft categories. Send photographs, swatches, sketches, outlines, charts, artwork by post or by email, but do not send actual designs or instructions unless requested. See website for full details.

Les Figues Press

PO Box 7736
Los Angeles, CA 90007
Tel: +1 (323) 734-4732
Email: info@lesfigues.com
Website: http://www.lesfigues.com

Publishes: Fiction; Poetry; *Areas:* Short Stories; *Markets:* Adult

Publishes fiction and poetry. Accepts submissions through its annual contest only ($25 entry fee). Accepts poetry, novellas, innovative novels, anti-novels, short story collections, lyric essays, hybrids, and all forms not otherwise specified. Submit via form on website.

Lethe Press

Email: editor@lethepressbooks.com
Website: http://www.lethepressbooks.com

Publishes: Fiction; Nonfiction; Poetry; *Markets:* Adult

Small press publisher of gay and lesbian fiction, nonfiction, and poetry. Send query by email in first instance.

LexisNexis

230 Park Avenue, Suite 7
New York, NY 10169
Tel: +1 (212) 309-8100
Fax: +1 (800) 437-8674
Website: http://www.lexisnexis.com

Publishes: Nonfiction; Reference; *Areas:* Legal; *Markets:* Professional

Publishes books and online materials for the professional legal market.

Lillenas Drama Resources

PO Box 419527
Kansas City, MO 64141
Tel: +1 (800) 877-0700
Fax: +1 (816) 412-8390
Email: drama@lillenas.com
Website: http://www.lillenas.com

Publishes: Scripts; *Areas:* Religious; *Markets:* Adult; Children's; Family; Youth

Accepts creatively conceived and practically producible resources for church and school programs. Not currently accepting full-length plays. See website for more details.

Linden Publishing

2006 South Mary
Fresno, CA 93721
Tel: +1 (559) 233-6633
Fax: +1 (559) 233-6933
Email: richard@lindenpub.com
Website: http://www.lindenpub.com

Publishes: Nonfiction; *Areas:* Arts; Crafts; Historical; Hobbies; How-to; *Markets:* Adult

Publishes books on woodworking. Send email for full submission guidelines.

Liquid Silver Books

10509 Sedgegrass Drive
Indianapolis, IN 46235
Email: submissions@liquidsilverbooks.com
Website: http://www.lsbooks.com

Publishes: Fiction; *Areas:* Romance; *Markets:* Adult

Considers all romance genres and romance subgenres. Send query by email with complete ms as a .doc, .docx, or .rtf attachment. Manuscripts must be at least 15,000 words. See website for full guidelines.

Listen & Live Audio, Inc.

PO Box 817
Roseland, New Jersey 07068
Tel: +1 (201) 558-9000
Fax: +1 (201) 558-9800
Email: alisa@listenandlive.com
Website: http://www.listenandlive.com

Publishes: Fiction; Nonfiction; *Areas:* Adventure; Autobiography; Biography; Culture; Fantasy; Health; Humour; Lifestyle; Military; Mystery; Politics; Religious; Romance; Sci-Fi; Self-Help; Sport; *Markets:* Adult; Children's; Youth

Independent audiobook publisher based in Roseland, New Jersey. Describes itself as "the premier independent audiobook publishing company in the US."

Lonely Planet Publications

150 Linden Street
Oakland, CA 94607
Tel: +1 (510) 250-6400
Fax: +1 (510) 893-8572
Email: info@lonelyplanet.com
Website: http://www.lonelyplanet.com

Publishes: Nonfiction; Reference; *Areas:* Travel; *Markets:* Adult

Publisher of travel guides and other travel-related material.

Loose Id

Email: submissions@loose-id.com
Website: http://www.loose-id.com

Publishes: Fiction; *Areas:* Erotic; Fantasy; Historical; Mystery; Romance; Sci-Fi; Suspense; Westerns; *Markets:* Adult; *Treatments:* Contemporary

Publisher of erotic romance ebooks, which are occasionally also released in print. Send query by email with synopsis and first three chapters as RTF attachments only (no .doc files or submissions in the body of the email). See website for full guidelines.

Lucent Books

Attn: Publisher – Lucent Books
27500 Drake Road
Farmington Hills, MI 48331
Email: betz.deschenes@cengage.com
Website:
http://www.gale.cengage.com/greenhaven

Publishes: Nonfiction; *Markets:* Academic; Children's

Publishes educational, nonfiction books that support middle school curriculum and national standards. Send query by email with CV and list of previous publications.

Lucky Marble Books

Email: yaeditor@pagespringpublishing.com
Website: http://luckymarblebooks.com

Publishes: Fiction; *Areas:* Adventure; Culture; Fantasy; Historical; Humour; Mystery; Romance; Sci-Fi; Sport; Suspense; *Markets:* Children's; Youth; *Treatments:* Contemporary; Literary; Mainstream

Publishes Young Adult and Middle Grade novels. All material must be age appropriate and avoid content that might put off schools. No nonfiction. Send query by email with synopsis and first thirty pages in the body of the email, and the word "SUBMISSION" and the title of your book in the subject line. See website for full details.

The Lyons Press Inc.

The Globe Pequot Press, Inc.
Box 480
246 Goose Lane
Guilford, CT 06437
Tel: +1 (203) 458-4500
Fax: +1 (203) 458-4668
Email: info@globepequot.com
Website: http://www.lyonspress.com

Publishes: Nonfiction; Reference; *Areas:* Autobiography; Cookery; Culture; Current Affairs; Historical; Nature; Sport; *Markets:* Adult; *Treatments:* Popular

Publishes history, current affairs, popular culture, memoir, sports, cooking, nature, pets, fishing, hunting, reference and equestrian books. Not accepting submissions or proposals as at January 2015. Check website for current situation.

M P Publishing USA

Email: mark@mpassociates.co.uk
Website: http://mppublishingusa.com

Publishes: Fiction; Nonfiction; *Areas:* Adventure; Crime; Fantasy; Gothic; Literature; Mystery; Romance; Sci-Fi; Short Stories; Suspense; Thrillers; Women's Interests; *Markets:* Adult; Youth; *Treatments:* Commercial; Contemporary; Dark; Experimental; In-depth; Light; Literary; Mainstream; Niche; Popular; Progressive; Satirical; Serious; Traditional

Contact: Mark Pearce

Publishes fiction and nonfiction. Not accepting submissions for print publication or American distribution as at March 2015. Submitters should have bought or borrowed one of the publisher's books prior to submitting. Accepts submissions by post, but prefers electronic submissions via form on website.

Magination Press

American Psychological Association
750 First Street, NE
Washington, DC 20002-4242
Email: magination@apa.org
Website: http://www.apa.org

Publishes: Fiction; Nonfiction; *Areas:* Psychology; *Markets:* Children's; Youth

Publishes psychology-based books covering a broad range of topics of concern to children and teens, including everyday situations, such as starting school and the growing family, and more serious psychological, clinical, or medical problems, such as divorce, depression, anxiety, asthma, attention disorders, bullying, death, etc. Most books written by PhD psychologists, school counselors, mental health professionals, and MD physicians. Doctorate-level credentials are not a requirement, but the author should have expertise in the topic area. See website for full submission guidelines. No submissions by email or on disk.

Mandala Earth

10 Paul Drive
San Rafael CA 94903
Tel: +1 (415) 526-1370
Email: info@mandalapublishing.com
Website:
http://www.mandalaeartheditions.com

Publishes: Fiction; Nonfiction; *Areas:* Arts; Culture; Nature; Philosophy; Photography; Spiritual; Travel; *Markets:* Adult; Children's

Publisher aiming to "bring to its readers authentic and accessible renderings of thousands of years of wisdom and philosophy" from the culture of the East. Publishes adult nonfiction and fiction for children. Send query with SASE.

Martin Sisters Publishing

Email:
submissions@martinsisterspublishing.com
Website:
http://www.martinsisterspublishing.com

Publishes: Fiction; Nonfiction; *Areas:* Fantasy; Religious; Sci-Fi; Self-Help; Short Stories; *Markets:* Adult; Children's; Family; Youth

Accepts queries for all genres of fiction, including science fiction and fantasy, and nonfiction, including self-help. Submissions may include Christian fiction, inspirational, collections of stories. Send query by email with marketing plan and (for fiction) 5-10 pages in the body of the email. No attachments. See website for full guidelines.

Master Books

PO Box 726
Green Forest, AR 72638
Tel: +1 (800) 999-3777
Email: nlp@newleafpress.net
Website: http://www.masterbooks.net

Publishes: Nonfiction; *Areas:* Religious; *Markets:* Adult; Children's; Family; Youth

Publishes Christian and creation-based books.

Maverick Duck Press

Email: maverickduckpress@yahoo.com
Website: http://www.maverickduckpress.com

Publishes: Poetry; *Markets:* Adult; *Treatments:* Literary

Contact: Kendall A. Bell

Publishes poetry chapbooks of 18-24 pages. Submit by email only.

McBooks Press

ID Booth Building
520 North Meadow Street
Ithaca NY 14850
Tel: +1 (607) 272-2114
Fax: +1 (607) 273-6068
Email: jackie@mcbooks.com
Website: http://www.mcbooks.com

Publishes: Fiction; Nonfiction; *Areas:* Cookery; Historical; Military; Sport; *Markets:* Adult

Contact: Jackie Swift, Editorial Director

Publishes historical and military / nautical / naval historical fiction, plus historical, sports, and vegetarian nonfiction. Closed to submissions as at August 2014. Check website for current status.

McFarland & Company, Inc.

Box 611
Jefferson, NC 28640
Tel: +1 (336) 246-4460
Fax: +1 (336) 246-5018
Email: info@mcfarlandpub.com
Website: http://www.mcfarlandpub.com

Publishes: Nonfiction; Reference; *Areas:* Architecture; Arts; Culture; Current Affairs; Film; Health; Historical; Leisure; Literature; Medicine; Military; Music; Sport; Women's Interests; *Markets:* Adult

Publishes Pop Culture, Sports, Military History, Transportation, Body & Mind, History, Literature, Medieval Studies, and Graphic Novels. Send query with SASE, outline, and sample chapters. No fiction, poetry, or children's.

Medallion Media Group

100 S. River Street
Aurora, IL 60506
Tel: +1 (630) 513-8316
Fax: +1 (630) 513-8362
Email: submissions@medallionmediagroup.com
Website: http://medallionmediagroup.com

Publishes: Fiction; Nonfiction; *Areas:* Arts; Autobiography; Biography; Design; Fantasy; Health; Historical; Horror; Mystery; Religious; Romance; Sci-Fi; Suspense; Thrillers; *Markets:* Adult; Youth; *Treatments:* Literary; Mainstream

Contact: Emily Steele

Publishes fiction and nonfiction for adults and young adults. No children's books, short stories, or erotica. Accepts nonfiction proposals through agents only. Submit via submission form on website. No hard copy submissions.

Medical Group Management Association (MGMA)

104 Inverness Terrace East
Englewood, CO 80112-5306
Tel: +1 (303) 799-1111
Email: support@mgma.com
Website: http://www.mgma.com

Publishes: Nonfiction; *Areas:* Business; Medicine; *Markets:* Professional

Publishes books for professionals, aimed at the business side of medicine. Submit complete ms, or proposal including outline and three sample chapters.

Messianic Jewish Publishers

6120 Day Long Lane
Clarksville, MD 21029
Tel: +1 (410) 531-6644
Email: editor@messianicjewish.net
Website: http://www.messianicjewish.net

Publishes: Fiction; Nonfiction; *Areas:* Religious; *Markets:* Adult

Publishes books which address Jewish evangelism; the Jewish roots of Christianity; Messianic Judaism; Israel; the Jewish People. Publishes mainly nonfiction, but some fiction. See website for full submission guidelines.

Metal Powder Industries Federation (MPIF)

105 College Road East
Princeton, NJ 08540
Tel: +1 (609) 452-7700
Fax: +1 (609) 987-8523
Email: info@mpif.org
Website: http://www.mpif.org

Publishes: Nonfiction; *Areas:* Technology; *Markets:* Professional

Publishes books on powder metallurgy and particulate materials.

Mitchell Lane Publishers, Inc.

PO Box 196
Hockessin, DE 19707
Tel: +1 (302) 234-9426
Fax: +1 (302) 234-4742
Email: customerservice@mitchelllane.com
Website: http://www.mitchelllane.com

Publishes: Nonfiction; *Areas:* Arts; Biography; Crafts; Health; Historical; Literature; Music; Politics; Science; Technology; *Markets:* Children's

Publishes nonfiction for children. No unsolicited mss. Send query by post with SASE.

Morgan Kaufmann Publishers

30 Corporate Drive, Suite 400
Burlington, MA 01803-4252
Tel: +1 (781) 663-5200
Email: a.dierna@elsevier.com
Website: http://mkp.com

Publishes: Nonfiction; *Areas:* Science; Technology; *Markets:* Professional

Publishes books for the computer science community. Complete New Book Proposal Questionnaire (available on website) and send it by email to the appropriate editor (list available on website).

Mountain Press Publishing Company

PO Box 2399
Missoula, MT 59806
Tel: +1 (406) 728-1900
Email: Info@mtnpress.com
Website: http://mountain-press.com

Publishes: Nonfiction; *Areas:* Historical; Nature; Science; *Markets:* Adult; Children's

Publishes books on natural history, western US history, and earth science. Send query by post only, with proposal including outline or table of contents and sample (one or two chapters). See website for full submission guidelines.

Museum of Northern Arizona

3101 North Fort Valley Road
Flagstaff, AZ 86001
Tel: +1 (928) 774-5213
Email: publications@mna.mus.az.us
Website: http://musnaz.org

Publishes: Nonfiction; *Areas:* Historical; Nature; *Markets:* Adult

Publishes natural history relating to Northern Arizona.

NavPress

PO Box 35002
Colorado Springs, CO 80935
Tel: +1 (800) 366-7788
Fax: +1 (800) 343-3902
Email: CustomerService@NavPress.com
Website: http://www.navpress.com

Publishes: Nonfiction; *Areas:* Culture; How-to; Lifestyle; Religious; Sociology; Spiritual; *Markets:* Adult

Christian publisher based in Colorado Springs. Aims to publish products that are biblically rooted, culturally relevant, and highly practical.

NBM

160 Broadway, Suite 700 East Wing
New York, NY 10038
Email: tnantier@nbmpub.com
Website: http://nbmpub.com

Publishes: Fiction; *Areas:* Erotic; Fantasy; Horror; Humour; Mystery; Sci-Fi; *Markets:* Adult; Youth; *Treatments:* Satirical

Contact: Terry Nantier

Publisher of graphic novels, interested in general fiction, humour, satire of fantasy and horror, erotica, and mystery. No superheroes. Accepting approaches from previously published authors only (including those with proven success in online comics). No submissions from authors outside North America, except for adult. See website for full submission guidelines.

New Issues Poetry & Prose

1903 West Michigan Avenue
Kalamazoo, MI 49008-5463
Email: new-issues@wmich.edu
Website: http://wmich.edu/newissues

Publishes: Poetry; *Markets:* Adult

Publishes poetry books submitted through its poetry contests only – entry fee of $20-$25 applies. Submit by post or via online submission system. See website for more details.

New York University (NYU) Press

838 Broadway, 3rd Floor
New York, NY 10003-4812
Email: information@nyupress.org
Website: http://nyupress.org

Publishes: Nonfiction; *Areas:* Anthropology; Crime; Culture; Historical; Legal; Literature; Media; Politics; Psychology; Religious; Sociology; Women's Interests; *Markets:* Academic

Publishes mainly for the academic market. Send proposals by post only. See website for full guidelines.

Nicolas Hays Publishers

PO Box 540206
Lake Worth, FL 33454-0206
Email: info@nicolas hays.com
Website: http://www.nicolashays.com

Publishes: Nonfiction; *Areas:* Biography; Health; Historical; Mystery; Politics; Psychology; Religious; Self-Help; *Markets:* Adult

Publishes books on topics such as Eastern and Western mysteries, magick and occultism, alchemy, astrology, etc. See website for more details.

The Ninety-Six Press

Department of English
Furman University
3300 Poinsett Highway
Greenville, SC 29613
Tel: +1 (864) 294-3152
Email: gil.allen@furman.edu
Website:
http://library.furman.edu/specialcollections/96Press

Publishes: Poetry; *Markets:* Adult

Contact: Gilbert Allen

Focuses on publishing collections of poetry by poets from South Carolina. Accepts submissions by invitation only – see website for any current calls.

Nolo

950 Parker Street
Berkeley, CA 94710
Tel: +1 (510) 549-1976
Fax: +1 (510) 859-0025
Email: mantha@nolo.com
Website: http://www.nolo.com

Publishes: Nonfiction; Reference; *Areas:* Business; Finance; How-to; Legal; Self-Help; *Markets:* Adult; Professional

Publishes books that help individuals, small businesses, and other organisations handle their own legal matters.Send query with SASE, outline, and sample chapter.

Nova Press

9058 Lloyd P,ace
West Hollywood CA 90069
Email: sales@novapress.net
Website: http://novapress.net

Publishes: Nonfiction; Reference; *Markets:* Academic

Publishes test prep books for college entrance exams, and related reference books.

NursesBooks

American Nurses Association
8515 Georgia Avenue, Suite 400
Silver Spring, MD 20910-3492
Tel: +1 (800) 637-0323
Email: joseph.vallina@ana.org
Website: http://www.nursesbooks.org

Publishes: Nonfiction; *Areas:* Health; *Markets:* Professional

Publishes books for nurses. Send proposal, saved as a Word file, by email.

Oceanview Publishing

CEO Center at Mediterranean Plaza
595 Bay Isles Road, Suite 120-G
Longboat Key, FL 34228
Tel: +1 (941) 387-8500
Fax: +1 (941) 387-0039
Email: submissions@oceanviewpub.com
Website: http://oceanviewpub.com

Publishes: Fiction; *Areas:* Mystery; Thrillers; *Markets:* Adult

Publishes adult fiction, with a primary interest in the mystery/thriller genre. No children's or young adult literature, poetry, memoirs, cookbooks, technical manuals, or short stories. Accepts submissions only from authors who either have a literary agent; have been previously published by a traditional publishing house; or have been specifically invited to submit by a representative or author of the publishing house. See website for more details.

Ooligan Press

369 Neuberger Hall
724 SW Harrison Street
Portland, Oregon 97201
Tel: +1 (503) 725-9748
Fax: +1 (503) 725-3561
Email: acquisitions@ooliganpress.pdx.edu
Website: http://www.ooliganpress.pdx.edu

Publishes: Fiction; Nonfiction; Poetry; *Areas:* Historical; Sociology; *Markets:* Adult; Youth; *Treatments:* Literary

Publishes works of historical and social value, or significance to the Pacific Northwest region (Northern California, Oregon, Idaho, Washington, British Columbia, and Alaska). Accepts queries by email and proposals via onlnie submission system. See website for full details.

Open Court Publishing Company

Attn: Acquisitions Editor
70 East Lake Street, Suite 300
Chicago, IL 60601
Tel: +1 (800) 815-2280
Fax: +1 (312) 701-1728
Email: opencourt@caruspub.com
Website: http://www.opencourtbooks.com

Publishes: Nonfiction; *Areas:* Culture; Philosophy; *Markets:* Adult; *Treatments:* Popular

Accepts approaches for its Popular Culture and Philosophy series only. Send query by post only, with SASE, outline, and sample chapter. No approaches by fax or email. See website for full guidelines.

Open Idea Publishing, LLC

PO Box 1060
Owings Mills, MD 21117
Tel: +1 (410) 356-7014
Email: editors@openideapublishing.com
Website:
http://www.openideapublishing.com

Publishes: Fiction; Poetry; *Areas:* Adventure; Arts; Drama; Erotic; Fantasy; Leisure; Literature; Mystery; Romance; Short Stories; Theatre; *Markets:* Adult; Family; Youth; *Treatments:* Contemporary; Literary; Popular; Positive; Progressive; Satirical; Traditional

Contact: K Jones

Publishing company founded in 2012 whose mission is to get talented writers successfully published. There is no specialty at this time. Mainly interested in true life emotions and events.

The Overlook Press

141 Wooster Street
New York, NY 10012
Tel: +1 (212) 673-2210
Fax: +1 (212) 673-2296
Email: sales@overlookny.com
Website: http://www.overlookpress.com

Publishes: Fiction; Nonfiction; *Areas:* Architecture; Arts; Current Affairs; Design; Film; Health; Historical; How-to; Lifestyle; Theatre; Translations; *Markets:* Adult; *Treatments:* Commercial; Literary

Independent general-interest publisher. Eclectic list, with areas of strength in fiction, history, biography, drama, design, and other visual media. Submissions via literary agents only.

The Overmountain Press

PO Box 1261
Johnson City, TN 37605
Tel: +1 (423) 926-2691
Fax: +1 (423) 232-1252
Email: submissions@overmtn.com
Website: http://overmtn.com

Publishes: Fiction; Nonfiction; *Areas:* Cookery; Historical; Travel; *Markets:* Adult; Children's; Youth

Contact: Beth Wright (Publisher); Daniel Lewis (Managing Editor)

Primarily a publisher of Southern Appalachian nonfiction. Publishes fiction in the form of picture books for children only. Publishes nonfiction for children and adults, including histories, cookery, guidebooks, ghost lore and folk lore. No email submissions.

P&R Publishing

PO Box 817
Phillipsburg, NJ 08865-0817
Tel: +1 (908) 454-0505
Fax: +1 (908) 859-2390
Email: editorial@prpbooks.com
Website: http://www.prpbooks.com

Publishes: Fiction; Nonfiction; *Areas:* Biography; Historical; Lifestyle; Religious; Women's Interests; *Markets:* Academic; Adult; Children's; Youth; *Treatments:* Popular

Publishes books that promote biblical understanding and godly living, ranging from books aimed at the popular market to academic works that advance biblical and theological scholarship. Submit 2-3 chapters as Word or .rtf files by email, along with completed submission form (available from website).

Parenting Press, Inc.

PO Box 75267
Seattle, WA 98175-0267
Tel: +1 (206) 364-2900
Fax: +1 (206) 364-0702
Website: http://www.parentingpress.com

Publishes: Nonfiction; *Areas:* How-to; Lifestyle; *Markets:* Adult; Children's

Contact: Carolyn Threadgill, Acquisitions

Publishes books that teach practical life skills to parents, children, and the people who care for them. No fiction or poetry. See website for submission guidelines.

Papercutz

160 Broadway, Suite 700E
New York, NY 10038
Tel: +1 (646) 559-4681
Email: nantier@papercutz.com
Website: http://www.papercutz.com

Publishes: Fiction; *Areas:* Adventure; Horror; Humour; Mystery; *Markets:* Children's; Youth

Publisher dedicated to graphic novels for children, tweens, and teens. Publishes a wide range of genres, including humour, action adventure, mystery, horror, and favourite characters.

Paragon House

3600 Labore Road, Suite 1
St Paul, Minnesota 55110-4144
Tel: +1 (651) 644-3087
Fax: +1 (651) 644-0997
Email: submissions@paragonhouse.com
Website: http://www.paragonhouse.com

Publishes: Nonfiction; Reference; *Areas:* Biography; Current Affairs; Finance; Historical; Philosophy; Politics; Psychology; Religious; Spiritual; *Markets:* Academic; Adult

Submit by email only, as an attachment. Include abstract of your project (summary of your premise, main arguments, and conclusions); table of contents; sample chapter; CV; estimated number of diagrams, figures, pictures or drawings; estimated number of double-spaced manuscript pages, in your completed project; tentative schedule for completion; copies of any endorsements or reviews; list of competing books, and a brief note on how your book compares to each; and SASE for entire MS.

Parallax Press

PO Box 7355
Berkeley, CA 94707
Tel: +1 (510) 540-6411
Email: rachel.neumann@parallax.org
Website: http://www.parallax.org

Publishes: Nonfiction; Markets

Buddhist publisher of books on mindfulness in daily life. Committed to making these teachings accessible to everyone and preserving them for future generations. Proposals accepted by post or by email. See website for full guidelines.

Paul Dry Books, Inc.

1700 Sansom Street, Suite 700
Philadelphia, PA 19103
Tel: +1 (215) 231-9939
Fax: +1 (215) 231-9942
Email: editor@pauldrybooks.com
Website: http://pauldrybooks.com

Publishes: Fiction; Nonfiction; Poetry; *Areas:* Architecture; Autobiography; Biography; Criticism; Culture; Historical; Philosophy; Science; Short Stories; Translations; Travel; *Markets:* Adult; Youth; *Treatments:* Contemporary; Literary

Publisher with the aim to publish lively books "to awaken, delight, and educate"—and to spark conversation. Publishes fiction, including both novels and short stories; and nonfiction, including biography, memoirs, history, and essays.

Pauline Books and Media

50 St Paul's Avenue
Boston, MA 02130
Tel: +1 (617) 522-8911
Email: editorial@paulinemedia.com
Website: http://www.pauline.org

Publishes: Fiction; Nonfiction; *Areas:* Biography; Religious; Self-Help; Spiritual; *Markets:* Adult; Children's; Family; Youth

Catholic publisher, publishing nonfiction for children and adults of all ages, as well as fiction for children and teens only. Send complete manuscript or table of contents with sample chapter by email or by post. See website for full guidelines.

Penny-Farthing Press

2000 West Sam Houston Parkway South,
Suite 550
Houston, Texas 77042
Tel: +1 (713) 780-0300
Fax: +1 (713) 780-4004
Email: corp@pfpress.com
Website: http://www.pfpress.com

Publishes: Fiction; *Markets:* Adult; Children's

Award-winning publisher of comics and children's books. Send query with synopsis by post only. If submitting one single-issue story (standard 32 pp.), include full script. If submitting a story for a series or graphic novel send only first chapter. No submissions by fax or email. See website for full guidelines.

Persea Books

277 Broadway, Suite 708
New York, NY 10007
Tel: +1 (212) 260-9256
Fax: +1 (212) 267-3165
Email: info@perseabooks.com
Website: http://www.perseabooks.com

Publishes: Fiction; Nonfiction; Poetry; *Areas:* Autobiography; Biography; Criticism; Short Stories; Translations; *Markets:* Adult; Youth; *Treatments:* Literary

Publishes literary fiction and nonfiction manuscripts, including novels, novellas, short story collections, biography, essays, literary criticism, literature in translation, memoir. Encourages submissions to growing YA list in nonfiction, fiction, and poetry, aimed at the literary reader. No social science, psychology, self-help, textbooks, or children's books. Accepts submissions by post or by email. See website for full guidelines. For poetry, query by email in first instance.

Peter Lang Publishing, Inc.

29 Broadway
New York, NY 10006
Tel: +1 (212) 647-7706
Fax: +1 (212) 647-7707
Email: CustomerService@plang.com
Website: http://www.peterlang.com

Publishes: Nonfiction; *Markets:* Academic

International academic publisher. Submit query via web form.

Pflaum Publishing Group

2621 Dryden Road
Dayton, OH 45439
Tel: +1 (800) 543-4383
Email: Service@Pflaum.com
Website: http://www.pflaum.com

Publishes: Nonfiction; *Areas:* Religious; *Markets:* Academic

Publisher of religious education material, mainly catholic. Send query with SASE.

Piano Press

P.O. Box 85
Del Mar, CA 92014-0085
Tel: +1 (619) 884-1401
Fax: +1 (858) 755-1104
Email: pianopress@pianopress.com

Publishes: Fiction; Nonfiction; Poetry; *Areas:* Music; *Markets:* Children's; Youth

Publishes books related to music for young readers, middle readers and young adults. Includes fiction, nonfiction, poetry, colouring books, and songbooks. Send query by email only.

Picador USA

175 Fifth Avenue
New York, NY 10010
Tel: +1 (646) 307-5421
Fax: +1 (212) 388-9065
Email: publicity@picadorusa.com
Website: http://www.picadorusa.com

Publishes: Fiction; Nonfiction; *Markets:* Adult; *Treatments:* Literary

Publishes literary fiction and nonfiction. Submissions via a literary agent only.

Piccadilly Books Ltd

PO Box 25203

Colorado Springs, CO 80936
Tel: +1 (719) 550-9887
Fax: +1 (719) 550-8810
Email: info@piccadillybooks.com
Website: http://www.piccadillybooks.com

Publishes: Nonfiction; *Areas:* Cookery; Health; Nature; *Markets:* Adult

Publishes books on natural health, nutrition, diet, physical fitness, and related topics. Send query with a minimum of three sample chapters, however prefers to see complete ms. Include cover letter with overview of the book and market, and your qualifications in writing the book. Pitches accepted by email. See website for full guidelines.

Picton Press

814 East Elkcam Circle
Marco Island, FL 34145
Email: sales@pictonpress.com
Website: http://www.pictonpress.com

Publishes: Nonfiction; Reference; *Areas:* Historical; Hobbies; *Markets:* Adult

Publishes genealogical and historical books, specialising in research tools for the 17th-19th centuries. Send query with SASE and outline.

Plan B Press

PO Box 4067
Alexandria, VA 22303
Tel: +1 (215) 732-2663
Email: planbpress@gmail.com
Website: http://www.planbpress.com

Publishes: Poetry; *Markets:* Adult; *Treatments:* Literary

Small, independent publishing company primarily producing limited-run poetry chapbooks. Send 20-30 poems between June 1 and November 30, only, by post or by email. See website for full guidelines.

Possibility Press

One Oakglade circle
Hummelstown, PA 17036
Tel: +1 (717) 566-0468
Fax: +1 (717) 566-6423
Email: info@possibilitypress.com
Website: http://www.possibilitypress.com

Publishes: Fiction; Nonfiction; *Areas:* Business; Finance; Health; How-to; Lifestyle; Psychology; Religious; Self-Help; Spiritual; Technology; *Markets:* Adult

Contact: Mike Markowski; Marjie Markowski

Publishes mainly nonfiction books on personal improvement, covering finances, religion, relationships, self-esteem, public speaking, leadership, etc. Also considers fiction that teaches lessons about life and success. See website for detailed guide on preparing a submission.

Presa Press

PO Box 792
Rockford, MI 49341
Email: presapress@aol.com
Website: http://www.presapress.com

Publishes: Nonfiction; Poetry; *Areas:* Criticism; Literature; *Markets:* Adult; *Treatments:* Literary

Publishes poetry paperbacks and literary magazine, including poetry, reviews, essays, and criticism. Query for guidelines.

Press 53

411 West Fourth Street, Suite 101A
Winston-Salem, NC 27101
Tel: +1 (336) 770-5353
Email: kevin@press53.com
Website: http://www.press53.com

Publishes: Fiction; Poetry; *Areas:* Short Stories; *Markets:* Adult; *Treatments:* Literary

Contact: Kevin Morgan Watson

Publishes collections of poetry and short stories. No novels or book length fiction. Finds authors through its competitions, and through writers being active in the literary community and literary magazines.

Princeton University Press

41 William Street
Princeton, NJ 08540
Tel: +1 (609) 258-4900
Fax: +1 (609) 258-6305
Email: front_desk@press.princeton.edu
Website: http://press.princeton.edu

Publishes: Nonfiction; Poetry; Reference; *Areas:* Anthropology; Archaeology; Architecture; Arts; Film; Finance; Historical; Legal; Literature; Medicine; Music; Nature; Philosophy; Photography; Politics; Psychology; Religious; Science; Self-Help; Sociology; Spiritual; Technology; *Markets:* Academic

Scholarly publisher. Send brief proposals fitting the scholarly profile and the composition of their current lists, 1-2 pages maximum. No unsolicited mss.

Pro Lingua Associates ESL

PO Box 1348
Brattleboro, VT 05302-1348
Tel: +1 (802) 257-7779
Fax: +1 (802) 257-5117
Email: Ray@ProLinguaAssociates.com
Website: http://www.prolinguaassociates.com

Publishes: Nonfiction; *Markets:* Academic

Contact: Raymond C. Clark, Senior Editor

Small publisher dedicated to producing "superior language teaching materials". Will respond to enquiries made by email, but no proposals by email. See website for full submission guidelines.

Professional Publications, Inc. (PPI)

1250 Fifth Ave
Belmont, CA 94002
Tel: +1 (650) 593-9119
Fax: +1 (650) 592-4519
Email: acquisitions@ppi2pass.com
Website: http://ppi2pass.com

Publishes: Nonfiction; Reference; *Areas:* Architecture; Design; Science; *Markets:* Professional

Publishes books relating to architecture, engineering, design, matematics, science etc. and provides products and information for FE/EIT, PE, FS/PS, ARE, NCIDQ and LARE exam preparation. Send proposal with MS and market analysis, etc. Seeks technical, detailed material.

Prometheus Books

59 John Glenn Drive
Amherst, New York 14228-2197
Tel: +1 (716) 691-0133
Fax: +1 (716) 691-0137
Email: editorial@prometheusbooks.com
Website: http://www.prometheusbooks.com

Publishes: Nonfiction; *Areas:* Business; Current Affairs; Health; Philosophy; Science; Sociology; *Markets:* Adult

Send query by email in first instance. Do not send full proposal or complete MS unless requested, and then only by post. See website for full details.

Quarto Publishing Group USA

400 First Avenue North, Suite 400
Minneapolis, MN 55401
Tel: +1 (612) 344-8100
Fax: +1 (612) 344-8691
Website: http://www.quartous.com

Publishes: Nonfiction; Reference; *Areas:* Arts; Cookery; Crafts; Current Affairs; Design; Health; Historical; Hobbies; How-to; Military; Music; Politics; Science; Self-Help; Sport; Technology; Travel; *Markets:* Adult

Nonfiction publisher with offices in the US and UK. See website for specific interests and guidelines for different imprints.

Quest Books

306 West Geneva Road
PO Box 270
Wheaton, IL 60187-0270
Tel: +1 (630) 665-0130
Email: submissions@questbooks.net
Website: http://www.questbooks.net

Publishes: Nonfiction; *Areas:* Arts; Health;

Music; Mystery; Philosophy; Psychology; Religious; Science; Self-Help; Spiritual; *Markets:* Adult

Contact: Submissions Department

Publishes books of intelligence, readability, and insight for the contemporary spiritual seeker, exploring ancient wisdom, modern science, world religions, philosophy, the arts, and the inner meaning of life to "provide dynamic tools for spiritual healing and self-transformation". See website for full submission guidelines.

Quill Driver Books

2006 South Mary Street
Fresno, CA 93721
Email: kent@lindenpub.com
Website: http://quilldriverbooks.com

Publishes: Nonfiction; *Areas:* Architecture; Arts; Biography; Business; Crime; Health; Hobbies; Humour; Lifestyle; Self-Help; Spiritual; Technology; Travel; *Markets:* Adult

Contact: Kent Sorsky

Publishes nonfiction only. Send a book proposal including synopsis; commercial info; author platform; and sample chapters or supporting materials. See website for full guidelines.

Ragged Sky Press

PO Box 312
Annandale, NJ 08801
Email: info@raggedsky.com
Website: http://www.raggedsky.com

Publishes: Poetry; *Areas:* Women's Interests; *Markets:* Adult; *Treatments:* Literary

Small and selective co-operative press publishing collections of poetry. Has historically focused on mature voices, overlooked poets, and women's perspectives. Does no accept unsolicited mss. Poets are encouraged to join the community. Submissions by invitation.

Rainbow Books, Inc.

PO Box 430
Highland City, FL 33846-0430
Tel: +1 (863) 648-4420
Email: Submissions@RainbowBooksInc.com
Website: http://www.rainbowbooksinc.com

Publishes: Fiction; Nonfiction; *Areas:* How-to; Mystery; Self-Help; *Markets:* Adult

Publishes self-help, how-to, and cozy murder mysteries. Send query by post with SASE, one-page synopsis, up to three sample chapters, outline, details of any photos or illustrations, author background and credentials, and your email address. Queries may also be sent by email, however attachments will not be opened. See website for full guidelines.

Rainbow Publishers

PO Box 261129
San Diego, CA 92196
Email: info@rainbowpublishers.com
Website: http://www.rainbowpublishers.com

Publishes: Nonfiction; *Areas:* Religious; *Markets:* Children's

Publishes reproducible classroom resource books for Sunday School. See website for submission guidelines. No academics, poetry, picture books, or fiction.

RainTown Press

1111 E. Burnside St. #309
Portland, OR 97214
Email: submissions@raintownpress.com
Website: http://raintownpress.com

Publishes: Fiction; *Markets:* Children's; Youth

Independent press dedicated to publishing literature for middle grade and young adults in any genre. No short stories or novellas – young adult novels should be at least 60,000 words and Middle Grade novels should be at least 45,000 words. No poems or poetry chapbooks; picture books; memoirs; nonfiction; or incomplete manuscripts. See website for full submission guidelines.

Reading Harbor

Lansdale, PA
Email: ReadingHarborCo@gmail.com
Website: http://www.readingharbor.com

Publishes: Fiction; Nonfiction; *Areas:* Autobiography; Culture; Current Affairs; Entertainment; Literature; Philosophy; Psychology; Self-Help; Short Stories; Women's Interests; *Markets:* Adult; Family; Youth; *Treatments:* Commercial; Literary; Mainstream; Niche; Popular; Positive

Contact: Grace C

An American-based Publication Company, founded in 2014. Our goal is to bring quality literature to the public. Reading should be a passtime that not only informs the mind but stirs the spirit and inspires the heart. A good book is a treasured find. We want to provide you memories you will share.

Redleaf Press

10 Yorkton Court
St. Paul, MN 55117-1065
Tel: +1 (800) 423-8309
Fax: +1 (800) 641-0115
Email: acquisitions@redleafpress.org
Website: http://www.redleafpress.org

Publishes: Nonfiction; *Markets:* Professional

Publishes resources for early childhood professionals. Send proposals by post or by email. See website for guidelines.

Reference Service Press

2310 Homestead Road, Suite C1 #219
Los Altos, CA 94024
Tel: +1 (650) 861-3170
Fax: +1 (650) 861-3171
Email: info@rspfunding.com
Website: http://www.rspfunding.com

Publishes: Nonfiction; Reference; *Areas:* Architecture; Arts; Business; Culture; Health; Historical; Medicine; Religious; Science; Sociology; Women's Interests; *Markets:* Professional

Contact: Stuart Hauser, Acquisitions Editor

Publishes financial aid publications for librarians, counselors, researchers, students, re-entry women, scholars, and other fundseekers. Send outline with sample chapters.

Regnery Publishing, Inc.

One Massachusetts Avenue, NW
Washington, DC 20001
Tel: +1 (202) 216-0600
Fax: +1 (202) 216-0612
Email: editorial@regnery.com
Website: http://www.regnery.com

Publishes: Nonfiction; *Areas:* Historical; Military; Politics; Science; *Markets:* Adult; Children's

Publisher of conservative books. Accepts submissions via agents only.

Renaissance House

465 Westview Avenue
Englewood, NY 07631
Tel: +1 (201) 408-4048
Email: info@renaissancehouse.net
Website: http://renaissancehouse.net

Publishes: Fiction; Nonfiction; *Markets:* Adult; Children's

Creates books in English and in Spanish. Offers e-publishing. Send ideas by email.

Richard C. Owen Publishers, Inc.

PO Box 585
Katonah, NY 10536
Tel: +1 (914) 232-3903
Fax: +1 (914) 232-3977
Email: richardowen@rcowen.com
Website: http://www.rcowen.com

Publishes: Nonfiction; *Markets:* Academic; Children's; Professional

Publishes books on literacy education, including classroom materials for for grades PK-8, and books for teachers and administrators.

Rio Nuevo Publishers

PO Box 5250
Tucson, AZ 85703
Tel: +1 (520) 623-9558
Fax: +1 (520) 624-5888
Email: info@rionuevo.com
Website: http://www.rionuevo.com

Publishes: Fiction; Nonfiction; *Areas:* Architecture; Arts; Autobiography; Biography; Cookery; Culture; Design; Gardening; Historical; Nature; Photography; Spiritual; Travel; *Markets:* Adult; Children's

Publishes books for adults and children relating to the West and Southwest. Publishes only nonfiction for adults. Publishes fiction and nonfiction for children, via imprint. Send query and proposal by post or by email for adult titles; for children's books submit complete ms by email to address provided on website. See website for full submission guidelines.

Ripple Grove Press

PO Box 491
Hubbardston, MA 01452
Email: submit@ripplegrovepress.com
Website: http://www.ripplegrovepress.com

Publishes: Fiction; *Markets:* Children's

Publishes picture-driven stories for children aged 2-6. No early readers, middle grade, young adult, religious, or holiday-themed stories. Send submissions by post with SASE or by email, including cover letter with summary; age range of audience; brief bio; contact info; and full ms (as a PDF attachment if submitting by email). See website for full guidelines.

Roberts Press

685 Spring Street, PMB 161
Friday Harbor, WA 98250
Email: submit-robertspress@falsebaybooks.com
Website: https://robertsbookpressdotcom.wordpress.com

Publishes: Fiction; *Areas:* Fantasy; Mystery; Short Stories; Suspense; Women's Interests; *Markets:* Adult; Children's; Youth;

Treatments: Literary; Mainstream

Small indie book publisher, publishing works of fiction only. Publishes novels between 45,000 and 80,000 words. Also has specific calls for anthologies. Send complete ms by email. See website for full guidelines.

Rose Alley Press

4203 Brooklyn Avenue NE, #103A, Seattle, WA 98105-5911
Tel: +1 (206) 633-2725
Email: rosealleypress@juno.com
Website: http://www.rosealleypress.com

Publishes: Poetry; *Markets:* Adult

Contact: David D. Horowitz, Publisher

Publisher contacts authors whose work he wants to publish. Does not accept or consider unsolicited mss.

The Rosen Publishing Group, Inc.

29 East 21st Street
New York, NY 10010
Tel: +1 (800) 237-9932
Fax: +1 (888) 436-4643
Website: http://www.rosenpublishing.com

Publishes: Nonfiction; *Areas:* Arts; Biography; Crafts; Culture; Health; Historical; Religious; Science; Self-Help; Sociology; Sport; *Markets:* Academic; Children's; Youth

Independent educational publishing house serving the needs of students in grades Pre-K -12 with high interest, curriculum-correlated materials.

Rowman & Littlefield Publishing Group

4501 Forbes Boulevard, Suite 200
Lanham, MD 20706
Tel: +1 (301) 459-3366
Fax: +1 (301) 429-5748
Email: jsisk@rowmanlittlefield.com
Website: https://rowman.com

Publishes: Nonfiction; *Areas:* Crime;

Health; Historical; Legal; Nature; Philosophy; Politics; Psychology; Religious; Sociology; *Markets:* Academic; Adult; Professional

Publishes books on subjects throughout the humanities and social sciences, both for general readers and professional and scholarly titles. See website for submission guidelines.

Ruka Press

PO Box 1409
Washington, DC 20013
Tel: +1 (202) 546-8049
Email: submissions@rukapress.com
Website: http://www.rukapress.com

Publishes: Nonfiction; *Areas:* Finance; Nature; Science; *Markets:* Adult

Publishes books on economics, science, nature, climate change and sustainability. No fiction or poetry. Send query by post or email. See website for full guidelines.

Running Press

2300 Chestnut Street
Philadelphia, PA 19103
Tel: +1 (215) 567-5080
Fax: +1 (215) 568-2919
Email: perseus.promos@perseusbooks.com
Website: http://www.runningpress.com

Publishes: Fiction; Nonfiction; *Areas:* Arts; Beauty and Fashion; Cookery; Crafts; Culture; Health; Hobbies; Humour; Leisure; Lifestyle; Self-Help; Sport; *Markets:* Adult

Publisher of nonfiction and fiction. No unsolicited submissions.

Saddleback Educational Publishing

Submissions
3120-A Pullman Street
Costa Mesa, CA 92626
Email: contact@sdlback.com
Website: http://www.sdlback.com

Publishes: Fiction; *Markets:* Children's; Youth

Publishes books in all genres and subjects for children aged 12-18, but focusses on original fiction. No K-3 elementary submissions. Submit by post or email. See website for full guidelines.

Sakura Publishing & Technologies

PO BOX 1681
Hermitage,PA 16148
Tel: +1 (330) 360-5131
Email: skpublishing124@gmail.com
Website: http://sakura-publishing.com

Publishes: Fiction; Nonfiction; Poetry; *Markets:* Adult

Publishes fiction, nonfiction, and poetry, but shies away from YA novels, vampires or zombies, and poorly written science-fiction and fantasy. Accepts queries by post or via online form. See website for details.

Saturnalia Books

105 Woodside Road
Ardmore, PA 19003
Tel: +1 (267) 278-9541
Email: info@saturnaliabooks.com
Website: http://www.saturnaliabooks.org

Publishes: Poetry; *Markets:* Adult

Poetry publisher and non-profit organisation. Accepts submissions only via annual poetry competition running Feb 1 to April 15; entry fee: $30; first prize: $2,000 and publication. No other unsolicited mss accepted.

Scarecrow Press Inc.

4501 Forbes Blvd, Suite 200
Lanham, MD 20706
Tel: +1 (717) 794-3800 ext. 3557
Email: asnider@scarecrowpress.com
Website: http://www.scarecrowpress.com

Publishes: Nonfiction; Reference; *Areas:* Culture; Film; Historical; Literature; Music; Philosophy; Religious; Sport; Theatre; *Markets:* Academic

Contact: April Snider, Acquisitions Editor

Publishes historical dictionaries; reference and general interest in history, philosophy, religion and related areas.

School Guide Publications

606 Halstead Avenue
Mamaroneck, NY 10543
Tel: +1 (800) 433-7771
Email: mridder@schoolguides.com
Website: http://www.schoolguides.com

Publishes: Nonfiction; Reference; *Markets:* Adult

Publishes directories and guides on 4 & 2-year colleges, Nursing Schools, Business Schools and Military Programs.

Seriously Good Books

999 Vanderbilt Beach Road
Naples, FL 34119
Tel: +1 (800) 431-1579
Email: seriouslygoodbks@aol.com
Website: http://www.seriouslygoodbooks.net

Publishes: Fiction; *Areas:* Historical; *Markets:* Adult

Publishes historical fiction only. Send query up to one and a half pages in the body of an email, plus one-page synopsis and/or first ten pages and/or bibliography of sources consulted. No attachments. See website for full submission guidelines. Response in 30-60 days if interested. Mss must be professionally edited prior to submission.

Sierra Club Books

85 Second Street, 2nd Floor
San Francisco, CA 94105
Tel: +1 (415) 977-5500
Fax: +1 (415) 977-5797
Email: books.publishing@sierraclub.org
Website: http://www.sierraclub.org

Publishes: Nonfiction; Nature; Travel; *Markets:* Adult

Publishes books on the natural world, exploring nature, and environmental issues. Send query with SASE.

Silverfish Review Press

PO Box 3541
Eugene, OR 97403
Tel: +1 (541) 344-5060
Email: sfrpress@earthlink.net
Website: http://www.silverfishreviewpress.com

Publishes: Poetry; *Markets:* Adult; *Treatments:* Literary

Non-profit independent literary press, publishing poetry and sponsoring an annual poetry competition.

Skinner House Books

25 Beacon Street
Boston, MA 02108
Email: bookproposals@uua.org
Website: http://www.uua.org/publications/skinnerhouse/

Publishes: Nonfiction; *Areas:* Religious; Spiritual; *Markets:* Adult

Contact: Betsy Martin

Book publisher of the Unitarian Universalist faith. See website for current requirements and details on how to approach.

Small Beer Press

150 Pleasant Street, #306
Easthampton, MA 01027
Email: info@smallbeerpress.com
Website: http://smallbeerpress.com

Publishes: Fiction; *Areas:* Humour; Sci-Fi; Short Stories; *Markets:* Adult; *Treatments:* Experimental; Literary

Publishes literary and experimental fiction and short story collections. Does not publish poetry collections or chapbooks. No email queries or unsolicited mss. Familiarise yourself with books already published before approaching. Send query with SASE and first 10-20 pages. See website for full guidelines.

Soft Skull Press

1919 Fifth Street

Berkeley, CA 94710
Email: info@softskull.com
Website: http://softskull.com

Publishes: Fiction; Nonfiction; *Areas:* Arts; Autobiography; Biography; Cookery; Crime; Culture; Current Affairs; Fantasy; Film; Health; Historical; Humour; Lifestyle; Literature; Media; Mystery; Philosophy; Politics; Religious; Sociology; Thrillers; Travel; TV; Women's Interests; *Markets:* Adult; *Treatments:* Literary; Popular

Seeks books that are "new, fun, smart, revelatory, quirky, groundbreaking, cage-rattling and/or/otherwise unusual." Send query describing your project with proposal and two sample chapters (nonfiction), or complete manuscript (fiction). Material will not be returned, and response only if interested. No electronic submissions, and no follow-ups by phone or email.

St Augustine's Press

PO Box 2285
South Bend, IN 46680-2285
Tel: +1 (574) 291-3500
Email: bruce@staugustine.net
Website: http://www.staugustine.net

Publishes: Nonfiction; *Areas:* Culture; Historical; Philosophy; Religious; *Markets:* Academic

Contact: Bruce Fingerhut

Publishes scholarly works in the fields of philosophy, theology, and cultural and intellectual history. Send query by post or electronically; see website for full guidelines. No unsolicited mss.

St. Johann Press

PO Box 241
Haworth, NJ 07641
Email: d.biesel@verizon.net
Website: http://stjohannpress.com

Publishes: Fiction; Nonfiction; Poetry; *Areas:* Autobiography; Biography; Hobbies; Religious; Short Stories; Sport; *Markets:* Adult

Contact: David Biesel

Small, independent press located in Northern New Jersey specialising in niche publishing of nonfiction titles, though also some poetry and fiction collections. Send query with SASE.

Steel Toe Books

Department of English
Western Kentucky University
1906 College Heights Blvd. #11086
Bowling Green, KY 42101-1086
Email: tom.hunley@wku.edu
Website: http://www.steeltoebooks.com

Publishes: Poetry; *Markets:* Adult; *Treatments:* Literary

Contact: Tom C. Hunley

Publishes single-author poetry collections. No reading fee, but asks those who submit to purchase one of their titles directly from them. See website for full submission guidelines and details of reading periods, etc.

Stemmer House Publishers

PO Box 89
4 White Brook Road
Gilsum, NH 03448
Tel: +1 (603) 357-0236
Fax: +1 (603) 357-2073
Email: pbs@pathwaybook.com
Website: http://www.stemmer.com

Publishes: Fiction; Nonfiction; Poetry; Reference; *Areas:* Arts; Culture; Hobbies; Nature; Science; Short Stories; *Markets:* Adult; Children's

Publishes nonfiction and reference for adults and children on nature, science, hobbies, culture, and arts. Also publishes stories and poetry for children. Send query with SASE in first instance.

Stone Bridge Press

PO Box 8208
Berkeley, CA 94707

STREET ADDRESS:

1393 Solano Avenue, Suite C
Albany, CA 94706
Tel: +1 (510) 524-8732
Fax: +1 (888) 411-8527
Email: sbpedit@stonebridge.com
Website: http://www.stonebridge.com

Publishes: Fiction; Nonfiction; Reference; *Areas:* Business; Crafts; Culture; Design; Film; Lifestyle; Literature; Spiritual; Translations; Travel; *Markets:* Adult; Children's

Publishes books about Asia and in particular Japan. Publishes mainly nonfiction and fiction in translation, but will in rare cases consider original fiction if appropriate. No poetry. Prefers submissions by email, but will accept submissions by post (use street address if sending by express mail or delivery service such as UPS). See website for full guidelines.

Stoneslide Books

Email: editors@stoneslidecorrective.com
Website: http://stoneslidecorrective.com

Publishes: Fiction; *Markets:* Adult

Publishes novels "with strong character development and narrative thrust, brought out with writing that's clear and expressive". Pays modest advance and offers competitive revenue sharing arrangement after publication. Submit using submission form on website.

Strategic Media Books

782 Wofford Street
Rock Hill, SC 29730
Email: contact@strategicmediabooks.com
Website: http://strategicmediabooks.com

Publishes: Fiction; Nonfiction; *Areas:* Crime; Current Affairs; Politics; *Markets:* Adult

Publishes true crime, crime and mystery fiction, southern interest, international politics, and "books that have a compelling story line and a riveting narrative". Send query by post or email with cover letter outlining the story or theme, how long it will take to complete, brief bio, one or two chapters, and marketing plan. See website for full guidelines.

Sunbury Press

PO BOX 548
Boiling Springs, PA 17007
Tel: +1 (855) 338-8359
Fax: +1 (855) 338-8359
Email: proposals@sunburypress.com
Website: http://www.sunburypress.com

Publishes: Fiction; Nonfiction; Reference; *Areas:* Arts; Current Affairs; Historical; Humour; Religious; Science; *Markets:* Adult; Children's

Rapidly growing publisher, actively seeking new material. Receives about 1,000 manuscripts a year, and publishes around 70. No hard copy submissions or phone calls. Submit using form on website.

Sunscribe

1735 Heckle Blvd
Suite 103
Rock Hill, SC 29732
Tel: +1 (704) 467-4067
Email: sunscribepublishers@gmail.com
Website: http://sunscribe.net

Publishes: Fiction; Nonfiction; Poetry; Reference; Scripts; *Areas:* Adventure; Anthropology; Antiques; Archaeology; Architecture; Arts; Autobiography; Beauty and Fashion; Biography; Business; Cookery; Crafts; Crime; Criticism; Culture; Current Affairs; Design; Drama; Entertainment; Fantasy; Film; Finance; Gardening; Gothic; Health; Historical; Hobbies; How-to; Humour; Legal; Leisure; Lifestyle; Literature; Media; Medicine; Men's Interests; Military; Music; Mystery; Nature; New Age; Philosophy; Photography; Politics; Psychology; Radio; Religious; Romance; Science; Sci-Fi; Self-Help; Short Stories; Sociology; Spiritual; Sport; Suspense; Technology; Theatre; Thrillers; Translations; Travel; TV; Westerns; Women's Interests; *Markets:* Academic; Adult; Children's; Family; Professional; Youth; *Treatments:* Commercial; Contemporary; Experimental; In-depth;

Light; Literary; Mainstream; Niche; Popular; Positive; Progressive; Serious; Traditional

Contact: Roxanne Hanna

Traditional publishing company with three imprints, partnering with writers: we are proud members of AAP and IBPA. Our works adhere to our philosophy of pairing our expertise with excellent writing by establishing a culture of collaboration, focusing on talent and text. Our mission is to offer writers an opportunity to write: we handle editing, marketing, and distribution. Our standard is excellence, and we strive to team with writers passionate about their craft.

Swan Isle Press

PO Box 408790
Chicago, IL 60640-8790
Email: info@swanislepress.com
Website: http://www.swanislepress.com

Publishes: Fiction; Nonfiction; Poetry; *Areas:* Arts; Culture; Literature; Translations; *Markets:* Adult; *Treatments:* Literary

Independent, not-for-profit, literary publisher publishing works of poetry, fiction and nonfiction intended to inspire and educate while advancing the knowledge and appreciation of literature, art, and culture. Particularly interested in books related to Spanish and Latin American literature, art, and culture. Welcomes queries, but no unsolicited submissions. No queries by email.

Swan Scythe Press

1468 Mallard Way
Sunnyvale, CA 94087
Email: robert.pesich@gmail.com
Website: http://www.swanscythe.com

Publishes: Poetry; *Areas:* Translations; *Markets:* Adult

Contact: Robert Pesich

Publishes poetry collections and anthologies, including translations from Spanish and indigenous languages of the Americas into English. Send query before submitting ms.

SynergEbooks

948 New Highway 7
Columbia, TN 38401
Tel: +1 (931) 223-5990
Email: synergebooks@aol.com
Website: http://www.synergebooks.com

Publishes: Fiction; Nonfiction; Poetry; Reference; *Areas:* Business; Cookery; Crime; Fantasy; Horror; Humour; Music; Mystery; New Age; Religious; Romance; Sci-Fi; Self-Help; Spiritual; Suspense; Thrillers; Travel; Westerns; *Markets:* Adult; Children's; Youth

A non-subsidy digital publishing house. See website for full guidelines and current status regarding submissions.

Tantor Audio

2 Business Park Road
Old Saybrook, CT 06475
Tel: +1 (860) 395-1155
Fax: +1 (888) 782-7821
Email: rights@tantor.com
Website: http://www.tantor.com

Publishes: Fiction; Nonfiction; *Areas:* Adventure; Anthropology; Autobiography; Biography; Business; Cookery; Criticism; Culture; Current Affairs; Entertainment; Erotic; Fantasy; Finance; Gothic; Health; Historical; Horror; How-to; Humour; Legal; Leisure; Lifestyle; Military; Music; Mystery; Nature; New Age; Philosophy; Politics; Psychology; Religious; Romance; Science; Self-Help; Short Stories; Sociology; Spiritual; Sport; Suspense; Westerns; Women's Interests; *Markets:* Academic; Adult; Youth; *Treatments:* Contemporary; Experimental; Literary; Mainstream

Publisher of fiction and nonfiction audiobooks. Send query by post with SASE, or submit proposal with three sample chapters, plus synopsis for fiction.

Tarpaulin Sky Press

PO Box 189

Grafton, VT 05146
Email: editors@tarpaulinsky.com
Website: http://tarpaulinsky.com

Publishes: Fiction; Poetry; *Markets:* Adult; *Treatments:* Literary

Contact: Resh Daily

Accepts works of full-length prose and poetry during specific reading periods only. See website for details and join mailing list to be notified when these occur. Describes itself as "cross-genre, trans-genre, anti-genre".

Tate Publishing and Enterprises, LLC

127 East Trade Center Terrace
Mustang, OK 73064
Tel: +1 (405) 376-4900
Fax: +1 (405) 376-4401
Website: https://www.tatepublishing.com

Publishes: Fiction; Nonfiction; Poetry; *Areas:* Adventure; Arts; Biography; Business; Cookery; Entertainment; Fantasy; Health; Historical; Humour; Lifestyle; Military; Mystery; Philosophy; Politics; Religious; Romance; Sci-Fi; Self-Help; Short Stories; Spiritual; Sport; Suspense; Thrillers; Westerns; *Markets:* Adult; Children's

Describes itself as "a Christian-based, family-owned, mainline publishing organization with a mission to discover unknown authors." Aims to combine high royalties with good author relations, but accepts less than 10% of submissions. Submit proposals or manuscripts online using web form, or by post. See website for full details.

Tebot Bach

PO Box 7887
Huntington Beach, CA 92615-7887
Email: info@tebotbach.org
Website: http://www.tebotbach.org

Publishes: Poetry; *Markets:* Adult; *Treatments:* Literary

Poetry publisher. Send query by email with sample poems and brief bio.

Texas Tech University Press

Box 41037
Lubbock, TX 79409-1037
Tel: +1 (806) 742-2982
Fax: +1 (806) 742-2979
Email: ttup@ttu.edu
Website: http://universitypress.texastech printanddesign.com

Publishes: Fiction; Nonfiction; Poetry; *Areas:* Autobiography; Biography; Culture; Historical; Legal; Literature; Nature; Technology; *Markets:* Academic; Adult

University press, publishing all subject areas relating to Texas, the Great Plains, and the American West, particularly history, biography, and memoir; American and European history; American Indian studies; American legal studies; Costume and textile history; Environmental studies and literature of place; Fiction rooted in the American West and Southwest; and Jewish literature, culture, and history. Also publishes an invited first book of poetry each year, but no unsolicited submissions of poetry. See website for full details.

•Latin American and Latino fiction, in translation or English
•Natural history and natural science
•Sport in the American West
•Technical communication and rhetoric
•Vietnam and Southeast Asia, particularly during and after the Vietnam War

The Poisoned Pencil

6962 E. First Avenue, Suite 103
Scottsdale, AZ 85251
Tel: +1 (480) 945-3375
Email: ellen@thepoisonedpencil.com
Website: http://thepoisonedpencil.com

Publishes: Fiction; *Areas:* Mystery; *Markets:* Youth

Publishes young adult mystery by authors from the US and Canada. Avoid serial killers, excessive gore or horror, or heavy SF, supernatural, or fantasy content. No short story collections or middle grade fiction. Submit online via submission manager on website.

Tia Chucha Press

PO Box 328
San Fernando, CA 91341
Tel: +1 (818) 528-4511
Fax: +1 (818) 367-5600
Email: tcpress@tiachucha.org
Website: http://www.tiachucha.com

Publishes: Poetry; *Areas:* *Markets:* Adult

Contact: Luis J. Rodriguez, Editor

Publishes all types of poetic expression and are not bound by poetic style, form, school, or era. Cross-cultural – published poets have included Chicano, African American, Jamaican American, Native American, Irish American, Italian American, Korean American, Japanese American, Puerto Rican, Cuban American, and more. All ages, genders, sexual orientations, disabilities, and spiritual persuasions are welcome, but publishes only two books per year (1% of submissions). Send complete poetry ms between 60 and 120 pages by hard copy only. See website for full guidelines.

Top Cow Productions, Inc

Email: betsy@topcow.com
Website: http://www.topcow.com

Publishes: Fiction; *Areas:* Adventure; Fantasy; Sci-Fi; *Markets:* Adult; Youth

Contact: Betsy Gonia

Publishes comic books.

Torquere Press

1380 Rio Rancho Blvd #1319
Rio Rancho, NM 87124
Email: submissions@torquerepress.com
Website: http://www.torquerepress.com

Publishes: Fiction; *Areas:* Romance; Short Stories; *Markets:* Adult

Publisher of GLBT romance and all its sub-genres. Publishes works from 3,000 words up, including short stories, novelettes, novellas, and novels. A happy ending is required. See website for full submission guidelines.

Tristan Publishing

2355 Louisiana Avenue North
Golden Valley, MN 55427
Tel: +1 (763) 545-1383
Fax: +1 (763) 545-1387
Email: manuscripts@tristanpublishing.com
Website: http://www.tristanpublishing.com

Publishes: Fiction; Nonfiction; *Areas:* Lifestyle; Self-Help; Short Stories; *Markets:* Adult; Children's; *Treatments:* Positive

Contact: Brett Waldman; Sheila Waldman

Publishes uplifting, inspirational gift books of typically 36-42 pages and up to 1,000 words. Books should take readers fewer than 10 minutes to read, but should leave a lasting message of hope. Send submissions by email or by post. See website for full details.

Tsaba House

2252 12th Street
Reedley, CA 93654
Tel: +1 (559) 643-8575
Fax: +1 (559) 638-2640
Website: http://www.TsabaHouse.com

Publishes: Fiction; Nonfiction; *Areas:* Adventure; Autobiography; Beauty and Fashion; Biography; Current Affairs; Fantasy; Finance; How-to; Leisure; Lifestyle; Literature; Men's Interests; Mystery; Nature; Psychology; Religious; Romance; Science; Self-Help; Spiritual; Suspense; Thrillers; Women's Interests; *Markets:* Adult; Family; Youth; *Treatments:* Contemporary; Mainstream; Positive

Contact: Corrie Schwagerl

Dedicated to promoting the Gospel through the written word by producing quality, family friendly literature that covers a myriad of topics ranging from educational nonfiction to entertaining fiction and providing Christian based reading entertainment for all ages.

We accept unsolicited submissions once a year during the month of January ONLY. Full Submission guidelines are on our website. We are not a subsidy publisher and take full financial responsibility for publishing and marketing but we do require that our authors be willing to do a book tour and be actively involved in our Marketing Plan.

Tu Books

95 Madison Avenue, Suite #1205
New York, NY 10016
Tel: +1 (212) 779-4400
Fax: +1 (212) 683-1894
Email: tu@leeandlow.com
Website:
https://www.leeandlow.com/writers-illustrators/writing-guidelines-tu-books

Publishes: Fiction; *Areas:* Culture; Fantasy; Mystery; Sci-Fi; *Markets:* Children's; Youth

Publishes speculative fiction for children and young adults featuring diverse characters and settings. Focusses on well-told, exciting, adventurous fantasy, science fiction, and mystery novels featuring people of colour set in worlds inspired by non-Western folklore or culture. Publishes books for ages 8-12 and 12-18. No picture books, chapter books, or short stories. Send submissions by post only, with synopsis and first three chapters. Response only if interested, so do not include SASE. See website for full guidelines.

Turn the Page Publishing LLC

PO Box 3179
Upper Montclair, NJ 07043
Email: inquiry@turnthepagepublishing.com
Website: http://turnthepagepublishing.com

Publishes: Fiction; Nonfiction; *Areas:* Autobiography; Cookery; Finance; Humour; Lifestyle; Military; New Age; Spiritual; Suspense; Women's Interests; *Markets:* Adult; Youth; *Treatments:* Contemporary; Literary; Mainstream

Describes itself as "an independent press staffed by professional editors and artists dedicated to offering quality fiction and non-fiction to discerning readers". Publishes hardcover, softcover, and digital formats. May not be open to submissions at all times. See website for details.

Tuttle Publishing

Airport Business Part
364 Innovation Drive
North Clarendon, VT 05759-9436
Tel: +1 (800) 526-2778
Fax: +1 (800) 329-8885
Email: submissions@tuttlepublishing.com
Website: http://www.tuttlepublishing.com

Publishes: Fiction; Nonfiction; *Areas:* Architecture; Arts; Business; Cookery; Culture; Design; Gardening; Health; Historical; Literature; Nature; Religious; Spiritual; Sport; Travel; *Markets:* Adult; Children's

Publishes books on Asian cultures, Language and Martial Arts, including graphic novels. Accepts queries by post or by email, but prefers email approaches. See website for full submission guidelines.

Twilight Times Books

P O Box 3340
Kingsport, TN 37664
Fax: +1 (423) 323-0183
Email: publisher@twilighttimes.com
Website: http://www.twilighttimesbooks.com

Publishes: Fiction; *Areas:* Fantasy; Historical; Mystery; New Age; Romance; Sci-Fi; Suspense; Women's Interests; *Markets:* Adult; Children's; Youth; *Treatments:* Dark; Literary; Mainstream

Contact: Lida E. Quillen, Publisher

Send query by email only, including author bio, publishing credits, estimated word count, and marketing plan. Do not send complete ms.

Tyrus Books

1213 N. Sherman Ave. #306
Madison, WI 53704

Tel: +1 (508) 427-7100
Email: submissions@tyrusbooks.com
Website: http://www.tyrusbooks.com

Publishes: Fiction; *Areas:* Crime; *Markets:* Adult; *Treatments:* Literary

Publishes crime and literary fiction. Not interested in books that are heavy on explosions, violence, or cliched plots or characters. Stories should be approximately 60,000 to 100,000 words. See website for full guidelines. Send query by email with synopsis and optionally up to 20 pages in the body of the email. No attachments. If no response after a few months, assume rejection.

University of Nebraska Press

1111 Lincoln Mall
Lincoln NE 68588-0630
Tel: +1 (402) 472-3581
Fax: +1 (402) 472-6214
Email: pressmail@unl.edu
Website: http://nebraskapress.unl.edu

Publishes: Fiction; Nonfiction; Poetry; Translations; *Markets:* Academic; Adult; *Treatments:* Contemporary; Literary; Serious

Primarily publishes serious nonfiction books and scholarly journals. Publishes a few titles of regional poetry and prose each season, and occasional reprints of fiction with an established reputation. Also publishes literary woks in translation. Submit proposal in first instance. See website for more details.

University of Tampa Press

401 W. Kennedy Blvd
Tampa, FL 33606
Tel: +1 (813) 253-6266
Fax: +1 (813) 258-7593
Email: utpress@ut.edu
Website: http://www.ut.edu/tampapress/pressmain.aspx

Publishes: Fiction; Nonfiction; Poetry; *Areas:* Arts; Historical; *Markets:* Academic; Adult; *Treatments:* Literary

Has been dedicated to the publication of books and periodicals featuring poetry, fiction and nonfiction from Florida and around the globe for more than 50 years. Publishes poetry, Florida history, supernatural literature, book arts, and other titles. Also publishes literary journal and runs annual poetry and fiction competitions.

Vanderbilt University Press

Vanderbilt University
PMB 351813 2301 Vanderbilt Place
Nashville, TN 37235-1813
Tel: +1 (615) 322-3585
Email: vupress@vanderbilt.edu
Website:
http://www.vanderbilt.edu/university-press/

Publishes: Nonfiction; *Areas:* Anthropology; Archaeology; Culture; Health; Historical; Literature; Medicine; Music; Nature; Philosophy; Politics; Women's Interests; *Markets:* Academic; Adult

Contact: Michael Ames, Director

Publishes books in most areas of the humanities and social sciences, as well as health care and education. See website for full submission guidelines.

Vernon Press (an imprint of Vernon Art and Science Inc.)

Vernon Art and Science Inc.
1000 N West Street, Suite 1200
Wilmington, Delaware 19801
Tel: +1 (302) 250-4440
Email: info@vernonpress.com
Website: http://www.vernonpress.com

Publishes: Nonfiction; Reference; *Areas:* Arts; Biography; Business; Criticism; Culture; Current Affairs; Finance; Historical; Literature; Music; Philosophy; Politics; Psychology; Science; Sociology; Technology; *Markets:* Academic; Professional; *Treatments:* Experimental; Niche; Progressive

Contact: Rosario Batana

An independent publisher of scholarly books in the social sciences and humanities.

Our mission is to serve the community of academic and professional scholars by providing a visible, quality platform for the dissemination of emergent ideas.

We welcome academic book proposals from both experienced and first time authors.

Our acquisition process has as its central criterion the contribution of a work to knowledge. It is necessary for such a contribution to be scientifically rigorous and of current interest to the academic communities to which it belongs, but saleability is not as central to our commitment to scholarship as has widely become the case over the last few years. Peer-review and close collaboration with academic associations and other research communities ensure our titles are meaningful and relevant.

We have a particular interest in the following subjects:

- Economics (including economic history)
- Sociology and social psychology
- Politics and public policy
- Finance, Business and Management
- Philosophy
- Fine art (including the history of art)
- Statistics and mathematics
- Education and pedagogy
- Linguistics

Please send a short book proposal (5 pages maximum) or abstract by email. To speed up initial screening, you may include a brief overview of competing titles and the names of two possible reviewers who are (academically/professionally) qualified to comment on the originality, rigor and potential impact of your work.

We commit to reply to all complete proposals and endeavor to offer constructive feedback whenever possible.

Voyageur Press

Book Proposals—Voyageur Press
Quayside Publishing Group
400 First Avenue North, Suite 300
Minneapolis, MN 55401
Tel: +1 (800) 458-0454
Fax: +1 (612) 344-8691
Email: customerservice@quaysidepub.com
Website: http://www.voyageurpress.com

Publishes: Nonfiction; *Areas:* Culture; Historical; Lifestyle; Music; Nature; Photography; Travel; *Markets:* Adult

Publishes books on nature and the environment; country living and farming heritage; regional and cultural history; music; travel and photography. See website for full submission guidelines.

Waveland Press, Inc.

4180 IL Route 83, Suite 101
Long Grove, Illinois 60047
Tel: +1 (847) 634-0081
Fax: +1 (847) 634-9501
Email: info@waveland.com
Website: http://www.waveland.com

Publishes: Nonfiction; *Areas:* Anthropology; Archaeology; Architecture; Arts; Business; Design; Finance; Health; Historical; Legal; Literature; Music; Nature; Philosophy; Politics; Psychology; Religious; Science; Sociology; Technology; Theatre; Women's Interests; *Markets:* Academic

Publisher of college textbooks and supplements, providing reasonably priced teaching materials for the classroom. See website for submission guidelines.

Western Psychological Services

625 Alaska Avenue
Torrance, CA 90503-5124
Tel: +1 (800) 648-8857
Email: review@wpspublish.com
Website: http://www.wpspublish.com

Publishes: Fiction; Nonfiction; Reference; *Areas:* Psychology; Sociology; *Markets:* Children's; Professional

Publishes books for professionals in the areas of psychology and education, and children's fiction dealing with feelings, anger, social skills, autism, family problems, etc. for use by professionals when dealing with children. Send complete ms.

Westminster John Knox Press (WJK)

100 Witherspoon Street
Louisville, KY 40202-1396
Tel: +1 (800) 523-1631
Fax: +1 (800) 541-5113
Email: submissions@wjkbooks.com
Website: http://www.wjkbooks.com

Publishes: Nonfiction; *Areas:* Culture; Religious; Spiritual; *Markets:* Academic; Adult; Professional

Publishes books specifically related to the Presbyterian Church (USA), including theology, biblical studies, preaching, worship, ethics, religion and culture, and other related fields. Serves four main markets: scholars and students in colleges, universities, seminaries, and divinity schools; preachers, educators, and counselors working in churches; members of mainline Protestant congregations; and general readers. See website for detailed submission guidelines.

Whitaker House

1030 Hunt Valley Circle
New Kensington, PA 15068
Tel: +1 (724) 334-7000
Fax: +1 (724) 334-1200
Email: publisher@whitakerhouse.com
Website: http://www.whitakerhouse.com

Publishes: Fiction; Nonfiction; *Areas:* Autobiography; Biography; Historical; How-to; Lifestyle; Men's Interests; Religious; Self-Help; Spiritual; Women's Interests; *Markets:* Adult

Publisher of inspiring and uplifting Christian fiction and nonfiction. Establish contact with a representative prior to submitting a manuscript or proposal.

William S. Hein & Co., Inc.

2350 North Forest Road
Getzville, NY 14068
Tel: +1 (716) 882-2600
Fax: +1 (716) 883-8100
Email: mail@wshein.com
Website: https://www.wshein.com

Publishes: Nonfiction; Reference; *Areas:* Legal; *Markets:* Professional

Publishes reference books for the law library community.

Williamson Books

2630 Elm Hill Pike, Suite 100
Nashville, TN 37214
Tel: +1 (615) 781-1451
Email: kwest@guideposts.org

Publishes: Nonfiction; Arts; Cookery; Crafts; Historical; Hobbies; Science; *Markets:* Children's

Publishes nonfiction titles for children aged 3 to 12 that emphasise hands-on learning through crafts and activities. Subject matter ranges from maths and science to geography, history, art, and cooking. Send query with SASE for guidelines.

Wilshire Book Company

9731 Variel Avenue
Chatsworth, CA 91311-4315
Tel: +1 (818) 700-1522
Fax: +1 (818) 700-1527
Email: mpowers@mpowers.com
Website: http://www.mpowers.com

Publishes: Fiction; Nonfiction; *Areas:* How-to; Humour; Psychology; Self-Help; Spiritual; *Markets:* Adult; *Treatments:* Commercial

Publishes psychology and self help nonfiction, plus adult allegories that teach principles of psychological and spiritual growth. Advises writers to read the bestsellers listed on their website and duplicate their winning elements in your own style with a creative new approach and fresh material. Submissions should be conceived and developed with market potential uppermost in your mind. Send synopsis for fiction or detailed chapter outline for nonfiction with three sample chapters, SASE, and contact email address (however no email submissions). Queries accepted by telephone for instant feedback on ideas.

WordSong

815 Church Street
Honesdale, PA 18431
Tel: +1 (570) 253-1164
Email: submissions@boydsmillspress.com
Website: https://www.boydsmillspress.com

Publishes: Poetry; *Markets:* Children's

Describes itself as "the only children's imprint in the United States specifically dedicated to poetry". Send book-length collection of poetry by post with SASE. Do not make initial query prior to submission.

Yale University Press

PO Box 209040
New Haven, CT 06520-9040
Tel: +1 (203) 432-0960
Fax: +1 (203) 432-0948
Email: Sarah.Miller@yale.edu
Website: http://yalepress.yale.edu/yupbooks

Publishes: Nonfiction; Poetry; *Areas:* Architecture; Arts; Current Affairs; Historical; Legal; Literature; Medicine; Nature; Philosophy; Politics; Psychology; Religious; Science; *Markets:* Academic; Adult

Publishes nonfiction and one book of poetry a year. Poetry must be submitted through annual contest. For nonfiction, see website for list of editors and submit to one editor only, by post or by email. See website for full guidelines.

Zebra

Kensington Publishing Corp.
119 West 40th Street
New York, New York, 10018
Tel: +1 (800) 221-2647
Email: esogah@kensingtonbooks.com
Website: http://www.kensingtonbooks.com

Publishes: Fiction; *Areas:* Romance; Women's Interests; *Markets:* Adult

Contact: Esi Sogah, Senior Editor

Publishes women's fiction, including romance. Send query only by email. No attachments or proposals. Response only if interested. See website for full guidelines.

UK Publishers

For the most up-to-date listings of these and hundreds of other publishers, visit http://www.firstwriter.com/publishers

*To claim your **free** access to the site, please see the back of this book.*

A Swift Exit

Email: aswiftexit@gmail.com
Website: http://aswiftexit.co.uk

Publishes: Fiction; Nonfiction; Poetry; *Areas:* Short Stories; *Markets:* Adult; *Treatments:* Literary

Contact: Jim Ladd and Will Vigar

Publishes new collections of poetry and prose from the finest new writers as ebooks and in print. Currently working on a strict back end profit share basis. See website for current calls for submissions and guidelines.

AA Publishing

The Automobile Association
Fanum House
Basingstoke
RG21 4EA
Tel: +44 (0) 1256 491524
Fax: +44 (0) 1614 887544
Email: AAPublish@TheAA.com
Website: http://www.theAA.com

Publishes: Nonfiction; Reference; *Areas:* Leisure; Lifestyle; Travel; *Markets:* Adult

Contact: David Watchus

Publishes motoring and travel books including atlases, maps, travel and leisure guides for the UK and the rest of the world. Also walking, cycling, lifestyle and driving test guides.

Absolute Press

Scarborough House
29 James Street West
Bath
BA1 2BT
Tel: +44 (0) 1225 316013
Fax: +44 (0) 1225 445836
Email: info@absolutepress.co.uk
Website: http://www.absolutepress.co.uk

Publishes: Nonfiction; *Areas:* Cookery; *Markets:* Adult

Contact: Jon Croft (Managing Director); Meg Avent (Commissioning Editor)

Publishes book relating to food and wine. No unsolicited MSS, but accepts synopses and ideas.

Akasha Publishing Ltd

145-157 St John Street
London
EC1V 4PW
Tel: +44 (0) 7436 849371
Email: info@akashapublishing.co.uk
Website: http://www.akashapublishing.co.uk

Publishes: Fiction; Nonfiction; *Areas:* Autobiography; Biography; Culture; Fantasy; Finance; Historical; Sci-Fi;

Spiritual; *Markets:* Adult; Children's

Independent publishing company located in the South London and Surrey area, publishing trade fiction and nonfiction and children's books in the areas of African and Caribbean interest, fantasy, science fiction, spirituality, metaphysical, Mind, Body and Spirit, ancient and classical history, alternative history, economics, Nuwaupian books, biographies and autobiographies. Send submissions by email. See website for guidelines.

Alastair Sawday Publishing Co. Ltd

The Old Farmyard
Yanley Lane
Long Ashton
Bristol
BS41 9LR
Tel: +44 (0) 1275 395430
Email: specialplaces@sawdays.co.uk
Website: http://www.sawdays.co.uk

Publishes: Nonfiction; *Areas:* Nature; Travel; *Markets:* Adult

Publishes guidebooks and books on environmental topics.

Ian Allan Publishing Ltd

Riverdene Business Park
Molesey Road
Hersham
KT12 4RG
Tel: +44 (0) 1932 266600
Fax: +44 (0) 1932 266601
Email: info@ianallanpublishing.co.uk
Website: http://www.ianallanpublishing.com

Publishes: Nonfiction; Reference; *Areas:* Historical; Hobbies; Military; Travel; *Markets:* Adult

Publishes nonfiction and reference books relating to transport, including aviation, military, road, rail, maps, and atalases. Also modelling, including railway modelling. Send query with SAE, synopsis, and sample chapter.

Alma Books Ltd

Hogarth House
32-34 Paradise Road
Richmond
TW9 1SE
Tel: +44 (0) 20 8940 6917
Fax: +44 (0) 20 8948 5599
Email: info@almabooks.com
Website: http://www.almabooks.co.uk

Publishes: Fiction; Nonfiction; *Areas:* Historical; Literature; *Markets:* Adult; *Treatments:* Contemporary; Literary

Publishes literary fiction and a small number of nonfiction titles with a strong literary or historical connotation. No novellas, short stories, children's books, poetry, academic works, science fiction, horror, or fantasy. Accepts unsolicited MSS by post with synopsis, two sample chapters, and SAE if return of material required. No submissions by email, or submissions from outside the UK. Submissions received from outside the UK will not receive a response.

Alma Classics

Hogarth House
32-34 Paradise Road
Richmond
TW9 1SE
Tel: +44 (0) 20 8940 6917
Fax: +44 (0) 20 8948 5599
Email: info@almabooks.com
Website: http://www.almaclassics.com

Publishes: Fiction; Poetry; Scripts; *Areas:* Arts; Autobiography; Biography; Literature; Sociology; Translations; *Markets:* Adult; *Treatments:* Literary

Publishes classic European literature. Welcomes suggestions and ideas for the list, as well as proposals from translators. Send proposals by post with SAE, CV, and sample from the original text.

Ammonite Press

166 High Street
Lewes
East Sussex
BN7 1XU
Tel: +44 (0) 1273 488006

Fax: +44 (0) 1273 472418
Email: richard.wiles@ammonitepress.com
Website: http://www.ammonitepress.com

Publishes: Nonfiction; *Areas:* Historical; Photography; Sociology; *Markets:* Adult

Contact: Richard Wiles (Managing Editor)

Publishes books on photography, social history, and also gift books.

Andersen Press Ltd

20 Vauxhall Bridge Road
London
SW1V 2SA
Tel: +44 (0) 20 7840 8701
Fax: +44 (0) 20 7233 6263
Email:
andersenneditorial@randomhouse.co.uk
Website: http://www.andersenpress.co.uk

Publishes: Fiction; *Markets:* Children's

Publishes picture books and longer children's fiction up to 75,000 words. Publishes rhyming stories, but no poetry, adult fiction, nonfiction, or short story collections. Send query with synopsis and first three chapters.

Antique Collectors' Club Ltd

Sandy Lane
Old Martlesham
Woodbridge
Suffolk
IP12 4SD
Tel: +44 (0) 1394 389950
Fax: +44 (0) 1394 389999
Email: submissions@antique-acc.com
Website:
http://www.antiquecollectorsclub.com

Publishes: Nonfiction; *Areas:* Antiques; Architecture; Arts; Beauty and Fashion; Business; Crafts; Design; Gardening; Historical; Photography; Travel; *Markets:* Adult; Children's

Publishes books on antiques and decorative arts. Send queries or submit manuscripts by post or by email.

Appletree Press Ltd

Roycroft House
164 Malone Road
Belfast
BT9 5LL
Tel: +44 (0) 28 90 243074
Fax: +44 (0) 28 90 246756
Email: editorial@appletree.ie
Website: http://www.appletree.ie

Publishes: Nonfiction; *Markets:* Adult

Send query with synopsis, descriptive chapter list, and two or three chapters by email. Publishes small-format gift books and general nonfiction books of Irish and Scottish interest. No unsolicited MSS.

Arc Publications

Nanholme Mill
Shaw Wood Road
Todmorden
Lancs
OL14 6DA
Tel: +44 (0) 1706 812338
Fax: +44 (0) 1706 818948
Email: info@arcpublications.co.uk
Website: http://www.arcpublications.co.uk/submissions

Publishes: Poetry; *Areas:* Music; Translations; *Markets:* Adult; *Treatments:* Contemporary

Send 16-24 poems by email as a Word / PDF attachment, maximum one poem per page. Submissions from outside the UK and Ireland should be sent to specific address for international submissions, available on website. Cover letter should include short bio and details of the contemporary poets you read.

Ashgate Publishing Limited

Wey Court East
Union Road
Farnham
Surrey
GU9 7PT
Tel: +44 (0) 1252 736600
Fax: +44 (0) 1252 736736
Email: info@ashgatepublishing.com
Website: http://www.ashgate.com

Publishes: Nonfiction; *Areas:* Architecture; Arts; Business; Culture; Historical; Legal; Literature; Music; Philosophy; Politics; Religious; Sociology; *Markets:* Academic; Professional

Actively seeking new book proposals. See website for appropriate submission guidelines.

Atlantic Europe Publishing

The Barn
Bottom Farm
Bottom Lane
Henley-on-Thames
Oxon
RG8 0NR
Tel: +44 (0) 1491 684028
Email: info@atlanticeurope.com
Website: http://www.atlanticeurope.com

Publishes: Nonfiction; *Areas:* Historical; Science; Sociology; Technology; *Markets:* Academic; Children's

Publisher of illustrated nonfiction books for children, mainly National Curriculum titles. Accepts approaches by email only – no postal approaches and no attachments.

Aureus Publishing Limited

Email: info@aureus.co.uk
Website: http://www.aureus.co.uk

Publishes: Nonfiction; *Areas:* Autobiography; Biography; Music; Sport; *Markets:* Adult

Publishes books on music and sport. Not accepting new material as at August 2014.

Aurora Metro Press

67 Grove Avenue
Twickenham
TW1 4HX
Tel: +44 (0) 20 3261 0000
Fax: +44 (0) 20 8898 0735
Email: submissions@aurorametro.com
Website: http://www.aurorametro.com

Publishes: Fiction; Nonfiction; Scripts; *Areas:* Arts; Biography; Cookery; Drama; Humour; Short Stories; Theatre; Translations; Women's Interests; *Markets:* Adult; Children's; Youth

Contact: Neil Gregory (Submissions Manager)

Publisher set up to promote new writing by women. Specialises in anthologising new drama, fiction, and work in translation. Send synopsis and three chapters of the finished book by post or by email. For play submissions, if a production is scheduled then the full script must be sent at least 6 weeks before opening night.

Aurum Press Ltd

74-77 White Lion Street
London
N1 9PF
Tel: +44 (0) 20 7284 9300
Fax: +44 (0) 20 7485 0490
Email: sales@aurumpress.co.uk
Website: http://www.aurumpress.co.uk

Publishes: Nonfiction; *Areas:* Arts; Biography; Crafts; Current Affairs; Film; Historical; Lifestyle; Military; Music; Photography; Sport; Travel; *Markets:* Adult

Publishes adult nonfiction in the above areas, both illustrated and not.

Barefoot Books Ltd

294 Banbury Road
Oxford
OX2 7ED
Tel: +44 (0) 1865 311100
Fax: +44 (0) 1865 514965
Email: help@barefootbooks.com
Website: http://www.barefootbooks.com

Publishes: Fiction; *Markets:* Children's

Publishing program currently full as at June 2015. Check website for current status.

Publishes high-quality picture-books for children. Particularly interested in both new and traditional stories from a variety of cultures. Submit material via submission form on website.

Barrington Stoke

18 Walker Street
Edinburgh
EH3 7LP
Tel: +44 (0) 131 225 4113
Fax: +44 (0) 131 225 4140
Email: info@barringtonstoke.co.uk
Website: http://www.barringtonstoke.co.uk

Publishes: Fiction; Nonfiction; Reference; *Markets:* Children's; Professional

Commissions books via literary agents only. No unsolicited material. Publishes books for "reluctant, dyslexic, disenchanted and under-confident" readers and their teachers.

Berlitz Publishing

1st Floor West
Magdalen House
136-148 Tooley Street
London
SE1 2TU
Tel: +44 (0) 20 7403 0284
Email: london@berlitzpublishing.com
Website: http://www.berlitzpublishing.com

Publishes: Nonfiction; Reference; *Areas:* Travel; *Markets:* Adult

Publishes books on travel and language.

Bernard Babani (publishing) Ltd

The Grampians
Shepherds Bush Road
London
W6 7NF
Email: enquiries@babanibooks.com
Website: http://www.babanibooks.com

Publishes: Nonfiction; *Areas:* Technology; *Markets:* Adult

Publishes books on robotics, computing, and electronics. Always interested in hearing from potential authors. Send query by email with synopsis and details of your qualifications for writing on hte topic.

BFI Publishing

Palgrave Macmillan Ltd
Houndmills
Basingstoke
Hampshire
RG21 6XS
Tel: +44 (0) 1256 302994
Fax: +44 (0) 1256 479476
Email: j.burnell@palgrave.com
Website: http://www.palgrave.com/bfi

Publishes: Nonfiction; Reference; *Areas:* Film; Media; TV; *Markets:* Academic

Contact: Jenni Burnell, Commissioning Editor: BFI and Theatre & Performance

Welcomes book proposals. Publishes film and television-related books and resources, both for schools and academic readerships, and more generally. See website for publishing proposal forms, and lists of editorial contacts to submit them to.

Black & White Publishing Ltd

29 Ocean Drive
Edinburgh
EH6 6JL
Tel: +44 (0) 01316 254500
Email: mail@blackandwhitepublishing.com
Website:
http://www.blackandwhitepublishing.com

Publishes: Fiction; Nonfiction; *Areas:* Autobiography; Biography; Cookery; Crime; Humour; Romance; Sport; *Markets:* Academic; Adult; Children's; Youth

Contact: Campbell Brown; Alison McBride

Publisher of general fiction and nonfiction. See website for an idea of the kind of books normally published. Send query with brief synopsis and sample chapters up to 30 pages, in a single Word file by email.

Blackline Press

15 Lister Road
Ipswich
IP1 5EQ
Email: author@blacklinepress.com
Website: http://www.blacklinepress.com

Publishes: Nonfiction; *Areas:* Sport; *Markets:* Adult

Publishes books about football. Particularly interested in groundhopping tours and challenges, club histories and non-league autobiographies, but welcomes all ideas. Actively seeking new authors. Send query by email.

Blackstaff Press Ltd

4D Weavers Court Business Park
Linfield Road
Belfast
BT12 5GH
Tel: +44 (0) 28 9034 7510
Fax: +44 (0) 28 9034 7508
Email: info@blackstaffpress.com
Website: http://www.blackstaffpress.com

Publishes: Fiction; Nonfiction; Poetry; *Areas:* Autobiography; Biography; Cookery; Historical; Humour; Nature; Politics; Short Stories; Sport; Travel; *Markets:* Adult

Contact: Patsy Horton

Publishes full length fiction and nonfiction, plus one or two collections of short stories and poetry per year. Send query with SAE, synopsis, and three sample chapters in first instance. For nonfiction, include market information. No unsolicited MSS or electronic submissions. Only considers submissions of Northern Ireland/Irish interest. Queries or submissions without SAE will not be considered.

Blink Publishing

Deepdene Lodge
Deepdene Avenue
Dorking
RH5 4AT
Tel: +44 (0) 1306 876361
Email: info@blinkpublishing.co.uk
Website: http://www.blinkpublishing.co.uk

Publishes: Nonfiction; *Areas:* Autobiography; Cookery; Culture; Historical; Humour; Lifestyle; Military; Music; Sport; *Markets:* Adult; *Treatments:* Popular

Publishes illustrated and non-illustrated adult nonfiction. No fiction. Send queries with ideas or synopses. No unsolicited mss.

Bloodaxe Books Ltd

Highgreen
Tarset
Northumberland
NE48 1RP
Tel: +44 (0) 1434 240500
Fax: +44 (0) 1434 240505
Email: editor@bloodaxebooks.com
Website: http://www.bloodaxebooks.com

Publishes: Nonfiction; Poetry; *Areas:* Criticism; Literature; *Markets:* Adult

Contact: Neil Astley, Managing/Editorial Director

Submit poetry only if you have a track record of publication in magazines. If so, send sample of up to a dozen poems with SAE or IRCs. No submissions by email or on disk. Poems sent without return postage will be recycled unread. Will not respond to postal submissions by email. As at December 2013, closed to submissions from American poets as American list is full for the foreseeable future. Check website for current situation.

Bloomsbury Publishing Plc

50 Bedford Square
London
WC1B 3DP
Tel: +44 (0) 20 7631 5600
Fax: +44 (0) 20 7631 5800
Email: contact@bloomsbury.com
Website: http://www.bloomsbury.com

Publishes: Fiction; Nonfiction; Reference; *Areas:* Arts; Historical; Hobbies; Music; Nature; Sport; *Markets:* Academic; Adult; Children's; Professional

No longer accepting submissions of fiction, or nonfiction other than in the following areas: Education, Music, Military History, Natural History, Nautical and Sport. See website for full submission guidelines.

Bloomsbury Spark

Email: BloomsburySparkUK@bloomsbury.com
Website: http://www.bloomsbury.com/spark

Publishes: Fiction; *Areas:* Historical; Mystery; Romance; Sci-Fi; Thrillers; *Markets:* Adult; Children's; Youth; *Treatments:* Contemporary

Global, digital imprint from a major international publisher. Publishes ebooks for teen, young adult, and new adult readers. Willing to consider all genres, including romance, contemporary, dystopian, paranormal, sci-fi, mystery, and thrillers. Accepts unsolicited mss between 25,000 and 60,000 words. Submit by email (see website for specific email addresses for different geographic locations) along with query and author bio. See website for full details.

Blue Guides Limited
27 John Street
London
WC1N 2BX
Email: editorial@blueguides.com
Website: http://blueguides.com

Publishes: Nonfiction; *Areas:* Culture; Travel; *Markets:* Adult

Publishes travel guides. Always on the lookout for new authors. Contact by email in first instance, giving an indication of your areas of interest.

Bodleian Library
Commissioning Editor
Communications & Publishing Office
Broad Street
Oxford
OX1 3BG
Tel: +44 (0) 1865 277108
Fax: +44 (0) 1865 277218
Email: publishing@bodleian.ox.ac.uk
Website:
http://www.bodleianbookshop.co.uk

Publishes: Nonfiction; *Areas:* Arts; Historical; Literature; *Markets:* Academic; Adult

Publishes books relating to the library collections only. Send synopses and ideas by post. No unsolicited MSS.

Booth-Clibborn Editions
Studio 83
235 Earls Court Road
London
SW5 9FE
Tel: +44 (0) 20 7565 0688
Fax: +44 (0) 20 7244 1018
Email: info@booth-clibborn.com
Website: http://www.booth-clibborn.com

Publishes: Nonfiction; *Areas:* Arts; Culture; Design; Media; Photography; *Markets:* Adult

Publishes books on the fine, media, and decorative arts.

Bowker (UK) Ltd
5th Floor
3 Dorset Rise
London
EC4Y 8EN
Tel: +44 (0) 20 7832 1770
Fax: +44 (0) 20 7832 1710
Email: sales@bowker.co.uk
Website: http://www.bowker.co.uk

Publishes: Reference; *Areas:* Biography; Business; *Markets:* Academic; Professional

Publishes reference books; professional and business directories; bibliographies and biographies.

Brown, Son & Ferguson, Ltd
4-10 Darnley Street
Glasgow
G41 2SD
Tel: +44 (0) 141 429 1234
Fax: +44 (0) 141 420 1694
Email: info@skipper.co.uk
Website: http://www.skipper.co.uk

Publishes: Nonfiction; Reference; *Areas:* Crafts; Historical; Hobbies; Technology; *Markets:* Adult; Professional

Nautical publishers, printers and ships' stationers since 1850. Publishes technical and non-technical nautical textbooks, books about the sea, historical books, information on old sailing ships and how to build model ships. Welcomes ideas, synopses, and unsolicited MSS.

Bryntirion Press

Waterton Cross Business Park
South Road
Bridgend
CF31 3UL
Tel: +44 (0) 1656 655886
Fax: +44 (0) 1656 665919
Email: office@emw.org.uk
Website: http://www.emw.org.uk

Publishes: Nonfiction; *Areas:* Religious; *Markets:* Adult

Welcomes synopses and ideas, but no unsolicited MSS. Publishes Christian books both in English and in Welsh.

Canongate Books

14 High Street
Edinburgh
EH1 1TE
Tel: +44 (0) 1315 575111
Fax: +44 (0) 1315 575211
Email: info@canongate.co.uk
Website: http://www.canongate.net

Publishes: Fiction; Nonfiction; *Areas:* Autobiography; Biography; Culture; Historical; Humour; Politics; Science; Translations; Travel; *Markets:* Adult; *Treatments:* Literary

Contact: Jamie Byng, Publisher

Publisher of a wide range of literary fiction and nonfiction, with a traditionally Scottish slant but becoming increasingly international. Publishes fiction in translation under its international imprint. No children's books, poetry, or drama. Send synopsis with three sample chapters and info about yourself. No submissions by fax, email or on disk.

Canopus Publishing Ltd

15 Nelson Parade
Bdeminster
Bristol
BS3 4HY
Email: robin@canopusbooks.com
Website: http://www.canopusbooks.com

Publishes: Nonfiction; *Areas:* Science; *Markets:* Academic; Adult; *Treatments:* Popular

Welcomes book proposals for both academic and popular branches of physics and astronomy. Send query by email with author bio, two-page summary outlining concept, coverage, and readership level. See website for more details.

Carlton Publishing Group

20 Mortimer Street
London
W1T 3JW
Tel: +44 (0) 20 7612 0400
Fax: +44 (0) 20 7612 0401
Email: pmurrayhill@carltonbooks.co.uk
Website: http://www.carltonbooks.co.uk

Publishes: Nonfiction; Reference; *Areas:* Architecture; Arts; Beauty and Fashion; Biography; Culture; Design; Entertainment; Film; Historical; Humour; Music; Sport; *Markets:* Adult; Children's; *Treatments:* Commercial; Mainstream; Popular

Publishes illustrated reference, sport, entertainment and children's books. Synopses and ideas for suitable books are welcomed, but no unsolicited MSS, academic, fiction, or poetry. Send query by email only with short synopsis, author bio, market info, and up to two chapters up to a maximum of 20 pages. See website for full guidelines.

Chartered Institute of Personnel and Development (CIPD) Publishing

151 The Broadway
London
SW19 1JQ
Tel: +44 (0) 20 8612 6202
Fax: +44 (0) 20 8612 6201
Email: publish@cipd.co.uk
Website: http://www.cipd.co.uk

Publishes: Nonfiction; Reference; *Areas:*

Business; How-to; *Markets:* Academic; Professional

Contact: Stephen Dunn, Head of Publishing

Publishes professional and academic books, looseleafs, and online subscription products, covering topics relating to personnel, training, and management. Submit proposal by email or by post.

Christian Education

1020 Bristol Road
Selly Oak
Birmingham
B29 6LB
Email: sales@christianeducation.org.uk
Website:
http://shop.christianeducation.org.uk

Publishes: Nonfiction; *Areas:* Religious; *Markets:* Adult; Family; Professional

Publishes Christian resources for use by individuals, families and churches.

Classical Comics Limited

PO Box 16310
Birmingham
B30 9EL
Tel: +44 (0) 845 812 3000
Fax: +44 (0) 845 812 3005
Email: info@classicalcomics.com
Website: http://www.classicalcomics.com

Publishes: Fiction; *Areas:* Literature; *Markets:* Children's

Publishes graphic novel adaptations of classical literature.

Co & Bear Productions

63 Edith Grove
London
SW10 0LB
Email: info@cobear.co.uk
Website: http://www.scriptumeditions.co.uk

Publishes: Nonfiction; *Areas:* Arts; Beauty and Fashion; Design; Lifestyle; Nature; Photography; *Markets:* Adult

Publishes illustrated books on interior design, fashion and photography, botanical art, natural history and exploration.

Compelling Books

Compelling Ideas Ltd
Basepoint Centre
Metcalf Way
RH11 7XX
Email: info@compellingbooks.com
Website: http://www.compellingbooks.com

Publishes: Fiction; Nonfiction; *Areas:* Adventure; Autobiography; Biography; Crime; Culture; Fantasy; Gothic; Historical; Horror; How-to; Humour; Literature; Mystery; Philosophy; Psychology; Science; Sci-Fi; Short Stories; Technology; Translations; *Markets:* Adult; Youth; *Treatments:* Commercial; Contemporary; Cynical; Dark; Light; Literary; Mainstream; Niche; Popular; Progressive; Serious; Traditional

Contact: Peter J Allen

Innovative independent publisher of compelling new fiction and non-fiction across all genres. Offers groundbreaking support for authors, with creative marketing, international scope, excellent royalty rates and uniquely ethical contracts.

We welcome new material – send a synopsis and first chapter via the submissions page of our website. (Hardcopy/print mss are NOT accepted.)

Corazon Books

Wyndham Media Ltd
27 Old Gloucester Street
London
WC1N 3AX
Email: editor@greatstorieswithheart.com
Website:
http://www.greatstorieswithheart.com

Publishes: Fiction; *Areas:* Gothic; Historical; Romance; Thrillers; Women's Interests; *Markets:* Adult; *Treatments:* Contemporary

Publishes contemporary romance, historical

romance (including family sagas), chick lit, gothic romance and romantic thrillers. Historical imprint launching autumn 2014 will welcome all historical fiction submissions, but will be particularly interested in historical novels and novellas with a romantic element.

In early 2014 will be considering submissions from published authors only, but in later 2014 will consider submissions from unpublished authors.

Crescent Moon Publishing

PO Box 393
Maidstone
Kent
ME14 5XU
Tel: +44 (0) 1622 729593
Email: cresmopub@yahoo.co.uk
Website: http://www.crescentmoon.org.uk

Publishes: Fiction; Nonfiction; Poetry; *Areas:* Arts; Criticism; Culture; Film; Literature; Media; Music; Philosophy; Politics; Women's Interests; *Markets:* Adult; *Treatments:* Contemporary; Literary

Contact: Jeremy Robinson

Publishes nonfiction on literature, culture, media, and the arts; as well as poetry and some fiction. Non-rhyming poetry is preferred. Send query with one or two sample chapters or up to six poems, with author bio and appropriate return postage for response. Material is only returned if requested and if adequate postage is provided.

Cressrelles Publishing Co. Ltd

10 Station Road Industrial Estate
Colwall
Malvern
WR13 6RN
Tel: +44 (0) 1684 540154
Fax: +44 (0) 1684 540154
Email: simon@cressrelles.co.uk

Publishes: Nonfiction; Scripts; *Areas:* Drama; *Markets:* Academic; Adult

Welcomes submissions. Publishes plays, theatre and drama textbooks, and local interest books.

The Crowood Press

The Stable Block
Crowood Lane
Ramsbury
Marlborough
Wiltshire
SN8 2HR
Tel: +44 (0) 1672 520320
Fax: +44 (0) 1672 520280
Email: enquiries@crowood.com
Website: http://www.crowood.com

Publishes: Nonfiction; Reference; *Areas:* Architecture; Arts; Crafts; Film; Gardening; Health; Historical; Hobbies; Leisure; Military; Nature; Photography; Sport; Theatre; Travel; *Markets:* Adult; Professional

Publishes instructional books on sports, crafts, gardening and DIY; information and reference books on motoring, aviation and military history; animal care and husbandry. Books are aimed at hobbyists, enthusiasts and professionals. Send query by email, fax, or post. No unsolicited mss.

DC Thomson

2 Albert Square
Dundee
DD1 9QJ
Tel: +44 (0) 1382 223131
Email: innovation@dcthomson.co.uk
Website: http://www.dcthomson.co.uk

Publishes: Fiction; Nonfiction; *Markets:* Adult; Children's

Publisher of newspapers, magazines, comics, and books, with offices in Dundee, Aberdeen, Glasgow, and London. For fiction guidelines send large SAE marked for the attention of the Central Fiction Department.

Dedalus Ltd

Langford Lodge
St Judith's Lane
Sawtry
PE28 5XE

Tel: +44 (0) 1487 832382
Fax: +44 (0) 1487 832382
Email: info@dedalusbooks.com
Website: http://www.dedalusbooks.com

Publishes: Fiction; *Areas:* Literature; Translations; *Markets:* Adult; *Treatments:* Contemporary; Literary

Send query letter describing yourself along with SAE, synopsis, three sample chapters, and explanation of why you think this publisher in particular is right for you – essential to be familiar with and have read other books on this publisher's list before submitting, as most material received is entirely inappropriate. Welcomes submissions of suitable original fiction and is particularly interested in intellectually clever and unusual fiction. No email or disk submissions, or collections of short stories by unknown authors. Novels should be over 40,000 words – ideally over 50,000. Most books are translations.

Dovecote Press

Stanbridge
Wimborne Minster
Dorset
BH21 4JD
Tel: +44 (0) 1258 840549
Email: online@dovecotepress.com
Website: http://www.dovecotepress.com

Publishes: Nonfiction; *Areas:* Architecture; Biography; Historical; Nature; *Markets:* Adult

Contact: David Burnett

Publishes books on architecture, local history, and natural history. List is expanding; welcomes ideas for new titles. Prefers to be approached at an early stage of the project. Send query by post with SAE and detailed synopsis or outline. Offers small advance.

Egmont UK Ltd

First Floor
The Yellow Building
1 Nicholas Road
London
W11 4AN
Tel: +44 (0) 20 3220 0400
Fax: +44 (0) 20 3220 0401
Email: service@egmont.co.uk
Website: http://www.egmont.co.uk

Publishes: Fiction; *Markets:* Children's

Publishes picture books and children's fiction. Agented submissions only.

Eland Publishing Ltd

61 Exmouth Market
Clerkenwell
London
EC1R 4QL
Tel: +44 (0) 20 7833 0762
Fax: +44 (0) 20 7833 4434
Email: info@travelbooks.co.uk
Website: http://www.travelbooks.co.uk

Publishes: Nonfiction; Poetry; *Areas:* Travel; *Markets:* Adult

Contact: Rose Baring; John Hatt; Barnaby Rogerson; Stephanie Allen

Specialises in keeping the classics of travel literature in print. Also publishes books of poetry relating to particular places.

Enitharmon Press

10 Bury Place
London
WC1A 2JL
Tel: +44 (0) 20 7430 0844
Email: info@enitharmon.co.uk
Website: http://www.enitharmon.co.uk

Publishes: Fiction; Poetry; *Areas:* Arts; Criticism; Photography; *Markets:* Adult; *Treatments:* Literary

One of Britain's leading literary publishers, specialising in poetry and in high-quality artists' books and original prints. It is divided into two companies: the press, which publishes poetry and general literature in small-format volumes and anthologies, and the editions, which produces de luxe artists' books in the tradition of the livre d'artiste. Send a preliminary enquiry to the editor before submitting material.

Euromonitor

60-61 Britton Street
London
EC1M 5UX
Tel: +44 (0) 20 7251 8024
Fax: +44 (0) 20 7608 3149
Email: info@euromonitor.com
Website: http://www.euromonitor.com

Publishes: Nonfiction; Reference; *Areas:* Business; *Markets:* Professional

International publisher of business reference and nonfiction, including market reports, directories, etc. for the professional market.

Ex-L-Ence Publishing

Deepfurrow Bungalow
Main Road
Minsterworth
Gloucestershire
GL2 8JH
Tel: +44 (0) 1452 751 276
Email: robert@winghigh.co.uk
Website: http://www.kindlebook.me

Publishes: Fiction; Nonfiction; Poetry; Reference; *Areas:* Adventure; Anthropology; Antiques; Archaeology; Architecture; Arts; Autobiography; Beauty and Fashion; Biography; Business; Cookery; Crafts; Crime; Criticism; Culture; Current Affairs; Design; Drama; Entertainment; Fantasy; Film; Finance; Gardening; Gothic; Health; Historical; Hobbies; How-to; Humour; Leisure; Lifestyle; Literature; Media; Medicine; Men's Interests; Military; Music; Mystery; Nature; New Age; Philosophy; Photography; Politics; Psychology; Religious; Romance; Science; Sci-Fi; Self-Help; Short Stories; Sociology; Spiritual; Sport; Suspense; Technology; Theatre; Thrillers; Travel; TV; Westerns; Women's Interests; *Markets:* Family; Professional; *Treatments:* Commercial; Contemporary; Experimental; In-depth; Light; Literary; Mainstream; Niche; Popular; Positive; Progressive; Satirical; Serious; Traditional

Contact: Robert Agar-Hutton

We get your manuscript ready for publication without it costing you any money, and then we pay you 50% of net royalties. Please visit our website then call or email to discuss how we can work together.

F&W Media International Ltd

Brunel House
Forde Close
Newton Abbot
TQ12 4PU
Tel: +44 (0) 1626 323200
Fax: +44 (0) 1626 323319
Email: ali.myer@fwmedia.com
Website: http://fwmedia.co.uk

Publishes: Nonfiction; *Areas:* Arts; Business; Crafts; Gardening; Historical; Hobbies; Humour; Lifestyle; Military; Nature; Photography; Travel; *Markets:* Adult

Contact: Ali Myer (Editorial and Design)

Publishes books for hobbyists and enthusiasts.

Faber & Faber Ltd

Bloomsbury House
74-77 Great Russell Street
London
WC1B 3DA
Tel: +44 (0) 20 7927 3800
Fax: +44 (0) 20 7927 3801
Website: http://www.faber.co.uk

Publishes: Fiction; Nonfiction; Poetry; Scripts; *Areas:* Biography; Drama; Film; Music; Politics; Theatre; *Markets:* Adult; Children's

Originally published poetry and plays but has expanded into other areas. Has published some of the most prominent writers of the twentieth century, including several poet laureates. No longer accepting unsolicited MSS in any areas other than poetry. Submit 6 poems in first instance, with adequate return postage. Submissions of material other than poetry will neither be read nor returned. No submissions by email, fax, or on disk.

Fabian Society

61 Petty France
Westminster
London

SW1H 9EU
Tel: +44 (0) 20 7227 4900
Email: info@fabians.org.uk
Website: http://www.fabians.org.uk

Publishes: Nonfiction; *Areas:* Current Affairs; Finance; Nature; Politics; Sociology; *Markets:* Adult

Left-leaning political think tank publishing books on current affairs, politics, economics, environment, social policy, etc.

Fingerpress UK

Email: firstwriter@fingerpress.co.uk
Website: http://www.fingerpress.co.uk

Publishes: Fiction; *Areas:* Historical; Sci-Fi; Thrillers; *Markets:* Adult; *Treatments:* Commercial

*** Please read the submissions page on our website before submitting anything... ***

Only open to submissions at certain times. Check website for current status. When open to submissions, this will be announced on our Facebook and Twitter pages.

We're an independent publisher based in London; we publish high quality Historical Fiction and Science Fiction. We're building a range of savvy, entertaining titles that are both thought-provoking and a good read. The ideal novel will have memorable characters with good plot development and pacing.

If your book isn't either Historical Fiction or Science Fiction, please don't submit it to us -- many thanks for your understanding.

We look for:

* submissions of completed, professionally edited, commercial-grade novels

Please check out our sister website – a virtual reality Facebook for authors, publishers and readers.

Fitzrovia Press Limited

10 Grafton Mews
London
W1T 5JG
Tel: +44 (0) 20 7380 0749
Email: info@fitzroviapress.co.uk
Website: http://www.fitzroviapress.com

Publishes: Fiction; Nonfiction; *Areas:* Philosophy; Spiritual; *Markets:* Adult

Contact: Ranchor Prime

Publishes fiction and nonfiction on Hinduism, spirituality, and Eastern philosophy. No unsolicited mss. Send query with outline and sample chapter.

Flame Tree Publishing

Crabtree Hall
Crabtree Lane
London
SW6 6TY
Tel: +44 (0) 20 7386 4700
Fax: +44 (0) 20 7386 4701
Email: info@flametreepublishing.com
Website:
http://www.flametreepublishing.com

Publishes: Nonfiction; *Areas:* Cookery; Culture; Lifestyle; Music; *Markets:* Adult; *Treatments:* Popular

Publihses practical cookbooks, music, popular culture and lifestyle books. Very rarely accepts unsolicited mss or book proposals.

Floris Books

15 Harrison Gardens
Edinburgh
EH11 1SH
Tel: +44 (0) 1313 372372
Fax: +44 (0) 1313 479919
Email: floris@florisbooks.co.uk
Website: http://www.florisbooks.co.uk

Publishes: Fiction; Nonfiction; *Areas:* Architecture; Arts; Biography; Crafts; Health; Historical; Literature; Philosophy; Religious; Science; Self-Help; Sociology; Spiritual; *Markets:* Adult; Children's; Youth

Publishes a wide range of books including adult nonfiction, picture books and children's novels. No poetry or verse, fiction for people over the age of 15, or autobiography, unless it specifically relates to a relevant nonfiction subject area. No submissions by email. See website for full details of areas covered and submission guidelines.

George Ronald Publisher

3 Rosecroft Lane
Welwyn
Herts
AL6 0UB
Tel: +44 (0) 1438 716062
Email: sales@grbooks.com
Website: http://grbooks.com

Publishes: Nonfiction; *Areas:* Religious; *Markets:* Adult

Religious publisher, concentrating solely on books of interest to Bahá'ís. Send email for copy of submission guidelines.

Ghostwoods Books

Email: ghostwoodsbooks@gmail.com
Website: http://www.gwdbooks.com

Publishes: Fiction; *Areas:* Crime; Fantasy; Gothic; Historical; Horror; Romance; Sci-Fi; Short Stories; Thrillers; Women's Interests; *Markets:* Adult; *Treatments:* Dark

Contact: Tim Dedopulos; Salome Jones

In the process of expanding. In order to do that we need to publish good books that attract readers. Providing information about your target market is helpful in your approach.

From personal interest, we like smart, funny, or dark fiction. Answering one of our specific calls for submissions, especially for an anthology, is a good way to get in.

Gibson Square Books Ltd

47 Lonsdale Square
London
N1 1EW
Tel: +44 (0) 20 7096 1100
Fax: +44 (0) 20 7993 2214
Email: info@gibsonsquare.com
Website: http://www.gibsonsquare.com

Publishes: Fiction; Nonfiction; *Areas:* Arts; Biography; Criticism; Culture; Current Affairs; Historical; Philosophy; Politics; Psychology; Travel; Women's Interests; *Markets:* Adult

Synopses, and ideas welcomed. Send query by email only. Publishes books which contribute to a general debate. Almost exclusively nonfiction, but does publish a small amount of fiction. See website for full guidelines.

Gingko Library

70 Cadogan Place
London
SW1X 9AH
Tel: +44 (0) 20 7838 9055
Email: aran@thegingkolibrary.com
Website: http://www.gingkolibrary.com

Publishes: Nonfiction; *Areas:* Architecture; Arts; Biography; Finance; Historical; Literature; Music; Philosophy; Politics; Religious; Science; Technology; *Markets:* Academic; Adult

Publisher promoting dialogue between the West and the Middle East and North Africa. Publishes collected articles and academic monographs, peer-reviewed by scholars and academic advisors. See website for submission guidelines.

Gomer Press

Llandysul Enterprise Park
Llandysul
Ceredigion
SA44 4JL
Tel: +44 (0) 1559 362371
Fax: +44 (0) 1559 363758
Email: gwasg@gomer.co.uk
Website: http://www.gomer.co.uk

Publishes: Fiction; Nonfiction; Poetry; Reference; Scripts; *Areas:* Arts; Autobiography; Biography; Culture; Drama; Historical; Leisure; Literature; Music; Nature; Religious; Sport; Theatre; Travel; *Markets:* Academic; Adult; Children's

Publishes fiction, nonfiction, plays, poetry, language books, and educational material, for adults and children, in English and in Welsh. See website for contact details of editors and query appropriate editor with sample chapter, synopsis, CV, and sales strengths of your proposal. Do not send complete MS in first instance.

Goss & Crested China Club

62 Murray Road
Horndean
Waterlooville
PO8 9JL
Tel: +44 (0) 23 9259 7440
Fax: +44 (0) 23 9259 7440
Email: info@gosschinaclub.co.uk
Website: http://www.gosschinaclub.co.uk

Publishes: Nonfiction; Reference; *Areas:* Antiques; *Markets:* Adult; Professional

Publishes books on crested heraldic china and antique porcelain.

Green Bottle Press

83 Grove Avenue
London
N10 2AL
Website: http://greenbottlepress.com

Publishes: Poetry; *Markets:* Adult; *Treatments:* Literary

Publishes poetry by poets writing in English who have not yet published a pamphlet or full collection. Will also consider new work by more established poets. Do not submit unless already published by several poetry journals. See website for full submission guidelines and online submission form, or send submission by post.

Grey Hen Press

PO Box 450
Keighley
West Yorkshire
BD22 9WS
Email: contact@greyhenpress.com
Website: http://www.greyhenpress.com

Publishes: Poetry; *Markets:* Adult

Publishes anthologies of poetry by women over 60. Aims to give less well-known poets the opportunity of having their work published alongside that of established writers.

Grub Street Publishing

4 Rainham Close
London
SW11 6SS
Tel: +44 (0) 20 7924 3966 / 20 7738 1008
Fax: +44 (0) 20 7738 1009
Email: post@grubstreet.co.uk
Website: http://www.grubstreet.co.uk

Publishes: Nonfiction; Reference; *Areas:* Cookery; Health; Historical; Military; *Markets:* Adult

Contact: John Davies (Military); Anne Dolamore (Cookery)

Publishes books on cookery and military aviation history only. No fiction or poetry. Accepts synopses and unsolicited MSS by post only with SASE. No email queries or submissions. See website for full submission guidelines.

Halban Publishers

22 Golden Square
London
W1F 9JW
Tel: +44 (0) 20 7437 9300
Fax: +44 (0) 20 7437 9512
Email: books@halbanpublishers.com
Website: http://www.halbanpublishers.com

Publishes: Fiction; Nonfiction; *Areas:* Autobiography; Biography; Criticism; Historical; Literature; Philosophy; Politics; Religious; *Markets:* Adult

Contact: Peter Halban; Martine Halban

Independent publisher of fiction, memoirs, history, biography, and books of Jewish interest. Send query by post or by email. No unsolicited MSS. Unsolicited emails deleted unread.

Haldane Mason Ltd

PO Box 34196
London
NW10 3YB
Tel: +44 (0) 20 8459 2131
Fax: +44 (0) 20 8728 1216
Email: sfrancis@haldanemason.com
Website: http://haldanemason.com

Publishes: Nonfiction; *Areas:* Crafts; Health; Historical; Lifestyle; Science; *Markets:* Adult; Children's; Youth

Publishes books and box-sets – mainly for children through children's imprint, but also for adults, covering such topics as alternative health, yoga, henna body art, Feng Shui, etc. Children's books include crafts, puzzles, history, science, maths, etc. Send query by email in first instance.

Halsgrove

Halsgrove House
Ryelands Business Park
Bagley Road
Wellington
Somerset
TA21 9PZ
Tel: +44 (0) 1823 653777
Fax: +44 (0) 1823 216796
Email: sales@halsgrove.com
Website: http://www.halsgrove.com

Publishes: Nonfiction; *Areas:* Arts; Biography; Historical; Photography; *Markets:* Adult

Publishes regional material covering various regions in the areas of history, biography, photography, and art. No fiction or poetry. Send query by email with brief synopsis in first instance.

Harlequin Mills & Boon Ltd

Eton House
18-24 Paradise Road
Richmond
Surrey
TW9 1SR
Tel: +44 (0) 20 8288 2800
Fax: +44 (0) 20 8288 2899
Email: submissions@hqnuk.co.uk
Website: http://www.millsandboon.co.uk

Publishes: Fiction; *Areas:* Crime; Historical; Romance; *Markets:* Adult; *Treatments:* Commercial; Contemporary

Major publisher with extensive romance list and various romance imprints. Send synopsis and three sample chapters in one Word document by email. See website for full submission guidelines.

Also includes digital imprint accepting submissions in any genre, and particularly interested in authors from rapidly expanding digital markets in the UK, Ireland, South Africa and India. See website for separate submission guidelines and specific email address for this imprint. Commercial fiction and crim imprint accepts submissions via literary agents only.

HarperCollins Publishers Ltd

The News Building
1 London Bridge Street
London
SE1 9GF
Tel: +44 (0) 20 8741 7070
Fax: +44 (0) 20 8307 4440
Email: enquiries@harpercollins.co.uk
Website: http://www.harpercollins.co.uk

Publishes: Fiction; Nonfiction; Reference; *Areas:* Autobiography; Biography; Cookery; Crafts; Crime; Entertainment; Fantasy; Film; Gardening; Health; Historical; Leisure; Lifestyle; Media; Military; Science; Sci-Fi; Sport; Thrillers; *Markets:* Adult; Children's; *Treatments:* Literary

One of the UK's three largest publishers, with one of the broadest ranges of material published. Authors include many award-winning bestsellers, and significant figures of literary history. Accepts approaches through agents and from published authors only, or if accompanied by a positive assessment from a manuscript assessment agency. No unsolicited MSS.

HarperImpulse

Email: romance@harpercollins.co.uk
Website:
http://www.harperimpulseromance.com

Publishes: Fiction; *Areas:* Erotic; Historical; Romance; Short Stories; *Markets:* Adult; *Treatments:* Contemporary; Experimental; Mainstream

Contact: Kimberley Young, Publishing Director

Digital-first romance publisher publishing fun and fast Adult and New Adult genre fiction to more mainstream novels; particularly contemporary, historical, paranormal and erotic fiction. Will consider work of any length (including short form fiction targetted at mobile devices), and is keen to see work that experiements with length, genre, and form, etc. Submit complete ms with covering letter and synopsis by email. See website for full guidelines.

Hart Publishing Ltd

16c Worcester Place
Oxford
OX1 2JW
Tel: +44 (0) 1865 517530
Fax: +44 (0) 1865 510710
Email: sinead@hartpub.co.uk
Website: http://www.hartpub.co.uk

Publishes: Nonfiction; *Areas:* Legal; *Markets:* Academic; Professional

Contact: Sinead Moloney; Bill Asquith; Rachel Turner

Publisher or legal books and journals for the professional and academic markets. See website for submission guidelines and specific editor subject areas and contact details.

Hawthorn Press

1 Lansdown Lane
Stroud
Gloucestershire
GL5 1BJ
Tel: +44 (0) 1453 757040
Fax: +44 (0) 1453 751138
Email: info@hawthornpress.com
Website: http://www.hawthornpress.com

Publishes: Nonfiction; *Areas:* Lifestyle; Self-Help; *Markets:* Adult

Publisher aiming to contribute to a more creative, peaceful and sustainable world through its publishing. Publishes mainly commissioned work, but will consider approaches. Send first two chapters with introduction, full table of contents/book plan, brief author biography and/or CV, and SAE. Allow at least 2–4 months for response. Accepts email enquiries, but full submissions should be made by post.

Headland Publications

38 York Avenue
West Kirby
Wirral
CH48 3JF
Tel: +44 (0) 01516 259128
Email: headlandpublications@hotmail.co.uk
Website: http://www.headlandpublications.co.uk

Publishes: Fiction; Nonfiction; Poetry; *Areas:* Biography; Short Stories; *Markets:* Adult

Specialises in poetry, but has expanded scope to include short stories and biography.

Headline Publishing Group

338 Euston Road
London
NW1 3BH
Tel: +44 (0) 20 7873 6000
Fax: +44 (0) 20 7873 6024
Email: enquiries@headline.co.uk
Website: http://www.hodderheadline.co.uk

Publishes: Fiction; Nonfiction; *Areas:* Autobiography; Biography; Cookery; Gardening; Historical; Science; Sport; TV; *Markets:* Adult; *Treatments:* Commercial; Literary; Popular

Contact: Jane Morpeth

Publishes hardback and paperback commercial and literary fiction, as well as popular nonfiction.

The History Press

The Mill,
Brimscombe Port
Stroud
Gloucestershire
GL5 2QG
Email: web@thehistorypress.co.uk
Website: http://www.thehistorypress.co.uk

Publishes: Nonfiction; *Areas:* Archaeology; Biography; Crime; Historical; Military; Sport; *Markets:* Adult

Publishes books on history, from local to international. Send query by email. No unsolicited mss. See website for full guidelines.

Hodder Education

338 Euston Road
London
NW1 3BH
Tel: +44 (0) 20 7873 6000
Fax: +44 (0) 20 7873 6299
Email: educationenquiries@hodder.co.uk
Website: http://www.hoddereducation.co.uk

Publishes: Nonfiction; Reference; *Areas:* Health; Medicine; Science; Self-Help; *Markets:* Academic; Adult

Publishes educational and reference books including home learning and school textbooks. See website for more details and for specific submission addresses for different types of books.

Honno Welsh Women's Press

Honno
Unit 14, Creative Units
Aberystwyth Arts Centre
Aberystwyth
Ceredigion
SY23 3GL
Tel: +44 (0) 1970 623150
Fax: +44 (0) 1970 623150
Email: post@honno.co.uk
Website: http://www.honno.co.uk

Publishes: Fiction; Nonfiction; Poetry; *Areas:* Autobiography; Crime; Fantasy; Short Stories; Women's Interests; *Markets:* Adult; Children's; Youth; *Treatments:* Literary

Contact: Caroline Oakley

Welcomes MSS and ideas for books from women born in, living in, or significantly connected to Wales, only. Publishes fiction, autobiographical writing and reprints of classic titles in English and Welsh, as well as anthologies of poetry and short stories. Particularly looking for more literary, crime, and fantasy titles, among others. All submissions must be sent as hard copy; no email submissions. Send query with synopsis and first 50 pages. Not currently accepting children/teenage novels or poetry or short story collections by a single author.

Hopscotch

Jesses Farm
Snow Hill
Dinton
Salisbury
Wiltshire
SP3 5HN
Tel: +44 (0) 1722 716 935
Email: info@hopscotchbooks.com
Website: http://www.hopscotchbooks.com

Publishes: Nonfiction; *Markets:* Professional

Publishes teaching resources for primary school teachers. Happy to hear from authors both new and established, with completed mss or just ideas. Contact editorial department by phone or submit complete ms.

House of Lochar

Isle of Colonsay
PA61 7YR
Tel: +44 (0) 1951 200232
Fax: +44 (0) 1951 200232
Email: sales@houseoflochar.com
Website: http://www.houseoflochar.com

Publishes: Fiction; Nonfiction; *Areas:* Biography; Historical; Literature; Travel; *Markets:* Adult; Children's

Welcomes unsolicited MSS for fiction and nonfiction related to Scotland and / or Celtic themes, including history, fiction, transport, maritime, genealogy, Gaelic, and books for children. No poetry or books unrelated to Scottish or Celtic themes.

Icon Books Ltd

Omnibus Business Centre
39-41 North Road
London
N7 9DP
Tel: +44 (0) 20 7697 9695
Fax: +44 (0) 20 7697 9501
Email: submissions@iconbooks.net
Website: http://www.iconbooks.co.uk

Publishes: Nonfiction; *Areas:* Arts; Historical; Humour; Philosophy; Politics; Psychology; Religious; Science; Sport; *Markets:* Adult; *Treatments:* Popular

Submit by email only. See website for full guidelines. Has in the past tended to publish series of books, including an ongoing series of graphic introductions to key figure and ideas in history, science, psychology, philosophy, religion, and the arts, but increasingly publishing individual nonfiction titles in such areas as politics, popular philosophy and psychology, history, sport, humour and, especially, popular science.

Igloo Books Limited

Cottage Farm
Mears Ashby Road
Sywell
Northants
NN6 0BJ
Tel: +44 (0) 1604 741116
Fax: +44 (0) 1604 670495
Email: customerservice@igloobooks.com
Website: http://igloobooks.com

Publishes: Fiction; Nonfiction; Reference; *Areas:* Cookery; Hobbies; Lifestyle; *Markets:* Adult; Children's

Publishes nonfiction and gift and puzzle books for adults, and fiction, nonfiction, and novelty books for children.

The Ilex Press

Tel: +44 (0) 1273 403124
Email: jones@ilex-press.com
Website: http://www.ilex-press.com

Publishes: Nonfiction; Reference; *Areas:* Arts; Culture; Photography; *Markets:* Adult

Contact: Nick Jones

Publishes high quality illustrated reference books which cover all aspects of creativity and popular culture. Send query by email in first instance.

Independent Music Press

PO Box 69
Church Stretton
Shropshire
SY6 6WZ
Email: info@impbooks.com
Website: http://www.impbooks.com

Publishes: Nonfiction; *Areas:* Biography; Culture; Music; *Markets:* Adult; Youth

Contact: Martin Roach

Publishes biographies of music stars, and books on youth culture.

Indigo Dreams Publishing

132 Hinckley Road
Stoney Stanton
Leics
LE9 4LN
Tel: +44 (0) 1455 272861
Email: publishing@indigodreams.co.uk
Website: http://www.indigodreams.co.uk

Publishes: Fiction; Nonfiction; Poetry; *Areas:* Adventure; Antiques; Arts; Autobiography; Biography; Crime; Entertainment; Erotic; Fantasy; Film; Gothic; Historical; Hobbies; Horror; How-to; Humour; Leisure; Lifestyle; Literature; Media; Men's Interests; Music; Mystery; Nature; New Age; Photography; Romance; Science; Sci-Fi; Spiritual; Sport; Suspense; Theatre; Thrillers; Translations; Travel; Westerns; Women's Interests; *Markets:* Adult; Family; Professional; *Treatments:* Commercial; Contemporary; Cynical; Dark; Experimental; In-depth; Light; Literary; Mainstream; Niche; Popular; Positive;

Progressive; Satirical; Serious; Traditional

Contact: Ronnie Goodyer

IDP are an independant publisher of fiction, nonfiction, and poetry. They have a speedy decision process through frequent Acquisition Meetings and an established method of approach, initially via a form on their website. Interesting proposals are then contacted for complete manuscripts in a second stage process and these are read and considered at the relevant Acquisitions Meetings. Books are distributed through Central Books, London. IDP are free to choose whatever material they wish as they have independant finance and no restrictions other than those which are self-imposed. No children's or religious subject matter and no short story collections.

Influx Press

Unit 25
Heartspace Hackney Downs Studios 17
Amhurst Terrace
London
E8 2BT
Email: submissions@influxpress.com
Website: http://www.influxpress.com

Publishes: Fiction; Nonfiction; Poetry; *Areas:* Literature; Short Stories; *Markets:* Adult; *Treatments:* Literary

Publishes novels, novellas, creative nonfiction, and themed collections of poetry and short stories. Accepts submissions only during specific submission windows – see website for details.

Iron Press

5 Marden Terrace
Cullercoats
North Shields
Northumberland
NE30 4PD
Tel: +44 (0) 191 253 1901
Fax: +44 (0) 191 253 1901
Email: contact@ironpress.co.uk
Website: http://www.ironpress.co.uk

Publishes: Fiction; Poetry; *Areas:* Short Stories; *Markets:* Adult; *Treatments:* Literary

Contact: Peter Mortimer

Poetry and fiction publisher championing quality new writing since 1973. Publishes poetry, (including haiku), collections of short stories, and anthologies of verse and prose. No novels or unsolicited mss. Send query by email in first instance.

Jordan Publishing

21 St Thomas Street
Bristol
BS1 6JS

20-22 Bedford Row
London
WC1R 4JS
Tel: +44 (0) 1179 230600
Fax: +44 (0) 1179 250486
Email: editor@jordanpublishing.co.uk
Website: http://www.jordanpublishing.co.uk

Publishes: Nonfiction; *Areas:* Legal; *Markets:* Professional

Legal publisher specialising in family law, company and commercial, insolvency, private client, civil litigation and personal injury. Welcomes proposals in these and other areas of legal practice. Submit query via website.

Josef Weinberger Ltd

12-14 Mortimer Street
London
W1T 3JJ
Tel: +44 (0) 20 7580 2827
Fax: +44 (0) 20 7436 9616
Email: general.info@jwmail.co.uk
Website: http://www.josef-weinberger.com

Publishes: Scripts; *Areas:* Theatre; *Markets:* Adult

Publishes theatre scripts for musicals, plays, pantomimes, operas, and operettas.

Kindred Rainbow Publishing

Tel: +44 (0) 20 8133 3751
Email: submissions@kindredrainbow.com
Website: http://kindredrainbow.com

Publishes: Fiction; Nonfiction; *Areas:* Adventure; Entertainment; Fantasy; Humour; Mystery; Science; Sci-Fi; *Markets:* Children's; Youth; *Treatments:* Commercial; Contemporary; Experimental; Light; Niche; Popular; Positive

Contact: Alexandra Mercury

We look for picture books, fiction, non-fiction and illustration for children of aged three to eight approx. We will consider books of all genres. It's all about the story, and if we feel that it is amazing and catchy we will consider for publishing.

What works best:
- Stories that are very visual with robust characterisations – not too long-winded
- Humorous plots
- Scary parts – not too scary though!
- Stories with a message – but not too moralistic
- Unusual styles to non-fiction material
- Diverse themes

Knox Robinson Publishing (UK)

34 New House
67-68 Hatton Garden
London
EC1N 8JY
Tel: +44 (0) 20 8816 8630
Fax: +44 (0) 20 8711 2334
Email: subs@knoxrobinsonpublishing.com
Website: http://www.knoxrobinsonpublishing.com

Publishes: Fiction; *Areas:* Fantasy; Historical; Romance; *Markets:* Adult

Publishes historical fiction, historical romance (pre-1960), and medieval fantasy. No science fiction, time travel, or fantasy with children and/or animal protagonists. Send query by email only, with detailed synopsis and the first three chapters. No approaches by fax or post. See website for full details.

Kube Publishing

MCC, Ratby Lane
Markfield
Leicestershire
LE67 9SY
Tel: +44 (0) 1530 249230
Fax: +44 (0) 1530 249656
Email: manuscript@kubepublishing.com
Website: http://www.kubepublishing.com

Publishes: Fiction; Nonfiction; *Areas:* Biography; Culture; Historical; Lifestyle; Religious; *Markets:* Academic; Adult; Children's; Youth

Independent publisher of general interest, academic, and children's books on Islam and the Muslim experience. Publishes nonfiction for children, young people, and adults, but fiction for children and teens only. See website for full guidelines.

Kyle Books

192-198 Vauxhall Bridge Road
London
SW1V 1DX
Tel: +44 (0) 20 7692 7215
Fax: +44 (0) 20 7692 7260
Email: general.enquiries@kylebooks.com
Website: http://www.kylebooks.com

Publishes: Nonfiction; Reference; *Areas:* Beauty and Fashion; Cookery; Gardening; Health; Lifestyle; *Markets:* Adult

Describes itself as "one of the UK's leading publishers in the areas of cookery, health, lifestyle and gardening."

Legend Press

2 London Wall Buildings
London
EC2M 5UU
Tel: +44 (0) 20 7448 5137
Email: submissions@legend-paperbooks.co.uk
Website: http://www.legendpress.co.uk

Publishes: Fiction; *Markets:* Adult;

Treatments: Commercial; Contemporary; Mainstream

Contact: Tom Chalmers

Publishes a diverse list of contemporary adult novels. No historical fiction, children's books, poetry or travel writing. See website for full submission guidelines and online submission system.

Frances Lincoln Ltd

74-77 White Lion Street
Islington
London
N1 9PF
Tel: +44 (0) 20 7284 9300
Fax: +44 (0) 20 7485 0490
Email: fl@frances-lincoln.com
Website: http://www.franceslincoln.com

Publishes: Fiction; Nonfiction; Poetry; *Areas:* Architecture; Arts; Design; Gardening; Leisure; Lifestyle; Nature; Travel; *Markets:* Adult; Children's

Publishers of illustrated nonfiction books for adults, particularly on gardening, walking and the outdoors, art, architecture, design and landscape. In the area of children's books, publishes picture books, multicultural books, poetry, and information books. No poetry or novel submissions for adults. See website for full submission guidelines.

Lion Hudson Plc

Wilkinson House
Jordan Hill Road
Oxford
OX2 8DR
Tel: +44 (0) 1865 302750
Fax: +44 (0) 1865 302757
Email: info@lionhudson.com
Website: http://www.lionhudson.com

Publishes: Fiction; Nonfiction; Reference; *Areas:* Autobiography; Biography; Health; Religious; Spiritual; *Markets:* Adult; Children's; *Treatments:* Positive

Publishes books that reflect Christian values or are inspired by a Christian world view, including adult nonfiction / reference, and children's fiction and nonfiction. See website for specific submission guidelines for different imprints.

Liverpool University Press

4 Cambridge Street
Liverpool
L69 7ZU
Tel: +44 (0) 1517 942233
Fax: +44 (0) 1517 942235
Email: lup@liv.ac.uk
Website:
http://www.liverpooluniversitypress.co.uk

Publishes: Nonfiction; *Areas:* Archaeology; Architecture; Arts; Culture; Historical; Literature; Politics; Sci-Fi; Sociology; *Markets:* Academic

Contact: Alison Welsby; Anthony Cond

Publishes books and journals, specialising in Modern Languages, Postcolonial, Slavery and Migration Studies, Irish History, Labour History, Science Fiction Studies and Art History. Download proposal submission form from website.

Logaston Press

Little Logaston
Woonton
Almeley
Herefordshire
HR3 6QH
Tel: +44 (0) 1544 327344
Email: logastonpress@phonecoop.coop
Website: http://www.logastonpress.co.uk

Publishes: Nonfiction; *Areas:* Archaeology; Biography; Historical; Sociology; Travel; *Markets:* Adult

Contact: Andy and Karen Johnson

Publishes biographies and books on the rural West Midlands and mid and South Wales. Welcomes ideas: submit synopsis in first instance.

Lost Tower Publications

Email: losttowerpublications@yahoo.com
Website:

http://losttowerpublications.jigsy.com

Publishes: Fiction; Poetry; *Areas:* Adventure; Autobiography; Crime; Fantasy; Gothic; Horror; Leisure; Lifestyle; Mystery; Sci-Fi; Spiritual; Suspense; Thrillers; Women's Interests; *Markets:* Adult; Children's; Family; Youth; *Treatments:* Contemporary; Dark; Experimental; Niche; Positive; Progressive

Contact: Harry Yang

Formed in 2011 as part of a poetry book publishing campaign to promote poetry world wide as an attractive and entertaining art form for the twenty first century. We print 3-4 books a year collecting the best photographs and poetry from around the world, to produce high quality books for people to enjoy. Our books are available to buy worldwide either from Amazon or to order through your local bookshop.

In March 2013 we published a journey of hope through poems and photographs which have been collected from around the world. The work in this anthology has been collected from every continent of our planet and illustrates ideas of hope from many of the world religions; looks at the different forms hope can take and how hope can always be found if you look carefully into the world which surrounds you.

Luath Press Ltd

543/2 Castlehill
The Royal Mile
Edinburgh
EH1 2ND
Tel: +44 (0) 131 225 4326
Fax: +44 (0) 131 225 4324
Email: sales@luath.co.uk
Website: http://www.luath.co.uk

Publishes: Fiction; Nonfiction; Poetry; *Areas:* Arts; Beauty and Fashion; Biography; Crime; Current Affairs; Drama; Historical; Leisure; Lifestyle; Nature; Photography; Politics; Sociology; Sport; Thrillers; Travel; *Markets:* Adult; Children's; Youth

Contact: G.H. MacDougall, Managing Editor

Publishes a range of books, usually with a Scottish connection. Check upcoming publishing schedule on website, and – if you think your book fits – send query with SAE, synopsis up to 250 words, manuscript or sample chapters, author bio, and any other relevant material. See website for full submission guidelines. Approaches by email will not be considered.

Macmillan

The Macmillan Building
4 Crinan Street
London
N1 9XW
Tel: +44 (0) 20 7833 4000
Fax: +44 (0) 20 7843 4640
Website: http://www.macmillan.com

Publishes: Fiction; Nonfiction; Poetry; Reference; *Areas:* Autobiography; Biography; Business; Cookery; Crime; Culture; Current Affairs; Fantasy; Film; Finance; Gardening; Health; Historical; Horror; Humour; Military; Music; Nature; Philosophy; Politics; Psychology; Romance; Science; Sci-Fi; Sport; Theatre; Thrillers; Travel; TV; *Markets:* Academic; Adult; Children's; Family; Professional; Youth; *Treatments:* Commercial; Literary; Popular

Large publishing company publishing a wide range of titles through its various divisions and imprints. Policies towards submissions and material published varies across these divisions and imprints (as does the address to contact), so further research essential.

Mainstream Publishing Co. (Edinburgh) Ltd

7 Albany Street
Edinburgh
EH1 3UG
Tel: +44 (0) 131 557 2959
Fax: +44 (0) 131 556 8720
Email: admin@mainstreampublishing.com
Website: http://www.mainstreampublishing.com

Publishes: Nonfiction; *Areas:* Arts; Autobiography; Biography; Culture; Current Affairs; Health; Historical; Politics; Sport; *Markets:* Adult

Nonfiction publisher based in Scotland, with particular emphasis on biography, history, politics, art, popular culture, sport, health and current affairs.

Manchester University Press

Floor J, Renold Building
Altrincham Street
Manchester
M1 7JA
Tel: +44 (0) 1612 752310
Fax: +44 (0) 1612 757711
Email: mup@manchester.ac.uk
Website: http://www.manchesteruniversitypress.co.uk

Publishes: Nonfiction; Reference; *Areas:* Arts; Business; Criticism; Culture; Design; Film; Finance; Historical; Legal; Literature; Media; Politics; Theatre; TV; *Markets:* Academic

Publishes mainly textbooks for undergraduates and A-level students, plus research monographs.

Mandrake of Oxford

PO Box 250
Oxford
OX1 1AP
Email: mandrake@mandrake.uk.net
Website: http://mandrake.uk.net

Publishes: Fiction; Nonfiction; *Areas:* Arts; Crime; Culture; Erotic; Health; Horror; Lifestyle; Mystery; Philosophy; Sci-Fi; Self-Help; Spiritual; *Markets:* Adult

Send query by post or by email. May also include synopsis. See website for full guidelines, and for examples of the kind of material published.

Marion Boyars Publishers

26 Parke Road
London
SW13 9NG
Tel: +44 (0) 20 8788 9522
Fax: +44 (0) 20 8789 8122
Email: catheryn@marionboyars.com
Website: http://www.marionboyars.co.uk

Publishes: Fiction; Nonfiction; *Areas:* Anthropology; Autobiography; Biography; Criticism; Culture; Drama; Film; Literature; Music; Philosophy; Psychology; Sociology; Theatre; Women's Interests; *Markets:* Adult

Contact: Catheryn Kilgarriff (Director), catheryn@marionboyars.com; Rebecca Gillieron (Fiction Editor), rebecca@marionboyars.com; Amy Christian (Nonfiction Editor), amy@marionboyars.com

Note: Not accepting new submissions as at June 2015. Check website for current status.

For nonfiction, send synopses and ideas with SAE. Particularly interested in music, film, and contemporary culture. Fiction submissions via a literary agent only. No poetry submissions or approaches by email.

Kevin Mayhew Publishers

Buxhall
Stowmarket
Suffolk
IP14 3BW
Tel: +44 (0) 845 3881634
Fax: +44 (0) 1449 737834
Email: info@kevinmayhew.com
Website: http://www.kevinmayhew.com

Publishes: Nonfiction; *Areas:* Music; Religious; Spiritual; *Markets:* Academic; Adult; Children's

Contact: Manuscript Submissions Department

Publishes books relating to Christiantity and music, for adults, children, schools, etc. Send query with synopsis and one or two sample chapters. No approaches by telephone. See website for full guidelines.

Meadowside Children's Books

185 Fleet Street
London
EC4A 2HS
Tel: +44 (0) 20 7400 1084
Fax: +44 (0) 20 7400 1037

Email: queries@dctbooks.co.uk
Website: http://www.meadowsidebooks.com

Publishes: Fiction; *Markets:* Children's; Youth

Contact: Submissions Editor

Publishes picture and novelty books, and junior fiction. Send complete MS with cover letter, and SAE if return of samples required. Prefers to receive material digitally, but do also send a printed copy of the story. Only replies to successful submissions.

Merlin Unwin Books

Palmers House
7 Corve Street
Ludlow
Shropshire
SY8 1DB
Tel: +44 (0) 1584 877456
Fax: +44 (0) 1584 877457
Email: books@merlinunwin.co.uk
Website: http://www.merlinunwin.co.uk

Publishes: Nonfiction; *Areas:* Autobiography; Cookery; Humour; Leisure; Nature; Sport; *Markets:* Adult

Publishes books on the countryside and countryside pursuits, covering such topics as nature, fishing, shooting, etc.

Merrell Publishers Limited

70 Cowcross Street
London
EC1M 6EJ
Tel: +44 (0) 20 7928 8880
Fax: +44 (0) 20 7928 1199
Email: hm@merrellpublishers.com
Website: http://www.merrellpublishers.com

Publishes: Nonfiction; *Areas:* Architecture; Arts; Beauty and Fashion; Culture; Design; Photography; *Markets:* Adult

Contact: Hugh Merrell, Publisher

Send query, preferably by email, with one-page synopsis of the project, highlighting its subject-matter, scope, approach and purpose, and indicating why you believe it to be commercially viable; an annotated table of contents to indicate how the book will be structured and what each chapter will contain in terms of subject-matter, numbers of words and numbers of illustrations; a single chapter of sample text, if already written; photocopies or printouts of sample images from the book, if available; a brief (one-paragraph) biography of each author, which should highlight, in particular, why they are qualified to write on the subject of the proposed book and provide details of any previous publications; an annotated list of related or competing works currently in print, highlighting how the proposed book differs from anything already available.

Methodist Publishing

Methodist Church House
25 Marylebone Road
London
NW1 5JR
Tel: +44 (0) 20 7486 5502
Email: helpdesk@methodistchurch.org.uk
Website: http://www.mph.org.uk

Publishes: Nonfiction; *Areas:* Philosophy; Religious; *Markets:* Adult

Publishes resources for the Methodist Church in Britain. No unsolicited mss.

Methuen Publishing Ltd

35 Hospital Fields Road
York
YO10 4DZ
Tel: +44 (0) 1904 624730
Fax: +44 (0) 1904 624733
Email: editorial@methuen.co.uk
Website: http://www.methuen.co.uk

Publishes: Fiction; Nonfiction; Poetry; Scripts; *Areas:* Architecture; Autobiography; Biography; Culture; Current Affairs; Film; Historical; Hobbies; How-to; Humour; Literature; Military; Philosophy; Politics; Sport; Theatre; Travel; *Markets:* Adult

No unsolicited submissions. Send query by email for information about manuscript submission policy. No children's books.

Michelin Maps and Guides

Hannay House
39 Clarendon Road
Watford
Hertfordshire
WD17 1JA
Tel: +44 (0) 1923 205247
Email: themichelinguide-gbirl@uk.michelin.com
Website: http://travel.michelin.co.uk

Publishes: Nonfiction; Reference; *Areas:* Travel; *Markets:* Adult

Publishes travel guides; maps; atlases; and hotel and restaurant guides.

Milo Books Ltd

The Old Weighbridge
Station Road
Wrea Green
Lancashire
PR4 2PH
Email: publish@milobooks.com
Website: http://www.milobooks.com

Publishes: Nonfiction; *Areas:* Autobiography; Biography; Crime; Culture; Current Affairs; Sport; *Markets:* Adult; Youth

Will consider books in any nonfiction genre, but specialises in true crime, autobiography/biography, sports, current affairs and youth culture. Send query by post (with return postage if return required) or by email, with first couple of chapters.

Monarch Books

Lion Hudson Plc.
Wilkinson House
Jordan Hill Road
Oxford
OX2 8DR
Tel: +44 (0) 1865 302750
Fax: +44 (0) 1865 302757
Email: SubmissionstoLionBooks
MonarchLionFiction@LionHudson.com
Website:
http://www.lionhudson.com/page.asp?pid=monarch_books

Publishes: Fiction; Nonfiction; *Areas:* Politics; Psychology; Religious; Spiritual; *Markets:* Adult

Publishes a wide range of Christian books. Accepts unsolicited MSS, synopses, and ideas. Accepts submissions by email. See website for full guidelines. Response not guaranteed unless interested. If no response after three months assume rejection.

Mudfog Press

C/o Arts and Events
Culture and Tourism
P.O Box 99A
Civic Centre
Middlesbrough
TS1 2QQ
Email: contact@mudfog.co.uk
Website: http://www.mudfog.co.uk

Publishes: Fiction; Poetry; *Areas:* Short Stories; *Markets:* Adult

Publishes poetry and short fiction by writers in the Tees Valley area. Send query with 15-20 poems or 2-3 stories. See website for full details. No email submissions.

Myriad Editions

59 Lansdowne Place
Brighton
BN3 1FL
Tel: +44 (0) 1273 720000
Fax: +44 (0) 1273 720000
Email: info@MyriadEditions.com
Website: http://www.myriadeditions.com

Publishes: Fiction; Nonfiction; Reference; *Markets:* Adult

Contact: Vicky Blunden

Publishes atlases, works or graphical nonfiction, and fiction. Send synopsis and first three chapters by post only. No email approaches. Include SASE if return required. No short stories, poetry, plays, children's books, teenage/young adult fiction or general nonfiction.

National Museum Wales

Cathays Park

Cardiff
CF10 3NP
Email: books@museumwales.ac.uk
Website: http://www.museumwales.ac.uk

Publishes: Nonfiction; *Areas:* Archaeology; Arts; Historical; Nature; Sociology; *Markets:* Academic; Adult; Children's

Publishes books based on the collections and research of the museum, aimed at adults, children, and schools. Publishes in both Welsh and English.

Neil Wilson Publishing Ltd

226 King Street
Castle Douglas
DG7 1DS
Tel: +44 (0) 1556 504119
Fax: +44 (0) 1556 504065
Email: submissions@nwp.co.uk
Website: http://www.nwp.co.uk

Publishes: Nonfiction; Reference; *Areas:* Biography; Cookery; Crime; Culture; Historical; Humour; Music; Nature; Travel; *Markets:* Adult

Welcomes approaches by email only. Publishes books of Scottish interest through a variety of imprints, including history, hill-walking, humour, food and drink (including whisky), biography, true crime, and reference. Has published fiction in the past, but longer does so. No academic, political, fiction, or technical. See website for full guidelines.

Neon

Email: info@neonmagazine.co.uk
Website: http://neonmagazine.co.uk

Publishes: Fiction; Poetry; *Areas:* Short Stories; *Markets:* Adult; *Treatments:* Literary

Publishes chapbooks and pamphlets of poetry and fiction. Chapbooks and pamphlets contain the work of a single author and may be a collection of poetry, a single long story, or a collection of short stories, but the material should be thematically linked. Authors will receive payment for chapbooks but not for pamphlets, as these are given away free and distributed as widely as possible. Send query via form on website.

New Beacon Books, Ltd

76 Stroud Green Road
Finsbury Park
London
N4 3EN
Tel: +44 (0) 20 7272 4889
Fax: +44 (0) 20 7281 4662
Email: newbeaconbooks@btconnect.com

Publishes: Fiction; Nonfiction; Poetry; *Areas:* Culture; Historical; Politics; *Markets:* Adult

Publishes a range of fiction, nonfiction, and poetry, all concerning black people. No unsolicited MSS.

New Cavendish Books

3 Denbigh Road
London
W11 2SJ
Tel: +44 (0) 20 7229 6765
Fax: +44 (0) 20 7792 0027
Email: sales@newcavendishbooks.co.uk
Website:
http://www.newcavendishbooks.co.uk

Publishes: Nonfiction; Reference; *Areas:* Antiques; Arts; Hobbies; *Markets:* Adult

Independent publisher publishing books on collectable items.

The New Curiosity Shop

Edinburgh
Tel: +44 (0) 1312 081900
Email: contact@newcurioshop.com
Website: http://www.newcurioshop.com

Publishes: Nonfiction; Reference; *Areas:* Adventure; Anthropology; Antiques; Archaeology; Architecture; Arts; Beauty and Fashion; Biography; Business; Cookery; Crafts; Crime; Criticism; Culture; Current Affairs; Design; Drama; Fantasy; Film; Gardening; Gothic; Historical; Hobbies; Horror; Humour; Literature; Medicine; Men's Interests; Military; Music; Mystery;

Nature; Philosophy; Photography; Politics; Psychology; Radio; Religious; Science; Sci-Fi; Sociology; Sport; Technology; Theatre; Travel; Women's Interests; *Markets:* Academic; Adult; Professional; *Treatments:* Commercial; Contemporary; Mainstream; Niche; Positive; Progressive; Traditional

Contact: Noel Chidwick

We're looking for informative and entertaining ebooks on topics you know and love well. We're not looking for dry and dusty, we're looking for nonfiction page turners to grab your readers; leave them wanting more. Above all, bring your subject screaming to life. Your ebook will be between 13,000 to 17,000 words in length, just right for someone with a Kindle tucked into their travel bag.

Full information available on the website

Queries by email, initial submissions preferred via form on website.

New Holland Publishers (UK) Ltd

The Chandlery Unit 009
50 Westminster Road
London
SE1 7QY
Tel: +44 (0) 20 7953 7565
Email: enquiries@nhpub.co.uk
Website: http://www.newhollandpublishers.com

Publishes: Nonfiction; Reference; *Areas:* Arts; Biography; Cookery; Crafts; Design; Gardening; Health; Historical; How-to; Humour; Lifestyle; Nature; Photography; Self-Help; Spiritual; Sport; Travel; *Markets:* Adult

International publisher of nonfiction and reference. Send query with SAE, synopsis, CV, and sample chapters.

New Playwrights' Network (NPN)

10 Station Road Industrial Estate
Colwall
Herefordshire
WR13 6RN
Tel: +44 (0) 1684 540154
Email: simon@cressrelles.co.uk
Website: http://www.cressrelles.co.uk

Publishes: Scripts; *Areas:* Drama; Theatre; *Markets:* Adult

Contact: Simon Smith

Established in the 1970s to promote scripts by new writers. Send scripts by email or by post.

Nick Hern Books Ltd

The Glasshouse
49a Goldhawk Road
London
W12 8QP
Tel: +44 (0) 20 8749 4953
Fax: +44 (0) 20 8735 0250
Email: matt@nickhernbooks.co.uk
Website: http://www.nickhernbooks.co.uk

Publishes: Nonfiction; Scripts; *Areas:* Film; Theatre; *Markets:* Adult; Professional

Contact: Matt Applewhite, Commissioning Editor

Publishes plays attached to significant professional productions in major theatres only. No unsolicited scripts. Also publishes books by theatre practitioners and for theatre practitioners. No critical, analytical or historical studies.

Nightingale Press

Manning Partnership
7 Green Park Station
Green Park Road
Bath
BA1 1JB
Tel: +44 (0) 1225 478444
Fax: +44 (0) 1225 478440
Email: karen@manning-partnership.co.uk
Website: http://www.manning-partnership.co.uk

Publishes: Nonfiction; *Areas:* Humour; Lifestyle; *Markets:* Adult

Contact: Karen Twissell

Publishes health, lifestyle, humour, gift, and language and learning.

Michael O'Mara Books Ltd

9 Lion Yard
Tremadoc Road
London
SW4 7NQ
Tel: +44 (0) 20 7720 8643
Fax: +44 (0) 20 7627 4900
Email: enquiries@mombooks.com
Website: http://www.mombooks.com

Publishes: Nonfiction; *Areas:* Biography; Historical; Humour; *Markets:* Adult; Children's

Independent publisher dealing in general nonfiction, royal and celebrity biographies, humour, and anthologies, and books for children through its imprint (including quirky nonfiction, humour, novelty, picture, and board books). Welcomes ideas, and prefers synopses and sample text to unsolicited mss. No fiction. See website for full details.

Oberon Books

521 Caledonian Road
London
N7 9RH
Tel: +44 (0) 20 7607 3637
Fax: +44 (0) 20 7607 3629
Email: andrew@oberonbooks.com
Website: http://www.oberonbooks.com

Publishes: Nonfiction; Scripts; *Areas:* Drama; Theatre; *Markets:* Adult; Professional

Contact: Andrew Walby, Senior Editor

Publishes play texts, and books on dance and theatre. Specialises in translations of European classics and contemporary plays, though also publishes edited performance versions of classics including Shakespeare. Play texts are usually published in conjunction with a production. Play scripts may be submitted by post or by email. Book proposals for trade and professional titles should include summary, table of contents, estimate word count, and sample chapter.

Omnibus Press

14/15 Berners Street
London
W1T 3LJ
Tel: +44 (0) 20 7612 7400
Fax: +44 (0) 20 7612 7545
Email: info@omnibuspress.com
Website: http://www.omnibuspress.com

Publishes: Nonfiction; *Areas:* Biography; Music; *Markets:* Adult

Contact: Chris Charlesworth

Publisher of music books, including song sheets and rock and pop biographies. Welcomes ideas, synopses, and unsolicited MSS for appropriate books.

Oneworld Publications

10 Bloomsbury Street
London
WC1B 3SR
Tel: +44 (0) 20 7307 8900
Email: submissions@oneworld-publications.com
Website: http://www.oneworld-publications.com

Publishes: Fiction; Nonfiction; *Areas:* Biography; Business; Current Affairs; Historical; Nature; Philosophy; Politics; Psychology; Religious; Science; Self-Help; *Markets:* Adult; *Treatments:* Commercial; Literary; Popular

Nonfiction authors must be academics and/or experts in their field. Approaches for fiction must provide a clear and concise synopsis, outlining the novel's main themes. See website for full submission guidelines, and forms for fiction and nonfiction, which may be submitted by email.

The Orion Publishing Group Limited

Orion House
5 Upper Saint Martin's Lane
London
WC2H 9EA
Tel: +44 (0) 20 7240 3444
Fax: +44 (0) 20 7240 4822
Website: http://www.orionbooks.co.uk

Publishes: Fiction; Nonfiction; Reference; *Areas:* Adventure; Archaeology; Arts; Autobiography; Beauty and Fashion; Biography; Cookery; Culture; Current Affairs; Design; Fantasy; Gardening; Health; Historical; Lifestyle; Literature; Military; Nature; Sci-Fi; Sport; Travel; *Markets:* Adult; Children's; Youth; *Treatments:* Commercial

One of the UK's leading commercial publishers. Accepts approaches through agents only.

Osprey Publishing Ltd

Commissioning Editor
Editorial Department
Osprey Publishing
Kemp House
Chawley Park
Cumnor Hill
Oxford
OX2 9PH
Tel: +44 (0) 1865 757022
Fax: +44 (0) 1865 242009
Email: editorial@ospreypublishing.com
Website: http://www.ospreypublishing.com

Publishes: Nonfiction; *Areas:* Historical; Military; *Markets:* Adult

Publishes illustrated books on military history and aviation. Welcomes synopses and ideas for books by post or by email, but no unsolicited MSS. See website for full guidelines.

Ouen Press

Email: submissions@ouenpress.com
Website: http://www.ouenpress.com

Publishes: Fiction; Nonfiction; *Areas:* Biography; Short Stories; Travel; *Markets:* Adult; *Treatments:* Contemporary

Publishes contemporary fiction, travel literature, short story collections and biography, if edgy. No genre, children's books, poetry, single short stories, guide books or recipe books. Send query by email only with outline, brief resume of your writing experience, and first 4,000 words, all in the body of the email. Do not include a cover letter. No attachments, or submissions by post. If no reponse within 60 days, assume rejection.

Oversteps Books

6 Halwell House
South Pool
Nr Kingsbridge
Devon
TQ7 2RX
Email: alwynmarriage@overstepsbooks.com
Website: http://www.overstepsbooks.com

Publishes: Poetry; *Markets:* Adult

Poetry publisher. Send email with copies of six poems that have been published in magazines or won competitions, along with details of dates or issue numbers and email addresses of the editors. Include poems and information in the body of your email. No submissions by post.

Peter Owen Publishers

81 Ridge Road
London
N8 9NP
Tel: +44 (0) 20 8350 1775
Fax: +44 (0) 20 8340 9488
Email: info@peterowen.com
Website: http://www.peterowen.com

Publishes: Fiction; Nonfiction; *Areas:* Arts; Biography; Criticism; Historical; Literature; Translations; *Markets:* Adult; *Treatments:* Literary

Contact: Antonia Owen (Editorial Director)

Publishes general nonfiction and international literary fiction. No first novels, short stories, poetry, plays, sport, spirituality, self-help, or children's or genre fiction. Prefers query by email or alternatively by post with return postage, including cover letter, synopsis, and one or two sample chapters. Prefers fiction to come from an agent or translator as appropriate.

Oxford University Press

Great Clarendon Street
Oxford

OX2 6DP
Tel: +44 (0) 1865 556767
Fax: +44 (0) 1865 556646
Email: webenquiry.uk@oup.com
Website: http://www.oup.com

Publishes: Fiction; Nonfiction; Reference; *Areas:* Current Affairs; Drama; Finance; Historical; Legal; Literature; Medicine; Music; Philosophy; Politics; Religious; Science; Sociology; *Markets:* Academic; Adult; Children's; Professional

Publishes academic works including journals, schoolbooks, dictionaries, reference works, classics, and children's fiction, and nonfiction. Email addresses for editorial available on website.

PaperBooks

The Old Fire Station
140 Tabernacle Street
London
EC2A 4SD
Tel: +44 (0) 20 7300 7370
Email: submissions@legend-paperbooks.co.uk
Website: http://www.legendtimesgroup.co.uk/paperbooks

Publishes: Nonfiction; *Areas:* Autobiography; Cookery; *Markets:* Adult

Former fiction publisher now relaunched as a nonfiction publisher. Publishes cookery and memoir, and looking to extend this list. Submit online using online submission system.

Parthian Books

426 Grove Extension
Swansea University
Singleton Park
Swansea
SA2 8PP
Tel: +44 (0) 1792 606605
Email: susieparthian@gmail.com
Website: http://www.parthianbooks.co.uk

Publishes: Fiction; Poetry; Scripts; *Areas:* Drama; Short Stories; Translations; *Markets:* Adult

Contact: Susie Wild

Publisher of poetry, drama, and fiction, of Welsh origin, in the English language. Also publishes English language translations of Welsh language work. Not accepting poetry submissions as at June 2015 (check website for current situation). Send query with SAE, one-page synopsis, and first 30 pages. No email submissions. See website for full submission guidelines.

Pavilion Publishing

Rayford House
School Road
Hove
East Sussex
BN3 5HX
Tel: +44 (0) 1273 434943
Fax: +44 (0) 1273 227308
Email: info@pavpub.com
Website: http://www.pavpub.com

Publishes: Nonfiction; Reference; *Areas:* Health; Sociology; *Markets:* Professional

Publishes books and resources for public, private and voluntary workers in the health, social care, education and community safety sectors.

Pearson UK

Edinburgh Gate
Harlow
CM20 2JE
Tel: +44 (0) 845 313 6666
Fax: +44 (0) 845 313 7777
Website: http://www.pearsoned.co.uk

Publishes: Nonfiction; *Markets:* Academic; Professional

World's largest publisher of educational material, inclusing books for primary school pupils through to professionals. See website for appropriate imprint to approach, and specific submission guidelines.

Pen & Sword Books Ltd

47 Church Street
Barnsley
South Yorkshire

S70 2AS
Tel: +44 (0) 1226 734555
Fax: +44 (0) 1226 734438
Email: editorialoffice@pen-and-sword.co.uk
Website: http://www.pen-and-sword.co.uk

Publishes: Fiction; Nonfiction; *Areas:* Adventure; Archaeology; Autobiography; Biography; Crime; Historical; Military; Sociology; Travel; *Markets:* Adult

Submissions of unsolicited synopses and ideas welcomed, but no unsolicited MSS. Publishes across a number of areas including military, aviation, maritime, family, local, true crime and transport history. Also launching historical fiction, adventure and discovery, archaeology and social history imprints. Send query by email with synopsis and sample chapter.

Persephone Books

59 Lamb's Conduit Street
London
WC1N 3NB
Tel: +44 (0) 20 7242 9292
Fax: +44 (0) 20 7242 9272
Email: info@persephonebooks.co.uk
Website: http://www.persephonebooks.co.uk

Publishes: Fiction; Nonfiction; *Areas:* Women's Interests; *Markets:* Adult

Publishes mainly forgotten fiction and non-fiction by women, for women and about women. Publishes reprints, so no unsolicited material.

Phaidon Press Limited

Regent's Wharf
All Saints Street
London
N1 9PA
Tel: +44 (0) 20 7843 1000
Fax: +44 (0) 20 7843 1010
Email: submissions@phaidon.com
Website: http://www.phaidon.com

Publishes: Nonfiction; *Areas:* Architecture; Arts; Beauty and Fashion; Cookery; Culture; Design; Film; Historical; Music; Photography; Travel; *Markets:* Academic; Adult; Children's

Publishes books in the areas of art, architecture, design, photography, film, fashion, contemporary culture, decorative arts, music, performing arts, cultural history, food and cookery, travel and books for children. No fiction or approaches by post. Send query by email only, with CV and short description of the project. Response only if interested.

Phoenix Yard Books

65 King's Cross Road
London
WC1X 9LW
Tel: +44 (0) 20 7239 4968
Email: submissions@phoenixyardbooks.com
Website: http://www.phoenixyardbooks.com

Publishes: Fiction; Nonfiction; Poetry; *Markets:* Children's; Youth; *Treatments:* Literary

Contact: Emma Langley

Publishes picture books, fiction, poetry, nonfiction and illustration for children aged around three to thirteen. Considers books of all genres, but leans more towards the literary and of the fiction spectrum. Particularly interested in character-based series, and fiction appealing to boys aged 6-9. Does not concentrate on young adult fiction, but will consider older fiction as part of epic series, sagas or trilogies. Send query by email only – no exceptions. See website for full submission guidelines. Replies to email queries only if interested.

Piatkus Books

Piatkus Submissions
Little, Brown Book Group
100 Victoria Embankment
London
EC4Y 0DY
Tel: +44 (0) 20 7911 8030
Fax: +44 (0) 20 7911 8100
Email: info@littlebrown.co.uk
Website: http://www.piatkus.co.uk

Publishes: Fiction; Nonfiction; *Areas:* Autobiography; Biography; Business; Crime; Health; Historical; Humour; Lifestyle; Psychology; Self-Help; Spiritual; Thrillers;

Markets: Adult; *Treatments:* Light; Popular; Serious

Contact: Gill Bailey (Nonfiction); Emma Beswetherick (Fiction)

No longer accepts unsolicited submissions. Accepts material through a literary agent only.

Piccadilly Press

5 Castle Road
London
NW1 8PR
Tel: +44 (0) 20 7267 4492
Fax: +44 (0) 20 7267 4493
Email: books@piccadillypress.co.uk
Website: http://www.piccadillypress.co.uk

Publishes: Fiction; Nonfiction; *Areas:* Humour; *Markets:* Children's; Youth; *Treatments:* Contemporary; Light

Publishes a range of titles, including parental books, but for new titles focuses on three main areas: picture books for children aged 2 to 5; teen fiction; and teen nonfiction.

Picture books should be character led and between 500 and 1,000 words. No novelty books. Prefers authors to be familiar with other books published before submitting – a catalogue is available upon request.

Publishes teen fiction and nonfiction which is contemporary, humorous, and deals with the issues faced by teenagers. Usually 25,000-35,000 words.

Send query by email with Word or Doc attachments of up to 5MB only.

Plexus Publishing Limited

25 Mallinson Road
London
SW11 1BW
Tel: +44 (0) 20 7924 4662
Fax: +44 (0) 20 7924 5096
Email: info@plexusuk.demon.co.uk
Website: http://www.plexusbooks.com

Publishes: Nonfiction; *Areas:* Biography; Culture; Film; Music; *Markets:* Adult; *Treatments:* Popular

Publishes illustrated nonfiction books specialising in biography, popular culture, movies and music.

Pluto Publishing Ltd

345 Archway Road
London
N6 5AA
Tel: +44 (0) 20 8348 2724
Fax: +44 (0) 20 8340 8252
Email: pluto@plutobooks.com
Website: http://www.plutobooks.com

Publishes: Nonfiction; *Areas:* Anthropology; Culture; Current Affairs; Finance; Historical; Legal; Media; Nature; Politics; Sociology; *Markets:* Academic

Contact: Anne Beech; David Castle; David Shulman

Academic press publishing books for students and academics in higher education. Consult website for appropriate commissioning editor to submit your proposal to, then contact by email giving outline of book, synopsis and table of contents, format and delivery estimate, plus market info (see website for more information).

Princeton University Press Europe

3 Market Place
Woodstock
Oxfordshire
OX20 1SY
Tel: +44 (0) 1993 814500
Fax: +44 (0) 1993 814504
Email: admin@pupress.co.uk
Website: http://www.pupress.co.uk

Publishes: Nonfiction; Reference; *Areas:* Anthropology; Archaeology; Architecture; Arts; Film; Finance; Historical; Legal; Literature; Media; Medicine; Music; Nature; Philosophy; Photography; Politics; Religious; Science; Self-Help; Sociology; *Markets:* Academic

Contact: Richard Baggaley, Publishing Director, Europe

European office of US academic publisher.

Professional and Higher Partnership

4 The Links
Cambridge Road
Newmarket
Suffolk
CB8 0TG
Tel: +44 (0) 1638 663456
Email: info@frontinus.org.uk
Website: http://pandhp.com

Publishes: Nonfiction; *Markets:* Academic; Professional

Publishes nonfiction for the academic and professional markets, including books on higher education and creative writing studies.

Profile Books

3A Exmouth House
Pine Street
Exmouth Market
London
EC1R OJH
Tel: +44 (0) 20 7841 6300
Fax: +44 (0) 20 7833 3969
Email: info@profilebooks.co.uk
Website: http://www.profilebooks.co.uk

Publishes: Nonfiction; *Areas:* Biography; Business; Culture; Current Affairs; Finance; Historical; Humour; Politics; Psychology; Science; *Markets:* Adult

Award-winning small publisher noted for author-friendly relations. Published the number-one Christmas bestseller in 2003. Recommends approaches be through a literary agent.

Pure Indigo Limited

Publishing Department
17 The Herons
Cottenham
Cambridge
CB24 8XX
Tel: +44 (0) 7981 395258
Email: submissions@pureindigo.co.uk
Website: http://www.pureindigo.co.uk/publishing

Publishes: Fiction; Nonfiction; *Areas:* Fantasy; Sci-Fi; *Markets:* Children's

Publishes books for children, including single-player role-playing gamebooks and books designed to support early readers. Prefers submissions by email. See website for guidelines.

Pushkin Press

71-75 Shelton Street
London
WC2H 9JQ
Tel: +44 (0) 20 7470 8830
Email: books@pushkinpress.com
Website: http://pushkinpress.com

Publishes: Fiction; Nonfiction; *Areas:* Autobiography; *Markets:* Adult; Children's; *Treatments:* Contemporary; Traditional

Publishes novels, essays, memoirs, children's books, including timeless classics and contemporary.

Quadrille Publishing Ltd

Pentagon House
52-54 Southwark Street
London
SE1 1UN
Tel: +44 (0) 20 7601 7500
Email: enquiries@quadrille.co.uk
Website: http://www.quadrille.co.uk

Publishes: Nonfiction; *Areas:* Beauty and Fashion; Cookery; Crafts; Design; Gardening; Health; Humour; *Markets:* Adult

Publishes quality illustrated nonfiction. No fiction or books for children.

Quarto Publishing Group UK

The Old Brewery
6 Blundell Street
London
N7 9BH
Tel: +44 (0) 20 7700 6700

Fax: +44 (0) 20 7700 8066
Email: info@quarto.com
Website: http://www.quarto.com

Publishes: Nonfiction; *Areas:* Arts; Beauty and Fashion; Cookery; Crafts; Design; Entertainment; Gardening; Health; Historical; Hobbies; How-to; Lifestyle; Sport; *Markets:* Adult; Children's

Publisher of illustrated nonfiction books for adults and children.

Quercus Books

55 Baker Street, 7th Floor
South Block
London
W1U 8EW
Tel: +44 (0) 20 7291 7200
Email: enquiries@quercusbooks.co.uk
Website: http://www.quercusbooks.co.uk

Publishes: Fiction; Nonfiction; *Areas:* Crime; Fantasy; Sci-Fi; *Markets:* Adult; Children's

Publishes fiction and nonfiction. Does not accept unsolicited submissions at this time.

Quiller Publishing Ltd

Wykey House
Wykey
Shrewsbury
Shropshire
SY4 1JA
Tel: +44 (0) 1939 261616
Fax: +44 (0) 1939 261606
Email: admin@quillerbooks.com
Website:
http://www.countrybooksdirect.com

Publishes: Nonfiction; Reference; *Areas:* Architecture; Biography; Business; Cookery; Gardening; Humour; Sport; Travel; *Markets:* Adult

Contact: John Beaton

Publishes books for all lovers of fishing, shooting, equestrian and country pursuits. Accepts unsolicited MSS from authors. Send submissions as hard copy only, with email address for reply or SAE if return of ms is required.

Radcliffe Publishing Ltd

5 Thomas More Square
London
E1W 1YW
Tel: +44 (0) 844 887 1380
Email:
jonathan.mckenna@radcliffepublishing.com
Website: http://www.radcliffehealth.com

Publishes: Nonfiction; *Areas:* Health; Medicine; *Markets:* Professional

Contact: Jonathan McKenna; Katrina Hulme-Cross

Publishes books on medicine, including health care policy and management, and also training materials. Welcomes synopses, ideas, and unsolicited MSS.

Ragged Bears Limited

Unit 14A
Bennett's Field Trading Estate
Southgate Road
Wincanton
Somerset
BA9 9DT
Tel: +44 (0) 1963 34300
Email: books@ragged-bears.co.uk
Website: http://www.ragged-bears.co.uk

Publishes: Fiction; *Markets:* Children's; Youth

Publishes picture books and novelty books, up to young teen fiction. Accepts submissions by post with SAE (no original artwork), but prefers submissions by email.

Ransom Publishing Ltd

Radley House
8 St Cross Road
Winchester
Hampshire
SO23 9HX
Tel: +44 (0) 1962 862307
Fax: +44 (0) 5601 148881
Email: ransom@ransom.co.uk
Website: http://www.ransom.co.uk

Publishes: Fiction; Nonfiction; *Markets:* Adult; Children's; Professional; Youth

An independent specialist publisher of high quality, inspirational books that encourage and help children, young adults, and adults to develop their reading skills. Books are intended to have content which is age appropriate and engaging, but reading levels that would normally be appropriate for younger readers. Also publishes resources for both the library and classroom. Will consider unsolicited mss. Email in first instance.

Reader's Digest Association Ltd

PO Box 7853
Ringwood
BH24 9FH
Tel: +44 (0) 330 333 2220
Email:
customer_service@readersdigest.co.uk
Website: http://www.readersdigest.co.uk

Publishes: Nonfiction; *Markets:* Adult

Publishes monthly magazine and condensed and series books. See website for more details.

Reality Street Editions

63 All Saints Street
Hastings
East Sussex
TN34 3BN
Tel: +44 (0) 7706 189253
Email: info@realitystreet.co.uk
Website: http://www.realitystreet.co.uk

Publishes: Fiction; Poetry; *Markets:* Adult; *Treatments:* Experimental; Literary

Contact: Ken Edwards

Not planning to publish any new titles after 2016, when existing commitments are fulfilled. Not accepting any new material.

Small poetry press which has in recent years also published experimental prose, both narrative and non-narrative. Publishes only a few books each year, so usually heavily committed: "if you are not familiar with any of those writers we have published and/or are unwilling to research further by buying and reading our books, then it's highly unlikely you have anything to interest us."

Red Rattle Books

Email: editor@redrattlebooks.co.uk
Website: http://www.redrattlebooks.co.uk

Publishes: Fiction; Nonfiction; *Areas:* Crime; Horror; *Markets:* Adult

Independent, family run company, publishing new crime, horror and nonfiction books. Submit via website using online submission form.

Richard Dennis Publications

The New Chapel
Shepton Beauchamp
Ilminster
Somerset
TA19 0JT
Tel: +44 (0) 1460 240044
Email:
books@richarddennispublications.com
Website:
http://www.richarddennispublications.com

Publishes: Nonfiction; *Areas:* Arts; Crafts; Design; *Markets:* Adult

Publisher of arts and crafts books, including books on ceramics, glass, sculpture, etc.

Robert Hale Publishers

Clerkenwell House
45-47 Clerkenwell Green
London
EC1R 0HT
Tel: +44 (0) 20 7251 2661
Fax: +44 (0) 20 7490 4958
Email: submissions@halebooks.com
Website: http://www.halebooks.com

Publishes: Fiction; Nonfiction; Reference; *Areas:* Arts; Autobiography; Biography; Cookery; Crime; Historical; Hobbies;

Humour; Leisure; Military; Spiritual; Westerns; *Markets:* Adult

See website for full submission guidelines, and list of material not currently being accepted. Send query with synopsis and three sample chapters.

Rose and Crown Books

36 Salmons Leap
Calne
Wiltshire
SN11 9EU
Tel: +44 (0) 1508 480087
Email: query@roseandcrownbooks.com
Website:
http://www.roseandcrownbooks.com/

Publishes: Fiction; *Areas:* Historical; Military; Religious; Romance; Travel; *Markets:* Adult; Family; *Treatments:* Commercial; Contemporary; Light; Literary; Mainstream; Niche; Popular; Positive; Serious; Traditional

Imprint with launch date in 2009. Our focus is on romance with an inspirational flavour. Intended to complement American brands such as the Steeple Hill, Thorndike and Bethany House imprints, we would seem to be the first publisher in the United Kingdom to take up the banner for this genre.

We believe strongly that Inspirational Romance has a role to play in the lives of today's women, of all ages, races and creeds around the world – a role of pure reading enjoyment as well as food for their imaginations and their feminine spirits and minds. We are concentrating on strong writing and intelligent stories that speak to women across the board, with characters and situations they can identify with – tales that fit many age groups and categories: tender young love, later life meetings, families, and romance for the more senior of us, too.

Some will have more Christian influence than others; some will be contemporary, others historical, with locations all around the world. They will vary in style from straight romance to historical fiction, contemporary novels, humour, travel, adventure, crime/detective, Western, military, etc. As long as they have a romance at their heart and Christian characters, with a greater or lesser Christian implication, they fit what we are looking for.

Query first please, with single para description of book, brief author bio, email address and postal address, and synopsis. For full guidelines and more information on how we work as a company, please visit the web site, and please take the time to read and follow the guidelines. If you want us to show interest in you, please show enough interest in us to submit correctly; we thank you!

Roundhouse Group

Unit B
18 Marine Gardens
Brighton
BN2 1AH
Tel: +44 (0) 1273 603717
Fax: +44 (0) 1273 697494
Email: sandy@roundhousegroup.co.uk
Website:
https://www.roundhousegroup.co.uk

Publishes: Nonfiction; Reference; *Areas:* Architecture; Arts; Business; Cookery; Crafts; Design; Film; Health; Historical; Lifestyle; Literature; Medicine; Music; Nature; Photography; Self-Help; Spiritual; Sport; Travel; *Markets:* Adult; Children's; Youth

Publisher of nonfiction and reference for adults, children, and young adults.

Route Publishing

PO Box 167
Pontefract
WF8 4WW
Tel: +44 (0) 845 158 1565
Email: info@route-online.com
Website: http://www.route-online.com

Publishes: Fiction; Poetry; *Areas:* Culture; Short Stories; *Markets:* Adult; *Treatments:* Contemporary

Contact: Ian Daley; Isabel Galan

Publisher of novels, short stories, and poetry. Open door for new writing submissions is currently unsupported. Any new books considered must be self-supporting. This consideration must be addressed in any proposals.

Saffron Books

EAPGROUP
PO Box 13666
London
SW14 8WF
Tel: +44 (0) 20 8392 1122
Fax: +44 (0) 20 8392 1422
Email: info@eapgroup.com
Website: http://www.saffronbooks.com

Publishes: Fiction; Nonfiction; *Areas:* Archaeology; Arts; Business; Culture; Current Affairs; Finance; Historical; Sociology; *Markets:* Adult

Publishes books on art, archaeology and architecture, art history, current affairs and linguistics, with a particular emphasis on Asia, Africa, and the Middle East. Also publishes fiction. Welcomes proposals for books and monongraphs from new or established authors. Send query by email, post, or fax (not preferred for long documents). See website for full guidelines.

The Salariya Book Company

25 Marlborough Place
Brighton
East Sussex
BN1 1UB
Tel: +44 (0) 1273 603306
Fax: +44 (0) 1273 621619
Email: salariya@salariya.com
Website: http://www.salariya.com

Publishes: Fiction; Nonfiction; *Areas:* Adventure; Fantasy; Historical; Nature; Science; *Markets:* Children's

Publishes books of fiction and nonfiction for children.

Salt Publishing Ltd

12 Norwich Road
CROMER
Norfolk
NR27 0AX
Tel: +44 (0) 1263 511011
Email: submissions@saltpublishing.com
Website: http://www.saltpublishing.com

Publishes: Fiction; *Areas:* Crime; Gothic; Literature; Thrillers; *Markets:* Adult; *Treatments:* Dark; Literary; Mainstream; Traditional

Accepts print fiction submissions via agents only. Accepts direct submissions from authors for ebooks – novellas 20,000 to 30,000 words long, dealing explicitly with lives of young people in modern Britain and the US. Full submission guidelines on website. No poetry (adult or children's), biography or autobiography, plays or nonfiction.

Samuel French Ltd

Performing Rights Department
52 Fitzroy Street
London
W1T 5JR
Tel: +44 (0) 20 7387 9373
Fax: +44 (0) 20 7387 2161
Email: submissions@samuelfrench-london.co.uk
Website: http://www.samuelfrench-london.co.uk

Publishes: Scripts; *Areas:* Drama; *Markets:* Adult

Publishes plays only. Send query by email only, following the guidelines in the FAQ section of the website. No unsolicited MSS.

Sandstone Press Ltd

PO Box 5725
One High Street
Dingwall
Ross-shire
IV15 9WJ
Tel: +44 (0) 1349 862583
Fax: +44 (0) 1349 862583
Email: moira@sandstonepress.com
Website: http://www.sandstonepress.com

Publishes: Fiction; Nonfiction; *Areas:* Crime; Thrillers; *Markets:* Adult; *Treatments:* Literary

Contact: Moira Forsyth, Commissioning Editor

Publishes fiction and nonfiction and adults. Interested in literary fiction, crime novels, and thrillers, set in the past, present, or future. Welcomes proposals – send introductory email query in first instance, including outline and bio, including publishing history. No children's, young adult, poetry, short story collections, science fiction, fantasy, general historical fiction, or horror. See website for more details and submission form.

Scala Arts & Heritage Publishers

21 Queen Anne's Gate
London
SW1H 9BU
Tel: +44 (0) 20 7808 1550
Email: info@scalapublishers.com
Website: http://www.scalapublishers.com

Publishes: Nonfiction; *Areas:* Antiques; Architecture; Arts; Historical; *Markets:* Adult

Specialises in producing books for museums, galleries, libraries, heritage organisations, cathedrals and other religious sites.

SCM-Canterbury Press

Hymns Ancient and Modern Ltd
3rd Floor
Invicta House
108-114 Golden Lane
London
EC1Y 0TG
Tel: +44 (0) 20 7776 7540
Fax: +44 (0) 20 7776 7556
Email: christine@hymnsam.co.uk
Website: http://www.canterburypress.co.uk

Publishes: Nonfiction; Reference; *Areas:* Philosophy; Religious; Spiritual; *Markets:* Adult

Publisher of religious nonfiction and reference. No dissertations, fiction, poetry, drama, children's books, books of specialist local interest, or (as a general rule) multi-authored collections of essays or symposium papers.

Seafarer Books

102 Redwald Road
Rendlesham
Woodbridge
Suffolk
IP12 2TE
Tel: +44 (0) 1394 420789
Fax: +44 (0) 1394 461314
Email: info@seafarerbooks.com
Website: http://www.seafarerbooks.com

Publishes: Fiction; Nonfiction; *Areas:* Arts; Crafts; Historical; How-to; Military; Music; Travel; *Markets:* Adult; *Treatments:* Traditional

Contact: Patricia Eve

Publishes fiction and nonfiction books on sailing, including maritime history, practical seamanship and boatbuilding, etc. Also music CDs, cards, and calendars. No unsolicited MSS. Send query in first instance.

Seren Books

57 Nolton Street
Bridgend
Wales
CF31 3AE
Tel: +44 (0) 1656 663018
Fax: +44 (0) 1656 649226
Email: Seren@SerenBooks.com
Website: http://www.serenbooks.com

Publishes: Fiction; Nonfiction; Poetry; *Areas:* Anthropology; Arts; Biography; Criticism; Current Affairs; Drama; Historical; Music; Photography; Politics; Sport; Translations; Travel; *Markets:* Adult; Children's; *Treatments:* Literary

Contact: Penny Thomas (Fiction Editor); Amy Wack (Poetry Editor); Mick Felton (Nonfiction Editor)

Publishes fiction, nonfiction, and poetry. Specialises in English-language writing from Wales and aims to bring Welsh culture, art, literature, and politics to a wider audience.

Accepts nonfiction submissions only by email; no poetry or fiction submissions by email. See website for complete submission guidelines.

Severn House Publishers

Salatin House
19 Cedar Road
Sutton
Surrey
SM2 5DA
Tel: +44 (0) 20 8770 3930
Fax: +44 (0) 20 8770 3850
Email: sales@severnhouse.com
Website: http://severnhouse.com

Publishes: Fiction; *Areas:* Crime; Historical; Horror; Mystery; Romance; Sci-Fi; Thrillers; Markets

Accepts submissions via literary agents only. Targets the UK and US fiction library markets, and considers only authors with a significant background in these markets.

Shearsman Books

50 Westons Hill Drive
Emersons Green
Bristol
BS16 7DF
Tel: +44 (0) 1179 572957
Email: editor@shearsman.com
Website: http://www.shearsman.com

Publishes: Nonfiction; Poetry; *Areas:* Autobiography; Criticism; Literature; Translations; *Markets:* Adult

Contact: Tony Frazer

Publishes poetry books of at least 64 A5 pages. Publishes mainly poetry by British, Irish, North American and Australian/New Zealand poets, plus poetry in translation from any language—although particular interest in German, Spanish and Latin American poetry.

Submit only if MS is of appropriate length and most of it has already appeared in UK or US magazines of some repute. Send selection of 6-10 pages by post with SASE or by email with material embedded in the text or as PDF attachment. No other kind of attachments accepted.

Also sometimes publishes literary criticism on poetry, and essays or memoirs by poets.

Shepheard-Walwyn (Publishers) Ltd

107 Parkway House
Sheen Lane
London
SW14 8LS
Tel: +44 (0) 20 8241 5927
Email: books@shepheard-walwyn.co.uk
Website: http://www.shepheard-walwyn.co.uk

Publishes: Nonfiction; Poetry; *Areas:* Biography; Finance; Historical; Philosophy; Politics; *Markets:* Adult

Publishes mainly nonfiction, particularly the areas listed above and also books of Scottish interest, and gift books in calligraphy and / or illustrated. Also some poetry.

Shire Publications Ltd

Editorial Department
Shire & Old House
Midland House
West Way
Botley,
Oxford
OX2 0PH
Tel: +44 (0) 1865 811332
Fax: +44 (0) 1865 242009
Email: shireeditorial@shirebooks.co.uk
Website: http://www.shirebooks.co.uk

Publishes: Nonfiction; *Areas:* Antiques; Archaeology; Architecture; Beauty and Fashion; Biography; Crafts; Design; Film; Gardening; Historical; Hobbies; Military; Music; Photography; Sociology; Sport; Technology; Theatre; Travel; *Markets:* Adult

Send query by post or by email, with short synopsis up to 2,000 words. Publishes inexpensive, nonfiction paperbacks on a wide range of subjects: the obscure, the unusual, the collectable, the historical; main subject areas include, but are not limited, to: Archaeology; Architecture; Biographies;

Canals; Ceramics; Church History; Coins and Medals; Costume and Fashion Accessories; Egyptology; Ephemera; Ethnography; Furniture and Furnishings; Garden History; Genealogy and local history; Glass; Guide and Walking Books; Household Bygones; Industrial History; London; Maritime; Mechanical & Electrical Bygones; Military History; Motoring; Music; Natural History; Needlecrafts and Accessories; Photography; Railways & Steam; Rural Crafts; Scottish Heritage; Social History; Textile History; Toys and Sporting Collectables...

Short Books

Unit 316
ScreenWorks
22 Highbury Grove
London
N5 2EF
Tel: +44 (0) 20 7833 9429
Email: info@shortbooks.co.uk
Website: http://shortbooks.co.uk

Publishes: Fiction; Nonfiction; *Markets:* Adult

Send submissions via literary agent only. Send cover letter with synopsis and first three chapters / roughly 30 pages.

Sigma Press

Stobart House
Pontyclerc
Penybanc Road
Ammanford
Carmarthenshire
SA18 3HP
Tel: +44 (0) 1269 593100
Fax: +44 (0) 1269 596116
Email: info@sigmapress.co.uk
Website: http://www.sigmapress.co.uk

Publishes: Nonfiction; *Areas:* Adventure; Biography; Historical; Leisure; Travel; *Markets:* Adult

Contact: Nigel Evans; Jane Evans

Publishes books mainly in the leisure area, including the outdoors, adventure, local heritage and biography. No poetry or fiction.

Souvenir Press Ltd

43 Great Russell Street
London
WC1B 3PA
Tel: +44 (0) 20 7580 9307 / +44 (0) 20 7637 5711
Fax: +44 (0) 20 7580 5064
Email: souvenirpress@souvenirpress.co.uk
Website: http://www.souvenirpress.co.uk

Publishes: Fiction; Nonfiction; *Areas:* Antiques; Archaeology; Autobiography; Beauty and Fashion; Biography; Business; Cookery; Crafts; Crime; Gardening; Health; Historical; Hobbies; Humour; Lifestyle; Literature; Medicine; Military; Music; Mystery; Nature; Philosophy; Politics; Psychology; Religious; Science; Self-Help; Sociology; Spiritual; Sport; Theatre; Travel; Women's Interests; *Markets:* Academic; Adult

Contact: Ernest Hecht

Independent publisher publishing an eclectic mixture of bestsellers and books intended for more limited audiences. Send query letter with outline in first instance.

SportsBooks Limited

1 Evelyn Court
Malvern Road
Cheltenham
GL50 2JR
Tel: +44 (0) 1242 256755
Fax: +44 (0) 0560 310 8126
Email: info@sportsbooks.ltd.uk
Website: http://www.sportsbooks.ltd.uk

Publishes: Nonfiction; *Areas:* Biography; Sport; *Markets:* Adult

Welcomes submissions by hard copy or email as .txt or .rtf attachments. Send query with synopsis and up to three sample chapters, plus information on market and marketing. No fiction.

Stacey International

128 Kensington Church Street
London
W8 4BH
Tel: +44 (0) 20 7221 7166

Fax: +44 (0) 20 7792 9288
Email: editorial@stacey-international.co.uk
Website: http://www.stacey-international.co.uk

Publishes: Fiction; Nonfiction; Poetry; Reference; *Areas:* Archaeology; Historical; Literature; Nature; Photography; Travel; *Markets:* Adult; Children's

Publishes nonfiction, fiction, and poetry, for adults and children. Submit manuscripts and proposals by email. See website for more information.

Stainer & Bell Ltd

PO Box 110
Victoria House
23 Gruneisen Road
London, England
N3 1DZ
Tel: +44 (0) 20 8343 3303
Fax: +44 (0) 20 8343 3024
Email: post@stainer.co.uk
Website: http://www.stainer.co.uk

Publishes: Nonfiction; *Areas:* Music; Religious; *Markets:* Adult

Independent, family run business, specialising in the publication of printed music and books on music and religious communication, including hymns.

Stairwell Books

Email: rose@stairwellbooks.com
Website: http://www.stairwellbooks.co.uk

Publishes: Fiction; Poetry; *Areas:* Short Stories; *Markets:* Adult

Contact: Rose Drew

Small press publisher specialising in poetry anthologies, short stories, and novels from new writers. Send query by email. See website for full details.

Stripes Publishing

1 The Coda Centre
189 Munster Road
London
SW6 6AW
Tel: +44 (0) 20 7385 6333
Fax: +44 (0) 20 7385 7333
Website: http://www.stripespublishing.co.uk

Publishes: Fiction; *Markets:* Children's

Publishes fiction for children over 5 and young teens. Send query by post with SASE, synopsis, and first three chapters. No submissions by email or on disk.

Sussex Academic Press

PO Box 139
Eastbourne
East Sussex
BN24 9BP
Tel: +44 (0) 1323 479220
Fax: +44 (0) 1323 478185
Email: edit@sussex-academic.com
Website: http://www.sussex-academic.com

Publishes: Nonfiction; *Areas:* Anthropology; Archaeology; Arts; Biography; Criticism; Culture; Drama; Finance; Historical; Literature; Media; Music; Nature; Philosophy; Politics; Psychology; Religious; Sociology; Theatre; Women's Interests; *Markets:* Academic

Contact: Anthony V. P. Grahame, Editorial Director

Academic publisher. Send query by post. Book proposal form available on website. No unsolicited MSS.

Sweet & Maxwell

Friars House
160 Blackfriars Road
London
SE1 8EZ
Tel: +44 (0) 20 7542 6664
Email: TRLUKI.CS@thomsonreuters.com
Website: http://www.sweetandmaxwell.co.uk

Publishes: Nonfiction; Reference; *Areas:* Legal; *Markets:* Academic; Professional

Contact: Tania Quan; Katherine Brewer; Steven Warriner; Nicola Thurlow; Simon Smith; Cassi Waddy

Publishes legal material only, for professionals, academics, and students. Products include looseleafs, CDs, books, newsletters, and online services. Ideas from writers for legal / professional projects are welcomed. See website for list of managers for different subject areas, and their email addresses.

Sweet Cherry Publishing

Unit E Vulcan Business Complex
Vulcan Road
Leicester
LE5 3EB
Email:
submissions@sweetcherrypublishing.com
Website:
http://www.sweetcherrypublishing.com

Publishes: Fiction; *Markets:* Children's; Youth

Contact: Abdul Thadha

Publishes books for children of all ages and young adults. Send submissions by post or by email, or through online form. Postal submissions accepted from UK authors only. See website for full submission guidelines.

TSO (The Stationery Office)

St Crispins
Duke Street
Norwich
NR3 1PD
Tel: +44 (0) 1603 622211
Email: customer.services@tso.co.uk
Website: http://www.tso.co.uk

Publishes: Nonfiction; Reference; *Areas:* Business; Current Affairs; Medicine; *Markets:* Professional

One of the largest publishers by volume in the UK, publishing more than 9,000 titles a year in print and digital formats.

Tango Books Ltd

PO Box 32595
London
W4 5YD
Tel: +44 (0) 20 8996 9970
Fax: +44 (0) 20 8996 9977
Email: info@tangobooks.co.uk
Website: http://www.tangobooks.co.uk

Publishes: Fiction; Nonfiction; *Markets:* Children's

Contact: David Fielder; Sheri Safran

Publisher of children's fiction (ages 1-8), nonfiction (ages 1-15), and novelty books, up to 1,000 words. Send query by email or by post with complete text, bio, and SAE. No poetry or verse, or texts that are very British in content or style. See website for complete guidelines.

The Templar Company Limited

Deepdene Lodge
Deepdene Avenue
Dorking
Surrey
RH5 4AT
Tel: +44 (0) 1306 876361
Fax: +44 (0) 1306 889097
Email: submissions@templarco.co.uk
Website: http://www.templarco.co.uk

Publishes: Fiction; Nonfiction; *Markets:* Children's

Publishes children's fiction and picture and novelty books. Currently closed to fiction submissions, but welcomes novelty and picture book submissions, in hard copy by post only. Include SAE if return of work required. Artwork submissions accepted by email.

Templar Poetry

58 Dale Road
Matlock
Derbyshire
DE4 3NB
Tel: +44 (0) 1629 582500
Email: info@templarpoetry.com
Website: http://templarpoetry.com

Publishes: Poetry; *Markets:* Adult; *Treatments:* Contemporary; Literary

Publishes poetry acquired through a numebr of competitions, ranging from short selections of poems up to a full collection. See website for guidelines and to submit online. Note that entering the competitions requires the payment of an entry fee.

Thames and Hudson Ltd

181A High Holborn
London
WC1V 7QX
Tel: +44 (0) 20 7845 5000
Fax: +44 (0) 20 7845 5050
Email: editorial@thameshudson.co.uk
Website: http://www.thamesandhudson.com

Publishes: Nonfiction; Reference; *Areas:* Archaeology; Architecture; Arts; Beauty and Fashion; Biography; Culture; Design; Gardening; Historical; Photography; Religious; Travel; *Markets:* Adult

Publishes illustrated nonfiction only. No fiction. Send query by email with short outline and CV in the body of the email. No attachments.

Titan Books

Titan House
144 Southwark Street
London
SE1 0UP
Tel: +44 (0) 20 7620 0200
Fax: +44 (0) 20 7620 0032
Email: editorial@titanemail.com
Website: http://www.titanbooks.com

Publishes: Fiction; Nonfiction; *Areas:* Entertainment; Film; Humour; Sci-Fi; Short Stories; TV; *Markets:* Adult; Youth

Contact: Commissioning Editor

Publisher of graphic novels, particularly with film or television tie-ins, and books related to film and TV. No unsolicited fiction or books for children, but will consider ideas for licensed projects they have already contracted. Send query with synopsis by post only. No email submissions.

Top That! Publishing

Marine House
Tide Mill Way
Woodbridge
Suffolk
IP12 1AP
Tel: +44 (0) 1394 386651
Email: dan@topthatpublishing.com
Website: http://topthatpublishing.com

Publishes: Fiction; Nonfiction; Reference; *Areas:* Cookery; Humour; *Markets:* Adult; Children's

Contact: Dan Graham, Editorial Director

Publishes Activity Books, Character Books, Cookery Books, Felt Books, Fiction, Humour, Magnetic Books, Novelty Books, Phonics Books, Picture Storybooks, Pop-Up Books, Press Out & Play, Reference Books, and Sticker Books. Does not currently publish "regular" children's or adults fiction. See online book catalogue for the kinds of books published. If suitable for the list, send submissions by email (preferred), ideally under 1MB, or by post (mss not returned). See website for full guidelines. Responds within 8 weeks if interested. No simultaneous submissions.

Trentham Books Limited

Institute of Education
University of London
20 Bedford Way
London
WC1H 0AL
Tel: +44 (0) 20 7911 5563
Email: g.klein@ioe.ac.uk
Website: http://www.trentham-books.co.uk

Publishes: Nonfiction; *Areas:* Culture; Humour; Legal; Sociology; Women's Interests; *Markets:* Academic; Professional

Contact: Dr Gillian Klein

Publishes academic and professional books. No fiction, biography, or poetry. No unsolicited MSS, but accepts queries by post with SASE, or by email. See website for full guidelines.

Ulverscroft Large Print Books Ltd

The Green
Bradgate Road
Anstey
Leicester
LE7 7FU
Tel: +44 (0) 1162 364325
Fax: +44 (0) 1162 340205
Email: m.merrill@ulverscroft.co.uk
Website: http://www.ulverscroft.com

Publishes: Fiction; Nonfiction; *Markets:* Adult

Contact: Mark Merrill

Publishes a wide variety of large print titles in hard and soft cover formats, as well as abridged and unabridged audio books. Many titles are written by the world's favourite authors.

Unicorn Press Ltd

66 Charlotte Street
LONDON
W1T 4QE
Tel: +44 (0) 7836 633377
Email: ian@unicornpress.org
Website: http://unicornpress.org

Publishes: Nonfiction; Reference; *Areas:* Architecture; Arts; Biography; Historical; *Markets:* Adult

Contact: Ian Strathcarron (Publisher)

Works with artists, authors, museums, and galleries to publish high-quality fine and decorative art reference books, guides and monographs.

Unthank Books

PO Box 3506
Norwich
Norfolk
NR7 7QP
Tel: +44 (0) 1603 471300
Email: robin.jones@unthankbooks.com
Website: http://www.unthankbooks.com

Publishes: Fiction; Nonfiction; *Markets:* Adult; *Treatments:* Literary

Contact: Robin Jones (Publisher); Ashley Stokes (Editorial Director)

Publishes adult literary fiction and nonfiction. Send query with SAE, synopsis, and 50 double spaced pages.

Usborne Publishing

83-85 Saffron Hill
London
EC1N 8RT
Tel: +44 (0) 20 7430 2800
Fax: +44 (0) 20 7430 1562
Email: mail@usborne.co.uk
Website: http://www.usborne.co.uk

Publishes: Fiction; Nonfiction; Reference; *Markets:* Children's

Publisher of children's reference now expanding into children's fiction. All nonfiction written in-house and fiction submissions accepted via literary agents only.

Virago Press

Carmelite House
50 Victoria Embankment
LONDON
EC4Y 0DZ
Tel: +44 (0) 20 3122 7000
Email: virago@littlebrown.co.uk
Website: http://www.virago.co.uk

Publishes: Fiction; Nonfiction; *Areas:* Literature; Women's Interests; *Markets:* Adult; *Treatments:* Literary

Publishes fiction and nonfiction women's literature. No poetry. Accepts approaches via literary agents only.

Virtue Books

Edward House
Tenter Street
Rotherham
S60 1LB
Tel: +44 (0) 845 094 2030
Fax: +44 (0) 845 094 2060
Email: info@russums.co.uk
Website: http://www.virtuebooks.co.uk

Publishes: Nonfiction; *Areas:* Cookery; *Markets:* Professional

Publishes books for professional chefs.

Wooden Books

8A Market Place
Glastonbury
BA6 8LT
Email: info@woodenbooks.com
Website: http://www.woodenbooks.com

Publishes: Nonfiction; *Areas:* Historical; Science; Spiritual; *Markets:* Adult

Publishes illustration-heavy books on such topics as ancient sciences, magic, mathematics, etc. Prospective authors will need to provide high quality illustrations. Essential to query before commencing work. Send query by email or by post. See website for full details.

Wallflower Press

4 Eastern Terrace Mews
Brighton
BN2 1EP
Email: yoram@wallflowerpress.co.uk
Website: http://www.wallflowerpress.co.uk

Publishes: Nonfiction; *Areas:* Culture; Entertainment; Film; Media; *Markets:* Academic; Adult

Contact: Yoram Allon, Consulting Editor to Columbia

Publisher of books relating to film, plus related media and culture, for both popular and academic markets. Contact by email in first instance. No fiction, or academic nonfiction which is not related to the moving image.

Acquired by a US publisher in 2011, the previous editorial and pre-production team continue to work directly with authors as an imprint of the US firm.

Waverley Books

Academy Park
Building 4000
Glasgow
G51 1PR
Email: info@waverley-books.co.uk
Website: http://www.waverley-books.co.uk

Publishes: Fiction; Nonfiction; *Areas:* Cookery; Historical; Humour; *Markets:* Adult; Children's

Publishes history, fiction, nostalgia, food and drink, humour, children's, graphic novels, and Scottish interest.

Whittet Books Ltd

1 St John's Lane
Stansted
Essex
CM24 8JU
Tel: +44 (0) 1279 815871
Fax: +44 (0) 1279 647564
Email: mail@whittetbooks.com
Website: http://www.whittetbooks.com

Publishes: Nonfiction; *Areas:* Nature; *Markets:* Adult

Publishes books of rural interest, including horses, pets, poultry, livestock, horticulture, natural history, etc. Send query with outline in first instance; preferably by email.

William Reed Business Media

Broadfield Park
Crawley
West Sussex
RH11 9RT
Tel: +44 (0) 1293 613400
Website: http://www.william-reed.com

Publishes: Nonfiction; Reference; *Areas:* Business; *Markets:* Professional

Publishes business to business directories and reports.

Wolters Kluwer (UK) Ltd

145 London Road
Kingston upon Thames
Surrey
KT2 6SR
Tel: +44 (0) 20 8547 3333
Fax: +44 (0) 20 8547 2637

Email: info@croner.co.uk
Website: http://www.wolterskluwer.co.uk

Publishes: Nonfiction; Reference; *Areas:* Business; Finance; Health; Legal; *Markets:* Professional

Publishes books, looseleafs, and online services for professionals. Areas of expertise include: Human Resources, Health and Safety, Tax and Accountancy, Education and Healthcare, Manufacturing and Construction.

The X Press

PO Box 25694
London
N17 6FP
Tel: +44 (0) 20 8801 2100
Fax: +44 (0) 20 8885 1322
Email: vibes@xpress.co.uk
Website: http://www.xpress.co.uk

Publishes: Fiction; *Areas:* Culture; *Markets:* Adult; Children's; *Treatments:* Contemporary; Literary; Popular

Contact: Dotun Adebayo (Editorial Director); Steve Pope (Marketing Director)

Europe's largest publisher of Black interest books. Publishes popular contemporary fiction, children's fiction, and black classics, though scope is expanding. Send SAE with MS, rather than synopses or ideas. No poetry.

Zambezi Publishing Ltd

PO Box 221
Plymouth
PL2 2YJ
Tel: +44 (0) 1752 367300
Fax: +44 (0) 1752 350453
Email: pubscripts@zampub.com
Website: http://www.zampub.com

Publishes: Nonfiction; *Areas:* Business; Finance; Health; Lifestyle; New Age; Self-Help; Spiritual; *Markets:* Adult

Publisher of books on mind, body, and spirit, including self-publishing division. Send synopsis and sample chapter by mail, or brief email query. No attachments.

Zero to Ten Limited

327 High Street
Slough
Berkshire
SL1 1TX
Tel: +44 (0) 1753 578 499
Email: annamcquinn@zerototen.co.uk

Publishes: Nonfiction; *Markets:* Children's

Contact: Anna McQuinn

Publishes nonfiction for children up to 10 years old, including board books and toddler books. Welcomes submissions, but responds only if interested.

Canadian Publishers

For the most up-to-date listings of these and hundreds of other publishers, visit http://www.firstwriter.com/publishers

*To claim your **free** access to the site, please see the back of this book.*

Annick Press

15 Patricia Avenue
Toronto, ON
M2M 1H9
Email: annickpress@annickpress.com
Website: http://www.annickpress.com

Publishes: Fiction; Nonfiction; *Markets:* Children's; Youth

Canadian publisher committed to publishing Canadian authors. Publishes fiction and nonfiction for children aged six months to twelve years and young adults. Not currently accepting picture book submissions. No submissions by fax or email. See website for full submission guidelines.

Brine Books Publishing

Email: Help@BrineBooks.com
Website: http://BrineBooks.com

Publishes: Fiction; Nonfiction; Poetry; *Areas:* Adventure; Arts; Crime; Criticism; Culture; Current Affairs; Drama; Entertainment; Fantasy; Historical; Horror; Humour; Literature; Men's Interests; Military; Mystery; New Age; Philosophy; Photography; Politics; Psychology; Religious; Romance; Sci-Fi; Short Stories; Sociology; Spiritual; Suspense; Thrillers; Translations; Westerns; Women's Interests; *Markets:* Adult; *Treatments:* Commercial; Contemporary; Cynical; Dark; Experimental; In-depth; Light; Literary; Mainstream; Niche; Popular; Positive; Progressive; Satirical; Serious; Traditional

Contact: Chris Brine and Olga Brine

We are an activist publishing house trying to raise awareness for human rights issues from all around the world. In doing so, we also will donate a fair portion of our earnings to these causes. Our hopes are to create a steady stream of funds to numerous human rights problems from human trafficking to domestic violence to racial or LGBT equality and many more. We will depend on our writers and readers to make this happen.

The Brucedale Press

Box 2259
Port Elgin, Ontario N0H 2C0
Tel: +1 (519) 832-6025
Email: info@brucedalepress.ca
Website: http://www.brucedalepress.ca

Publishes: Fiction; Nonfiction; *Areas:* Historical; *Markets:* Adult; *Treatments:* Literary

Publishes literary, historical, and pictorial works focusing on the Bruce Peninsula and Queen's Bush area of Ontario. Publishes books by Canadian authors only. Query by post in first instance. See website for full details.

Central Avenue Publishing

Delta, British Columbia
Email:
meghan@centralavenuepublishing.com
Website:
http://www.centralavenuepublishing.com

Publishes: Fiction; Poetry; *Areas:* Adventure; Arts; Autobiography; Beauty and Fashion; Biography; Crime; Culture; Current Affairs; Drama; Entertainment; Erotic; Fantasy; Gothic; Historical; Horror; Humour; Leisure; Lifestyle; Literature; Media; Men's Interests; Military; Music; Mystery; Nature; New Age; Philosophy; Photography; Politics; Psychology; Religious; Romance; Science; Sci-Fi; Self-Help; Short Stories; Sociology; Spiritual; Sport; Suspense; Technology; Theatre; Thrillers; Translations; Travel; Westerns; Women's Interests; *Markets:* Adult; Children's; Family; Youth; *Treatments:* Commercial; Contemporary; Cynical; Dark; Experimental; In-depth; Light; Literary; Mainstream; Niche; Popular; Positive; Progressive; Satirical; Serious; Traditional

Contact: Michelle Halket

Press specialising in electronic books (with select books going into print). Fiction, poetry, short stories. Email with query, agent not necessary.

Everheart Books

Email:
meghan@centralavenuepublishing.com
Website: http://www.everheartbooks.com

Publishes: Fiction; Poetry; *Areas:* Erotic; Romance; *Markets:* Adult; Family; *Treatments:* Commercial; Contemporary; Cynical; Dark; Experimental; In-depth; Light; Literary; Mainstream; Niche; Popular; Positive; Progressive; Satirical; Serious; Traditional

Contact: Meg

We publish erotica and all subgenres of romance. Send us your query and first three chapters of your story. We pay royalties quarterly. We handle everything from cover design to distribution. We'd love to take a look at your romance or erotic novel.

Groundwood Books

Attention: Submissions
110 Spadina Avenue, Suite 801
Toronto, Ontario
M5V 2K4
Email:
submissions@groundwoodbooks.com
Website: http://www.houseofanansi.com

Publishes: Fiction; Nonfiction; *Markets:* Children's; Youth; *Treatments:* Literary

Publishes picture books and novel-length fiction and nonfiction for children of all ages. Publishes character-driven literary fiction; no stories with obvious moral messages, or genre fiction such as thrillers or fantasy. Closed to approaches for picture books. Send query with brief synopsis and several sample chapters. See website for full guidelines.

House of Anansi Press

110 Spadina Ave., Suite 801
Toronto, ON
M5V 2K4
Tel: +1 (416) 363-4343
Fax: +1 (416) 363-1017
Email: customerservice@houseofanansi.com
Website: http://www.houseofanansi.com

Publishes: Fiction; Nonfiction; Poetry; *Markets:* Adult; *Treatments:* Literary; Serious

Publishes literary fiction, poetry, and serious nonfiction. Particular interest in Canadian writers; attitude towards international writers seems potentially contradictory:

"publishes Canadian and international writers..."

Yet further down the same page of their website:

"does not accept unsolicited materials from non-Canadian writers."

Kindred Productions

1310 Taylor Avenue
Winnipeg, MB R3M 3Z6
Tel: +1 (204) 669-6575
Fax: +1 (204) 654-1865
Email: custserv@kindredproductions.com
Website:
https://www.kindredproductions.com

Publishes: Nonfiction; *Areas:* Historical; Religious; *Markets:* Adult; Children's; Youth

Religious book publisher. Send query by email for a copy of the full submission guidelines. See website for more details.

Kids Can Press

Corus Quay
25 Dockside Drive
Toronto, Ontario
M5A 0B5
Tel: +1 (416) 479-7000
Fax: +1 (416) 960-5437
Email: customerservice@kidscan.com
Website: http://www.kidscanpress.com

Publishes: Fiction; Nonfiction; *Markets:* Children's

Publishes quality picture books and nonfiction manuscripts for children, as well as chapter books for ages 7–10. No young adult fiction or fantasy novels for any age. No unsolicited manuscripts from children or teenagers, or from authors outside of Canada. No submissions by disk, fax, or email.

Magenta Publishing for the Arts

151 Winchester Street
Toronto, Ontario
M4X 1B5
Email: info@magentafoundation.org
Website: http://www.magentafoundation.org

Publishes: Nonfiction; *Areas:* Arts; Photography; *Markets:* Adult

Established to publish works of art by Canadian and International artists.

Manor House Publishing

452 Cottingham Crescent
Ancaster ON L9G 3V6
Email: mbdavie@manor-house.biz
Website: http://manor-house.biz

Publishes: Fiction; Nonfiction; Poetry; *Areas:* Biography; Business; Fantasy; New Age; Politics; Short Stories; *Markets:* Adult; Youth

Send query by email only. See website for full guidelines. Response only if interested.

On The Mark Press

15 Dairy Avenue
Napanee, ON, K7R 1M4
Tel: +1 (800) 463-6367
Email:
productdevelopment@onthemarkpress.com
Website: http://www.onthemarkpress.com

Publishes: Nonfiction; *Markets:* Academic; Professional

Publishes workbooks and resources to support teachers in the classroom. Send samples with resume by post or by email.

Pedlar Press

113 Bond Street
St John's NL
A1C 1T6
Email: feralgrl@interlog.com
Website: http://www.pedlarpress.com

Publishes: Fiction; Poetry; *Markets:* Adult; *Treatments:* Contemporary; Experimental; Literary

Publishes innovative contemporary Canadian poetry and fiction. Particularly interested in work that preserves and extends the literary tradition that values experimentation in style and form. Send query by email in first instance. No attachments.

Penguin Canada

Penguin Group (Canada)
90 Eglinton Avenue East, Suite 700
Toronto, Ontario M4P 2Y3
Tel: +1 (416) 925-2249

Fax: +1 (416) 925-0068
Email: customerservicescanada@penguinrandomhouse.com
Website: http://penguinrandomhouse.ca

Publishes: Fiction; Nonfiction; *Markets:* Adult

Publishes fiction and nonfiction by Canadian authors on Canadian subjects. Accepts submissions through literary agents only.

Red Deer Press

195 Allstate Parkway
Markham, Ontario
L3R 4T8
Tel: +1 (905) 477-9700
Fax: +1 (905) 477-9179
Email: rdp@reddeerpress.com
Website: http://www.reddeerpress.com

Publishes: Fiction; Nonfiction; *Areas:* Biography; Drama; Fantasy; Historical; Sci-Fi; *Markets:* Adult; Children's; Youth; *Treatments:* Contemporary

Publishes fiction and nonfiction for adults and children of all ages, though currently less interested in picture books and more interested in middle grade and young adult fiction. See website for full submission guidelines.

Ronsdale Press

3350 West 21st Avenue
Vancouver, B.C.
V6S 1G7
Tel: +1 (604) 738-4688
Fax: +1 (604) 731-4548
Email: ronsdale@shaw.ca
Website: http://www.ronsdalepress.com

Publishes: Fiction; Nonfiction; Poetry; *Areas:* Biography; Historical; Short Stories; Theatre; *Markets:* Adult; Children's; *Treatments:* Literary

Contact: Ronald B. Hatch (General Acquisition Editor); Veronica Hatch (Children's Acquisition Editor)

Literary publishing house, publishing fiction, poetry, biography, regional history, and children's literature. Particularly interested in young adult historical novels. No mass-market, pulp, mystery stories, or fiction that is entirely plot-driven. MSS considered only from writers who have had work published in literary magazines. See website for full submission guidelines.

All prospective authors are encouraged to familiarise themselves with the list (perusing the catalogue; reading published titles) to assess suitability before submitting. Send query with sample or full MS with SASE for response, with brief bio and list of writing credits (if any).

Second Story Press

20 Maud Street, Suite 401
Toronto ON
M5V 2M5
Tel: +1 (416) 537-7850
Fax: +1 (416) 537-0588
Email: info@secondstorypress.ca
Website: http://secondstorypress.ca

Publishes: Fiction; Nonfiction; *Areas:* Women's Interests; *Markets:* Adult; Children's

Canadian feminist press publishing fiction, nonfiction and children's books of special interest to women. Tries to focus on Canadian authors. No poetry, rhyming picture books, or books with anthropomorphised animals. Send query by post with SASE, synopsis, and up to three chapters. No submissions on disk or by email. See website for full guidelines.

Stonehouse Publishing

PO Box 68092
Bonnie Doon Shopping Centre
Edmonton, Alberta
T6C 4N6
Email: editor@stonehousepublishing.ca
Website: http://www.stonehousepublishing.ca

Publishes: Fiction; *Markets:* Adult; *Treatments:* Commercial; Literary

Contact: Julie Yerex, Editor; Netta Johnson, Publisher

Publishes literary fiction with commercial appeal, and non-formulaic fiction in general – initially by Canadian authors only, but with the intention of opening to international writers in future. No nonfiction, formulaic genre fiction, sci-fi, horror, mysteries, thrillers, erotica, picture books, or children's books. Send query by post only with 30 sample pages. No submissions by email – these will not be read or responded to. See website for full guidelines.

Thistledown Press

410 2nd Avenue North
Saskatoon, SK S7K 2C3
Tel: +1 (306) 244-1722
Fax: +1 (306) 244-1762
Email: editorial@thistledownpress.com
Website: http://www.thistledownpress.com

Publishes: Fiction; Poetry; *Areas:* Short Stories; *Markets:* Adult

Contact: Allan Forrie

Accepts work by Canadian citizens or landed immigrants only. Publishes novels, poetry, and short story collections, but no romance, science fiction, horror, westerns, or fiction in verse. Not currently accepting juvenile fiction or children's manuscripts. Reading period from August 1 to November 30. See website for full submission guidelines.

Turnstone Press

Artspace Building
206-100 Arthur Street
Winnipeg, Manitoba
Canada R3B 1H3
Tel: +1 (204) 947-1555
Fax: +1 (204) 947-1556
Email: editor@turnstonepress.com
Website: http://www.turnstonepress.com

Publishes: Fiction; Nonfiction; Poetry; *Areas:* Criticism; Fantasy; Literature; Mystery; Short Stories; Thrillers; *Markets:* Adult; *Treatments:* Literary

Contact: Submissions Assistant

Literary publisher publishing the work of Canadian authors or landed immigrants only. Publishes literary fiction, literary non-fiction – including literary criticism – and poetry. Publishes literary mysteries, thrillers, noir, speculative fiction, and fantasy under imprint. No contact by email. All submissions must be by post with SASE. Mss without SASE will be recycled without response, as will submissions requesting response by email. See website for full guidelines.

Irish Publishers

For the most up-to-date listings of these and hundreds of other publishers, visit http://www.firstwriter.com/publishers

*To claim your **free** access to the site, please see the back of this book.*

Columba Press

55a Spruce Avenue
Stillorgan Industrial Park
Blackrock
Co. Dublin
Tel: +353 (1) 2942556
Email: Fearghal@columba.ie
Website: http://www.columba.ie

Publishes: Nonfiction; *Areas:* Arts; Biography; Historical; Music; Nature; Religious; Spiritual; *Markets:* Adult

Religious publisher publishing across a broad range of areas, including pastoral resources, spirituality, theology, the arts, and history.

Cork University Press

Tel: +353 (0) 21 490 2980
Email: corkuniversitypress@ucc.ie
Website: http://www.corkuniversitypress.com

Publishes: Nonfiction; *Areas:* Architecture; Arts; Cookery; Culture; Current Affairs; Film; Historical; Legal; Literature; Music; Philosophy; Politics; Travel; Women's Interests; *Markets:* Academic

Publishes distinctive and distinguished scholarship in the broad field of Irish Cultural Studies.

The Educational Company of Ireland

Ballymount Road
Walkinstown
Dublin 12
Email: amulloy@edco.ie
Website: http://www.edco.ie

Publishes: Nonfiction; *Markets:* Academic; Adult; Children's; Professional

Contact: Áine Mulloy

Publishes textbooks and ancillary educational materials for the Primary and Post-Primary markets. Submit proposals by post or by email. See website for full guidelines.

Flyleaf Press

4 Spencer Villas
Glenageary
Co. Dublin
Tel: +353 1 2854658
Email: books@flyleaf.ie
Website: http://flyleaf.ie

Publishes: Nonfiction; Reference; *Areas:* Historical; How-to; *Markets:* Adult

Publishes family history and genealogy titles, how-to guides for researching family history, and reference workds on Church Records, Census records and wills.

The Gallery Press

Loughcrew
Oldcastle
County Meath
Tel: +353 (0) 49 8541779
Fax: +353 (0) 49 8541779
Email: gallery@indigo.ie
Website: http://www.gallerypress.com

Publishes: Fiction; Nonfiction; Poetry; Scripts; *Areas:* Theatre; *Markets:* Adult; *Treatments:* Literary

Contact: Peter Fallon

Publishes poetry, drama, and prose by Ireland's leading contemporary writers. See website for submission guidelines. No submissions by fax or email.

Gill & Macmillan

Hume Avenue
Park West
Dublin 12
Tel: +353 (01) 500 9500
Email: dmarsh@gillmacmillan.ie
Website: http://www.gillmacmillanbooks.ie

Publishes: Fiction; Nonfiction; Reference; *Areas:* Biography; Cookery; Crime; Current Affairs; Historical; Hobbies; Humour; Leisure; Lifestyle; Nature; Sport; *Markets:* Adult; Children's

Contact: Deborah Marsh, Editorial Administrator

Publishes adult nonfiction and children's fiction and nonfiction. No adult fiction, poetry, short stories or plays. Prefers proposals by email, but will also accept proposals by post. See website for full submission guidelines.

Institute of Public Administration (IPA)

57-61 Lansdowne Road
Ballsbridge
Dublin 4
Tel: +353 1 240 3600
Fax: +353 1 668 9135
Email: information@ipa.ie

Publishes: Nonfiction; *Areas:* Current Affairs; Finance; Health; Legal; Politics; Sociology; *Markets:* Academic; Professional

Irish publisher specialising in texts on public service administration and management.

Liberties Press

140 Terenure Road North
Terenure
Dublin 6W
Tel: +353 01 405 5703
Email: editorial@libertiespress.com
Website: http://www.libertiespress.com

Publishes: Fiction; Nonfiction; Poetry; *Areas:* Architecture; Arts; Autobiography; Biography; Business; Cookery; Crime; Current Affairs; Finance; Health; Historical; Hobbies; Humour; Lifestyle; Music; Politics; Sport; *Markets:* Adult; *Treatments:* Literary

Publishes fiction, nonfiction, and poetry primarily for the Irish market. Focusses on Irish interest nonfiction in such areas as history, memoir, politics, current affairs, sport and lifestyle. Accepts submissions between January 1 and March 31 each year only. Prefers hard copy submissions (include SAE if return required) but will also accept email submissions. See website for full details.

The Lilliput Press

62-63 Sitric Road
Arbour Hill
Dublin 7
Tel: +353 (01) 671 16 47
Fax: +353 (01) 671 12 33
Email: info@lilliputpress.ie
Website: http://www.lilliputpress.ie

Publishes: Fiction; Nonfiction; Poetry; Reference; Scripts; *Areas:* Architecture; Arts; Autobiography; Biography; Business; Cookery; Criticism; Culture; Current Affairs; Drama; Historical; Literature; Music; Nature; Philosophy; Photography; Politics; Sociology; Sport; Travel; *Markets:* Adult; *Treatments:* Literary; Popular

Contact: Submissions Editor

Publishes books broadly focused on Irish themes. Send query by post with one-page synopsis and complete ms or three sample chapters. Include SASE if response required. No submissions by email. See website for full guidelines.

Mentor Books

43 Furze Road
Sandyford Industrial Estate
Dublin 18
Tel: 01 2952112
Fax: 01 295 2114
Email: admin@mentorbooks.ie
Website: http://www.mentorbooks.ie

Publishes: Nonfiction; *Areas:* Biography; Business; Crime; Historical; Humour; Politics; Science; Sport; *Markets:* Academic; Adult

Publishes educational books and general nonfiction of Irish interest.

Mercier Press

Unit 3b
Oak House
Bessboro Road
Blackrock
Cork
Tel: +353 21-4614700
Email: commissioning@mercierpress.ie
Website: http://www.mercierpress.ie

Publishes: Fiction; Nonfiction; *Areas:* Autobiography; Biography; Business; Cookery; Current Affairs; Health; Historical; Humour; Lifestyle; Military; Politics; Religious; Sport; *Markets:* Adult; Children's

Contact: Mary Feehan

Publishes Irish-interest fiction and nonfiction for adults and children. Prefers approaches by email. See website for full submission guidelines.

New Island

16 Priory Hall Office Park
Stillorgan
County Dublin
Tel: + 353 1 278 42 25
Email: editor@newisland.ie
Website: http://www.newisland.ie

Publishes: Fiction; Nonfiction; Poetry; Scripts; *Areas:* Autobiography; Biography; Cookery; Crime; Criticism; Current Affairs; Drama; Historical; Humour; Literature; Politics; Short Stories; Sociology; Travel; Women's Interests; *Markets:* Adult; *Treatments:* Literary; Popular

Contact: Editorial Manager

Committed to literature and literary publishing. Publishes in all literary areas, from fiction to drama to poetry. Also publishes nonfiction of Irish interest, especially social affairs and biographies. No children's books. Not currently accepting drama and poetry. Seeking submissions of literary fiction, general fiction, crime fiction, short stories, history, biography, memoir, autobiography, and food and drink. Accepts submissions by email only. Send query with one-page synopsis and sample of the text as Word .doc or .docx attachments. Include details of any previous publications. No submissions by post. See website for full details.

The O'Brien Press

12 Terenure Road East
Rathgar
Dublin 6
Tel: +353-1-4923333
Fax: +353-1-4922777
Email: books@obrien.ie
Website: http://www.obrien.ie

Publishes: Fiction; Nonfiction; Reference; *Areas:* Architecture; Arts; Autobiography; Biography; Business; Cookery; Crafts; Crime; Drama; Historical; Humour; Lifestyle; Literature; Music; Nature; Photography; Politics; Religious; Sport; Travel; *Markets:* Adult; Children's; Youth

Mainly publishes children's fiction, children's nonfiction and adult nonfiction. Generally doesn't publish poetry, academic works or adult fiction. Send synopsis and two or three sample chapters. If fewer than 1,000 words, send complete ms. See website for full guidelines.

Oak Tree Press

33 Rochestown Rise
Rochestown
Cork
Tel: +353 86 244 1633
Fax: +353 86 330 7694
Email: info@oaktreepress.com
Website: http://oaktreepress.eu

Publishes: Nonfiction; *Areas:* Business; Finance; Legal; *Markets:* Professional

Publishes books on business, particularly for small business owners and managers.

Onstream Publications Ltd

Currabaha
Cloghroe
Blarney
Co. Cork
Tel: +353 21 4385798
Email: info@onstream.ie
Website: http://www.onstream.ie

Publishes: Fiction; Nonfiction; *Areas:* Cookery; Historical; Travel; *Markets:* Academic; Adult

Publisher of mainly nonfiction, although some fiction published. Also offers services to authors.

Poolbeg

123 Grange Hill
Baldoyle Industrial Estate
Baldoyle
Dublin 13
Tel: +353 1 832 1477
Email: info@poolbeg.com
Website: http://www.poolbeg.com

Publishes: Fiction; Nonfiction; *Areas:* Cookery; Gardening; Travel; *Markets:* Adult; Children's

Contact: Paula Campbell, publisher

Accepts submissions of nonfiction, and fiction up to 100,000 words. Send query by post with SASE, CV, short bio, first six chapters in hard copy, and full ms as Word file on CD. See website for full submission guidelines.

Round Hall

43 Fitzwilliam Place
Dublin 2
Tel: + 353 1 662 5301
Fax: + 353 1 662 5302
Email: frieda.donohue@thomsonreuters.com
Website: http://www.roundhall.ie

Publishes: Nonfiction; Reference; *Areas:* Legal; *Markets:* Academic; Professional

Publishes information on Irish law in the form of books, journals, periodicals, looseleaf services, CD-ROMs and online services. See website for submission guidelines and appropriate contacts / proposal forms to complete.

Somerville Press

Dromore
Bantry
Co. Cork
Tel: 353 (0) 28 32873
Fax: 353 (0) 28 328
Email: somervillepress@eircom.net
Website: http://www.somervillepress.com

Publishes: Fiction; Nonfiction; *Markets:* Adult

Publishes fiction and nonfiction of Irish interest.

Tirgearr Publishing

Email: info@tirgearrpublishing.com
Website: http://www.tirgearrpublishing.com

Publishes: Fiction; *Areas:* Adventure; Anthropology; Biography; Business; Cookery; Crafts; Crime; Culture; Current Affairs; Drama; Entertainment; Erotic; Fantasy; Film; Gothic; Health; Historical; Hobbies; Horror; How-to; Humour; Legal; Leisure; Lifestyle; Literature; Media; Men's Interests; Military; Nature; New Age; Romance; Science; Sci-Fi; Self-Help; Suspense; Technology; Thrillers; Westerns; Women's Interests; *Markets:* Adult; Family; Commercial; Contemporary; Popular

Contact: Kemberlee Shortland

A small independently-owned digital-only

publishing company of adult genre fiction.

They offer full-circle services, working with authors on a one-on-one basis to ensure each book we publish is of the highest quality.

University College Dublin (UCD) Press

UCD Humanities Institute Room H103
Belfield
Dublin 4

Tel: + 353 1 4716 4680
Email: ucdpress@ucd.ie
Website: http://www.ucdpress.ie

Publishes: Nonfiction; *Areas:* Historical; Literature; Music; Nature; Politics; Science; Sociology; *Markets:* Academic

Contact: Noelle Moran, Executive Editor

Peer-reviewed publisher of contemporary scholarship with a reputation for publications relating to historic and contemporary Ireland. Send synopsis with market description, a paragraph about the career and publications of the author(s), and two specimen chapters in hard copy (not email attachments). See website for full guidelines.

Australian Publishers

For the most up-to-date listings of these and hundreds of other publishers, visit http://www.firstwriter.com/publishers

*To claim your **free** access to the site, please see the back of this book.*

Hinkler Books

45-55 Fairchild Street
Heatherton
Victoria 3202
Tel: +61 (0) 3 9552 1333
Fax: +61 (0) 3 9558 2566
Email: editor@hinkler.com.au
Website: http://www.hinklerbooks.com

Publishes: Nonfiction; Reference; *Areas:* Cookery; Crafts; Health; Humour; Lifestyle; Music; Spiritual; Sport; *Markets:* Adult; Children's; Family

Book publisher and packager – creates and produces books for publishers and consumers around the world. Specialises in nonfiction for adults and children. Send one-page query by fax, post, or email in first instance. No unsolicited mss. See website for full details.

Scribe Publications Pty Ltd

18–20 Edward Street
Brunswick 3056
Victoria
Tel: +61 (0) 3 9388 8780
Fax: +61 (0) 3 9388 8787
Email: info@scribepub.com.au
Website: http://scribepublications.com.au

Publishes: Fiction; Nonfiction; *Areas:* Architecture; Arts; Autobiography; Biography; Business; Crime; Culture; Current Affairs; Finance; Health; Historical; Humour; Literature; Medicine; Military; Nature; Philosophy; Politics; Psychology; Religious; Sociology; *Markets:* Adult

Publishes general trade fiction and nonfiction. No unsolicited poetry, writing for children or young adults, or individual short stories. Only accepts approaches from writers who do not have a literary agent if they have a previous track record of being published by trade publishers, or have had articles or short stories published in magazines, or if they have received awards or have a recommendation from a published author. See website for full submission guidelines.

Publishers Subject Index

This section lists publishers by their subject matter, with directions to the section of the book where the full listing can be found.

You can create your own customised lists of publishers using different combinations of these subject areas, plus over a dozen other criteria, instantly online at http://www.firstwriter.com.

*To claim your **free** access to the site, please see the back of this book.*

Sunscribe (*US*)
Archaeology
Alondra Press (*US*)
Ex-L-Ence Publishing (*UK*)
Geostar Publishing & Services LLC (*US*)
Hadley Rille Books (*US*)
The History Press (*UK*)
Liverpool University Press (*UK*)
Logaston Press (*UK*)
National Museum Wales (*UK*)
The New Curiosity Shop (*UK*)
The Orion Publishing Group Limited (*UK*)
Pen & Sword Books Ltd (*UK*)
Princeton University Press (*US*)
Princeton University Press Europe (*UK*)
Saffron Books (*UK*)
Shire Publications Ltd (*UK*)
Souvenir Press Ltd (*UK*)
Stacey International (*UK*)
Sunscribe (*US*)
Sussex Academic Press (*UK*)
Thames and Hudson Ltd (*UK*)
Vanderbilt University Press (*US*)
Waveland Press, Inc. (*US*)
Architecture
American Press (*US*)
Antique Collectors' Club Ltd (*UK*)
Ashgate Publishing Limited (*UK*)
Carlton Publishing Group (*UK*)
Cork University Press (*Ire*)
The Crowood Press (*UK*)
Dovecote Press (*UK*)
Ex-L-Ence Publishing (*UK*)
Floris Books (*UK*)
Geostar Publishing & Services LLC (*US*)
Gibbs Smith, Publisher (*US*)
Gingko Library (*UK*)
Harry N. Abrams, Inc. (*US*)
Homestead Publishing (*US*)
Liberties Press (*Ire*)
The Lilliput Press (*Ire*)
Frances Lincoln Ltd (*UK*)
Liverpool University Press (*UK*)
McFarland & Company, Inc. (*US*)
Merrell Publishers Limited (*UK*)
Methuen Publishing Ltd (*UK*)
The New Curiosity Shop (*UK*)
The O'Brien Press (*Ire*)
The Overlook Press (*US*)
Paul Dry Books, Inc. (*US*)
Phaidon Press Limited (*UK*)
Princeton University Press (*US*)
Princeton University Press Europe (*UK*)
Professional Publications, Inc. (PPI) (*US*)
Quill Driver Books (*US*)
Quiller Publishing Ltd (*UK*)
Reference Service Press (*US*)
Rio Nuevo Publishers (*US*)
Roundhouse Group (*UK*)
Scala Arts & Heritage Publishers (*UK*)
Scribe Publications Pty Ltd (*Aus*)
Shire Publications Ltd (*UK*)
Sunscribe (*US*)
Thames and Hudson Ltd (*UK*)
Tuttle Publishing (*US*)
Unicorn Press Ltd (*UK*)
Waveland Press, Inc. (*US*)
Yale University Press (*US*)
Arts
Alma Classics (*UK*)
American Press (*US*)
Antique Collectors' Club Ltd (*UK*)
Arcade Publishing (*US*)
Arch Street Press (*US*)
Ashgate Publishing Limited (*UK*)
Aurora Metro Press (*UK*)
Aurum Press Ltd (*UK*)
Barron's Educational Series, Inc. (*US*)
Bick Publishing House (*US*)
Bloomsbury Publishing Plc (*UK*)
Bodleian Library (*UK*)
Booth-Clibborn Editions (*UK*)
Brine Books Publishing (*Can*)
Carlton Publishing Group (*UK*)
Central Avenue Publishing (*Can*)
Co & Bear Productions (*UK*)
Columba Press (*Ire*)
Continental (*US*)
Cork University Press (*Ire*)
Crescent Moon Publishing (*UK*)
The Crowood Press (*UK*)
Enitharmon Press (*UK*)
Ex-L-Ence Publishing (*UK*)
F&W Media International Ltd (*UK*)
Floris Books (*UK*)
Geostar Publishing & Services LLC (*US*)
Gibbs Smith, Publisher (*US*)
Gibson Square Books Ltd (*UK*)
Gingko Library (*UK*)
Gomer Press (*UK*)
Halsgrove (*UK*)
Harry N. Abrams, Inc. (*US*)
Homestead Publishing (*US*)
HOW Books (*US*)
IBEX Publishers, Inc. (*US*)
Icon Books Ltd (*UK*)
The Ilex Press (*UK*)
Impact Books (*US*)
Indigo Dreams Publishing (*UK*)
Liberties Press (*Ire*)
The Lilliput Press (*Ire*)
Frances Lincoln Ltd (*UK*)
Linden Publishing (*US*)
Liverpool University Press (*UK*)
Luath Press Ltd (*UK*)
Magenta Publishing for the Arts (*Can*)
Mainstream Publishing Co. (Edinburgh) Ltd (*UK*)
Manchester University Press (*UK*)
Mandala Earth (*US*)
Mandrake of Oxford (*UK*)
McFarland & Company, Inc. (*US*)
Medallion Media Group (*US*)
Merrell Publishers Limited (*UK*)
Mitchell Lane Publishers, Inc. (*US*)
National Museum Wales (*UK*)

Shire Publications Ltd (*UK*)
Souvenir Press Ltd (*UK*)
Sunscribe (*US*)
Thames and Hudson Ltd (*UK*)
Tsaba House (*US*)

Biography

Akasha Publishing Ltd (*UK*)
Alma Classics (*UK*)
Amakella Publishing (*US*)
Arch Street Press (*US*)
Aureus Publishing Limited (*UK*)
Aurora Metro Press (*UK*)
Aurum Press Ltd (*UK*)
Black & White Publishing Ltd (*UK*)
Black Lawrence Press (*US*)
Blackstaff Press Ltd (*UK*)
Bowker (UK) Ltd (*UK*)
Canongate Books (*UK*)
Capstone (*US*)
Carlton Publishing Group (*UK*)
Centerstream Publishing (*US*)
Central Avenue Publishing (*Can*)
Chicago Review Press (*US*)
Columba Press (*Ire*)
Compelling Books (*UK*)
Dovecote Press (*UK*)
Dufour Editions (*US*)
Eakin Press (*US*)
Ex-L-Ence Publishing (*UK*)
Faber & Faber Ltd (*UK*)
Floris Books (*UK*)
Frederic C. Beil, Publisher (*US*)
Geostar Publishing & Services LLC (*US*)
Gibson Square Books Ltd (*UK*)
Gill & Macmillan (*Ire*)
Gingko Library (*UK*)
Gomer Press (*UK*)
Halban Publishers (*UK*)
Halsgrove (*UK*)
HarperCollins Publishers Ltd (*UK*)
Headland Publications (*UK*)
Headline Publishing Group (*UK*)
The History Press (*UK*)
Homestead Publishing (*US*)
House of Lochar (*UK*)
Independent Music Press (*UK*)
Indigo Dreams Publishing (*UK*)
Kamehameha Publishing (*US*)
Kube Publishing (*UK*)
Liberties Press (*Ire*)
The Lilliput Press (*Ire*)
Lion Hudson Plc (*UK*)
Listen & Live Audio, Inc. (*US*)
Logaston Press (*UK*)
Luath Press Ltd (*UK*)
Macmillan (*UK*)
Mainstream Publishing Co. (Edinburgh) Ltd (*UK*)
Manor House Publishing (*Can*)
Marion Boyars Publishers (*UK*)
Medallion Media Group (*US*)
Mentor Books (*Ire*)
Mercier Press (*Ire*)
Methuen Publishing Ltd (*UK*)
Milo Books Ltd (*UK*)
Mitchell Lane Publishers, Inc. (*US*)
Neil Wilson Publishing Ltd (*UK*)
The New Curiosity Shop (*UK*)
New Holland Publishers (UK) Ltd (*UK*)
New Island (*Ire*)
Nicolas Hays Publishers (*US*)
The O'Brien Press (*Ire*)
Michael O'Mara Books Ltd (*UK*)
Omnibus Press (*UK*)
Oneworld Publications (*UK*)
The Orion Publishing Group Limited (*UK*)
Ouen Press (*UK*)
Peter Owen Publishers (*UK*)
P&R Publishing (*US*)
Paragon House (*US*)
Paul Dry Books, Inc. (*US*)
Pauline Books and Media (*US*)
Pen & Sword Books Ltd (*UK*)
Persea Books (*US*)
Piatkus Books (*UK*)
Plexus Publishing Limited (*UK*)
Profile Books (*UK*)
Quill Driver Books (*US*)
Quiller Publishing Ltd (*UK*)
Red Deer Press (*Can*)
Rio Nuevo Publishers (*US*)
Robert Hale Publishers (*UK*)
Ronsdale Press (*Can*)
The Rosen Publishing Group, Inc. (*US*)
Scribe Publications Pty Ltd (*Aus*)
Seren Books (*UK*)
Shepheard-Walwyn (Publishers) Ltd (*UK*)
Shire Publications Ltd (*UK*)
Sigma Press (*UK*)
Soft Skull Press (*US*)
Souvenir Press Ltd (*UK*)
SportsBooks Limited (*UK*)
St. Johann Press (*US*)
Sunscribe (*US*)
Sussex Academic Press (*UK*)
Tirgearr Publishing (*Ire*)
Tantor Audio (*US*)
Tate Publishing and Enterprises, LLC (*US*)
Texas Tech University Press (*US*)
Thames and Hudson Ltd (*UK*)
Tsaba House (*US*)
Unicorn Press Ltd (*UK*)
Vernon Press (an imprint of Vernon Art and Science Inc.) (*US*)
Whitaker House (*US*)

Business

Alexander Hamilton Institute (*US*)
Amakella Publishing (*US*)
American Press (*US*)
Antique Collectors' Club Ltd (*UK*)
Arcade Publishing (*US*)
Arch Street Press (*US*)
Ashgate Publishing Limited (*UK*)
Barron's Educational Series, Inc. (*US*)
Bowker (UK) Ltd (*UK*)

Cork University Press (*Ire*)
Crescent Moon Publishing (*UK*)
Eakin Press (*US*)
Ex-L-Ence Publishing (*UK*)
Flame Tree Publishing (*UK*)
Geostar Publishing & Services LLC (*US*)
Gibson Square Books Ltd (*UK*)
Gival Press, LLC (*US*)
Gomer Press (*UK*)
Harry N. Abrams, Inc. (*US*)
HOW Books (*US*)
Ig Publishing (*US*)
The Ilex Press (*UK*)
Independent Music Press (*UK*)
Kamehameha Publishing (*US*)
Kube Publishing (*UK*)
The Lilliput Press (*Ire*)
Listen & Live Audio, Inc. (*US*)
Liverpool University Press (*UK*)
Lucky Marble Books (*US*)
The Lyons Press Inc. (*US*)
Macmillan (*UK*)
Mainstream Publishing Co. (Edinburgh) Ltd (*UK*)
Manchester University Press (*UK*)
Mandala Earth (*US*)
Mandrake of Oxford (*UK*)
Marion Boyars Publishers (*UK*)
McFarland & Company, Inc. (*US*)
Merrell Publishers Limited (*UK*)
Methuen Publishing Ltd (*UK*)
Milo Books Ltd (*UK*)
NavPress (*US*)
Neil Wilson Publishing Ltd (*UK*)
New Beacon Books, Ltd (*UK*)
The New Curiosity Shop (*UK*)
New York University (NYU) Press (*US*)
Open Court Publishing Company (*US*)
The Orion Publishing Group Limited (*UK*)
Paul Dry Books, Inc. (*US*)
Phaidon Press Limited (*UK*)
Plexus Publishing Limited (*UK*)
Pluto Publishing Ltd (*UK*)
Profile Books (*UK*)
Reading Harbor (*US*)
Reference Service Press (*US*)
Rio Nuevo Publishers (*US*)
The Rosen Publishing Group, Inc. (*US*)
Route Publishing (*UK*)
Running Press (*US*)
Saffron Books (*UK*)
Scarecrow Press Inc. (*US*)
Scribe Publications Pty Ltd (*Aus*)
Soft Skull Press (*US*)
St Augustine's Press (*US*)
Stemmer House Publishers (*US*)
Stone Bridge Press (*US*)
Sunscribe (*US*)
Sussex Academic Press (*UK*)
Swan Isle Press (*US*)
Tirgearr Publishing (*Ire*)
Tantor Audio (*US*)
Texas Tech University Press (*US*)
Thames and Hudson Ltd (*UK*)
Trentham Books Limited (*UK*)
Tu Books (*US*)
Tuttle Publishing (*US*)
Vanderbilt University Press (*US*)
Vernon Press (an imprint of Vernon Art and Science Inc.) (*US*)
Voyageur Press (*US*)
Wallflower Press (*UK*)
Westminster John Knox Press (WJK) (*US*)
The X Press (*UK*)

Current Affairs

Amakella Publishing (*US*)
Arcade Publishing (*US*)
Aurum Press Ltd (*UK*)
Brine Books Publishing (*Can*)
Central Avenue Publishing (*Can*)
Cork University Press (*Ire*)
Ex-L-Ence Publishing (*UK*)
Fabian Society (*UK*)
Geostar Publishing & Services LLC (*US*)
Gibson Square Books Ltd (*UK*)
Gill & Macmillan (*Ire*)
Institute of Public Administration (IPA) (*Ire*)
Liberties Press (*Ire*)
The Lilliput Press (*Ire*)
Luath Press Ltd (*UK*)
The Lyons Press Inc. (*US*)
Macmillan (*UK*)
Mainstream Publishing Co. (Edinburgh) Ltd (*UK*)
McFarland & Company, Inc. (*US*)
Mercier Press (*Ire*)
Methuen Publishing Ltd (*UK*)
Milo Books Ltd (*UK*)
The New Curiosity Shop (*UK*)
New Island (*Ire*)
Oneworld Publications (*UK*)
The Orion Publishing Group Limited (*UK*)
The Overlook Press (*US*)
Oxford University Press (*UK*)
Paragon House (*US*)
Pluto Publishing Ltd (*UK*)
Profile Books (*UK*)
Prometheus Books (*US*)
Quarto Publishing Group USA (*US*)
Reading Harbor (*US*)
Saffron Books (*UK*)
Scribe Publications Pty Ltd (*Aus*)
Seren Books (*UK*)
Soft Skull Press (*US*)
Strategic Media Books (*US*)
Sunbury Press (*US*)
Sunscribe (*US*)
TSO (The Stationery Office) (*UK*)
Tirgearr Publishing (*Ire*)
Tantor Audio (*US*)
Tsaba House (*US*)
Vernon Press (an imprint of Vernon Art and Science Inc.) (*US*)
Yale University Press (*US*)

Design

Antique Collectors' Club Ltd (*UK*)

Booth-Clibborn Editions (*UK*)
Carlton Publishing Group (*UK*)
Co & Bear Productions (*UK*)
Ex-L-Ence Publishing (*UK*)
Geostar Publishing & Services LLC (*US*)
Gibbs Smith, Publisher (*US*)
Gulf Publishing Company (*US*)
Harry N. Abrams, Inc. (*US*)
Homestead Publishing (*US*)
HOW Books (*US*)
Kansas City Star Books (*US*)
Frances Lincoln Ltd (*UK*)
Manchester University Press (*UK*)
Medallion Media Group (*US*)
Merrell Publishers Limited (*UK*)
The New Curiosity Shop (*UK*)
New Holland Publishers (UK) Ltd (*UK*)
The Orion Publishing Group Limited (*UK*)
The Overlook Press (*US*)
Phaidon Press Limited (*UK*)
Professional Publications, Inc. (PPI) (*US*)
Quadrille Publishing Ltd (*UK*)
Quarto Publishing Group UK (*UK*)
Quarto Publishing Group USA (*US*)
Richard Dennis Publications (*UK*)
Rio Nuevo Publishers (*US*)
Roundhouse Group (*UK*)
Shire Publications Ltd (*UK*)
Stone Bridge Press (*US*)
Sunscribe (*US*)
Thames and Hudson Ltd (*UK*)
Tuttle Publishing (*US*)
Waveland Press, Inc. (*US*)

Drama

American Press (*US*)
Anaiah Press, LLC (*US*)
Aurora Metro Press (*UK*)
Blurbeo (*US*)
Brine Books Publishing (*Can*)
Bronze Man Books (*US*)
Capstone (*US*)
Central Avenue Publishing (*Can*)
Cressrelles Publishing Co. Ltd (*UK*)
Ex-L-Ence Publishing (*UK*)
Faber & Faber Ltd (*UK*)
Geostar Publishing & Services LLC (*US*)
Gomer Press (*UK*)
The Lilliput Press (*Ire*)
Luath Press Ltd (*UK*)
Marion Boyars Publishers (*UK*)
The New Curiosity Shop (*UK*)
New Island (*Ire*)
New Playwrights' Network (NPN) (*UK*)
The O'Brien Press (*Ire*)
Oberon Books (*UK*)
Open Idea Publishing, LLC (*US*)
Oxford University Press (*UK*)
Parthian Books (*UK*)
Red Deer Press (*Can*)
Samuel French Ltd (*UK*)
Seren Books (*UK*)
Sunscribe (*US*)
Sussex Academic Press (*UK*)
Tirgearr Publishing (*Ire*)

Entertainment

Blurbeo (*US*)
Brine Books Publishing (*Can*)
Carlton Publishing Group (*UK*)
Central Avenue Publishing (*Can*)
Ex-L-Ence Publishing (*UK*)
Geostar Publishing & Services LLC (*US*)
HarperCollins Publishers Ltd (*UK*)
Harry N. Abrams, Inc. (*US*)
Indigo Dreams Publishing (*UK*)
Kindred Rainbow Publishing (*UK*)
Quarto Publishing Group UK (*UK*)
Reading Harbor (*US*)
Sunscribe (*US*)
Tirgearr Publishing (*Ire*)
Tantor Audio (*US*)
Tate Publishing and Enterprises, LLC (*US*)
Titan Books (*UK*)
Wallflower Press (*UK*)

Erotic

Amira Press (*US*)
Bold Strokes Books (*US*)
Central Avenue Publishing (*Can*)
Everheart Books (*Can*)
Geostar Publishing & Services LLC (*US*)
HarperImpulse (*UK*)
Indigo Dreams Publishing (*UK*)
Jupiter Gardens Press (*US*)
Loose Id (*US*)
Mandrake of Oxford (*UK*)
NBM (*US*)
Open Idea Publishing, LLC (*US*)
Tirgearr Publishing (*Ire*)
Tantor Audio (*US*)

Fantasy

Akasha Publishing Ltd (*UK*)
AMG Publishers (*US*)
Amira Press (*US*)
Anaiah Press, LLC (*US*)
Arrow Publications, LLC (*US*)
Barbarian Books (*US*)
BelleBooks (*US*)
Bethany House Publishers (*US*)
Bold Strokes Books (*US*)
Brine Books Publishing (*Can*)
By Light Unseen Media (*US*)
Capstone (*US*)
Central Avenue Publishing (*Can*)
Compelling Books (*UK*)
Dragonfairy Press (*US*)
Ex-L-Ence Publishing (*UK*)
Geostar Publishing & Services LLC (*US*)
Ghostwoods Books (*UK*)
Hadley Rille Books (*US*)
HarperCollins Publishers Ltd (*UK*)
Highland Press (*US*)
Honno Welsh Women's Press (*UK*)
Indigo Dreams Publishing (*UK*)
Jupiter Gardens Press (*US*)
Kane Miller Books (*US*)
Kelly Point Publishing LLC (*US*)
Kindred Rainbow Publishing (*UK*)

Honno Welsh Women's Press (*UK*)
Hopewell Publications (*US*)
House of Anansi Press (*Can*)
House of Lochar (*UK*)
Ideals Publications (*US*)
Ig Publishing (*US*)
Igloo Books Limited (*UK*)
Indigo Dreams Publishing (*UK*)
Influx Press (*UK*)
Ion Imagination Entertainment, Inc. (*US*)
Iron Press (*UK*)
Jewish Lights Publishing (*US*)
Jupiter Gardens Press (*US*)
Just Us Books (*US*)
Kamehameha Publishing (*US*)
Kane Miller Books (*US*)
Kearney Street Books (*US*)
Kelly Point Publishing LLC (*US*)
Kids Can Press (*Can*)
Kind of a Hurricane Press (*US*)
Kindred Rainbow Publishing (*UK*)
Knox Robinson Publishing (UK) (*UK*)
Knox Robinson Publishing (US) (*US*)
Kube Publishing (*UK*)
Legacy Press (*US*)
Leapfrog Press (*US*)
Ledge Hill Publishing (*US*)
Legend Press (*UK*)
Les Figues Press (*US*)
Lethe Press (*US*)
Liberties Press (*Ire*)
The Lilliput Press (*Ire*)
Frances Lincoln Ltd (*UK*)
Lion Hudson Plc (*UK*)
Liquid Silver Books (*US*)
Listen & Live Audio, Inc. (*US*)
Loose Id (*US*)
Lost Tower Publications (*UK*)
Luath Press Ltd (*UK*)
Lucky Marble Books (*US*)
M P Publishing USA (*US*)
Macmillan (*UK*)
Magination Press (*US*)
Mandala Earth (*US*)
Mandrake of Oxford (*UK*)
Manor House Publishing (*Can*)
Marion Boyars Publishers (*UK*)
Martin Sisters Publishing (*US*)
McBooks Press (*US*)
Meadowside Children's Books (*UK*)
Medallion Media Group (*US*)
Mercier Press (*Ire*)
Messianic Jewish Publishers (*US*)
Methuen Publishing Ltd (*UK*)
Monarch Books (*UK*)
Mudfog Press (*UK*)
Myriad Editions (*UK*)
NBM (*US*)
Neon (*UK*)
New Beacon Books, Ltd (*UK*)
New Island (*Ire*)
The O'Brien Press (*Ire*)
Oceanview Publishing (*US*)
Oneworld Publications (*UK*)
Onstream Publications Ltd (*Ire*)
Ooligan Press (*US*)
Open Idea Publishing, LLC (*US*)
The Orion Publishing Group Limited (*UK*)
Ouen Press (*UK*)
The Overlook Press (*US*)
The Overmountain Press (*US*)
Peter Owen Publishers (*UK*)
Oxford University Press (*UK*)
P&R Publishing (*US*)
Papercutz (*US*)
Parthian Books (*UK*)
Paul Dry Books, Inc. (*US*)
Pauline Books and Media (*US*)
Pedlar Press (*Can*)
Pen & Sword Books Ltd (*UK*)
Penguin Canada (*Can*)
Penny-Farthing Press (*US*)
Persea Books (*US*)
Persephone Books (*UK*)
Phoenix Yard Books (*UK*)
Piano Press (*US*)
Piatkus Books (*UK*)
Picador USA (*US*)
Piccadilly Press (*UK*)
Poolbeg (*Ire*)
Possibility Press (*US*)
Press 53 (*US*)
Pure Indigo Limited (*UK*)
Pushkin Press (*UK*)
Quercus Books (*UK*)
Ragged Bears Limited (*UK*)
Rainbow Books, Inc. (*US*)
RainTown Press (*US*)
Ransom Publishing Ltd (*UK*)
Reading Harbor (*US*)
Reality Street Editions (*UK*)
Red Deer Press (*Can*)
Red Rattle Books (*UK*)
Renaissance House (*US*)
Rio Nuevo Publishers (*US*)
Ripple Grove Press (*US*)
Robert Hale Publishers (*UK*)
Roberts Press (*US*)
Ronsdale Press (*Can*)
Rose and Crown Books (*UK*)
Route Publishing (*UK*)
Running Press (*US*)
Saddleback Educational Publishing (*US*)
Saffron Books (*UK*)
Sakura Publishing & Technologies (*US*)
The Salariya Book Company (*UK*)
Salt Publishing Ltd (*UK*)
Sandstone Press Ltd (*UK*)
Scribe Publications Pty Ltd (*Aus*)
Seafarer Books (*UK*)
Second Story Press (*Can*)
Seren Books (*UK*)
Seriously Good Books (*US*)
Severn House Publishers (*UK*)
Short Books (*UK*)
Small Beer Press (*US*)

The Crowood Press (*UK*)
Ex-L-Ence Publishing (*UK*)
F&W Media International Ltd (*UK*)
Geostar Publishing & Services LLC (*US*)
HarperCollins Publishers Ltd (*UK*)
Harry N. Abrams, Inc. (*US*)
Headline Publishing Group (*UK*)
Kyle Books (*UK*)
Frances Lincoln Ltd (*UK*)
Macmillan (*UK*)
The New Curiosity Shop (*UK*)
New Holland Publishers (UK) Ltd (*UK*)
The Orion Publishing Group Limited (*UK*)
Poolbeg (*Ire*)
Quadrille Publishing Ltd (*UK*)
Quarto Publishing Group UK (*UK*)
Quiller Publishing Ltd (*UK*)
Rio Nuevo Publishers (*US*)
Shire Publications Ltd (*UK*)
Souvenir Press Ltd (*UK*)
Sunscribe (*US*)
Thames and Hudson Ltd (*UK*)
Tuttle Publishing (*US*)

Gothic

Central Avenue Publishing (*Can*)
Compelling Books (*UK*)
Corazon Books (*UK*)
Ex-L-Ence Publishing (*UK*)
Geostar Publishing & Services LLC (*US*)
Ghostwoods Books (*UK*)
Indigo Dreams Publishing (*UK*)
Lost Tower Publications (*UK*)
M P Publishing USA (*US*)
The New Curiosity Shop (*UK*)
Salt Publishing Ltd (*UK*)
Sunscribe (*US*)
Tirgearr Publishing (*Ire*)
Tantor Audio (*US*)

Health

American Press (*US*)
Barron's Educational Series, Inc. (*US*)
Bick Publishing House (*US*)
Conari Press (*US*)
The Crowood Press (*UK*)
Ex-L-Ence Publishing (*UK*)
Filbert Publishing (*US*)
Floris Books (*UK*)
Geostar Publishing & Services LLC (*US*)
Grub Street Publishing (*UK*)
Haldane Mason Ltd (*UK*)
HarperCollins Publishers Ltd (*UK*)
Harvest House Publishers (*US*)
Hinkler Books (*Aus*)
Hodder Education (*UK*)
Institute of Public Administration (IPA) (*Ire*)
International Foundation of Employee Benefit Plans (*US*)
Kyle Books (*UK*)
Liberties Press (*Ire*)
Lion Hudson Plc (*UK*)
Listen & Live Audio, Inc. (*US*)
Macmillan (*UK*)
Mainstream Publishing Co. (Edinburgh) Ltd (*UK*)
Mandrake of Oxford (*UK*)
McFarland & Company, Inc. (*US*)
Medallion Media Group (*US*)
Mercier Press (*Ire*)
Mitchell Lane Publishers, Inc. (*US*)
New Holland Publishers (UK) Ltd (*UK*)
Nicolas Hays Publishers (*US*)
NursesBooks (*US*)
The Orion Publishing Group Limited (*UK*)
The Overlook Press (*US*)
Pavilion Publishing (*UK*)
Piatkus Books (*UK*)
Piccadilly Books Ltd (*US*)
Possibility Press (*US*)
Prometheus Books (*US*)
Quadrille Publishing Ltd (*UK*)
Quarto Publishing Group UK (*UK*)
Quarto Publishing Group USA (*US*)
Quest Books (*US*)
Quill Driver Books (*US*)
Radcliffe Publishing Ltd (*UK*)
Reference Service Press (*US*)
The Rosen Publishing Group, Inc. (*US*)
Roundhouse Group (*UK*)
Rowman & Littlefield Publishing Group (*US*)
Running Press (*US*)
Scribe Publications Pty Ltd (*Aus*)
Soft Skull Press (*US*)
Souvenir Press Ltd (*UK*)
Sunscribe (*US*)
Tirgearr Publishing (*Ire*)
Tantor Audio (*US*)
Tate Publishing and Enterprises, LLC (*US*)
Tuttle Publishing (*US*)
Vanderbilt University Press (*US*)
Waveland Press, Inc. (*US*)
Wolters Kluwer (UK) Ltd (*UK*)
Zambezi Publishing Ltd (*UK*)

Historical

Akasha Publishing Ltd (*UK*)
Ian Allan Publishing Ltd (*UK*)
Alma Books Ltd (*UK*)
Alondra Press (*US*)
Amakella Publishing (*US*)
American Press (*US*)
Amira Press (*US*)
Ammonite Press (*UK*)
Anaiah Press, LLC (*US*)
Antique Collectors' Club Ltd (*UK*)
Arcade Publishing (*US*)
Arch Street Press (*US*)
Ashgate Publishing Limited (*UK*)
Atlantic Europe Publishing (*UK*)
Aurum Press Ltd (*UK*)
Barbarian Books (*US*)
BelleBooks (*US*)
Bethany House Publishers (*US*)
Black Lyon Publishing, LLC (*US*)
Blackstaff Press Ltd (*UK*)
Blink Publishing (*UK*)
Bloomsbury Publishing Plc (*UK*)

Bloomsbury Spark (*UK*)
Bodleian Library (*UK*)
Bold Strokes Books (*US*)
Brine Books Publishing (*Can*)
Brown, Son & Ferguson, Ltd (*UK*)
The Brucedale Press (*Can*)
By Light Unseen Media (*US*)
Canongate Books (*UK*)
Capstone (*US*)
Carlton Publishing Group (*UK*)
The Catholic University of America Press (*US*)
Central Avenue Publishing (*Can*)
Chicago Review Press (*US*)
Columba Press (*Ire*)
Compelling Books (*UK*)
Corazon Books (*UK*)
Cork University Press (*Ire*)
The Crowood Press (*UK*)
Dovecote Press (*UK*)
Dufour Editions (*US*)
Eakin Press (*US*)
William B. Eerdmans Publishing Co. (*US*)
Ex-L-Ence Publishing (*UK*)
F&W Media International Ltd (*UK*)
Fingerpress UK (*UK*)
Floris Books (*UK*)
Flyleaf Press (*Ire*)
Foreign Policy Association (*US*)
Frederic C. Beil, Publisher (*US*)
Geostar Publishing & Services LLC (*US*)
Ghostwoods Books (*UK*)
Gibson Square Books Ltd (*UK*)
Gill & Macmillan (*Ire*)
Gingko Library (*UK*)
Gomer Press (*UK*)
Grub Street Publishing (*UK*)
Gun Digest Books (*US*)
Heritage Books, Inc. (*US*)
Hadley Rille Books (*US*)
Halban Publishers (*UK*)
Haldane Mason Ltd (*UK*)
Halsgrove (*UK*)
Harlequin Mills & Boon Ltd (*UK*)
HarperCollins Publishers Ltd (*UK*)
HarperImpulse (*UK*)
Harvest House Publishers (*US*)
Headline Publishing Group (*UK*)
Highland Press (*US*)
Hill and Wang (*US*)
The History Press (*UK*)
House of Lochar (*UK*)
IBEX Publishers, Inc. (*US*)
Icon Books Ltd (*UK*)
Indigo Dreams Publishing (*UK*)
Jewish Lights Publishing (*US*)
Kindred Productions (*Can*)
Kamehameha Publishing (*US*)
Kane Miller Books (*US*)
Kelly Point Publishing LLC (*US*)
Knox Robinson Publishing (UK) (*UK*)
Knox Robinson Publishing (US) (*US*)
Kube Publishing (*UK*)
Liberties Press (*Ire*)
The Lilliput Press (*Ire*)
Linden Publishing (*US*)
Liverpool University Press (*UK*)
Logaston Press (*UK*)
Loose Id (*US*)
Luath Press Ltd (*UK*)
Lucky Marble Books (*US*)
The Lyons Press Inc. (*US*)
Macmillan (*UK*)
Mainstream Publishing Co. (Edinburgh) Ltd (*UK*)
Manchester University Press (*UK*)
McBooks Press (*US*)
McFarland & Company, Inc. (*US*)
Medallion Media Group (*US*)
Mentor Books (*Ire*)
Mercier Press (*Ire*)
Methuen Publishing Ltd (*UK*)
Mitchell Lane Publishers, Inc. (*US*)
Mountain Press Publishing Company (*US*)
Museum of Northern Arizona (*US*)
National Museum Wales (*UK*)
Neil Wilson Publishing Ltd (*UK*)
New Beacon Books, Ltd (*UK*)
The New Curiosity Shop (*UK*)
New Holland Publishers (UK) Ltd (*UK*)
New Island (*Ire*)
New York University (NYU) Press (*US*)
Nicolas Hays Publishers (*US*)
The O'Brien Press (*Ire*)
Michael O'Mara Books Ltd (*UK*)
Oneworld Publications (*UK*)
Onstream Publications Ltd (*Ire*)
Ooligan Press (*US*)
The Orion Publishing Group Limited (*UK*)
Osprey Publishing Ltd (*UK*)
The Overlook Press (*US*)
The Overmountain Press (*US*)
Peter Owen Publishers (*UK*)
Oxford University Press (*UK*)
P&R Publishing (*US*)
Paragon House (*US*)
Paul Dry Books, Inc. (*US*)
Pen & Sword Books Ltd (*UK*)
Phaidon Press Limited (*UK*)
Piatkus Books (*UK*)
Picton Press (*US*)
Pluto Publishing Ltd (*UK*)
Princeton University Press (*US*)
Princeton University Press Europe (*UK*)
Profile Books (*UK*)
Quarto Publishing Group UK (*UK*)
Quarto Publishing Group USA (*US*)
Red Deer Press (*Can*)
Reference Service Press (*US*)
Regnery Publishing, Inc. (*US*)
Rio Nuevo Publishers (*US*)
Robert Hale Publishers (*UK*)
Ronsdale Press (*Can*)
Rose and Crown Books (*UK*)
The Rosen Publishing Group, Inc. (*US*)
Roundhouse Group (*UK*)
Rowman & Littlefield Publishing Group (*US*)

Saffron Books (*UK*)
The Salariya Book Company (*UK*)
Scala Arts & Heritage Publishers (*UK*)
Scarecrow Press Inc. (*US*)
Scribe Publications Pty Ltd (*Aus*)
Seafarer Books (*UK*)
Seren Books (*UK*)
Seriously Good Books (*US*)
Severn House Publishers (*UK*)
Shepheard-Walwyn (Publishers) Ltd (*UK*)
Shire Publications Ltd (*UK*)
Sigma Press (*UK*)
Soft Skull Press (*US*)
Souvenir Press Ltd (*UK*)
St Augustine's Press (*US*)
Stacey International (*UK*)
Sunbury Press (*US*)
Sunscribe (*US*)
Sussex Academic Press (*UK*)
Tirgearr Publishing (*Ire*)
Tantor Audio (*US*)
Tate Publishing and Enterprises, LLC (*US*)
Texas Tech University Press (*US*)
Thames and Hudson Ltd (*UK*)
Tuttle Publishing (*US*)
Twilight Times Books (*US*)
Unicorn Press Ltd (*UK*)
University College Dublin (UCD) Press (*Ire*)
University of Tampa Press (*US*)
Vanderbilt University Press (*US*)
Vernon Press (an imprint of Vernon Art and Science Inc.) (*US*)
Voyageur Press (*US*)
Wooden Books (*UK*)
Waveland Press, Inc. (*US*)
Waverley Books (*UK*)
Whitaker House (*US*)
Williamson Books (*US*)
Yale University Press (*US*)

Hobbies

Ian Allan Publishing Ltd (*UK*)
Amakella Publishing (*US*)
Barron's Educational Series, Inc. (*US*)
Bloomsbury Publishing Plc (*UK*)
Brown, Son & Ferguson, Ltd (*UK*)
The Crowood Press (*UK*)
Ex-L-Ence Publishing (*UK*)
F&W Media International Ltd (*UK*)
Geostar Publishing & Services LLC (*US*)
Gill & Macmillan (*Ire*)
Gun Digest Books (*US*)
Harry N. Abrams, Inc. (*US*)
Igloo Books Limited (*UK*)
Indigo Dreams Publishing (*UK*)
Kalmbach Publishing Co. (*US*)
Kansas City Star Books (*US*)
Leisure Arts, Inc. (*US*)
Liberties Press (*Ire*)
Linden Publishing (*US*)
Methuen Publishing Ltd (*UK*)
New Cavendish Books (*UK*)
The New Curiosity Shop (*UK*)
Picton Press (*US*)
Quarto Publishing Group UK (*UK*)
Quarto Publishing Group USA (*US*)
Quill Driver Books (*US*)
Robert Hale Publishers (*UK*)
Running Press (*US*)
Shire Publications Ltd (*UK*)
Souvenir Press Ltd (*UK*)
St. Johann Press (*US*)
Stemmer House Publishers (*US*)
Sunscribe (*US*)
Tirgearr Publishing (*Ire*)
Williamson Books (*US*)

Horror

Amira Press (*US*)
Anaiah Press, LLC (*US*)
BelleBooks (*US*)
Blurbeo (*US*)
Bold Strokes Books (*US*)
Brine Books Publishing (*Can*)
By Light Unseen Media (*US*)
Central Avenue Publishing (*Can*)
Compelling Books (*UK*)
Geostar Publishing & Services LLC (*US*)
Ghostwoods Books (*UK*)
Indigo Dreams Publishing (*UK*)
Lost Tower Publications (*UK*)
Macmillan (*UK*)
Mandrake of Oxford (*UK*)
Medallion Media Group (*US*)
NBM (*US*)
The New Curiosity Shop (*UK*)
Papercutz (*US*)
Red Rattle Books (*UK*)
Severn House Publishers (*UK*)
SynergEbooks (*US*)
Tirgearr Publishing (*Ire*)
Tantor Audio (*US*)

How-to

Amakella Publishing (*US*)
Centerstream Publishing (*US*)
Chartered Institute of Personnel and Development (CIPD) Publishing (*UK*)
Compelling Books (*UK*)
Ex-L-Ence Publishing (*UK*)
Filbert Publishing (*US*)
Flyleaf Press (*Ire*)
Free Spirit Publishing (*US*)
Geostar Publishing & Services LLC (*US*)
Gun Digest Books (*US*)
Humanics Publishing Group (*US*)
Impact Books (*US*)
Indigo Dreams Publishing (*UK*)
JIST Publishing (*US*)
Kalmbach Publishing Co. (*US*)
Leisure Arts, Inc. (*US*)
Linden Publishing (*US*)
Methuen Publishing Ltd (*UK*)
NavPress (*US*)
New Holland Publishers (UK) Ltd (*UK*)
Nolo (*US*)
The Overlook Press (*US*)
Parenting Press, Inc. (*US*)
Possibility Press (*US*)

Gomer Press (*UK*)
HarperCollins Publishers Ltd (*UK*)
Harry N. Abrams, Inc. (*US*)
Indigo Dreams Publishing (*UK*)
Frances Lincoln Ltd (*UK*)
Lost Tower Publications (*UK*)
Luath Press Ltd (*UK*)
McFarland & Company, Inc. (*US*)
Merlin Unwin Books (*UK*)
Open Idea Publishing, LLC (*US*)
Robert Hale Publishers (*UK*)
Running Press (*US*)
Sigma Press (*UK*)
Sunscribe (*US*)
Tirgearr Publishing (*Ire*)
Tantor Audio (*US*)
Tsaba House (*US*)

Lifestyle

AA Publishing (*UK*)
Amakella Publishing (*US*)
AMG Publishers (*US*)
Anaiah Press, LLC (*US*)
Aurum Press Ltd (*UK*)
Barron's Educational Series, Inc. (*US*)
Blink Publishing (*UK*)
Blurbeo (*US*)
Central Avenue Publishing (*Can*)
Chicago Review Press (*US*)
Co & Bear Productions (*UK*)
Conari Press (*US*)
Ex-L-Ence Publishing (*UK*)
F&W Media International Ltd (*UK*)
Filbert Publishing (*US*)
Flame Tree Publishing (*UK*)
Free Spirit Publishing (*US*)
Geostar Publishing & Services LLC (*US*)
Gill & Macmillan (*Ire*)
Haldane Mason Ltd (*UK*)
HarperCollins Publishers Ltd (*UK*)
Harry N. Abrams, Inc. (*US*)
The Harvard Common Press (*US*)
Harvest House Publishers (*US*)
Hawthorn Press (*UK*)
Hinkler Books (*Aus*)
Igloo Books Limited (*UK*)
Indigo Dreams Publishing (*UK*)
Kube Publishing (*UK*)
Kyle Books (*UK*)
Leisure Arts, Inc. (*US*)
Liberties Press (*Ire*)
Frances Lincoln Ltd (*UK*)
Listen & Live Audio, Inc. (*US*)
Lost Tower Publications (*UK*)
Luath Press Ltd (*UK*)
Mandrake of Oxford (*UK*)
Mercier Press (*Ire*)
NavPress (*US*)
New Holland Publishers (UK) Ltd (*UK*)
Nightingale Press (*UK*)
The O'Brien Press (*Ire*)
The Orion Publishing Group Limited (*UK*)
The Overlook Press (*US*)
P&R Publishing (*US*)
Parenting Press, Inc. (*US*)
Piatkus Books (*UK*)
Possibility Press (*US*)
Quarto Publishing Group UK (*UK*)
Quill Driver Books (*US*)
Roundhouse Group (*UK*)
Running Press (*US*)
Soft Skull Press (*US*)
Souvenir Press Ltd (*UK*)
Stone Bridge Press (*US*)
Sunscribe (*US*)
Tirgearr Publishing (*Ire*)
Tantor Audio (*US*)
Tate Publishing and Enterprises, LLC (*US*)
Tristan Publishing (*US*)
Tsaba House (*US*)
Turn the Page Publishing LLC (*US*)
Voyageur Press (*US*)
Whitaker House (*US*)
Zambezi Publishing Ltd (*UK*)

Literature

Alma Books Ltd (*UK*)
Alma Classics (*UK*)
Amakella Publishing (*US*)
Anaiah Press, LLC (*US*)
Arch Street Press (*US*)
Ashgate Publishing Limited (*UK*)
Black Lawrence Press (*US*)
Bloodaxe Books Ltd (*UK*)
Blurbeo (*US*)
Bodleian Library (*UK*)
Brine Books Publishing (*Can*)
The Catholic University of America Press (*US*)
Central Avenue Publishing (*Can*)
Classical Comics Limited (*UK*)
Compelling Books (*UK*)
Cork University Press (*Ire*)
Crescent Moon Publishing (*UK*)
Dedalus Ltd (*UK*)
Ex-L-Ence Publishing (*UK*)
Floris Books (*UK*)
Geostar Publishing & Services LLC (*US*)
Gingko Library (*UK*)
Gomer Press (*UK*)
Halban Publishers (*UK*)
Homestead Publishing (*US*)
House of Lochar (*UK*)
IBEX Publishers, Inc. (*US*)
Indigo Dreams Publishing (*UK*)
Influx Press (*UK*)
The Lilliput Press (*Ire*)
Liverpool University Press (*UK*)
M P Publishing USA (*US*)
Manchester University Press (*UK*)
Marion Boyars Publishers (*UK*)
McFarland & Company, Inc. (*US*)
Methuen Publishing Ltd (*UK*)
Mitchell Lane Publishers, Inc. (*US*)
The New Curiosity Shop (*UK*)
New Island (*Ire*)
New York University (NYU) Press (*US*)
The O'Brien Press (*Ire*)
Open Idea Publishing, LLC (*US*)

The Orion Publishing Group Limited (*UK*)
Peter Owen Publishers (*UK*)
Oxford University Press (*UK*)
Presa Press (*US*)
Princeton University Press (*US*)
Princeton University Press Europe (*UK*)
Reading Harbor (*US*)
Roundhouse Group (*UK*)
Salt Publishing Ltd (*UK*)
Scarecrow Press Inc. (*US*)
Scribe Publications Pty Ltd (*Aus*)
Shearsman Books (*UK*)
Soft Skull Press (*US*)
Souvenir Press Ltd (*UK*)
Stacey International (*UK*)
Stone Bridge Press (*US*)
Sunscribe (*US*)
Sussex Academic Press (*UK*)
Swan Isle Press (*US*)
Tirgearr Publishing (*Ire*)
Texas Tech University Press (*US*)
Tsaba House (*US*)
Turnstone Press (*Can*)
Tuttle Publishing (*US*)
University College Dublin (UCD) Press (*Ire*)
Vanderbilt University Press (*US*)
Vernon Press (an imprint of Vernon Art and Science Inc.) (*US*)
Virago Press (*UK*)
Waveland Press, Inc. (*US*)
Yale University Press (*US*)

Media

Amakella Publishing (*US*)
BFI Publishing (*UK*)
Booth-Clibborn Editions (*UK*)
Central Avenue Publishing (*Can*)
Crescent Moon Publishing (*UK*)
Ex-L-Ence Publishing (*UK*)
Geostar Publishing & Services LLC (*US*)
HarperCollins Publishers Ltd (*UK*)
Indigo Dreams Publishing (*UK*)
Manchester University Press (*UK*)
New York University (NYU) Press (*US*)
Pluto Publishing Ltd (*UK*)
Princeton University Press Europe (*UK*)
Soft Skull Press (*US*)
Sunscribe (*US*)
Sussex Academic Press (*UK*)
Tirgearr Publishing (*Ire*)
Wallflower Press (*UK*)

Medicine

Ex-L-Ence Publishing (*UK*)
Geostar Publishing & Services LLC (*US*)
Hodder Education (*UK*)
Lawyers & Judges Publishing Co. (*US*)
McFarland & Company, Inc. (*US*)
Medical Group Management Association (MGMA) (*US*)
The New Curiosity Shop (*UK*)
Oxford University Press (*UK*)
Princeton University Press (*US*)
Princeton University Press Europe (*UK*)
Radcliffe Publishing Ltd (*UK*)
Reference Service Press (*US*)
Roundhouse Group (*UK*)
Scribe Publications Pty Ltd (*Aus*)
Souvenir Press Ltd (*UK*)
Sunscribe (*US*)
TSO (The Stationery Office) (*UK*)
Vanderbilt University Press (*US*)
Yale University Press (*US*)

Men's Interests

Amakella Publishing (*US*)
Blurbeo (*US*)
Brine Books Publishing (*Can*)
Central Avenue Publishing (*Can*)
Ex-L-Ence Publishing (*UK*)
Geostar Publishing & Services LLC (*US*)
Harvest House Publishers (*US*)
Indigo Dreams Publishing (*UK*)
Jewish Lights Publishing (*US*)
The New Curiosity Shop (*UK*)
Sunscribe (*US*)
Tirgearr Publishing (*Ire*)
Tsaba House (*US*)
Whitaker House (*US*)

Military

Ian Allan Publishing Ltd (*UK*)
Arcade Publishing (*US*)
Aurum Press Ltd (*UK*)
Blink Publishing (*UK*)
Blurbeo (*US*)
Brine Books Publishing (*Can*)
Capstone (*US*)
Central Avenue Publishing (*Can*)
The Crowood Press (*UK*)
Eakin Press (*US*)
Ex-L-Ence Publishing (*UK*)
F&W Media International Ltd (*UK*)
Geostar Publishing & Services LLC (*US*)
The Glencannon Press (*US*)
Grub Street Publishing (*UK*)
Heritage Books, Inc. (*US*)
HarperCollins Publishers Ltd (*UK*)
The History Press (*UK*)
Listen & Live Audio, Inc. (*US*)
Macmillan (*UK*)
McBooks Press (*US*)
McFarland & Company, Inc. (*US*)
Mercier Press (*Ire*)
Methuen Publishing Ltd (*UK*)
The New Curiosity Shop (*UK*)
The Orion Publishing Group Limited (*UK*)
Osprey Publishing Ltd (*UK*)
Pen & Sword Books Ltd (*UK*)
Quarto Publishing Group USA (*US*)
Regnery Publishing, Inc. (*US*)
Robert Hale Publishers (*UK*)
Rose and Crown Books (*UK*)
Scribe Publications Pty Ltd (*Aus*)
Seafarer Books (*UK*)
Shire Publications Ltd (*UK*)
Souvenir Press Ltd (*UK*)
Sunscribe (*US*)
Tirgearr Publishing (*Ire*)
Tantor Audio (*US*)

Bloomsbury Publishing Plc (*UK*)
Central Avenue Publishing (*Can*)
Co & Bear Productions (*UK*)
Columba Press (*Ire*)
Craigmore Creations (*US*)
The Crowood Press (*UK*)
Dog-Eared Publications (*US*)
Dovecote Press (*UK*)
Ex-L-Ence Publishing (*UK*)
F&W Media International Ltd (*UK*)
Fabian Society (*UK*)
Geostar Publishing & Services LLC (*US*)
Gill & Macmillan (*Ire*)
Gomer Press (*UK*)
Harry N. Abrams, Inc. (*US*)
Homestead Publishing (*US*)
Indigo Dreams Publishing (*UK*)
The Lilliput Press (*Ire*)
Frances Lincoln Ltd (*UK*)
Luath Press Ltd (*UK*)
The Lyons Press Inc. (*US*)
Macmillan (*UK*)
Mandala Earth (*US*)
Merlin Unwin Books (*UK*)
Mountain Press Publishing Company (*US*)
Museum of Northern Arizona (*US*)
National Museum Wales (*UK*)
Neil Wilson Publishing Ltd (*UK*)
The New Curiosity Shop (*UK*)
New Holland Publishers (UK) Ltd (*UK*)
The O'Brien Press (*Ire*)
Oneworld Publications (*UK*)
The Orion Publishing Group Limited (*UK*)
Piccadilly Books Ltd (*US*)
Pluto Publishing Ltd (*UK*)
Princeton University Press (*US*)
Princeton University Press Europe (*UK*)
Rio Nuevo Publishers (*US*)
Roundhouse Group (*UK*)
Rowman & Littlefield Publishing Group (*US*)
Ruka Press (*US*)
The Salariya Book Company (*UK*)
Scribe Publications Pty Ltd (*Aus*)
Sierra Club Books (*US*)
Souvenir Press Ltd (*UK*)
Stacey International (*UK*)
Stemmer House Publishers (*US*)
Sunscribe (*US*)
Sussex Academic Press (*UK*)
Tirgearr Publishing (*Ire*)
Tantor Audio (*US*)
Texas Tech University Press (*US*)
Tsaba House (*US*)
Tuttle Publishing (*US*)
University College Dublin (UCD) Press (*Ire*)
Vanderbilt University Press (*US*)
Voyageur Press (*US*)
Waveland Press, Inc. (*US*)
Whittet Books Ltd (*UK*)
Yale University Press (*US*)

New Age

Anaiah Press, LLC (*US*)
Barron's Educational Series, Inc. (*US*)
Brine Books Publishing (*Can*)
Central Avenue Publishing (*Can*)
Ex-L-Ence Publishing (*UK*)
Geostar Publishing & Services LLC (*US*)
Humanics Publishing Group (*US*)
Indigo Dreams Publishing (*UK*)
Jupiter Gardens Press (*US*)
Manor House Publishing (*Can*)
Sunscribe (*US*)
SynergEbooks (*US*)
Tirgearr Publishing (*Ire*)
Tantor Audio (*US*)
Turn the Page Publishing LLC (*US*)
Twilight Times Books (*US*)
Zambezi Publishing Ltd (*UK*)

Nonfiction

A Swift Exit (*UK*)
AA Publishing (*UK*)
Abrams ComicArts (*US*)
Absolute Press (*UK*)
Akasha Publishing Ltd (*UK*)
Alastair Sawday Publishing Co. Ltd (*UK*)
Alexander Hamilton Institute (*US*)
Ian Allan Publishing Ltd (*UK*)
Alma Books Ltd (*UK*)
Alondra Press (*US*)
Amadeus Press (*US*)
Amakella Publishing (*US*)
American Press (*US*)
AMG Publishers (*US*)
Ammonite Press (*UK*)
Anaiah Press, LLC (*US*)
Ankerwycke (*US*)
Annick Press (*Can*)
Antique Collectors' Club Ltd (*UK*)
Appletree Press Ltd (*UK*)
Arcade Publishing (*US*)
Arch Street Press (*US*)
Ashgate Publishing Limited (*UK*)
Atlantic Europe Publishing (*UK*)
Aureus Publishing Limited (*UK*)
Aurora Metro Press (*UK*)
Aurum Press Ltd (*UK*)
Barrington Stoke (*UK*)
Barron's Educational Series, Inc. (*US*)
Bellevue Literary Press (*US*)
Berlitz Publishing (*UK*)
Bernard Babani (publishing) Ltd (*UK*)
Bethany House Publishers (*US*)
BFI Publishing (*UK*)
Bick Publishing House (*US*)
Bilingual Review Press (*US*)
Black & White Publishing Ltd (*UK*)
Black Lawrence Press (*US*)
Black Lyon Publishing, LLC (*US*)
Blackline Press (*UK*)
Blackstaff Press Ltd (*UK*)
Blink Publishing (*UK*)
Bloodaxe Books Ltd (*UK*)
Bloomsbury Publishing Plc (*UK*)
Blue Guides Limited (*UK*)
Bodleian Library (*UK*)
Bold Strokes Books (*US*)

Booth-Clibborn Editions (*UK*)
Bracket Books (*US*)
Brine Books Publishing (*Can*)
Brown, Son & Ferguson, Ltd (*UK*)
The Brucedale Press (*Can*)
Bryntirion Press (*UK*)
By Light Unseen Media (*US*)
Canongate Books (*UK*)
Canopus Publishing Ltd (*UK*)
Canterbury House Publishing, Ltd (*US*)
Capstone (*US*)
Carlton Publishing Group (*UK*)
The Catholic University of America Press (*US*)
Centerstream Publishing (*US*)
Chartered Institute of Personnel and Development (CIPD) Publishing (*UK*)
Chicago Review Press (*US*)
Christian Education (*UK*)
Church Publishing Incorporated (*US*)
Co & Bear Productions (*UK*)
Columba Press (*Ire*)
Compelling Books (*UK*)
Conari Press (*US*)
Continental (*US*)
Cork University Press (*Ire*)
Craigmore Creations (*US*)
Crescent Moon Publishing (*UK*)
Cressrelles Publishing Co. Ltd (*UK*)
The Crowood Press (*UK*)
Cyclotour Guide Books (*US*)
DC Thomson (*UK*)
Dog-Eared Publications (*US*)
Dovecote Press (*UK*)
Dufour Editions (*US*)
Eakin Press (*US*)
The Educational Company of Ireland (*Ire*)
William B. Eerdmans Publishing Co. (*US*)
Eland Publishing Ltd (*UK*)
Enete Enterprises (*US*)
Euromonitor (*UK*)
Ex-L-Ence Publishing (*UK*)
F&W Media International Ltd (*UK*)
Faber & Faber Ltd (*UK*)
Fabian Society (*UK*)
Facts on File, Inc. (*US*)
Farrar, Straus & Giroux, Inc. (*US*)
Filbert Publishing (*US*)
Fitzrovia Press Limited (*UK*)
Flame Tree Publishing (*UK*)
Floris Books (*UK*)
Flyleaf Press (*Ire*)
Fodor's Travel Publications (*US*)
Foreign Policy Association (*US*)
Frederic C. Beil, Publisher (*US*)
Free Spirit Publishing (*US*)
George Ronald Publisher (*UK*)
The Gallery Press (*Ire*)
Geostar Publishing & Services LLC (*US*)
Gibbs Smith, Publisher (*US*)
Gibson Square Books Ltd (*UK*)
Gill & Macmillan (*Ire*)
Gingko Library (*UK*)
Gival Press, LLC (*US*)
The Glencannon Press (*US*)
Gomer Press (*UK*)
Goss & Crested China Club (*UK*)
Great Potential Press, Inc. (*US*)
Groundwood Books (*Can*)
Grub Street Publishing (*UK*)
Gulf Publishing Company (*US*)
Gun Digest Books (*US*)
Heritage Books, Inc. (*US*)
Halban Publishers (*UK*)
Haldane Mason Ltd (*UK*)
Halsgrove (*UK*)
HarperCollins Publishers Ltd (*UK*)
Harry N. Abrams, Inc. (*US*)
Hart Publishing Ltd (*UK*)
The Harvard Common Press (*US*)
Harvest House Publishers (*US*)
Hawthorn Press (*UK*)
Hayes School Publishing Co., Inc. (*US*)
Headland Publications (*UK*)
Headline Publishing Group (*UK*)
Hearts 'N Tummies Cookbook Co. / Quixote Press (*US*)
Highland Press (*US*)
Hill and Wang (*US*)
Hinkler Books (*Aus*)
The History Press (*UK*)
Hodder Education (*UK*)
Homestead Publishing (*US*)
Honno Welsh Women's Press (*UK*)
Hopewell Publications (*US*)
Hopscotch (*UK*)
House of Anansi Press (*Can*)
House of Lochar (*UK*)
HOW Books (*US*)
Humanics Publishing Group (*US*)
IBEX Publishers, Inc. (*US*)
Icon Books Ltd (*UK*)
Ideals Publications (*US*)
Ig Publishing (*US*)
Igloo Books Limited (*UK*)
Ignatius Press (*US*)
The Ilex Press (*UK*)
Impact Books (*US*)
Impact Publishers (*US*)
Independent Music Press (*UK*)
Indigo Dreams Publishing (*UK*)
Influx Press (*UK*)
Institute of Public Administration (IPA) (*Ire*)
International Foundation of Employee Benefit Plans (*US*)
International Press (*US*)
Jewish Lights Publishing (*US*)
JIST Publishing (*US*)
Jordan Publishing (*UK*)
Jupiter Gardens Press (*US*)
Just Us Books (*US*)
Kindred Productions (*Can*)
Kalmbach Publishing Co. (*US*)
Kamehameha Publishing (*US*)
Kansas City Star Books (*US*)
Kids Can Press (*Can*)
Kindred Rainbow Publishing (*UK*)

Kirkbride Bible Company (*US*)
Kube Publishing (*UK*)
Kyle Books (*UK*)
Legacy Press (*US*)
Lawyers & Judges Publishing Co. (*US*)
Leapfrog Press (*US*)
Ledge Hill Publishing (*US*)
Leisure Arts, Inc. (*US*)
Lethe Press (*US*)
LexisNexis (*US*)
Liberties Press (*Ire*)
The Lilliput Press (*Ire*)
Frances Lincoln Ltd (*UK*)
Linden Publishing (*US*)
Lion Hudson Plc (*UK*)
Listen & Live Audio, Inc. (*US*)
Liverpool University Press (*UK*)
Logaston Press (*UK*)
Lonely Planet Publications (*US*)
Luath Press Ltd (*UK*)
Lucent Books (*US*)
The Lyons Press Inc. (*US*)
M P Publishing USA (*US*)
Macmillan (*UK*)
Magenta Publishing for the Arts (*Can*)
Magination Press (*US*)
Mainstream Publishing Co. (Edinburgh) Ltd (*UK*)
Manchester University Press (*UK*)
Mandala Earth (*US*)
Mandrake of Oxford (*UK*)
Manor House Publishing (*Can*)
Marion Boyars Publishers (*UK*)
Martin Sisters Publishing (*US*)
Master Books (*US*)
Kevin Mayhew Publishers (*UK*)
McBooks Press (*US*)
McFarland & Company, Inc. (*US*)
Medallion Media Group (*US*)
Medical Group Management Association (MGMA) (*US*)
Mentor Books (*Ire*)
Mercier Press (*Ire*)
Merlin Unwin Books (*UK*)
Merrell Publishers Limited (*UK*)
Messianic Jewish Publishers (*US*)
Metal Powder Industries Federation (MPIF) (*US*)
Methodist Publishing (*UK*)
Methuen Publishing Ltd (*UK*)
Michelin Maps and Guides (*UK*)
Milo Books Ltd (*UK*)
Mitchell Lane Publishers, Inc. (*US*)
Monarch Books (*UK*)
Morgan Kaufmann Publishers (*US*)
Mountain Press Publishing Company (*US*)
Museum of Northern Arizona (*US*)
Myriad Editions (*UK*)
National Museum Wales (*UK*)
NavPress (*US*)
Neil Wilson Publishing Ltd (*UK*)
New Beacon Books, Ltd (*UK*)
New Cavendish Books (*UK*)
The New Curiosity Shop (*UK*)
New Holland Publishers (UK) Ltd (*UK*)
New Island (*Ire*)
New York University (NYU) Press (*US*)
Nick Hern Books Ltd (*UK*)
Nicolas Hays Publishers (*US*)
Nightingale Press (*UK*)
Nolo (*US*)
Nova Press (*US*)
NursesBooks (*US*)
The O'Brien Press (*Ire*)
Michael O'Mara Books Ltd (*UK*)
Oak Tree Press (*Ire*)
Oberon Books (*UK*)
Omnibus Press (*UK*)
On The Mark Press (*Can*)
Oneworld Publications (*UK*)
Onstream Publications Ltd (*Ire*)
Ooligan Press (*US*)
Open Court Publishing Company (*US*)
The Orion Publishing Group Limited (*UK*)
Osprey Publishing Ltd (*UK*)
Ouen Press (*UK*)
The Overlook Press (*US*)
The Overmountain Press (*US*)
Peter Owen Publishers (*UK*)
Oxford University Press (*UK*)
P&R Publishing (*US*)
Parenting Press, Inc. (*US*)
PaperBooks (*UK*)
Paragon House (*US*)
Parallax Press (*US*)
Paul Dry Books, Inc. (*US*)
Pauline Books and Media (*US*)
Pavilion Publishing (*UK*)
Pearson UK (*UK*)
Pen & Sword Books Ltd (*UK*)
Penguin Canada (*Can*)
Persea Books (*US*)
Persephone Books (*UK*)
Peter Lang Publishing, Inc. (*US*)
Pflaum Publishing Group (*US*)
Phaidon Press Limited (*UK*)
Phoenix Yard Books (*UK*)
Piano Press (*US*)
Piatkus Books (*UK*)
Picador USA (*US*)
Piccadilly Books Ltd (*US*)
Piccadilly Press (*UK*)
Picton Press (*US*)
Plexus Publishing Limited (*UK*)
Pluto Publishing Ltd (*UK*)
Poolbeg (*Ire*)
Possibility Press (*US*)
Presa Press (*US*)
Princeton University Press (*US*)
Princeton University Press Europe (*UK*)
Pro Lingua Associates ESL (*US*)
Professional and Higher Partnership (*UK*)
Professional Publications, Inc. (PPI) (*US*)
Profile Books (*UK*)
Prometheus Books (*US*)
Pure Indigo Limited (*UK*)

Pushkin Press (*UK*)
Quadrille Publishing Ltd (*UK*)
Quarto Publishing Group UK (*UK*)
Quarto Publishing Group USA (*US*)
Quercus Books (*UK*)
Quest Books (*US*)
Quill Driver Books (*US*)
Quiller Publishing Ltd (*UK*)
Radcliffe Publishing Ltd (*UK*)
Rainbow Books, Inc. (*US*)
Rainbow Publishers (*US*)
Ransom Publishing Ltd (*UK*)
Reader's Digest Association Ltd (*UK*)
Reading Harbor (*US*)
Red Deer Press (*Can*)
Red Rattle Books (*UK*)
Redleaf Press (*US*)
Reference Service Press (*US*)
Regnery Publishing, Inc. (*US*)
Renaissance House (*US*)
Richard C. Owen Publishers, Inc. (*US*)
Richard Dennis Publications (*UK*)
Rio Nuevo Publishers (*US*)
Robert Hale Publishers (*UK*)
Ronsdale Press (*Can*)
The Rosen Publishing Group, Inc. (*US*)
Round Hall (*Ire*)
Roundhouse Group (*UK*)
Rowman & Littlefield Publishing Group (*US*)
Ruka Press (*US*)
Running Press (*US*)
Saffron Books (*UK*)
Sakura Publishing & Technologies (*US*)
The Salariya Book Company (*UK*)
Sandstone Press Ltd (*UK*)
Scala Arts & Heritage Publishers (*UK*)
Scarecrow Press Inc. (*US*)
School Guide Publications (*US*)
SCM-Canterbury Press (*UK*)
Scribe Publications Pty Ltd (*Aus*)
Seafarer Books (*UK*)
Second Story Press (*Can*)
Seren Books (*UK*)
Shearsman Books (*UK*)
Shepheard-Walwyn (Publishers) Ltd (*UK*)
Shire Publications Ltd (*UK*)
Short Books (*UK*)
Sierra Club Books (*US*)
Sigma Press (*UK*)
Skinner House Books (*US*)
Soft Skull Press (*US*)
Somerville Press (*Ire*)
Souvenir Press Ltd (*UK*)
SportsBooks Limited (*UK*)
St Augustine's Press (*US*)
St. Johann Press (*US*)
Stacey International (*UK*)
Stainer & Bell Ltd (*UK*)
Stemmer House Publishers (*US*)
Stone Bridge Press (*US*)
Strategic Media Books (*US*)
Sunbury Press (*US*)
Sunscribe (*US*)
Sussex Academic Press (*UK*)
Swan Isle Press (*US*)
Sweet & Maxwell (*UK*)
SynergEbooks (*US*)
TSO (The Stationery Office) (*UK*)
Tango Books Ltd (*UK*)
Tantor Audio (*US*)
Tate Publishing and Enterprises, LLC (*US*)
The Templar Company Limited (*UK*)
Texas Tech University Press (*US*)
Thames and Hudson Ltd (*UK*)
Titan Books (*UK*)
Top That! Publishing (*UK*)
Trentham Books Limited (*UK*)
Tristan Publishing (*US*)
Tsaba House (*US*)
Turn the Page Publishing LLC (*US*)
Turnstone Press (*Can*)
Tuttle Publishing (*US*)
Ulverscroft Large Print Books Ltd (*UK*)
Unicorn Press Ltd (*UK*)
University College Dublin (UCD) Press (*Ire*)
University of Nebraska Press (*US*)
University of Tampa Press (*US*)
Unthank Books (*UK*)
Usborne Publishing (*UK*)
Vanderbilt University Press (*US*)
Vernon Press (an imprint of Vernon Art and Science Inc.) (*US*)
Virago Press (*UK*)
Virtue Books (*UK*)
Voyageur Press (*US*)
Wooden Books (*UK*)
Wallflower Press (*UK*)
Waveland Press, Inc. (*US*)
Waverley Books (*UK*)
Western Psychological Services (*US*)
Westminster John Knox Press (WJK) (*US*)
Whitaker House (*US*)
Whittet Books Ltd (*UK*)
William Reed Business Media (*UK*)
William S. Hein & Co., Inc. (*US*)
Williamson Books (*US*)
Wilshire Book Company (*US*)
Wolters Kluwer (UK) Ltd (*UK*)
Yale University Press (*US*)
Zambezi Publishing Ltd (*UK*)
Zero to Ten Limited (*UK*)

Philosophy

Alondra Press (*US*)
American Press (*US*)
Arch Street Press (*US*)
Ashgate Publishing Limited (*UK*)
Bick Publishing House (*US*)
Brine Books Publishing (*Can*)
The Catholic University of America Press (*US*)
Central Avenue Publishing (*Can*)
Compelling Books (*UK*)
Cork University Press (*Ire*)
Crescent Moon Publishing (*UK*)
William B. Eerdmans Publishing Co. (*US*)
Ex-L-Ence Publishing (*UK*)
Fitzrovia Press Limited (*UK*)

Floris Books (*UK*)
Geostar Publishing & Services LLC (*US*)
Gibson Square Books Ltd (*UK*)
Gingko Library (*UK*)
Gival Press, LLC (*US*)
Halban Publishers (*UK*)
IBEX Publishers, Inc. (*US*)
Icon Books Ltd (*UK*)
Jewish Lights Publishing (*US*)
The Lilliput Press (*Ire*)
Macmillan (*UK*)
Mandala Earth (*US*)
Mandrake of Oxford (*UK*)
Marion Boyars Publishers (*UK*)
Methodist Publishing (*UK*)
Methuen Publishing Ltd (*UK*)
The New Curiosity Shop (*UK*)
Oneworld Publications (*UK*)
Open Court Publishing Company (*US*)
Oxford University Press (*UK*)
Paragon House (*US*)
Paul Dry Books, Inc. (*US*)
Princeton University Press (*US*)
Princeton University Press Europe (*UK*)
Prometheus Books (*US*)
Quest Books (*US*)
Reading Harbor (*US*)
Rowman & Littlefield Publishing Group (*US*)
Scarecrow Press Inc. (*US*)
SCM-Canterbury Press (*UK*)
Scribe Publications Pty Ltd (*Aus*)
Shepheard-Walwyn (Publishers) Ltd (*UK*)
Soft Skull Press (*US*)
Souvenir Press Ltd (*UK*)
St Augustine's Press (*US*)
Sunscribe (*US*)
Sussex Academic Press (*UK*)
Tantor Audio (*US*)
Tate Publishing and Enterprises, LLC (*US*)
Vanderbilt University Press (*US*)
Vernon Press (an imprint of Vernon Art and Science Inc.) (*US*)
Waveland Press, Inc. (*US*)
Yale University Press (*US*)

Photography

Ammonite Press (*UK*)
Antique Collectors' Club Ltd (*UK*)
Aurum Press Ltd (*UK*)
Barron's Educational Series, Inc. (*US*)
Booth-Clibborn Editions (*UK*)
Bracket Books (*US*)
Brine Books Publishing (*Can*)
Central Avenue Publishing (*Can*)
Co & Bear Productions (*UK*)
The Crowood Press (*UK*)
Enitharmon Press (*UK*)
Ex-L-Ence Publishing (*UK*)
F&W Media International Ltd (*UK*)
Geostar Publishing & Services LLC (*US*)
Halsgrove (*UK*)
Harry N. Abrams, Inc. (*US*)
Homestead Publishing (*US*)
The Ilex Press (*UK*)
Indigo Dreams Publishing (*UK*)
The Lilliput Press (*Ire*)
Luath Press Ltd (*UK*)
Magenta Publishing for the Arts (*Can*)
Mandala Earth (*US*)
Merrell Publishers Limited (*UK*)
The New Curiosity Shop (*UK*)
New Holland Publishers (UK) Ltd (*UK*)
The O'Brien Press (*Ire*)
Phaidon Press Limited (*UK*)
Princeton University Press (*US*)
Princeton University Press Europe (*UK*)
Rio Nuevo Publishers (*US*)
Roundhouse Group (*UK*)
Seren Books (*UK*)
Shire Publications Ltd (*UK*)
Stacey International (*UK*)
Sunscribe (*US*)
Thames and Hudson Ltd (*UK*)
Voyageur Press (*US*)

Poetry

A Swift Exit (*UK*)
Ahsahta Press (*US*)
Alice James Books (*US*)
Alma Classics (*UK*)
Arc Publications (*UK*)
The Backwater Press (*US*)
Bilingual Review Press (*US*)
Black Lawrence Press (*US*)
Black Ocean (*US*)
Blackstaff Press Ltd (*UK*)
Bloodaxe Books Ltd (*UK*)
Brine Books Publishing (*Can*)
Bronze Man Books (*US*)
Capstone (*US*)
Central Avenue Publishing (*Can*)
Crescent Moon Publishing (*UK*)
Dufour Editions (*US*)
Eland Publishing Ltd (*UK*)
Enitharmon Press (*UK*)
Everheart Books (*Can*)
Ex-L-Ence Publishing (*UK*)
Faber & Faber Ltd (*UK*)
Farrar, Straus & Giroux, Inc. (*US*)
The Gallery Press (*Ire*)
Gival Press, LLC (*US*)
Gomer Press (*UK*)
Green Bottle Press (*UK*)
Grey Hen Press (*UK*)
Headland Publications (*UK*)
Honno Welsh Women's Press (*UK*)
House of Anansi Press (*Can*)
IBEX Publishers, Inc. (*US*)
Indigo Dreams Publishing (*UK*)
Influx Press (*UK*)
Iron Press (*UK*)
Just Us Books (*US*)
Kind of a Hurricane Press (*US*)
Leapfrog Press (*US*)
Ledge Hill Publishing (*US*)
Les Figues Press (*US*)
Lethe Press (*US*)
Liberties Press (*Ire*)

Stacey International (*UK*)
Stemmer House Publishers (*US*)
Stone Bridge Press (*US*)
Sunbury Press (*US*)
Sunscribe (*US*)
Sweet & Maxwell (*UK*)
SynergEbooks (*US*)
TSO (The Stationery Office) (*UK*)
Thames and Hudson Ltd (*UK*)
Top That! Publishing (*UK*)
Unicorn Press Ltd (*UK*)
Usborne Publishing (*UK*)
Vernon Press (an imprint of Vernon Art and Science Inc.) (*US*)
Western Psychological Services (*US*)
William Reed Business Media (*UK*)
William S. Hein & Co., Inc. (*US*)
Wolters Kluwer (UK) Ltd (*UK*)

Religious

American Press (*US*)
AMG Publishers (*US*)
Anaiah Press, LLC (*US*)
Ashgate Publishing Limited (*UK*)
Bethany House Publishers (*US*)
Blurbeo (*US*)
Brine Books Publishing (*Can*)
Bryntirion Press (*UK*)
The Catholic University of America Press (*US*)
Central Avenue Publishing (*Can*)
Christian Education (*UK*)
Church Publishing Incorporated (*US*)
Columba Press (*Ire*)
William B. Eerdmans Publishing Co. (*US*)
Ex-L-Ence Publishing (*UK*)
Floris Books (*UK*)
George Ronald Publisher (*UK*)
Geostar Publishing & Services LLC (*US*)
Gingko Library (*UK*)
Gomer Press (*UK*)
Halban Publishers (*UK*)
Harry N. Abrams, Inc. (*US*)
Harvest House Publishers (*US*)
Humanics Publishing Group (*US*)
IBEX Publishers, Inc. (*US*)
Icon Books Ltd (*UK*)
Ignatius Press (*US*)
Jewish Lights Publishing (*US*)
Kindred Productions (*Can*)
Kelly Point Publishing LLC (*US*)
Kirkbride Bible Company (*US*)
Kube Publishing (*UK*)
Legacy Press (*US*)
Lillenas Drama Resources (*US*)
Lion Hudson Plc (*UK*)
Listen & Live Audio, Inc. (*US*)
Martin Sisters Publishing (*US*)
Master Books (*US*)
Kevin Mayhew Publishers (*UK*)
Medallion Media Group (*US*)
Mercier Press (*Ire*)
Messianic Jewish Publishers (*US*)
Methodist Publishing (*UK*)
Monarch Books (*UK*)
NavPress (*US*)
The New Curiosity Shop (*UK*)
New York University (NYU) Press (*US*)
Nicolas Hays Publishers (*US*)
The O'Brien Press (*Ire*)
Oneworld Publications (*UK*)
Oxford University Press (*UK*)
P&R Publishing (*US*)
Paragon House (*US*)
Pauline Books and Media (*US*)
Pflaum Publishing Group (*US*)
Possibility Press (*US*)
Princeton University Press (*US*)
Princeton University Press Europe (*UK*)
Quest Books (*US*)
Rainbow Publishers (*US*)
Reference Service Press (*US*)
Rose and Crown Books (*UK*)
The Rosen Publishing Group, Inc. (*US*)
Rowman & Littlefield Publishing Group (*US*)
Scarecrow Press Inc. (*US*)
SCM-Canterbury Press (*UK*)
Scribe Publications Pty Ltd (*Aus*)
Skinner House Books (*US*)
Soft Skull Press (*US*)
Souvenir Press Ltd (*UK*)
St Augustine's Press (*US*)
St. Johann Press (*US*)
Stainer & Bell Ltd (*UK*)
Sunbury Press (*US*)
Sunscribe (*US*)
Sussex Academic Press (*UK*)
SynergEbooks (*US*)
Tantor Audio (*US*)
Tate Publishing and Enterprises, LLC (*US*)
Thames and Hudson Ltd (*UK*)
Tsaba House (*US*)
Tuttle Publishing (*US*)
Waveland Press, Inc. (*US*)
Westminster John Knox Press (WJK) (*US*)
Whitaker House (*US*)
Yale University Press (*US*)

Romance

Amakella Publishing (*US*)
Amira Press (*US*)
Anaiah Press, LLC (*US*)
Arrow Publications, LLC (*US*)
Barbarian Books (*US*)
BelleBooks (*US*)
Bethany House Publishers (*US*)
Black & White Publishing Ltd (*UK*)
Black Lyon Publishing, LLC (*US*)
Bloomsbury Spark (*UK*)
Blurbeo (*US*)
Bold Strokes Books (*US*)
Brine Books Publishing (*Can*)
Bullitt Publishing (*US*)
Canterbury House Publishing, Ltd (*US*)
Central Avenue Publishing (*Can*)
Corazon Books (*UK*)
Cup of Tea Books (*US*)
Dragonfairy Press (*US*)
Everheart Books (*Can*)

Lost Tower Publications (*UK*)
Lucky Marble Books (*US*)
M P Publishing USA (*US*)
Macmillan (*UK*)
Mandrake of Oxford (*UK*)
Martin Sisters Publishing (*US*)
Medallion Media Group (*US*)
NBM (*US*)
The New Curiosity Shop (*UK*)
The Orion Publishing Group Limited (*UK*)
Pure Indigo Limited (*UK*)
Quercus Books (*UK*)
Red Deer Press (*Can*)
Severn House Publishers (*UK*)
Small Beer Press (*US*)
Sunscribe (*US*)
SynergEbooks (*US*)
Tirgearr Publishing (*Ire*)
Tate Publishing and Enterprises, LLC (*US*)
Titan Books (*UK*)
Top Cow Productions, Inc (*US*)
Tu Books (*US*)
Twilight Times Books (*US*)

Scripts

Alma Classics (*UK*)
Aurora Metro Press (*UK*)
Bilingual Review Press (*US*)
Bronze Man Books (*US*)
Cressrelles Publishing Co. Ltd (*UK*)
Faber & Faber Ltd (*UK*)
The Gallery Press (*Ire*)
Gomer Press (*UK*)
Josef Weinberger Ltd (*UK*)
Lillenas Drama Resources (*US*)
The Lilliput Press (*Ire*)
Methuen Publishing Ltd (*UK*)
New Island (*Ire*)
New Playwrights' Network (NPN) (*UK*)
Nick Hern Books Ltd (*UK*)
Oberon Books (*UK*)
Parthian Books (*UK*)
Samuel French Ltd (*UK*)
Sunscribe (*US*)

Self-Help

Amakella Publishing (*US*)
Bick Publishing House (*US*)
Black Lyon Publishing, LLC (*US*)
Central Avenue Publishing (*Can*)
Conari Press (*US*)
Ex-L-Ence Publishing (*UK*)
Filbert Publishing (*US*)
Floris Books (*UK*)
Free Spirit Publishing (*US*)
Geostar Publishing & Services LLC (*US*)
Hawthorn Press (*UK*)
Hodder Education (*UK*)
Humanics Publishing Group (*US*)
Impact Publishers (*US*)
JIST Publishing (*US*)
Listen & Live Audio, Inc. (*US*)
Mandrake of Oxford (*UK*)
Martin Sisters Publishing (*US*)
New Holland Publishers (UK) Ltd (*UK*)
Nicolas Hays Publishers (*US*)
Nolo (*US*)
Oneworld Publications (*UK*)
Pauline Books and Media (*US*)
Piatkus Books (*UK*)
Possibility Press (*US*)
Princeton University Press (*US*)
Princeton University Press Europe (*UK*)
Quarto Publishing Group USA (*US*)
Quest Books (*US*)
Quill Driver Books (*US*)
Rainbow Books, Inc. (*US*)
Reading Harbor (*US*)
The Rosen Publishing Group, Inc. (*US*)
Roundhouse Group (*UK*)
Running Press (*US*)
Souvenir Press Ltd (*UK*)
Sunscribe (*US*)
SynergEbooks (*US*)
Tirgearr Publishing (*Ire*)
Tantor Audio (*US*)
Tate Publishing and Enterprises, LLC (*US*)
Tristan Publishing (*US*)
Tsaba House (*US*)
Whitaker House (*US*)
Wilshire Book Company (*US*)
Zambezi Publishing Ltd (*UK*)

Short Stories

A Swift Exit (*UK*)
Amakella Publishing (*US*)
Aurora Metro Press (*UK*)
BelleBooks (*US*)
Bilingual Review Press (*US*)
Black Lawrence Press (*US*)
Blackstaff Press Ltd (*UK*)
Blurbeo (*US*)
Brine Books Publishing (*Can*)
Bronze Man Books (*US*)
Central Avenue Publishing (*Can*)
Compelling Books (*UK*)
Darkhouse Books (*US*)
Dufour Editions (*US*)
Ex-L-Ence Publishing (*UK*)
Geostar Publishing & Services LLC (*US*)
Ghostwoods Books (*UK*)
HarperImpulse (*UK*)
Headland Publications (*UK*)
Hearts 'N Tummies Cookbook Co. / Quixote Press (*US*)
Honno Welsh Women's Press (*UK*)
Influx Press (*UK*)
Iron Press (*UK*)
Jupiter Gardens Press (*US*)
Kelly Point Publishing LLC (*US*)
Kind of a Hurricane Press (*US*)
Ledge Hill Publishing (*US*)
Les Figues Press (*US*)
M P Publishing USA (*US*)
Manor House Publishing (*Can*)
Martin Sisters Publishing (*US*)
Mudfog Press (*UK*)
Neon (*UK*)
New Island (*Ire*)

Wooden Books (*UK*)
Westminster John Knox Press (WJK) (*US*)
Whitaker House (*US*)
Wilshire Book Company (*US*)
Zambezi Publishing Ltd (*UK*)

Sport

American Press (*US*)
Aureus Publishing Limited (*UK*)
Aurum Press Ltd (*UK*)
Barron's Educational Series, Inc. (*US*)
Black & White Publishing Ltd (*UK*)
Blackline Press (*UK*)
Blackstaff Press Ltd (*UK*)
Blink Publishing (*UK*)
Bloomsbury Publishing Plc (*UK*)
Capstone (*US*)
Carlton Publishing Group (*UK*)
Central Avenue Publishing (*Can*)
Chicago Review Press (*US*)
The Crowood Press (*UK*)
Cyclotour Guide Books (*US*)
Eakin Press (*US*)
Ex-L-Ence Publishing (*UK*)
Geostar Publishing & Services LLC (*US*)
Gill & Macmillan (*Ire*)
Gomer Press (*UK*)
HarperCollins Publishers Ltd (*UK*)
Harry N. Abrams, Inc. (*US*)
Headline Publishing Group (*UK*)
Hinkler Books (*Aus*)
The History Press (*UK*)
Icon Books Ltd (*UK*)
Indigo Dreams Publishing (*UK*)
Kelly Point Publishing LLC (*US*)
Liberties Press (*Ire*)
The Lilliput Press (*Ire*)
Listen & Live Audio, Inc. (*US*)
Luath Press Ltd (*UK*)
Lucky Marble Books (*US*)
The Lyons Press Inc. (*US*)
Macmillan (*UK*)
Mainstream Publishing Co. (Edinburgh) Ltd (*UK*)
McBooks Press (*US*)
McFarland & Company, Inc. (*US*)
Mentor Books (*Ire*)
Mercier Press (*Ire*)
Merlin Unwin Books (*UK*)
Methuen Publishing Ltd (*UK*)
Milo Books Ltd (*UK*)
The New Curiosity Shop (*UK*)
New Holland Publishers (UK) Ltd (*UK*)
The O'Brien Press (*Ire*)
The Orion Publishing Group Limited (*UK*)
Quarto Publishing Group UK (*UK*)
Quarto Publishing Group USA (*US*)
Quiller Publishing Ltd (*UK*)
The Rosen Publishing Group, Inc. (*US*)
Roundhouse Group (*UK*)
Running Press (*US*)
Scarecrow Press Inc. (*US*)
Seren Books (*UK*)
Shire Publications Ltd (*UK*)
Souvenir Press Ltd (*UK*)
SportsBooks Limited (*UK*)
St. Johann Press (*US*)
Sunscribe (*US*)
Tantor Audio (*US*)
Tate Publishing and Enterprises, LLC (*US*)
Tuttle Publishing (*US*)

Suspense

Amira Press (*US*)
Anaiah Press, LLC (*US*)
Arrow Publications, LLC (*US*)
Barbarian Books (*US*)
BelleBooks (*US*)
Bethany House Publishers (*US*)
Blurbeo (*US*)
Brine Books Publishing (*Can*)
Canterbury House Publishing, Ltd (*US*)
Central Avenue Publishing (*Can*)
Ex-L-Ence Publishing (*UK*)
Geostar Publishing & Services LLC (*US*)
Harvest House Publishers (*US*)
Highland Press (*US*)
Indigo Dreams Publishing (*UK*)
Loose Id (*US*)
Lost Tower Publications (*UK*)
Lucky Marble Books (*US*)
M P Publishing USA (*US*)
Medallion Media Group (*US*)
Roberts Press (*US*)
Sunscribe (*US*)
SynergEbooks (*US*)
Tirgearr Publishing (*Ire*)
Tantor Audio (*US*)
Tate Publishing and Enterprises, LLC (*US*)
Tsaba House (*US*)
Turn the Page Publishing LLC (*US*)
Twilight Times Books (*US*)

Technology

American Press (*US*)
Atlantic Europe Publishing (*UK*)
Bernard Babani (publishing) Ltd (*UK*)
Brown, Son & Ferguson, Ltd (*UK*)
Central Avenue Publishing (*Can*)
Compelling Books (*UK*)
Continental (*US*)
Ex-L-Ence Publishing (*UK*)
Geostar Publishing & Services LLC (*US*)
Gingko Library (*UK*)
Gulf Publishing Company (*US*)
Gun Digest Books (*US*)
HOW Books (*US*)
Metal Powder Industries Federation (MPIF) (*US*)
Mitchell Lane Publishers, Inc. (*US*)
Morgan Kaufmann Publishers (*US*)
The New Curiosity Shop (*UK*)
Possibility Press (*US*)
Princeton University Press (*US*)
Quarto Publishing Group USA (*US*)
Quill Driver Books (*US*)
Shire Publications Ltd (*UK*)
Sunscribe (*US*)
Tirgearr Publishing (*Ire*)

The Lilliput Press (*Ire*)
Frances Lincoln Ltd (*UK*)
Logaston Press (*UK*)
Lonely Planet Publications (*US*)
Luath Press Ltd (*UK*)
Macmillan (*UK*)
Mandala Earth (*US*)
Methuen Publishing Ltd (*UK*)
Michelin Maps and Guides (*UK*)
Neil Wilson Publishing Ltd (*UK*)
The New Curiosity Shop (*UK*)
New Holland Publishers (UK) Ltd (*UK*)
New Island (*Ire*)
The O'Brien Press (*Ire*)
Onstream Publications Ltd (*Ire*)
The Orion Publishing Group Limited (*UK*)
Ouen Press (*UK*)
The Overmountain Press (*US*)
Paul Dry Books, Inc. (*US*)
Pen & Sword Books Ltd (*UK*)
Phaidon Press Limited (*UK*)
Poolbeg (*Ire*)
Quarto Publishing Group USA (*US*)
Quill Driver Books (*US*)
Quiller Publishing Ltd (*UK*)
Rio Nuevo Publishers (*US*)
Rose and Crown Books (*UK*)
Roundhouse Group (*UK*)
Seafarer Books (*UK*)
Seren Books (*UK*)
Shire Publications Ltd (*UK*)
Sierra Club Books (*US*)
Sigma Press (*UK*)
Soft Skull Press (*US*)
Souvenir Press Ltd (*UK*)
Stacey International (*UK*)
Stone Bridge Press (*US*)
Sunscribe (*US*)
SynergEbooks (*US*)
Thames and Hudson Ltd (*UK*)
Tuttle Publishing (*US*)
Voyageur Press (*US*)

TV

BFI Publishing (*UK*)
Ex-L-Ence Publishing (*UK*)
Geostar Publishing & Services LLC (*US*)
Headline Publishing Group (*UK*)
Macmillan (*UK*)
Manchester University Press (*UK*)
Soft Skull Press (*US*)
Sunscribe (*US*)
Titan Books (*UK*)

Westerns

Amira Press (*US*)
Barbarian Books (*US*)
Brine Books Publishing (*Can*)
Central Avenue Publishing (*Can*)
Ex-L-Ence Publishing (*UK*)
Geostar Publishing & Services LLC (*US*)
Harvest House Publishers (*US*)
Indigo Dreams Publishing (*UK*)
Kelly Point Publishing LLC (*US*)
Loose Id (*US*)
Robert Hale Publishers (*UK*)
Sunscribe (*US*)
SynergEbooks (*US*)
Tirgearr Publishing (*Ire*)
Tantor Audio (*US*)
Tate Publishing and Enterprises, LLC (*US*)

Women's Interests

Amakella Publishing (*US*)
Anaiah Press, LLC (*US*)
Arch Street Press (*US*)
Arrow Publications, LLC (*US*)
Aurora Metro Press (*UK*)
BelleBooks (*US*)
Bethany House Publishers (*US*)
Black Lyon Publishing, LLC (*US*)
Blurbeo (*US*)
Brine Books Publishing (*Can*)
Central Avenue Publishing (*Can*)
Chicago Review Press (*US*)
Conari Press (*US*)
Corazon Books (*UK*)
Cork University Press (*Ire*)
Crescent Moon Publishing (*UK*)
Cup of Tea Books (*US*)
Ex-L-Ence Publishing (*UK*)
Geostar Publishing & Services LLC (*US*)
Ghostwoods Books (*UK*)
Gibson Square Books Ltd (*UK*)
Gival Press, LLC (*US*)
Harvest House Publishers (*US*)
Honno Welsh Women's Press (*UK*)
Indigo Dreams Publishing (*UK*)
Jewish Lights Publishing (*US*)
Kelly Point Publishing LLC (*US*)
Lost Tower Publications (*UK*)
M P Publishing USA (*US*)
Marion Boyars Publishers (*UK*)
McFarland & Company, Inc. (*US*)
The New Curiosity Shop (*UK*)
New Island (*Ire*)
New York University (NYU) Press (*US*)
P&R Publishing (*US*)
Persephone Books (*UK*)
Ragged Sky Press (*US*)
Reading Harbor (*US*)
Reference Service Press (*US*)
Roberts Press (*US*)
Second Story Press (*Can*)
Soft Skull Press (*US*)
Souvenir Press Ltd (*UK*)
Sunscribe (*US*)
Sussex Academic Press (*UK*)
Tirgearr Publishing (*Ire*)
Tantor Audio (*US*)
Trentham Books Limited (*UK*)
Tsaba House (*US*)
Turn the Page Publishing LLC (*US*)
Twilight Times Books (*US*)
Vanderbilt University Press (*US*)
Virago Press (*UK*)
Waveland Press, Inc. (*US*)
Whitaker House (*US*)
Zebra (*US*)

US Magazines

For the most up-to-date listings of these and hundreds of other magazines, visit http://www.firstwriter.com/magazines

*To claim your **free** access to the site, please see the back of this book.*

The Alembic

Providence College
English Department
Attn: The Alembic Editors
1 Cunningham Square
Providence, RI 02918-0001
Email: Alembic@providence.edu
Website: http://www.providence.edu/english/creative-writing/Pages/alembic.aspx

Publishes: Fiction; Poetry; Scripts; *Areas:* Drama; Short Stories; *Markets:* Adult; *Treatments:* Literary

Publishes poetry, drama, and fiction – including short stories and self-contained excerpts of novels. Send up to 5 poems or prose up to 6,000 words by post with return postage if return of material required. Accepts submissions from August 1 to November 30 annually.

A&U

Main Office
25 Monroe Street, Suite 205
Albany, New York 12210
Tel: +1 (518) 426-9010
Fax: +1 (518) 436-5354
Email: mailbox@aumag.org
Website: http://www.aumag.org

Articles; Essays; Fiction; Interviews; News; Nonfiction; Poetry; Reviews; *Areas:* Culture; Health; Medicine; Politics; Short Stories; *Markets:* Adult

Editors: David Waggoner

Publishes material covering the medical, cultural, and political responses to AIDS **only**. Does not publish material unconnected to AIDS so please do not send any. For fiction, and poetry, send complete MS. For nonfiction send query with published clips. Accepts approaches by email.

American Indian Art Magazine

7314 East Osborn Drive
Scottsdale, AZ 85251
Tel: +1 (480) 994-5445
Fax: +1 (480) 945-9533
Email: editorial@aiamagazine.com
Website: http://www.aiamagazine.com

Publishes: Articles; Nonfiction; *Areas:* Arts; *Markets:* Adult; Professional

Publishes articles covering the art of all native Americans. Articles should be of interest to both casual readers and professionals. See website for full guidelines.

Able Muse

467 Saratoga Avenue, #602
San Jose, CA 95129
Email: submission@ablemuse.com
Website: http://www.ablemuse.com

Publishes: Essays; Fiction; Interviews; Nonfiction; Poetry; Reviews; *Areas:* Short Stories; Translations; *Markets:* Adult; *Treatments:* Light; Literary

Editors: Alex Pepple

Publishes mainly metrical poetry and poetry in translation. All forms of formal poetry welcome. Also publishes fiction, and nonfiction relating to metrical poetry, including book reviews and interviews. Accepts electronic submissions only – preferably using online submission system, but will also accept submissions by email. Welcomes humorous and light poetry. See website for full details.

The Adirondack Review

Email: editors@theadirondackreview.com
Website: http://adirondackreview.homestead.com

Publishes: Fiction; Nonfiction; Poetry; Reviews; *Areas:* Arts; Photography; Short Stories; Translations; Markets

Editors: Angela Leroux-Lindsey

Publishes poetry, fiction, translation, art, photography, and book reviews. Submit through online system via website.

Adventure Cyclist

150 East Pine Street
Missoula, MT 59802
Tel: +1 (406) 532-2762
Email: mdeme@adventurecycling.org
Website: http://www.adventurecycling.org/adventure-cyclist

Publishes: Articles; Essays; Features; Nonfiction; *Areas:* How-to; Technology; Travel; *Markets:* Adult

Editors: Mike Deme

Magazine dedicated to bicycle travel and adventure. See website for full submission guidelines, and submit using online submission system.

African-American Career World

Equal Opportunity Publications, Inc.
445 Broad Hollow Road, Suite 425
Melville, NY 11747
Tel: +1 (631) 421-9421
Fax: +1 (631) 421-1352
Email: info@eop.com
Website: http://www.eop.com

Publishes: Articles; Nonfiction; Reference; *Areas:* How-to; Self-Help; *Markets:* Adult; Professional

Careers magazine aimed at African Americans.

Akron Life

1653 Merriman Road, Suite 116
Akron OH 44313
Tel: +1 (330) 253-0056
Fax: +1 (330) 253-5868
Email: editor@bakermediagroup.com
Website: http://www.akronlife.com

Publishes: Articles; Features; Interviews; Nonfiction; *Areas:* Arts; Beauty and Fashion; Culture; Entertainment; Gardening; Health; Historical; How-to; Humour; Leisure; Lifestyle; Travel; *Markets:* Adult

Editors: Abby Cymerman

Monthly regional lifestyle publication committed to providing information that enhances and enriches the experience of living in or visiting Akron and the surrounding region of Summit, Portage, Medina and Stark Counties.

Alimentum

PO Box 210028
Nashville, TN 37221
Email: editor@alimentumjournal.com
Website: http://www.alimentumjournal.com

Publishes: Essays; Fiction; Nonfiction; Poetry; Reviews; *Areas:* Cookery; Short Stories; *Markets:* Adult; *Treatments:* Literary

Editors: Peter Selgin, fiction and nonfiction editor; Cortney Davis, poetry editor

Publishes poetry, fiction, creative nonfiction, book reviews, and art, related to food. Send submissions by post with SAE in specific submission windows. See website for more details.

The Allegheny Review

Allegheny College Box 32
520 North Main Street
Meadville, PA 16335
Email: review@allegheny.edu
Website:
https://alleghenyreview.wordpress.com

Publishes: Fiction; Nonfiction; Poetry; *Areas:* Short Stories; *Markets:* Adult; *Treatments:* Literary

National magazine publishing the work of enrolled undergraduate students. Submit fiction or creative nonfiction up to 20 double-spaced pages, or up to five poems. Submissions via online form only. See website for details.

Allegory

Email: submissions@allegoryezine.com
Website: http://www.allegoryezine.com

Publishes: Articles; Fiction; Nonfiction; *Areas:* Fantasy; Horror; Humour; Sci-Fi; Short Stories; *Markets:* Adult

Editors: Ty Drago

Online magazine specialising in science fiction, fantasy and horror, but also willing to consider humour and general interest fiction. No specific length restrictions for fiction, but stories under 500 words or over 5,000 may be hard sells. Also publishes articles up to 2,000 words on the art or business of writing. All submissions must be as attachments by email. See website for full guidelines.

Alligator Juniper

Prescott College
220 Grove Avenue
Prescott, AZ 86301
Email: alligatorjuniper@prescott.edu
Website: http://www.alligatorjuniper.org

Publishes: Fiction; Nonfiction; Poetry; *Areas:* Short Stories; *Markets:* Adult; *Treatments:* Literary

Annual magazine publishing winners and finalists from its annual competitions only. $18 entry fee. Open August 15 – October 15 each year. Submit through online submission system. Winner in each category receives $1,000. Submit up to 5 poems, or a piece of fiction or creative nonfiction up to 30 pages. No children's literature or strict genre work. All entrants receive a copy of the magazine.

American Careers

6701 West 64th Street, Suite 210
Overland Park, KS 66202
Tel: +1 (800) 669-7795
Email: ccinfo@carcom.com
Website: http://www.carcom.com

Publishes: Articles; Nonfiction; *Areas:* How-to; Self-Help; *Markets:* Children's

Publishes career information for middle and high school students. Send query with sample and CV in first instance.

American Turf Monthly

747 Middle Neck Road
Great Neck, NY 11024
Tel: +1 (516) 773-4075
Fax: +1 (516) 773-2944
Email: editor@americanturf.com
Website: http://www.americanturf.com

Publishes: Articles; Nonfiction; *Areas:* Sport; *Markets:* Adult

Editors: Joe Girardi

Horse racing magazine aimed at horseplayers, focusing on handicapping and wagering. Not aimed at owners or breeders. Send query in first instance.

Amulet

PO Box 761495
San Antonio, CA 78245

or

PO Box 884223
San Francisco, CA 94188-4223
Email: amulet20032003@yahoo.com
Website:
https://sites.google.com/site/conceitmagazine/home/amulet

Publishes: Poetry; *Markets:* Adult

Editors: Perry Terrell

Publishes 16 writers each month – both new and established writers. Unsolicited, simultaneous, and previously published manuscripts are welcomed. No reading fee. Submit by post or by email.

Analog Science Fiction & Fact

44 Wall Street, Suite 904
New York, NY 10005-2401
Email: analog@dellmagazines.com
Website: http://www.analogsf.com

Publishes: Articles; Fiction; Poetry; *Areas:* Science; Sci-Fi; Short Stories; *Markets:* Adult

Editors: Trevor Quachri

Publishes short stories with few restrictions: the story must have some aspect of science or technology as an integral part of it (i.e. the story can't happen without it), and the characters must be believable (though not necassarily human), regardless of how fantastic the setting. For fiction, between 2,000 and 7,000 words for shorts is preferred, 10,000–20,000 words for novelettes, and 40,000–80,000 for serials. For serials, send query in first instance. Otherwise send complete MS.

Also publishes articles of current and future interest (i.e. at the cutting edge of research). Though subscribers tend to have a high level of technical knowledge they come from a wide variety of backgrounds, and therefore specialised jargon should be kept to a minimum. Contributors should also remember that the magazine is read largely for entertainment, and your style should reflect this.

Submit using online submission system on website. If absolutely necessary, accepts submissions by post with return postage. No submissions by fax or email. See website for full guidelines.

Ancient Paths

Email: skylarburris@yahoo.com
Website:
http://www.editorskylar.com/magazine/table.html

Publishes: Fiction; Poetry; *Areas:* Religious; Short Stories; *Markets:* Adult; *Treatments:* Literary

Editors: Skylar Hamilton Burris

Contains writing and art that makes the reader both think and feel. The poems, stories, and art celebrate God, depict the consequences of sin, and explore man's struggle with faith. The editor favors works that convey a message subtly without directly telling the reader what to think. This magazine is a Christian publication, but works by non-Christian authors will be considered provided that the themes, values, and issues explored are appropriate in a Christian context.

As of 2012, this publication is online only.

Angus Beef Bulletin

3201 Frederick Avenue
St Joseph, MO 64506-2997
Tel: +1 (816) 383-5270
Email: shermel@angusjournal.com
Website: http://www.angusbeefbulletin.com

Publishes: Articles; Interviews; Nonfiction; *Areas:* Business; How-to; Nature; Technology; *Markets:* Professional; *Treatments:* Commercial

Editors: Shauna Rose Hermel

Publishes material aimed at commercial cattle owners of Angus bulls.

Another Chicago Magazine (ACM)

Email: editors@anotherchicagomagazine.net

Website: http://www.anotherchicagomagazine.net

Publishes: Fiction; Nonfiction; Poetry; *Areas:* Short Stories; *Markets:* Adult; *Treatments:* Literary

Literary magazine publishing work by both new and established writers. Send up to 5 poems; fiction up to 7,500 words; or nonfiction up to 25 pages. Submit via website using online submission system only. $3 fee per submission.

Apalachee Review

PO Box 10469
Tallahassee, FL 32302
Email: ARsubmissions@gmail.com
Website: http://apalacheereview.org

Publishes: Fiction; Nonfiction; Poetry; *Areas:* Short Stories; *Markets:* Adult; *Treatments:* Literary

Editors: Michael Trammell; Jenn Bronson

Publishes fiction, poetry, and creative nonfiction. Send one story (or more, if very short), or 3-5 poems, with SASE. Will consider chapters of novels if they work by themselves, but no short story collections or novels. Accepts simultaneous submissions. Aims to reply within four months. Send query by email for details of submissions policies for writers outside the US. See website for full details.

Appalachian Heritage

Borea College
101 Chestnut Street
Berea, KY 40403
Email: appalachianheritage@berea.edu
Website: http://appalachianheritage.net

Publishes: Essays; Fiction; Nonfiction; Poetry; Reviews; *Areas:* Short Stories; *Markets:* Adult; Youth; *Treatments:* Literary

Strives to be a literary sanctuary for the finest contemporary writing. Publishes previously unpublished fiction, creative nonfiction, poetry, writing for young adults, literary craft essays, book reviews, and visual art. No genre fiction.

Apple Valley Review

Email: editor@leahbrowning.net
Website: http://applevalleyreview.com

Publishes: Essays; Fiction; Nonfiction; Poetry; *Areas:* Short Stories; *Markets:* Adult; *Treatments:* Literary; Positive

Editors: Leah Browning

Online literary journal, publishing poetry, short fiction, and essays. Prose should be between 100 and 4,000 words. Preference is given to non-rhyming poetry under two pages in length. No genre fiction, scholarly, critical, inspirational, children's, erotica, explicit, violent, or depressing. Submit up to three prose pieces or up to six poems, by email. See website for full submission guidelines.

Aquatics International

6222 Wilshire Boulevard, Suite 600
Los Angeles, CA 90048
Tel: +1 (972) 536-6439
Email: etaylor@hanleywood.com
Website: http://www.aquaticsintl.com

Publishes: Articles; Interviews; Nonfiction; *Areas:* Business; How-to; Technology; Theatre; *Markets:* Professional

Editors: Erika Taylor, Editorial Director

Magazine aimed at professionals in the commercial and public swimming pool industries. Send query with published clips.

Aries

c/o Dr. Price
McMurray, General Editor
Texas Wesleyan University
Department of Languages and Literature
1201 Wesleyan
Fort Worth, TX 76105-1536
Email: aries@txwes.edu
Website: http://ariesjournal.wix.com/aries

Publishes: Essays; Fiction; Nonfiction; Poetry; Scripts; *Areas:* Drama; Short Stories; Theatre; *Markets:* Adult; *Treatments:* Literary

Editors: Dr Price McMurray (General Editor); Rolandra West (Managing Editor)

Literary journal inviting submissions of original, unpublished poetry (including poetry written by the author in Spanish and then translated to English); fiction; essays; one-act plays; and black-and-white photography and art. Submit up to 5 poems or one piece of prose up to 4,000 words, between August 15 and December 15 annually. See website for full submission guidelines.

Arms Control Today

1313 L Street, NW, Suite 130
Washington, DC 20005
Tel: +1 (202) 463-8270
Fax: +1 (202) 463-8273
Email: aca@armscontrol.org
Website: https://www.armscontrol.org

Publishes: Articles; Nonfiction; *Areas:* Military; *Markets:* Adult; Professional

Publishes articles providing information and ideas to solve global nuclear, biological, chemical, and conventional weapons-related security challenges. Articles should be aimed at both experts and non-experts. Send query with outline in first instance.

Artifact Nouveau

Delta College, Shima 310
5151 Pacific Avenue
Stockton, CA 95207
Tel: +1 (209) 954-5533
Email: artifactsjdc@gmail.com
Website: https://www.deltacollege.edu/org/wrtrsgld/pubinfo.htm

Publishes: Essays; Fiction; Nonfiction; Poetry; *Areas:* Adventure; Arts; Autobiography; Criticism; Culture; Current Affairs; Drama; Entertainment; Erotic; Fantasy; Horror; Humour; Leisure; Lifestyle; Literature; Media; Music; Mystery; Nature; New Age; Philosophy; Photography; Politics; Romance; Sci-Fi; Short Stories; Spiritual; Suspense; Theatre; Thrillers; TV; Westerns; Women's Interests; *Markets:* Academic; Adult; *Treatments:* Contemporary; Experimental; In-depth; Literary; Popular; Progressive; Satirical; Serious; Traditional

A magazine of works by students, faculty, alumni, and employees of the college and Writers' Guild. Currently in its first year of publication, it is a re-branding of a previous publication (2007-2014). With a new advisor, officers, and editors, the magazine was re-booted to reflect its new beginnings. Its current format is 5.5 x 8.5 in a full color presentation. Works by writers and artists unaffiliated with the College may be selected for publication for up to 15% of the overall content. We accept submissions year round. All genres and mediums are welcome. Submit by email.

Asheville Poetry Review

PO Box 7086
Asheville, NC 28802
Email: editor@ashevillepoetryreview.com
Website: http://www.ashevillepoetryreview.com

Publishes: Essays; Interviews; Nonfiction; Poetry; Reviews; *Areas:* Translations; *Markets:* Adult; *Treatments:* Literary

Editors: Keith Flynn

Accepts regular submissions between January 15 and July 15 each year. Send 3-6 poems of any length or style, with SASE. Between July 15 and January 15 each year, accepts submissions through its annual poetry competition: $1,000 prize and $20 entry fee. No submissions by email.

Astronomy

Kalmbach Publishing
21027 Crossroads Circle
PO Box 1612
Waukesha, WI 53187-1612
Tel: +1 (800) 533-6644
Fax: +1 (262) 798-6468
Website: http://www.astronomy.com

Publishes: Articles; *Areas:* Hobbies; How-to; Science; *Markets:* Adult

Magazine publishing articles on the science and hobby of astronomy. Send query by post or via form on website.

ATV Rider Magazine

GrindMedia, LLC
1733 Alton Parkway
Irvine, CA 92606
Tel: +1 (763) 383-4499
Website: http://www.atvrider.com

Publishes: Articles; Features; Interviews; Nonfiction; *Areas:* Hobbies; Technology; Travel; *Markets:* Adult

Editors: John Prusak

Magazine for all-terain vehicle enthusiasts. Send query with published clips.

Autograph Collector

Odyssey Publications
510-A South Corona Mall
Corona, CA 92879
Email: editorev@telus.net
Website: http://autographmagazine.com

Publishes: Articles; Interviews; Nonfiction; *Areas:* Historical; Hobbies; How-to; *Markets:* Adult

Magazine for collectors of autographs.

Backpacker

2520 55th Street, Suite 210
Boulder, CO 80301
Email: dlewon@backpacker.com
Website: http://www.backpacker.com

Publishes: Articles; Essays; Features; Interviews; Nonfiction; *Areas:* Hobbies; How-to; Travel; *Markets:* Adult

Editors: Dennis Lewon, Editor-in-Chief

Hiking magazine covering destinations, personality, skills, and gear. Send query by email (preferred) or by post with SASE, with published clips. See website for full guidelines.

Baltimore Magazine

1000 Lancaster Street, Suite 400 Baltimore, MD 21202
Tel: +1 (410) 752-4200
Fax: +1 (410) 625-0280
Email: frontdesk@baltimoremagazine.net
Website: http://www.baltimoremagazine.net

Publishes: Articles; Features; News; Nonfiction; *Markets:* Adult

Editors: Max Weiss; Suzanne Loudermilk; Ken Iglehart; John Lewis; Amy Mulvihill

Regional magazine serving the Baltimore metropolitan area, focussing on local people, events, trends, and ideas. See website for writer's guidelines.

Bartleby Snopes

Website: http://www.bartlebysnopes.com

Publishes: Fiction; *Areas:* Short Stories; *Markets:* Adult; *Treatments:* Literary

Publishes short stories between 1,000 and 3,000 words, and flash fiction up to 1,200 words (stories between 1,000 and 1,200 can be either). Submit online via website submission system.

Bee Culture

PO Box 706
Medina, OH 44256-0706
Tel: +1 (330) 725-6677
Fax: +1 (330) 725-5624
Email: info@BeeCulture.com
Website: http://www.beeculture.com

Publishes: Articles; Interviews; Nonfiction; *Areas:* Hobbies; Nature; Science; Technology; *Markets:* Adult; Professional; *Treatments:* In-depth

Magazine of beekeeping. See website for writers' guidelines.

Bible Advocate

PO Box 33677

Denver, CO 80233
Tel: +1 (303) 452-7973
Email: bibleadvocate@cog7.org
Website: http://baonline.org

Publishes: Articles; Features; Nonfiction; Poetry; *Areas:* Current Affairs; Lifestyle; Religious; Sociology; *Markets:* Adult

Christian magazine publishing articles on Bible doctrine, current social and religious issues, Christian living, Bible topics, textual/biblical book studies, prophecy, personal experience, and poetry (traditional, free, and blank verse). Prefers email submissions. See website for full guidelines.

Big Fiction

Email: info@bigfictionmagazine.com
Website:
http://www.bigfictionmagazine.com

Publishes: Fiction; *Areas:* Short Stories; *Markets:* Adult; *Treatments:* Literary

Literary magazine devoted to longer short fiction, between 7,500 and 30,000 words. Accepts submissions online via competition ($20 entry fee).

BirdWatching Magazine

25 Braintree Hill Office Park, Suite 404
Braintree, MA 02184
Tel: +1 (617) 706-9098
Email: mail@birdwatchingdaily.com
Website: http://www.birdwatchingdaily.com

Publishes: Essays; Features; Interviews; Nonfiction; *Areas:* Hobbies; How-to; Nature; Photography; Travel; *Markets:* Adult

Editors: Matt Mendenhall

Magazine for bird watchers. Send query with published clips.

Black Heart Magazine

Email: laura@blackheartmagazine.com
Website: http://blackheartmagazine.com

Publishes: Fiction; Interviews; Nonfiction; Poetry; Reviews; *Areas:* Arts; Crime; Criticism; Fantasy; Humour; Literature; Mystery; Philosophy; Sci-Fi; Short Stories; Suspense; *Markets:* Adult; *Treatments:* Contemporary; Cynical; Dark; Experimental; Light; Literary; Positive; Progressive; Satirical

Editors: Laura Roberts

An independent online literary magazine, transmitting our tenacious texts around the world at the speed of wifi. Tthe site has been combating clichés and berating boring wordslinging since 2004. Our objective can be summarised in three short words:

Reading. Writing. Rebellion.

That's LITERARY rebellion, so ease off the trigger there, tiger.

In brief, we publish fiction that breaks the rules. Join us, if you dare.

Bow & Arrow Hunting

Beckett Media LLC
22840 Savi Ranch Parkway, Suite 200
Yorba Linda, CA 92887
Tel: +1 (714) 200-1900
Fax: +1 (800) 249-7761
Email: editorial@bowandarrowhunting.com
Website:
http://www.bowandarrowhunting.com

Publishes: Articles; Features; News; Nonfiction; Reviews; *Areas:* Nature; Sport; *Markets:* Adult

Editors: Joe Bell

Magazine for bow-hunting enthusiasts. Send complete ms.

Brew Your Own

PO Box 469121
Escondido, CA 92046
Tel: +1 (800) 900-7594
Fax: +1 (760) 738-4805
Email: edit@byo.com
Website: http://byo.com

Publishes: Articles; Interviews; Nonfiction; *Areas:* Cookery; Hobbies; How-to;

Technology; *Markets:* Adult

Magazine for home brewing enthusiasts. Send query with published clips, or details of brewing expertise, in first instance.

Burnside Review

Portland, Oregon
Email: sid@burnsidereview.org
Website: http://burnsidereview.org

Publishes: Fiction; Poetry; *Areas:* Short Stories; *Markets:* Adult

Editors: Sid Miller

Publishes poetry and fiction. Send 3-5 poems and brief bio, or fiction up to 5,000 words (can be collections of flash fiction or a single story), using online submission system only. $3 fee.

Business NH Magazine

55 South Commercial Street
Manchester, NH 03101

Tel: +1 (603) 626-6354
Fax: +1 (603) 626-6359
Email: edit@BusinessNHmagazine.com
Website: http://millyardcommunications.com

Publishes: Articles; Features; Interviews; News; Nonfiction; *Areas:* Business; How-to; *Markets:* Professional

Editors: Matthew J. Mowry

New Hampshire business magazine aimed at the business owners and managers of New Hampshire.

B'nai B'rith Magazine

2020 K Street, NW, 7th Floor
Washington, DC 20006
Tel: +1 (202) 857-6539
Email: bbmag@bnaibrith.org
Website: http://www.bnaibrith.org

Publishes: Articles; Features; Interviews; Nonfiction; *Areas:* Culture; Current Affairs; Historical; Lifestyle; Politics; Religious; Sociology; Travel; *Markets:* Adult

Jewish magazine focussing on the North American and Isreali Jewish communities. Send query with published clips.

California Lawyer

44 Montgomery Street, Suite 500
San Francisco, CA 94104
Tel: +1 (415) 296-2400
Fax: +1 (415) 296-2440
Email: Chuleenan_Svetvilas@dailyjournal.com
Website: http://www.callawyer.com

Publishes: Articles; Features; News; Nonfiction; *Areas:* Legal; *Markets:* Professional

Editors: Chuleenan Svetvilas

Magazine aimed at professionals working in the Californian legal market.

Cape Cod Life

13 Steeple Street
Mashpee, MA 02649
Tel: +1 (508) 419-7381
Fax: +1 (508) 477-1225
Email: info@capecodlife.com
Website: http://capecodlife.com

Publishes: Articles; Features; Interviews; Nonfiction; *Areas:* Business; Culture; Historical; Lifestyle; Nature; Travel; *Markets:* Adult

Lifestyle magazine covering the area of Cape Cod, sold locally, nationally, and internationally. Freelances have a good chance of publication. Send query with wide selection of writers' clips in first instance.

Carbon Culture Review

PO Box 1643
Moriarty, NM 87035
Email: editorial@carbonculturereview.com
Website: http://www.carbonculturereview.com

Publishes: Articles; Essays; Features; Fiction; Interviews; Nonfiction; Poetry; Reviews; *Areas:* Adventure; Anthropology; Architecture; Arts; Business; Crafts; Crime;

Criticism; Culture; Design; Drama; Entertainment; Fantasy; Film; Gothic; Hobbies; Humour; Literature; Media; Medicine; Military; Mystery; Philosophy; Photography; Radio; Science; Sci-Fi; Short Stories; Sociology; Suspense; Technology; Thrillers; Translations; *Markets:* Adult; *Treatments:* Commercial; Contemporary; Dark; Experimental; Literary; Mainstream; Niche; Popular

Editors: Jessica Housand-Weaver

A journal at the intersection of technology and literature and art. Available in bookstores in the United States, we feature monthly creative work, literature and art as well as articles and reviews on exciting new tech online alongside our annual print edition.

For more information, please visit our website or Submittable page.

Carve Magazine

PO Box 701510
Dallas, TX 75370
Email: managingeditor@carvezine.com
Website: http://carvezine.com

Publishes: Fiction; *Areas:* Short Stories; *Markets:* Adult; *Treatments:* Literary

Editors: Kristin S. vanNamen, PhD

Publishes literary fiction up to 10,000 words, and poetry/fiction crossovers: poetry that tells a story; or flash fiction that has a lyrical feel, etc. No genre fiction or previously published fiction. Submit by post for free, or via online submission system for $3. See website for full guidelines.

Cat Fancy

I-5 Publishing
PO Box 6050
Mission Viejo, CA 92690
Tel: +1 (949) 855-8822
Fax: +1 (949) 855-3045
Email: query@catfancy.com
Website: http://www.catfancy.com

Publishes: Articles; Features; Nonfiction; *Areas:* Health; How-to; Lifestyle; Nature; Markets

Magazine covering the subjects of cats and cat ownership. No unsolicited mss. Send query by post or email between January and May only.

Cemetery Moon

Email: cemeterymoon@yahoo.com
Website: http://www.fortresspublishinginc.com

Publishes: Fiction; Poetry; *Areas:* Gothic; Horror; Short Stories; Suspense; *Markets:* Adult

Editors: Chris Pisano

Publishes horror, suspense, and/or gothc short stories and poetry. Send submissions as Word documents by email.

Chamber Music Magazine

12 West 32nd Street, 7th Floor
New York, NY 10001-3813
Tel: +1 (212) 242-2022
Fax: +1 (212) 967-9747
Email: egoldensohn@chamber-music.org
Website: http://www.chamber-music.org

Publishes: Articles; Essays; Nonfiction; *Areas:* Music; *Markets:* Adult

Editors: Ellen Goldensohn

Magazine publishing material on chamber music. Send query with published clips in first instance.

Chef Magazine

704 North Wells Sreet, 2nd Floor
Chicago, IL 60654
Tel: +1 (312) 849-2220
Fax: +1 (312) 849-2174
Email: cjohnson@talcott.com
Website: http://www.chefmagazine.com

Publishes: Articles; Features; News; Nonfiction; *Areas:* Business; Cookery; How-to; Technology; *Markets:* Professional

Editors: Claire Johnson

Magazine aimed at foodservice professionals, providing food and equipment articles; industry news; case studies; business solutions, etc.

China Grove

Website: http://www.chinagrovepress.com

Publishes: Essays; Fiction; Nonfiction; Poetry; *Areas:* Short Stories; *Markets:* Adult; *Treatments:* Literary

Literary journal publishing fiction, poetry, and essays. Submit via online submission system only – small fee ($2-$3) to cover expenses. Also offers prizes.

The Christian Century

104 S. Michigan Ave., Suite 1100
Chicago, IL 60603-5901
Tel: +1 (312) 263-7510
Fax: +1 (312) 263-7540
Email: submissions@christiancentury.org
Website: http://www.christiancentury.org

Publishes: Articles; Essays; Interviews; Nonfiction; Poetry; Reviews; *Areas:* Culture; Humour; Politics; Religious; *Markets:* Adult

Christian magazine seeking to apply religious traditions to modern questions such as poverty, human rights, international relations, etc. For articles, send query by email. For poetry, submit poetry by email to separate address on website. See website for full submission guidelines.

Cincy

30 Garfield Place, Suite 440 Cincinnati OH 45202
Tel: +1 (513) 421-2533
Fax: +1 (513) 421-2542
Email: cminard@cincymagazine.com
Website: http://www.cincymagazine.com

Publishes: Articles; Features; Interviews; News; Nonfiction; *Areas:* Business; Health; Lifestyle; Travel; *Markets:* Professional

Editors: Corinne Minard, Managing Editor

Magazine aimed at business professionals both at work and away from work, publishing features and news related to business, as well as lifestyle pieces on dining, shopping, health, home, travel, etc.

Common Ground Review

H-5132
Western New England University
1215 Wilbraham Road, Springfield, MA 01119
Tel: +1 (413) 782-1729
Email: submissions@cgreview.org
Website: http://www.cgreview.org

Publishes: Fiction; Nonfiction; Poetry; *Areas:* Short Stories; *Markets:* Adult; *Treatments:* Literary

Editors: Janet Bowdan

Publishes two issues a year, with deadlines of August 31 and March 31. Submit up to three poems per issue. Publishes one piece of creative nonfiction in the Autumn/Winter issue, and one short story in the Spring/Summer issue. Prose may be up to 12 double-spaced pages. Accepts submissions by post or by email. See website for full guidelines.

Conceit Magazine

PO Box 761495
San Antonio, CA 78245

or

PO Box 884223
San Francisco, CA 94188-4223
Email: Conceitmagazine2007@yahoo.com
Website:
https://sites.google.com/site/conceitmagazine

Publishes: Articles; Essays; Fiction; News; Nonfiction; Poetry; *Areas:* Short Stories; *Markets:* Adult; *Treatments:* Literary

Editors: Perry Terrell

Publishes poetry, short stories, articles, essays, and new book and magazine announcements. Material must be family-friendly. Submit by post or by email. See website for more details.

Consumer Goods Technology

4 Middlebury Boulevard
Randolph, NJ 07869
Tel: +1 (973) 607-1300
Fax: +1 (973) 607-1395
Email: aackerman@edgellmail.com
Website: http://consumergoods.edgl.com

Publishes: Articles; Features; Interviews; News; Nonfiction; *Areas:* Business; Technology; *Markets:* Professional

Editors: Alliston Ackerman Orr

Publishes material aimed at businesses in the consumer good sector and techologies used by the industry. Always on the lookout for freelances. Send query with published clips.

Cosmopolitan

Hearst Corporation
300 West 57th Street
New York, NY 10019-3791
Tel: +1 (212) 649-2000
Email: inbox@cosmopolitan.com
Website: http://www.cosmopolitan.com

Publishes: Articles; Essays; Features; Nonfiction; *Areas:* Beauty and Fashion; Entertainment; Health; Lifestyle; Women's Interests; *Markets:* Adult

Women's lifestyle magazine. This is the largest magazine in the world, and generally a hard market to break into – however, is looking to build a "network of talented and eager contributors" and is looking for personal essays up to 800 words on college experiences, or what you did instead of college, etc. Submit online via website. For other areas of the magazine, approach by email with published clips and "story pitch" in the subject line.

Creating Keepsakes

Creative Crafts Group, LLC
14850 Pony Express Road
Bluffdale, UT 84065
Tel: +1 (801) 984-2070
Email: editorial@CreatingKeepsakes.com
Website: http://www.creatingkeepsakes.com

Publishes: Articles; Nonfiction; *Areas:* Crafts; Hobbies; *Markets:* Adult

Magazine for scrapbook enthusiasts. Send query with two images to illustrate your topic.

Cruising Outpost Magazine

Box 100,
Berry Creek, 95916
Tel: +1 (510) 900-3616
Email: submissions@cruisingoutpost.com
Website: http://cruisingoutpost.com

Publishes: Articles; Essays; Interviews; Nonfiction; *Areas:* Cookery; How-to; Technology; Travel; *Markets:* Adult

Magazine covering boats/cruising. Submit via form on website.

Cura – A Literary Magazine of Art and Action

Email: curamag@fordham.edu
Website: http://curamag.com

Publishes: Articles; Essays; Fiction; Nonfiction; Poetry; *Areas:* Short Stories; Markets

Publishes prose and poetry based in some way on the theme: Borderlands. Accepts online submissions only. Reading period runs from October to March. See website for full guidelines and to submit via online submission system.

Current Nursing in Geriatric Care

Freiberg Press, Inc.
PO Box 612
Cedar Falls, IA 50613
Tel: +1 (319) 553-0642
Fax: +1 (319) 553-0644
Email: kfreiberg@cfu.net
Website: http://www.care4elders.com

Publishes: Articles; Nonfiction; *Areas:* Health; *Markets:* Professional

Magazine for geriatric care professionals. Query in first instance.

Dance Teacher

Email: khildebrand@dancemedia.com
Website: http://www.dance-teacher.com

Publishes: Articles; Nonfiction; *Areas:* Business; Health; How-to; Legal; Music; *Markets:* Professional

Editors: Karen Hildebrand

Magazine for professional teachers of dance. Send query in the first instance.

DASH Journal

Department of English and Comparative Literature
California State University Fullerton
800 North State College Boulevard
Fullerton, CA 92831
Email: DASHLiteraryJournal@gmail.com
Website: http://dashliteraryjournal.com

Publishes: Essays; Fiction; Nonfiction; Poetry; *Areas:* Criticism; Short Stories; *Markets:* Adult; *Treatments:* Literary

Submit one piece of prose or up to five poems, between January 1 and March 1 annually. Prefers email submissions. Any submissions not conforming to the guidelines will be immediately discarded. See website for full details.

Dime (Designs in Machine Embroidery)

2517 Manana Drive
Dallas, TX 75220
Tel: +1 (888) 739-0555
Fax: +1 (214) 352-3102
Email: dholguin@dzgns.com
Website: http://www.dzgns.com

Publishes: Articles; Interviews; Nonfiction; *Areas:* Crafts; Hobbies; How-to; *Markets:* Adult

Editors: Denise Holguin

Project-based magazine covering embroidery. Send submissions by post or by email. See website for more details.

Dollars & Sense

One Milk Street
Boston, MA 02109
Tel: +1 (617) 447-2177
Fax: +1 (617) 447-2179
Email: dollars@dollarsandsense.org
Website: http://www.dollarsandsense.org

Publishes: Articles; Features; Nonfiction; Reviews; *Areas:* Finance; *Markets:* Adult; Treatments

Magazine explaining economics in a popular way. Send queries in the first instance, by post or by email.

Drunken Boat

Email: editor@drunkenboat.com
Website: http://www.drunkenboat.com

Publishes: Fiction; Nonfiction; Poetry; *Areas:* Arts; Short Stories; Translations; *Markets:* Adult; *Treatments:* Literary

Online journal of art and literature, publishing fiction, poetry, and creative nonfiction. Submit online via website submission system ($3 charge).

Early American Life

Firelands Media Group LLC
Post Office Box 221228
Shaker Heights, OH 44122-0996
Tel: +1 (440) 543-8566
Email: queries@firelandsmedia.com
Website: http://www.ealonline.com

Publishes: Articles; Nonfiction; *Areas:* Antiques; Architecture; Crafts; Historical; *Markets:* Adult

Magazine aimed at people with an interest in the style of the period 1600-1840 in America, and its use in their modern homes and lives. Covers architecture, antiques, etc. Will consider unsolicited mss but prefers initial queries by email.

18 Wheels & Heels

Email: Photos@18wheelsandheels.com
Website:
http://18wheelsandheelsmagazine.com

Publishes: Articles; Interviews; Nonfiction; Poetry; *Areas:* Beauty and Fashion; Business; Cookery; Culture; Hobbies; How-to; Leisure; Lifestyle; Men's Interests; Music; *Markets:* Adult; Family; *Treatments:* Contemporary; Niche; Positive

Editors: Tina Foca

Female truckers magazine. Articles and stories are related to the trucking industry. Product reviews have to be for products or services for people on the go. Music reviews are for driving conditions.

El Restaurante

Maiden Name Press, LLC
PO Box 2249
Oak Park, IL 60303-2249
Tel: +1 (708) 267-0023
Email: kfurore@restmex.com
Website: http://elrestaurante.com

Publishes: Articles; Features; Nonfiction; *Areas:* Business; Cookery; *Markets:* Professional

Editors: Kathleen Furore

Magazine for the owners and operators of restaurants interested in Mexican, Tex-Mex, Southwestern, and Latin cuisine. Send query with published clips.

Electrical Apparatus

Barks Publications, Inc.
500 North Michigan Avenue, Suite 901
Chicago, IL 60611-4299
Tel: +1 (312) 321-9440
Fax: +1 (312) 321-1288
Email: eamagazine@barks.com
Website: http://www.barks.com/eacurr.html

Publishes: Articles; Features; Nonfiction; *Areas:* Technology; *Markets:* Professional

Magazine for professionals working with and maintaining electronic machinery including motors, transformers, etc. technical expertise required. Send query with CV and article outline.

Enchanted Conversation

Email: enchantedconversation@gmail.com
Website: http://www.fairytalemagazine.com

Publishes: Essays; Fiction; Nonfiction; Poetry; *Areas:* Fantasy; *Markets:* Adult

Editors: Kate Wolford

Magazine for lovers of fairy tales. Publishes fiction, poetry, and scholarly essays. Each issue has a theme and a specific submission window. See website for details. Send complete MS by email only as an attachment, with the title of the work and your name in the subject line. Include brief bio and PayPal address for payment. Considers work up to 2,500 words but prefers up to 1,500. Aimed at adults but should not be unsuitable for children.

Epoch

251 Goldwin Smith Hall
Cornell University
Ithaca, NY 14853
Website: http://english.arts.cornell.edu/publications/epoch

Publishes: Essays; Fiction; Nonfiction; Poetry; Scripts; *Areas:* Drama; Film; Short Stories; TV; *Markets:* Adult; *Treatments:* Literary

Editors: Michael Koch

Publishes literary fiction, poetry, essays, screenplays, cartoons, graphic art, and graphic fiction. Previously unpublished material only. Accepts submissions between September 15 and April 15 annually. Submit up to 5 poems, one short story, or upt to three short short stories. Submit by post only. See website for full details.

Equal Opportunity

445 Broad Hollow Road, Suite 425
Melville, NY 11747
Tel: +1 (631) 421-9421

Fax: +1 (631) 421-1352
Email: jschneider@eop.com
Website: http://www.eop.com

Publishes: Articles; Nonfiction; *Areas:* Business; Finance; How-to; Self-Help; *Markets:* Academic; Professional

Editors: James Schneider (Director, Editorial & Production)

Career-guidance and recruitment magazine aimed at minority college students and professionals in career disciplines. Send complete ms.

Escapees Magazine

100 Rainbow Drive
Livingston, TX 77351
Tel: +1 (888) 757-2582
Fax: +1 (936) 327-4388
Email: editor@escapees.com
Website: http://escapees.com

Publishes: Articles; Nonfiction; *Areas:* Lifestyle; Travel; *Markets:* Adult

Editors: Allyssa Dyson

Magazine covering the RV community and lifestyle.

Evansville Living

Tucker Publishing Group
223 NW Second Street, Suite 200
Evansville, IN 47708
Tel: +1 (812) 426-2115
Email: webmaster@evansvilleliving.com
Website: http://www.evansvilleliving.com

Publishes: Articles; Features; Nonfiction; *Areas:* Design; Gardening; Historical; Lifestyle; Sport; Travel; *Markets:* Adult

Regional magazine covering Evansville, Indiana, and the greater area. Send query with published clips.

Evening Street Review

7652 Sawmill Road, #352
Dublin, Ohio 43016-9296
Email: editor@eveningstreetpress.com
Website: http://www.eveningstreetpress.com

Publishes: Essays; Fiction; Nonfiction; Poetry; *Areas:* Short Stories; *Markets:* Adult; *Treatments:* Literary

Editors: Gordon Grigsby

Publishes poetry, short stories, essays, and creative nonfiction. Prefers to receive submissions by email as a single Word or .rtf file attachment. See website for full guidelines.

The Fabricator

833 Featherstone Road
Rockford, IL 61107
Tel: +1 (815) 227-8281
Email: dand@thefabricator.com
Website: http://www.thefabricator.com

Publishes: Articles; News; Nonfiction; *Areas:* How-to; Technology; *Markets:* Professional

Editors: Dan Davis

Magazine covering metal forming and the fabricating industry. Publishes news, technical articles, and case histories. Send query with published clips.

Fast Company

7 World Trade Center
New York, NY 10007-2195
Tel: +1 (212) 389-5300
Fax: +1 (212) 389-5496
Email: pr@fastcompany.com
Website: http://www.fastcompany.com

Publishes: Articles; Nonfiction; *Areas:* Business; Design; Finance; Technology; *Markets:* Professional

Publishes business articles, with a focus on innovation in technology, ethonomics (ethical economics), leadership, and design. See website for submission guidelines.

Fence

Science Library 320
University at Albany

1400 Washington Avenue
Albany, NY 12222
Tel: +1 (518) 591-8162
Email: peter.n.fence@gmail.com
Website: http://www.fenceportal.org

Publishes: Fiction; Nonfiction; Poetry; *Areas:* Arts; Criticism; Literature; Short Stories; *Markets:* Adult; *Treatments:* Literary

Biannual journal of poetry, fiction, art, and criticism. Submit online using web-based submission system. Submit no more than five poems at any one time, and up to twenty-five pages of fiction.

Field & Stream

Email: fsletters@bonniercorp.com
Website: http://www.fieldandstream.com

Publishes: Articles; Essays; Nonfiction; *Areas:* Hobbies; How-to; Leisure; Nature; Sport; *Markets:* Adult

Magazine aimed at hunters and fishermen. Send query by email to propose article ideas.

Film Comment

70 Lincoln Center Plaza
New York, NY 10023
Tel: +1 (212) 875-5610
Email: editor@filmlinc.com
Website: http://www.filmlinc.com/fcm

Publishes: Articles; Essays; Interviews; Nonfiction; *Areas:* Criticism; Film; Historical; *Markets:* Adult

Editors: Gavin Smith

Magazine of film criticism and history. Publishes good writing relating about films the writer feels passionately about, rather than focusing currently popular stars or upcoming blockbusters. No unsolicited submissions. Accepts queries, but cannot guarantee a response.

FineScale Modeler

21027 Crossroads Circle
PO Box 1612
Waukesha, WI 53187
Website: http://www.finescale.com

Publishes: Articles; Nonfiction; *Areas:* Crafts; Hobbies; How-to; *Markets:* Adult

Magazine for modeling enthusiasts. Most articles come from modelers, rather than professional writers. Prefers queries describing proposed article in first instance. See website for full guidelines.

Food Product Design

Tel: +1 (480) 990-1101 ext. 1241
Email: lkuntz@vpico.com
Website: http://www.foodproductdesign.com

Publishes: Articles; News; Nonfiction; *Areas:* Business; Cookery; How-to; *Markets:* Professional

Editors: Lynn A. Kuntz

Magazine for professionals working in the food processing industry.

Freelance Writer's Report (FWR)

CNW Publishing, Editing & Promotion Inc.
PO Box A
North Stratford, NH 03590
Tel: +1 (603) 922-8338
Email: info@writers-editors.com
Website: http://www.writers-editors.com

Publishes: Articles; Nonfiction; *Areas:* Business; How-to; *Markets:* Professional

Magazine for freelance writers. Publishes how-to articles. No articles on freelancing basics. Submit complete ms by email.

Fruit Growers News Magazine

Great American Media Services
PO Box 128
Sparta, Michigan 49345
Tel: +1 (616) 887-9008
Fax: +1 (616) 887-2666
Email: fgnedit@fruitgrowersnews.com
Website: http://fruitgrowersnews.com

Publishes: Articles; Interviews; News;

Nonfiction; *Areas:* Business; Nature; *Markets:* Professional

Magazine for commercial growers of fruit.

Girlfriendz Magazine

6 Brookville Drive
Cherry Hill, NJ 08003
Tel: +1 (856) 751-2997
Email: tobi@girlfriendzmag.com
Website: http://www.girlfriendzmag.com

Publishes: Articles; *Areas:* Beauty and Fashion; Business; Health; Historical; How-to; Humour; Self-Help; Women's Interests; *Markets:* Adult

Editors: Tobi Schwartz-Cassell, Editor-in-Chief

Publishes well-researched articles for the thinking woman, from credentialed professionals. Aimed at women born between 1946 and 1964. Prefers not to be pitched ideas, but interested in baby-boom women writers who can be assigned to write articles, make-over tips, business articles, and fitness programmes. No poetry, personal essays, or community calendar announcements. Send query by email including published clips. No queries by fax. See website for full guidelines.

Golf News Magazine

PO Box 1040
Rancho Mirage, CA 92270
Tel: +1 (760) 321-8800
Fax: +1 (760) 328-3013
Email: dan@golfnewsmag.com
Website: http://golfnewsmag.com

Publishes: Articles; Features; Interviews; News; Nonfiction; *Areas:* Health; How-to; Sport; *Markets:* Adult

Magazine covering the sport of golf. Send query with published clips.

Grain Journal

Country Journal Publishing Co.
3065 Pershing Court
Decatur, IL 62526
Tel: +1 (800) 728-7511
Email: ed@grainnet.com
Website: http://www.grainnet.com

Publishes: Articles; Interviews; Nonfiction; *Areas:* Business; How-to; Technology; *Markets:* Professional

Editors: Ed Zdrojewski

Trade magazine for the North American grain industry.

GuestLife

303 North Indian Canyon Drive
Palm Springs, CA 92262
Tel: +1 (760) 325-2333
Fax: +1 (760) 325-7008
Email: Sales@GuestLife.com
Website: http://www.guestlife.com

Publishes: Articles; Features; Nonfiction; *Areas:* Culture; Entertainment; Historical; Leisure; Travel; *Markets:* Adult

Magazine placed in hotel rooms, covering activities, attractions, and history of the specific area being covered. See website for details.

Gyroscope Review

Website: http://www.gyroscopereview.com

Publishes: Poetry; *Markets:* Adult; *Treatments:* Contemporary; Literary

Publishes fine contemporary poetry in a variety of forms and themes. Welcomes both new and established writers. Submit online via website submission system.

Hard Hat News

PO Box 121
Palatine Bridge, NY 13428
Tel: +1 (717) 497-7616
Fax: +1 (518) 673-2381
Email: jcasey@leepub.com
Website: http://hardhat.com

Publishes: Articles; Interviews; News; Nonfiction; *Markets:* Professional

Editors: Jon Casey

Magazine for construction workers. Send complete ms.

Hill Country Sun

Email: melissa@hillcountrysun.com
Website: http://www.hillcountrysun.com

Publishes: Articles; Nonfiction; *Areas:* Travel; *Markets:* Adult

Editors: Melissa Maxwell Ball

Magazine covering interesting people, places, and things to do in Central Texas Hill Country from Austin to Leakey, from San Antonio to Burnet. Aimed at both residents and visitors. All topics must be pre-approved by editor. Send query by email.

Home Energy Magazine

1250 Addison Street, Suite 211B
Berkeley, CA 94702
Tel: +1 (510) 524-5405
Fax: +1 (510) 981-1406
Email: contact@homeenergy.org
Website: http://www.homeenergy.org

Publishes: Articles; Nonfiction; *Areas:* Architecture; Design; *Markets:* Professional

Editors: Jim Gunshinan

Magazine for the construction industry, publishing articles that disseminate objective and practical information on residential energy efficiency, performance, comfort, and affordability. Query with published clips.

The Horn Book Magazine

300 The Fenway
Palace Road Building, Suite P-311
Boston, MA 02115
Tel: +1 (617) 628-0225
Fax: +1 (617) 628-0882
Email: magazine@hbook.com
Website: http://www.hbook.com

Publishes: Articles; Nonfiction; *Areas:* Criticism; Literature; *Markets:* Academic; Professional

Magazine aimed at professionals and academics involved with children's literature, publishing critical articles on the same. No fiction or work by children.

Houston Press

2603 La Branch Street
Houston, TX 77004
Tel: +1 (713) 280-2400
Fax: +1 (713) 280-2444
Website: http://www.houstonpress.com

Publishes: Articles; News; Nonfiction; *Areas:* Arts; Entertainment; *Markets:* Adult

Covers news, arts, and entertainment specific to Houston.

Hyde Park Living

179 Fairfield Avenue
Bellevue, KY 41073
Tel: +1 (859) 291-1412
Email: hydepark@livingmagazines.com
Website: http://www.livingmagazines.com/Hyde_Park_Living/Hyde_Park_Living.html

Publishes: Articles; Essays; Features; Interviews; Nonfiction; Poetry; Reviews; *Areas:* Historical; Humour; Travel; *Markets:* Adult

Editors: Grace DeGregorio

Publishes material related to Hyde Park, Ohio, only. Query in first instance.

Indianapolis Monthly

1 Emmis Plaza
40 Monument Circle Suite 100
Indianapolis, IN 46204
Tel: +1 (317) 237-9288
Fax: +1 (317) 684-2080
Email: khannel@indianapolismonthly.com
Website: http://www.indianapolismonthly.com

Publishes: Articles; Essays; Features; Interviews; Nonfiction; *Areas:* Lifestyle; *Markets:* Adult

Editors: Kim Hannel

Regional magazine publishing material related to Indiana. No fiction or poetry. Send query with published clips.

InTents

Industrial Fabrics Association International
1801 County Road, B W
Roseville MN 55113
Email: editorial@ifai.com
Website: http://intentsmag.com

Publishes: Interviews; Nonfiction; *Areas:* How-to; Technology; *Markets:* Professional

Magazine covering event tents, providing information on renting tents and staging tented events. Query in first instance.

Interweave Knits

201 East Fourth Street
Loveland, CO 80537
Website: http://www.knittingdaily.com

Publishes: Articles; Features; Nonfiction; *Areas:* Beauty and Fashion; Crafts; Design; Hobbies; How-to; *Markets:* Adult

Knitting magazine. Send query by post.

Iron Horse Literary Review

Texas Tech University
English Department
Mail Stop 43091
Lubbock, TX 79409-3091
Tel: +1 (806) 742-2500
Fax: +1 (806) 742-0989
Email: ihlr.mail@gmail.com
Website: http://www.ironhorsereview.com

Publishes: Essays; Fiction; Nonfiction; Poetry; *Areas:* Short Stories; *Markets:* Adult; *Treatments:* Literary

Publishes stories, poetry, and essays. Pays for published pieces, but submission fee charged. Subject matter, length restrictions, and submission fees vary from issue to issue. See website for details for upcoming issues.

The Journal of Adventist Education

12501 Old Columbia Pike
Silver Spring, MD 20904-6600
Tel: +1 (301) 680-5069
Fax: +1 (301) 622-9627
Email: mcgarrellf@gc.adventist.org
Website: http://jae.adventist.org

Publishes: Articles; Nonfiction; *Areas:* Religious; *Markets:* Professional

Editors: Faith-Ann McGarrell

Magazine aimed at Seventh-day Adventist teachers and educational administrators. See website for full submission guidelines.

Kashrus Magazine

PO Box 204
Brooklyn, NY 11204
Tel: +1 (718) 336-8544
Fax: +1 (718) 336-8550
Email: editorial@kashrusmagazine.com
Website: http://www.kashrusmagazine.com

Publishes: Articles; Nonfiction; *Areas:* Health; Religious; Travel; *Markets:* Adult

Magazine publishing information on Kosher.

KNOWAtlanta

9040 Roswell Road, Suite 210
Atlanta, GA 30350
Tel: +1 (770) 650-1102
Fax: +1 (770) 650.2848
Email: lindsay@knowatlanta.com
Website: http://www.knowatlanta.com

Publishes: Articles; Interviews; Nonfiction; *Areas:* Business; Culture; Finance; Health; How-to; Lifestyle; Self-Help; Travel; *Markets:* Adult; Professional

Magazine for businesses and individuals looking to relocate to Atlanta.

Lakeland Boating

O'Meara-Brown Publications
630 Davis Street, Suite 301
Evanston, IL 60201
Tel: +1 (312) 276-0610

Email: ljohnson@lakelandboating.com
Website: http://www.lakelandboating.com

Publishes: Articles; Essays; Features; Interviews; Nonfiction; *Areas:* Historical; How-to; Leisure; Technology; Travel; *Markets:* Adult

Editors: Lindsey Johnson

Magazine covering boating in the Great Lakes.

Launch Pad: Where Young Authors and Illustrators Take Off!

PO Box 80578
Baton Rouge, LA 70898
Email: editor@launchpadmag.com
Website: http://www.launchpadmag.com

Publishes: Articles; Fiction; Nonfiction; Poetry; Reviews; *Areas:* Adventure; Arts; Fantasy; Sci-Fi; *Markets:* Children's; *Treatments:* Niche; Positive

Editors: Paul Kelsey

An online magazine that publishes fiction, nonfiction, poetry, book reviews, and art by kids ages 6 through 14. Founded by a librarian, has been recognised by the American Library Association with the Scholastic Library Publishing Award.

Leisure Group Travel

621 Plainfield Road, Suite 406
Willowbrook, IL 60527
Tel: +1 (630) 794-0696
Fax: +1 (630) 794-0652
Email: editor@ptmgroups.com
Website: http://leisuregrouptravel.com

Publishes: Articles; News; Nonfiction; *Areas:* Business; Travel; *Markets:* Professional

Magazine aimed at group travel buyers. Send query with published clips in first instance.

Little Patuxent Review

PO Box 6084
Columbia, MD 21045
Email: editor@littlepatuxentreview.org
Website: http://littlepatuxentreview.org

Publishes: Fiction; Nonfiction; Poetry; *Areas:* Short Stories; *Markets:* Adult; *Treatments:* Literary

Editors: Steven Leyva

A community-based publication focused on writers and artists from the Mid-Atlantic region, but will consider work originating from anywhere in the United States. Submit fiction up to 5,000 words; creative nonfiction up to 3,500 words, or up to three poems of up to 100 lines. No submissions from writers outside the US. Submit online using website submission system.

LONE STARS Magazine

4219 Flinthill
San Antonio, TX 78230
Email: lonestarsmagazine@yahoo.com

Publishes: Poetry; *Areas:* Arts; Culture; Current Affairs; Fantasy; Literature; Music; *Markets:* Adult; *Treatments:* Commercial; Contemporary; In-depth; Literary; Mainstream; Popular; Progressive; Serious; Traditional

Editors: Milo Rosebud

8 1/2 x 11, 25+ pages, Saddle stapled. Graphic Art accepted for Cover and Illustration. Authors retain All Rights. Limit 5 poems per submission. Single spaced Camera ready, the way you want to see it in print.

Lost Treasure, Inc.

PO Box 451589
Grove, OK 74345
Tel: +1 (918) 786-2182
Email: managingeditor@losttreasure.com
Website: http://new.losttreasure.com

Publishes: Articles; Nonfiction; *Areas:* Hobbies; *Markets:* Adult

Editors: Carla Nielsen

Magazine for treasure hunting hobbyists.

The Maine Review

Email: editor@themainereview.com
Website: http://www.themainereview.com

Publishes: Essays; Fiction; Nonfiction; Poetry; *Areas:* Short Stories; *Markets:* Adult; *Treatments:* Literary

Editors: Katherine Mayfield

Publishes creative nonfiction, poetry, short fiction, essays, and prose. See website for full details.

NextStepU Magazine

Next Step Publishing Inc.
2 W. Main St., Suite 200
Victor, NY 14564
Tel: +1 (800) 771-3117
Email: info@NextStepU.com
Website: http://www.nextstepu.com

Publishes: Articles; Features; Interviews; Nonfiction; *Areas:* Finance; How-to; Self-Help; Travel; *Markets:* Youth

Magazine aimed at preparing students for life after school; covering careers, college, finance, etc. Send query by email.

Northern Woodlands

1776 Center Road
PO Box 471
Corinth, Vermont 05039
Tel: +1 (802) 439-6292
Fax: +1 (802) 368-1053
Email: mail@northernwoodlands.org
Website: http://northernwoodlands.org

Publishes: Articles; Nonfiction; *Areas:* Nature; *Markets:* Adult

Publishes nonfiction relating to natural history, conservation, and forest management. Send query with published clips.

O&A (Oil & Automotive Service) Marketing News

KAL Publications, Inc.
559 South Harbor Boulevard, Suite A
Anaheim, CA 92805-4525
Tel: +1 (714) 563-9300
Fax: +1 (714) 563-9310
Email: kathy@kalpub.com
Website: http://www.kalpub.com

Publishes: Articles; Features; Interviews; News; Nonfiction; *Areas:* Business; *Markets:* Professional

Trade magazine covering the petroleum marketing industry in the 13 Western states.

One

Catholic Near East Welfare Association
1011 First Avenue
New York, NY 10022
Tel: +1 (212) 826-1480
Fax: +1 (212) 838-1344
Email: cnewa@cnewa.org
Website: http://www.cnewa.org

Publishes: Articles; News; Nonfiction; *Areas:* Culture; Current Affairs; Politics; Religious; *Markets:* Adult

Catholic magazine covering political, cultural, and religious affairs in the Near East. Send query by fax or by post.

The Ottawa Object

Email: threwlinebooks@gmail.com
Website:
https://theottawaobject.wordpress.com

Publishes: Fiction; *Areas:* Short Stories; *Markets:* Adult; *Treatments:* Literary

Editors: Joshua Hjalmer Lind

Print literary journal with a particular interest in speculative fiction. Submit online through website.

Overdrive

Randall-Reilly Publishing
3200 Rice Mine Road NE
Tuscaloosa, AL 35406

Tel: +1 (205) 349-2990
Fax: +1 (205) 750-8070
Email: mheine@randallreilly.com
Website: http://www.overdriveonline.com

Publishes: Essays; Features; Interviews; Nonfiction; *Areas:* Business; How-to; Technology; Travel; *Markets:* Professional

Editors: Max Heine, Editorial Director

Magazine for self-employed truck drivers. Send complete ms.

Pulse

International SPA Association
2365 Harrodsburg Road, Suite A325
Lexington, KY 40504
Tel: +1 (859) 226-4326
Fax: +1 (859) 226-4445
Email: mae.manacap-johnson@ispastaff.com
Website: http://www.experienceispa.com/media/pulse-magazine

Publishes: Articles; News; Nonfiction; *Areas:* Business; *Markets:* Professional

Magazine for spa professionals. Send query with published clips.

PRISM Magazine

PO Box 367
Wayne PA 19087
Email: kkomarni@eastern.edu
Website: http://prismmagazine.org

Publishes: Articles; Essays; Features; Interviews; Nonfiction; Reviews; *Areas:* Religious; *Markets:* Adult

Editors: Kristyn Komarnicki

Evangelical magazine. Aims to be a prophetic, consistently biblical voice in the North American church. Submit by post or by email, with email address or SAE for response. See website for full guidelines.

Painted Cave

Email: paintedcavesubmissions@gmail.com
Website: http://paintedcave.net

Publishes: Fiction; Nonfiction; Poetry; *Areas:* Short Stories; *Markets:* Adult; *Treatments:* Literary

Online literary magazine publishing submissions from community college students. Submit up to three pieces of flash fiction or flash creative nonfiction up to 750 words; one piece of fiction or creative nonfiction up to 5,000 words; or 3-5 poems up to 50 lines each. Include short, third-person biography. See website for full submission guidelines.

Pakn Treger

The Yiddish Book Center
Harry and Jeanette Weinberg Building
1021 West Street
Amherst, MA 01002
Tel: +1 (413) 256-4900
Fax: +1 (413) 256-4700
Email: pt@bikher.org
Website: http://www.yiddishbookcenter.org

Publishes: Articles; Essays; Features; Fiction; Interviews; Nonfiction; *Areas:* Culture; Historical; Humour; Literature; Mystery; Religious; Travel; *Markets:* Adult

Publishes fiction and nonfiction for a secular audience interested in Yiddish and Jewish history, literature, and culture. Send query by email in first instance.

Pallet Enterprise

Industrial Reporting, Inc.
10244 Timber Ridge Dr.
Ashland, VA 23005
Tel: +1 (804) 550-0323
Fax: +1 (804) 550-2181
Email: edb@ireporting.com
Website: http://www.palletenterprise.com

Publishes: Articles; Interviews; Nonfiction; *Areas:* Business; How-to; Nature; Technology; *Markets:* Professional

Editors: Edward C. Brindley, Jr., Ph.D.

Describes itself as the leading pallet and sawmill magazine in America. Send query with published clips.

Pennsylvania Heritage

The Pennsylvania Heritage Society
Commonwealth Keystone Building
400 North Street
Harrisburg, PA 17120
Tel: +1 (717) 787-2407
Fax: +1 (717) 346-9099
Email: miomalley@state.pa.us
Website: http://www.paheritage.org/pa-magazine.html

Publishes: Articles; Essays; Interviews; Nonfiction; *Areas:* Culture; Historical; *Markets:* Adult

Editors: Michael J. O'Malley III

Publishes material relating to Pennsylvania history and/or culture. Send query by email.

Perfume River Poetry Review

Tourane Poetry Press
PO Box 2192
Cupertino, CA 95015-2192
Website: http://touranepoetrypress.wordpress.com/about-4/

Publishes: Poetry; *Markets:* Adult; *Treatments:* Literary

Submit 3-5 poems during specific reading periods only, relating to the subject of the upcoming issue (see website for details). No email submissions, unless outside of the US (in which case query by email in first instance).

The Photo Review

140 East Richardson Avenue, Suite 301, Langhorne, PA 19047-2824
Email: info@photoreview.org
Website: http://www.photoreview.org

Publishes: Essays; Interviews; Nonfiction; Reviews; *Areas:* Criticism; Photography; *Markets:* Adult

Photography magazine publishing critical reviews, essays, and interviews. No how-to or technical. Submit complete ms.

Pipeline & Gas Journal

Oildom Publishing Company of Texas, Inc.
PO Box 941669
Houston, TX 77094-8669
Tel: +1 (281) 558-6930, ext. 218
Email: jshare@oildompublishing.com
Website: http://www.pgjonline.com

Publishes: Articles; Features; Nonfiction; *Areas:* Business; Design; Technology; *Markets:* Professional

Editors: Jeff Share

Publishes articles and features relating to the pipeline business: natural gas, crude oil, or products. See website for full submission guidelines.

Pointe Magazine

333 7th Avenue, 11th Floor
New York, NY 10001
Tel: +1 (212) 979-4862
Fax: +1 (646) 459-4848
Email: pointe@dancemedia.com
Website: http://www.pointemagazine.com

Publishes: Articles; Features; Interviews; News; Nonfiction; *Areas:* Drama; Historical; How-to; Music; *Markets:* Adult; Professional

Editors: Amy Cogan, Vice President and Group Publisher

Ballet magazine. Send query with published clips.

Popular Woodworking Magazine

F+W Media, Inc.
8469 Blue Ash Road, Suite 100
Cincinnati, OH 45236
Email: popwood@fwmedia.com
Website:
http://www.popularwoodworking.com

Publishes: Articles; Nonfiction; *Areas:* Crafts; Design; Hobbies; How-to; Humour; Technology; *Markets:* Adult; Professional

Editors: Megan Fitzpatrick

Publishes articles on woodworking as a profession and as a hobby, including how-to and technical guides. Also publishes relevant humour. Does not consider reviews of tools. Send complete ms.

Postcard Poems and Prose

Website: https://postcardpoemsandprose.wordpress.com

Publishes: Fiction; Poetry; *Areas:* Short Stories; *Markets:* Adult

Publishes postcard-sized combinations of images and poems (12-20 lines) or prose (up to 190 words). Text and images should be sent as separate attachments. Will consider text without images.

Produce Business

5400 Broken Sound Boulevard NW, Suite 400
Boca Raton, FL 33487
Tel: +1 (561) 994-1118
Fax: +1 (561) 994-1610
Email: info@producebusiness.com
Website: http://www.producebusiness.com

Publishes: Nonfiction; *Areas:* Business; *Markets:* Professional

Trade magazine concentrating on the buying end of the produce/floral industry.

Promo

Tel: +1 (203) 899-8442
Email: podell@accessintel.com
Website: http://www.chiefmarketer.com/promotional-marketing

Publishes: Articles; Interviews; Nonfiction; *Areas:* Business; How-to; *Markets:* Professional

Editors: Patty Odell, Senior Editor

Magazine for marketing professionals. Send query with published clips.

Quilter's World

306 E PARR RD
BERNE, IN 46711
Email: Editor@QuiltersWorld.com
Website: http://www.quiltersworld.com

Publishes: Articles; Features; Interviews; Nonfiction; *Areas:* Crafts; Hobbies; How-to; *Markets:* Adult

Magazine covering quilting. Send query or manuscript by post or email.

Romance Flash

Email: submissions@romanceflash.com
Website: http://www.romanceflash.com

Publishes: Fiction; *Areas:* Romance; Short Stories; *Markets:* Adult

Editors: Kat de Falla; Rachel Green

Publishes romance flash fiction up to 1,000 words. No heavy erotica or postal submissions. Submit by email or through form on website only.

Rappahannock Review

University of Mary Washington
1301 College Avenue
Fredericksburg, VA 22401
Tel: +1 (540) 654-1033
Fax: +1 (540) 654-1569
Email: editor@rappahannockreview.com
Website: http://www.rappahannockreview.com

Publishes: Essays; Fiction; Nonfiction; Poetry; *Areas:* Short Stories; *Markets:* Adult; *Treatments:* Experimental; Literary

Editors: Avery Kopp; Sarah Palmer

Online literary journal publishing poetry of any length (submit up to five poems), plus creative nonfiction and fiction up to 8,000 words (or three pieces up to 1,000 words each). Encourages experimental pieces. See website for reading periods and any special topics.

The Realm Beyond

Email: realm.beyond@yahoo.com
Website:

http://www.fortresspublishinginc.com

Publishes: Fiction; *Areas:* Horror; Sci-Fi; Short Stories; Suspense; *Markets:* Adult; Youth

Editors: Brian Koscienski

Magazine publishing exciting and suspenseful stories of science fiction, fantasy and horror. Send submissions by email as Word file attachments. No profanity or graphic scenes.

Red Paint Hill Poetry Journal

Email: submissions@redpainthill.com
Website: http://redpainthill.com

Publishes: Essays; Nonfiction; Poetry; Reviews; *Markets:* Adult; *Treatments:* Literary

Editors: Stephanie Bryant Anderson

Send 3-5 poems in a single Word document by email. No PDF files. Work must be unpublished. Simultaneous submissions accepted, provide immediate notification given of acceptance elsewhere. No rhyming poetry, poetry about poems or the writing process, or melodramatic love poems. Also publishes reviews, essays, and interviews. See website for full submission guidelines.

Reed Magazine

San Jose State University
English Department
One Washington Square
San Jose, CA 95192-0090
Email: reed@email.sjsu.edu
Website: http://www.reedmag.org

Publishes: Essays; Fiction; Nonfiction; Poetry; *Areas:* Short Stories; *Markets:* Adult; *Treatments:* Literary

Submit up to five poems, or as many stories or essays as you like. Work must be sent as .doc or .rtf formats. No paper submissions. Accepts work between June 1 and November 1, only. See website for full submission guidelines.

Rhino Poetry

PO Box 591
Evanston, IL 60204
Email: editors@rhinopoetry.org
Website: http://rhinopoetry.org

Publishes: Fiction; Poetry; *Areas:* Short Stories; Translations; *Markets:* Adult; *Treatments:* Literary

Accepts submissions between April 1 and October 1 annually. Publishes poetry, poetry translations, and flash fiction up to 1,000 words. Submissions accepted via online submissions manager, or by post with SASE. See website for full guidelines.

Road King

Parthenon Publishing
102 Woodmont Boulevard, Suite 450
Nashville, TN 37205
Website: http://roadking.com

Publishes: Articles; Nonfiction; *Areas:* Business; Travel; *Markets:* Professional

Magazine publishing articles of interest to those in the trucking industry. Send query with published clips.

The Rockford Review

Rockford Writers' Guild
Attn: Connie Kuntz
PO Box 858
Rockford, IL 61105
Email: editor@rockfordwritersguild.com
Website:
http://www.rockfordwritersguild.com

Publishes: Fiction; Poetry; *Areas:* Short Stories; *Markets:* Adult; *Treatments:* Literary

Publishes two issues per year: one is open to submissions from members only, the other is open to submissions from all writers. Publishes poetry up to 50 lines and prose up to 1,300 words which express fresh insights into the human condition.

RTJ's Creative Catechist

PO Box 6015

New London, CT 06320
Tel: +1 (800) 321-0411
Email:
creativesubs@rtjscreativecatechist.com
Website:
http://www.rtjscreativecatechist.com

Publishes: Articles; Nonfiction; *Areas:* How-to; Religious; *Markets:* Professional

Magazine for Catholic Directors of Religious Education. Send complete ms. No response without SASE.

RV Business

2901 E. Bristol Street, Suite B
Elkhart, IN 46514
Tel: +1 (800) 831-1076
Fax: +1 (574) 266-7984
Email: bhampson@rvbusiness.com
Website: http://www.rvbusiness.com

Publishes: Articles; News; Nonfiction; *Areas:* Business; Design; Finance; Technology; Travel; *Markets:* Professional

Editors: Bruce Hampson

Magazine for professionals in the recreational vehicle industry. Send query with published clips.

Symphony

33 West 60th Street, Fifth Floor
New York, NY 10023
Tel: +1 (212) 262-5161
Fax: +1 (212) 262-5198
Email: clane@americanorchestras.org
Website: http://www.symphony.org

Publishes: Articles; Essays; Features; Nonfiction; *Areas:* Historical; Music; *Markets:* Adult; Professional

Editors: Chester Lane

Magazine publishing items reflecting the concerns and interests of the orchestra field. General interest classical-music subjects may also be of interest. Prefers to receive queries rather than completed articles. See website for full guidelines.

Salmagundi Magazine

Skidmore College
815 North Broadway
Saratoga Springs, NY 12866
Tel: +1 (518) 580-5000
Email: salsubmit@skidmore.edu
Website:
http://cms.skidmore.edu/salmagundi/

Publishes: Essays; Fiction; Nonfiction; Reviews; *Areas:* Criticism; Culture; *Markets:* Adult

Publishes poetry, fiction, personal essays, cultural criticism, and book reviews. Submit five or six poems or up to 12,000 words of prose as an attachment to an email only. Book reviews generally by commission only. No hard copy submissions. See website for dates of reading periods.

Salt Hill Journal

Creative Writing Program, Syracuse University
English Deptartment
401 Hall of Languages, Syracuse University
Syracuse, NY 13244
Email: salthilljournal@gmail.com
Website: http://www.salthilljournal.com

Publishes: Essays; Fiction; Interviews; Nonfiction; Poetry; Reviews; *Areas:* Short Stories; Translations; *Markets:* Adult; *Treatments:* Literary

Reads submissions for the magazine between August 1 and April 1 of each year and for the Poetry Award between May 15 and August 1. Send up to five poems or up to 30 pages of prose. No submissions by email – submit via online submission system.

Salt Water Sportsman

Email: Editor@saltwatersportsman.com
Website:
http://www.saltwatersportsman.com

Publishes: Articles; Nonfiction; *Areas:* Leisure; Sport; *Markets:* Adult

Editors: John Brownlee

Magazine for serious marine sport fishermen. Send articles etc. by email.

Sandy River Review

111 South Street
Farmington, ME 04938
Tel: +1 (207) 778-7000
Fax: +1 (207) 778-7000
Email: SRReview@gmail.com
Website:
http://sandyriverreview.umf.maine.edu

Publishes: Fiction; Nonfiction; Poetry; *Areas:* Short Stories; *Markets:* Adult; *Treatments:* Literary

Publishes poetry, literary fiction, and nonfiction. No horror, fantasy, sci-fi, or romance. Submit up to five poems or up to three pieces of prose, by email, as Word attachments. See website for full guidelines.

Santa Clara Review

PO Box 3212
500 El Camino Real
Santa Clara, CA 95053-3212
Tel: +1 (408) 554-4484
Email: santaclarareview@gmail.com
Website: http://www.santaclarareview.com

Publishes: Essays; Fiction; Nonfiction; Poetry; Scripts; *Areas:* Drama; Short Stories; *Markets:* Adult; *Treatments:* Literary

For poetry send up to three poems, up to ten pages in length. Fiction, nonfiction, and scripts should be less than 5,000 words. 2,000-4,000 is more normal. Accepts submissions by post, but prefers electronic submissions.

Santa Monica Review

Santa Monica College
1900 Pico Boulevard
Santa Monica, CA 90405
Website: http://www2.smc.edu/sm_review

Publishes: Essays; Fiction; Interviews; Nonfiction; *Areas:* Short Stories; *Markets:* Adult; *Treatments:* Literary

Publishes literary short stories, essays and interviews by established and emerging writers. Makes a special effort to present and promote writers from Southern California. Include SASE with submissions.

Saranac Review

CVH, Dept of English
SUNY Plattsburgh
101 Broad Street
Plattsburgh, NY 12901
Email: saranacreview@plattsburgh.edu
Website:
http://research.plattsburgh.edu/saranacreview

Publishes: Essays; Fiction; Nonfiction; Poetry; *Areas:* Short Stories; Translations; *Markets:* Adult; *Treatments:* Literary

Publishes poetry and literary fiction and nonfiction. Accepts submissions between September 1 and May 15 each year. Submit one story or essay, or 3-5 poems by post only with SASE. No genre fiction (science fiction, etc.) or light verse. See website for full submission guidelines.

The Saturday Evening Post

1100 Waterway Boulevard
Indianapolis, IN 46202
Tel: +1 (317) 634-1100
Email: editor@saturdayeveningpost.com
Website:
http://www.saturdayeveningpost.com

Publishes: Articles; Features; Fiction; Interviews; Nonfiction; *Areas:* Beauty and Fashion; Entertainment; Finance; Gardening; Health; How-to; Humour; Lifestyle; Medicine; Short Stories; Technology; Travel; *Markets:* Adult; *Treatments:* Light

Publishes articles, features, and new fiction with a light, humorous touch. Send complete ms with SASE for return or response. See website for full details.

Scary Monsters Magazine

Email: Scaremail@aol.com
Website:
http://www.scarymonstersmagazine.com

Publishes: Fiction; *Areas:* Horror; Short

Stories; *Markets:* Adult

Horror magazine focusing on monsters. Send query in first instance.

School Nurse News

Franklin Communications, Inc.
71 Redner Road
Morristown, NJ 07960
Tel: +1 (973) 644-4003
Fax: +1 (973) 644-4062
Email: editor@schoolnursenews.org
Website: http://www.schoolnursenews.org

Publishes: Articles; Interviews; News; Nonfiction; *Areas:* Medicine; *Markets:* Professional

Editors: Deb Ilardi, RN, BSN

Magazine aimed at school nurses and other healthcare professionals serving children. Send query by email.

Sea Magazine

17782 Cowan, Suite C
Irvine, CA 92614
Tel: +1 (949) 660-6150
Fax: +1 (949) 660-6172
Email: editorial@seamagazine.com
Website: http://www.seamag.com

Publishes: Articles; Features; Nonfiction; *Areas:* How-to; Technology; Travel; *Markets:* Adult

Describes itself as "America's western boating magazine". Aims to provide up-to-date information on boating trends, new boat and equipment reports and new product news; electronics, accessory and gear features; maintenance tips and how-to project ideas; anchorages, places to fish, and cruising destinations. Regional editions for California and the Pacific Northwest.

Seek

Standard Publishing
8805 Governor's Hill Drive, Suite 400
Cincinnati, OH 45249
Tel: +1 (800) 543-1353
Email: seek@standardpub.com
Website: http://www.standardpub.com

Publishes: Articles; Fiction; Nonfiction; *Areas:* Religious; Short Stories; *Markets:* Adult

Publishes religious articles and short stories for adults. See website for list of upcoming topics and submit complete ms by email.

Sequestrum

Email: sequr.info@gmail.com
Website: http://www.sequestrum.org

Publishes: Articles; Essays; Features; Fiction; Nonfiction; Poetry; *Areas:* Arts; Criticism; Culture; Drama; Fantasy; Horror; Literature; Mystery; Philosophy; Sci-Fi; Short Stories; *Markets:* Adult; Youth; *Treatments:* Commercial; Contemporary; Literary; Mainstream; Progressive; Satirical

Editors: Ralph Cooper

Founded by graduates of creative writing programs. This magazine has faithfully published award-winning writers and new voices alike for its 1,000+ monthly readership since its advent.

We accept and publish manuscripts on a rolling basis, and maintain our archives for the public free of charge. We only accept submissions through our online submission system. Hard copy or otherwise emailed submissions will not be read.

Sew News

Creative Crafts Group
741 Corporate Circle, Suite A
Golden, CO 80401
Tel: +1 (303) 215-5600
Fax: +1 (303) 215-5601
Email: sewnews@sewnews.com
Website: http://www.sewnews.com

Publishes: Articles; Features; News; Nonfiction; *Areas:* Crafts; Hobbies; *Markets:* Adult; Professional

Sewing magazine for amateurs and professionals. Send query with published clips.

The Sewanee Review

University of the South
735 University Avenue
Sewanee, TN 37383-1000
Email: Lcouch@sewanee.edu
Website:
http://www.sewanee.edu/sewanee_review

Publishes: Articles; Essays; Fiction; Nonfiction; Poetry; Reviews; *Areas:* Short Stories; *Markets:* Adult; *Treatments:* Literary

Editors: George Core

For fiction and poetry send complete ms with SASE for response. Stories should be at least 3,500 words. Submit a maximum of six poems per submission. For reviews, query first; for essays a query is acceptable, but the complete ms preferred. No submissions between June 1 and August 31. See website for full guidelines.

Shadows Express

Email:
managingeditor@shadowexpress.com
Website: http://www.shadowexpress.com

Publishes: Articles; Essays; Fiction; Nonfiction; Poetry; *Areas:* Short Stories; *Markets:* Adult; *Treatments:* Literary

Online literary magazine publishing short stories, novel excerpts, poetry, and articles. Submit complete ms by email to specific addresses listed on website if under 2,500 words. For works over 2,500 words, query. See website for full guidelines.

Short Story America

2121 Boundary Street, Suite 204
Beaufort, SC 29902
Tel: +1 (843) 597-3220
Email: editors@shortstoryamerica.com
Website: http://www.shortstoryamerica.com

Publishes: Fiction; *Areas:* Short Stories; *Markets:* Adult; *Treatments:* Literary

Editors: Tim Johnston

Online magazine. Submit short stories and flash fiction using form on website only.

The Sierra Nevada Review

999 Tahoe Boulevard
Incline Village, NV 89451
Tel: +1 (775) 831-1314
Email: sncreview@sierranevada.edu
Website: http://www.sierranevada.edu/academics/humanities-social-sciences/english/the-sierra-nevada-review/

Publishes: Fiction; Poetry; *Markets:* Adult; *Treatments:* Literary

Submit up to five poems or fiction up to ten pages at a time. Particularly interested in flash fiction. Accepts submissions between September 1 and March 1 annually. Use submission manager on website to submit.

Sign Builder Illustrated

Simmons-Boardman Publishing Corporation
55 Broad Street, 26th floor
New York, NY 10004
Tel: +1 (212) 620-7200
Fax: +1 (212) 633-1863
Email: jwooten@sbpub.com
Website: http://www.signshop.com

Publishes: Articles; Features; Interviews; Nonfiction; *Areas:* Design; How-to; Technology; *Markets:* Professional

Editors: Jeff Wooten

Magazine aimed at professionals in the signage industry. Query in first instance.

Sixpenny Magazine

Email: elizabeth@sixpenny.org
Website: http://www.sixpenny.org

Publishes: Fiction; *Areas:* Arts; Literature; Short Stories; *Markets:* Adult; *Treatments:* Contemporary; Dark; Experimental; Literary; Popular; Progressive; Satirical; Serious; Traditional

Editors: Elizabeth Leonard, Kate Thomas

A digital and print magazine of illustrated

short stories. Our stories will be classified as literary fiction, but they'll also be entertaining as a rule. Each issue has six stories that take six minutes to read: three by established authors, and three by emerging authors.

Skin Deep

Associated Skin Care Professionals
25188 Genesee Trail Road, Suite 200
Golden, CO 80401
Tel: +1 (800) 789-0411
Fax: +1 (800) 790-0299
Email: getconnected@ascpskincare.com
Website: http://www.ascpskincare.com

Publishes: Articles; Nonfiction; *Areas:* Beauty and Fashion; Business; Health; *Markets:* Professional

Industry magazine for professional skin care practitioners. Query in first instance.

Skipping Stones

PO BOX 3939
Eugene, OR 97403-0939
Email: editor@skippingstones.org

Publishes: Articles; Essays; Features; Fiction; Interviews; Nonfiction; Poetry; *Areas:* Biography; Cookery; Culture; Historical; Humour; Nature; Sociology; Sport; Travel; *Markets:* Children's

Aimed at children aged 7-17 from diverse cultural and socioeconomic backgrounds. Publishes creative informational stories by adults, and fiction, poetry, and nonfiction from children.

Slate & Style

National Federation of the Blind Writers' Division
504 South 57th Street
Omaha, Nebraska 68106-1202
Tel: +1 (402) 556-3216
Email: newmanrl@cox.net
Website: http://www.nfb-writers-division.net/slate_style/slate_style.cfm

Publishes: Articles; Essays; Fiction; Nonfiction; Poetry; Reviews; *Areas:* Autobiography; Literature; Short Stories; *Markets:* Adult; *Treatments:* Literary

Magazine aimed at visually impaired writers. Publishes fiction, poetry, and nonfiction related to writing. Send submissions by email between January 1 and September 1 only, as Word or .rtf attachments. Do not include submissions within the body of the email.

Sling Magazine

Email: SlingMag@gmail.com
Website: http://www.slingmag.com

Publishes: Essays; Fiction; Interviews; Poetry; *Areas:* Short Stories; *Markets:* Adult; *Treatments:* Literary

Editors: Hope Johnson; Bonita Lee Penn; Kaela Danielle McNeil

Publishes essays, fiction, poetry, art / photography and interviews. See website for current requirements and deadlines. Submit one piece of prose, or up to two poems, by email.

Slow Trains

Email: editor@slowtrains.com
Website: http://www.slowtrains.com

Publishes: Essays; Fiction; Nonfiction; Poetry; *Markets:* Adult; *Treatments:* Literary

Publishes fiction, essays, and poetry reflecting the spirit of adventure, the exploration of the soul, the energies of imagination, and the experience of Big Fun. Music, travel, sex, humour, love, loss, art, spirituality, childhood/coming of age, baseball, and dreams. No sci-fi, erotica, horror, or romance. Email submissions only. Prefers material pasted into the body of the email, but will accept .rtf attachments. See website for full details.

Smithsonian Magazine

Capital Gallery, Suite 6001
MRC 513, PO Box 37012
Washington, DC 20013
Tel: +1 (202) 275-2000

Email: smithsonianmagazine@si.edu
Website: http://www.smithsonianmag.com

Publishes: Articles; Nonfiction; *Areas:* Anthropology; Archaeology; Arts; Culture; Historical; Lifestyle; Nature; Science; Technology; *Markets:* Adult

Publishes articles on archaeology, arts, different lifestyles, cultures and peoples, nature, science and technology. Submit proposal through online form on website.

Snowy Egret

PO Box 9265
Terre Haute, IN 47808
Website: http://www.snowyegret.net

Publishes: Articles; Essays; Fiction; Nonfiction; Poetry; Reviews; *Areas:* Nature; Short Stories; *Markets:* Adult

Publishes fiction, nonfiction, and poetry, relating to the natural world and human interactions with it. Submit by post only.

Sorry We're Booked

8 Ogden Avenue
White Plains, NY 10605
Tel: +1 (914) 610-0132
Fax: +1 (914) 610-0132
Email: swbooked@gmail.com
Website: http://www.sorrywerebooked.com

Publishes: Essays; Fiction; Nonfiction; Poetry; Reviews; *Areas:* Arts; Autobiography; Biography; Criticism; Culture; Entertainment; Historical; Literature; Philosophy; Politics; Short Stories; Theatre; Women's Interests; *Markets:* Adult; Children's; Family; Youth; *Treatments:* Contemporary; Literary; Positive; Satirical; Serious

Editors: Zach Borenstein; Dagny Leonard

There are three things we know to be true:

(1) All people are writers. It isn't even that all people have the ability to be writers; all acting humans influence each other, shape each others' consciousness, leave their lives written upon the world. For those that are writers in the more literal sense, we present another chance to have your words reach a wider audience. Writing is a form of expression that helps us to understand the human condition; so, as a human, you have a right (a write! -- we like puns) to be a writer; the term "humanities" is not so accidental. So, send us anything you've written, and we'll put forth an honest effort to publish it.

(2) All people are readers, influenced by world around them. Everything is free, not only because it would be unfeasible to charge access, but also because of a hazy moral line from which we are choosing to steer clear. If someone were to have written something that could be of dire importance to the greater world, would it not be our obligation to make it accessible to as many people as possible?

(3) Language is metaphorical -- nonexistent ideas being rearranged and restructured to convey meaning. You might even say that all writing is playing around with words. The term "wordplay" is also not so accidental, and we hope you'll contribute to what we hope will be the greatest list of puns ever assembled.

Now, for the five Ws, or four Ws and an H, or really, two Ws, an H, and then another two Ws.

What we publish: Poetry, fiction, nonfiction, reviews -- respecting the work we did not personally make vailable -- original book cover designs, and puns. We're also open to new ideas, so if there is a form of expression relevant to the literary world that we do not yet accommodate here, please let us know.

Why we publish: In addition to our ideological quest to support all we know this may just be a place where we publish our own work, our friends' work, and where only the parents of each individual author actually read the content. We're cool with that. We also may have hidden aspirations to publish anthologies of this work, and lay a foundation for further literary ambitions we may have down the road.

How we publish: You may have noticed that

we're not using a blog CMS, the most common online publishing format. We wanted a little more creative control, to keep the site clean, and honor the idea of the permanence of the written word. Perhaps you can think of this as a repository of expression, knowledge, inquisition.

Where we belong: The community will decide what literary works are of importance, and we're comfortable with having just a small say (for now). Your humble editors are aware that our contributions pale in comparison to the works of greater minds, or of those privy to as yet under-appreciated human experiences; those who have something greater to offer should receive greater attention. But every writer deserves some attention, some care, some love.

Who we are: We have used strong language to convey a moral basis for this site's existence, but we are, largely, deplorable people. While the written word can have a positive impact on the globe, we could spend time trying to more directly engage the world in efforts to fix it. We'll get on that eventually, but until then, sorry, we're booked.

South Carolina Review

Clemson University
Strode Tower Room 611, Box 340522
Clemson SC 29634-0522
Tel: +1 (864) 656-5399
Fax: +1 (864) 656-1345
Email: cwayne@clemson.edu
Website: http://www.clemson.edu/cedp/cudp/journals.htm

Publishes: Essays; Fiction; Nonfiction; Poetry; Reviews; *Areas:* Literature; Short Stories; *Markets:* Adult; *Treatments:* Literary; Mainstream

Editors: Wayne Chapman

Publishes fiction, poetry, essays, and reviews. No previously published or simultaneous submissions. Submit 3-10 poems at a time. No submissions accepted in December or June to August.

South Dakota Review

The University of South Dakota
Department of English
414 East Clark Street
Vermillion, SD 57069
Email: sdreview@usd.edu
Website: http://southdakotareview.com

Publishes: Essays; Fiction; Interviews; Nonfiction; Poetry; Reviews; *Areas:* Short Stories; Translations; *Markets:* Adult; *Treatments:* Literary

Publishes fiction, poetry, essays (and mixed/hybrid-genre work), literary reviews, interviews, and translations. Accepts submission by post, or online via form on website (no submissions by email). No length limits, but prose is generally no longer than 6,000 words. Accepts simultaneous submissions, provided notification is given. See website for full guidelines.

South Florida Parenting

1701 Green Road, Suite B
Deerfield Beach, FL 33064
Tel: +1 (954) 698-6397
Fax: +1 (954) 421-9002
Email: klcamarena@tribune.com
Website: http://www.sun-sentinel.com

Publishes: Articles; Essays; Features; News; Nonfiction; *Markets:* Adult

Editors: Kyara Lomer-Camarena

Magazine aimed at parents living in the South of Florida, publishing features on topics of interest to local families, including personal essays, advice (maternity, baby, toddler/preschool, child and preteen), local news, deals, travel, and health and safety. Send queries by email. Preference given to local writers.

Southeast Review

Email: southeastreview@gmail.com
Website: http://southeastreview.org

Publishes: Essays; Fiction; Interviews; Nonfiction; Poetry; Reviews; *Areas:* Autobiography; Short Stories; Travel; *Markets:* Adult; *Treatments:* Literary

Editors: Katie Cortese

Publishes poetry, literary fiction, creative nonfiction (including personal essays, autobiography, and travel writing), book reviews, interviews, and art. Accepts submissions via online web system only. See website for more details. For interviews, query by email in first instance.

Southern California Review

Master of Professional Writing Program
University of Southern California
3501 Trousdale Parkway
Mark Taper Hall of Humanities, THH 355J
Los Angeles, CA 90089-0355
Email: scr@dornsife.usc.edu
Website: http://southerncaliforniareview.wordpress.com

Publishes: Essays; Fiction; Nonfiction; Poetry; Scripts; *Areas:* Drama; Short Stories; *Markets:* Adult; *Treatments:* Literary

Literary magazine, publishing fiction, poetry, nonfiction, and dramatic forms. See website for more details and to submit via online submissions manager. Also accepts submissions by post. Only open to submissions between September 1 and December 1.

Southwestern American Literature

Center for the Study of the Southwest
Texas State University
Brazos Hall
601 University Drive
San Marcos, TX 78666-4616
Tel: +1 (512) 245-2224
Fax: +1 (512) 245-7462
Email: swpublications@txstate.edu
Website: http://www.txstate.edu/cssw/publications/sal.html

Publishes: Fiction; Nonfiction; Poetry; Reviews; *Areas:* Criticism; Short Stories; *Markets:* Adult; *Treatments:* Literary

Scholarly journal publishing literary criticism, fiction, poetry, and book reviews concerning the Greater Southwest. Submit online via online submission system.

Sou'wester

Department of English
Box 1438
Southern Illinois University Edwardsville
Edwardsville, IL 62026-1438
Website: http://souwester.org

Publishes: Fiction; Poetry; *Areas:* Short Stories; *Markets:* Adult; Literary

Submit up to five poems, or one piece of prose (or up to three pieces of flash fiction) via submission system on website. No submissions by post.

SpeciaLiving magazine

PO Box 1000
Bloomington, IL 61702-1000
Tel: +1 (309) 962-2003
Email: gareeb@aol.com
Website: http://www.specialiving.com

Publishes: Articles; Interviews; Nonfiction; Reviews; *Areas:* How-to; Humour; Lifestyle; Technology; Travel; *Markets:* Adult

Online magazine publishing articles, interviews, and product reviews etc. of interest to the physically disabled / mobility impaired.

Spider

Submissions Editor
Spider
Carus Publishing
70 E. Lake Street, Suite 800
Chicago, IL 60601
Tel: +1 (800) 821-0115
Email: customerservice@caruspub.com
Website: http://www.cricketmag.com

Publishes: Articles; Fiction; Nonfiction; Poetry; *Areas:* Nature; Science; Short Stories; *Markets:* Children's

Magazine for children aged 6-9. Publishes fiction, poetry, and articles on such topics as animals, cool scientific discoveries, and kids of the reader's own age doing amazing things. See website for full details. Submit by post with SASE, or using online web submission system. No submissions in emails.

Springs

2001 Midwest Road, Suite 106
Oak Brook, IL 60523-1335
Tel: +1 (630) 495-8588
Fax: +1 (630) 495-8595
Email: lynne@smihq.org
Website: http://www.smihq.org

Publishes: Articles; Interviews; Nonfiction; *Areas:* How-to; Technology; *Markets:* Professional

Editors: Lynne Carr

Magazine for spring manufacturers.

Star 82 Review

Email: editor@star82review.com
Website: http://star82review.com

Publishes: Essays; Fiction; Nonfiction; *Areas:* Short Stories; *Markets:* Adult; *Treatments:* Literary

Publishes short fiction, creative fiction, mini essays, and work that combines words with visual art. Especially looks for humanity, humility and humour. Submit through website via online submission system.

Steamboat Magazine

Ski Town Publications, Inc.
1120 South Lincoln Avenue, Suite F
Steamboat Springs, CO 80487
Tel: +1 (970) 871-9413
Fax: +1 (970) 871-1922
Email: info@steamboatmagazine.com
Website:
http://www.steamboatmagazine.com

Publishes: Articles; Essays; Interviews; Nonfiction; *Areas:* Historical; Humour; Leisure; Lifestyle; Travel; *Markets:* Adult

Magazine covering Steamboat Springs and the Yampa Valley. Send query with published clips.

Stirring : A Literary Collection

Email: eesmith81@gmail.com
Website: http://www.sundresspublications.com/stirring/

Publishes: Fiction; Nonfiction; Poetry; Reviews; *Areas:* Short Stories; *Markets:* Adult; *Treatments:* Literary

Editors: Erin Elizabeth Smith (Poetry); Josh Webster (fiction)

Describes itself as one of the oldest continuously publishing journals on the internet. Publishes poetry, short fiction, creative nonfiction, book reviews, and photography. Submit by email. See website for more details.

storySouth

Email: terry@storysouth.com
Website: http://www.storysouth.com

Publishes: Essays; Fiction; Nonfiction; Poetry; *Markets:* Adult; *Treatments:* Experimental; Literary

Editors: Terry Kennedy

Publishes poetry, fiction, and creative nonfiction from the "new south". The exact definition of "new south" varies from person to person, but if you can make a case for why you consider yourself part of the new south, then you can submit. Accepts work March 15 to June 15, and September 15 to December 15. Submit 3-5 poems or one piece of fiction or nonfiction. No length limits and longer pieces are encouraged. See website for more details.

The Stray Branch

Email: thestraybranchlitmag@yahoo.com
Website: http://www.thestraybranch.org

Publishes: Fiction; Poetry; *Areas:* Short Stories; Suspense; *Markets:* Adult; *Treatments:* Dark; Literary

Editors: Debbie Berk

Submit up to 6 poems or up to 2 pieces of fiction up to two and a half pages each. Shorter pieces stand a better chance of publication. Looking for edgy, dark, suspense, and anything on the paranormal or after life. Topics include depression, mental illness, loss, sorrow, addiction, recovery, abuse, survival, daily existence, self struggles and discovery through words. No stories by or for children. Submissions by email only. See website for full submission guidelines.

Straylight

English Department
University of Wisconsin-Parkside
900 Wood Road
Kenosha, WI 53141
Email: submissions@straylightmag.com
Website: http://www.straylightmag.com

Publishes: Fiction; Poetry; *Areas:* Short Stories; *Markets:* Adult; *Treatments:* Literary

Literary magazine with separate print and online editions, with different content. Accepts stories of 1,000-5,000 words for the print edition (but prefers 1,500-3,000), and up to 1,000 for online. Also publishes novellas up to 45,000 words online only. Poems may be submitted for both print and online editions. See website for specific submission guidelines.

Struggle

Box 28536
Detroit, MI 48228
Email: timhall11@yahoo.com
Website: http://www.strugglemagazine.net

Publishes: Fiction; Poetry; Scripts; *Areas:* Drama; Politics; Short Stories; *Markets:* Adult; *Treatments:* Literary; Progressive

Magazine publishing progressive and revolutionary literature and art expressing the "anti-establishment struggles of the working class and oppressed people in the U.S. and worldwide". Publishes poems, songs, stories, short plays, drawings, cartoons. See website for full details.

The Summerset Review

25 Summerset Drive
Smithtown, New York 11787
Email: editor@summersetreview.org
Website: http://www.summersetreview.org

Publishes: Essays; Fiction; Nonfiction; Poetry; *Areas:* Short Stories; *Markets:* Adult; *Treatments:* Literary

Editors: Joseph Levens

Submit literary fiction and nonfiction up to 8,000 words or up to five poems. Prefers to receive submissions by email. Will accept prose by post but no hard copy poetry submissions. See website for full details.

The Sun

107 N. Roberson Street
Chapel Hill, NC 27516
Tel: +1 (919) 942-5282
Fax: +1 (919) 932-3101
Website: http://thesunmagazine.org

Publishes: Essays; Fiction; Interviews; Nonfiction; Poetry; *Areas:* Culture; Philosophy; Politics; Short Stories; *Markets:* Adult; *Treatments:* Literary

Publishes essays, interviews, fiction, and poetry. Favours personal writing, but also looking for thoughtful, well-written essays on political, cultural, and philosophical themes. No journalistic features, academic works, or opinion pieces.

Sun Valley Magazine

111 1st Avenue North #1M,
Meriwether Building
Hailey, ID 83333
Tel: +1 (208) 788-0770
Fax: +1 (208) 788-3881
Email: michael@sunvalleymag.com
Website: http://www.sunvalleymag.com

Publishes: Articles; Features; Interviews; News; Nonfiction; *Areas:* Arts; Culture; Historical; Leisure; Travel; *Markets:* Adult

Editors: Mike McKenna

Regional magazine covering the Sun Valley area and the Wood River Valley. Send query with published clips.

Suspense Magazine

26500 Agoura Road, #102-474

Calabasas, CA 91302
Email: editor@suspensemagazine.com
Website: http://www.suspensemagazine.com

Publishes: Fiction; Nonfiction; Reviews; *Areas:* Horror; Mystery; Short Stories; Suspense; Thrillers; *Markets:* Adult

Magazine of suspense, mystery, horror, and thriller fiction. Send stories up to 5,000 words in the body of an email. No attachments. Response not guaranteed unless story is accepted.

T. Gene Davis's Speculative Blog

Email: tgenedavis@gmail.com
Website: http://tgenedavis.com/submission-guidelines/

Publishes: Fiction; *Areas:* Fantasy; Gothic; Horror; Sci-Fi; Short Stories; *Markets:* Adult; Family; *Treatments:* Dark; Experimental; Light; Literary; Mainstream; Popular; Satirical; Serious

Editors: T. Gene Davis

A web-based magazine releasing a family-friendly speculative story every Monday, mostly by guest authors. Speculative stories include horror, fantasy, science fiction and other related genres.

The stories accepted are for adults with mature themes, but safe to read out loud with children in the room. All stories MUST be written so that adults will enjoy them.

Stories can be of any length. This includes flash fiction, short stories, novelettes, and novellas. Preference is given to flash fiction and short stories. Formatting should be in standard manuscript format.

Payment for accepted stories is made upon my receipt of the signed author agreement.

Tales of the Talisman

Hadrosaur Productions
PO Box 2194
Mesilla Park, NM 88047-2194
Email: hadrosaur@zianet.com
Website: http://www.talesofthetalisman.com

Publishes: Fiction; Poetry; *Areas:* Fantasy; Horror; Sci-Fi; Short Stories; *Markets:* Adult

Editors: David L. Summers

Publishes Science Fiction, fantasy, and horror short stories up to 6,000 words and poems up to 50 lines. Accepts submissions by post and by email. See website for full guidelines.

Talking River

Lewis-Clark State College
500 8th Avenue
Lewiston, ID 83501
Email: talkingriver@lcmail.lcsc.edu
Website: http://www.lcsc.edu/talking-river/

Publishes: Fiction; Nonfiction; Poetry; Reviews; *Areas:* Short Stories; *Markets:* Adult; *Treatments:* Literary

Submit fiction or creative nonfiction up to 4,000 words, or up to five poems at a time. Also publishes reviews between 500 and 1,000 words. Accepts submissions between August 1 and April 1. Include cover letter, email address for correspondence, and SASE for return of material. See website for full guidelines.

Tattoo Highway

Email: submissions@tattoohighway.org
Website: http://www.tattoohighway.org

Publishes: Fiction; Poetry; *Areas:* Short Stories; *Markets:* Adult; *Treatments:* Literary

Online magazine publishing fiction and poetry. Submit by email as RTF attachments, or as plain text in the body of your email.

The Teacher's Voice

PO Box 150384
Kew Gardens, NY 11415
Email: editor@the-teachers-voice.org
Website: http://www.the-teachers-voice.org

Publishes: Fiction; Nonfiction; Poetry;

Scripts; *Areas:* Drama; Short Stories; *Markets:* Professional; *Treatments:* Experimental; Literary

Litetary magazine for poets and writers in education. Publishes poems, flash fiction, flash creative nonfiction, flash plays, and flash experimental. Simultaneous submissions accepted if immediate notification of acceptance elsewhere is given. Send query with up to 5 pages of poetry, or prose pieces no longer than 1,500 words. Prefers shorter work. See website for full submission guidelines, and/or to submit using online submission system.

Teaching Music

National Association for Music Education
1806 Robert Fulton Drive
Reston, VA 20191
Tel: +1 (703) 860-4000
Fax: +1 (703) 860-1531
Email: lindab@nafme.org
Website: http://www.nafme.org

Publishes: Articles; Nonfiction; *Areas:* How-to; Music; *Markets:* Academic; Professional

Publishes articles aimed at music teachers. Send complete ms.

Telluride Magazine

PO Box 3488
Telluride, CO 81435
Tel: +1 (970) 728-4245
Fax: +1 (866) 936-8406
Email: deb@telluridemagazine.com
Website: http://www.telluridemagazine.com

Publishes: Articles; Nonfiction; *Areas:* Historical; Humour; Leisure; Lifestyle; Nature; Travel; *Markets:* Adult

Editors: Deb Dion Kees

Magazine publishing material relating to the immediate surrounding area and mountain life in general. Send query with published clips.

Textile World

2100 RiverEdge Parkway, Suite 1200
Atlanta, Georgia 30328
Tel: +1 (678) 569-4876
Fax: +1 (770) 952-0669
Email: editor@textileworld.com
Website: http://www.textileworld.com

Publishes: Articles; Nonfiction; *Areas:* Business; Crafts; Design; Technology; *Markets:* Professional

Magazine for the textile industry, covering manufacturing processes, products, technology, etc. Query in first instance.

The Health Journal

4808 Courthouse Street, Suite 204
Williamsburg, VA 23188
Tel: +1 (757) 645-4475
Email: editorial@thehealthjournals.com
Website: http://www.thehealthjournals.com

Publishes: Articles; Nonfiction; *Areas:* Health; *Markets:* Adult

Health magazine focussing on Virginia, but willing to publish articles of both local and national interest.

The Rejected Quarterly

PO Box 1351
Cobb, CA 95426
Email: bplankton@yahoo.com
Website: http://www.rejectedq.com

Publishes: Features; Fiction; Nonfiction; Poetry; Reviews; *Areas:* Humour; Short Stories; *Markets:* Adult

Editors: Daniel Weiss, Jeff Ludecke

Magazine publishing fiction that has been rejected at least 5 times elsewhere, poetry about rejection, plus humour, opinions, and reviews. See website for full submission guidelines.

The Vehicle

600 Lincoln Avenue
Charleston, IL
Email: vehicleeiu@gmail.com

Website: http://www.thevehiclemagazine.com

Publishes: Essays; Fiction; Interviews; Nonfiction; Poetry; Scripts; *Areas:* Adventure; Arts; Crime; Drama; Fantasy; Gothic; Historical; Horror; Humour; Literature; Mystery; Photography; Romance; Sci-Fi; Short Stories; Suspense; Theatre; Thrillers; Westerns; *Markets:* Adult

Editors: Hannah Green

A biannual literary magazine produced by students. Since 1959, the magazine has been publishing poetry, short stories, creative nonfiction, and artwork by the university's students but now has opened its doors to submissions from anyone, anywhere, and has moved online to facilitate the transition.

The Write Place at the Write Time

Email: submissions@thewriteplaceatthewritetime.org
Website: http://www.thewriteplaceatthewritetime.org

Publishes: Essays; Fiction; Nonfiction; Poetry; *Areas:* Short Stories; *Markets:* Adult; *Treatments:* Literary

Editors: Nicole M. Bouchard

Online magazine publishing fiction, poetry, and personal essays in a memoir style. Send up to three short stories, up to five poems, or up to three essays per issue. Send submissions in the body of an email – no attachments. See website for full guidelines.

34th Parallel

Email: 34thParallel@gmail.com
Website: http://www.34thparallel.net

Publishes: Essays; Fiction; Nonfiction; Poetry; Scripts; *Areas:* Short Stories; *Markets:* Adult; *Treatments:* Literary

Editors: Tracey Boone Swan; Martin Chipperfield

Publishes fiction, creative nonfiction, essays, scripts, poetry, and artwork. Submit via online submission system. $6 fee includes download of latest digital edition.

Timber

Email: timberjournal@gmail.com
Website: http://www.timberjournal.com

Publishes: Fiction; Nonfiction; Poetry; *Areas:* Short Stories; *Markets:* Adult; *Treatments:* Literary

Editors: Matthew Treon

Publishes innovative fiction, flash fiction, poetry, nonfiction, visual art and webcomics. Accepts prose up to 5,000 words and 3-5 poems. One submission per reading period (August to March) only. Submit using submission system on website.

TimberLine

10244 Timber Ridge Drive
Ashland, VA 23005
Tel: +1 (804) 550-0323
Fax: +1 (804) 550-2181
Email: edb@ireporting.com
Website: http://www.timberlinemag.com

Publishes: Articles; News; Nonfiction; *Areas:* Business; How-to; Technology; *Markets:* Professional

Editors: Edward C. Brindley, Jr., Ph.D

Online newspaper for the forest products industry including loggers, sawmills, remanufacturers and secondary wood processors. Send query with published clips.

Timeline

1982 Velma Avenue
Columbus, Ohio 43211-2497
Tel: +1 (614) 297-2360
Fax: +1 (614) 297-2367
Email: timeline@ohiohistory.org
Website: http://ww2.ohiohistory.org/resource/publicat/timeline/

Publishes: Articles; Features; Nonfiction; *Areas:* Anthropology; Archaeology; Architecture; Arts; Biography; Finance;

Historical; Military; Nature; Politics; Science; Sociology; Technology; *Markets:* Adult

Publishes historical articles and features, particularly focusing on Ohio, but also willing to consider pieces of regional or national relevance. Suitable topics include the traditional fields of political, economic, military, and social history; biography; the history of science and technology; archaeology and anthropology; architecture; the fine and decorative arts; and the natural sciences including botany, geology, zoology, ecology, and paleontology. If unsure of suitability, send query in first instance.

Toad Suck Review

Email: toadsucksubmit@gmail.com
Website: http://www.toadsuckreview.org

Publishes: Fiction; Interviews; Nonfiction; Poetry; Reviews; Scripts; *Areas:* Autobiography; Culture; Literature; Nature; Politics; Short Stories; *Markets:* Adult

Editors: Mark Spitzer

Publishes a wide range of fiction, nonfiction, and poetry. Offers open and ambiguous guidelines: "Don't send us too much and don't make it too long". See website for more details.

Toasted Cheese Literary Journal

Email: submit@toasted-cheese.com
Website: http://www.toasted-cheese.com

Publishes: Fiction; *Areas:* Short Stories; *Markets:* Adult; *Treatments:* Literary

Quarterly e-zine. Submit flash fiction up to 500 words; fiction up to 5,000 words; creative nonfiction up to 5,000 words; or up to five poems. See website for full submission guidelines.

Toledo Area Parent

1120 Adams Street
Toledo, OH 43604
Tel: +1 (419) 244-9859
Fax: +1 (419) 244-9871
Email: cjacobs@toledocitypaper.com
Website: http://www.toledoparent.com

Publishes: Articles; Features; Interviews; News; Nonfiction; *Areas:* How-to; Humour; Lifestyle; *Markets:* Adult

Editors: Collette Jacobs, Editor in Chief

Magazine aimed at parents living in Northwest Ohio/Southeast Michigan. Send queries by email, post, or fax.

Tradicion Revista Magazine

925 Salamanca NW
Los Ranchos de ABQ, NM 87107-5647
Tel: +1 (505) 344-9382
Fax: +1 (505) 345-5129
Email: LPDPress@q.com
Website: http://www.LPDPress.com

Publishes: Articles; Essays; Features; Nonfiction; *Areas:* Arts; Culture; Historical; Travel; *Markets:* Adult

Editors: Barbe Awalt and Paul Rhetts

Magazine with a focus on the art and culture of the American Southwest. Query in first instance.

Trail of Indiscretion

Email: realm.beyond@yahoo.com
Website:
http://www.fortresspublishinginc.com

Publishes: Fiction; *Areas:* Short Stories; *Markets:* Adult; Youth

Editors: Brian Koscienski

Magazine publishing short stories and graphic novel storytelling in the genres of science fiction, fantasy, and horror. No profanity or graphic scenes. Send submissions as Word documents by email.

Trajectory

PO Box 655
Frankfort, KY 40602
Tel: +1 (502) 330-4746

Email: adobechris@hotmail.com
Website: http://www.trajectoryjournal.com

Publishes: Fiction; Interviews; Nonfiction; Poetry; Reviews; *Areas:* Autobiography; Short Stories; *Markets:* Adult; Literary

Editors: Chris Helvey

Publishes fiction, poetry, creative nonfiction, memoirs, book reviews, and author interviews. No fiction or poetry for young children, young adult, fantasy, romance, sci-fi, or horror. Send submissions by post with SASE and 25-75 word bio. No electronic submissions.

Transition Magazine

Hutchins Center for African & African American Research
Harvard University
104 Mount Auburn Street, 3R
Cambridge, MA 02138
Tel: +1 (617) 495-8508
Fax: +1 (617) 495-8511
Email: HutchinsCenter@fas.harvard.edu
Website: http://hutchinscenter.fas.harvard.edu/transition

Publishes: Essays; Fiction; Interviews; Nonfiction; Poetry; Reviews; *Areas:* Culture; Short Stories; *Markets:* Adult; *Treatments:* Literary

Magazine publishing material from and about Africa and the Diaspora. Publishes short stories, novel extracts, poetry, creative nonfiction, essays, reviews, and interviews. See website for full submission guidelines and online submission system.

Traverse

Prism Publications / MyNorth Media
148 East Front Street
Traverse City, MI 49684
Tel: +1 (231) 941-8174
Email: smith@traversemagazine.com
Website: http://www.mynorth.com

Publishes: Articles; Essays; Nonfiction; *Areas:* Arts; Crafts; Culture; Gardening; Historical; Leisure; Lifestyle; Nature; Sport; *Markets:* Adult

Editors: Jeff Smith

Regional magazine for Northern Michigan. Prefers submissions by email. See website for full guidelines.

TriQuarterly

Email: triquarterly@northwestern.edu
Website: http://www.triquarterly.org

Publishes: Essays; Features; Fiction; Interviews; Nonfiction; Poetry; Reviews; Scripts; *Areas:* Drama; Literature; *Markets:* Adult; *Treatments:* Literary

University online literary magazine. Accepts submissions of fiction, creative nonfiction, poetry, short drama, video essays and hybrid work from established and emerging writers between October 15 and July 15 only. Accepts interviews, reviews and other features year-round. See website for full submission guidelines and online submission manager.

True West

PO Box 8008
Cave Creek, AZ 85327
Tel: +1 (888) 687-1881
Fax: +1 (480) 575-1903
Email: editor@twmag.com
Website: http://www.truewestmagazine.com

Publishes: Articles; Features; Nonfiction; *Areas:* Historical; Westerns; *Markets:* Adult

Editors: Meghan Saar

Magazine covering the history of the American West. Send query with hard copy ms and copy on CD or DVD. See website for more details.

Tulane Review

122 Norman Mayer
Tulane University
New Orleans, LA 70118
Email: litsoc@tulane.edu
Website: http://www.tulane.edu/~litsoc/treview.html

Publishes: Fiction; Poetry; *Areas:* Arts;

Literature; Short Stories; *Markets:* Adult; *Treatments:* Literary

Literary arts journal publishing poetry, prose, and artwork. Submit up to five poems or prose up 4,000 words by email, or by post with SASE. See website for full guidelines.

Ultimate MMA

Beckett Media, LLC
22840 Savi Ranch Parkway, Suite 200
Yorba Linda, CA 92887
Tel: +1 (714) 200-1930
Fax: +1 (714) 456-0146
Email: DJeffrey@Beckett.com
Website: http://www.ultimatemmamag.com

Publishes: Articles; Nonfiction; *Areas:* Men's Interests; Sport; *Markets:* Adult

Editors: Doug Jeffrey

Magazine covering mixed martial arts fighting. Query in first instance.

US Catholic

205 West Monroe Street
Chicago, IL 60606
Email: submissions@uscatholic.org
Website: http://www.uscatholic.org

Publishes: Articles; Essays; Features; Fiction; Nonfiction; Poetry; Reviews; *Areas:* Religious; Short Stories; Spiritual; *Markets:* Adult

Religious magazine aimed at Catholics. See website for detailed submission guidelines and separate email address for submissions of short stories and poetry.

Validation Times

19-B Wirt Street SW
Leesburg, VA 20175
Email: publisher@FDAINFO.com
Website: http://www.fdainfo.com

Publishes: Articles; News; Nonfiction; *Areas:* Business; Legal; Medicine; Technology; *Markets:* Professional

Newsletter covering the regulation of medical and pharmaceutical devices. Send query by post in first instance.

Vanillerotica

Email: talentdripseroticpublishing@yahoo.com
Website: http://eroticatalentdrips.wordpress.com

Publishes: Fiction; *Areas:* Erotic; Romance; *Markets:* Adult

Editors: Kimberly Steele

Print and electronic magazine publishing erotic and romantic short fiction between 10,000 and 15,000 words, plus poetry up to 30 lines.

Verse

English Department, University of Richmond, Richmond, VA 23173
Website: http://versemag.blogspot.com

Publishes: Fiction; Nonfiction; Poetry; *Areas:* Short Stories; *Markets:* Adult; *Treatments:* Literary

Editors: Brian Henry and Andrew Zawacki

Magazine publishing poetry, fiction, nonfiction, and visual art. Originally founded in England in 1984, it moved to its current US home in 2005. Submissions should be chapbook-length (20-40 pages long), and entirely unpublished. Current subscribers may submit for free; non-subscribers must pay a $10 reading fee.

Veterinary Economics

Advanstar Communications, Veterinary Group
8033 Flint
Lenexa, KS 66214

Tel: +1 (800) 255-6864
Fax: +1 (913) 871-3808
Email: ve@advanstar.com
Website: http://veterinarybusiness.dvm360.com

Publishes: Articles; Interviews; Nonfiction;

Areas: Business; Finance; How-to; Medicine; *Markets:* Professional

Magazine for vets, focusing on the business side of managing a practice.

VMSD

ST Media Group International
11262 Cornell Park Drive
Cincinnati, OH 45242
Tel: +1 (513) 263-9386
Email: robin.donovan@stmediagroup.com
Website: http://vmsd.com

Publishes: Articles; Nonfiction; *Areas:* Business; Design; *Markets:* Professional

Editors: Robin Donovan

Magazine covering retail store design. Query editor by email with details of your project in first instance. See website for full guidelines.

Wag's Revue

Email: editors@wagsrevue.com
Website: http://www.wagsrevue.com

Publishes: Essays; Fiction; Interviews; Nonfiction; Poetry; *Markets:* Adult

Reading periods run from the beginning of March to the end of May, and from the start of September to the end of November. In addition to these reading periods, accepts submissions via competitions, for which there is a reading fee and a prize of $1,000. See website for full details. All submissions to made via system on website.

Washington Square Review

Creative Writing Program
New York University
58 West 10th St.
New York, NY 10011
Email: washingtonsquarereview@gmail.com
Website: http://washingtonsquarereview.com

Publishes: Fiction; Poetry; *Areas:* Short Stories; Translations; *Markets:* Adult; *Treatments:* Literary

Nationally distributed literary journal publishing fiction and poetry by emerging and established writers. Submit fiction up to 50 pages, or up to 5 poems up to 10 pages total. Reading periods run August 1 to October 15 and December 15 to February 1. Accepts submissions by post or online using website submission system.

Wesleyan Life

PO Box 50434
Indianapolis, IN 46250
Tel: +1 (317) 774-7900
Email: info@wesleyan.org
Website: http://www.wesleyanlifeonline.com

Publishes: Articles; Nonfiction; *Areas:* Religious; *Markets:* Adult

Magazine publishing inspirational and religious articles. No poetry. Send complete ms.

Whole Life Times

Whole Life Media, LLC
23705 Vanowen Street, #306
West Hills, CA 91307
Tel: +1 (877) 807-2599
Fax: +1 (310) 933-1693
Email: abigail@wholelifemagazine.com
Website: http://www.wholelifemagazine.com

Publishes: Articles; Interviews; Nonfiction; *Areas:* Finance; Health; Lifestyle; Medicine; Nature; New Age; Sociology; Spiritual; *Markets:* Adult

Publishes stories that deal with a progressive, healthy lifestyle, including stories on natural health, alternative healing, green living, sustainable and local food, social responsibility, conscious business, the environment, spirituality and personal growth. Relies heavily on freelances. See website for full submission guidelines.

Willow Review

19351 West Washington Street
Grayslake, IL 60030-1198
Tel: +1 (847) 543-2956
Email: com426@clcillinois.edu
Website: http://www.clcillinois.edu/campus-life/arts/literary-arts/willow-review

Publishes: Fiction; Nonfiction; Poetry; *Areas:* Short Stories; *Markets:* Adult; *Treatments:* Literary

Send up to five poems, or short fiction or creative nonfiction up to 7,000 words, with SASE. Prize money for the best poetry and prose in the issue. See website for full details.

Windhover

UMHB Box 8008
900 College Street
Belton, TX 76513
Email: windhover@umhb.edu
Website: http://undergrad.umhb.edu/english/windhover-journal

Publishes: Fiction; Nonfiction; Poetry; *Areas:* Religious; Short Stories; Spiritual; *Markets:* Adult

Editors: Dr Nathaniel Hansen

Magazine publishing poetry, fiction, and creative nonfiction that considers Christian and spiritual perspectives and themes. Submit via online submission system between Feb 1 and Aug 1 annually.

Wine Press Northwest

333 West Canal Drive
Kennewick, WA 99336
Tel: +1 (509) 582-1443
Email: gmcconnell@winepressnw.com
Website: http://www.winepressnw.com

Publishes: Articles; Features; Interviews; Nonfiction; *Areas:* Historical; Travel; *Markets:* Adult

Editors: Gregg McConnell

Wine magazine focusing on wines of Washington, Oregon, Idaho and British Columbia.

Wine Spectator

M. Shanken Communications
387 Park Avenue South
New York, NY 10016
Tel: +1 (212) 684-4224
Email: wsonline@mshanken.com
Website: http://www.winespectator.com

Publishes: Articles; Features; Interviews; News; Nonfiction; *Areas:* Hobbies; Travel; *Markets:* Adult

Consumer magazine publishing news, interviews, features, and articles aimed at wine enthusiasts. Send query in first instance.

Wisconsin Review

University of Wisconsin Oshkosh
800 Algoma Boulevard
Oshkosh, WI 54901
Tel: +1 (920) 424-2267
Email: wisconsinreview@uwosh.edu
Website:
http://www.uwosh.edu/wisconsinreview

Publishes: Essays; Fiction; Nonfiction; Poetry; *Areas:* Short Stories; *Markets:* Adult; *Treatments:* Literary

Publishes fiction, poetry, and essays. Submit 3-5 poems or up to 15 double-spaced pages of fiction or nonfiction. Submit by post or online for $2 fee (free for subscribers).

Witches & Pagans

BBI Media
PO Box 687
Forest Grove, OR 97116
Tel: +1 (503) 430-8817
Email: editor2@bbimedia.com
Website: http://www.witchesandpagans.com

Publishes: Articles; Essays; Fiction; Interviews; Nonfiction; Poetry; Reviews; *Areas:* Religious; Short Stories; Spiritual; *Markets:* Adult

Magazine of pagan spirituality. Submit by email. See website for full details.

Woodshop News

10 Bokum Road
Essex, CT 06426
Tel: +1 (860) 767-8227
Fax: +1 (860) 767-1048
Email: editorial@woodshopnews.com

Website: http://www.woodshopnews.com

Publishes: Articles; Features; Interviews; News; Nonfiction; *Areas:* Business; Crafts; How-to; *Markets:* Professional

Magazine for professional woodworkers. Send query or complete ms.

The Worcester Review

1 Ekman St
Worcester, MA 01602
Email: twr.diane@gmail.com
Website: http://www.theworcesterreview.org

Publishes: Articles; Fiction; Nonfiction; Poetry; *Areas:* Literature; Short Stories; *Markets:* Adult; *Treatments:* Literary

Editors: Diane Mulligan

Publishes poetry, fiction, and literary articles. No submissions by email. Submit by post only, including email address and telephone number for response. Do not send SASE, as responses will be electronic only. See website for full guidelines.

Word Riot

PO Box 414
Middletown, NJ 07748-3143
Email: wr.submissions@gmail.com
Website: http://www.wordriot.org

Publishes: Fiction; Interviews; Nonfiction; Poetry; Reviews; *Areas:* Short Stories; *Markets:* Adult; *Treatments:* Experimental; Literary

Online magazine publishing short stories, flash fiction, novel excerpts, creative nonfiction, poetry, reviews, and interviews. Likes edgy and experimental material. Maximum one entry per writer per quarter across all genres. Submit online via website.

Wordpeace

Email: editors.wordpeace@gmail.com
Website: http://wordpeace.co

Publishes: Articles; Fiction; Interviews; Nonfiction; Poetry; *Areas:* Short Stories; *Markets:* Adult; *Treatments:* Literary

Editors: Monica A. Hand, Poetry; Joanna Eleftheriou, Nonfiction; Oonagh C. Doherty, Fiction

Online journal of literary response to world events in the spirit of promoting peace and hope for all people. Seeks poems, stories and articles or interviews that reflect or are in conversation with world events. Submit using online submission system.

Workers Write

Blue Cubicle Press
PO Box 250382
Plano, TX 75025-0382
Email: coliseum@workerswritejournal.com
Website:
http://www.workerswritejournal.com

Publishes: Fiction; Poetry; *Areas:* Short Stories; *Markets:* Adult

Magazine publishing stories and poems from the world of work. Each issue concentrates on one specific industry – see website for current focus, submission deadlines, and details on how to submit.

Writer's Bloc

MSC 162, Fore Hall 110
700 University Boulevard
Texas A&M University-Kingsville
Kingsville, Texas 78363
Email: WritersBlocLitMag@hotmail.com
Website: http://www.tamuk.edu/artsci/langlit/index4.html

Publishes: Essays; Fiction; Interviews; Nonfiction; Poetry; Scripts; *Areas:* Drama; Short Stories; Translations; *Markets:* Adult; *Treatments:* Literary

Editors: Dr Octavio Quintanilla

Publishes poetry, short fiction, flash fiction, one-act plays, interviews, and essays from around the world. Publishes in multiple languages, with or without translation. All work must be submitted by February. No new work accepted February to May. See website for more details and for submission form.

The Writing Disorder

PO Box 93613
Los Angeles, CA 90093-0613
Email: submit@thewritingdisorder.com
Website: http://www.thewritingdisorder.com

Publishes: Articles; Nonfiction; Poetry; Reviews; *Areas:* Short Stories; *Markets:* Adult; *Treatments:* Experimental; Literary; Traditional

Editors: C.E. Lukather

Publishes: Fiction, Poetry, Nonfiction, Art, Reviews, Comic Art, Experimental. Send prose or poetry to appropriate email addresses (see website) as MS Word attachments, or submit by post or via online form. No specific guidelines regarding subject matter, and no length limits. Traditional accepted as well as experimental.

Written By

7000 West Third Street
Los Angeles, CA 90048
Tel: +1 (323) 782-4699
Website: http://www.wga.org/writtenby/writtenby.aspx

Publishes: Articles; Essays; Features; Interviews; Nonfiction; *Areas:* Business; Film; TV; *Markets:* Professional

Magazine for screen and TV writers, aimed at those already inside the industry rather than those trying to break in.

Xavier Review

Xavier University of Louisiana
1 Drexel Drive Box 89
New Orleans, LA 70125
Email: radamo@xula.edu
Website: http://www.xula.edu/review

Publishes: Essays; Fiction; Nonfiction; Poetry; *Areas:* Criticism; Religious; Short Stories; Spiritual; *Markets:* Adult; *Treatments:* Literary

Editors: Ralph Adamo

Publishes poetry, fiction, translations, personal essays, and critical essays. Willing to consider all themes, but particularly interested in African American, Caribbean and Southern literature, as well as works that touch on issues of religion and spirituality. Rarely publishes mss over 20 pages. Send complete ms by post with SASE. No simultaneous submissions. See website for full guidelines.

Yachting Magazine

55 Hammarlund Way
Middletown, RI 02842
Fax: +1 (401) 845-5180
Email: letters@yachtingmagazine.com
Website: http://www.yachtingmagazine.com

Publishes: Articles; Nonfiction; *Areas:* Hobbies; Travel; *Markets:* Adult

Magazine on yachting, aimed at an experienced and knowledgeable audience. Send query with published clips in first instance.

Zeek

125 Maiden Lane, 8th Floor
New York, NY 10038
Email: zeek@zeek.net
Website: http://zeek.forward.com

Publishes: Articles; Essays; Fiction; Nonfiction; Poetry; *Areas:* Arts; Culture; Religious; Spiritual; *Markets:* Adult; *Treatments:* Progressive

Editors: Erica Brody

Jewish online magazine launched in 2001 and relaunched in 2013 as a hub for the domestic Jewish social justice movement. Publishes first-person essays, commentary, reporting, fiction, and poetry. Send query by email in first instance. Not accepting fiction submissions as at January 2015.

Zink

Email: fashion@zinkmediagroup.com
Website: http://www.zinkmagazine.com

Publishes: Articles; Features; Nonfiction; *Areas:* Beauty and Fashion; *Markets:* Adult

Editors: Leila Cole; Jennifer Stevens

Fashion magazine. Like edgy material. Submission must be in line with the theme of the issue. See website for upcoming themes and detailed submission guidelines.

ZYZZYVA

57 Post Street, Suite 604
San Francisco, CA 94104
Tel: +1 (415) 752-4393
Fax: +1 (415) 752-4391
Email: editor@zyzzyva.org
Website: http://www.zyzzyva.org

Publishes: Fiction; Nonfiction; Poetry; *Areas:* Short Stories; Translations; *Markets:* Adult; *Treatments:* Literary

Publishes material by writers living on the West Coast, in Alaska and Hawaii only. Submit one piece of fiction or nonfiction or up to five poems at a time, with SASE for response. No restrictions as to length of item or number of items submitted. Accepts simultaneous submissions, but notify if accepted elsewhere. No submissions by email. Accepts submissions from January 1 to May 31 and from August 1 to November 30 only. See website for full guidelines.

UK Magazines

For the most up-to-date listings of these and hundreds of other magazines, visit http://www.firstwriter.com/magazines

To claim your ***free*** *access to the site, please see the back of this book.*

Accounting and Business

ACCA
29 Lincoln's Inn Fields
London
WC2A 3EE
Tel: +44 (0) 20 7059 5000
Fax: +44 (0) 20 7059 5050
Email: chris.quick@accaglobal.com
Website:
http://www.accaglobal.com/en/member/accounting-business.html

Publishes: Articles; Nonfiction; *Areas:* Business; Finance; *Markets:* Professional

Editors: Chris Quick

Magazine aimed at accountants and finance directors.

Acumen

6 The Mount
Higher Furzeham
Brixham
South Devon
TQ5 8QY
Tel: +44 (0) 1803 851098
Email: patriciaoxley6@gmail.com
Website: http://www.acumen-poetry.co.uk

Publishes: Articles; Features; Interviews; Nonfiction; Poetry; Reviews; *Areas:* Criticism; Literature; *Markets:* Adult; *Treatments:* Literary

Editors: Patricia Oxley

Magazine publishing poetry and articles, features, and reviews connected to poetry. Send submissions with SAE and author details on each page, or submit by email as Word attachment. See website for full submission guidelines.

Aesthetica: A Review of Contemporary Artists

PO Box 371
York
YO23 1WL
Tel: +44 (0) 1904 629137
Email: info@aestheticamagazine.com
Website:
http://www.aestheticamagazine.com

Publishes: Articles; Essays; Features; Fiction; Interviews; News; Nonfiction; Poetry; Reviews; *Areas:* Arts; Culture; Current Affairs; Drama; Film; Humour; Literature; Music; Short Stories; Theatre; Women's Interests; *Markets:* Adult; *Treatments:* Literary

Editors: Cherie Federico

I am the founder and editor of a literary and arts magazine that I actually began with my MA fee money (I eventually paid the fees and received my MA). I started the magazine because I believe that there are too many closed doors in the literary and art world. I believe in making the arts accessible and available for all. My convictions are deep because I believe that in this modern, some say, post-modern world that we live in it is important to remember the essentials about being human. There are too many reality TV shows that mock existence. As a culture we are slipping away from the arts. Writing has too many stigmas attached and people believe that there are too many rules. My aim was to bring a magazine to life that would challenge some of these notions and make a difference.

This writing and artistic platform is spreading across the UK and making it to places like Israel, Italy, Ireland, New Zealand, Australia, America, Canada, Bulgaria, and Switzerland. We started in York and are now selling at Borders in York, Leeds, Brighton, Islington, and Oxford Street as well as in some local York bookshops and direct either from the website or by post.

I believe that art and literature is something that is found within all of us. We need to believe in ourselves and see the beauty of the moment to take this concept further. With my literary magazine I have created a space for new ideas and fresh opinions. I believe in creativity, diversity, and equality.

Africa-Asia Confidential

73 Farringdon Road
London
EC1M 3JQ
Tel: +44 (0) 20 7831 3511
Fax: +44 (0) 20 7831 6778
Email: editorial@africa-asia-confidential.com
Website: http://www.africa-asia-confidential.com

Publishes: Articles; Features; News; Nonfiction; *Areas:* Current Affairs; *Markets:* Adult

Editors: Clare Tauben

Publishes news articles and features focussing on the Africa-Asia axis. Welcomes unsolicited mss, but must be unpublished and offered exclusively.

African Business

IC Publications Ltd
7 Coldbath Square
EC1R 4LQ
London
Tel: +44 (0) 20 7841 3210
Fax: +44 (0) 20 7841 3211
Email: editorial@icpublications.com
Website: http://africanbusinessmagazine.com

Publishes: Articles; Nonfiction; *Areas:* Business; Finance; *Markets:* Professional

Editors: Anver Versi

Bestselling pan-African business magazine. Special reports profile a wide range of sectors and industries including transport, energy, mining, construction, aviation and agriculture.

Agenda

The Wheelwrights
Fletching Street
Mayfield
East Sussex
TN20 6TL
Tel: +44 (0) 1435 873703
Email: submissions@agendapoetry.co.uk
Website: http://www.agendapoetry.co.uk

Publishes: Essays; Poetry; Reviews; *Areas:* Criticism; Literature; *Markets:* Adult; *Treatments:* Literary

Editors: Patricia McCarthy

Publishes poems, critical essays, and reviews. Send up to five poems or up to two essays / reviews with email address, age, and short bio. No previously published material. Submit by email only, with each piece in a separate Word attachment. Accepts work only during specific submission windows – see website for current status.

Ambit

Staithe House
Main Road
Brancaster Staithe
Norfolk
PE31 8BP
Tel: +44 (0) 7503 633601

Email: info@ambitmagazine.co.uk
Website: http://ambitmagazine.co.uk

Publishes: Fiction; Poetry; *Areas:* Arts; Short Stories; *Markets:* Adult; *Treatments:* Literary

An international magazine. Potential contributors are advised to read a copy before submitting work to us. Send up to 5 poems, a story up to 5,000 words, or flash fiction up to 1,000 words. Submit via online portal on website, or by post (see website for full details). No submissions by email. Two reading periods per year: Feb 1 to April 1; and Sep 1 to Nov 1.

Android Magazine

Richmond House
33 Richmond Hill
Bournemouth
Dorset
BH2 6EZ
Tel: +44 (0) 1202 586200
Email: enquiries@imagine-publishing.co.uk
Website: http://www.littlegreenrobot.co.uk

Publishes: Articles; Features; News; Nonfiction; Reviews; *Areas:* How-to; Technology; *Markets:* Adult

Magazine covering the Android operating system, including news, features, reviews, and tips. Send query by email. No unsolicited mss.

Angling Times

1 Lincoln Court
Lincoln Road
Peterborough
PE1 2RF
Tel: +44 (0) 1733 395097
Email: steve.fitzpatrick@bauermedia.co.uk
Website:
http://www.gofishing.co.uk/Angling-Times

Publishes: Articles; News; Nonfiction; *Areas:* Hobbies; Nature; Sport; *Markets:* Adult

Editors: Steve Fitzpatrick

Magazine for fishing enthusiasts.

Aquila

Studio 2
67A Willowfield Road
Eastbourne
East Sussex
BN22 8AP
Tel: +44 (0) 1323 431313
Fax: +44 (0) 1323 731136
Email: info@aquila.co.uk
Website: https://www.aquila.co.uk

Publishes: Features; Fiction; Nonfiction; *Areas:* Short Stories; *Markets:* Children's

Magazine for children aged 8-13. Publishes fiction 1,000-1,150 words; serials 1,050-1,150 words per episode; and features between 600 and 800 words. See website for full submission guidelines.

Arc

c/o New Scientist
Lacon House
84 Theobald's Road
London
WC1X 8NS
Tel: +44 (0) 20 7611 1205
Email: simon.ings@arcfinity.org
Website: http://www.arcfinity.org

Publishes: Essays; Features; Fiction; Nonfiction; *Areas:* Science; Sci-Fi; Short Stories; *Markets:* Adult

Editors: Simon Ings

"Journal of the future". Publishes features, essays, and speculative fiction about the world to come. Most work is commissioned.

Architecture Today

34 Pentonville Road
London
N1 9HF
Tel: +44 (0) 20 7837 0143
Email: editorial@architecturetoday.co.uk
Website: http://www.architecturetoday.co.uk

Publishes: Articles; Features; Nonfiction; *Areas:* Architecture; *Markets:* Professional

Monthly magazine for architects, presenting

the most important current projects in the UK and the rest of Europe.

Areopagus Magazine

48 Cornwood Road
Plympton
Plymouth
PL7 1AL
Fax: +44 (0) 870 1346384
Email: editor@areopagus.org.uk
Website: http://www.areopagus.org.uk

Publishes: Articles; Fiction; Poetry; Reviews; *Areas:* Religious; Short Stories; *Markets:* Adult

Editors: Julian Barritt

A Christian-based arena for creative writers. A forum for debate on contemporary issues relating to Christianity and wider issues. A chance for new writers to have their work published for the first time. Writers' workshop's and market news also help inform both new and established writers. This press produce a range of small publications and have recently produced their first royalty-paying book. We can only consider MSS which are submitted by subscribers to the magazine however. Subscribers may submit by email.

Art Business Today

16-18 Empress Place
London
SW6 1TT
Tel: +44 (0) 20 7381 6616
Email: info@fineart.co.uk
Website: http://www.fineart.co.uk

Publishes: Articles; News; Nonfiction; *Areas:* Arts; Business; Technology; *Markets:* Professional

Magazine aimed at professionals in the fine art and framing industries.

Artificium

Email: editor@artificium.co.uk
Website: http://www.artificium.co.uk

Publishes: Fiction; Poetry; *Areas:* Short Stories; *Markets:* Adult; *Treatments:* Literary

Publishes short fiction between 2,000 and 6,000 words; three-part serials up to a total of 12,000 words; very short fiction between 400 and 1,250 words; and poetry of any length. All work must be in English and submitted by email during open reading periods: see website for details.

Assent

Room E701
Kedelston Road
University of Derby
Derby
DE22 1GB
Email: editorassent@gmail.com
Website: http://assentpoetry.com

Publishes: Essays; Interviews; Nonfiction; Poetry; Reviews; *Areas:* Criticism; Literature; *Markets:* Adult; *Treatments:* Literary

Editors: Julia Gaze

A leading small press magazine with a world wide circulation and readership. Publishes poetry, critical essays, interviews and reviews of contemporary collections.

Athletics Weekly

Athletics Weekly Limited
PO Box 614
Farnham
Surrey
GU9 1GR
Tel: +44 (0) 1733 808531
Fax: +44 (0) 1733 808530
Email: jason.henderson@athleticsweekly.com
Website: http://www.athletics-weekly.com

Publishes: Features; News; Nonfiction; *Areas:* Sport; *Markets:* Adult

Editors: Jason Henderson

Publishes features, news, and fixtures relating to track and field, race walking, sport politics, etc. Send query in writing in first instance.

Attitude

Attitude Media Ltd
33 Pear Tree Street
London
EC1V 3AG
Email: matthew.todd@attitude.co.uk
Website: http://attitude.co.uk

Publishes: Articles; Features; News; Nonfiction; *Areas:* Beauty and Fashion; Entertainment; Lifestyle; Men's Interests; Travel; *Markets:* Adult

Editors: Matthew Todd (Editorial Director)

Magazine for gay men.

BackTrack

PO Box No.3
Easingwold
York
YO61 3YS
Tel: +44 (0) 1347 824397
Email: pendragonpublishing@btinternet.com
Website:
http://www.pendragonpublishing.co.uk

Publishes: Articles; Features; Nonfiction; *Areas:* Historical; Travel; *Markets:* Adult

Editors: Michael Blakemore

Publishes articles on British railway history. See website for full guidelines.

Baptist Times

Baptist House
PO Box 44
129 Broadway
Didcot
Oxon
OX11 8RT
Email: editor@baptisttimes.co.uk
Website: http://www.baptisttimes.co.uk

Publishes: Articles; Features; News; Nonfiction; Reviews; *Areas:* Religious; *Markets:* Adult

Religious magazine. Welcomes direct submissions. Approach via contact form on website.

Bare Fiction Magazine

177 Copthorne Road
Shrewsbury
Shropshire
SY3 8NA
Email: info@barefiction.co.uk
Website:
http://www.barefictionmagazine.co.uk

Publishes: Essays; Fiction; Interviews; Nonfiction; Poetry; Reviews; Scripts; *Areas:* Drama; Literature; Short Stories; Theatre; *Markets:* Adult; *Treatments:* Literary

Publishes poetry, fiction and plays, literary review, interviews and commentary. Does not accept submissions at all times – check website for current status and sign up to newsletter to be notified when submissions next open.

The Beano

185 Fleet Street
London
EC4A 2HS
Tel: +44 (0) 1382 575580
Fax: +44 (0) 1382 575413
Email: beano@dcthomson.co.uk
Website: http://www.beano.com

Publishes: Fiction; *Areas:* Humour; Short Stories; *Markets:* Children's

Publishes comic strips for children aged 6-12. Accepts artwork and scripts.

The Big Issue

43 Bath Street
Glasgow
G2 1HW
Tel: +44 (0) 1413 527280
Email: editorial@bigissue.com
Website: http://www.bigissue.com

Publishes: Articles; Features; Interviews; News; Reviews; *Areas:* Arts; Culture; Sociology; *Markets:* Adult

General interest magazine focusing on social issues, culture, the arts, etc. No short stories or poetry.

Bird Watching

Media House
Lynch Wood
Peterborough
PE2 6EA
Tel: +44 (0) 1733 468000
Email: birdwatching@bauermedia.co.uk
Website: http://www.birdwatching.co.uk

Publishes: Articles; Features; Nonfiction; Reviews; *Areas:* Hobbies; Nature; *Markets:* Adult

Editors: Matthew Merritt

Magazine publishing articles, features, photography and reviews relating to birds. Send query with synopsis in first instance.

Bizarre

Dennis Publishing
30 Cleveland Street
London
W1T 4JD
Tel: +44 (0) 20 7907 6000
Email: bizarre@dennis.co.uk
Website: http://www.bizarremag.com

Publishes: Articles; Features; Interviews; News; Nonfiction; *Markets:* Adult

Describes itself as one of the most shocking magazines in the world. Publishes features, interviews, and uncensored photos of the weird, freakish, and outrageous. No fiction.

Black Static

TTA Press
5 Martins Lane
Witcham
Ely
Cambs
CB6 2LB
Website: http://ttapress.com

Publishes: Fiction; *Areas:* Fantasy; Horror; Short Stories; *Markets:* Adult; *Treatments:* Dark

Editors: Andy Cox

Publishes short stories of horror and dark fantasy. See website for full guidelines.

BMA News

BMA House
Tavistock Square
London
WC1H 9JP
Tel: +44 (0) 20 7387 4499
Email: bmanews@bma.org.uk
Website: http://bma.org.uk

Publishes: Features; News; Nonfiction; *Areas:* Medicine; *Markets:* Professional

Publishes medical news and analysis.

British Journal of Photography

Apptitude Media Ltd
Unit A, Zetland House
5-25 Scrutton Street
Shoreditch
London
EC2A 4HJ
Tel: +44 (0) 20 8123 6873
Email: bjp.editor@bjphoto.co.uk
Website: http://www.bjp-online.com

Publishes: Articles; News; Nonfiction; Reviews; *Areas:* Arts; Beauty and Fashion; Photography; Technology; *Markets:* Professional

Editors: Simon Bainbridge

Magazine for professional photographers, publishing articles and reviews.

Building

Ludgate House
245 Blackfriars Road
London
SE1 9UY
Tel: +44 (0) 20 7560 4000
Email: sarah.richardson@ubm.com
Website: http://www.building.co.uk

Publishes: Articles; News; Nonfiction; *Areas:* Architecture; Business; *Markets:* Professional

Editors: Sarah Richardson

Magazine for the construction industry.

Buses

PO Box 14644
Leven
KY9 1WX
Tel: +44 (0) 1780 755131
Fax: +44 (0) 1780 751323
Email: buseseditor@btconnect.com
Website: http://www.busesmag.com

Publishes: Articles; Nonfiction; *Areas:* Travel; *Markets:* Adult; Professional

Editors: Alan Millar

The UK's highest circulation magazine covering the bus and coach industries. Aimed at both industry professionals and interested enthusiasts. Query in first instance.

Caravan Magazine

Warners Group Publications
The Maltings
Bourne
Lincs
PE10 9PH
Tel: +44 (0) 1778 392450
Email: johns@warnersgroup.co.uk
Website: http://www.caravanmagazine.co.uk

Publishes: Articles; Nonfiction; *Areas:* Hobbies; Leisure; Travel; *Markets:* Adult

Editors: John Sootheran

Magazine for those interested in caravanning.

Carousel

The Saturn Centre
54-76 Bissell Street
Birmingham
B5 7HP
Tel: +44 (0) 1216 227458
Email: carousel.guide@virgin.net
Website: http://www.carouselguide.co.uk

Publishes: Articles; Interviews; Nonfiction; Reviews; *Areas:* Literature; *Markets:* Children's

Editors: David Blanch

Magazine publishing reviews of fiction, poetry, and nonfiction books for children. Also publishes articles, author profiles, and interviews.

The Casket of Fictional Delights

Email: joanna@thecasket.co.uk
Website: http://www.thecasket.co.uk

Publishes: Fiction; *Areas:* Short Stories; *Markets:* Adult

Editors: Joanna Sterling

Online magazine. Publishes flash fiction up to 300 words and short stories between 1,200 and 3,000 words. No children's stories, science fiction, excessive swearing, sex or violence. See website for full guidelines and to submit online.

The Catholic Herald

Herald House
15 Lamb's Passage
Bunhill Row
London
EC1Y 8TQ
Tel: +44 (0) 20 7448 3607
Fax: +44 (0) 20 7448 3603
Email: editorial@catholicherald.co.uk
Website: http://www.catholicherald.co.uk

Publishes: Articles; News; Nonfiction; *Areas:* Religious; *Markets:* Adult

Editors: Luke Coppen

Weekly magazine publishing articles and news for Catholics.

Ceramic Review

63 Great Russell Street
London
WC1B 3BF
Tel: +44 (0) 20 7183 5583
Fax: +44 (0) 20 3137 0924
Email: editorial@ceramicreview.com
Website: http://www.ceramicreview.com

Publishes: Articles; Features; Nonfiction; Reviews; *Areas:* Crafts; *Markets:* Adult

Magazine covering ceramics and clay art. See website for full submission guidelines.

Chapman

4 Broughton Place
Edinburgh
EH1 3RX
Tel: +44 (0) 131 557 2207
Email: chapman-pub@blueyonder.co.uk
Website: http://www.chapman-pub.co.uk

Publishes: Articles; Essays; Features; Fiction; Nonfiction; Poetry; Reviews; *Areas:* Arts; Criticism; Culture; Literature; Short Stories; Theatre; *Markets:* Adult; *Treatments:* Literary

Editors: Joy Hendry

Describes itself as Scotland's leading literary magazine, publishing new creative writing – poetry, fiction, discussion of cultural affairs, theatre, reviews and the arts in general, plus critical essays. It publishes international as well as Scottish writers and is a dynamic force for artistic and cultural change and development. Always open to new writers and ideas.

Fiction may be of any length, but average is around 3,000 words. Send one piece at a time. Poetry submissions should contain between four and ten poems. Single poems are not usually published.

Articles and reviews are usually commissioned and ideas should be discussed with the editor in advance.

All submissions must include an SAE or IRCs or email address for response. No submissions by email.

Classic Boat

The Chelsea Magazine Company
Jubilee House
2 Jubilee Place
London
SW3 3TQ
Tel: +44 (0) 20 7349 3700
Fax: +44 (0) 20 7349 3701
Email:
Dan.Houston@chelseamagazines.com
Website: http://www.classicboat.co.uk

Publishes: Articles; Features; News; Nonfiction; Reviews; *Areas:* Crafts; Historical; Hobbies; Travel; *Markets:* Adult

Editors: Dan Houston

Showcases classic yachts and traditionally designed workboats, plus news, opinions and reviews. Read at least three previous issues then query for guidelines if appropriate.

Classic Cars

Bauer
Lynch Wood
Peterborough Business Park
Peterborough
Cambridgeshire
PE2 6EA
Tel: +44 (0) 1733 468582
Email: classic.cars@bauermedia.co.uk
Website:
http://www.classiccarsmagazine.co.uk

Publishes: Articles; Nonfiction; *Areas:* Historical; Technology; Travel; *Markets:* Adult

Publishes articles on classic cars and related events.

Closer

Tel: +44 (0) 20 7859 8463
Email: closer@closermag.co.uk
Website: http://www.closeronline.co.uk

Publishes: Articles; Features; News; Nonfiction; *Areas:* Beauty and Fashion; Entertainment; Health; Lifestyle; Women's Interests; *Markets:* Adult

Women's lifestyle magazine publishing news, articles, and features on style and beauty, body and wellbeing, celebrities, and real life stories.

Commando

185 Fleet Street
London
EC4A 2HS
Email: webmaster@commandocomics.com

Website: http://www.commandocomics.com

Publishes: Fiction; *Areas:* Adventure; Military; Short Stories; *Markets:* Adult; Children's; Youth

Publishes stories of action and adventure set in times of war, told in graphic novel format. May be wars of the modern age or ancient wars, or even occasionally wars of the future. Encourages new writers. Send synopsis in first instance.

Cook Vegetarian

25 Phoenix Court
Hawkins Road
Colchester
Essex
CO2 8JY
Tel: +44 (0) 1206 508627
Email: fae@cookveg.co.uk
Website:
http://www.vegetarianrecipesmag.com

Publishes: Nonfiction; *Areas:* Cookery; *Markets:* Adult

Editors: Fae Gilfillan

Publishes recipes for meat-free cooking.

craft&design Magazine

PO Box 5
Driffield
East Yorkshire
YO25 8JD
Tel: +44 (0) 1377 255213
Email: info@craftanddesign.net
Website: http://www.craftanddesign.net

Publishes: Articles; Features; News; Nonfiction; *Areas:* Crafts; Design; *Markets:* Adult

Editors: Angie Boyer

Publishes material for those interested in crafts and design. Ideas for articles and features welcome.

Crafts

44a Pentonville Road
Islington
N1 9BY
Tel: +44 (0) 20 7806 2538
Email: editorial@craftscouncil.org.uk
Website: http://www.craftsmagazine.org.uk

Publishes: Articles; Features; News; Nonfiction; Reviews; *Areas:* Crafts; *Markets:* Adult

Magazine covering crafts. Send query by email with brief outline and example of previous work. Response not guaranteed.

Crystal Magazine

3 Bowness Avenue
Prenton
Birkenhead
CH43 0SD
Tel: +44 (0) 1516 089736
Email: christinecrystal@hotmail.com
Website:
http://www.christinecrystal.blogspot.com

Publishes: Articles; Fiction; Nonfiction; Poetry; *Areas:* Fantasy; Humour; Literature; Mystery; Nature; Romance; Sci-Fi; Short Stories; Suspense; Thrillers; Travel; Westerns; *Markets:* Adult; *Treatments:* Light; Literary; Mainstream; Popular; Positive; Traditional

Editors: Christine Carr

A Popular Publication for Creative Writers. Your poems, your stories, your articles and more. FOR SUBSCRIBERS ONLY.

A4. Spiral-bound and easy to lie open. 40 pages. Bi-monthly. Part colour. Stories (true and fiction), articles, poems. Work is only considered from subscribers. Submissions from subscribers can be any length and theme except erotica. Work can be sent by email or post. Handwritten material is acceptable.

Under normal circumstances you will not have to wait weeks and weeks for a reply.

Readers' Letters (usually pages and pages).

Subscribers' News.

Wordsmithing – Titters, Tips, Titillations.

Each issue the writer of the most popular piece will win £10.

I have received a lot of positive feedback over the years. Here are just two comments:

"The magazine is good value for money and worth every penny." Alan Jones

"Thanks for providing us with such a great and friendly magazine." Heather Buswell

The current May magazine is now out. This is number 87 which means November 2015 will be the 90th.

2015 is 150 years since Lewis Carroll wrote Alice's Adventures in Wonderland and Jules Verne wrote From the Earth to the Moon. From subscribers I am looking for Science Fiction and children's stories/poems/articles to feature in a bumper November issue which will be the 90th issue.

Cycle Sport

IPC Focus Network
Leon House
233 High Street
Croydon
CR9 1HZ
Tel: +44 (0) 20 8726 8453
Email: cyclesport@ipcmedia.com
Website: http://www.cyclesportmag.com

Publishes: Articles; Features; Interviews; News; Nonfiction; *Areas:* Sport; *Markets:* Adult; Professional

Editors: Robert Garbutt

Magazine on professional cycle racing. Includes coverage of events such as the Tour de France, and interviews with the big names in the field. Most material commissioned, but will consider unsolicited materia. Welcomes ideas for articles and features.

Dare

Ground Floor
16 Connaught Place
London
W2 2ES
Tel: +44 (0) 20 7420 7000
Email: info@therivergroup.co.uk
Website: http://www.therivergroup.co.uk

Publishes: Articles; Features; Nonfiction; *Areas:* Beauty and Fashion; Women's Interests; *Markets:* Adult

Free magazine published on behalf of high street chain.

The Dawntreader

24 Forest Houses
Cookworthy Moor
Halwill
Beaworthy
Devon
EX21 5UU
Email: dawnidp@indigodreams.co.uk
Website: http://www.indigodreams.co.uk

Publishes: Articles; Features; Fiction; Nonfiction; Poetry; *Areas:* Fantasy; Nature; Short Stories; *Markets:* Adult

Editors: Ronnie Goodyer

A quarterly publication specialising in the landscape; myth and legend... nature; spirituality and pre-history... environment and ecology... the mystic.

Seeking poetry in all forms and also welcomes prose up to 1,000 words, articles and local legends.

Decanter

Blue Fin Building
110 Southwark Street
SE1 0SU
Tel: +44 (0) 20 3148 5000
Email: editor@decanter.com
Website: http://www.decanter.com

Publishes: Articles; Features; News; Nonfiction; *Areas:* Cookery; Travel; *Markets:* Adult

Magazine on wines publishing articles, features, and news relating to wine and related subjects of food, cookery, etc. Welcomes ideas by post or fax.

Decanto

PO Box 3257
Littlehampton
BN16 9AF
Email: masque_pub@btinternet.com
Website: http://myweb.tiscali.co.uk/masquepublishing/decanto.html

Publishes: Poetry; *Markets:* Adult

Editors: Lisa Stewart

Send up to six original poems, of which 1-3 may be published, by post with SAE or by email in the body of the message (no attachments). Poems of any subject or style are considered.

The Dickensian

The School of English
Rutherford College
University of Kent
Canterbury
Kent
CT2 7NX
Email: M.Y.Andrews@kent.ac.uk
Website: http://www.dickensfellowship.org/dickensian

Publishes: Articles; Nonfiction; *Areas:* Biography; Criticism; Historical; Literature; *Markets:* Adult

Editors: Professor Malcolm Andrews

Publishes articles on the life and works of Dickens. Send articles as hard copy by post with SAE and electronic copy in .doc format (not .docx). See website for full guidelines.

Digital Camera World

Quay House
The Ambury
Bath
BA1 1UA
Tel: +44 (0) 1225 442244
Website:
http://www.digitalcameraworld.com

Publishes: Articles; Features; Nonfiction; Reviews; *Areas:* How-to; Photography; *Markets:* Adult

How-to magazine for photographers, including reviews of equipment and software, etc.

Dogs Today

The Old Print House
62 The High Street
Chobham
Surrey
GU24 8AA
Tel: +44 (0) 1276 858880
Fax: +44 (0) 1276 858860
Email: enquiries@dogstodaymagazine.co.uk
Website:
http://www.dogstodaymagazine.co.uk

Publishes: Articles; Features; Interviews; Nonfiction; *Areas:* Entertainment; Health; Hobbies; Nature; Travel; *Markets:* Adult

Glossy monthly magazine for dog lovers. Send submissions by post with SAE, or by email with "Editorial Submission" in the subject line.

Dragon's Haul

Tel: +44 (0) 1303 720155
Email: editors@dragonshaul.com
Website: http://dragonshaul.com

Publishes: Fiction; *Areas:* Fantasy; *Markets:* Adult; Youth; *Treatments:* Commercial; Contemporary; Cynical; Dark; Experimental; Light; Literary; Mainstream; Popular; Progressive; Satirical; Serious; Traditional

Editors: Andy Coughlan and David Winstanley

A Fantasy Fiction short story anthology, and sister publication to a Sci-Fi anthology. Published bimonthly exclusively through Apple's Newsstand app and Google's Play Store, it will be available to billions of iOS and Android users.

The aim of the anthology is to bring cutting-edge fiction to an eager and discerning global Fantasy Fiction audience.

We welcome fiction submissions from around the globe (please refer to our submissions guidelines), and we look forward to publishing brilliant and astounding Fantasy Fiction to a worldwide readership.

Drapers

Telephone House
69-77 Paul St
London
EC2A 4NQ
Tel: +44 (0) 20 3033 2600
Email: eric.musgrave@emap.com
Website: http://www.drapersonline.com

Publishes: Articles; Nonfiction; *Areas:* Beauty and Fashion; Business; Design; *Markets:* Professional

Editors: Eric Musgrave

Magazine for fashion retailers and suppliers.

Dream Catcher

Stairwell Books
161 Lowther Street
York
YO31 7LZ
Tel: +44 (0) 1904 733767
Email: rose@stairwellbooks.com
Website:
http://www.dreamcatchermagazine.co.uk

Publishes: Fiction; Interviews; Nonfiction; Poetry; Reviews; *Areas:* Short Stories; Translations; *Markets:* Adult; *Treatments:* Literary

Editors: Paul Sutherland

Send submissions by post, following guidelines on website.

East Lothian Life

1 Beveridge Row
Belhaven
Dunbar
East Lothian
EH42 1TP
Tel: +44 (0) 1368 863593
Fax: +44 (0) 1368 863593
Email: info@eastlothianlife.co.uk
Website: http://www.eastlothianlife.co.uk

Publishes: Articles; Features; Nonfiction; *Markets:* Adult

Editors: Pauline Jaffray

Publishes articles and features relating to East Lothian.

The Edge

Unit 138
22 Notting Hill Gate
London
W11 3JE
Tel: +44 (0) 8454 569337
Email: enquiries@theedgemagazine.co.uk
Website: http://www.theedgemagazine.co.uk

Publishes: Features; Fiction; Interviews; Nonfiction; Reviews; *Areas:* Crime; Entertainment; Erotic; Fantasy; Gothic; Horror; Sci-Fi; *Markets:* Adult; *Treatments:* Contemporary; Experimental

Editors: Dave Clark

Not accepting submissions as at May 2014. See website for current status.

Education Journal

The Education Publishing Company
Devonia House
4 Union Terrace
Crediton
EX17 3DY
Tel: +44 (0) 1363 774455
Fax: +44 (0) 1363 776592
Email: ejw@educationpublishing.com
Website:
http://www.educationpublishing.com

Publishes: Articles; Features; News; Nonfiction; *Markets:* Professional

Magazine for education professionals, including news, features, analysis, conference and parliamentary reports, reviews of major documents and research reports on schools, colleges, universities and the full range of educational issues.

Energy Engineering

Media Culture
Office 46
Pure Offices
Plato Close
Leamington Spa
Warwickshire
CV34 6WE
Tel: +44 (0) 1926 671338
Email: info@energyengineering.co.uk
Website:
http://www.energyengineering.co.uk

Publishes: Articles; Features; News; Nonfiction; *Areas:* Design; Technology; *Markets:* Professional

Magazine covering the products and processes, innovation, technology and management of renewable energy and sustainability.

The English Garden

The Chelsea Magazine Company
Third Floor Offices
Cumberland House
Oriel Road
Cheltenham
GL50 1BB
Email:
theenglishgarden@chelseamagazines.com
Website: http://www.theenglishgarden.co.uk

Publishes: Articles; Features; Nonfiction; *Areas:* Gardening; How-to; *Markets:* Adult

Editors: Stephanie Mahon

Publishes features on gardens across the UK and Ireland, as well as gardening advice.

Envoi

Meirion House
Glan yr afon
Tanygrisiau
Blaenau Ffestiniog
LL41 3SU
Tel: +44 (0) 1766 832112
Email: jan@envoipoetry.com
Website:
http://www.cinnamonpress.com/envoi

Publishes: Articles; Nonfiction; Poetry; Reviews; *Areas:* Literature; Translations; *Markets:* Adult; *Treatments:* Literary

Editors: Dr Jan Fortune-Wood

Magazine of poems, poetry sequences, reviews, and competitions, now more than 50 years old. Occasional poetry related articles and poetry in translation. Submit up to 6 poems up to 40 lines each or one or two longer poems by email only (in the body of the email; attachments will not be read). No submissions by post.

What others say:

"Probably the best poetry magazine currently available" – The Writers' College

"Without a grant and obviously well read, this poetry magazine excels itself." – Ore

"The policy of giving poets space to show their skills is the right one." – Haiku Quarterly

"Good quality, lots of bounce, poems, comps, reviews, reader comeback" – iota

"If you haven't tried it yet, do so, you'll get your money's worth." – New Hope International

Erotic Review

Email: editorial@ermagazine.org
Website: http://eroticreviewmagazine.com

Publishes: Articles; Features; Fiction; Nonfiction; Reviews; *Areas:* Erotic; Lifestyle; Short Stories; *Markets:* Adult

Editors: Jamie Maclean

Literary lifestyle publication about sex and sexuality aimed at sophisticated, intelligent and mature readers. Print version has been retired and is now online only. Publishes features, articles, short stories, and reviews. See website for full submission guidelines.

Esquire

Hearst Magazines UK London
72 Broadwick Street

London
W1F 9EP
Tel: +44 (0) 20 7439 5000
Email: alex.bilmes@hearst.co.uk
Website: http://www.esquire.co.uk

Publishes: Articles; Features; Nonfiction; *Areas:* Beauty and Fashion; Culture; Lifestyle; Men's Interests; Technology; *Markets:* Adult

Editors: Alex Bilmes

Men's general interest magazine. Publishes features and articles on style, tech gadgets, food and drink, culture, and women.

Evergreen

The Lypiatts
Lansdown Road
Cheltenham
Gloucestershire
GL50 2JA
Tel: +44 (0) 1242 225780
Email: editor@evergreenmagazine.co.uk
Website: https://www.thisengland.co.uk

Publishes: Articles; *Areas:* Culture; Historical; Nature; Travel; *Markets:* Adult

Magazine which "takes readers on a gentle journey around the highways and byways of Britain", covering British history, culture, people, and places. Publishes articles and poetry.

Family Law Journal

Jordan Publishing Limited
21 St Thomas Street
Bristol
BS1 6JS
Tel: +44 (0) 1179 230600
Fax: +44 (0) 1179 250486
Email: sales@jordanpublishing.co.uk
Website: http://www.jordanpublishing.co.uk

Publishes: Articles; Nonfiction; *Areas:* Legal; *Markets:* Professional

Editors: Elizabeth Walsh

Legal journal publishing articles in the area of family law.

Feminist Review

c/o Women's Studies,
London Metropolitan University
166-220 Holloway Road
London
N7 8DB
Email: feminist-review@londonmet.ac.uk
Website: http://www.feminist-review.com

Publishes: Articles; Essays; Fiction; Interviews; Nonfiction; *Areas:* Politics; Sociology; Women's Interests; *Markets:* Academic; Adult; *Treatments:* Experimental

Editors: Joanna Hoare, Assistant Editor

Peer reviewed, interdisciplinary feminist journal. Publishes academic articles, experimental pieces, visual and textual media and political interventions, including, for example, interviews, short stories, poems and photographic essays. Submit via online submission system.

Fire Magazine

Ground Floor
Rayford House
School Road
Hove
BN3 5HX
Tel: +44 (0) 1273 434951
Email: andrew.lynch@pavpub.com
Website: http://www.fire-magazine.com

Publishes: Articles; Nonfiction; *Markets:* Professional

Editors: Andrew Lynch

Publishes expert articles and fire fighting and prevention. No unsolicited mss; query in first instance.

Fishing News

11th Floor
Nexus Place
25 Farringdon Street
London
EC4A 4AB
Tel: +44 (0) 1434 607375
Email: editor@fishingnews.co.uk
Website: http://fishingnews.co.uk

Publishes: Articles; News; Nonfiction; *Areas:* Business; Legal; Nature; *Markets:* Professional

Editors: Dave Linkie

Magazine for the fishing industry.

Flash: The International Short-Short Story Magazine

Department of English
University of Chester
Parkgate Road
Chester
CH1 4BJ
Email: flash.magazine@chester.ac.uk
Website:
http://www.chester.ac.uk/flash.magazine

Publishes: Fiction; *Areas:* Short Stories; *Markets:* Adult; *Treatments:* Literary

Editors: Dr Peter Blair; Dr Ashley Chantler

Publishes flash fiction up to 360 words, including the title. Send up to four pieces per issue. Attach submissions to a single email. See website for full submission guidelines.

France

Archant House
3 Oriel Road
Cheltenham
GL50 1BB
Tel: +44 (0) 1242 216050
Email: editorial@francemag.com
Website: http://www.francemag.com

Publishes: Articles; Features; Interviews; Nonfiction; *Areas:* Cookery; Culture; Film; Historical; Literature; Travel; *Markets:* Adult

Editors: Carolyn Boyd

Magazine about France, including articles on weekend getaways, destinations and holiday ideas, food and wine section, history and culture, guide to improving your French, book and film reviews, interviews with A-list French stars and France-loving celebrities.

Freelance Market News

8-10 Dutton Street
Manchester
M3 1LE
Tel: +44 (0) 161 819 9919
Fax: +44 (0) 161 819 2842
Email: fmn@writersbureau.com
Website:
http://www.freelancemarketnews.com

Publishes: Articles; News; Nonfiction; *Markets:* Adult; Professional

Editors: Angela Cox

Publishes well-researched notes for markets for writers (including the editor's full name with a complete address, telephone and fax number, email address and website, and preferably a quote from the editor or editorial office giving advice to potential contributors) and short articles around 700 words (one page) or 1500 words (two pages). Welcomes unsolicited MSS.

The Friend

173 Euston Road
London
NW1 2BJ
Tel: +44 (0) 20 7663 1010
Email: editorial@thefriend.org
Website: https://thefriend.org

Publishes: Articles; Features; Nonfiction; *Areas:* Arts; Humour; Nature; Politics; Religious; Sociology; *Markets:* Adult

Unofficial magazine of Quaker interest intended to propogate their religious teaching, and promote interest in their work.

Go Girl Magazine

239 Kensington High Street
Kensington
W8 6SA
Email: gogirlmag@euk.egmont.com
Website: http://www.gogirlmag.co.uk

Publishes: Articles; Features; Interviews; News; Nonfiction; *Areas:* Beauty and Fashion; Entertainment; Film; Lifestyle; Music; *Markets:* Children's

Magazine for girls aged 7-11, covering beauty, fashion, celebrity news and gossip, friends, pets, etc.

Gay Times (GT Magazine)

Millivres Prowler Group
Unit M, Spectrum House
32-34 Gordon House Road
London
NW5 1LP
Tel: +44 (0) 20 7424 7400
Email: edit@gaytimes.co.uk
Website: http://www.gaytimes.co.uk

Publishes: Articles; Features; Interviews; Nonfiction; *Areas:* Arts; Beauty and Fashion; Culture; Current Affairs; Entertainment; Film; Health; Lifestyle; Music; Technology; *Markets:* Adult

Editors: Darren Scott

Lifestyle magazine aimed at gay men.

The Good Book Guide

4A All Hallows Road
Bispham
Blackpool
Lancs
FY2 0AS
Tel: +44 (0) 1213 143539
Fax: +44 (0) 20 3070 0343
Email: enquiries@thegoodbookguide.com
Website: http://www.thegoodbookguide.com

Publishes: Nonfiction; Reviews; *Areas:* Literature; *Markets:* Adult

Publishes reviews of books published in the UK.

Graffiti Magazine

Email: graffiti.magazine@yahoo.co.uk
Website:
https://www.facebook.com/pages/Graffiti-Magazine/63653000411

Publishes: Fiction; Interviews; Poetry; Reviews; *Areas:* Short Stories; *Markets:* Adult; *Treatments:* Literary

Editors: Rona Laycock

Magazine produced by a writers group to help showcase local writing, and to publish commissioned items and competition winners. Publishes fiction, poetry, reviews, and interviews.

Granta

12 Addison Avenue
Holland Park
London
W11 4QR
Tel: +44 (0) 20 7605 1360
Fax: +44 (0) 20 7605 1361
Email: editorial@granta.com
Website: http://www.granta.com

Publishes: Fiction; Nonfiction; *Areas:* Autobiography; Culture; Politics; Short Stories; *Markets:* Adult; *Treatments:* Contemporary; Literary

Editors: Sigrid Rausing; Yuka Igarashi; Rachael Allen

Publishes fiction, memoirs, reportage, and photography. Issues tend to be themed and aim to be high-brow, diverse, and contemporary. No essays, book reviews, articles or news items that are topical and therefore transitory, genre fiction, poetry, or travel writing that does not have a particular focus. Accepts submissions between October 1 and April 1 only. No length limits, but pieces are generally between 3,000 and 6,000 words. Submit online through website submission system.

Greetings Today

1 Churchgates
The Wilderness
Berkhamsted
HP4 2UB
Tel: +44 (0) 1442 289930
Email: tracey@lemapublishing.co.uk
Website: http://www.greetingstoday.co.uk

Publishes: Articles; Features; News; Nonfiction; Reference; *Areas:* Business; *Markets:* Professional

Editors: Tracey Bearton

Trade magazine for the greetings card

industry, publishing articles, features, news, and a directory for artists seeking publishers.

The Grocer

William Reed Business Media Ltd
Broadfield Park
Crawley
RH11 9RT
Tel: +44 (0) 1293 610263
Email: adam.leyland@wrbm.com
Website: http://www.thegrocer.co.uk

Publishes: Articles; News; Nonfiction; *Areas:* Business; *Markets:* Professional

Editors: Adam Leyland

Magazine for professionals in the grocery trade.

Grow Your Own

25 Phoenix Court
Hawkins Road
Colchester
Essex
CO2 8JY
Tel: +44 (0) 1206 505979
Email: lucy.halsall@aceville.co.uk
Website: http://www.growfruitandveg.co.uk

Publishes: Articles; Features; News; Nonfiction; *Areas:* Gardening; How-to; *Markets:* Adult

Editors: Lucy Halsall

Magazine covering the growing of fruit and veg.

Health Club Management

The Leisure Media Company Ltd
Portmill House
Portmill Lane
Hitchin
Hertfordshire
SG5 1DJ
Tel: +44 (0) 1462 431385
Fax: +44 (0) 1462 433909
Email: lizterry@leisuremedia.com
Website:
http://www.healthclubmanagement.co.uk

Publishes: Articles; News; Nonfiction; *Areas:* Business; Health; Leisure; *Markets:* Professional

Editors: Liz Terry

Professional magazine for those involved in the running of health clubs, sports centres, etc.

Heat

Endeavour House
189 Shaftesbury Avenue
London
WC2H 8JG
Email: heatEd@heatmag.com
Website: http://www.heatworld.com

Publishes: Articles; Features; News; Nonfiction; *Areas:* Entertainment; *Markets:* Adult

Publishes news and features on celebrities.

Homes and Gardens

IPC Media Limited
Blue Fin Building
110 Southwark Street
London
SE1 0SU
Tel: +44 (0) 20 3148 5000
Email: housetohome@ipcmedia.com
Website: http://www.housetohome.co.uk/homesandgardens

Publishes: Articles; Nonfiction; *Areas:* Design; Gardening; How-to; *Markets:* Adult

Publishes articles on domestic design, both inside and out.

Horse & Hound

IPC Media
Blue Fin Building
110 Southwark Street
SE1 0SU
Tel: +44 (0) 20 3148 4562
Fax: +44 (0) 20 3148 8128
Email: lucy_higginson@ipcmedia.com
Website: http://www.horseandhound.co.uk

Publishes: Articles; News; Nonfiction;

Areas: Sport; *Markets:* Adult

Editors: Lucy Higginson

Weekly magazine publishing news and articles relating to equestrian sports.

I-70 Review

913 Joseph Drive
Lawrence, KS 66044
Email: i70review@gmail.com

Publishes: Fiction; Poetry; *Areas:* Short Stories; *Markets:* Adult; *Treatments:* Literary

Accepts submissions of fiction and flash fiction or 3-5 poems, by email, during the reading period that runs from July 1 to January 31. Maximum one submission per reading period. Accepts simultaneous submissions, but no previously published work. See website for full details.

ICIS Chemical Business Magazine

Reed Business Information
Quadrant House
The Quadrant
Sutton
Surrey
SM2 5AS
Tel: +44 (0) 20 8652 3500
Fax: +44 (0) 20 8652 3375
Email: icbeditorial@icis.com
Website: http://www.icis.com

Publishes: Articles; Features; News; Nonfiction; *Areas:* Business; Science; *Markets:* Professional

Business magazine covering the global chemical markets.

Icon Magazine

Tel: +44 (0) 20 3225 5200
Email: christopher@icon-magazine.co.uk
Website: http://www.iconeye.com

Publishes: Articles; Interviews; Reviews; *Areas:* Architecture; Arts; Design; *Markets:* Adult

Editors: Christopher Turner

Magazine of architecture and design. Includes interviews with architects and designers, visits to the best new buildings, analysis of new cultural movements and technologies, and reviews of an eclectic range of exhibitions, books, products and films.

Intermedia

The International Institute of Communications
2 Printers Yard
90a Broadway
London
SW19 1RD
Tel: +44 (0) 20 8417 0600
Fax: +44 (0) 20 8417 0800
Email: j.grimshaw@iicom.org
Website: http://www.iicom.org/intermedia

Publishes: Articles; Nonfiction; *Areas:* Media; Politics; Science; Technology; *Markets:* Academic; Professional

Editors: Joanne Grimshaw

Journal on media and telecom policy, aimed at regulators and policymakers, academics, lawyers, consultants and service providers around the world. Send query by email.

International Affairs

Email: csoper@chathamhouse.org
Website: http://www.chathamhouse.org/publications/ia

Publishes: Articles; Nonfiction; Reviews; *Areas:* Current Affairs; Politics; *Markets:* Academic

Editors: Caroline Soper

Publishes peer-reviewed articles on international current affairs and relevant book reviews. Send submissions by email as Word documents with abstract summarising the main points of the article and a note about the author. See website for full guidelines.

Interzone

TTA Press
5 Martins Lane
Witcham
Ely
Cambs
CB6 2LB
Website: http://ttapress.com

Publishes: Fiction; *Areas:* Fantasy; Sci-Fi; Short Stories; *Markets:* Adult

Editors: Andy Cox

Publishes science fiction and fantasy short stories up to about 10,000 words. See website for full guidelines and online submission system.

Irish Pages

129 Ormeau Road
Belfast
BT7 1SH
Tel: +44 (0) 2890 434800
Email: editor@irishpages.org
Website: http://www.irishpages.org

Publishes: Essays; Fiction; Nonfiction; Poetry; Reviews; *Areas:* Autobiography; Historical; Nature; Science; Short Stories; Translations; *Markets:* Adult; *Treatments:* Literary

Editors: Chris Agee

Non-partisan and non-sectarian literary journal publishing writing from the island of Ireland and elsewhere in equal measure. Publishes work in English, and in the Irish Language or Ulster Scots with English translations or glosses. Welcomes submissions throughout the year by post only with SAE or IRCs. See website for more details.

The Irish Post

Suite A
1 Lindsey Street
Smithfield
London
EC1A 9HP
Tel: +44 (0) 20 8900 4193
Email: editor@irishpost.co.uk
Website: http://www.irishpost.co.uk

Publishes: Articles; News; Nonfiction; *Areas:* Business; Entertainment; Lifestyle; Politics; Sport; Travel; *Markets:* Adult

Editors: Siobhán Breatnach

Magazine aimed at the Irish community in Britain, covering social events, sports, politics, and entertainment.

Jewish Quarterly

93 South Hill Park
London
NW3 2SP
Tel: +44 (0) 20 7443 5155
Email: info@jewishquarterly.org
Website: http://www.jewishquarterly.org

Publishes: Essays; Fiction; Nonfiction; Poetry; *Areas:* Arts; Culture; Current Affairs; Historical; Literature; Music; Philosophy; Politics; Religious; Short Stories; *Markets:* Adult; *Treatments:* Literary

Says of itself it "leads the field in Jewish writing, covering a wide spectrum of subjects including art, criticism, fiction, film, history, Judaism, literature, poetry, philosophy, politics, theatre, the Shoah, Zionism and much more". Submissions welcomed by email or post with SAE.

The Journal

17 High Street
Maryport
Cumbria
CA15 6BQ
Email: smithsssj@aol.com
Website:
http://www.freewebs.com/thesamsmith/

Publishes: Articles; Interviews; Poetry; Reviews; *Areas:* Translations; *Markets:* Adult

Editors: Sam Smith

This publication continues to keep up its Scandinavian connections, especially with the diaspora. Keen to sustain its international flavour, I favour dual text publication where possible. Regards the criteria for acceptance for those poems written in English, I think it best to quote from the editorial for issue 1 – the aim being .... "to publish those poems ... written with thought to what the poem is saying and to how it is being said." The magazine is A4, stapled, about 40 pages long, a third of the pages given over to articles and/or reviews.

Email submissions accepted in the body of the email only, not as attached files. See website for full details.

Junior

Immediate Media Co. Ltd
(Formerly Magicalia Publishing Ltd)
15-18 White Lion Street
London
N1 9PG

Immediate Media Co.
Vineyard House
44 Brook Green
Hammersmith
W6 7BT
Tel: +44 (0) 20 7150 5000
Email: editorial@juniormagazine.co.uk
Website: http://www.juniormagazine.co.uk

Publishes: Articles; Features; Nonfiction; *Areas:* Beauty and Fashion; Cookery; Entertainment; Health; Lifestyle; Travel; *Markets:* Adult; Family

Editors: Catherine O'Dolan

Glossy, family lifestyle magazine aimed at parents of children 0-8, including informative features and expert advice on child development, education and health, as well as children's fashion, inspirational interiors and child-friendly travel suggestions.

Kent Life

Apple Barn
Hythe Road, Smeeth
Ashford
Kent
TN25 6SS
Tel: +44 (0) 1303 817000
Email: sarah.sturt@archant.co.uk
Website: http://www.kent-life.co.uk

Publishes: Articles; Features; Nonfiction; *Areas:* Entertainment; Historical; Leisure; Lifestyle; Travel; *Markets:* Adult

Editors: Sarah Sturt

Local lifestyle magazine for Kent. Publishes articles and features on local people, events, walks, and heritage, etc. Send query with ideas for articles and features in first instance.

Kids Alive!

The Salvation Army
101 Newington Causeway
London
SE1 6BN
Tel: +44 (0) 20 7367 4911
Fax: +44 (0) 20 7367 4710
Email: kidsalive@salvationarmy.org.uk
Website:
http://www.salvationarmy.org.uk/kidsalive

Publishes: Fiction; Nonfiction; *Areas:* Religious; *Markets:* Children's

Editors: Justin Reeves

Christian children's magazine publishing puzzles, comic strips, etc.

Lancashire Magazine

Seasiders Way
Blackpool
Lancashire
FY1 6NZ
Tel: +44 (0) 1253 336588
Fax: +44 (0) 1253 336587
Email: website@lancashiremagazine.co.uk
Website: http://thelancashiremagazine.com

Publishes: Articles; Nonfiction; *Areas:* Leisure; Lifestyle; *Markets:* Adult

Publishes articles relating to Lancashire and the North West.

Legal Week

Incisive Media

Haymarket House
28-29 Haymarket
London
SW1Y 4RX
Tel: +44 (0) 20 7316 9755
Email: georgina.stanley@incisivemedia.com
Website: http://www.legalweek.com

Publishes: Articles; Features; News; Nonfiction; *Areas:* Business; Legal; *Markets:* Professional

Editors: Georgina Stanley

Magazine dedicated exclusively to commercial lawyers in the UK and major international jurisdictions.

Leopard Magazine

24 Cairnaquheen Gardens
Aberdeen
AB15 5HJ
Email: editor@leopardmag.co.uk
Website: http://www.leopardmag.co.uk

Publishes: Articles; Fiction; News; Nonfiction; Poetry; *Areas:* Culture; Historical; Short Stories; *Markets:* Adult

Editors: Judy Mackie

Magazine celebrating the people, places, history, and heritage of North-East Scotland. For articles, send query in first instance. For poetry and fiction, send complete ms.

The List

14 High Street
Edinburgh
EH1 1TE
Tel: +44 (0) 1315 503050
Email: newwriters@list.co.uk
Website: http://www.list.co.uk

Publishes: Articles; Features; Nonfiction; *Areas:* Arts; Entertainment; Film; Literature; Music; Theatre; TV; *Markets:* Adult

Magazine intended to publicise and promote arts, events and entertainment taking place in Scotland.

Living France Magazine

Archant House
Oriel Road
Cheltenham
Glos
GL50 1BB
Tel: +44 (0) 1242 216050
Email: karen.tait@archant.co.uk
Website: http://www.livingfrance.com

Publishes: Articles; Features; Interviews; Nonfiction; *Areas:* Culture; How-to; Leisure; Lifestyle; Travel; *Markets:* Adult

Editors: Karen Tait

Magazine for poeple looking to relocate to France. Includes advice on buying property, starting a business, and stories from ex-pats.

Lunar Poetry

Email: editor@lunarpoetry.co.uk
Website: http://www.lunarpoetry.co.uk

Publishes: Articles; Nonfiction; Poetry; Reviews; *Areas:* Criticism; Literature; *Markets:* Adult; *Treatments:* Literary

Publishes poems of any kind or style, articles on poetry up to 1,000 words, and reviews. Send up to six poems in the body of an email or as attachments, with 50-word bio. See website for full submission guidelines.

Magma

23 Pine Walk
Carshalton
SM5 4ES
Email: contributions@magmapoetry.com
Website: http://www.magmapoetry.com

Publishes: Nonfiction; Poetry; Reviews; *Areas:* Literature; *Markets:* Adult; *Treatments:* Literary

Editors: Laurie Smith

Prefers submissions by email. Postal submissions accepted from the UK only, and must include SAE. Accepts poems and artwork. Poems are considered for one issue only – they are not held over from one issue to the next. Seeks poems that give a direct sense of what it is to live today – honest about feelings, alert about world, sometimes funny, always well crafted. Strongly prefers poems to be in the body of the email, rather than an attachment. If, for formatting reasons, you feel you must use an attachment include all the poems you are submitting in one file. Also publishes reviews of books and pamphlets of poetry. See website for details and separate contact details.

Market Newsletter

Bureau of Freelance Photographers
Focus House
497 Green Lanes
London
N13 4BP
Tel: +44 (0) 20 8882 3315
Email: info@thebfp.com
Website: http://www.thebfp.com

Publishes: Articles; News; Nonfiction; *Areas:* Photography; *Markets:* Professional

Publishes stories and markets of interest to freelance photographers.

Media Week

Haymarket Publishing Ltd
174 Hammersmith Road
London
W6 7JP
Tel: +44 (0) 20 8267 8024
Email: arif.durrani@haymarket.com
Website: http://www.mediaweek.co.uk

Publishes: Articles; Features; Interviews; News; Nonfiction; *Areas:* Business; Media; *Markets:* Professional

Editors: Arif Durrani

Online magazine for the media industry.

Methodist Recorder

122 Golden Lane
London
EC1Y 0TL
Tel: +44 (0) 20 7793 0033
Fax: +44 (0) 20 7793 3459
Email: editorial@methodistrecorder.co.uk
Website: http://www.methodistrecorder.co.uk

Publishes: Articles; News; Nonfiction; *Areas:* Religious; *Markets:* Adult

Methodist newspaper with limited opportunities for freelances. Potential contributors are advised to query in first instance.

Mixmag

Development Hell Ltd
90-92 Pentonville Road
London
N1 9HS
Tel: +44 (0) 20 7078 8400
Fax: +44 (0) 20 7833 9900
Email: mixmag@mixmag.net
Website: http://www.mixmag.net

Publishes: Articles; Features; Interviews; News; Nonfiction; Reviews; *Areas:* Music; *Markets:* Adult

Dance music and clubbing magazine, publishing news, features, reviews, and interviews.

Modern Poetry in Translation

The Queens College
Oxford
OX1 4AW
Tel: +44 (0) 1865 244701
Email: submissions@mptmagazine.com
Website: http://www.mptmagazine.com

Publishes: Essays; Nonfiction; Poetry; *Areas:* Literature; Translations; *Markets:* Adult

Editors: David and Helen Constantine, The Editors

Respected poetry series originally founded by prominent poets in the sixties. New Series continues their editorial policy: translation of good poets by translators who are often themselves poets, fluent in the foreign language, and sometimes working with the original poet. See website for submission guidelines.

Modern Language Review

1 Carlton House Terrace
London
SW1Y 5AF
Email: mlr@mhra.org.uk
Website: http://www.mhra.org.uk/Publications/Journals/mlr.html

Publishes: Articles; Reviews; *Areas:* Literature; *Markets:* Academic

Publishes scholarly articles and reviews relating to modern languages. See website for full submission guidelines, including specific email addresses for different languages.

Monkey Kettle

Email: monkeykettle@hotmail.com
Website: http://www.monkeykettle.co.uk

Publishes: Articles; Fiction; Nonfiction; Poetry; *Areas:* Humour; Politics; Short Stories; *Markets:* Adult; *Treatments:* Dark; Satirical

Editors: Matthew Taylor

Send up between five and ten poems at a time, or a short story up to 1,500 words. Favours the funny, surreal, dark, poignant, and political. Not interested "whiny" material about no-one understanding you.

Monomyth

Atlantean Publishing
4 Pierrot Steps
71 Kursaal Way
Southend-on-Sea
Essex
SS1 2UY
Email: atlanteanpublishing@hotmail.com
Website: http://atlanteanpublishing.wikia.com/wiki/Monomyth

Publishes: Fiction; Poetry; *Areas:* Fantasy; Short Stories; *Markets:* Adult

Editors: David-John Tyrer

Publishes longer short stories and long poetry. Submit by post with SASE or by email with your submission in the body of the email (no attachments).

Mother & Baby Magazine

Bauer Consumer Media Ltd
1 Lincoln Court
Lincoln Road
Peterborough
PE1 2RF
Email: team@motherandbaby.co.uk
Website: http://www.motherandbaby.co.uk

Publishes: Articles; Features; Nonfiction; *Areas:* Health; How-to; Lifestyle; Women's Interests; *Markets:* Adult

Publishes articles and features offering advice on pregnancy, birth, and babycare.

Mslexia

PO Box 656
Newcastle upon Tyne
NE99 1PZ
Tel: +44 (0) 1912 048860
Email: submissions@mslexia.co.uk
Website: http://www.mslexia.co.uk

Publishes: Articles; Essays; Features; Fiction; Interviews; News; Nonfiction; Poetry; Reference; Reviews; *Areas:* Autobiography; Short Stories; Women's Interests; *Markets:* Adult

By women, for women who write, who want to write, who teach creative writing or who have an interest in womens' literature and creativity. It is a mixture of original work, features, news, views, advice and listings. The UK's only magazine devoted to women writers and their writing.

See website for themes of upcoming issues / competitions.

Publishes features, columns, reviews, flash fiction, and literature listings. Email submissions for themed new writing from overseas writers only. Email submissions for other contributions accepted from anywhere. See website for full details.

Music Teacher

Rhinegold House
20 Rugby Street
London
WC1N 3QZ
Tel: +44 (0) 7785 613145
Fax: +44 (0) 20 7333 1736
Email: music.teacher@rhinegold.co.uk
Website: http://www.rhinegold.co.uk

Publishes: Articles; Nonfiction; Reviews; *Areas:* How-to; Music; *Markets:* Professional

Magazine for both private and school music teachers.

The Musical Times

7 Brunswick Mews
Hove
East Sussex
BN3 1HD
Email: mted@gotadsl.co.uk
Website:
http://themusicaltimes.blogspot.com

Publishes: Articles; Nonfiction; *Areas:* Music; *Markets:* Adult

Editors: Antony Bye

Publishes articles on a wide variety of subjects pertaining to "classical" music, between 2,000 and 8,000 words. Send articles by email. See website for full submission guidelines.

Neon Highway Poetry Magazine

37 Grinshill Close
Liverpool
L8 8LD
Email: neonhighwaypoetry@yahoo.co.uk
Website:
http://neonhighwaypoetry.webstarts.com

Publishes: Poetry; *Markets:* Adult; *Treatments:* Literary

Editors: Alice Lenkiewicz

Avant-garde literary journal publishing poetry and art. Submissions accepted by post and by email. See website for details.

.net

30 Monmouth Street
Bath
BA1 2BW
Tel: +44 (0) 1225 442244
Fax: +44 (0) 1225 732295
Email: oliver.lindberg@futurenet.com
Website: http://www.netmagazine.com

Publishes: Articles; Features; News; Nonfiction; *Areas:* Technology; *Markets:* Professional

Editors: Oliver Lindberg

Magazine for web designers and developers, publishing articles, features, and news.

The New Accelerator

Email: editors@thenewaccelerator.com
Website: http://thenewaccelerator.com

Publishes: Fiction; *Areas:* Entertainment; Fantasy; Horror; Religious; Science; Sci-Fi; Short Stories; Spiritual; Technology; Thrillers; *Markets:* Adult; *Treatments:* Commercial; Contemporary; Dark; Experimental; Literary; Positive; Progressive; Satirical; Serious; Traditional

Editors: Andy Coughlan and David Winstanley

A Science Fiction short story anthology. Published monthly exclusively through Apple's Newsstand app, the anthology will be available to over half a billion iOS users worldwide.

The aim of the anthology is to bring cutting-edge fiction to an eager and discerning global Science Fiction audience.

New Humanist

Merchants House
5-7 Southwark Street
London
SE1 1RQ
Tel: +44 (0) 20 3117 0630

Email: editor@newhumanist.org.uk
Website: http://www.newhumanist.org.uk

Publishes: Articles; Nonfiction; *Areas:* Arts; Current Affairs; Historical; Literature; Philosophy; Religious; Science; *Markets:* Adult

Editors: Daniel Trilling; Samira Shackle

Publishes humanist articles on current affairs, history, humanism, human rights, literature, philosophy, and science. No fiction. Pitch articles by email.

New London Writers

Flat 34
67 Hatton Garden
London
EC1N 8JY
Tel: +44 (0) 07913 373870
Email: publish@newlondonwriters.com
Website: http://newlondonwriters.com

Publishes: Articles; Fiction; Reviews; *Areas:* Fantasy; Mystery; Philosophy; Sci-Fi; Short Stories; Suspense; *Markets:* Adult; Youth; *Treatments:* Commercial; Contemporary; Dark; Experimental; Literary; Mainstream; Niche; Satirical

Editors: Alice Wickham

A platform for new writing. We act as publisher and literary agent for emerging novelists. Work is published and promoted to our network of over 500 literary agents and publishers in the UK and overseas, mainly USA. Work published on our site is noticed by the people who count.

New Walk Magazine

c/o Nick Everett
School of English
Leicester University
University Road
Leicester
LE1 7RH
Email: newwalkmagazine@gmail.com
Website:
http://newwalkmagazine.wordpress.com

Publishes: Articles; Essays; Features; Fiction; Interviews; Nonfiction; Poetry; Reviews; *Areas:* Criticism; Literature; Short Stories; *Markets:* Adult; *Treatments:* Experimental; Literary

Editors: Rory Waterman and Nick Everett

Publishes poetry and poetry-related features; criticism; debate; short fiction; and art. Send up to six poems or one piece of prose in the body of an email.

New Welsh Review

PO Box 170
Aberystwyth
SY23 1WZ
Tel: +44 (0) 1970 628410
Email: submissions@newwelshreview.com
Website: http://www.newwelshreview.com

Publishes: Features; Fiction; Nonfiction; Poetry; Reviews; *Areas:* Short Stories; *Markets:* Adult; *Treatments:* Literary

Editors: Gwen Davies

Focus is on Welsh writing in English, but has an outlook which is deliberately diverse, encompassing broader UK and international contexts. For feature articles, send 300-word query by email. Submit fiction or up to 6 poems by email or by post with cover letter and SAE. Full details available on website.

Note: Not accepting fiction submissions as at September 2014 due to high volume of submissions. See website for current status.

Now

IPC Media
Blue Fin Building
110 Southwark Street
London
SE1 4SU
Tel: +44 (0) 20 3148 5000
Fax: +44 (0) 20 3148 8110
Email: nowfriends@ipcmedia.com
Website: http://www.nowmagazine.co.uk

Publishes: Articles; Features; News; Nonfiction; *Areas:* Beauty and Fashion; Entertainment; Lifestyle; Media; Women's

Interests; *Markets:* Adult

Women's lifestyle magazine, covering celebrity gossip, fashion, news, etc. Most articles are commissioned or originated in-house.

Nursery World

MA Education
St Jude's Church
Dulwich Road
London
SE24 0PB
Tel: +44 (0) 20 7501 6693
Email: liz.roberts@markallengroup.com
Website: http://www.nurseryworld.co.uk

Publishes: Articles; News; Nonfiction; *Markets:* Professional

Editors: Liz Roberts

Magazine aimed at professionals dealing with the care of children in nurseries, primary schools, childcare, etc.; nannies and foster parents; and those involved with caring for expectant mothers, babies, and young children.

Obsessed with Pipework

Flarestack Publishing
8 Abbot's Way
Pilton
Somerset
BA4 4BN
Tel: +44 (0) 1749 890019
Email: cannula.dementia@virgin.net
Website: http://www.flarestack.co.uk

Publishes: Poetry; *Markets:* Adult; *Treatments:* Experimental; Literary

Editors: Charles Johnson

Submit up to six poems of any length or style. Looking for poems that are original and display an element of creative risk, rather than things that are simply "clever". Nothing predictable or obvious. SAE essential unless submitting by fax or email. Prefers submissions by post, but if you do email your poems send them in the body of an email or in a single attached document.

Other Poetry

10 Prospect Bank Road
Edinburgh
EH6 7NR
Email: editors@otherpoetry.com
Website: http://www.otherpoetry.com

Publishes: Poetry; *Markets:* Adult

Send up to five poems by email, or by post if impossible to send by email. A live email address must be included for a response. No correspondence will be entered into by post and no SAE is required. Submissions should be sent in the body of the email, rather than as attachments. Any emails containing attachments will be deleted unread and without acknowledgement. Do not submit more than twice per calendar year, or within six months of any editorial decision.

Pony Magazine

Headley House
Headley Road
Grayshott
Surrey
GU26 6TU
Tel: +44 (0) 1428 601020
Fax: +44 (0) 1428 601030
Email: pony@djmurphy.co.uk
Website: http://www.ponymag.com

Publishes: Articles; Nonfiction; *Areas:* Hobbies; Nature; Sport; *Markets:* Children's; Youth

Editors: Janet Rising

Magazine for young horse-lovers aged 8-16.

PC Advisor

101 Euston Road
London
NW1 2RA
Tel: +44 (0) 20 7756 2800
Email: matt_egan@idg.co.uk
Website: http://www.pcadvisor.co.uk

Publishes: Articles; Features; Nonfiction; *Areas:* How-to; Technology; *Markets:* Adult

Editors: Matt Egan

PC magazine aimed at proficient users. May consider unsolicited material.

PC Pro

PC Pro Dennis Technology
30 Cleveland Street
London
W1T 4JD
Tel: +44 (0) 20 7907 6000
Fax: +44 (0) 20 7907 6304
Email: editor@pcpro.co.uk
Website: http://www.pcpro.co.uk

Publishes: Articles; Features; News; Nonfiction; Reviews; *Areas:* Technology; *Markets:* Adult; Professional; *Treatments:* In-depth

Editors: Barry Collins

IT magazine for professionals in the IT industry and enthusiasts.

Peace and Freedom

17 Farrow Road
Whaplode Drove
Spalding
Lincs
PE12 0TS
Tel: +44 (0) 1406 330242
Email: p_rance@yahoo.co.uk
Website:
http://pandf.booksmusicfilmstv.com

Publishes: Articles; Fiction; Interviews; Poetry; Reviews; *Areas:* Nature; Short Stories; Sociology; *Markets:* Adult; *Treatments:* Literary

Editors: Paul Rance

Magazine publishing poetry, fiction, and articles, with an emphasis on social, humanitarian and environmental issues. Also publishes interviews of animal welfare/environmental/human rights campaigners, writers, poets, artists, film, music and TV personalities, up to 1,000 words. Reviews of books / records / events etc. up to 50 words also considered. Email submissions accepted for reviews, short stories, and interviews ONLY. Accepts submissions from subscribers only.

Peace News

5 Caledonian Road
London
N1 9DY
Tel: +44 (0) 20 7278 3344
Email: editorial@peacenews.info
Website: http://peacenews.info

Publishes: Articles; News; Nonfiction; *Areas:* Politics; *Markets:* Adult

Newspaper covering peace and justice issues, focussing on non-violence. Draws on the traditions of pacifism, feminism, anarchism, socialism, human rights, animal rights and green politics.

The Penniless Press

100 Waterloo Road
Ashton
Preston
PR2 1EP
Tel: +44 (0) 1772 736421
Email: editor@pennilesspress.co.uk
Website: http://www.pennilesspress.co.uk

Publishes: Essays; Fiction; Nonfiction; Poetry; Reviews; *Areas:* Criticism; Literature; Philosophy; Short Stories; Translations; *Markets:* Adult; *Treatments:* Literary

Editors: Alan Dent

Eclectic magazine publishing material on a diverse range of subjects, as well as fiction, poetry, criticism, translations, and reviews. Prose should be restricted to 3,000 words or less. Send contributions with SAE by post or by email.

Pennine Platform

Frizingley Hall
Frizinghall Road
Bradford
BD9 4LD
Tel: +44 (0) 1274 541015
Email: nicholas.bielby@virgin.co.uk
Website: http://www.pennineplatform.co.uk

Publishes: Poetry; *Markets:* Adult

Editors: Nicholas Bielby

The pick of poetry from the Pennines and beyond. Hard copy submissions only.

The People's Friend

80 Kingsway East
Dundee
DD4 8SL
Tel: +44 (0) 1382 462276
Fax: +44 (0) 1382 452491
Email: peoplesfriend@dcthomson.co.uk
Website: http://www.thepeoplesfriend.co.uk

Publishes: Articles; Features; Fiction; Nonfiction; Poetry; *Areas:* Adventure; Cookery; Mystery; Romance; Short Stories; Women's Interests; *Markets:* Adult; Children's; Family; *Treatments:* Traditional

Publishes complete short stories (1,200-3,000 words (4,000 for specials)) and serials (total 60,000-70,000 words) focusing on character development rather than complex plots. Also considers children's stories and nonfiction on knitting and cookery. Send request with SAE for guidelines.

People's Friend Pocket Novels

80 Kingsway East
Dundee
DD4 8SL
Tel: +44 (0) 1382 223131
Email: tsteel@dcthomson.co.uk
Website: http://www.thepeoplesfriend.co.uk

Publishes: Fiction; *Areas:* Romance; *Markets:* Adult; Family

Editors: Sheelagh Heron

Publishes romance and family fiction between 40,000 and 42,000 words, aimed at adults aged over 30. Send query by email with synopsis and first three chapters in first instance. See website for more information.

Performance

Mediscript Ltd
1 Mountview Court
310 Friern Barnett Lane
London
Tel: +44 (0) 20 8369 5382
Fax: +44 (0) 20 8446 8898
Email: Fatima@mediscript.ltd.uk
Website: http://www.performancesport andfitness.co.uk

Publishes: Articles; Features; Interviews; News; Nonfiction; Reviews; *Areas:* Health; Sport; *Markets:* Academic; Adult; Professional; *Treatments:* Commercial; Contemporary; Popular

Editors: Fatima Patel

A research led magazine for professionals and sport enthusiasts. It is presented in an attractive easy to read style, covering a series of key issues in sport and fitness. These include training, nutrition, injury and rehabilitation. There are features on elite athletes with interviews and commentary on key research papers by our experts. The editorial board comprises sport training professionals and academics.

Planet

PO Box 44
Aberystwyth
Ceredigion
SY23 3ZZ
Tel: +44 (0) 1970 611255
Fax: +44 (0) 1970 611197
Email: emily.trahair@planetmagazine.org.uk
Website: http://www.planetmagazine.org.uk

Publishes: Articles; Features; Fiction; Nonfiction; Poetry; Reviews; *Areas:* Arts; Current Affairs; Literature; Music; Politics; Short Stories; Theatre; *Markets:* Adult; *Treatments:* Literary

Editors: Emily Trahair

Publishes one story and between eight and ten poems per issue. A range of styles and themes are accepted, but postal submissions will not be considered unless adequate return postage is provided. Submit 4-6 poems or fiction up to 2,750 words. Submissions are accepted by email.

Most articles, features, and reviews are commissioned, however if you have an idea for a relevant article send a query with brief synopsis.

PN Review

St John's College
Cambridge
CB2 1TP

4th Floor
Alliance House
Cross Street
Manchester
M2 7AP
Tel: +44 (0) 161 834 8730
Fax: +44 (0) 161 832 0084
Email: schmidt@carcanet.co.uk
Website: http://www.pnreview.co.uk

Publishes: Articles; Features; Interviews; News; Poetry; Reviews; *Areas:* Translations; *Markets:* Adult

Editors: Michael Schmidt

Send query with synopsis and sample pages, after having familiarised yourself with the magazine. Accepts prose up to 20 pages and poetry up to 10 pages.

Bimonthly magazine of poetry and poetry criticism. Includes editorial, letters, news, articles, interviews, features, poems, translations, and a substantial book review section. No short stories, children's prose / poetry, or non-poetry related work (academic, biography etc.). Accepts electronic submissions from individual subscribers only – otherwise only hard copy submissions are considered.

Poetic Licence

70 Aveling Close
Purley
Surrey
CR8 4DW
Email: poets@poetsanon.org.uk
Website: http://www.poetsanon.org.uk

Publishes: Poetry; *Markets:* Adult

Editors: Peter L. Evans (co-ordinator)

The editing is rotated through the membership to help ensure that each issue does not get stuck in a rut or 'house style'. Submit up to six poems per issue, by email.

The Poetry Church

Eldwick Crag Farm
High Eldwick
Bingley
Yorkshire
BD16 3BB
Email: reavill@globalnet.co.uk
Website: http://www.waddysweb.freeuk.com

Publishes: Poetry; *Areas:* Religious; *Markets:* Adult

Editors: Tony Reavill

Ecumenical Christian poetry magazine. Features the work of international Christian poets coming from a wide variety of backgrounds in the mainline churches.

Poetry Cornwall / Bardhonyeth Kernow

11a Penryn Street
Redruth
Cornwall/Kernow
TR15 2SP

1 Station Hill
Redruth
Cornwall
TR15 2PP
Tel: +44 (0) 1209 218209
Email: poetrycornwall@yahoo.com
Website:
http://www.poetrycornwall.freeservers.com

Publishes: Poetry; *Markets:* Adult; *Treatments:* Literary

Editors: Les Merton

Publishes poetry from around the world, in original language (including Kernewek and Cornish dialect) with English translation. Send up to three poems by post with SASE, or (if a subscriber) by email. Non-subscribers may not submit by email.

Poetry Express

Survivors' Poetry
Studio 11, Bickerton House
25-27 Bickerton Road
Archway
London

N19 5JT
Tel: +44 (0) 20 7281 4654
Fax: +44 (0) 20 7281 7894
Email: info@survivorspoetry.org
Website: http://www.survivorspoetry.org/the-poetry/publications/poetry-express/

Publishes: Articles; News; Nonfiction; Poetry; Reviews; *Areas:* Literature; *Markets:* Adult

Publishes poetry, articles, reviews, and news. Name and contact details on each sheet of submission.

Poetry London

The Albany
Douglas Way
Deptford
London
SE8 4AG
Tel: +44 (0) 20 8691 7260
Email: ahren@poetrylondon.co.uk
Website: http://www.poetrylondon.co.uk

Publishes: Features; Nonfiction; Poetry; Reviews; *Areas:* Translations; *Markets:* Adult; *Treatments:* Contemporary; Literary

Editors: Ahren Warner

Send up to six poems with SASE or adequate return postage, unless you do not require your poems returning, in which case you should make this clear. Considers poems by both new and established poets. Also publishes book reviews. No submissions by email.

The Poetry Review

The Poetry Society
22 Betterton Street
London
WC2H 9BX
Tel: +44 (0) 20 7420 9883
Fax: +44 (0) 20 7240 4818
Email: poetryreview@poetrysociety.org.uk
Website: http://www.poetrysociety.org.uk

Publishes: Essays; Nonfiction; Poetry; Reviews; *Markets:* Adult

Editors: Maurice Riordan

Describes itself as "one of the liveliest and most influential literary magazines in the world", and has been associated with the rise of the New Generation of British poets – Carol Ann Duffy, Simon Armitage, Glyn Maxwell, Don Paterson... though its scope extends beyond the UK, with special issues focusing on poetries from around the world. Poets from the UK must submit by post; those from elsewhere in the world may submit using online system. See website for details. Send up to 6 unpublished poems.

Poetry Scotland

91-93 Main Street
Callander
FK17 8BQ
Email: sallyevans35@gmail.com
Website: http://www.poetryscotland.co.uk

Publishes: Poetry; *Markets:* Adult

Editors: Sally Evans

Poetry broadsheet with Scottish emphasis. Considers poetry in English, Gaelic, Scots, and (on occasions) Welsh. Please see website for submission guidelines.

Poetry Wales

57 Nolton Street
Bridgend
CF31 3AE
Tel: +44 (0) 1656 663018
Email: info@poetrywales.co.uk
Website: http://poetrywales.co.uk

Publishes: Poetry; *Markets:* Adult

Editors: Nia Davies

Send up to six poems in one .doc file with your name, contact details, and short bio up to 50 words, via online submission system (see website).

The Political Quarterly

9600 Garsington Road
Oxford
OX4 2DQ
Tel: +44 (0) 1865 776868
Fax: +44 (0) 1865 714591

Website: http://www.wiley.com

Publishes: Articles; Features; Nonfiction; *Areas:* Politics; *Markets:* Adult; *Treatments:* Progressive

Magazine covering national and international politics. Accepts unsolicited articles.

Post

Incisive Financial Publishing Ltd
28-29 Haymarket
London
SW1Y 4RX
Tel: +44 (0) 20 7316 9134
Email: stephanie.denton@incisivemedia.com
Website: http://www.postonline.co.uk

Publishes: Articles; News; Nonfiction; *Areas:* Business; *Markets:* Professional

Editors: Stephanie Denton

Industry journal for insurance professionals.

PR Week

Tel: +44 (0) 20 8267 4429/4428
Email: prweek@haymarket.com
Website: http://www.prweek.com

Publishes: Articles; Features; News; Nonfiction; *Areas:* Business; *Markets:* Professional

Editors: Daniel Farey-Jones

Magazine publishing news and features on public relations and communications.

Practical Wireless

PW Publishing Limited
Tayfield House
38 Poole Road
Westbourne
Bournemouth
BH4 9DW
Tel: +44 (0) 845 803 1979
Email: rob@pwpublishing.ltd.uk
Website: http://www.pwpublishing.ltd.uk

Publishes: Articles; Nonfiction; *Areas:* How-to; Technology; *Markets:* Adult

Editors: Rob Mannion

Magazine covering amateur radio and communications. Send query by email in first instance.

Premonitions

13 Hazely Combe
Arreton
Isle of Wight
PO30 3AJ
Tel: +44 (0) 1983 865668
Email: mail@pigasuspress.co.uk
Website: http://www.pigasuspress.co.uk

Publishes: Fiction; Poetry; *Areas:* Fantasy; Horror; Sci-Fi; *Markets:* Adult

Editors: Tony Lee

Magazine of cutting edge science fiction and fantasy. Also publishes genre poetry, and horror, however this must have an SF element, and must be psychological rather than simply gory. Send submission with cover letter, bio, and publication credits, with SAE. No supernatural fantasy or swords n' sorcery. Study magazine before submitting.

Presence

90 D Fishergate Hill
Preston
PR1 8JD
Email: haikupresence@gmail.com
Website: http://haiku-presence.50webs.com/

Publishes: Poetry; *Markets:* Adult

Editors: Martin Lucas; Matthew Paul; Ian Storr

The UK's leading forum for the full range of haiku-related genres. Includes haiku of the highest standard from an international list of contributors, backed by insightful reviews and critical prose. Our mission is to encourage dialogue and build a sense of community among haiku poets – and we're definitely getting there!

See website for different submission addresses for specific forms.

Prima

33 Broadwick Street
London
W1F 9EP
Tel: +44 (0) 20 7439 5000
Email: prima@hearst.co.uk
Website: http://www.allaboutyou.com/prima/

Publishes: Articles; Features; Nonfiction; *Areas:* Beauty and Fashion; Cookery; Crafts; Health; Travel; Women's Interests; *Markets:* Adult

Women's magazine publishing articles and features on food, diet and wellbeing, fashion and beauty, homes, crafts, and country and travel.

Professional Photographer

Archant House
Oriel Road
Cheltenham
GL50 1BB
Website:
http://www.professionalphotographer.co.uk

Publishes: Articles; Nonfiction; *Areas:* Photography; Technology; *Markets:* Professional

Magazine aimed at professional photographers.

Prospect

25 Sackville Street
London
W1S 3HQ
Tel: +44 (0) 20 7255 1281
Fax: +44 (0) 20 7255 1279
Email: editorial@prospect-magazine.co.uk
Website: http://www.prospect-magazine.co.uk

Publishes: Essays; Features; Fiction; Nonfiction; Reviews; *Areas:* Arts; Culture; Current Affairs; Literature; Politics; Short Stories; *Markets:* Adult

Editors: David Goodhart

Intelligent magazine of current affairs and cultural debate. No news features. Almost all articles are commissioned from regular writers, but will consider unsolicited nonfiction submissions if suitable for the magazine, but no unsolicited fiction submissions. Does not publish any poetry. No postal submissions or telephone pitches. Submit by email only.

Pulsar Poetry Magazine

34 Lineacre
Grange Park
Swindon
Wiltshire
SN5 6DA
Tel: +44 (0) 1793 875941
Email: pulsar.ed@btopenworld.com
Website: http://www.pulsarpoetry.com

Publishes: Poetry; *Markets:* Adult

Editors: David Pike

From 2010 a webzine only. We seek interesting and stimulating unpublished work – thoughts, comments and observations, genial or sharp. Prefer hard-hitting work. We welcome poetry and constructive ideas from all areas of the world. Normal time taken to reply is no longer than four weeks, include a stamped addressed return envelope with your submission, (or include International Reply Coupons, if from overseas). Send no more than six poems at a time via conventional post, or three poems via email: note, email file attachments will not be read.

If your work is of a high standard it will be published – may take a few months to appear, though. Poets retain copyright of their poems. Poems which are simultaneously sent to other publications will not be considered.

Q Magazine

Endeavour House
189 Shaftesbury Avenue
London
WC2H 8JG
Tel: +44 (0) 20 7437 9011
Email: qmail@qthemusic.com
Website: http://www.qthemusic.com

Publishes: Articles; Features; Interviews;

News; Nonfiction; *Areas:* Music; *Markets:* Adult

UK's biggest selling music monthly magazine.

Quantum Leap

York House
15 Argyle Terrace
Rothesay
Isle of Bute
PA20 0BD
Tel: +44 (0) 1700 505422
Website: http://www.qqpress.co.uk

Publishes: Poetry; *Markets:* Adult

Editors: Alan J. Carter

A poetry magazine only – no short stories please! We have a four-page information leaflet – send SAE or 2 IRCs to 'Guidelines / Competitions' at the address below. We also provide a publication service for collections of people's poetry – send SAE or 2 IRCs to 'Collections' at address below.

We aim to run a 'user-friendly' magazine for our subscribers / contributors, so don't be afraid to ask for advice. We also pay for all poetry we use.

Reach

IDP
24 Forest Houses
Halwill
Beaworthy
Devon
EX21 5UU
Email: publishing@indigodreams.co.uk
Website: http://www.indigodreams.co.uk/#/reach-poetry/4536232470

Publishes: Poetry; *Markets:* Adult

Editors: Ronnie Goodyer

Publishes quality poetry from both experienced and new poets. Formal or free verse, haiku.. everything is considered. Subscribers can comment on and vote for poetry from the previous issue, the winner receiving £50, plus regular in-house anthologies and competitions. Receives no external funding and depends entirely on subscriptions.

Real People

Hearst Magazines UK London
72 Broadwick Street
London
W1F 9EP
Email: samm.taylor@hearst.co.uk
Website: http://www.realpeoplemag.co.uk

Publishes: Nonfiction; *Areas:* Lifestyle; Women's Interests; *Markets:* Adult

Editors: Samm Taylor

Publishes real life stories. See website for more details.

The Reater

Wrecking Ball Press
Office 9
Danish Buildings
44-46 High Street
Hull
East Yorkshire
HU1 1PS
Email: editor@wreckingballpress.com
Website: http://www.wreckingballpress.com

Publishes: Fiction; Poetry; *Areas:* Short Stories; *Markets:* Adult; *Treatments:* Literary

Editors: Shane Rhodes

Send up to six poems or up to two stories. Submissions can be digital or on paper. If submitting by email, include the word "Submission" in the subject box.

Red Pepper

44-48 Shepherdess Walk
London
N1 7JP
Tel: +44 (0) 20 7324 5068
Email: office@redpepper.org.uk
Website: http://www.redpepper.org.uk

Publishes: Articles; Features; News; Nonfiction; *Areas:* Politics; *Markets:* Adult

Political magazine aimed at the left and greens.

Red Poets

7 Stryt Gerallt
Wrecsam
LL11 1EH
Email: info@redpoets.org
Website: http://www.redpoets.org

Publishes: Poetry; *Areas:* Politics; *Markets:* Adult

Editors: Mike Jenkins; Marc Jones

Magazine of politically left-wing poetry. Submit poems via submission form on website or by email.

Resurgence & Ecologist

The Resurgence Trust
Ford House
Hartland
Bideford
Devon
EX39 6EE
Tel: +44 (0) 1237 441293
Fax: +44 (0) 1237 441203
Email: info@resurgence.org
Website: http://www.resurgence.org

Publishes: Articles; Features; News; Nonfiction; Poetry; Reviews; *Areas:* Arts; Humour; Nature; Philosophy; Spiritual; Markets

Publishes articles, features, news, book reviews, recipe columns, humour, poetry, and profiles, covering ecology, social justice, philosophy, spirituality, sustainable development and the arts. Send proposal in first instance.

The Rialto

PO Box 309
Aylsham
Norwich
NR11 6LN
Email: info@therialto.co.uk
Website: http://www.therialto.co.uk

Publishes: Articles; Nonfiction; Poetry; Reviews; *Markets:* Adult

Editors: Michael Mackmin

Send up to six poems with SASE or adequate return postage. Overseas contributors can include an email address for response instead of return postage, but poems must still be sent by post. No submissions online or by email. Reviews and articles commissioned.

Right Start Magazine

PO Box 481
Fleet
GU51 9FA
Tel: +44 (0) 7867 574590
Email: lynette@rightstartmagazine.co.uk
Website: http://www.rightstartmagazine.co.uk

Publishes: Articles; Nonfiction; *Areas:* Health; Lifestyle; Psychology; *Markets:* Adult

Editors: Lynette Lowthian

Magazine covering pre-school children's health, lifestyle, development, education, etc.

Royal Academy of Arts (RA) Magazine

Royal Academy of Arts
Burlington House
Piccadilly
London
W1J 0BD
Tel: +44 (0) 20 7300 5820
Fax: +44 (0) 20 7300 5032
Email: ramagazine@royalacademy.org.uk
Website: https://www.royalacademy.org.uk /ra-magazine

Publishes: Articles; News; Nonfiction; *Areas:* Architecture; Arts; Culture; *Markets:* Adult

Publishes articles relating to the academy, or to the wider British and international arts scene. No unsolicited MSS. Freelances who can write about art in an accessible way should approach by email or telephone. Articles are usually tied in to upcoming exhibitions, projects, or books.

Sable

Email: editorial@sablelitmag.org
Website: http://www.sablelitmag.org

Publishes: Essays; Fiction; Nonfiction; Poetry; Reviews; *Areas:* Autobiography; Historical; Short Stories; Translations; Travel; *Markets:* Adult

A showcase of new creative work by writers of colour. Submit short stories or a novel excerpt up to 5,000 words; 10-15 pages of poetry; or nonfiction up to 3,000 words, by email. See website for full guidelines.

Sarasvati

24 Forest Houses
Halwill
Beaworthy
Devon
EX21 5UU
Email: dawnidp@indigodreams.co.uk
Website: http://www.indigodreams.co.uk

Publishes: Fiction; Poetry; *Areas:* Short Stories; *Markets:* Adult

Editors: Dawn Bauling

Showcases poetry and prose. Each contributor will have three to four pages available to their poetry, up to 35 lines per page, or prose up to 1,000 words.

The Savage Kick

Murder Slim Press
29 Alpha Road
Gorleston
Norfolk
NR31 0LQ
Email: slim@murderslim.com
Website: http://www.murderslim.com

Publishes: Articles; Fiction; Interviews; Nonfiction; *Areas:* Crime; Literature; Military; Westerns; *Markets:* Adult; *Treatments:* Niche

Accepts only three or four stories per year. Publishes work dealing with any passionately held emotion and/or alternative viewpoints. Sleazy tales are encouraged. Prefers real-life stories. No genre fiction or poetry. See website for full submission guidelines. Also accepts articles and interviews relating to authors on the reading list provided on the website.

Scar Tissue

Pigasus Press
13 Hazely Combe
Arreton
Isle of Wight
PO30 3AJ
Email: mail@pigasuspress.co.uk
Website: http://www.pigasuspress.co.uk

Publishes: Fiction; News; Nonfiction; Poetry; Reviews; *Areas:* Horror; Humour; Short Stories; *Markets:* Adult; *Treatments:* Dark

Editors: Tony Lee

Free-sheet collage of horror and dark humour, featuring short fiction, genre prose, poetry, artwork, cartoons, lists, reviews, news, cuttings, trivia, and adverts.

The School Librarian

7 Clifton Bank
Rotherham
South Yorkshire
S60 2NA
Email: sleditor@sla.org.uk
Website: http://www.sla.org.uk/the-school-librarian.php

Publishes: Articles; Nonfiction; *Markets:* Professional

Editors: Steve Hird

Magazine for professionals working in the libraries of educational facilities from pre-school to adult.

Scientific Computing World

Europa Science Ltd
9 Clifton Court
Cambridge
CB1 7BN
Tel: +44 (0) 1223 275464
Fax: +44 (0) 1223 211107
Email: editor.scw@europascience.com

Website: http://www.scientific-computing.com

Publishes: Articles; Features; Interviews; News; Nonfiction; *Areas:* Science; Technology; *Markets:* Professional

Editors: Beth Harlen

Describes itself as "the only global publication dedicated to the computing and information technology needs of scientists and engineers". Covers computing for engineering, science, and technology. Publishes news, comment, feature articles, product news, white papers and webcasts. No research papers. Send submissions by email only. See website for full submission guidelines.

Scottish Memories

Celebrate Scotland
5th Floor
31-32 Park Row
Leeds
LS1 5JD
Email: matthewh@warnersgroup.co.uk
Website: https://www.celebrate-scotland.co.uk

Publishes: Articles; Features; Nonfiction; *Areas:* Historical; Military; *Markets:* Adult

Editors: Matthew Hill

Magazine of Scottish nostalgia, focussing on the period 1940-1980. War stories also considered if a Scottish connection.

Scribbler!

Remus House
Coltsfoot Drive
Peterborough
Cambridgeshire
PE2 9BF
Tel: +44 (0) 1733 890066
Email: info@scribblermagazine.com
Website: http://www.scribblermagazine.com

Publishes: Fiction; Poetry; Reviews; *Areas:* Short Stories; *Markets:* Children's

Educational magazine for 7–11 year-olds, encouraging them to submit their own poems, stories, and artwork. Email submissions accepted.

Sea Angler

Bauer Consumer Media Limited
1 Lincoln Court
Lincoln Road
0Peterborough
PE1 2RF
Tel: +44 (0) 01733 395147
Email: mel.russ@bauermedia.co.uk
Website: http://www.gofishing.co.uk/Sea-Angler

Publishes: Articles; News; Nonfiction; *Areas:* Hobbies; How-to; Sport; Technology; *Markets:* Adult

Editors: Mel Russ

Magazine for sea fishing enthusiasts.

The Seventh Quarry Swansea Poetry Magazine

8 Cherry Crescent
Parc Penderri
Penllergaer
Swansea
SA4 9FG
Email: requests@peterthabitjones.com
Website: http://www.peterthabitjones.com

Publishes: Poetry; *Markets:* Adult

Editors: Peter Thabit Jones

Poetry magazine with international outlook, publishing poems from around the world. Send up to four poems by email or by post with SASE.

Shearsman

50 Westons Hill Drive
Emersons Green
Bristol
BS16 7DF
Email: editor@shearsman.com
Website: http://www.shearsman.com

Publishes: Nonfiction; Poetry; Reviews; *Markets:* Adult

Editors: Tony Frazer

Now operates two reading windows for submissions: March and September.

Send submissions with SAE for return. If outside UK please send disposable MS and email address for response. Do not send IRCs. Email submissions accepted if submission is sent in body of email, not as an attachment. Please study magazine or at least website before deciding whether or not to submit your work.

Publishes poetry in the modernist tradition, plus some prose, including reviews. Reviews published on website only.

Shooting Times

Tel: +44 (0) 20 3148 4741
Email: steditorial@ipcmedia.com
Website: http://www.shootinguk.co.uk

Publishes: Articles; Nonfiction; *Areas:* Nature; Sport; *Markets:* Adult

Editors: Alistair Balmain

Magazine covering shooting and the countryside.

Shoreline of Infinity

8 Craiglockhart Bank
Edinburgh
EH14 1JH
Email: editor@shorelineofinfinity.com
Website: https://www.shorelineofinfinity.com

Publishes: Fiction; Interviews; Nonfiction; Reviews; *Areas:* Literature; Music; Sci-Fi; Short Stories; *Markets:* Adult; Family; Youth

Editors: Noel Chidwick

Science Fiction magazine from Scotland. We want stories that explore our unknown future. We want to play around with the big ideas and the little ones. We want writers to tell us stories to inspire us, give us hope, provide some laughs. Or to scare the stuffing out of us. We want good stories: we want to be entertained. We want to read how people cope in our exotic new world, we want to be in their minds, in their bodies, in their souls.

ShortStorySunday.com

27 Old Gloucester Street
London
WC1N 3AX
Email: submissions@shortstorysunday.com
Website: http://www.shortstorysunday.com

Publishes: Fiction; *Areas:* Adventure; Crime; Fantasy; Gothic; Historical; Horror; Humour; Literature; Mystery; Nature; New Age; Philosophy; Romance; Sci-Fi; Short Stories; Suspense; Thrillers; Westerns; *Markets:* Adult; Children's; Family; Youth; *Treatments:* Commercial; Contemporary; Dark; Experimental; Light; Literary; Mainstream; Niche; Popular; Positive; Progressive; Satirical; Traditional

A home for short stories and flash fiction online.

Launched in November 2014, this is a new 'boutique' experience for readers, authors, agents and publishers interested in reading and contributing world-class short stories. We wanted to create an experience for the reader so that every Sunday they can take half an hour and visit with a cup of tea and read through that week's story on their mobile, tablet or desktop either at home, at a coffee shop or on their lunch break.

To ensure we have the best stories we put together an editorial panel with an eye for a good story to pick the most interesting and original stories for our readers each Sunday.

Smallholder

3 Falmouth Business Park
Bickland Water Road
Falmouth
Cornwall
TR11 4SZ
Tel: +44 (0) 1326 213340
Fax: +44 (0) 1326 212084
Email: elizabeth.perry@packetseries.co.uk
Website: http://www.smallholder.co.uk

Publishes: Articles; Features; Nonfiction; *Areas:* Business; Nature; *Markets:* Adult; Professional

Editors: Elizabeth Perry

Magazine aimed at small-scale farmers. Publishes articles and features on poultry, livestock, bees, machinery, conservation, and will consider items on the countryside more generally. Send email for guidelines.

Smoke

MPAC
1-27 Bridport Street
Liverpool
L3 5QF
Tel: +44 (0) 7710 644325
Email: windowsproject@btinternet.com
Website: http://www.windowsproject.net/publish/smoke/wpinfs.htm

Publishes: Poetry; *Markets:* Adult

One of the highest selling small poetry magazines in the country. New writing, poetry and graphics by some of the best established names alongside new work from Merseyside, from all over the country and the world.

South

PO Box 4228
Bracknell
RG42 9PX
Email: south@southpoetry.org
Website: http://www.southpoetry.org

Publishes: Poetry; *Markets:* Adult

Editors: Anne Clegg, Andrew Curtis, Peter Keeble, Patrick Osada, and Chrissie Williams

Submit up to three poems by post (two copies of each), along with submission form available on website. No previously published poems (including poems that have appeared on the internet). Submissions are not returned. See website for full details. No submissions by email.

The Squash Player

Email: info1@squashplayer.co.uk
Website: http://www.squashplayer.co.uk

Publishes: Articles; Features; Nonfiction; *Areas:* Sport; *Markets:* Adult

Magazine covering all aspects of the game of squash. Query editor with ideas in first instance.

Stamp Magazine

MyTimeMedia Ltd
PO Box 718
Orpington
Kent
BR6 1AP
Email: julia.lee@mytimemedia.com
Website: http://www.stampmagazine.co.uk

Publishes: Articles; News; Nonfiction; *Areas:* Hobbies; *Markets:* Adult

Magazine publishing news and articles relating to classic stamps from the past and present. Send query in first instance.

Stand Magazine

School of English
Leeds University
Leeds
LS2 9JT
Tel: +44 (0) 113 233 4794
Fax: +44 (0) 113 233 2791
Email: stand@leeds.ac.uk
Website: http://standmagazine.org

Publishes: Fiction; Poetry; *Areas:* Short Stories; Translations; *Markets:* Adult; *Treatments:* Literary

A well established magazine of poetry and literary fiction. Has previously published the work of, among others, Samuel Beckett, Angela Carter, Seamus Heaney, Geoffrey Hill, and Andrew Motion. No electronic submissions. See website for submission guidelines and alternative US address for American submissions.

Stuff

Teddington Studios

Broom Road
Teddington
Middlesex
TW11 9BE
Tel: +44 (0) 20 8267 5036
Email: stuff@haymarket.com
Website: http://www.stuff.tv

Publishes: Articles; News; Nonfiction; Reviews; *Areas:* Lifestyle; Technology; *Markets:* Adult

Magazine publishing articles on technology, gadgets, lifestyle, news, and reviews.

Suffolk Norfolk Life

Email: editor@suffolknorfolklife.com
Website: http://www.suffolknorfolklife.com

Publishes: Articles; Features; Nonfiction; *Areas:* Arts; Current Affairs; Historical; Leisure; *Markets:* Adult

Editors: Richard Bryson

Magazine covering Suffolk and Norfolk. Welcomes ideas and accepts unsolicited mss. Contact by email.

Taxation

LexisNexis
Quadrant House
The Quadrant
Brighton Road
Sutton
SM2 5AS
Tel: +44 (0) 20 8212 1949
Email: taxation@lexisnexis.co.uk
Website: http://www.taxation.co.uk

Publishes: Articles; Nonfiction; *Areas:* Finance; Legal; *Markets:* Professional

Editors: Mike Truman

Publishes articles on tax for accountants and tax experts. All articles are written by professionals in the field. Send query by email – see website for full guidelines.

Tears in the Fence

Portman Lodge
Durweston
Blandford Forum
Dorset
DT11 0QA
Tel: +44 (0) 7824 618708
Email: tearsinthefence@gmail.com
Website: http://tearsinthefence.com

Publishes: Essays; Fiction; Interviews; Nonfiction; Poetry; Reviews; *Areas:* Short Stories; Translations; *Markets:* Adult; *Treatments:* Literary

Editors: David Caddy

International literary magazine publishing poetry, fiction, prose poems, essays, translations, interviews and reviews. Publishes fiction as short as 100 words or as long as 12,000, plus stories of the more normal 3,500 word length. Maximum 6 poems per poet per issue. No simultaneous submissions or previously published material. Send submissions by post or by email as an attachment and in the body of the email.

10th Muse

c/o October Books
243 Portswood Road
Southampton
SO17 2NG
Website:
http://www.nonism.org.uk/muse.html

Publishes: Articles; Nonfiction; Poetry; Humour; *Markets:* Adult; *Treatments:* Literary

Editors: Andrew Jordan

Looking for poetry, prose, and b&w artwork, combining lyrical with pastoral and experimental. Poetry is accepted in any style or form.

The Recusant

Email: therecusant@yahoo.co.uk
Website:
http://www.therecusant.moonfruit.com

Publishes: Articles; Essays; Nonfiction; Poetry; Reviews; *Areas:* Politics; *Markets:* Adult

Editors: Alan Morrison

Online magazine publishing poetry, articles, reviews, and polemic of a left-wing political viewpoint. Send submissions by email.

The Supplement

Atlantean Publishing
4 Pierrot Steps
71 Kursaal Way
Southend-on-Sea
Essex
SS1 2UY
Email: atlanteanpublishing@hotmail.com
Website: http://atlanteanpublishing.wikia.com/wiki/The_Supplement

Publishes: Articles; Fiction; News; Nonfiction; Poetry; Reviews; *Areas:* Literature; Short Stories; *Markets:* Adult; *Treatments:* Literary

Editors: DJ Tyrer

Magazine publishing news, reviews, and guidelines for the small press, plus competition details, etc. Occasional poem or very short piece of fiction. Requires news, reviews, and letters of content. Submissions by email must be pasted into the body of the email. No attachments.

The Teacher

NUT
Hamilton House
Mabledon Place
London
WC1H 9BD
Email: teacher@nut.org.uk
Website: http://www.teachers.org.uk/teacher-online/

Publishes: Articles; Features; News; Nonfiction; Reviews; *Markets:* Professional

Magazine aimed at teaching professionals. Submit news items and articles for regular columns by email. Rarely publishes unsolicited features, but accepts ideas by email. See website for full details.

The Voice

GV Media Group Ltd
The Elephant & Castle Shopping Centre
Unit 236
London
SE1 6TE
Tel: +44 (0) 20 7510 0383
Email: newsdesk@gvmedia.co.uk
Website: http://voice-online.co.uk

Publishes: Articles; Features; Interviews; News; Nonfiction; *Areas:* Arts; Business; Culture; Entertainment; Politics; Sport; *Markets:* Adult

Weekly newspaper aimed at black Britons, publishing a mixture of news, features, sports and celebrity interviews.

thesnailmagazine

Tel: +44 (0) 1314 415619
Email: ronfrancis.thesnailmagazine@gmail.com
Website: http://www.thesnailmagazine.com

Publishes: Articles; Essays; Features; Interviews; Nonfiction; *Areas:* Adventure; Arts; Business; Criticism; Culture; Current Affairs; Legal; Literature; Media; Sociology; *Markets:* Academic; Adult; Professional; *Treatments:* Contemporary; Literary; Progressive; Serious; Traditional

Editors: Ron Francis

A magazine specialising in longform narrative journalism. No memoir or family history. Stories should be fact-based, in-depth studies of events that will resonate with the reader. Avoid first-person singular narrative where possible.

Third Way

3rd Floor, Invicta House
108-114 Golden Lane
London
EC1Y 0TG
Tel: +44 (0) 20 7776 1071
Email: editor@thirdway.org.uk

Website:
http://www.thirdwaymagazine.co.uk

Publishes: Articles; Features; Nonfiction; Poetry; Reviews; *Areas:* Culture; Finance; Politics; Religious; Sociology; *Markets:* Adult

Magazine publishing a Christian perspective on culture, society, economics and politics. Also publishes poetry. Prefers to receive submissions by email.

Today's Golfer

Media House
Peterborough
PE2 6EA
Tel: +44 (0) 1733 468243
Fax: +44 (0) 1733 468843
Email: editorial@todaysgolfer.co.uk
Website: http://www.todaysgolfer.co.uk

Publishes: Articles; Features; Nonfiction; Reviews; *Areas:* How-to; Sport; Technology; *Markets:* Adult

Editors: Chris Jones

Publishes articles, features, and reviews on golf equipment, technique, and courses.

Total Off-Road

Assignment Media Ltd
Repton House G34
Bretby Business Park
Burton on Trent
Staffordshire
DE15 0YZ
Tel: +44 (0) 1283 741311
Email: alan.kidd@assignment-media.co.uk
Website: http://toronline.co.uk

Publishes: Articles; Features; Nonfiction; *Areas:* Hobbies; Sport; Technology; *Markets:* Adult

Editors: Alan Kidd

Publishes items on off-roading, including competitions, events, and vehicles. Send query by email in first instance.

Total Politics

21 Dartmouth Street
Westminster
London
SW1H 9BP
Tel: +44 (0) 20 7 593 5500
Email: sam.macrory@dods.co.uk
Website: http://www.totalpolitics.com

Publishes: Articles; Features; Nonfiction; *Areas:* Politics; *Markets:* Adult; Professional

Editors: Sam Macrory

Political magazine publishing articles and features up to 2,200 words.

25 Beautiful Homes

Blue Fin Building
110 Southwark Street
London
SE1 0SU
Tel: +44 (0) 20 3148 7154
Email: 25_beautiful_homes@ipcmedia.com
Website: http://www.housetohome.co.uk/25beautifulhomes

Publishes: Articles; Features; Nonfiction; *Areas:* Design; *Markets:* Adult

Editors: Deborah Barker

Introduces readers to real homes, from apartments to farmhouses, delivering real-life homes that inspire and inform.

Unthology

Unthank Submissions (Unthology)
PO Box 3506
Norwich
NR7 7QP
Email: unthology@unthankbooks.com
Website: http://www.unthankbooks.com

Publishes: Essays; Fiction; Nonfiction; *Areas:* Short Stories; *Markets:* Adult; *Treatments:* Experimental; Literary; Traditional

Publishes the work of new or established writers and can include short stories of any length, reportage, essays or novel extracts from anywhere in the world. Allows space for stories of different styles and subjects to rub up against each other, featuring classic slice-of-life alongside the experimental, the shocking and strange. Submit by post with SAE and personal contact details, or by email.

Viz

30 Cleveland Street
London
W1T 4JD
Tel: +44 (0) 20 7907 6000
Fax: +44 (0) 20 7907 6020
Email: viz@viz.co.uk
Website: http://www.viz.co.uk

Publishes: Articles; Fiction; *Areas:* Humour; *Markets:* Adult

Editors: Graham Dury; Simon Thorp

Magazine of adult humour, including cartoons, spoof articles, etc.

World Fishing

Mercator Media Ltd
The Old Mill
Lower Quay
Fareham
Hampshire
PO16 0RA
Tel: +44 (0) 1329 825335
Fax: +44 (0) 1329 825330
Email: editor@worldfishing.net
Website: http://www.worldfishing.net

Publishes: Articles; Nonfiction; *Areas:* Business; Nature; Technology; *Markets:* Professional

Magazine for fishing industry professionals. Publishes articles between 500 and 1,500 words.

The Warwick Review

Department of English
University of Warwick
Coventry
CV4 7AL
Email: m.w.hulse@warwick.ac.uk
Website: http://www2.warwick.ac.uk/fac/arts/english/writingprog/warwickreview/

Publishes: Essays; Fiction; Nonfiction; Poetry; Reviews; *Areas:* Historical; Politics; *Markets:* Adult; *Treatments:* Literary

Literary magazine with international scope, publishing poetry, prose fiction, essays and reviews, symposia and thematic sections. Particularly interested in history and politics. Send complete ms by post with SAE or send initial query by email. Does not read unsolicited submissions between July 1 and September 30.

Wasafiri

1-11 Hawley Crescent
Camden Town
London
NW1 8NP
Tel: +44 (0) 20 7556 6110
Fax: +44 (0) 20 7556 6187
Email: wasafiri@open.ac.uk
Website: http://www.wasafiri.org

Publishes: Articles; Essays; Fiction; Interviews; Nonfiction; Poetry; Reviews; *Areas:* Criticism; Culture; Literature; Short Stories; *Markets:* Adult; *Treatments:* Literary

Editors: Susheila Nasta

The indispensable journal of contemporary African, Asian Black British, Caribbean and transnational literatures.

In over fifteen years of publishing, this magazine has changed the face of contemporary writing in Britain. As a literary magazine primarily concerned with new and postcolonial writers, it continues to stress the diversity and range of black and diasporic writers world-wide. It remains committed to its original aims: to create a definitive forum for the voices of new writers and to open up lively spaces for serious critical discussion not available elsewhere. It is Britain's only international magazine for Black British, African, Asian and Caribbean literatures. Get the whole picture, get the magazine at the core of contemporary international literature today.

Wedding

Hubert Burda Media UK
The Tower
Phoenix Square
Colchester
Essex
CO4 9HU
Tel: +44 (0) 1206 851117 ext. 273
Email: emma.vince@burdamagazines.co.uk
Website:
http://www.weddingmagazine.co.uk

Publishes: Articles; Features; Nonfiction; *Areas:* Beauty and Fashion; How-to; Travel; *Markets:* Adult

Editors: Ciara Elliott; Editorial Contact: Emma Vince

Magazine aimed at brides, wedding planners and leading industry figures. Provides articles on weddings, gift ideas, honeymoon locations, etc.

The Week

30 Cleveland Street
London
W1T 4JD
Tel: +44 (0) 20 7907 6000
Email: holden_frith@dennis.co.uk
Website: http://www.theweek.co.uk

Publishes: News; Nonfiction; *Markets:* Adult

Editors: Holden Frith

Weekly magazine condensing the best of the British and international news from the week into 35 succinct pages.

The White Review

243 Knightsbridge
London
SW7 1DN
Email: editors@thewhitereview.org
Website: http://www.thewhitereview.org

Publishes: Essays; Fiction; Nonfiction; Poetry; Reviews; *Areas:* Arts; Culture; Literature; Short Stories; *Markets:* Adult; *Treatments:* Literary; Serious

Print and online quarterly arts and literature magazine. Publishes cultural analysis, reviews, and new fiction and poetry. See website for guidelines and submit by email.

Woman & Home Feel Good Food

Email: wandhmail@ipcmedia.com
Website: http://www.womanandhome.com

Publishes: Articles; Nonfiction; *Areas:* Cookery; Women's Interests; *Markets:* Adult

Editors: Jane Curran

Magazine covering cookery, recipes, ingredients, etc.

Woman Alive

Christian Publishing and Outreach
Garcia Estate
Canterbury Road
Worthing
West Sussex
BN13 1BW
Tel: +44 (0) 1903 264556
Fax: +44 (0) 1903 830066
Email: womanalive@cpo.org.uk
Website: http://www.womanalive.co.uk

Publishes: Articles; Features; Interviews; Nonfiction; *Areas:* Beauty and Fashion; Crafts; Entertainment; Health; Lifestyle; Religious; Travel; Women's Interests; *Markets:* Adult

Editors: Jackie Harris

Monthly lifestyle magazine for Christian women aged 25 and over. Welcomes unsolicited mss by post or by email. See website for full submission guidelines.

Woman's Weekly

IPC Media Ltd
Blue Fin Building
110 Southwark Street
London
SE1 0SU
Tel: +44 (0) 20 3148 5000
Email:
womansweeklypostbag@timeinc.com

Website: http://www.womansweekly.com

Publishes: Features; Fiction; News; Nonfiction; *Areas:* Short Stories; Women's Interests; *Markets:* Adult; *Treatments:* Contemporary

Editors: Diane Kenwood; Sue Pilkington (Features); Gaynor Davies (Fiction)

Publishes features of interest to women over forty, plus fiction between 1,000 and 2,000 words and serials in three, four, or five parts of 3,300 words each. Only uses experienced journalists for nonfiction. No submissions by email. Submit by post with SAE.

Woman's Weekly Fiction Special

IPC Media Ltd
The Blue Fin Building
110 Southwark Street
London
SE1 0SU
Tel: +44 (0) 20 3148 6600
Email: womansweeklypostbag@timeinc.com
Website: http://www.womansweekly.com

Publishes: Fiction; *Areas:* Short Stories; Women's Interests; *Markets:* Adult

Editors: Gaynor Davies

Publishes short stories for women up to 8,000 words. Send stories by post – no correspondence by email.

The World Today

The Royal Institute of International Affairs
Chatham House
10 St James's Square
London
SW1Y 4LE
Tel: +44 (0) 20 7957 5700
Fax: +44 (0) 20 7957 5710
Email: contact@chathamhouse.org
Website: http://www.theworldtoday.org

Publishes: Articles; News; Nonfiction; *Areas:* Current Affairs; Politics; *Markets:* Adult; *Treatments:* Serious

Bimonthly magazine providing authoritative analysis and commentary on current topics.

Writing Short Fiction

Email: bruceharris241@btinternet.com
Website: http://writingshortfiction.org

Publishes: Articles; Fiction; Nonfiction; *Areas:* Adventure; Architecture; Arts; Autobiography; Crime; Culture; Current Affairs; Entertainment; Historical; Humour; Leisure; Literature; Media; Nature; Politics; Short Stories; Travel; *Markets:* Adult; Youth; *Treatments:* Contemporary; Literary; Mainstream

Editors: Bruce Harris

The magazine offers advice, questionnaires and resources to new and established writers, and also publishes stories which have won prizes, commendations or listings in UK fiction competitions in its 'Champion Fiction' section.

Yoga and Health Magazine

PO Box 16969
London
E1W 1FY
Tel: +44 (0) 20 7480 5456
Email: Editor@yogaandhealthmag.co.uk
Website: http://www.yogaandhealthmag.co.uk

Publishes: Articles; Nonfiction; Reviews; *Areas:* Health; Hobbies; How-to; Leisure; Philosophy; *Markets:* Adult

Editors: Jane Sill

Publishes articles on yoga, Eastern philosophies, complementary therapies, healthy eating,vegetarian recipes, new products, book reviews, courses and classes.

Yorkshire Ridings Magazine

Seasiders Way
Blackpool
Lancashire
FY1 6NZ
Tel: +44 (0) 1253 336588
Fax: +44 (0) 1253 336587

Website: http://www.yorkshireridingsmagazine.com

Publishes: Articles; News; *Areas:* Beauty and Fashion; Business; Cookery; Entertainment; Finance; Gardening; Historical; Leisure; Lifestyle; Sport; Travel; *Markets:* Adult

County magazine for Yorkshire. All material must be related to the people and places of Yorkshire.

Your Cat

1-6 Buckminster Yard
Main Street
Buckminster
Grantham
Lincs
NG33 5SB
Tel: +44 (0) 1476 859820
Email: editorial@yourcat.co.uk
Website: http://www.yourcat.co.uk

Publishes: Articles; Fiction; Nonfiction; *Areas:* How-to; Short Stories; *Markets:* Adult

Editors: Chloë Hukin

Practical magazine covering the care of cats and kittens. No poetry and no articles written from the cat's viewpoint. Fiction by commission only. Send query by email with outline by post or by email.

Yours

Media House
Peterborough Business Park
Peterborough
PE2 6EA
Tel: +44 (0) 1733 468000
Email: yours@bauermedia.co.uk
Website: http://www.yours.co.uk

Publishes: Articles; Features; Fiction; Nonfiction; *Areas:* Lifestyle; Short Stories; Women's Interests; *Markets:* Adult; *Treatments:* Positive

Editors: Sharon Red

Lifestyle magazine aimed at women over 55. Welcomes nonfiction articles. Uses one or two pieces of fiction each issue. Send complete MS with SAE.

Canadian Magazines

For the most up-to-date listings of these and hundreds of other magazines, visit http://www.firstwriter.com/magazines

*To claim your **free** access to the site, please see the back of this book.*

Abilities

c/o Canadian Abilities Foundation
340 College Street, Suite 270
Toronto, Ontario M5T 3A9
Tel: +1 (416) 923-9829
Email: jennifer@abilities.ca
Website: http://abilities.ca

Publishes: Articles; Nonfiction; *Areas:* Health; Lifestyle; Self-Help; Sport; Travel; *Markets:* Adult

Editors: Jennifer Rivkin

Lifestyle magazine for the disabled. Covers areas such as travel, health, careers, education, relationships, parenting, new products, social policy, organisations, events and activities, sports, education, careers and more. No fiction, poetry, cartoons/comics or drama. Send query by email.

Alberta Views

208, 320 23rd Ave SW
Calgary AB, T2S 0J2
Tel: +1 (403) 243-5334
Fax: +1 (403) 243-8599
Email: queries@albertaviews.ab.ca
Website: https://albertaviews.ab.ca

Publishes: Articles; Features; Fiction; Nonfiction; Poetry; Reviews; *Areas:* Arts; Business; Culture; Finance; Politics; Short Stories; Sociology; *Markets:* Adult

Regional magazine for Alberta, publishing articles about the culture, politics and economy of Alberta; book reviews of books written or published in the province; poetry; and fiction. Accepted unsolicited poetry submissions. For nonfiction, query. Accepts fiction only through annual fiction competition. See website for full details.

Canadian Gardening

Transcontinental Media Inc.
25 Sheppard Avenue West, Suite 100
Toronto, ON M2N 6S7
Tel: +1 (416) 733-7600
Website: http://www.canadiangardening.com

Publishes: Articles; Nonfiction; *Areas:* Gardening; How-to; *Markets:* Adult

Magazine on gardening, covering all of Canada. Send query in first instance.

Coast & Kayak Magazine

PO Box 24
Stn A Nanaimo, BC
Tel: +1 (866) 984-6437
Fax: +1 (866) 654-1937
Email: kayak@coastandkayak.com
Website: http://www.coastandkayak.com

Publishes: Articles; Nonfiction; *Areas:* Hobbies; Leisure; Sport; Travel; *Markets:* Adult

Magazine for kayak enthusiasts, focussing on the Pacific coast. Queries accepted by post or by email.

Common Ground

Common Ground Publishing Corp
3152 West 8th Avenue
Vancouver, BC V6K 2C3
Tel: +1 (604) 733-2215
Fax: +1 (604) 733-4415
Email: editor@commonground.ca
Website: http://commonground.ca

Publishes: Articles; Features; Nonfiction; *Areas:* Health; Lifestyle; Nature; Self-Help; Travel; *Markets:* Adult

Publishes articles and features on health, wellness, the environment, transformational travel and personal growth. Send query by email including description of the proposed article, title, approximate length, and optionally the first paragraph, along with author bio and details of qualifications for writing on the subject. No attachments. See website for full guidelines.

Flare

Rogers Communications
One Mt Pleasant Road, 8th Floor
Toronto
Ontario
M4Y 2Y5
Tel: +1 (416) 764-1829
Fax: +1 (416) 764-2866
Email: editors@flare.com
Website: http://www.flare.com/about/writers-guidelines/

Publishes: Articles; News; Nonfiction; *Areas:* Beauty and Fashion; Entertainment; Women's Interests; *Markets:* Adult

Canada's best-selling fashion magazine, celebrating "smart fashion, Canadian style". Publishes articles on the home, fashion, beauty, celebrity, and weddings. Welcomes pitches from experienced writers familiar with the magazine's tone and content. Send query by email with published writing samples.

Pacific Yachting

200 West Esplanade, Suite 500
North Vancouver, BC V7M 1A4
Tel: +1 (604) 998-3310
Email: editor@pacificyachting.com
Website: http://www.pacificyachting.com

Publishes: Articles; Features; Nonfiction; *Areas:* How-to; Leisure; Travel; *Markets:* Adult

Editors: Dale Miller

Magazine for powerboaters and sailors sharing a common interest in recreational boating in British Columbia and the Pacific Northwest. Query by email in first instance.

Prairie Messenger

100 College Drive
Box 190
MUENSTER, SK S0K 2Y0
Tel: +1 (306) 682-1772
Fax: +1 (306) 682-5285
Email: pm.canadian@stpeterspress.ca
Website: http://www.prairiemessenger.ca

Publishes: Articles; Features; News; Nonfiction; Poetry; *Areas:* Current Affairs; Religious; *Markets:* Adult

Editors: Maureen Weber

16-20-page tabloid newspaper covering local, national and international religious news and current affairs. Send complete ms by post, email, or fax. Responds to postal submissions only if return Canadian postage is provided; responds to fax and email submissions only if interested.

Resources for Feminist Research

Ontario Institute for Studies in Education/University of Toronto
252 Bloor Street West
Toronto, Ontario
M5S 1V6
Email: rfrdrf@oise.utoronto.ca
Website: http://legacy.oise.utoronto.ca/rfr

Publishes: Articles; Nonfiction; *Areas:* Women's Interests; *Markets:* Academic

Editors: Philinda Masters

Bilingual (English/French) Canadian scholarly journal, covering Canadian and international feminist research, issues, and debates.

Riddle Fence

Email: contact@riddlefence.com
Website: http://www.riddlefence.com

Publishes: Fiction; Nonfiction; Poetry; *Areas:* Arts; Culture; Short Stories; *Markets:* Adult; *Treatments:* Literary

Newfoundland and Labrador-based journal of arts and culture. Publishes fiction, nonfiction, poetry, and artwork. Submit to appropriate email address listed on website.

Room Magazine

P.O. Box 46160, Station D
Vancouver, BC
V6J 5G5
Email: submissions@roommagazine.com
Website: http://www.roommagazine.com

Publishes: Fiction; Nonfiction; Poetry; *Areas:* Women's Interests; *Markets:* Adult; *Treatments:* Literary

Publishes fiction, creative nonfiction, and poetry, for, by, and about women. Submit prose up to 3,500 words or up to 5 poems, with cover letter, via online submission system.

subTerrain Magazine

PO Box 3008, MPO
Vancouver, BC V6B 3X5
Tel: +1 (604) 876-8710
Fax: +1 (604) 879-2667
Email: subter@portal.ca
Website: http://www.subterrain.ca

Publishes: Essays; Fiction; Nonfiction; Poetry; *Areas:* Short Stories; *Markets:* Adult; *Treatments:* Literary

Publishes fiction up to 3,000 words, creative nonfiction and commentary up to 4,000 words, and poetry. Each issue has a theme (see website for details of upcoming themes). Poetry only accepted if it relates directly to the theme, however prose may or may not make use of the theme. See website for full guidelines.

Today's Parent

Rogers Media, Inc.
One Mt Pleasant Road, 8th Floor
Toronto, ON
M4Y 2Y5
Tel: +1 (416) 764-2883
Fax: +1 (416) 764-2894
Email: editors@todaysparent.com
Website: http://www.todaysparent.com

Publishes: Articles; Features; Nonfiction; *Areas:* Health; Leisure; Lifestyle; *Markets:* Adult

Magazine aimed at Canadian parents of children aged up to 12. Concentrates on Canadian writers and content.

Irish Magazines

For the most up-to-date listings of these and hundreds of other magazines, visit http://www.firstwriter.com/magazines

*To claim your **free** access to the site, please see the back of this book.*

Africa

St Patrick's
Kiltegan
Co. Wicklow
Tel: +353 (0)59 647-3600
Fax: +353 (0)59 647-3622
Email: africa@spms.org
Website: http://www.spms.org

Publishes: Articles; Nonfiction; *Areas:* Religious; *Markets:* Adult

Editors: Fr. Tim Redmond

Catholic missionary magazine.

Books Ireland

Unit 9
78 Furze Road
Sandyford
Dublin 18
Tel: +353-1-2933568
Fax: +353-1-2939377
Email: office@wordwellbooks.com
Website: http://www.wordwellbooks.com

Publishes: Articles; Nonfiction; Reviews; *Areas:* Literature; *Markets:* Adult; Professional

Magazine publishing reviews of books by Irish authors or of Irish interest, plus articles aimed at booksellers, readers, and general readers.

The Caterpillar

Drummullen
Cavan
Co. Cavan
Tel: 353 49 4362677
Email: editor@thecaterpillarmagazine.com
Website: http://www.thecaterpillarmagazine.com

Publishes: Fiction; Poetry; *Areas:* Short Stories; *Markets:* Children's

Editors: Rebecca O'Connor

Magazine of stories and poems for children aged 7-11. Send up to six poems or short stories up to 1,000 words by email or by post. See website for full submission guidelines.

Cyphers

3 Selskar Terrace
Ranelagh
Dublin 6
Email: letters@cyphers.ie
Website: http://www.cyphers.ie

Publishes: Fiction; Poetry; *Areas:* Short Stories; Translations; *Markets:* Adult; *Treatments:* Literary

Publishes poetry and fiction in English and Irish, from Ireland and around the world. Translations are welcome. No unsolicited critical articles. Submissions by post only. Attachments sent by email will be deleted. See website for full guidelines.

The Dublin Review

PO Box 7948
Dublin 1
Email: enquiry@thedublinreview.com
Website: http://thedublinreview.com

Publishes: Essays; Fiction; Nonfiction; *Areas:* Criticism; Literature; Short Stories; *Markets:* Adult; *Treatments:* Literary

Publishes essays, criticism, reportage, and fiction for a general, intelligent readership. No poetry. Send submissions by post only with email address for response. Material is not returned, so do not include return postage. No response without email address.

Ireland's Own

Channing House
Rowe Street
Wexford
Email: irelands.own@peoplenews.ie
Website: https://irelandsown.ie

Publishes: Articles; Features; Fiction; Nonfiction; *Areas:* Short Stories; *Markets:* Adult; Children's; Family; Youth; *Treatments:* Literary; Traditional

Magazine publishing stories and articles of Irish interest for the whole family, plus puzzles and games.

Irish Printer

Tel: 01 432 2271
Email:
maeve.martin@ashvillemediagroup.com
Website: http://www.irishprinter.ie

Publishes: Articles; News; *Areas:* Business; Technology; *Markets:* Professional

Editors: Maev Martin

Magazine publishing news and articles for the printing industry.

The Moth

Drummullen
Cavan
Co. Cavan
Tel: 353 (0) 49 4362677
Email: editor@themothmagazine.com
Website: http://www.themothmagazine.com

Publishes: Fiction; Poetry; *Areas:* Short Stories; *Markets:* Adult; *Treatments:* Literary

Editors: Rebecca O'Connor

Closed to submissions as at August 2014, however status may change in September 2014. Check website for current situation.

Submit up to six poems or up to two short stories or novel extracts by post or by email. See website for full submission guidelines.

Poetry Ireland Review

Poetry Ireland
32 Kildare Street
Dublin 2
Tel: +353 (0)1 6789815
Fax: +353 (0)1 6789782
Email: info@poetryireland.ie
Website: http://www.poetryireland.ie

Publishes: Articles; Nonfiction; Poetry; Reviews; *Areas:* Literature; *Markets:* Adult

Editors: Vona Groarke

Send up to 6 poems with SASE / IRCs or email address for response. Poetry is accepted from around the world, but must be previously unpublished. No sexism or racism. No submissions by email. Articles and reviews are generally commissioned, however proposals are welcome. No unsolicited reviews or articles.

Reality Magazine

Redemptorist Communications
75 Orwell Road
Rathgar
Dublin 6
Tel: 353 1 492 2488
Email: sales@redcoms.org
Website: http://www.redcoms.org

Publishes: Articles; Nonfiction; *Areas:* Leisure; Religious; *Markets:* Adult; Youth

Catholic magazine, covering all aspects of modern life from a Christian perspective.

The Songwriter

International Songwriters Association (1967) Ltd
PO Box 46
Limerick City
Email: jliddane@songwriter.iol.ie
Website: http://www.songwriter.co.uk

Publishes: Articles; Interviews; *Areas:* Music; Markets

Magazine publishing articles and interviews of interest to songwriters.

The Stinging Fly

PO Box 6016
Dublin 1
Email: stingingfly@gmail.com
Website: http://www.stingingfly.org

Publishes: Essays; Fiction; Interviews; Nonfiction; Poetry; Reviews; *Areas:* Short Stories; *Markets:* Adult; *Treatments:* Literary

Editors: Declan Meade

Send submissions with SAE or international reply coupons sufficient for return of MS. Submit one story or up to four poems at a time. Poems and short stories should be as long or as short as they need to be. Has published stories over 5,000 words and as short as 600. Await response before making further submissions. For reviews, email editor with sample review as attachment. No submissions by email. Accepts submissions during specific months only. See website for details.

U Magazine

Harmonia Ltd
Rosemount House
Dundrum Road
Dundrum
Dublin 14
Tel: +353 1 240 5300
Fax: +353 1 661 9486
Email: webmaster@harmonia.ie
Website: http://umagazine.ie

Publishes: Articles; Features; Interviews; Nonfiction; *Areas:* Beauty and Fashion; Cookery; Design; Entertainment; Film; Health; Lifestyle; Music; Travel; Women's Interests; *Markets:* Adult

Magazine aimed at Irish women aged 18-25. Most material is commissioned.

Australian Magazines

For the most up-to-date listings of these and hundreds of other magazines, visit http://www.firstwriter.com/magazines

*To claim your **free** access to the site, please see the back of this book.*

Alternative Law Journal

c/- Law Faculty
Monash University
Victoria
3800
Tel: +61 (0) 3 9544 0974
Fax: +61 (0) 3 9905 5305
Email: altlj.org@monash.edu
Website: http://www.altlj.org

Publishes: Articles; Features; Nonfiction; *Areas:* Legal; *Markets:* Professional

Legal journal with the following goals:

-promotion of social justice, human rights and law reform issues

-critique of the legal system

-monitoring developments in alternative legal practice

-community legal education.

Meanjin

Melbourne University Publishing
Level 1, 11-15 Argyle Place South
Carlton Victoria 3053
Tel: +61 3 9342 0317
Email: meanjin@unimelb.edu.au
Website: http://meanjin.com.au

Publishes: Essays; Fiction; Nonfiction; Poetry; *Areas:* Autobiography; *Markets:* Adult

Editors: Jonathan Green; Catherine McInnis (Deputy Editor); Judith Beveridge (Poetry Editor)

Publishes fiction, essays, memoir, creative nonfiction, and poetry. May be open to different types of material at different times. See website for current status and online form for submission. $2 submission fee.

Verandah Literary Journal

Deakin University
221 Burwood Highway
Burwood Victoria 3125
Email: verandah@deakin.edu.au
Website: http://verandahjournal.wordpress.com

Publishes: Fiction; Nonfiction; Poetry; Scripts; *Areas:* Drama; Short Stories; *Markets:* Adult; *Treatments:* Literary

Submit fiction or nonfiction between 350 and 2,500 words; or poems / suites of poems up to 100 lines total. Also accepts scripts 5-7 minutes long. Submit by post or by email. Reading period each year runs from Februray 1 to June 10. Non-students must pay an entry fee of $10 for one submission or $15 for up to three submissions. See website for full details.

Magazines Subject Index

This section lists magazines by their subject matter, with directions to the section of the book where the full listing can be found.

You can create your own customised lists of magazines using different combinations of these subject areas, plus over a dozen other criteria, instantly online at http://www.firstwriter.com.

*To claim your **free** access to the site, please see the back of this book.*

The World Today (*UK*)
Writing Short Fiction (*UK*)

Design
Carbon Culture Review (*US*)
craft&design Magazine (*UK*)
Drapers (*UK*)
Energy Engineering (*UK*)
Evansville Living (*US*)
Fast Company (*US*)
Home Energy Magazine (*US*)
Homes and Gardens (*UK*)
Icon Magazine (*UK*)
Interweave Knits (*US*)
Pipeline & Gas Journal (*US*)
Popular Woodworking Magazine (*US*)
RV Business (*US*)
Sign Builder Illustrated (*US*)
Textile World (*US*)
25 Beautiful Homes (*UK*)
U Magazine (*Ire*)
VMSD (*US*)

Drama
The Alembic (*US*)
Aesthetica: A Review of Contemporary Artists (*UK*)
Aries (*US*)
Artifact Nouveau (*US*)
Bare Fiction Magazine (*UK*)
Carbon Culture Review (*US*)
Epoch (*US*)
Pointe Magazine (*US*)
Santa Clara Review (*US*)
Sequestrum (*US*)
Southern California Review (*US*)
Struggle (*US*)
The Teacher's Voice (*US*)
The Vehicle (*US*)
TriQuarterly (*US*)
Verandah Literary Journal (*Aus*)
Writer's Bloc (*US*)

Entertainment
Akron Life (*US*)
Artifact Nouveau (*US*)
Attitude (*UK*)
Carbon Culture Review (*US*)
Closer (*UK*)
Cosmopolitan (*US*)
Dogs Today (*UK*)
The Edge (*UK*)
Flare (*Can*)
Go Girl Magazine (*UK*)
Gay Times (GT Magazine) (*UK*)
GuestLife (*US*)
Heat (*UK*)
Houston Press (*US*)
The Irish Post (*UK*)
Junior (*UK*)
Kent Life (*UK*)
The List (*UK*)
The New Accelerator (*UK*)
Now (*UK*)
The Saturday Evening Post (*US*)
Sorry We're Booked (*US*)
The Voice (*UK*)
U Magazine (*Ire*)
Woman Alive (*UK*)
Writing Short Fiction (*UK*)
Yorkshire Ridings Magazine (*UK*)

Erotic
Artifact Nouveau (*US*)
The Edge (*UK*)
Erotic Review (*UK*)
Vanillerotica (*US*)

Fantasy
Allegory (*US*)
Artifact Nouveau (*US*)
Black Heart Magazine (*US*)
Black Static (*UK*)
Carbon Culture Review (*US*)
Crystal Magazine (*UK*)
The Dawntreader (*UK*)
Dragon's Haul (*UK*)
The Edge (*UK*)
Enchanted Conversation (*US*)
Interzone (*UK*)
Launch Pad: Where Young Authors and Illustrators Take Off! (*US*)
LONE STARS Magazine (*US*)
Monomyth (*UK*)
The New Accelerator (*UK*)
New London Writers (*UK*)
Premonitions (*UK*)
Sequestrum (*US*)
ShortStorySunday.com (*UK*)
T. Gene Davis's Speculative Blog (*US*)
Tales of the Talisman (*US*)
The Vehicle (*US*)

Fiction
The Alembic (*US*)
A&U (*US*)
Able Muse (*US*)
The Adirondack Review (*US*)
Aesthetica: A Review of Contemporary Artists (*UK*)
Alberta Views (*Can*)
Alimentum (*US*)
The Allegheny Review (*US*)
Allegory (*US*)
Alligator Juniper (*US*)
Ambit (*UK*)
Analog Science Fiction & Fact (*US*)
Ancient Paths (*US*)
Another Chicago Magazine (ACM) (*US*)
Apalachee Review (*US*)
Appalachian Heritage (*US*)
Apple Valley Review (*US*)
Aquila (*UK*)
Arc (*UK*)
Areopagus Magazine (*UK*)
Aries (*US*)
Artifact Nouveau (*US*)
Artificium (*UK*)
Bare Fiction Magazine (*UK*)
Bartleby Snopes (*US*)
The Beano (*UK*)
Big Fiction (*US*)

The Teacher's Voice (*US*)
Tears in the Fence (*UK*)
The Rejected Quarterly (*US*)
The Supplement (*UK*)
The Vehicle (*US*)
The Write Place at the Write Time (*US*)
34th Parallel (*US*)
Timber (*US*)
Toad Suck Review (*US*)
Toasted Cheese Literary Journal (*US*)
Trail of Indiscretion (*US*)
Trajectory (*US*)
Transition Magazine (*US*)
TriQuarterly (*US*)
Tulane Review (*US*)
Unthology (*UK*)
US Catholic (*US*)
Vanillerotica (*US*)
Verandah Literary Journal (*Aus*)
Verse (*US*)
Viz (*UK*)
Wag's Revue (*US*)
The Warwick Review (*UK*)
Wasafiri (*UK*)
Washington Square Review (*US*)
The White Review (*UK*)
Willow Review (*US*)
Windhover (*US*)
Wisconsin Review (*US*)
Witches & Pagans (*US*)
Woman's Weekly (*UK*)
Woman's Weekly Fiction Special (*UK*)
The Worcester Review (*US*)
Word Riot (*US*)
Wordpeace (*US*)
Workers Write (*US*)
Writer's Bloc (*US*)
Writing Short Fiction (*UK*)
Xavier Review (*US*)
Your Cat (*UK*)
Yours (*UK*)
Zeek (*US*)
ZYZZYVA (*US*)

Film

Aesthetica: A Review of Contemporary Artists (*UK*)
Carbon Culture Review (*US*)
Epoch (*US*)
Film Comment (*US*)
France (*UK*)
Go Girl Magazine (*UK*)
Gay Times (GT Magazine) (*UK*)
The List (*UK*)
U Magazine (*Ire*)
Written By (*US*)

Finance

Accounting and Business (*UK*)
African Business (*UK*)
Alberta Views (*Can*)
Dollars & Sense (*US*)
Equal Opportunity (*US*)
Fast Company (*US*)
KNOWAtlanta (*US*)
NextStepU Magazine (*US*)
RV Business (*US*)
The Saturday Evening Post (*US*)
Taxation (*UK*)
Third Way (*UK*)
Timeline (*US*)
Veterinary Economics (*US*)
Whole Life Times (*US*)
Yorkshire Ridings Magazine (*UK*)

Gardening

Akron Life (*US*)
Canadian Gardening (*Can*)
The English Garden (*UK*)
Evansville Living (*US*)
Grow Your Own (*UK*)
Homes and Gardens (*UK*)
The Saturday Evening Post (*US*)
Traverse (*US*)
Yorkshire Ridings Magazine (*UK*)

Gothic

Carbon Culture Review (*US*)
Cemetery Moon (*US*)
The Edge (*UK*)
ShortStorySunday.com (*UK*)
T. Gene Davis's Speculative Blog (*US*)
The Vehicle (*US*)

Health

A&U (*US*)
Abilities (*Can*)
Akron Life (*US*)
Cat Fancy (*US*)
Cincy (*US*)
Closer (*UK*)
Common Ground (*Can*)
Cosmopolitan (*US*)
Current Nursing in Geriatric Care (*US*)
Dance Teacher (*US*)
Dogs Today (*UK*)
Gay Times (GT Magazine) (*UK*)
Girlfriendz Magazine (*US*)
Golf News Magazine (*US*)
Health Club Management (*UK*)
Junior (*UK*)
Kashrus Magazine (*US*)
KNOWAtlanta (*US*)
Mother & Baby Magazine (*UK*)
Performance (*UK*)
Prima (*UK*)
Right Start Magazine (*UK*)
The Saturday Evening Post (*US*)
Skin Deep (*US*)
The Health Journal (*US*)
Today's Parent (*Can*)
U Magazine (*Ire*)
Whole Life Times (*US*)
Woman Alive (*UK*)
Yoga and Health Magazine (*UK*)

Historical

Akron Life (*US*)
Autograph Collector (*US*)
BackTrack (*UK*)
B'nai B'rith Magazine (*US*)
Cape Cod Life (*US*)

Classic Boat (*UK*)
Classic Cars (*UK*)
The Dickensian (*UK*)
Early American Life (*US*)
Evansville Living (*US*)
Evergreen (*UK*)
Film Comment (*US*)
France (*UK*)
Girlfriendz Magazine (*US*)
GuestLife (*US*)
Hyde Park Living (*US*)
Irish Pages (*UK*)
Jewish Quarterly (*UK*)
Kent Life (*UK*)
Lakeland Boating (*US*)
Leopard Magazine (*UK*)
New Humanist (*UK*)
Pakn Treger (*US*)
Pennsylvania Heritage (*US*)
Pointe Magazine (*US*)
Symphony (*US*)
Sable (*UK*)
Scottish Memories (*UK*)
ShortStorySunday.com (*UK*)
Skipping Stones (*US*)
Smithsonian Magazine (*US*)
Sorry We're Booked (*US*)
Steamboat Magazine (*US*)
Suffolk Norfolk Life (*UK*)
Sun Valley Magazine (*US*)
Telluride Magazine (*US*)
The Vehicle (*US*)
Timeline (*US*)
Tradicion Revista Magazine (*US*)
Traverse (*US*)
True West (*US*)
The Warwick Review (*UK*)
Wine Press Northwest (*US*)
Writing Short Fiction (*UK*)
Yorkshire Ridings Magazine (*UK*)

Hobbies

Angling Times (*UK*)
Astronomy (*US*)
ATV Rider Magazine (*US*)
Autograph Collector (*US*)
Backpacker (*US*)
Bee Culture (*US*)
Bird Watching (*UK*)
BirdWatching Magazine (*US*)
Brew Your Own (*US*)
Caravan Magazine (*UK*)
Carbon Culture Review (*US*)
Classic Boat (*UK*)
Coast & Kayak Magazine (*Can*)
Creating Keepsakes (*US*)
Dime (Designs in Machine Embroidery) (*US*)
Dogs Today (*UK*)
18 Wheels & Heels (*US*)
Field & Stream (*US*)
FineScale Modeler (*US*)
Interweave Knits (*US*)
Lost Treasure, Inc. (*US*)
Pony Magazine (*UK*)
Popular Woodworking Magazine (*US*)
Quilter's World (*US*)
Sea Angler (*UK*)
Sew News (*US*)
Stamp Magazine (*UK*)
Total Off-Road (*UK*)
Wine Spectator (*US*)
Yachting Magazine (*US*)
Yoga and Health Magazine (*UK*)

Horror

Allegory (*US*)
Artifact Nouveau (*US*)
Black Static (*UK*)
Cemetery Moon (*US*)
The Edge (*UK*)
The New Accelerator (*UK*)
Premonitions (*UK*)
The Realm Beyond (*US*)
Scar Tissue (*UK*)
Scary Monsters Magazine (*US*)
Sequestrum (*US*)
ShortStorySunday.com (*UK*)
Suspense Magazine (*US*)
T. Gene Davis's Speculative Blog (*US*)
Tales of the Talisman (*US*)
The Vehicle (*US*)

How-to

Adventure Cyclist (*US*)
African-American Career World (*US*)
Akron Life (*US*)
American Careers (*US*)
Android Magazine (*UK*)
Angus Beef Bulletin (*US*)
Aquatics International (*US*)
Astronomy (*US*)
Autograph Collector (*US*)
Backpacker (*US*)
BirdWatching Magazine (*US*)
Brew Your Own (*US*)
Business NH Magazine (*US*)
Canadian Gardening (*Can*)
Cat Fancy (*US*)
Chef Magazine (*US*)
Cruising Outpost Magazine (*US*)
Dance Teacher (*US*)
Digital Camera World (*UK*)
Dime (Designs in Machine Embroidery) (*US*)
18 Wheels & Heels (*US*)
The English Garden (*UK*)
Equal Opportunity (*US*)
The Fabricator (*US*)
Field & Stream (*US*)
FineScale Modeler (*US*)
Food Product Design (*US*)
Freelance Writer's Report (FWR) (*US*)
Girlfriendz Magazine (*US*)
Golf News Magazine (*US*)
Grain Journal (*US*)
Grow Your Own (*UK*)
Homes and Gardens (*UK*)
InTents (*US*)
Interweave Knits (*US*)
KNOWAtlanta (*US*)

Chef Magazine (*US*)
China Grove (*US*)
The Christian Century (*US*)
Cincy (*US*)
Classic Boat (*UK*)
Classic Cars (*UK*)
Closer (*UK*)
Coast & Kayak Magazine (*Can*)
Common Ground (*Can*)
Common Ground Review (*US*)
Conceit Magazine (*US*)
Consumer Goods Technology (*US*)
Cook Vegetarian (*UK*)
Cosmopolitan (*US*)
craft&design Magazine (*UK*)
Crafts (*UK*)
Creating Keepsakes (*US*)
Cruising Outpost Magazine (*US*)
Crystal Magazine (*UK*)
Cura – A Literary Magazine of Art and Action (*US*)
Current Nursing in Geriatric Care (*US*)
Cycle Sport (*UK*)
Dance Teacher (*US*)
Dare (*UK*)
DASH Journal (*US*)
The Dawntreader (*UK*)
Decanter (*UK*)
The Dickensian (*UK*)
Digital Camera World (*UK*)
Dime (Designs in Machine Embroidery) (*US*)
Dogs Today (*UK*)
Dollars & Sense (*US*)
Drapers (*UK*)
Dream Catcher (*UK*)
Drunken Boat (*US*)
The Dublin Review (*Ire*)
Early American Life (*US*)
East Lothian Life (*UK*)
The Edge (*UK*)
Education Journal (*UK*)
18 Wheels & Heels (*US*)
El Restaurante (*US*)
Electrical Apparatus (*US*)
Enchanted Conversation (*US*)
Energy Engineering (*UK*)
The English Garden (*UK*)
Envoi (*UK*)
Epoch (*US*)
Equal Opportunity (*US*)
Erotic Review (*UK*)
Escapees Magazine (*US*)
Esquire (*UK*)
Evansville Living (*US*)
Evening Street Review (*US*)
The Fabricator (*US*)
Family Law Journal (*UK*)
Fast Company (*US*)
Feminist Review (*UK*)
Fence (*US*)
Field & Stream (*US*)
Film Comment (*US*)
FineScale Modeler (*US*)
Fire Magazine (*UK*)
Fishing News (*UK*)
Flare (*Can*)
Food Product Design (*US*)
France (*UK*)
Freelance Market News (*UK*)
Freelance Writer's Report (FWR) (*US*)
The Friend (*UK*)
Fruit Growers News Magazine (*US*)
Go Girl Magazine (*UK*)
Gay Times (GT Magazine) (*UK*)
Golf News Magazine (*US*)
The Good Book Guide (*UK*)
Grain Journal (*US*)
Granta (*UK*)
Greetings Today (*UK*)
The Grocer (*UK*)
Grow Your Own (*UK*)
GuestLife (*US*)
Hard Hat News (*US*)
Health Club Management (*UK*)
Heat (*UK*)
Hill Country Sun (*US*)
Home Energy Magazine (*US*)
Homes and Gardens (*UK*)
The Horn Book Magazine (*US*)
Horse & Hound (*UK*)
Houston Press (*US*)
Hyde Park Living (*US*)
ICIS Chemical Business Magazine (*UK*)
Indianapolis Monthly (*US*)
InTents (*US*)
Intermedia (*UK*)
International Affairs (*UK*)
Interweave Knits (*US*)
Ireland's Own (*Ire*)
Irish Pages (*UK*)
The Irish Post (*UK*)
Iron Horse Literary Review (*US*)
Jewish Quarterly (*UK*)
The Journal of Adventist Education (*US*)
Junior (*UK*)
Kashrus Magazine (*US*)
Kent Life (*UK*)
Kids Alive! (*UK*)
KNOWAtlanta (*US*)
Lancashire Magazine (*UK*)
Lakeland Boating (*US*)
Launch Pad: Where Young Authors and Illustrators Take Off! (*US*)
Legal Week (*UK*)
Leisure Group Travel (*US*)
Leopard Magazine (*UK*)
The List (*UK*)
Little Patuxent Review (*US*)
Living France Magazine (*UK*)
Lost Treasure, Inc. (*US*)
Lunar Poetry (*UK*)
Magma (*UK*)
The Maine Review (*US*)
Market Newsletter (*UK*)
Meanjin (*Aus*)
Media Week (*UK*)

Methodist Recorder (*UK*)
Mixmag (*UK*)
Modern Poetry in Translation (*UK*)
Monkey Kettle (*UK*)
Mother & Baby Magazine (*UK*)
Mslexia (*UK*)
Music Teacher (*UK*)
The Musical Times (*UK*)
.net (*UK*)
New Humanist (*UK*)
New Walk Magazine (*UK*)
New Welsh Review (*UK*)
NextStepU Magazine (*US*)
Northern Woodlands (*US*)
Now (*UK*)
Nursery World (*UK*)
O&A (Oil & Automotive Service) Marketing News (*US*)
One (*US*)
Overdrive (*US*)
Pony Magazine (*UK*)
Pulse (*US*)
PRISM Magazine (*US*)
Pacific Yachting (*Can*)
Painted Cave (*US*)
Pakn Treger (*US*)
Pallet Enterprise (*US*)
PC Advisor (*UK*)
PC Pro (*UK*)
Peace News (*UK*)
The Penniless Press (*UK*)
Pennsylvania Heritage (*US*)
The People's Friend (*UK*)
Performance (*UK*)
The Photo Review (*US*)
Pipeline & Gas Journal (*US*)
Planet (*UK*)
Poetry Express (*UK*)
Poetry Ireland Review (*Ire*)
Poetry London (*UK*)
The Poetry Review (*UK*)
Pointe Magazine (*US*)
The Political Quarterly (*UK*)
Popular Woodworking Magazine (*US*)
Post (*UK*)
PR Week (*UK*)
Practical Wireless (*UK*)
Prairie Messenger (*Can*)
Prima (*UK*)
Produce Business (*US*)
Professional Photographer (*UK*)
Promo (*US*)
Prospect (*UK*)
Q Magazine (*UK*)
Quilter's World (*US*)
Rappahannock Review (*US*)
Real People (*UK*)
Reality Magazine (*Ire*)
Red Paint Hill Poetry Journal (*US*)
Red Pepper (*UK*)
Reed Magazine (*US*)
Resources for Feminist Research (*Can*)
Resurgence & Ecologist (*UK*)
The Rialto (*UK*)
Riddle Fence (*Can*)
Right Start Magazine (*UK*)
Road King (*US*)
Room Magazine (*Can*)
Royal Academy of Arts (RA) Magazine (*UK*)
RTJ's Creative Catechist (*US*)
RV Business (*US*)
Symphony (*US*)
Sable (*UK*)
Salmagundi Magazine (*US*)
Salt Hill Journal (*US*)
Salt Water Sportsman (*US*)
Sandy River Review (*US*)
Santa Clara Review (*US*)
Santa Monica Review (*US*)
Saranac Review (*US*)
The Saturday Evening Post (*US*)
The Savage Kick (*UK*)
Scar Tissue (*UK*)
The School Librarian (*UK*)
School Nurse News (*US*)
Scientific Computing World (*UK*)
Scottish Memories (*UK*)
Sea Angler (*UK*)
Sea Magazine (*US*)
Seek (*US*)
Sequestrum (*US*)
Sew News (*US*)
The Sewanee Review (*US*)
Shadows Express (*US*)
Shearsman (*UK*)
Shooting Times (*UK*)
Shoreline of Infinity (*UK*)
Sign Builder Illustrated (*US*)
Skin Deep (*US*)
Skipping Stones (*US*)
Slate & Style (*US*)
Slow Trains (*US*)
Smallholder (*UK*)
Smithsonian Magazine (*US*)
Snowy Egret (*US*)
Sorry We're Booked (*US*)
South Carolina Review (*US*)
South Dakota Review (*US*)
South Florida Parenting (*US*)
Southeast Review (*US*)
Southern California Review (*US*)
Southwestern American Literature (*US*)
SpeciaLiving magazine (*US*)
Spider (*US*)
Springs (*US*)
The Squash Player (*UK*)
Stamp Magazine (*UK*)
Star 82 Review (*US*)
Steamboat Magazine (*US*)
The Stinging Fly (*Ire*)
Stirring : A Literary Collection (*US*)
storySouth (*US*)
Stuff (*UK*)
subTerrain Magazine (*Can*)
Suffolk Norfolk Life (*UK*)
The Summerset Review (*US*)

The Sun (*US*)
Sun Valley Magazine (*US*)
Suspense Magazine (*US*)
Talking River (*US*)
Taxation (*UK*)
The Teacher's Voice (*US*)
Teaching Music (*US*)
Tears in the Fence (*UK*)
Telluride Magazine (*US*)
10th Muse (*UK*)
Textile World (*US*)
The Health Journal (*US*)
The Recusant (*UK*)
The Rejected Quarterly (*US*)
The Supplement (*UK*)
The Teacher (*UK*)
The Vehicle (*US*)
The Voice (*UK*)
The Write Place at the Write Time (*US*)
thesnailmagazine (*UK*)
Third Way (*UK*)
34th Parallel (*US*)
Timber (*US*)
TimberLine (*US*)
Timeline (*US*)
Toad Suck Review (*US*)
Today's Golfer (*UK*)
Today's Parent (*Can*)
Toledo Area Parent (*US*)
Total Off-Road (*UK*)
Total Politics (*UK*)
Tradicion Revista Magazine (*US*)
Trajectory (*US*)
Transition Magazine (*US*)
Traverse (*US*)
TriQuarterly (*US*)
True West (*US*)
25 Beautiful Homes (*UK*)
U Magazine (*Ire*)
Ultimate MMA (*US*)
Unthology (*UK*)
US Catholic (*US*)
Validation Times (*US*)
Verandah Literary Journal (*Aus*)
Verse (*US*)
Veterinary Economics (*US*)
VMSD (*US*)
World Fishing (*UK*)
Wag's Revue (*US*)
The Warwick Review (*UK*)
Wasafiri (*UK*)
Wedding (*UK*)
The Week (*UK*)
Wesleyan Life (*US*)
The White Review (*UK*)
Whole Life Times (*US*)
Willow Review (*US*)
Windhover (*US*)
Wine Press Northwest (*US*)
Wine Spectator (*US*)
Wisconsin Review (*US*)
Witches & Pagans (*US*)
Woman & Home Feel Good Food (*UK*)
Woman Alive (*UK*)
Woman's Weekly (*UK*)
Woodshop News (*US*)
The Worcester Review (*US*)
Word Riot (*US*)
Wordpeace (*US*)
The World Today (*UK*)
Writer's Bloc (*US*)
The Writing Disorder (*US*)
Writing Short Fiction (*UK*)
Written By (*US*)
Xavier Review (*US*)
Yachting Magazine (*US*)
Yoga and Health Magazine (*UK*)
Your Cat (*UK*)
Yours (*UK*)
Zeek (*US*)
Zink (*US*)
ZYZZYVA (*US*)

Philosophy

Artifact Nouveau (*US*)
Black Heart Magazine (*US*)
Carbon Culture Review (*US*)
Jewish Quarterly (*UK*)
New Humanist (*UK*)
New London Writers (*UK*)
The Penniless Press (*UK*)
Resurgence & Ecologist (*UK*)
Sequestrum (*US*)
ShortStorySunday.com (*UK*)
Sorry We're Booked (*US*)
The Sun (*US*)
Yoga and Health Magazine (*UK*)

Photography

The Adirondack Review (*US*)
Artifact Nouveau (*US*)
BirdWatching Magazine (*US*)
British Journal of Photography (*UK*)
Carbon Culture Review (*US*)
Digital Camera World (*UK*)
Market Newsletter (*UK*)
The Photo Review (*US*)
Professional Photographer (*UK*)
The Vehicle (*US*)

Poetry

The Alembic (*US*)
A&U (*US*)
Able Muse (*US*)
Acumen (*UK*)
The Adirondack Review (*US*)
Aesthetica: A Review of Contemporary Artists (*UK*)
Agenda (*UK*)
Alberta Views (*Can*)
Alimentum (*US*)
The Allegheny Review (*US*)
Alligator Juniper (*US*)
Ambit (*UK*)
Amulet (*US*)
Analog Science Fiction & Fact (*US*)
Ancient Paths (*US*)
Another Chicago Magazine (ACM) (*US*)
Apalachee Review (*US*)

Spider (*US*)
Stand Magazine (*UK*)
The Stinging Fly (*Ire*)
Stirring : A Literary Collection (*US*)
storySouth (*US*)
The Stray Branch (*US*)
Straylight (*US*)
Struggle (*US*)
subTerrain Magazine (*Can*)
The Summerset Review (*US*)
The Sun (*US*)
Tales of the Talisman (*US*)
Talking River (*US*)
Tattoo Highway (*US*)
The Teacher's Voice (*US*)
Tears in the Fence (*UK*)
10th Muse (*UK*)
The Recusant (*UK*)
The Rejected Quarterly (*US*)
The Supplement (*UK*)
The Vehicle (*US*)
The Write Place at the Write Time (*US*)
Third Way (*UK*)
34th Parallel (*US*)
Timber (*US*)
Toad Suck Review (*US*)
Trajectory (*US*)
Transition Magazine (*US*)
TriQuarterly (*US*)
Tulane Review (*US*)
US Catholic (*US*)
Verandah Literary Journal (*Aus*)
Verse (*US*)
Wag's Revue (*US*)
The Warwick Review (*UK*)
Wasafiri (*UK*)
Washington Square Review (*US*)
The White Review (*UK*)
Willow Review (*US*)
Windhover (*US*)
Wisconsin Review (*US*)
Witches & Pagans (*US*)
The Worcester Review (*US*)
Word Riot (*US*)
Wordpeace (*US*)
Workers Write (*US*)
Writer's Bloc (*US*)
The Writing Disorder (*US*)
Xavier Review (*US*)
Zeek (*US*)
ZYZZYVA (*US*)

Politics

A&U (*US*)
Alberta Views (*Can*)
Artifact Nouveau (*US*)
B'nai B'rith Magazine (*US*)
The Christian Century (*US*)
Feminist Review (*UK*)
The Friend (*UK*)
Granta (*UK*)
Intermedia (*UK*)
International Affairs (*UK*)
The Irish Post (*UK*)
Jewish Quarterly (*UK*)
Monkey Kettle (*UK*)
One (*US*)
Peace News (*UK*)
Planet (*UK*)
The Political Quarterly (*UK*)
Prospect (*UK*)
Red Pepper (*UK*)
Red Poets (*UK*)
Sorry We're Booked (*US*)
Struggle (*US*)
The Sun (*US*)
The Recusant (*UK*)
The Voice (*UK*)
Third Way (*UK*)
Timeline (*US*)
Toad Suck Review (*US*)
Total Politics (*UK*)
The Warwick Review (*UK*)
The World Today (*UK*)
Writing Short Fiction (*UK*)

Psychology

Right Start Magazine (*UK*)

Radio

Carbon Culture Review (*US*)

Reference

African-American Career World (*US*)
Greetings Today (*UK*)
Mslexia (*UK*)

Religious

Africa (*Ire*)
Ancient Paths (*US*)
Areopagus Magazine (*UK*)
Baptist Times (*UK*)
Bible Advocate (*US*)
B'nai B'rith Magazine (*US*)
The Catholic Herald (*UK*)
The Christian Century (*US*)
The Friend (*UK*)
Jewish Quarterly (*UK*)
The Journal of Adventist Education (*US*)
Kashrus Magazine (*US*)
Kids Alive! (*UK*)
Methodist Recorder (*UK*)
The New Accelerator (*UK*)
New Humanist (*UK*)
One (*US*)
PRISM Magazine (*US*)
Pakn Treger (*US*)
The Poetry Church (*UK*)
Prairie Messenger (*Can*)
Reality Magazine (*Ire*)
RTJ's Creative Catechist (*US*)
Seek (*US*)
Third Way (*UK*)
US Catholic (*US*)
Wesleyan Life (*US*)
Windhover (*US*)
Witches & Pagans (*US*)
Woman Alive (*UK*)
Xavier Review (*US*)

Zeek (*US*)
Romance
Artifact Nouveau (*US*)
Crystal Magazine (*UK*)
The People's Friend (*UK*)
People's Friend Pocket Novels (*UK*)
Romance Flash (*US*)
ShortStorySunday.com (*UK*)
The Vehicle (*US*)
Vanillerotica (*US*)
Science
Analog Science Fiction & Fact (*US*)
Arc (*UK*)
Astronomy (*US*)
Bee Culture (*US*)
Carbon Culture Review (*US*)
ICIS Chemical Business Magazine (*UK*)
Intermedia (*UK*)
Irish Pages (*UK*)
The New Accelerator (*UK*)
New Humanist (*UK*)
Scientific Computing World (*UK*)
Smithsonian Magazine (*US*)
Spider (*US*)
Timeline (*US*)
Sci-Fi
Allegory (*US*)
Analog Science Fiction & Fact (*US*)
Arc (*UK*)
Artifact Nouveau (*US*)
Black Heart Magazine (*US*)
Carbon Culture Review (*US*)
Crystal Magazine (*UK*)
The Edge (*UK*)
Interzone (*UK*)
Launch Pad: Where Young Authors and Illustrators Take Off! (*US*)
The New Accelerator (*UK*)
New London Writers (*UK*)
Premonitions (*UK*)
The Realm Beyond (*US*)
Sequestrum (*US*)
Shoreline of Infinity (*UK*)
ShortStorySunday.com (*UK*)
T. Gene Davis's Speculative Blog (*US*)
Tales of the Talisman (*US*)
The Vehicle (*US*)
Scripts
The Alembic (*US*)
Aries (*US*)
Bare Fiction Magazine (*UK*)
Epoch (*US*)
Santa Clara Review (*US*)
Southern California Review (*US*)
Struggle (*US*)
The Teacher's Voice (*US*)
The Vehicle (*US*)
34th Parallel (*US*)
Toad Suck Review (*US*)
TriQuarterly (*US*)
Verandah Literary Journal (*Aus*)
Writer's Bloc (*US*)
Self-Help
Abilities (*Can*)
African-American Career World (*US*)
American Careers (*US*)
Common Ground (*Can*)
Equal Opportunity (*US*)
Girlfriendz Magazine (*US*)
KNOWAtlanta (*US*)
NextStepU Magazine (*US*)
Short Stories
The Alembic (*US*)
A&U (*US*)
Able Muse (*US*)
The Adirondack Review (*US*)
Aesthetica: A Review of Contemporary Artists (*UK*)
Alberta Views (*Can*)
Alimentum (*US*)
The Allegheny Review (*US*)
Allegory (*US*)
Alligator Juniper (*US*)
Ambit (*UK*)
Analog Science Fiction & Fact (*US*)
Ancient Paths (*US*)
Another Chicago Magazine (ACM) (*US*)
Apalachee Review (*US*)
Appalachian Heritage (*US*)
Apple Valley Review (*US*)
Aquila (*UK*)
Arc (*UK*)
Areopagus Magazine (*UK*)
Aries (*US*)
Artifact Nouveau (*US*)
Artificium (*UK*)
Bare Fiction Magazine (*UK*)
Bartleby Snopes (*US*)
The Beano (*UK*)
Big Fiction (*US*)
Black Heart Magazine (*US*)
Black Static (*UK*)
Burnside Review (*US*)
Carbon Culture Review (*US*)
Carve Magazine (*US*)
The Casket of Fictional Delights (*UK*)
The Caterpillar (*Ire*)
Cemetery Moon (*US*)
Chapman (*UK*)
China Grove (*US*)
Commando (*UK*)
Common Ground Review (*US*)
Conceit Magazine (*US*)
Crystal Magazine (*UK*)
Cura – A Literary Magazine of Art and Action (*US*)
Cyphers (*Ire*)
DASH Journal (*US*)
The Dawntreader (*UK*)
Dream Catcher (*UK*)
Drunken Boat (*US*)
The Dublin Review (*Ire*)
Epoch (*US*)
Erotic Review (*UK*)

Evening Street Review (*US*)
Fence (*US*)
Flash: The International Short-Short Story Magazine (*UK*)
Graffiti Magazine (*UK*)
Granta (*UK*)
I-70 Review (*UK*)
Interzone (*UK*)
Ireland's Own (*Ire*)
Irish Pages (*UK*)
Iron Horse Literary Review (*US*)
Jewish Quarterly (*UK*)
Leopard Magazine (*UK*)
Little Patuxent Review (*US*)
The Maine Review (*US*)
Monkey Kettle (*UK*)
Monomyth (*UK*)
The Moth (*Ire*)
Mslexia (*UK*)
The New Accelerator (*UK*)
New London Writers (*UK*)
New Walk Magazine (*UK*)
New Welsh Review (*UK*)
The Ottawa Object (*US*)
Painted Cave (*US*)
Peace and Freedom (*UK*)
The Penniless Press (*UK*)
The People's Friend (*UK*)
Planet (*UK*)
Postcard Poems and Prose (*US*)
Prospect (*UK*)
Romance Flash (*US*)
Rappahannock Review (*US*)
The Realm Beyond (*US*)
The Reater (*UK*)
Reed Magazine (*US*)
Rhino Poetry (*US*)
Riddle Fence (*Can*)
The Rockford Review (*US*)
Sable (*UK*)
Salt Hill Journal (*US*)
Sandy River Review (*US*)
Santa Clara Review (*US*)
Santa Monica Review (*US*)
Saranac Review (*US*)
Sarasvati (*UK*)
The Saturday Evening Post (*US*)
Scar Tissue (*UK*)
Scary Monsters Magazine (*US*)
Scribbler! (*UK*)
Seek (*US*)
Sequestrum (*US*)
The Sewanee Review (*US*)
Shadows Express (*US*)
Shoreline of Infinity (*UK*)
Short Story America (*US*)
ShortStorySunday.com (*UK*)
Sixpenny Magazine (*US*)
Slate & Style (*US*)
Sling Magazine (*US*)
Snowy Egret (*US*)
Sorry We're Booked (*US*)
South Carolina Review (*US*)
South Dakota Review (*US*)
Southeast Review (*US*)
Southern California Review (*US*)
Southwestern American Literature (*US*)
Sou'wester (*US*)
Spider (*US*)
Stand Magazine (*UK*)
Star 82 Review (*US*)
The Stinging Fly (*Ire*)
Stirring : A Literary Collection (*US*)
The Stray Branch (*US*)
Straylight (*US*)
Struggle (*US*)
subTerrain Magazine (*Can*)
The Summerset Review (*US*)
The Sun (*US*)
Suspense Magazine (*US*)
T. Gene Davis's Speculative Blog (*US*)
Tales of the Talisman (*US*)
Talking River (*US*)
Tattoo Highway (*US*)
The Teacher's Voice (*US*)
Tears in the Fence (*UK*)
The Rejected Quarterly (*US*)
The Supplement (*UK*)
The Vehicle (*US*)
The Write Place at the Write Time (*US*)
34th Parallel (*US*)
Timber (*US*)
Toad Suck Review (*US*)
Toasted Cheese Literary Journal (*US*)
Trail of Indiscretion (*US*)
Trajectory (*US*)
Transition Magazine (*US*)
Tulane Review (*US*)
Unthology (*UK*)
US Catholic (*US*)
Verandah Literary Journal (*Aus*)
Verse (*US*)
Wasafiri (*UK*)
Washington Square Review (*US*)
The White Review (*UK*)
Willow Review (*US*)
Windhover (*US*)
Wisconsin Review (*US*)
Witches & Pagans (*US*)
Woman's Weekly (*UK*)
Woman's Weekly Fiction Special (*UK*)
The Worcester Review (*US*)
Word Riot (*US*)
Wordpeace (*US*)
Workers Write (*US*)
Writer's Bloc (*US*)
The Writing Disorder (*US*)
Writing Short Fiction (*UK*)
Xavier Review (*US*)
Your Cat (*UK*)
Yours (*UK*)
ZYZZYVA (*US*)

Sociology

Alberta Views (*Can*)
Bible Advocate (*US*)
The Big Issue (*UK*)

B'nai B'rith Magazine (*US*)
Carbon Culture Review (*US*)
Feminist Review (*UK*)
The Friend (*UK*)
Peace and Freedom (*UK*)
Skipping Stones (*US*)
thesnailmagazine (*UK*)
Third Way (*UK*)
Timeline (*US*)
Whole Life Times (*US*)

Spiritual

Artifact Nouveau (*US*)
The New Accelerator (*UK*)
Resurgence & Ecologist (*UK*)
US Catholic (*US*)
Whole Life Times (*US*)
Windhover (*US*)
Witches & Pagans (*US*)
Xavier Review (*US*)
Zeek (*US*)

Sport

Abilities (*Can*)
American Turf Monthly (*US*)
Angling Times (*UK*)
Athletics Weekly (*UK*)
Bow & Arrow Hunting (*US*)
Coast & Kayak Magazine (*Can*)
Cycle Sport (*UK*)
Evansville Living (*US*)
Field & Stream (*US*)
Golf News Magazine (*US*)
Horse & Hound (*UK*)
The Irish Post (*UK*)
Pony Magazine (*UK*)
Performance (*UK*)
Salt Water Sportsman (*US*)
Sea Angler (*UK*)
Shooting Times (*UK*)
Skipping Stones (*US*)
The Squash Player (*UK*)
The Voice (*UK*)
Today's Golfer (*UK*)
Total Off-Road (*UK*)
Traverse (*US*)
Ultimate MMA (*US*)
Yorkshire Ridings Magazine (*UK*)

Suspense

Artifact Nouveau (*US*)
Black Heart Magazine (*US*)
Carbon Culture Review (*US*)
Cemetery Moon (*US*)
Crystal Magazine (*UK*)
New London Writers (*UK*)
The Realm Beyond (*US*)
ShortStorySunday.com (*UK*)
The Stray Branch (*US*)
Suspense Magazine (*US*)
The Vehicle (*US*)

Technology

Adventure Cyclist (*US*)
Android Magazine (*UK*)
Angus Beef Bulletin (*US*)
Aquatics International (*US*)
Art Business Today (*UK*)
ATV Rider Magazine (*US*)
Bee Culture (*US*)
Brew Your Own (*US*)
British Journal of Photography (*UK*)
Carbon Culture Review (*US*)
Chef Magazine (*US*)
Classic Cars (*UK*)
Consumer Goods Technology (*US*)
Cruising Outpost Magazine (*US*)
Electrical Apparatus (*US*)
Energy Engineering (*UK*)
Esquire (*UK*)
The Fabricator (*US*)
Fast Company (*US*)
Gay Times (GT Magazine) (*UK*)
Grain Journal (*US*)
InTents (*US*)
Intermedia (*UK*)
Irish Printer (*Ire*)
Lakeland Boating (*US*)
.net (*UK*)
The New Accelerator (*UK*)
Overdrive (*US*)
Pallet Enterprise (*US*)
PC Advisor (*UK*)
PC Pro (*UK*)
Pipeline & Gas Journal (*US*)
Popular Woodworking Magazine (*US*)
Practical Wireless (*UK*)
Professional Photographer (*UK*)
RV Business (*US*)
The Saturday Evening Post (*US*)
Scientific Computing World (*UK*)
Sea Angler (*UK*)
Sea Magazine (*US*)
Sign Builder Illustrated (*US*)
Smithsonian Magazine (*US*)
SpeciaLiving magazine (*US*)
Springs (*US*)
Stuff (*UK*)
Textile World (*US*)
TimberLine (*US*)
Timeline (*US*)
Today's Golfer (*UK*)
Total Off-Road (*UK*)
Validation Times (*US*)
World Fishing (*UK*)

Theatre

Aesthetica: A Review of Contemporary Artists (*UK*)
Aquatics International (*US*)
Aries (*US*)
Artifact Nouveau (*US*)
Bare Fiction Magazine (*UK*)
Chapman (*UK*)
The List (*UK*)
Planet (*UK*)
Sorry We're Booked (*US*)
The Vehicle (*US*)

Thrillers

Artifact Nouveau (*US*)
Carbon Culture Review (*US*)

Crystal Magazine (*UK*)
The New Accelerator (*UK*)
ShortStorySunday.com (*UK*)
Suspense Magazine (*US*)
The Vehicle (*US*)

Translations
Able Muse (*US*)
The Adirondack Review (*US*)
Asheville Poetry Review (*US*)
Carbon Culture Review (*US*)
Cyphers (*Ire*)
Dream Catcher (*UK*)
Drunken Boat (*US*)
Envoi (*UK*)
Irish Pages (*UK*)
The Journal (*UK*)
Modern Poetry in Translation (*UK*)
The Penniless Press (*UK*)
PN Review (*UK*)
Poetry London (*UK*)
Rhino Poetry (*US*)
Sable (*UK*)
Salt Hill Journal (*US*)
Saranac Review (*US*)
South Dakota Review (*US*)
Stand Magazine (*UK*)
Tears in the Fence (*UK*)
Washington Square Review (*US*)
Writer's Bloc (*US*)
ZYZZYVA (*US*)

Travel
Abilities (*Can*)
Adventure Cyclist (*US*)
Akron Life (*US*)
Attitude (*UK*)
ATV Rider Magazine (*US*)
Backpacker (*US*)
BackTrack (*UK*)
BirdWatching Magazine (*US*)
Buses (*UK*)
B'nai B'rith Magazine (*US*)
Cape Cod Life (*US*)
Caravan Magazine (*UK*)
Cincy (*US*)
Classic Boat (*UK*)
Classic Cars (*UK*)
Coast & Kayak Magazine (*Can*)
Common Ground (*Can*)
Cruising Outpost Magazine (*US*)
Crystal Magazine (*UK*)
Decanter (*UK*)
Dogs Today (*UK*)
Escapees Magazine (*US*)
Evansville Living (*US*)
Evergreen (*UK*)
France (*UK*)
GuestLife (*US*)
Hill Country Sun (*US*)
Hyde Park Living (*US*)
The Irish Post (*UK*)
Junior (*UK*)
Kashrus Magazine (*US*)
Kent Life (*UK*)
KNOWAtlanta (*US*)
Lakeland Boating (*US*)
Leisure Group Travel (*US*)
Living France Magazine (*UK*)
NextStepU Magazine (*US*)
Overdrive (*US*)
Pacific Yachting (*Can*)
Pakn Treger (*US*)
Prima (*UK*)
Road King (*US*)
RV Business (*US*)
Sable (*UK*)
The Saturday Evening Post (*US*)
Sea Magazine (*US*)
Skipping Stones (*US*)
Southeast Review (*US*)
SpeciaLiving magazine (*US*)
Steamboat Magazine (*US*)
Sun Valley Magazine (*US*)
Telluride Magazine (*US*)
Tradicion Revista Magazine (*US*)
U Magazine (*Ire*)
Wedding (*UK*)
Wine Press Northwest (*US*)
Wine Spectator (*US*)
Woman Alive (*UK*)
Writing Short Fiction (*UK*)
Yachting Magazine (*US*)
Yorkshire Ridings Magazine (*UK*)

TV
Artifact Nouveau (*US*)
Epoch (*US*)
The List (*UK*)
Written By (*US*)

Westerns
Artifact Nouveau (*US*)
Crystal Magazine (*UK*)
The Savage Kick (*UK*)
ShortStorySunday.com (*UK*)
The Vehicle (*US*)
True West (*US*)

Women's Interests
Aesthetica: A Review of Contemporary Artists (*UK*)
Artifact Nouveau (*US*)
Closer (*UK*)
Cosmopolitan (*US*)
Dare (*UK*)
Feminist Review (*UK*)
Flare (*Can*)
Girlfriendz Magazine (*US*)
Mother & Baby Magazine (*UK*)
Mslexia (*UK*)
Now (*UK*)
The People's Friend (*UK*)
Prima (*UK*)
Real People (*UK*)
Resources for Feminist Research (*Can*)
Room Magazine (*Can*)
Sorry We're Booked (*US*)
U Magazine (*Ire*)
Woman & Home Feel Good Food (*UK*)
Woman Alive (*UK*)

Get Free Access to the firstwriter.com Website

To claim your free access to the firstwriter.com website simply go to the website at http://www.firstwriter.com/subscribe and begin the subscription process as normal. On the second page you will be asked to select your preferred payment processor, but don't worry – this doesn't mean you will have to make any payments!

Select whichever payment processor you prefer (we suggest using WorldPay unless you already have a PayPal account) and then continue to enter the requested details. When you are given the opportunity to enter a voucher / coupon reference number please enter the following promotional code:

- **LM12-D6WD**

This will reduce the cost of creating a subscription by up to $15 / £10 / €15, making it free to create a monthly, quarterly, or combination subscription. Alternatively, you can use the discount to take out an annual or life subscription at a reduced rate.

Select the subscription plan you prefer and proceed to complete the subscription process. Please note that you will need to provide your payment details, even if there is no up-front payment. This is in case you choose to leave your subscription running after the free initial period, but there is no obligation for you to do so.

When you use this code to take out a free subscription you are under no obligation to make any payments whatsoever and you are free to cancel your account before you make any payments if you wish.

If you need any assistance, please email support@firstwriter.com.

If you have found this book useful, please consider leaving a review on the website where you bought it!

What you get

Once you have set up access to ths site you will be able to benefit from all the following features:

Databases

All our databases are updated almost every day, and include powerful search facilities to help you find exactly what you need. Searches that used to take you hours or even days in print books or on search engines can now be done in seconds, and produce more accurate and up-to-date information. Our agents database also includes independent reports from at least three separate sources, showing you which are the top agencies and helping you avoid the scams that are all over the internet. You can try out any of our databases before you subscribe:

- Search **over 850 literary agencies**
- Search **over 1,700 book publishers**
- Search **over 2,000 magazines**
- Search between **100** and **250 current competitions**

PLUS advanced features to help you with your search:

- Save searches and save time – set up to 15 search parameters specific to your work, save them, and then access the search results with a single click whenever you log in. You can even save multiple different searches if you have different types of work you are looking to place.
- Add personal notes to listings, visible only to you and fully searchable – helping you to organise your actions.
- Set reminders on listings to notify you when to submit your work, when to follow up, when to expect a reply, or any other custom action.
- Track which listings you've viewed and when, to help you organise your search – any listings which have changed since you last viewed them will be highlighted for your attention!

Daily email updates

As a subscriber you will be able to take advantage of our email alert service, meaning you can specify your particular interests and we'll send you automatic email updates when we change or add a listing that matches them. So if you're interested in agents dealing in romantic fiction in the United States you can have us send you emails with the latest updates about them – keeping you up to date without even having to log in.

User feedback

Our agent, publisher, and magazine databases all include a user feedback feature that allows our subscribers to leave feedback on each listing – giving you not only the chance to have your say about the markets you contact, but giving a unique authors' perspective on the listings.

Save on copyright protection fees

If you're sending your work away to publishers, competitions, or literary agents, it's vital that you first protect your copyright. As a subscriber to firstwriter.com you can do this through our site and save 10% on the copyright registration fees normally payable for protecting your work internationally through the Intellectual Property Rights Office.

firstwriter.magazine

firstwriter.magazine showcases the best in new poetry and fiction from around the world. If you're interested in writing and want to get published, the most important thing you can do is read contemporary writing that's getting into print now. firstwriter.magazine helps you do that.

Half price competitions

As well as saving money on copyright registration, subscribers to firstwriter.com can also make further savings by entering writing competitions at a special reduced rate. Subscribers can enter the firstwriter.com International Poetry Competition and International Short Story Contest for half price.

Monthly newsletter

When you subscribe to firstwriter.com you also receive our monthly email newsletter – described by one publishing company as "the best in the business" – including articles, news, and interviews for writers. And the best part is that you can continue to receive the newsletter even after you stop your paid subscription – at no cost!

Terms and conditions

The promotional code contained in this publication may be used by the owner of the book only to create one subscription to firstwriter.com at a reduced cost, or for free. It may not be used by or disseminated to third parties. Should the code be misused then the owner of the book will be liable for any costs incurred, including but not limited to payment in full at the standard rate for the subscription in question. The code may be used at any time until the end of the calendar year named in the title of the publication, after which time it will become invalid. The code may be redeemed against the creation of a new account only – it cannot be redeemed against the ongoing costs of keeping a subscription open. In order to create a subscription a method of payment must be provided, but there is no obligation to make any payment. Subscriptions may be cancelled at any time, and if an account is cancelled before any payment becomes due then no payment will be made. Once a subscription has been created, the normal schedule of payments will begin on a monthly, quarterly, or annual basis, unless a life Subscription is selected, or the subscription is cancelled prior to the first payment becoming due. Subscriptions may be cancelled at any time, but if they are left open beyond the date at which the first payment becomes due and is processed then payments will not be refundable.

CPSIA information can be obtained
at www.ICGtesting.com
Printed in the USA
LVOW04s1115250116
472153LV00030B/635/P

9 781909 935099